fifth edition

Writing Arguments
A Rhetoric with Readings
Brief Edition

John D. Ramage

Arizona State University

John C. Bean

Seattle University

June Johnson

Seattle University

Allyn and Bacon

Boston ▪ *London* ▪ *Toronto* ▪ *Sydney* ▪ *Tokyo* ▪ *Singapore*

Vice President: Eben W. Ludlow
Editorial Assistant: Grace Trudow
Executive Marketing Manager: Lisa Kimball
Editorial Production Administrator: Susan Brown
Editorial-Production Service: Matrix Productions
Text Designer: Denise Hoffman
Composition Buyer: Linda Cox
Manufacturing Buyer: Suzanne Lareau
Compositor: Omegatype Typography, Inc.
Cover Administrator: Linda Knowles
Cover Designer: Susan Paradise

Copyright © 2001, 1998, 1995, 1992, and 1989 by Allyn & Bacon
A Pearson Education Company
160 Gould St.
Needham Heights, Mass. 02494
Internet: abacon.com

Library of Congress Cataloging-in-Publication Data

Ramage, John D.
    Writing arguments : a rhetoric with readings / John D. Ramage,
John C. Bean, June Johnson. — Brief ed., 5th ed.
      p.   cm.
    Includes index.
    ISBN 0-205-31746-4
    1. English language—Rhetoric. 2. Persuasion (Rhetoric)
3. College readers. 4. Report writing. I. Bean, John C.
II. Johnson, June. III. Title.
PE1431.R33 2000b
808'.0427—dc21
                                                 00–21662
                                                    CIP

brief contents

contents

PART TWO
PRINCIPLES OF ARGUMENT   73

CHAPTER 4   The Core of an Argument:
                    A Claim with Reasons   75

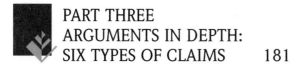

PART THREE
ARGUMENTS IN DEPTH:
SIX TYPES OF CLAIMS   181

CHAPTER 9   An Introduction to Types of Claims   183

CHAPTER 10   Categorical and Definitional Arguments: X Is (Is Not) a Y   192

CHAPTER 11   Causal Arguments: X Causes (Does Not Cause) Y   228

CHAPTER 12   Resemblance Arguments: X Is (Is Not) like Y   261

CHAPTER 13   Evaluation Arguments: X Is (Is Not) a Good Y   280

CHAPTER 15   Ethical Arguments   346

PART FOUR
WRITING FROM SOURCES: THE ARGUMENT
AS A FORMAL RESEARCH PAPER   359

APPENDIXES   431

preface

Overview

Through its first four editions, *Writing Arguments* has earned its place as the leading college textbook in argumentation. It has been especially praised for teaching the critical thinking that helps students *write* arguments: how to analyze the occasion for an argument; how to ground an argument in the values and beliefs of the targeted audience; how to develop and elaborate an argument; and how to respond sensitively to objections and alternative views. By treating argument as a means of discovery as well as persuasion, the text shows students how arguing involves productive dialog in search of the best solutions to problems rather than pro-con debate with winners and losers. Adopters of *Writing Arguments* testify that students using this text write better arguments—arguments that are more critically thoughtful, more fully developed and elaborated, and more in tune with the demands of their audience. Available in three versions—a regular edition, which includes an anthology of readings; a brief edition, which offers the complete rhetoric without the anthology; and a concise edition with fewer readings and examples—*Writing Arguments* has been used successfully at every level, from first-year composition to advanced argumentation courses.

For the fifth edition, we have made judicious changes that reflect our own evolving understanding of the theory and practice of argumentation and our awareness of what concepts and skills students need to write thoughtful and effective arguments. We also have increased the book's interest level for students by using examples and readings that connect more directly to their own lives. As in previous editions, our aim is to integrate a comprehensive study of argument with a process approach to writing and critical thinking. In both its treatment of argumentation and its approach to teaching writing, the text is rooted in current research and theory. Our emphasis throughout is on providing a teaching tool that really works in the classroom.

The fifth edition of *Writing Arguments* is particularly strengthened by the presence of a new coauthor, June Johnson, a colleague of John Bean's at Seattle University. Her background in contemporary literary and rhetorical theory and her research interests in popular culture and civic argument—along with extensive classroom experience and training in pedagogy—have made June an invaluable writing partner.

What's New in the Fifth Edition?

The fifth edition retains all the features that have made earlier editions successful. In addition, the fifth edition contains the following improvements:

- Substantial revision of Chapter 2, "Reading Arguments," aimed at shortening the chapter and increasing student interest. We have replaced the Charles Murray article on welfare reform with two arguments on gender pay equity. Besides teaching summary writing and critical analysis, the chapter shows students how to seek out alternative views, pose questions about facts and values, and use disagreement productively to prompt further investigation. Throughout, we treat the process of reading arguments as a step toward writing arguments.

- Increased focus on audience, on real-world occasions for argument, and on analyzing rhetorical context. Throughout the text, we have infused a philosophical view of argument that emphasizes audience and rhetorical context at every stage of the construction of an argument. Our revisions of Chapter 3, "Writing Arguments," particularly reflect this focus.

- Reconceptualization of Chapter 9, "An Introduction to the Types of Claims," to reflect our evolving understanding of stasis theory. Using lasik eye surgery as an extended example, we show how knowledge of the claim types—combined with an analysis of audience—can help writers focus an argument and generate ideas. Also, in this edition we have added a sixth claim type, called "simple categorical arguments."

- A revision of Chapter 10, now titled "Categorical and Definitional Arguments." This chapter now explains both simple categorical arguments and definitional arguments. The revised chapter makes it easy for students to appreciate the universality of these two claim types, to understand the argumentative moves they entail, and to produce their own categorical or definitional arguments. Additionally, Chapter 11, on causal arguments, is significantly streamlined and clarified.

- Six new student essays selected for the quality of their arguments and the appeal of their subject matter. Drawn from popular culture issues and other contemporary concerns, these readings connect effectively to the interests of today's students. For example, one student essay persuades readers to change their misconception of skateboarders ("'Half-Criminals' or Urban Athletes? A Plea for Fair Treatment of Skateboarders," pp. 129–31); another evaluates the marketing wizardry of the Spice Girls ("The Spice Girls: Good at Marketing but Not Good for Their Market," pp. 296–99); still another identifies high school cliques as a possible cause for the Columbine massacre ("The Monster That Is High School," pp. 247–49).

- Ten new professional essays, also chosen for the appeal of their subject matter and for the range of genres represented. Among the new professional essays are John Leo's analysis of racial stereotypes in the film *The*

Phantom Menace ("Stereotypes No Phantom in New *Star Wars* Movie," pp. 218–19); law professor Vicki Schultz's definitional argument on sexual harassment ("Sex Is the Least of It: Let's Focus Harassment Law on Work, Not Sex," pp. 223–27); and physician Ezekiel Emanuel's evaluation argument on fertility drugs ("Eight Is Too Many: The Case against Octuplets," pp. 303–06). In addition to new professional essays, we include screen captures from several Web sites (on gender pay equity, on sweatshops) and several examples of visual arguments (photographs on Kosovo and on Makah whaling; tables and graphs related to wealth and income distribution).

- The addition of discussion questions following each reading. These questions prompt students to analyze writers' persuasive strategies, including how writers frame their arguments and situate them in larger social conflicts. Also we now introduce each reading with a brief headnote describing the reading's rhetorical context.

- Attention to visual arguments, with a special section devoted to visual arguments in Chapter 7, "Moving Your Audience: Audience-Based Reasons, *Ethos,* and *Pathos.*"

- A new section on using humor to appeal to resistant audiences in Chapter 8, "Accommodating Your Audience: Treating Differing Views."

- Expanded treatment of electronic sources including explanations of how to evaluate Web sites and how to understand the logic of electronic searching—for example, the differences between licensed databases and the World Wide Web.

- More concise explanations throughout the text with the goal of making the style crisper and more engaging.

What Hasn't Changed? The Distinguishing Features of *Writing Arguments*

Building on earlier success, we have preserved all the features of earlier editions praised by students, instructors, and reviewers. The fifth edition provides the same teachable material but in a more streamlined and lively style. Specifically, the fifth edition retains the following successful features from the fourth edition:

- Focus throughout on writing arguments. Grounded in composition theory, this text combines explanations of argument with class-tested discussion tasks, exploratory writing tasks, and sequenced writing assignments aimed at developing skills of writing and critical thinking.

- Extensive treatment of invention including use of the Toulmin system of analyzing arguments combined with use of the enthymeme as a discovery and shaping tool.

- Detailed explanations of *logos, pathos,* and *ethos* as persuasive appeals.
- Comprehensive treatment of stasis theory identified for students as "types of claims."
- Focus on both the reading and the writing of arguments with emphasis on argument as inquiry and discovery as well as persuasion.
- Focus on the critical thinking that underlies effective arguments, particularly the skills of critical reading, of believing and doubting, of empathic listening, of active questioning, and of negotiating ambiguity and seeking synthesis.
- Focus on strategies for analyzing rhetorical context, for rooting arguments in the values and beliefs of the intended audience, and for basing decisions about content, structure, and style on analysis of audience and context.
- Copious treatment of the research paper, including two student examples—one using the MLA system and one using the APA system.
- Numerous "For Class Discussion" exercises and sequenced writing assignments designed to teach critical thinking and build argumentative skills. All "For Class Discussion" exercises can be used either for whole class discussions or for collaborative group tasks.
- Numerous student and professional arguments used to illustrate argumentative strategies and stimulate discussion, analysis, and debate. The fifth edition contains thirteen student essays of varied length and complexity as well as fourteen professional essays. Additionally, the fifth edition contains four letters to the editor from citizens, several screen captures from Web sites, and several examples of visual arguments.

Our Approaches to Argumentation

Our interest in argumentation grows out of our interest in the relationship between writing and thinking. When writing arguments, writers are forced to lay bare their thinking processes in an unparalleled way, grappling with the complex interplay between inquiry and persuasion, between issue and audience. In an effort to engage students in the kinds of critical thinking that argument demands, we draw on four major approaches to argumentation:

- *The enthymeme as a rhetorical and logical structure.* This concept, especially useful for beginning writers, helps students "nutshell" an argument as a claim with one or more supporting *because* clauses. It also helps them see how real-world arguments are rooted in assumptions granted by the audience rather than in universal and unchanging principles.
- *The three classical types of appeal*—**logos, ethos,** *and* **pathos.** These concepts help students place their arguments in a rhetorical context focusing on audience-based appeals; they also help students create an effective voice and style.

- *Toulmin's system of analyzing arguments.* Toulmin's system helps students see the complete, implicit structure that underlies an enthymeme and develop appropriate grounds and backing to support the claim. It also highlights the rhetorical, social, and dialectical nature of argument.
- *Stasis or claim-type theory.* This approach stresses the heuristic value of learning different patterns of support for different types of claims and often leads students to make surprisingly rich and full arguments.

Throughout the text these approaches are integrated and synthesized into generative tools for both producing and analyzing arguments.

Structure of the Text

The text has four main parts plus two appendixes. Part One gives an overview of argumentation. The first three chapters present our philosophy of argument, showing how argument helps writers clarify their own thinking and connect with the values and beliefs of a questioning audience. Throughout we link the process of arguing—articulating issue questions, formulating propositions, examining alternative points of view, and creating structures of supporting reasons and evidence—with the processes of reading and writing.

Part Two examines the principles of argument. Chapters 4 through 6 show that the core of an argument is a claim with reasons. These reasons are often stated as enthymemes, the unstated premise of which must sometimes be brought to the surface and supported. Discussion of Toulmin logic shows students how to discover the stated and unstated premises of their arguments and to provide structures of reasons and evidence to support them. Chapters 7 and 8 focus on the rhetorical context of arguments. These chapters discuss the writer's relationship with an audience, particularly with finding audience-based reasons, with using *pathos* and *ethos* effectively and responsibly, and with accommodating arguments to different kinds of audiences from sympathetic to neutral to resistant.

Part Three discusses six different types of argument: simple categorical arguments, definitional arguments, causal arguments, resemblance arguments, evaluation arguments, and proposal arguments. These chapters introduce students to two recurring strategies of argument that cut across the different category types: criteria-match arguing, in which the writer establishes criteria for making a judgment and argues whether a specific case does or does not meet those criteria, and causal arguing, in which the writer shows that one event or phenomenon can be linked to others in a causal chain. The last chapter of Part Three deals with the special complexities of moral arguments.

Part Four shows students how to incorporate research into their arguments. It explains how writers use sources, with a special focus on the skills of summary, paraphrase, and judicious quotation. Unlike standard treatments of the research paper, our discussion explains to students how the writer's meaning and purpose control the selection and shaping of source materials. Part Four explains both the MLA and the APA documentation systems, which are illustrated by two student examples of researched arguments. Throughout Chapters 16 and 17, we incorporate discussions of electronic searching and the challenges of detecting what is useful on the World Wide Web.

The appendixes provide important supplemental information useful for courses in argument. Appendix One gives an overview of informal fallacies. Appendix Two shows students how to get the most out of collaborative groups in an argument class. Appendix Two also provides a sequence of collaborative tasks that will help students learn to peer-critique their classmates' arguments-in-progress. The numerous "For Class Discussion" exercises within the text provide additional tasks for group collaboration.

Writing Assignments

The text provides a variety of sequenced writing assignments, including exploratory tasks for discovering and generating arguments, "microthemes" for practicing basic argumentative moves (for example, supporting a reason with statistical evidence), cases, and numerous other assignments calling for complete arguments. Thus the text provides instructors with a wealth of options for writing assignments on which to build a coherent course.

An Expanded and Improved Instructor's Manual

The Instructor's Manual has been revised and expanded to make it more useful for teachers and writing program administrators. Written by co-author June Johnson, the new Instructor's Manual has the following features:

- Discussion of planning decisions an instructor must make in designing an argument course: for example, how to use readings; how much to emphasize or de-emphasize Toulmin or claim-type theory; how much time to build into the course for invention, peer review of drafts, and other writing instruction; and how to select and sequence assignments.
- Three detailed sample syllabi showing how *Writing Arguments* can support a variety of course structures and emphases:

  Syllabus #1: This course emphasizes argumentative skills and strategies, uses readings for rhetorical analysis, and asks students to write on issues drawn from their own experience.

  Syllabus #2: This more rigorous course works intensely with the logical structure of argument, the classical appeals, the Toulmin schema, and claim-type theory. It uses readings for rhetorical analysis and for an introduction to the argumentative controversies that students will address in their papers.

Syllabus #3: This course asks students to experiment with genres of argument (for example, op-ed pieces, white papers, visual arguments, and researched freelance or scholarly arguments) and focuses on students' choice of topics and claim types.

- For instructors who include Toulmin, an independent, highly teachable introductory lesson on the Toulmin schema.

- For new teachers, a helpful discussion of how to sequence writing assignments and how to use a variety of collaborative tasks in the classroom to promote active learning and critical thinking.

- Chapter-by-chapter responses to the For Class Discussion exercises.

- Numerous teaching tips and suggestions placed strategically throughout the chapter material.

- Helpful suggestions for using the exercises on critiquing readings in Part Three, "Arguments in Depth: Six Types of Claims." By focusing on rhetorical context as well as the strengths and weaknesses of these arguments, our suggestions will help students connect their reading of arguments to their writing of arguments.

Companion Web Site

The *Writing Arguments* Companion Web Site, http://www.abacon.com/ramage, enables instructors to access online writing activities and Web links keyed to specific chapters, post and make changes to their syllabi, hold chat sessions with individual students or groups of students, and receive e-mail and essay assignments directly from students.

Acknowledgments

We are happy for this opportunity to give public thanks to the scholars, teachers, and students who have influenced our approach to composition and argument. We would especially like to thank Darlene Panvini of Vanderbilt University for her advice on our treatment of the wetlands controversy in Chapter 10. Additional thanks go to Seattle University librarian Sandra Brandt for her help with our explanations of library and Internet databases and retrieval and to Daniel Anderson of the University of North Carolina, Chapel Hill, for his material on electronic communication. Thanks also to Susan Meyer, Stephen Bean, and Sarah Bean for their research assistance in preparing the fifth edition.

Particular thanks go to the following reviewers, who gave us helpful and cogent advice at various stages of the revision process: Jonathan Ayres, the University of Texas at Austin; Linda Bensel-Meyers, University of Tennessee–Knoxville; Deborah Core, Eastern Kentucky University; Richard Fulkerson, Texas A&M University–Commerce; Carol A. Lowe, McLennan Community College; David Mair, University of Oklahoma; Tim McGee, the College of New Jersey; Thomas A. Wallis, North Carolina State University; and Irene Ward, Kansas State University, for their reviews of *Writing Arguments,* Fourth Edition, and draft chapters of this fifth edition.

We also would like to thank our editor of more than fifteen years, Eben Ludlow, who well deserves his reputation as a premier editor in college publishing. In fact, it has been a joy for us to work with the whole Allyn & Bacon English team: Lisa Kimball, English marketing manager; Susan Brown, editorial production administrator; and Doug Day, English sales specialist. Additional thanks go to Merrill Peterson of Matrix Productions, who professionally managed many key aspects of production.

Finally, we would like to thank our families. John Bean: Thanks to my wife, Kit, whose own work as an ESL instructor has produced wonderful discussions of argument and pedagogy in a multicultural setting, and to my children Matthew, Andrew, Stephen, and Sarah for their love and support. June Johnson: Thanks to my husband, Kenneth Bube, and my daughter, Jane Ellen, for their keen insights, loving encouragement, and inspirational humor.

Overview of Argument

1 Argument

An Introduction

At the outset of a book on argument, we ought to explain what an argument is. Instead, we're going to explain why no simple definition is possible. Philosophers and rhetoricians have disagreed over the centuries about the meaning of the term and about the goals that arguers should set for themselves. This opening chapter introduces you to some of these controversies. Our goal is to introduce you to various ways of thinking about argument as a way of helping you become a more powerful arguer yourself.

We begin by asking what we mean by argument and then proceed to three defining features: *Argument* requires justification of its claims, it is both a product and a process, and it combines elements of truth seeking and persuasion. We then explore more deeply the relationship between truth seeking and persuasion by asking questions about the nature of "truth" that arguments seek. Finally, we give you an example of a successful arguing process.

WHAT DO WE MEAN BY ARGUMENT?

Let's begin by examining the inadequacies of two popular images of argument—fight and debate.

Argument Is Not a Fight or a Quarrel

To many, the word *argument* connotes anger and hostility, as when we say, "I just got in a huge argument with my roommate," or "My mother and I argue all the time." What we picture here is heated disagreement, rising pulse rates, and an urge to slam doors. Argument imagined as fight conjures images of shouting talk-show guests, name-calling letter writers, or fist-banging speakers.

But to our way of thinking, argument doesn't imply anger. In fact, arguing is often pleasurable. It is a creative and productive activity that engages us at high levels of inquiry and critical thinking, often in conversation with persons we like and respect. For your primary image of argument, we invite you to think not of a fist-banging speaker but of a small group of reasonable persons seeking the best solution to a problem. We will return to this image throughout the chapter.

Argument Is Not Pro-Con Debate

Another popular image of argument is debate—a presidential debate, perhaps, or a high school or college debate tournament. According to one popular dictionary, *debate* is "a formal contest of argumentation in which two opposing teams defend and attack a given proposition." While formal debate can develop critical thinking, its weakness is that it can turn argument into a game of winners and losers rather than a process of cooperative inquiry.

For an illustration of this weakness, consider one of our former students, a champion high school debater who spent his senior year debating the issue of prison reform. Throughout the year he argued for and against propositions such as "The United States should build more prisons" and "Innovative alternatives to prison should replace prison sentences for most crimes." We asked him, "What do you personally think is the best way to reform prisons?" He replied, "I don't know. I haven't thought about what I would actually choose."

Here was a bright, articulate student who had studied prisons extensively for a year. Yet nothing in the atmosphere of pro-con debate had engaged him in truth-seeking inquiry. He could argue for and against a proposition, but he hadn't experienced the wrenching process of clarifying his own values and taking a personal stand. As we explain throughout this text, argument entails a desire for truth; it aims to find the best solutions to complex problems. We don't mean that arguers don't passionately support their own points of view or expose weaknesses in views they find faulty. Instead, we mean that their goal isn't to win a game but to find and promote the best belief or course of action.

Arguments Can Be Explicit or Implicit

Before proceeding to some defining features of argument, we should note also that arguments can be either explicit or implicit. An *explicit* argument states directly a controversial claim and supports it with reasons and evidence. An *implicit* argument, in contrast, doesn't look like an argument. It may be a poem or short story, a photograph or cartoon, a personal essay or an autobiographical narrative. But like an explicit argument, it persuades its audience toward a certain point of view. John Steinbeck's *Grapes of Wrath* is an implicit argument for the unionization of farm workers, just as the following poem is an implicit argument against the premise that it is sweet and fitting to die for one's country.

Dulce et Decorum Est

Bent double, like old beggars under sacks,
Knock-kneed, coughing like hags, we cursed through sludge
Till on the haunting flares we turned our backs,
And towards our distant rest began to trudge.
Men marched asleep. Many had lost their boots,
But limped on, blood-shod. All went lame, all blind;
Drunk with fatigue; deaf even to the hoots
Of gas-shells dropping softly behind.

Gas! Gas! Quick, boys—An ecstasy of fumbling,
Fitting the clumsy helmets just in time,
But someone still was yelling out and stumbling
And flound'ring like a man in fire or lime.
Dim through the misty panes and thick green light,
As under a green sea, I saw him drowning.

In all my dreams before my helpless sight
He plunges at me, guttering, choking, drowning.

If in some smothering dreams, you too could pace
Behind the wagon that we flung him in,
And watch the white eyes writhing in his face,
His hanging face, like a devil's sick of sin,
If you could hear, at every jolt, the blood
Come gargling from the froth-corrupted lungs
Bitter as the cud
Of vile, incurable sores on innocent tongues,—
My friend, you would not tell with such high zest
To children ardent for some desperate glory,
The old lie: *Dulce et decorum est*
*Pro patria mori.**

                                        —Wilfred Owen

Here Wilfred Owen makes a powerful case against the "old lie"—that war is honorable, that dying for one's country is sweet and fitting. But the argument is implicit: It is carried in the horrible image of a soldier drowning in his own fluids from a mustard gas attack rather than through an ordered structure of thesis, rea-

---

*"How sweet and fitting it is to die for one's country." Wilfred Owen (1893–1918) was killed in World War I and wrote many of his poems while in the trenches.

sons, and evidence. Visual images can also make implicit arguments, often by evoking powerful emotions in audiences. The perspective photos take, the stories they tell, or the vivid details of place and time they display compel viewers literally to see the issue from a particular angle. Take, for instance, the photo (Figure 1.1) of Albanian refugees during the Kosovo War. The photographer conveys the nightmare of this war by foregrounding the old woman, probably a grandmother, perched precariously atop a heavily loaded wheelbarrow, her canes or crutches sticking out from the pile, and the five other persons in the scene hastening down a stark road against an ominous gray background. Here *showing* the urgency of the Albanians' flight for their lives and the helplessness of the two who can't walk is an effective strategy to arouse sympathy for the Albanians. Photographs of this kind regularly appeared in American newspapers during the war, serving to heighten U.S. support of NATO bombing. Meanwhile, Serbs complained that no American newspapers showed photographs of KLA (Kosovo Liberation Army) atrocities against Serbs.

FIGURE 1.1   Albanian refugees during the Kosovo War

Newsweek, April 12, 1999, p. 33.

FOR CLASS DISCUSSION

1. In your own words, how do explicit and implicit arguments differ?

2. Imagine that you wanted to take a photograph that creates an implicit argument persuading (1) teenagers against smoking; (2) teenagers against becoming sexually active; (3) the general public toward banning handguns; (4) the general public against banning handguns; (5) the general public toward saving endangered species; (6) the general public toward supporting timber companies' desire to harvest old-growth forests. Working individually or in small groups, describe a photograph you might take that would create an appropriate implicit argument.

EXAMPLE: To create an implicit argument against legalizing hard drugs, you might photograph a blank-eyed, cadaverous teenager plunging a needle into her arm.

Although implicit arguments can be powerful, the predominant focus of this text is on explicit argument. We don't leave implicit arguments entirely, however, because their strategies—especially the persuasive power of stories and narratives—can often be incorporated into explicit arguments, as we discuss more fully in Chapter 7.

THE DEFINING FEATURES OF ARGUMENT

We turn now to examine argument in more detail. (From here on, when we say "argument," we mean "explicit argument.") This section examines three defining features.

Argument Requires Justification of Its Claims

To begin defining argument, let's turn to a humble but universal site of disagreement: the conflict between a parent and a teenager over rules. In what way and in what circumstances do such conflicts constitute arguments?

Consider the following dialogue:

YOUNG PERSON (*racing for the front door while putting coat on*):   Bye. See you later.

PARENT: Whoa! What time are you planning on coming home?

YOUNG PERSON (*coolly, hand still on doorknob*):   I'm sure we discussed this earlier. I'll be home around 2 A.M. (*The second sentence, spoken very rapidly, is barely audible.*)

PARENT (*mouth tightening*):   We did *not* discuss this earlier and you're *not* staying out till two in the morning. You'll be home at twelve.

At this point in the exchange, we have a quarrel, not an argument. Quarrelers exchange antagonistic assertions without any attempt to support them rationally. If the dialogue never gets past the "Yes-you-will/No-I-won't" stage, it either remains a quarrel or degenerates into a fight.

Let us say, however, that the dialogue takes the following turn:

YOUNG PERSON (*tragically*):   But I'm *sixteen years old*!

Now we're moving toward argument. Not, to be sure, a particularly well-developed or cogent one, but an argument all the same. It's now an argument because one of the quarrelers has offered a reason for her assertion. Her choice of curfew is satisfactory, she says, *because* she is sixteen years old, an argument that depends on the unstated assumption that sixteen-year-olds are old enough to make decisions about such matters.

The parent can now respond in one of several ways that will either advance the argument or turn it back into a quarrel. The parent can simply invoke parental authority ("I don't care—you're still coming home at twelve"), in which case argument ceases. Or the parent can provide a reason for his or her view ("You will be home at twelve because your dad and I pay the bills around here!"), in which case the argument takes a new turn.

So far we've established two necessary conditions that must be met before we're willing to call something an argument: (1) a set of two or more conflicting assertions and (2) the attempt to resolve the conflict through an appeal to reason.

But good argument demands more than meeting these two formal requirements. For the argument to be effective, an arguer is obligated to clarify and support the reasons presented. For example, "But I'm sixteen years old!" is not yet a clear support for the assertion "I should be allowed to set my own curfew." On the surface, Young Person's argument seems absurd. Her parent, of all people, knows precisely how old she is. What makes it an argument is that behind her claim lies an unstated assumption—all sixteen-year-olds are old enough to set their own curfews. What Young Person needs to do now is to support that assumption.* In doing so, she must anticipate the sorts of questions the assumption will raise in the minds of her parent: What is the legal status of sixteen-year-olds? How psychologically mature, as opposed to chronologically mature, is Young Person? What is the actual track record of Young Person in being responsible? and so forth. Each of these questions will force Young Person to reexamine and clarify her assumptions about the proper degree of autonomy for sixteen-year-olds. And her response to those questions should in turn force the parents to reexamine their

---

*Later in this text we will call the assumption underlying a line of reasoning its *warrant* (see Chapter 5).

assumptions about the dependence of sixteen-year-olds on parental guidance and wisdom. (Likewise, the parents will need to show why "paying the bills around here" automatically gives them the right to set Young Person's curfew.)

As the argument continues, Young Person and Parent may shift to a different line of reasoning. For example, Young Person might say: "I should be allowed to stay out until 2 A.M. because all my friends get to stay out that late." (Here the unstated assumption is that the rules in this family ought to be based on the rules in other families.) The parent might in turn respond, "But I certainly never stayed out that late when I was your age"—an argument assuming that the rules in this family should follow the rules of an earlier generation.

As Young Person and Parent listen to each other's points of view (and begin realizing why their initial arguments have not persuaded their intended audience), both parties find themselves in the uncomfortable position of having to examine their own beliefs and to justify assumptions that they have taken for granted. Here we encounter one of the earliest senses of the term *to argue*, which is "to clarify." As an arguer begins to clarify her own position on an issue, she also begins to clarify her audience's position. Such clarification helps the arguer see how she might accommodate her audience's views, perhaps by adjusting her own position or by developing reasons that appeal to her audience's values. Thus Young Person might suggest an argument like this:

> I should be allowed to stay out until 2 on a trial basis because I need enough space to demonstrate my maturity and show you I won't get into trouble.

The assumption underlying this argument is that it is good to give teenagers freedom to demonstrate their maturity. Because this reason is likely to appeal to her parent's own values (the parent wants to see his or her daughter grow in maturity) and because it is tempered by the qualifier "on a trial basis" (which reduces some of the threat of Young Person's initial demands), it may prompt productive discussion.

Whether or not Young Person and Parent can work out a best solution, the preceding scenario illustrates how argument leads persons to clarify their reasons and provide justifications that can be examined rationally. The scenario also illustrates two specific aspects of argument that we will explore in detail in the next sections: (1) Argument is both a process and a product. (2) Argument combines truth seeking and persuasion.

Argument Is Both a Process and a Product

As the preceding scenario revealed, argument can be viewed as a *process* in which two or more parties seek the best solution to a question or problem. Argument can also be viewed as a *product,* each product being any person's contribution to the conversation at a given moment. In an informal discussion, the products are usually short, whatever time a person uses during his or her turns in the conversation. Under more formal settings, an orally delivered product might be a short impromptu speech (say, during an open-mike discussion of a campus issue) or a longer, carefully prepared formal speech (as in an oral brief before a judge, a presentation to a legislative subcommittee, or an argument at a public hearing for or against a proposed city project).

Similar conversations occur in writing. Roughly analogous to a small-group discussion is an e-mail discussion of the kind that occurs regularly through informal chat groups or professional listservs. In an online discussion, participants have more thinking time to shape their messages than they do in a real-time oral discussion. Nevertheless, messages are usually short and informal, making it possible over the course of several days to see participants' ideas shift and evolve as conversants modify their initial views in response to others' views.

Roughly equivalent to a formal speech would be a formal written argument composed through multiple drafts over the course of days or weeks and submitted as a college essay assignment, a grant proposal, a guest column for the op-ed* section of a newspaper, a letter to a congressional representative, a legal brief for a judge, or an article for an organizational newsletter, popular magazine, or professional journal. In each of these instances, the written argument (a product) enters a conversation (a process)—in this case, a conversation of readers, many of whom will carry on the conversation by writing their own responses or by discussing the writer's views with others. The goal of the community of writers and readers is to find the best solution to the problem or issue under discussion.

Argument Combines Truth Seeking and Persuasion

In thinking about argument as a product, the writer will find herself continually moving back and forth between truth seeking and persuasion—that is, between questions about the subject matter (What is the best solution to this problem?) and about audience (What do my readers already believe or value? What reasons and evidence will most persuade them?). Back and forth she'll weave, alternately absorbed in the subject of her argument and in the audience for that argument.

Neither of the two focuses is ever completely out of mind, but their relative importance shifts during different phases of the development of a paper. Moreover, different rhetorical situations place different emphases on truth seeking versus persuasion. We could thus place arguments on a kind of continuum that

---

*Op-ed stands for "opposite-editorial." It is the generic name in journalism for a signed argument that voices the writer's opinion on an issue, as opposed to a news story that is supposed to report events objectively, uncolored by the writer's personal views. Op-ed pieces appear in the editorial-opinion section of newspapers, which generally feature editorials by the resident staff, opinion pieces by syndicated columnists, and letters to the editor from readers. The term op-ed is often extended to syndicated columns appearing in news magazines.

measures the degree of attention a writer gives to subject matter versus audience. At the far truth-seeking end of the continuum might be an exploratory piece that lays out several alternative approaches to a problem and weighs the strengths and weaknesses of each with no concern for persuasion. At the other end of the continuum would be outright propaganda, such as a political campaign advertisement that reduces a complex issue to sound bites and distorts an opponent's position through out-of-context quotations or misleading use of data. (At its most blatant, propaganda obliterates truth seeking; it will do anything, including the knowing use of bogus evidence, distorted assertions, and outright lies, to win over an audience.) In the middle ranges of the continuum, writers shift their focuses back and forth between truth seeking and persuasion but with varying degrees of emphasis.

As an example of a writer focusing primarily on truth seeking, consider the case of Kathleen, who, in her college argument course, addressed the definitional question "Is American Sign Language (ASL) a 'foreign language' for purposes of meeting the university's foreign language requirement?" Kathleen had taken two years of ASL at a community college. When she transferred to a four-year college, the chair of the foreign languages department at her new college would not allow her ASL proficiency to count for the foreign language requirement. ASL isn't a "language," the chair said summarily. "It's not equivalent to learning French, German, or Japanese."

Kathleen disagreed, so she immersed herself in developing her argument. While doing research, she focused almost entirely on subject matter, searching for what linguists, brain neurologists, cognitive psychologists, and sociologists had said about the language of deaf people. Immersed in her subject matter, she was only tacitly concerned with her audience, whom she thought of primarily as her classmates and the professor of her argument class—persons who were friendly to her views and interested in her experiences with the deaf community. She wrote a well-documented paper, citing several scholarly articles, that made a good case to her classmates (and the professor) that ASL was indeed a distinct language.

Proud of the big red A the professor had placed on her paper, Kathleen returned to the chair of the foreign languages department with a new request to count ASL for her language requirement. The chair read her paper, congratulated her on her good writing, but said her argument was not persuasive. He disagreed with several of the linguists she cited and with the general definition of *language* that her paper assumed. He then gave her some additional (and to her fuzzy) reasons why the college would not accept ASL as a foreign language.

Spurred by what she considered the chair's too-easy dismissal of her argument, Kathleen decided, for a subsequent assignment in her argument class, to write a second paper on ASL—but this time aiming it directly at the chair of foreign languages. Now her writing task falls closer to the persuasive end of our continuum. Kathleen once again immersed herself in research, but this time it focused not on subject matter (whether ASL is a distinct language) but on audience. She researched the history of the foreign language requirement at her college and discovered some of the politics behind it (an old foreign language requirement had been dropped in the 1970s and reinstituted in the 1990s, partly—a math professor told her—to boost enrollments in foreign language courses). She also interviewed foreign language teachers to find out what they knew and didn't know about ASL. She discovered that many teachers thought ASL was "easy to learn," so that accepting ASL would allow students a Mickey Mouse way to avoid the rigors of a "real" foreign language class. Additionally, she learned that foreign language teachers valued immersing students in a foreign culture; in fact, the foreign language requirement was part of her college's effort to create a multicultural curriculum.

This new understanding of her target audience helped Kathleen totally reconceptualize her argument. She condensed and abridged her original paper down to one line of reasoning in her new argument. She added sections showing the difficulty of learning ASL (to counter her audience's belief that learning ASL was easy), showing how the deaf community formed a distinct culture with its own customs and literature (to show how ASL met the goals of multiculturalism), and showing that the number of transfer students with ASL credits would be negligibly small (to allay fears that accepting ASL would threaten enrollments in language classes). She ended her argument with an appeal to her college's public emphasis (declared boldly in its mission statement) on eradicating social injustice and reaching out to the oppressed. She described the isolation of deaf people in a world where almost no hearing people learn ASL, and she argued that the deaf community on her campus could be integrated more fully into campus life if more students could "talk" with them. Thus the ideas included in her new argument—the reasons selected, the evidence used, the arrangement and tone—all were determined by her primary focus on persuasion.

Our point, then, is that all along the continuum writers are concerned both to seek truth and to persuade, but not necessarily with equal balance. Kathleen could not have written her second paper, aimed specifically at persuading the chair of foreign languages, if she hadn't first immersed herself in truth-seeking research that convinced her that ASL was indeed a distinct language. Nor are we saying that her second argument was better than her first. Both fulfilled their purposes and met the needs of their intended audiences. Both involved truth seeking and persuasion, but the first focused primarily on subject matter whereas the second focused primarily on audience.

ARGUMENT AND THE PROBLEM OF TRUTH

The tension that we have just examined between truth seeking and persuasion raises one of the oldest issues in the field of argument: Is the arguer's first obligation to truth or to winning the argument? And just what is the nature of the truth to which arguers are supposed to be obligated? To this second question we now turn.

When Does Argument Become Propaganda?
The Debate between Socrates and Callicles

One of the first great debates on the issue of truth versus victory occurs in Plato's dialogue the *Gorgias,* in which the philosopher Socrates takes on the rhetorician Callicles.

Socrates was a great philosopher known to us today primarily through his student Plato, whose "dialogues" depict Socrates debating various friends and antagonists. Socrates' stated goal in these debates was to "rid the world of error." In dialogue after dialogue, Socrates vanquishes error by skillfully leading people through a series of questions that force them to recognize the inconsistency and implausibility of their beliefs. He was a sort of intellectual judo master who takes opponents' arguments the way they want to go until they suddenly fall over.

Callicles, in contrast, is a shadowy figure in history. We know him only through his exchange with Socrates—hence only through Plato's eyes. But Callicles is easily recognizable to philosophers as a representative of the Sophists, a group of teachers who schooled ancient Greeks in the fine art of winning arguments. The Sophists were a favorite, if elusive, target of both Socrates and Plato. Indeed, opposition to the Sophists' approach to life lies at the core of Platonic philosophy. Having said all that, let's turn to the dialogue.

Early in the debate, Socrates is clearly in control. He easily—too easily, as it turns out—wins a couple of preliminary rounds against some less-determined Sophists before confronting Callicles. But in the long and arduous debate that follows, it's not at all clear that Socrates wins. In fact, one of the points being made in the *Gorgias* seems to be that philosophers committed to "clarifying" and discovering truth may occasionally have to sacrifice winning the debate in the name of their higher ends. Although Plato makes an eloquent case for enlightenment as the goal of argument, he may well contribute to the demise of this noble principle if he should happen to lose. Unfortunately, it appears that Socrates can't win the argument without sinning against the very principle he's defending.

The effectiveness of Callicles as a debater lies in his refusal to allow Socrates *any* assumptions. In response to Socrates' concern for virtue and justice, Callicles responds dismissively that such concepts are mere conventions, invented by the weak to protect themselves from the strong. In Callicles' world, "might makes right." The function of argument in such a world is to extend the freedom and power of the arguer, not to arrive at some vision of "truth." Indeed, the power to decide what's "true" belongs to the winner of the debate. For Callicles, a truth that never wins is no truth at all because it will soon disappear. In sum, Callicles sees the ends (winning the argument) as justifying the means (refusing to grant any assumptions, using ambiguous language, and so forth). Socrates, in contrast, believes that no good end can come from questionable means.

Based on what we've said up to this point about our belief in argument as truth seeking, you might guess that our sympathies are with Socrates. To a great extent they are. But Socrates lived in a much simpler world than we do, if by "simple" we mean a world where the True and the Good were, if not universally agreed-upon notions, at least ones around which a clear consensus formed. For Socrates, there was one True Answer to any important question. Truth resided in the ideal world of forms, and through philosophic rigor humans could transcend the changing, shadowlike world of everyday reality to perceive the world of universals where Truth, Beauty, and Goodness resided.

Callicles, however, rejects the notion that there is only one possible truth at which all arguments will necessarily arrive. For Callicles, there are different degrees of truth and different kinds of truths for different situations or cultures. In raising the whole nettlesome question—How "true" is a "truth" that you can't get anyone to agree to?—Callicles is probably closer to the modern world than is Plato. Let's expand on Callicles' view of truth by examining some contemporary illustrations.

What Is Truth? The Place of Argument in Contemporary Life

Although the debate between Socrates and Callicles appears to end inconclusively, many readers over the centuries conceded the victory to Socrates almost by default. Callicles was seen as cheating. The term *sophistry* came to be synonymous with trickery in argument. The Sophists' relativistic beliefs were so repugnant to most people that they refused to grant any merit to the Sophists' position. In our century, however, the Sophists have found a more sympathetic readership, one that takes some of the questions they raised quite seriously.

One way of tracing this shift in attitude toward truth is by looking at a significant shift in the definition of the verb *to argue* over the centuries. On the one hand, as we have seen, one of the earliest meanings of *to argue* was "to clarify," a definition focusing on truth seeking. Another early meaning was "to prove"—a definition that focuses simultaneously on truth seeking and on persuasion in that it implies that truth can be both known (truth seeking) and "proved" (persuasion). Argument in this sense was closely associated with mathematical demonstrations in which you move from axioms to proofs through formulae. An argument of this sort is nearly irrefutable—unless we play Callicles and reject the axioms.

Today, on the other hand, *to argue* is usually taken to mean something like "to provide grounds for inferring." The better the argument, the better the reasons and evidence one provides, the more likely is the audience to infer what the arguer has inferred. Instead of "proving" one's claim, the best an arguer can hope for is to make an audience *more likely to agree with* the arguer's claim. One contemporary philosopher says that argument can hope only to "increase adherence" to ideas, not absolutely convince an audience of the necessary truth of ideas.

In the twentieth century, absolute, demonstrable truth is seen by many thinkers, from physicists to philosophers, as an illusion. Some would argue that truth is merely a product of human beings' talking and arguing with each other.

These thinkers say that when considering questions of interpretation, meaning, or value one can never tell for certain whether an assertion is true—not by examining the physical universe more closely or by reasoning one's way toward some Platonic form or by receiving a mystical revelation. The closest one can come to truth is through the confirmation of one's views from others in a community of peers. "Truth" in any field of knowledge, say these thinkers, is simply an agreement of knowledgeable people in that field.

To illustrate the relevance of Callicles to contemporary society, suppose for the moment that we wanted to ask whether sexual fidelity is a virtue. A Socratic approach would assume a single, real Truth about the value of sexual fidelity, one that could be discovered through a gradual peeling away of wrong answers. Callicles, meanwhile, would assume that sexual morality is culturally relative; hence, he might point out all the societies in which monogamous fidelity for one or both sexes is not the norm. Clearly, our world is more like Callicles'. We are all exposed to multiple cultural perspectives directly and indirectly. Through television, newspapers, travel, and education we experience ways of thinking and valuing that are different from our own. It is difficult to ignore the fact that our personal values are not universally shared or even respected. Thus, we're all faced with the need to justify our views in such a diverse society.

It should be clear, then, that when we speak of the truth-seeking aim of argument, we mean not the discovery of an absolute "right answer," but the willingness to think through the complexity of an issue and to consider respectfully a wide range of views. The process of argument allows social groups, through the thoughtful exchange of ideas, to seek the best solution to a problem. The value of argument is its ability to help social groups make decisions in a rational and humane way without resorting to violence or to other assertions of raw power.

FOR CLASS DISCUSSION

On any given day, newspapers provide evidence of the complexity of living in a pluralistic culture. Issues that could be readily decided in a completely homogeneous culture raise many questions for us in a society that has few shared assumptions.

What follows are two brief news stories from the Associated Press wires. Choose one story or the other and conduct a "simulation game" in which various class members role play the points of view of the characters involved in the controversy. If you choose the first case, for example, one class member should role-play the attorney of the woman refusing the Caesarean section, another the "court-appointed representative of the woman's fetus," and another the doctor. If you wish, conduct a court hearing in which other members role-play a judge, cross-examining attorneys, and a jury. No matter which case you choose, your class's goal should be to represent each point of view as fully and sympathetically as possible to help you realize the complexity of the values in conflict.

Illinois Court Won't Hear Case
of Mom Who Refuses Surgery

1   CHICAGO—A complex legal battle over a Chicago woman's refusal to undergo a Caesarean section, even though it could save the life of her unborn child, essentially was settled yesterday when the state's highest court refused to hear the case.

2   The court declined to review a lower court's ruling that the woman should not be forced to submit to surgery in a case that pitted the rights of the woman, referred to in court as "Mother Doe," against those of her fetus.

3   The 22-year-old Chicago woman, now in the 37th week of her pregnancy, refused her doctors' advice to have the surgery because she believes God intended her to deliver the child naturally.

4   The woman's attorneys argued that the operation would violate her constitutional rights to privacy and the free exercise of her religious beliefs.

5   Cook County Public Guardian Patrick Murphy, the court-appointed representative of the woman's fetus, said he would file a petition with the U.S. Supreme Court asking it to hear the case. He has 90 days to file the petition, but he acknowledged future action would probably come too late.

6   Doctors say the fetus is not receiving enough oxygen from the placenta and will either die or be retarded unless it is delivered by Caesarean section. Despite that diagnosis, the mother has stressed her faith in God's healing powers and refused doctors' advice to submit to the operation.

Homeless Hit the Streets
to Protest Proposed Ban

1   SEATTLE—The homeless stood up for themselves by sitting down in a peaceful but vocal protest yesterday in Seattle's University District.

2   About 50 people met at noon to criticize a proposed set of city ordinances that would ban panhandlers from sitting on sidewalks, put them in jail for repeatedly urinating in public, and crack down on "intimidating" street behavior.

3   "Sitting is not a crime," read poster boards that feature mug shots of Seattle City Attorney Mark Sidran, who is pushing for the new laws. [. . .] "This is city property; the police want to tell us we can't sit here," yelled one man named R.C. as he sat cross-legged outside a pizza establishment.

4   Marsha Shaiman stood outside the University Book Store holding a poster and waving it at passing cars. She is not homeless, but was one of many activists in the crowd. "I qualify as a privileged white yuppie," she said. "I'm offended that the privileged people in this country are pointing at the poor, and people of color, and say they're causing problems. They're being used as scapegoats."

Many local merchants support the ban saying that panhandlers hurt business by in-   5
timidating shoppers and fouling the area with the odor of urine, vomited wine, and sometimes even feces.

A SUCCESSFUL PROCESS
OF ARGUMENTATION:
THE WELL-FUNCTIONING COMMITTEE

We have said that neither the fist-banging speaker nor the college debate team
represents our ideal image of argument. The best image for us, as we have implied,
is a well-functioning small group seeking a solution to a problem. In professional
life such small groups usually take the form of committees.

We must acknowledge that many people find committee deliberations hopelessly muddled and directionless—the very antithesis of good argumentation. Our
collective suspicion of committees is manifest in the many jokes we make about
them. (For example, do you know the definition of the word *committee*? It's a place
where people keep minutes and waste hours. Or: What is a zebra? A horse designed by a committee.)

Our society relies on committees, however, for the same reason that Winston
Churchill preferred democracy: However imperfect it may be, the alternatives are
worse. A single individual making decisions may be quirky, idiosyncratic, and in-
sensitive to the effects of a decision on different groups of people; worse yet, he or
she may pursue self-interests to the detriment of an entire group. But too large a
group makes argumentative discussion impossible. Hence, people have generally
found it useful to delegate many decision- and policy-making tasks to a smaller,
representative group—a committee.

We use the word *committee* in its broadest sense to indicate all sorts of important work that grows out of group conversation and debate. The Declaration of
Independence is essentially a committee document with Thomas Jefferson as the
chair. Similarly, the U.S. Supreme Court is in effect a committee of nine judges who
rely heavily, as numerous books and articles have demonstrated, on small-group
decision-making processes to reach their judgments and formulate their legal
briefs.

To illustrate our committee model for argument, let's briefly consider the
workings of a university committee on which coauthor John Ramage once served,
the University Standards Committee. The Arizona State University (ASU) Standards Committee plays a role in university life analogous to that of the Supreme
Court in civic life. It's the final court of appeal for ASU students seeking exceptions to various rules that govern their academic lives (such as registering under
a different catalog, waiving a required course, or being allowed to retake a course
for the third time).

The Standards Committee is a large committee, comprising nearly two dozen members who represent the whole spectrum of departments and offices across campus. Every two weeks, the committee meets for two or more hours to consider between twenty and forty appeals. Several days before each meeting, committee members receive a hefty packet of materials relevant to the cases (such as, originals of the students' appeals, including the responses of those who've heard the appeal earlier, complete transcripts of each student's grades, and any supporting material or new information the student might wish to provide). Students may, if they choose, appear before the committee personally to make their cases.

The issues that regularly come before the committee draw forth all the argumentative strategies discussed in detail throughout this text. For example, all of the argument types discussed in Part Three regularly surface during committee deliberations. The committee deals with definition issues ("Is math anxiety a 'learning disability' for purposes of exempting a student from a math requirement? If so, what criteria can we establish for math anxiety?"); cause/consequence issues ("What were the causes of this student's sudden poor performance during spring semester?" "What will be the consequences of approving or denying her appeal?"); resemblance issues ("How is this case similar to an earlier case that we considered?"); evaluation issues ("Which criteria should take precedence in assessing this sort of appeal?"); and proposal issues ("Should we make it a policy to allow course X to substitute for course Y in the General Studies requirements?").

On any given day, the committee's deliberations showed how dialogue can lead to clarification of thinking. On many occasions, committee members' initial views shifted as they listened to opposing arguments. In one case, for example, a student petitioned to change the catalog under which she was supposed to graduate because the difference in requirements would let her graduate a half-year sooner. Initially, most committee members opposed the petition. They reminded the committee that in several earlier cases it had denied petitions to change catalogs if the petitioner's intent was to evade the more rigorous graduation requirements imposed by a new General Studies curriculum. Moreover, the committee was reminded that letting one student change catalogs was unfair to other students who had to meet the more rigorous graduation standards.

However, after emphatic negative arguments had been presented, a few committee members began to voice support for the student's case. While acknowledging the truth of what other committee members had said, they pointed out reasons to support the petition. The young woman in question had taken most of the required General Studies courses; it was mostly changes in the requirements for her major that delayed her graduation. Moreover, she had performed quite well in what everyone acknowledged to be a demanding course of study. Although the committee had indeed turned down previous petitions of this nature, in none of those cases had the consequences of denial been so dire for the student.

After extended negotiations between the two sides on this issue, the student was allowed to change catalogs. Although the committee was reluctant to set a bad precedent (those who resisted the petition foresaw a deluge of similar petitions from less worthy candidates), it recognized unique circumstances that legitimately made this petitioner's case different. Moreover, the rigor of the student's curriculum, the primary concern of those who opposed the change, was shown to be greater than the rigor of many who graduated under the newer catalog.

As the previous illustration suggests, what allowed the committee to function as well as it did was the fundamental civility of its members and their collective concern that their decisions be just. Unlike some committees, this committee made many decisions, the consequences of which were not trivial for the people involved. Because of the significance of these outcomes, committee members were more willing than they otherwise might have been to concede a point to another member in the name of reaching a better decision and to view their deliberations as an ongoing process of negotiation rather than a series of win-lose debates.

To give you firsthand experience at using argument as a process of clarification, we conclude this chapter with an actual case that came before the University Standards Committee. We invite you to read the following letter, pretending that you are a member of the University Standards Committee, and then proceed to the exercises that follow.

Petition to Waive the University Mathematics Requirement

Standards Committee Members,

1   I am a 43-year-old member of the Pawnee Tribe of Oklahoma and a very nontraditional student currently pursuing Justice Studies at the Arizona State University (ASU) College of Public Programs. I entered college as the first step toward completion of my goal—becoming legal counsel for my tribe, and statesman.

2   I come before this committee in good faith to request that ASU suspend, in my special case, its mathematics requirement for undergraduate degree completion so I may enter the ASU college of Law during Fall 1993. The point I wish to make to this committee is this: I do not need algebraic skills; I will never use algebra in my intended profession; and, if forced to comply with ASU's algebra requirement, I will be needlessly prevented from graduating in time to enter law school next fall and face an idle academic year before my next opportunity in 1994. I will address each of these points in turn, but a few words concerning my academic credentials are in order first.

3   Two years ago, I made a vow of moral commitment to seek out and confront injustice. In September of 1990, I enrolled in college. Although I had only the benefit of a ninth grade education, I took the General Equivalency Diploma (GED) examination and placed in the top ten percent of those, nationwide, who took the test. On the basis of this score I was accepted into Scottsdale Community College (SCC). This step made me the first in my entire family, and practically in my tribe, to enter college. During my first year at SCC I maintained a 4.0 GPA, I was placed on the President's list twice, was active in the Honors Program,

received the Honors Award of Merit in English Humanities, and was conferred an Honors Scholarship (see attached) for the Academic year of 1991–1992 which I declined, opting to enroll in ASU instead.

4   At the beginning of the 1991 summer semester, I transferred to ASU. I chose to graduate from ASU because of the courses offered in American Indian studies, an important field ignored by most other Universities but necessary to my commitment. At ASU I currently maintain a 3.6 GPA, although my cumulative GPA is closer to 3.9, I am a member of the Honors and Justice Colleges, was appointed to the Dean's List, and awarded ASU's prestigious Maroon and Gold Scholarship twice. My academic standing is impeccable. I will enter the ASU College of Law to study Indian and criminal law during the Fall of 1993—if this petition is approved. Upon successful completion of my juris doctorate I will return to Oklahoma to become active in the administration of Pawnee tribal affairs as tribal attorney and advisor, and vigorously prosecute our right to sovereignty before the Congress of the United States.

5   When I began my "college experience," I set a rigid time schedule for the completion of my goal. By the terms of that self-imposed schedule, founded in my belief that I have already wasted many productive years, I allowed myself thirty-five months in which to achieve my Bachelor of Science degree in Justice Studies, for indeed justice is my concern, and another thirty-six months in which to earn my juris doctorate—summa cum laude. Consistent with my approach to all endeavors, I fell upon this task with zeal. I have willingly assumed the burden of carrying substantial academic loads during fall, spring and summer semesters. My problem now lies in the fact that in order to satisfy the University's math requirement to graduate I must still take MAT-106 and MAT-117. I submit that these mathematics courses are irrelevant to my goals, and present a barrier to my fall matriculation into law school.

6   Upon consideration of my dilemma, the questions emerged: Why do I need college algebra (MAT-117)? Is college algebra necessary for studying American Indian law? Will I use college algebra in my chosen field? What will the University gain or lose, from my taking college algebra—or not? I decided I should resolve these questions.

7   I began my inquiry with the question: "Why do I need college algebra (MAT-117)?" I consulted Mr. Jim _____ of the Justice College and presented this question to him. He referred to the current ASU catalog and delineated the following answer: I need college algebra (1) for a minimum level of math competency in my chosen field, and (2) to satisfy the university math requirement in order to graduate. My reply to the first answer is this: I already possess ample math skills, both practical and academic; and, I have no need for algebra in my chosen field. How do I know this? During the spring 1992 semester at ASU I successfully completed introductory algebra (MAT-077), scoring the highest class grade on one test (see attached transcript and test). More noteworthy is the fact that I was a machine and welding contractor for fifteen years. I used geometry and algebra commonly in the design of many welded structures. I am proficient in the use of Computer Assisted Design (CAD) programs, designing and drawing all my own blueprints for jobs. My blueprints and designs are always approved by city planning departments. For example, my most recent job consisted of the manufacture, transportation and installation of one linear mile of anodized, aluminum handrailing at a luxury resort condo on Maui, Hawaii. I applied extensive use of

math to calculate the amount of raw materials to order, the logistics of mass production and transportation for both men and materials from Mesa to Maui, the job site installation itself, and cash flow. I have successfully completed many jobs of this nature—all without a mathematical hitch. As to the application of math competency in my chosen field, I can guarantee this committee that there will not be a time in my practice of Indian law that I will need algebra. If an occasion ever occurs that I need algebra, I will hire a mathematician, just as I would an engineer if I need engineering, or a surgeon if I need an operation.

I then contacted Dr. _____ of the ASU Mathematics Department and presented him   8
with the same question: "Why do I need college algebra?" He replied: (1) for a well rounded education; (2) to develop creative thinking; and (3) to satisfy the university math requirement in order to graduate. Responding to the first answer, I have a "well rounded education." My need is for a specific education in justice and American Indian law. In fact, I do not really need the degree to practice Indian law as representative of my tribe, just the knowledge. Regarding the second, I do not need to develop my creative thinking. It has been honed to a keen edge for many years. For example, as a steel contractor, I commonly create huge, beautiful and intricate structures from raw materials. Contracting is not my only experience in creative thinking. For twenty-five years I have also enjoyed the status of being one of this country's foremost designers and builders of racebikes. Machines I have designed and brought into existence from my imagination have topped some of Japan and Europe's best engineering efforts. To illustrate this point, in 1984 I rode a bike of my own design to an international victory over Honda, Suzuki, Laverda, BMW and Yamaha. I have excelled at creative thinking my entire life—I called it survival.

Expanding on the question of why I need college algebra, I contacted a few friends who   9
are practicing attorneys. All responded to my question in similar manner. One, Mr. Billy _____, Esq., whose law firm is in Tempe, answered my two questions as follows: "When you attended law school, were there any courses you took which required algebra?" His response was "no." "Have you ever needed algebra during the many years of your practice?" Again, his response was "no." All agreed there was not a single occasion when they had need for algebra in their professional careers.

Just to make sure of my position, I contacted the ASU College of Law, and among   10
others, spoke to Ms. Sierra _____. I submitted the question "What law school courses will I encounter in which I will need algebra?" The unanimous reply was, they knew of none.

I am not proposing that the number of credit hours I need for graduation be lowered.   11
In fact, I am more than willing to substitute another course or two in its place. I am not trying to get out of anything hard or distasteful, for that is certainly not my style. I am seeking only to dispose of an unnecessary item in my studies, one which will prevent me from entering law school this fall—breaking my stride. So little holds up so much.

I agree that a young adult directly out of high school may not know that he needs   12
algebraic skills. Understandably, he does not know what his future holds—but I am not that young adult. I claim the advantage. I know precisely what my future holds and that future holds no possibility of my needing college algebra.

Physically confronting injustice is my end. On reservations where government apathy   13
allows rapacious pedophiles to pose as teachers; in a country where a million and a half American Indians are held hostage as second rate human beings whose despair results in a

suicide, alcohol and drug abuse rate second to no other people; in prisons where helpless inmates are beaten like dogs by sadistic guards who should be the inmates—this is the realm of my chosen field—the disenfranchised. In this netherworld, algebra and justice exist independently of one another.

14   In summary, I am convinced that I do not need college algebra for a minimum level of math competency in my chosen field. I do not need college algebra for a well rounded education, nor to develop my creative thinking. I do not need algebra to take the LSAT. I do not need algebra for any courses in law school, nor will I for any purpose in the practice of American Indian law. It remains only that I need college algebra in order to graduate.

15   I promise this committee that ASU's integrity will not be compromised in any way by approving this waiver. Moreover, I assure this committee that despite not having a formal accreditation in algebra, I will prove to be nothing less than an asset to this University and its Indian community, both to which I belong, and I will continue to set a standard for integrity, excellence and perseverance for all who follow. Therefore, I ask this committee, for all the reasons described above, to approve and initiate the waiver of my University mathematics requirement.

[Signed: Gordon Adams]

FOR CLASS DISCUSSION

1. Before class discussion, decide how you would vote on this issue. Should this student be exempted from the math requirement? Write out the reasons for your decision.

2. Working in small groups or as a whole class, pretend that you are the University Standards Committee, and arrive at a group decision on whether to exempt this student from the math requirement.

3. After the discussion, write for five to ten minutes in a journal or notebook describing how your thinking evolved during the discussion. Did any of your classmates' views cause you to rethink your own? Class members should share with each other their descriptions of how the process of argument led to clarification of their own thinking.

We designed this exercise to help you experience argument as a clarifying process. But we had another purpose. We also designed the exercise to stimulate thinking about a problem we introduced at the beginning of this chapter: the difference between argument as clarification and argument as persuasion. Is a good argument necessarily a persuasive argument? In our opinion, this student's letter to the committee is a *good* argument. The student writes well, takes a clear stand, offers good reasons for his position, and supports his reasons with effective evidence. To what extent, however, is the letter a *persuasive* argument? Did it win its case? You know how you and your classmates stand on this issue. But what do you think the University Standards Committee at ASU actually decided during its deliberations?

We will return to this case again in Chapter 7.

CONCLUSION

In this chapter we have explored some of the complexities of argument, showing you why we believe that argument is a matter not of fist banging or of win-lose debate but of finding, through a process of rational inquiry, the best solution to a problem or issue. What is our advice for you at the close of this introductory chapter? Briefly, to see the purpose of argument as truth seeking as well as persuasion. We suggest that throughout the process of argument you seek out a wide range of views, that you especially welcome views different from your own, that you treat these views respectfully, and that you see them as intelligent and rationally defensible. (Hence you must look carefully at the reasons and evidence on which they are based).

Our goal in this text is to help you learn skills of argument. If you choose, you can use these skills, like Callicles, to argue any side of any issue. Yet we hope you won't. We hope that, like Socrates, you will use argument for truth seeking and that you will consequently find yourselves, on at least some occasions, changing your position on an issue while writing a rough draft (a sure sign that the process of arguing has complicated your views). We believe that the skills of reason and inquiry developed through the writing of arguments can help you get a clearer sense of who you are. If our culture sets you adrift in pluralism, argument can help you take a stand, to say, "These things I believe." In this text we will not pretend to tell you what position to take on any given issue. But as responsible beings, you will often need to take a stand, to define yourself, to say, "Here are the reasons that choice A is better than choice B, not just for me but for you also." If this text helps you base your commitments and actions on reasonable grounds, then it will have been successful.

2 Reading Arguments

WHY READING ARGUMENTS IS IMPORTANT FOR WRITERS

In the previous chapter we explained how reading and writing arguments is a social phenomenon growing out of people's search for the best answers to questions. In this chapter we'll focus on the first half of that social dynamic—the thoughtful reading of arguments.

Much of the advice we offer about reading applies equally to listening. In fact, it is often helpful to think of reading as a conversation. We like to tell students that a college library is not so much a repository of information as a discussion frozen in time until you as reader bring it to life. Those books and articles, stacked neatly on library shelves or stored in Web sites or databases, are arguing with each other, carrying on a great extended conversation. As you read, you bring those conversations to life. And when you write in response to your reading, you enter those conversations.

SUGGESTIONS FOR IMPROVING YOUR READING PROCESS

Before we offer specific strategies for reading arguments, let's examine some general reading strategies applicable to most complex texts.

1. *Slow down.* Ads for speed-reading courses misleadingly suggest that expert readers read rapidly. In fact, experts read difficult texts slowly, often rereading them two or three times, treating their first readings like first drafts. They hold confusing passages in mental suspension, hoping that later parts of the essay will clarify earlier parts. They "nutshell" or summarize passages in the margins. They interact with the text by asking questions, expressing disagreements, linking the text with other readings or with personal experience.

2. *Get the dictionary habit.* When you can't tell a word's meaning from context, get in the habit of looking it up. One strategy is to make small check marks next to words you're unsure of; then look them up after you're done so as not to break your concentration.

3. *Lose your highlighter/find your pen.* Relying on yellow highlighters makes you too passive. Next time you get the urge to highlight a passage, write in the margin why you think it's important. Is it a major new point in the argument? A significant piece of support? A summary of the opposition? A particularly strong or particularly weak point? Use the margins to summarize the text, protest vehemently, ask questions, give assent—don't just color the pages.

4. *Reconstruct the rhetorical context.* Train yourself to ask questions such as these: Who is this author? What audience is he or she writing for? What occasion prompted this writing? What is the author's purpose? Any piece of writing makes more sense if you think of its author as a real person writing for some real purpose out of real historical context.

5. *Continue the conversation after your reading.* After you've read a text, try completing the following statements in a journal: "The most significant question this essay raises is. . . ." "The most important thing I learned from this essay is. . . ." "I agree with the author about. . . ." "However, I have doubts about. . . ." These questions help you remember the reading and urge you to respond actively to it.

6. *Try "translating" difficult passages.* When you stumble over a difficult passage, try "translating" it into your own words. Converting the passage into your own language forces you to focus on the precise meanings of words. Although your translation may not be exactly what the author intended, you see more clearly where the sources of confusion lie and what the likely range of meanings might be.

STRATEGIES FOR READING ARGUMENTS: AN OVERVIEW

Whereas the preceding suggestions can be applied to all sorts of reading tasks, the rest of this chapter focuses on reading strategies specific to arguments. Because argument begins in disagreements within a social community, we recommend that you examine any argument as if it were only one voice in a larger conversation. We therefore recommend the following strategies in sequence:

1. Read as a believer.
2. Read as a doubter.
3. Consider alternative views and analyze sources of disagreement.
4. Use disagreement productively to prompt further investigation.

Let's now explore each of these strategies in turn.

STRATEGY 1: READING AS A BELIEVER

When you read as a believer, you practice what psychologist Carl Rogers calls *empathic listening*. Empathic listening requires you to see the world through the author's eyes, to adopt temporarily the author's beliefs and values, and to suspend your skepticism and biases long enough to hear what the author is saying.

Because empathic listening is such a vital skill, we will invite you shortly to try it on a controversial op-ed piece from conservative columnist George Will on the subject of equal pay for men and women. First, though, here is some background.

Each year, the federal government, using data collected by the Census Bureau and other sources, publishes wage data showing earnings broken down by state, region, profession, ethnicity, gender, and other categories. One of the most controversial statistics is the wage gap between the average earnings of men and women. The figure widely published in 1999, based on 1996 census data, was that women, on average, earn 74 cents to a man's dollar. When President Bill Clinton, in his 1999 State of the Union address, vowed to enforce equal-pay laws, he received hearty bipartisan applause. However, the issue is being hotly debated in both state legislatures and the United States Congress.

FOR CLASS DISCUSSION

Working individually or in groups, respond to the following questions:

1. Do you think the pay gap between women and men is a small, moderate, or major social and economic problem?

2. Has this problem affected you or your family? How might this problem affect you in the future? (Think ahead to your career and possible plans for a family.)

Now individually or in groups, examine Figure 2.1, which reproduces a Web page from the site of the nation's largest labor organization, the AFL-CIO (American Federation of Labor and Congress of Industrial Organizations). This advocacy Web site presents one of the main perspectives on the issue of pay equity. It aims to persuade workers to join the cause of pay equity for women. After looking at this site's examples of the wage gap in different occupational categories, respond to the following questions:

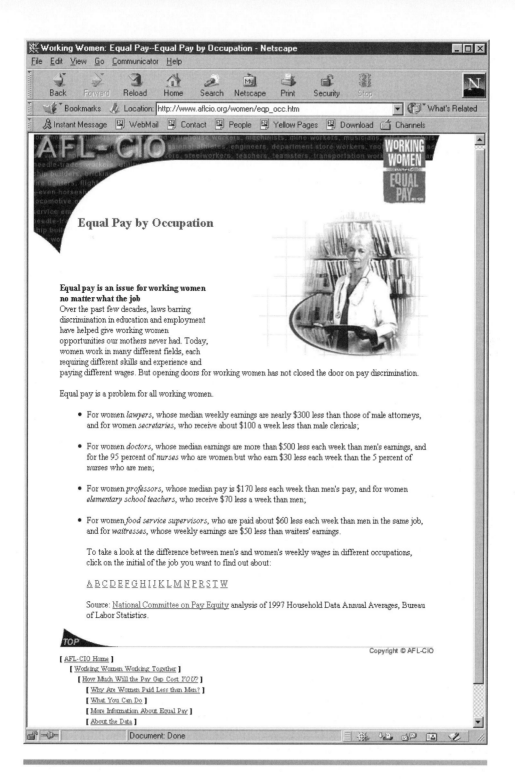

Equal Pay by Occupation

Equal pay is an issue for working women no matter what the job
Over the past few decades, laws barring discrimination in education and employment have helped give working women opportunities our mothers never had. Today, women work in many different fields, each requiring different skills and experience and paying different wages. But opening doors for working women has not closed the door on pay discrimination.

Equal pay is a problem for all working women.

- For women *lawyers*, whose median weekly earnings are nearly $300 less than those of male attorneys, and for women *secretaries*, who receive about $100 a week less than male clericals;

- For women *doctors*, whose median earnings are more than $500 less each week than men's earnings, and for the 95 percent of *nurses* who are women but who earn $30 less each week than the 5 percent of nurses who are men;

- For women *professors*, whose median pay is $170 less each week than men's pay, and for women *elementary school teachers*, who receive $70 less a week than men;

- For women *food service supervisors*, who are paid about $60 less each week than men in the same job, and for *waitresses*, whose weekly earnings are $50 less than waiters' earnings.

To take a look at the difference between men's and women's weekly wages in different occupations, click on the initial of the job you want to find out about:

A B C D E F G H I J K L M N P R S T W

Source: National Committee on Pay Equity analysis of 1997 Household Data Annual Averages, Bureau of Labor Statistics.

TOP

Copyright © AFL-CIO

[AFL-CIO Home]
[Working Women Working Together]
[How Much Will the Pay Gap Cost *YOU?*]
[Why Are Women Paid Less than Men?]
[What You Can Do]
[More Information About Equal Pay]
[About the Data]

FIGURE 2.1 Web page from the AFL-CIO Web site

1. What do you think are the causes of pay gaps between men and women?

2. Supporters of pay equity legislation generally have two areas of concern: First, they desire "equal pay for equal work." This idea means that female mechanics should receive the same pay as male mechanics or female college professors the same pay as male college professors. Second, they desire "equal pay for comparable work." This idea means that jobs held mostly by women, such as social workers, should pay the same wages as comparable jobs held mostly by men, such as parole officers. Supporters propose to measure comparable worth by using criteria such as education and training required for entry into the field, the levels of stress and responsibility demanded by the work, and the social value of the work. Based on these criteria, do you think an elementary teacher with an M.A. degree should earn more or less than an accountant with a B.A. degree? Do you think a secretary with an A.A. degree should earn more or less than an auto mechanic with an A.A. degree?

3. Who, if anyone, should be responsible for establishing fair pay? Businesses and employers alone? The government?

Now that you have some background on the pay equity issue, you are ready to read George Will's argument.

Lies, Damned Lies, and . . .

George F. Will

1   With the Dow Average nearing a fifth digit, Americans are cheerful. However, soon the women's division of the Great American Grievance Industry will weigh in, saying women remain trapped beneath the "glass ceiling" and in the "pink ghetto." Brace yourself for a blizzard of statistics purporting to prove that women are suffering a "wage gap" primarily caused by discrimination that requires government actions like affirmative action, quotas and set-asides.

2   But a counterblizzard has blown in from Diana Furchtgott-Roth and Christine Stolba, authors of "Women's Figures: An Illustrated Guide to the Economic Progress of Women in America." Furchtgott-Roth is a fellow at The American Enterprise Institute and Stolba is a historian living in Washington, and both had better mind their manners. Feminists are not famous for their sense of humor and may frown at the authors' dedication of their book to their husbands "who have always appreciated our figures."

3   The National Committee On Pay Equity and other participants in the theatrics of Equal Pay Day will not appreciate the figures Furchtgott-Roth and Stolba marshal. The premise of Equal Pay Day is that women work from Jan. 1 until early April essentially for no pay because women earn only 74 cents for every dollar men earn. That uninformative number is the basis for the allegation that the average woman loses approximately $420,000 in wages

and benefits during her working life. The 74 cents factoid is prima facie proof of "the de-meaning practice of wage discrimination," according to President Clinton, who opposes everything demeaning to women.

Furchtgott-Roth and Stolba argue that the 74 cents statistic is the product of faulty methodology that serves the political agenda of portraying women as victims needing yet more government intervention in the workplace. The authors demonstrate that income dis-parities between men and women have been closing rapidly and that sex discrimination, which has been illegal for 30 years, is a negligible cause of those that remain, which are largely the result of rational personal choices by women.   4

Between 1960 and 1994 women's wages grew 10 times faster than men's, and today, among people 27 to 33, women who have never had a child earn about 98 cents for every dollar men earn. Children change the earnings equations. They are the main reason that meaningful earnings contrasts must compare men and women who have similar experi-ences and life situations. Earnings differentials often reflect different professional paths that are cheerfully chosen because of different preferences, motivations, and expectations.   5

The "adjusted wage gap," adjusted for age, occupation, experience, education and time in the work force, is primarily the product of personal choices women make outside the work environment. Eighty percent of women bear children and 25 percent of working women work part-time, often to accommodate child rearing. Many women who expect to have chil-dren choose occupations where job flexibility compensates for somewhat lower pay, and occupations (e.g., teaching) in which job skills deteriorate slower than in others (e.g., engi-neering). And it is not sex discrimination that accounts for largely male employment in some relatively high-paying occupations (e.g., construction, oil drilling and many others) which place a premium on physical strength. (Workers in some such occupations pay a price: the 54 percent of all workers who are male account for 92 percent of all job-related deaths.)   6

Still, between 1974 and 1993 women's wages have been rising relative to men's in all age groups, and most dramatically among the youngest workers. The rise would be more dramatic if many women did not make understandable decisions to favor family over higher pay and more rapid job advancement purchased by 60-hour weeks on the fast track.   7

Some victimization theorists say the fast track is pointless for women because they are held down by the "glass ceiling" that limits their rise in business hierarchies. In 1995 the government's Glass Ceiling Commission (the propagandistic title prejudged the subject) saw proof of sex discrimination in the fact that women are only 5 percent of senior managers at Fortune 1000 industrial and Fortune 500 service companies. But Furchtgott-Roth and Stolba note that typical qualifications for such positions include an M.B.A. and 25 years' work experience. The pool of women with those qualifications is small, not because of cur-rent discrimination but because of women's expectations in the 1950s and 1960s. In 1970 women received only 4 percent of all M.B.A. degrees, 5 percent of law degrees.   8

Which lends support to the optimistic "pipeline" theory: women are rising in economic life as fast as they pour from the educational pipeline—which is faster than men. Since 1984 women have outnumbered men in undergraduate and graduate schools. Women are receiving a majority of two-year postsecondary degrees, bachelor's and master's degrees, almost 40 percent of M.B.A degrees, 40 percent of doctorates, more than 40 percent of law and medical degrees. Education improves economic opportunities—and opportunities   9 encourage education, which has higher rewards for women than for men because men without college degrees or even high-school diplomas can get those high-paying, physically demanding—and dangerous—jobs.

10   The supposed "pink ghetto" is where women are, in the Glass Ceiling Commission's words, "locked into" low-wage, low-prestige, dead-end jobs. Such overheated rhetoric ignores many women's rational sacrifices of pay and prestige for job flexibility in occupations in which skills survive years taken off for raising children. Women already predominate in the two economic sectors expected to grow fastest in the near future, service/trade/retail and finance/insurance/real estate.

11   The 74 cents statistic and related propaganda masquerading as social science are arrows in the quivers of those waging the American left's unending struggle to change the American premise, which stresses equality of opportunity, not equality of outcomes. Furchtgott-Roth and Stolba have better figures.

Summary Writing as a Way of Reading to Believe

Now that you have finished the article, ask yourself how well you "listened" to it. If you listened well, you should be able to write a summary of Will's argument in your own words. A *summary* (also called an *abstract*, a *précis*, or a *synopsis*) presents only a text's major points and eliminates supporting details. Writers often incorporate summaries of other writers' views into their own arguments, either to support their own claims or to represent alternative views that they intend to address. Summaries can be any length, depending on the writer's purposes, but usually they range from several sentences to one or two paragraphs.

Practicing the following steps should help you be a better summary writer:

Step 1:   Read the argument first for general meaning. Don't judge it; put your objections aside; just follow the writer's meaning, trying to see the issue from the writer's perspective. Try to adopt the writer's values and belief system. Walk in the writer's shoes.

Step 2:   Read the argument slowly a second and a third time, writing in the margins brief *does* and *says* statements for each paragraph (or group of closely connected paragraphs). A *does* statement identifies a paragraph's function, such as "summarizes an opposing view," "introduces a supporting reason," "gives an example," or "uses statistics to support the previous point." A *says* statement summarizes a paragraph's content. Figure 2.2 shows a page from a passage from Will's article with *does* and *says* statements intermixed in the margins. What follows are our *does* and *says* statements for the first six paragraphs of Will's article.

DOES/SAYS ANALYSIS OF WILL'S ARTICLE

Paragraph 1:   *Does:* Introduces issue by summarizing the wage gap argument that Will opposes. *Says:* Although most Americans are cheerful about the

Furchtgott-Roth and Stolba argue that the 74 cents statistic is the product of faulty methodology that serves the political agenda of portraying women as victims needing yet more government intervention in the workplace. The authors demonstrate that income disparities between men and women have been closing rapidly and that sex discrimination, which has been illegal for 30 years, is a negligible cause of those that remain, which are largely the result of rational personal choices by women.   [4]

74¢ statistic is faulty. Sex discrimination is negligible. Gap caused by personal choices.

Between 1960 and 1994 women's wages grew 10 times faster than men's, and today, among people 27 to 33, women who have never had a child earn about 98 cents for every dollar men earn. Children change the earnings equations. They are the main reason that meaningful earnings contrasts must compare men and women who have similar experiences and life situations. Earnings differentials often reflect different professional paths that are cheerfully chosen because of different preferences, motivations, and expectations.   [5]

Women's wages in general rising faster than men's.
Main cause of women's lower pay is children.

The "adjusted wage gap," adjusted for age, occupation, experience, education and time in the work force, is primarily the product of personal choices women make outside the work environment. Eighty percent of women bear children and 25 percent of working women work part-time, often to accommodate child rearing. Many women who expect to have children choose occupations where job flexibility compensates for somewhat lower pay, and occupations (e.g., teaching) in which job skills deteriorate slower than in others (e.g., engineering). And it is not sex discrimination that accounts for largely male employment in some relatively high-paying occupations (e.g., construction, oil drilling and many others) which place a premium on physical strength. (Workers in some such occupations pay a price: the 54 percent of all workers who are male account for 92 percent of all job-related deaths.)   [6]

Women choose careers that accommodate child-rearing.

Some lower paying female jobs result of work flexibility   Many higher paying male jobs result of danger

Still, between 1974 and 1993 women's wages have been rising relative to men's in all age groups, and most dramatically among the youngest workers. The rise would be more dramatic if many women did not make understandable decisions to favor family over higher pay and more rapid job advancement purchased by 60-hour weeks on the fast track.   [7]

Dramatic rise in women's wages would be higher if women didn't favor family.

Some victimization theorists say the fast track is pointless for women because they are held down by the "glass ceiling" that limits their rise in business hierarchies. In 1995 the government's Glass Ceiling Commission (the propagandistic title prejudged the subject) saw proof of sex discrimination in the fact that women are only 5 percent of senior managers at Fortune 1000 industrial and Fortune 500 service companies. But Furchtgott-Roth and Stolba note that typical qualifications for such positions include an M.B.A. and 25 years' work experience. The pool of women with those qualifications is small, not because of current discrimination but because of women's expectations in the 1950s and 1960s. In 1970 women received only 4 percent of all M.B.A. degrees, 5 percent of law degrees.   [8]

Refutes glass ceiling argument. Women haven't been in professional jobs long enough to reach highest levels.

FIGURE 2.2   Reading-to-believe notes for Will argument

boom economy, the "American Grievance Industry" will soon complain that women suffer a wage gap that will require government intervention.

Paragraph 2: *Does:* Introduces two authors whose research debunks the wage gap argument. *Says:* Diana Furchtgott-Roth and Christine Stolba provide a very different interpretation of the data on men's and women's wages.

Paragraph 3: *Does:* Summarizes the wage gap argument of the National Committee on Pay Equity. *Says:* According to the National Committee on Pay Equity, women earn only 74 cents for every dollar that men earn, so the average woman loses $420,000 in wages over a career, thus proving wage discrimination.

Paragraph 4: *Does:* Summarizes the counterargument of Diana Furchtgott-Roth and Christine Stolba. *Says:* The 74-cent "factoid" is not proof of wage discrimination; the pay gap has been closing rapidly, and whatever pay gap remains can be explained by women's personal career choices.

Paragraph 5: *Does:* Further develops this argument by focusing on the impact on children. *Says:* Women's pay has risen ten times faster than men's since 1960, and childless women ages 27 to 33 earn 98 percent of men's wages; having children makes the difference, causing women to choose different career paths.

Paragraph 6: *Does:* Further develops the child-raising explanation. *Says:* The lower wages of women are the result of women's choosing jobs with flexibility in occupations from which they can take time off.

FOR CLASS DISCUSSION

Working individually or in groups, make *does* and *says* statements for the remaining paragraphs in Will's article.

Step 3: Examine your *does* and *says* statements to determine the major sections of the argument, and create a list of major points and subpoints. If you are visually oriented, you may prefer to make a flowchart or diagram of the article. (See Figure 2.3 for our flowchart of Will's article.)

Step 4: Turn your list, outline, flowchart, or diagram into a prose summary. Typically, writers do this in one of two ways. Some start by joining all their *says* statements into a lengthy paragraph-by-paragraph summary and then prune it. Others start with a one-sentence summary of the argument's thesis and major supporting reasons and then gradually flesh it out with more supporting ideas.

Step 5: Revise your summary until it is the desired length and is sufficiently clear, concise, and complete. When you incorporate a summary of someone else's argument into your own essay, you must distinguish that author's

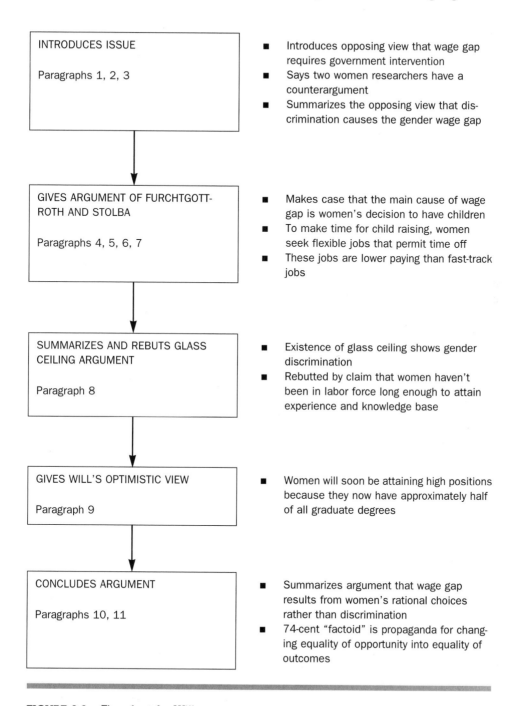

FIGURE 2.3   Flowchart for Will argument

words and ideas from your own by using *attributive tags* (expressions like "Will says," "according to Will," or "Will further explains"), by putting any directly borrowed language in quotation marks, and by citing the original author using appropriate conventions for documenting sources.*

As illustrations, we will show you our summaries of Will's article—a one-paragraph version and a single-sentence version. In the one-paragraph version we illustrate the MLA documentation system in which page numbers for direct quotations are placed in parentheses after the quotation and complete bibliographic information is placed in a Works Cited list at the end of the paper. See Chapter 17 for a complete explanation of the MLA and APA documentation systems.

ONE-PARAGRAPH SUMMARY OF WILL'S ARGUMENT

Identification of author and source

Insertion of a short quotation; MLA documentation style shows page number in parentheses

attributive tag

main claim of the article

attributive tag

attributive tag

attributive tag with transition

another short quotation

attributive tag

attributive tag

        In a recent *Newsweek* editorial entitled "Lies, Damned Lies and . . .," conservative columnist George Will questions the claim that women, in earning 74 cents to a man's dollar, are victims of gender-based wage discrimination that "requires government actions like affirmative action, quotas, and set-asides" (28). Citing a recent book by Diana Furchtgott-Roth and Christine Stolba, Will argues that the 74-cents statistic is a "factoid" (29) that indicates personal career choices, not wage discrimination. Arguing that the wage gap is rapidly closing and has virtually disappeared for childless women between ages 27 and 33, Will claims that the remaining wage gap results from women's sacrificing pay and prestige for flexible jobs that allow time off for child raising. Women's dramatic increases in pay, Will asserts, would be even more dramatic if women desiring children didn't drop out of the fast track. Will then examines the objection made by "victimization theorists" (29) that the absence of high-level women executives in Fortune 1000 companies reveals a glass ceiling. He rebuts this argument by claiming that women haven't occupied professional jobs long enough to gain the experience and qualifications to attain upper-level positions, a situation that will soon end now that half of advanced degrees are earned by women. Will concludes that the 74-cent statistic is mere propaganda aimed at changing the traditional American value of equal opportunity into the leftist value of equal outcomes. (236 words)

---

*The most frequently used documentation systems in academic writing are those of the Modern Language Association (MLA) and the American Psychological Association (APA). Both systems are explained in detail in Chapter 17.

Will article cited completely in MLA documentation format; in a formal paper the Works Cited list begins a new page

Work Cited

Will, George F. "Lies, Damned Lies and . . . " *Newsweek* 29 Mar. 1999: 84. Rpt. in *Writing Arguments: A Rhetoric with Readings.* John D. Ramage, John C. Bean, and June Johnson. 5th ed. Needham: Allyn, 2001. 28–30.

ONE-SENTENCE SUMMARY OF WILL'S ARGUMENT

In a recent *Newsweek* editorial, conservative columnist George Will argues that the supposed wage gap between men and women is the result not of wage discrimination but of women's rational choices to sacrifice the pay and prestige of fast-track careers for flexible jobs that allow time off for child raising. (51 words)

Whether you write a very short summary or a more detailed one, your goal should be to come as close as possible to a fair, accurate, and balanced condensation of the author's argument and to represent the relationships among the parts fairly and accurately. We don't want to pretend that summary writing is easy; often it's not, especially if the argument is complex and if the author doesn't explicitly highlight his or her thesis and main supporting reasons. Nonetheless, being able to summarize the arguments of others in your own words is an important skill for arguers.

Suspending Doubt: Willing Your Own Belief in the Writer's Views

Summarizing an argument is only the first step in your effort to believe it. You must also suspend doubt and will yourself to adopt the writer's view. Suspending doubt is easy if you already agree with the author. But if an author's views affront your own values, then "believing" can be a hard but valuable exercise. By struggling to believe strange, threatening, or unfamiliar views, we can grow as learners and thinkers.

To believe an author, search your mind for personal experiences, values, and beliefs that affirm his or her argument. Here is how one female student wrote a journal entry trying to believe Will's argument.

JOURNAL ENTRY SHOWING STUDENT'S ATTEMPT TO BELIEVE WILL

When I first read the Web page from the AFL-CIO, I was outraged at the low pay women got. I thought that this was outright discrimination against women. I thought of all the money that women lost during their careers because men automatically got more pay than women just because people don't think women's work is worth as much. But then when I read George Will I saw that maybe there was another explanation. It is really true that many women worry how they are going to balance a career with having children, and I can see how women might seek out jobs that don't demand 80-hour workweeks and that give them some flexibility in hours so that they can spend more time with their children. Although I think dads ought to make the same sacrifices, I can see how women are more likely to focus on family issues. So if enough women are opting for less prestigious jobs, then the average wages of all women would be lower. It's a shame that women rather than men have to sacrifice their careers for children, but I can see Will's point that their lower earnings are a result of personal choices rather than discrimination.

STRATEGY 2: READING AS A DOUBTER

Reading as a believer is only half of being a powerful reader. You must also read as a doubter by raising objections, asking questions, expressing skepticism, and withholding assent. In the margins of the text, as a doubter, you add a new layer of notes demanding more proof, doubting evidence, challenging the author's assumptions and values, and so forth. Figure 2.4 shows one reader's marginal notes doubting Will's argument. (For purposes of illustration, this reader's believing notes—efforts to map and summarize the argument—aren't shown. Marginal notes usually intermingle believing and doubting commentary.)

▼ FOR CLASS DISCUSSION

Return now to Will's article, reading it skeptically. Raise questions, offer objections, and express doubts. Then, working as a class or in small groups, list all doubts you have about Will's argument.

Now that you've doubted Will's article, compare your doubts to some of those raised by our students.

- Are all Americans happy about the healthy stock market, as Will suggests? Does this mean economic prosperity for everyone? What about all those people who don't own stocks?
- Will implies that mainly feminists believe that a gender wage gap exists. Who exactly is protesting the gender wage gap?
- What is the background of the two authors—Diana Furchtgott-Roth and Christine Stolba?
- What is the source of Will's claim that in the last thirty years women's wages have been rising ten times faster than men's? The AFL-CIO Web page doesn't agree at all with this claim. We wonder what jobs and careers he is describing.
- Will automatically assumes that if a job is flexible it ought to pay less. What's wrong with good-paying jobs being flexible? Also, can you really

Furchtgott-Roth and Stolba argue that the 74 cents statistic is the product of faulty methodology that serves the political agenda of portraying women as victims needing yet more government intervention in the workplace. The authors demonstrate that income disparities between men and women have been closing rapidly and that sex discrimination, which has been illegal for 30 years, is a negligible cause of those that remain, which are largely the result of rational personal choices by women.   [4]

Between 1960 and 1994 women's wages grew 10 times faster than men's, and today, among people 27 to 33, women who have never had a child earn about 98 cents for every dollar men earn. Children change the earnings equations. They are the main reason that meaningful earnings contrasts must compare men and women who have similar experiences and life situations. Earnings differentials often reflect different professional paths that are (cheerfully) chosen because of different preferences, motivations, and expectations.   [5]

Why do these figures not jibe with AFL/CIO data from Web site?

Are these choices really "cheerful"??!

The "adjusted wage gap," adjusted for age, occupation, experience, education and time in the work force, is primarily the product of personal choices women make outside the work environment. Eighty percent of women bear children and 25 percent of working women work part-time, often to accommodate child rearing. Many women who expect to have children choose occupations where job flexibility compensates for somewhat lower pay, and occupations (e.g., teaching) in which job skills deteriorate slower than in others (e.g., engineering). And it is not sex discrimination that accounts for largely male employment in some relatively high-paying occupations (e.g., construction, oil drilling and many others) which place a premium on physical strength. (Workers in some such occupations pay a price: the 54 percent of all workers who are male account for 92 percent of all job-related deaths.)   [6]

Why should job flexibility have to mean lower pay?

Seems to justify low pay of teachers because job skills don't deteriorate rapidly. Doesn't seem right.

Still, between 1974 and 1993 women's wages have been rising relative to men's in all age groups, and most dramatically among the youngest workers. The rise would be more dramatic if many women did not make understandable decisions to favor family over higher pay and more rapid job advancement purchased by 60-hour weeks on the fast track.   [7]

What percentage of men actually work 60 hours per week?

Some victimization theorists say the fast track is pointless for women because they are held down by the "glass ceiling" that limits their rise in business hierarchies. In 1995 the government's Glass Ceiling Commission (the propagandistic title prejudged the subject) saw proof of sex discrimination in the fact that women are only 5 percent of senior managers at Fortune 1000 industrial and Fortune 500 service companies. But Furchtgott-Roth and Stolba note that typical qualifications for such positions include an M.B.A. and 25 years' work experience. The pool of women with those qualifications is small, not because of current discrimination but because of women's expectations in the 1950s and 1960s. In 1970 women received only 4 percent of all M.B.A. degrees, 5 percent of law degrees.   [8]

Interesting explanation. But what about all the examples we hear about outright discrimination against women? Old boys club?

FIGURE 2.3   Reading-to-doubt notes for Will argument

justify paying teachers less because teaching skills don't deteriorate rapidly if you take time off?

- Will assumes that if a job is dangerous (he mentions construction and others) it ought to pay more. What about jobs in athletic-shoe sweatshops in Asia and Mexico where women workers are exposed to dangerous chemicals? By Will's argument, they ought to be making a mint.

- Will assumes a two-parent family where the father has the main career. He completely ignores mothers who must work and single mothers who can't afford to take time off from work and who must pay for child care.

- He also ignores working-class women. His optimistic picture involves college-educated women who are willing to forgo having children.

These are only some of the objections that might be raised against Will's argument. Perhaps you and your classmates have other objections that are equally important. Our point is that you should practice "doubting" an argument as well as "believing" it. Both skills are essential. *Believing* helps you expand your view of the world or modify your arguments and beliefs in response to others. *Doubting* helps protect you from becoming overpowered by others' arguments and teaches you to stand back, consider, and weigh points carefully.

STRATEGY 3: SEEKING OUT ALTERNATIVE VIEWS AND ANALYZING SOURCES OF DISAGREEMENT

When you analyze an argument, you shouldn't isolate it from the general conversation of differing views that form its context. If you were an arbitrator, you wouldn't think of settling a dispute between A and B on the basis of A's testimony only. You would also insist on hearing B's side of the story. In analyzing an argument, therefore, you should try to seek out the views of those who disagree with the author to appreciate the full context of the issue.

As you listen to differing views, try to identify sources of disagreement, which often fall into two categories: (1) disagreement about the facts or reality of the case and (2) disagreement about underlying beliefs, values, or assumptions, including assumptions about definitions or appropriate analogies. Let's look at each in turn.

Disagreement about Facts or Reality

Theoretically, a fact is a piece of empirical data on which everyone agrees. Often, however, what one person takes as fact another takes as a misconception or an opinionated misinterpretation. Thus in the 1996 presidential elections, Bob Dole claimed that President Clinton had pushed through "the largest tax increase in U.S. history," whereas Clinton claimed in turn that an earlier tax increase passed during President Bush's administration (and voted for by Senator Dole) was in "adjusted dollars" much higher. Here Dole and Clinton disagree about "facts"—in this case, the truth represented by raw numbers that can be selected and arranged in a variety of ways. Other examples of disagreements about facts or reality include the following:

- In arguing whether silver-mercury amalgam tooth fillings should be banned, dental researchers disagree on the amount of mercury vapor released by older fillings; they also disagree on how much mercury vapor has to be present before it is harmful.

- In arguing about the legalization of drugs, writers disagree about the degree to which Prohibition reduced alcohol consumption; they also disagree on whether crack cocaine is "crimogenic" (has chemical properties that induce violent behavior).

Disagreement about Values, Beliefs, or Assumptions

A second source of disagreement concerns differences in values, beliefs, or assumptions. Here are some examples:

- Persons A and B might agree that a huge tax on gasoline would cut down on the consumption of petroleum. They might agree further that the world's supply of petroleum will eventually run out. Thus Persons A and B agree at the level of facts. But they might disagree about whether the United States should enact a huge gas tax. Person A might support the law in order to conserve oil. Person B might oppose it, perhaps because B believes that scientists will find alternative energy sources before the petroleum runs out or because B believes the short-term harm of such a tax outweighs distant benefits.

- Person A and Person B might agree that capital punishment deters potential murderers (an agreement on facts). Person A supports capital punishment for this reason, but Person B opposes it, believing that the taking of a human life is always wrong in principle even if the state does it legally (a disagreement about basic beliefs).

Sometimes differing beliefs or values present themselves as disagreements about definitions or appropriate analogies.

- Social Theorist A and Social Theorist B disagree about whether the covers of some women's magazines like *Cosmopolitan* are pornographic. This disagreement turns on the definition of *pornography,* with different definitions reflecting different underlying values and beliefs.

- In supporting a Texas law forbidding flag burning, Chief Justice William Rehnquist argued that desecration of a flag in the name of free speech is similar to desecrating the Washington Monument. He thus makes this analogy: Just as we would forbid desecration of a national monument, so should we forbid desecration of the flag. Opposing justices did not think the analogy was valid.

■ Person A and Person B disagree on whether it is ethically acceptable to have Down's syndrome children undergo plastic surgery to correct some of the facial abnormalities associated with this genetic condition. Person A supports the surgery, arguing that it is analogous to any other cosmetic surgeries done to improve appearance. Person B argues against such surgery, saying it is analogous to the racial self-hatred of some minority persons who have tried to change their ethnic appearance and become lily white. (The latter analogy argues that Down's syndrome is nothing to be ashamed of and that persons should take pride in their difference.)

FOR CLASS DISCUSSION

As discussed in Chapter 1, we live in a pluralistic world wherein many differing systems of values and beliefs compete for our allegiance. It is not surprising, therefore, that people disagree on the issue of pay equity. What follows is a syndicated column by journalist Ellen Goodman, written about the same time as George Will's *Newsweek* piece. Read Goodman's column carefully. Then, working as a whole class or in small groups, answer the following questions:

1. To what extent do Will and Goodman disagree about the basic facts concerning men's and women's wages?

2. In what ways are the disagreements between Will and Goodman related to their differing values, beliefs, and underlying assumptions?

A New Campaign for Pay Equity

Ellen Goodman

1   Somewhere in the recesses of my desk drawer there is a battered old pink pin bearing the message: 59 cents. This was not the price of the pin. It was the price of being a working woman circa 1969.

2   When these pins first began to appear at political conferences and conventions, women were earning 59 cents for every male dollar. Today, after 30 years of change, guess what? Women are earning 74 cents for every male dollar.

3   We have, in short, made economic progress at roughly half a cent a year. And before you choke over this breakneck pace, consider that three-fifths of the "progress" in closing the gender gap has come from men's falling wages, not women's rising wages.

Somehow or other the unsexy issue of the paycheck—equal pay for the same or equivalent work— dropped off the economic agenda. But it never left the minds of women. In surveys, women workers went on rating pay equity as "very important," and a third said they didn't have it. These are the same women who worry about balancing work and family, but many said, if we get a fair paycheck, we'll work it out.   4

Now, without a whole lot of fanfare, the issue of pay equity is back.   5

Remember that moment in the State of the Union address when the president told Congress to "make sure women and men get equal pay by strengthening enforcement of the equal pay laws"? To everyone's surprise he got a bipartisan Standing O. Since then the president proposed a $14 million equal pay initiative with most of the money going to better enforcement of the existing laws.   6

Now, as spring rolls in, new legislation for pay equity is being planted in 24 statehouses. This campaign has a two-part strategy. Part One: Get the old laws enforced. Part Two: Expand the notion of equal pay to include work of equal value.   7

As for Part One, if you have any doubts that the old laws aren't enforced enough, click onto the depressing union Web page, www.aflcio.org/women/. There's a lot of bad news.   8

The gender gap between male and female accountants is $201 a week. The gap between bartenders is $48. And, to pick another occupation out of a hat, the gap between male and female reporters and editors—ahem—is $163. The Web site will also help you figure out your own lifetime net loss.   9

As for Part Two, if you have any doubts that the old laws are too narrow, even if women were paid equally for the same job, most don't hold the same jobs. The jobs held primarily by women are "worth less" than the ones held primarily by men. That's true even if they involve roughly the same skills, effort, responsibility and working conditions.   10

For this reason, a 911 dispatcher is paid less in many places than an emergency operator at the Fire Department. A social worker is paid less than a probation officer. And in some states we have the tale of two nursery workers, one working with plants, the other with children. Guess who gets paid more?   11

Underlying the new campaign for pay equity are attitudes that are changing faster than wages. When the 59-cent button first appeared, it was assumed that any woman who wanted to get paid "like a man" had to do a "man's job."   12

At the Center for Policy Alternatives, Linda Tarr-Whelan says, "In this economy we have a diminished sense that the work women do with people is worth the same amount as the work men do with machines and dollars." Many are finally asking why "women's jobs" should be "worth less"?   13

For a long time, the glib excuse for the gender values gap has been market values: "the marketplace." Now it's being reframed as a matter of fairness and discrimination.   14

Not surprisingly, the legislative campaign will begin at the state level—where the percentage of women legislators is twice as high as in Congress—and build momentum before it goes to Washington.   15

In the meantime, there is a figure from the new survey to keep in mind: $200 billion. That's the amount families of working women lose every year to the gender gap. At that rate, half a cent a year just won't hack it.   16

Writing an Analysis of a Disagreement

A common writing assignment in argument courses asks students to analyze the sources of disagreement between two or more writers who take different positions on an issue. In writing such an analysis, you need to determine whether the writers disagree primarily about facts/reality or values (or both). Specifically, you should pose the following questions:

1. Where do the writers disagree about facts and/or the interpretation of facts?
2. Where do the writers disagree about underlying beliefs, values, or assumptions?
3. Where do the writers disagree about key definitions or about appropriate analogies? How do these differences imply differences in values, beliefs, or assumptions?

To illustrate how these three questions can help you write an analysis, we've constructed the following model: our own brief analysis of the sources of disagreement between Will and Goodman written as a short, formal essay.

An Analysis of the Sources of Disagreement
between Will and Goodman

1   The op-ed pieces of George Will and Ellen Goodman on the gender pay gap show disagreements of both fact and value. Will and Goodman agree that there is a gender wage gap reflected in the statistic that women earn only 74 cents to a man's dollar. However, they disagree about the causes of this pay gap. Goodman attributes the gap to gender discrimination in the workplace, whereas Will attributes it to women's personal choices in opting for flexible jobs that permit time off for child raising. Will therefore calls the 74-cent statistic a meaningless "factoid" rather than a meaningful fact.

2   This basic disagreement about cause explains each author's choice of data for framing the issue. Goodman accepts the statistics disseminated on the AFL-CIO web site. She believes that women have made little progress in closing the wage gap in the last thirty years and argues that "three-fifths of the 'progress' in closing the gender gap has come from men's falling wages, not women's rising wages" (40). Goodman sees discrimination operating at two levels—in the disparate wages paid to men and women in the same jobs and in the lower worth placed on women's jobs.

3   In contrast, Will's selection of data paints an optimistic picture of women's progress. Drawing statistics from Furchtgott-Roth and Stolba, Will asserts that the 74-cents figure is not accurate for all women, citing instead the data that women's wages grew ten times faster than men's in the last thirty years and that "today, among people 27 to 33, women

who have never had a child earn about 98 cents for every dollar men earn" (29). Thus Goodman and Will disagree on which "facts" are significant. Their selection of data creates different views of reality.

Will's and Goodman's different views of the facts reflect deep differences in values. Will, a political conservative, upholds the free market and opposes "government actions like affirmative action, quotas and set-asides" (28). Will claims that the American left is trying to "change the American premise, which stresses equality of opportunity, not equality of outcomes" (30). Underneath Will's belief that women "cheerfully" opt for lower-paying jobs in order to raise children is a belief in the two-parent, nuclear family and in traditional gender roles that make child rearing primarily the mother's responsibility. In contrast, Goodman, a political liberal, sees the gender wage gap as an unfair, discriminatory situation that should be corrected by government. Moreover, she sees it as a problem for men and for families as well as for women.

4

Typical of many op-ed pieces, both Will and Goodman adopt a breezy, joking style, but the different ways they joke also reflect and convey their values. Will adopts a flippant, trivializing "guess who is complaining now?" tone. His frequent use of the phrase "women's figures" and his statement that women are just making up the problem ("victimization theorists") and that feminists like to complain ("the Great American Grievance Industry") suggest an anger directed at feminists rather than a concern for the social consequences of low-paying jobs for women. Although less filled with loaded words, Goodman's piece is also a little sarcastic. Her "guess what—the problem isn't going away" tone conveys her impatience with free-market proponents and with people who don't acknowledge the discrimination that seems so clear to her: "We have, in short, made economic progress at roughly half a cent a year. And before you choke over this breakneck pace [. . .]" (40). Both writers risk alienating readers, but both appear to decide that their tone fits with their aims and perceptions of their audiences. At least, both writers whip up the enthusiasm of readers who already share their values.

5

Not surprisingly, both Will's and Goodman's different interpretations of facts and their different values lead to different proposals for action. Believing that women are making progress through higher education and more professional experience, Will asserts that the gender wage gap is correcting itself. In contrast, Goodman calls for immediate political action and change. She is concerned with working-class jobs as well as professional, white-collar careers and supports enactment of new laws to "expand the notion of equal pay to include work of equal value" (41).

6

In sum, Will and Goodman disagree about both facts and values.

7

Works Cited

Goodman, Ellen. "A New Campaign for Pay Equity." *Buffalo News* 16 Mar. 1999: 3B. Rpt. in *Writing Arguments: A Rhetoric with Readings.* John D. Ramage, John C. Bean, and June Johnson. 5th ed. Needham: Allyn, 2001. 40–41.

Will, George F. "Lies, Damned Lies and . . ." *Newsweek* 29 Mar. 1999: 84. Rpt. in *Writing Arguments: A Rhetoric with Readings.* John D. Ramage, John C. Bean, and June Johnson. 5th ed. Needham: Allyn, 2001. 28–30.

STRATEGY 4: USING DISAGREEMENT PRODUCTIVELY TO PROMPT FURTHER INVESTIGATION

Our fourth strategy—using disagreement productively to prompt further investigation—is both a powerful strategy for reading arguments and a bridge toward constructing your own arguments. Our goal is to suggest ways to help you proceed when the experts disagree. Encountering divergent points of view, such as the disagreement between Will and Goodman, can create intense intellectual pressure. Inexperienced arguers sometimes opt for easy escape routes. Either they throw up their hands, claim that "everyone has a right to his own opinion," and leave the argumentative arena, or they latch on to one of the competing claims, defend it against all comers, and shut off opportunity for growth and change. What our fourth strategy invites you to do is stay in the argumentative arena. It urges you to become an active questioner and thinker—to seek answers where possible to disputed questions of fact and value and to articulate and justify your own beliefs and assumptions, which will ultimately inform the positions you take on issues.

As you sort through conflicting viewpoints, your goal is not to identify one of them as "correct" but to ask what is the best solution to the problem being debated here. You may eventually decide that one of the current viewpoints is indeed the best solution. Or you may develop a synthesis that combines strengths from several divergent viewpoints. In either case, you will emerge from the process with an enlarged, informed understanding. You will have developed the ability to remain intellectually flexible while listening to alternative viewpoints. Most important, you will have learned how to avoid falling into a valueless relativism. Responding productively to disagreement thus becomes part of your preparation for writing ethically responsible arguments.

To try to illustrate the process of responding to disagreements, we now show you how we responded to the disagreement between Will and Goodman over pay equity.

Accepting Ambiguity and Uncertainty as a Prompt for Further Investigation

When confronted with conflicting positions, you must learn to cope with ambiguity. If there were no disagreements, of course, there would be no need for argument. It is important to realize that experts can look at the same data, can analyze the same arguments, can listen to the same authorities, and still reach different conclusions. Seldom will one expert's argument triumph over another's in a field of dissenting claims. More often, one expert's argument will modify another's and in turn will be modified by yet another. Accepting ambiguity is a way of suspending judgment as you enter the complexity of an issue. A willingness to live with ambiguity enables you to delve deeply into an issue and to resist easy answers.

Seeking Out Sources of Facts and More Complete Versions of Alternative Views

After analyzing the sources of disagreement between Will and Goodman (see our sample essay on pp. 42–43), we next attempted to use these disagreements productively by striving for a more complete understanding of alternative views. We began by pursuing the sources cited by Will and Goodman. We needed to determine whether the book by Furchtgott-Roth and Stolba cited by Will or the data compiled by the AFL-CIO cited by Goodman seemed more reliable and persuasive. We also hoped to determine if there is a majority position among commentators.

Our searching for sources helped us see a pattern in the views of experts. We discovered that Will's perspective is endorsed by the American Enterprise Institute (a conservative think tank of which Furchtgott-Roth is a fellow) and by the Senate Republican Committee. Because conservatives tend to favor free markets, these endorsements seemed understandable. Numerous other organizations, however, believe that the gender pay gap is a serious problem: the Bureau of Labor Statistics, the Institute for Women's Policy Research, Catalyst (a women's research group), and the National Committee on Pay Equity. Furthermore, the results of the AFL-CIO's 1997 "Ask A Working Woman" survey, which strongly argues that a gender pay gap exists, are presented very clearly in their Web site (www.aflcio.org). Because these organizations are aligned with labor or with women's advocacy groups, they understandably favor proactive policies to boost wages of low-pay workers.

However, these pro-labor groups did provide strong evidence to confirm the reality of a gender pay gap. These sources gave extensive national and state data, based on what seemed to us factual information about wages, to show that a wage gap exists, that it varies by state, and that the gap is bigger for women of color.

Our search for fuller understanding inspired us to seek out information on the Fair Pay Act and the Paycheck Fairness Act currently before Congress to see how the legislators propose to deal with this problem. We discovered that pro-business commentators think that new laws could lead to costly litigation as women sue for back pay and could lead to government micro-management of corporations. These concerns are valid, but we also found that one main goal of the legislation is to encourage corporations and institutions to self-audit for internal equity in hiring and in establishing equitable policies for evaluations for salaries, promotions, and benefits.

We were also drawn to arguments that framed the gender pay gap as an issue affecting women, men, children, and families. The families of working women, and particularly of single mothers, are suffering the most from the inequity in wages of wives and mothers. These sources persuasively widened their concerns to show that equal pay for women affects children's security, health care, the poverty rate, domestic violence, Social Security, pensions, and family stability. The issue thus has enormous social repercussions.

Determining What Values Are at Stake for You in the Issue and Articulating Your Own Values

In responding to disagreement, you need to articulate your own values and to try to justify them by explaining the reasons you hold them. The authors of this text, for example, tend to support the need for greater pay equity and question Will's emphasis on women's choices as a complete explanation for lower pay for women. We know that for many women and families, working isn't a choice; it is a necessity. We have seen that women often sacrifice salaries and advancements when they have to take time off for children and that these choices are not always "cheerfully" made, as Will claims, but involve agonizing conflicts between job and family. Thinking about the fairness of pay reminds us that the United States has the highest poverty rate, the highest rate of children in poverty, and the biggest disparity of income distribution among industrialized nations. Therefore, we tend to favor government policies that boost the earnings of people at the bottom of the economic ladder.

Considering Ways to Synthesize Alternative Views

As a final step in your evaluation of conflicting sources, you should consider what you have gained from the different perspectives. How do the alternative views modify each other or otherwise "speak to each other"? If conflicting views don't lead to a synthesis, how do the different perspectives at least lead to an informed, enlarged vision of the issue?

What valuable points could we take from the opposing stands on this topic if we were to write our own argument on pay equity? What perspective could we synthesize from the free-market optimism of Will and the need for reform voiced by Goodman? Will claims that more women are earning college and graduate degrees and that these qualifications will equip them for better jobs; basically, he argues, the situation for women is improving and any inequalities will fix themselves. Yet Goodman believes that rigorous enforcement of pay equity laws *and* the enactment of new ones are needed. Could an argument on pay equity acknowledge the progress that Will cites and the urgency of the problems that Goodman discusses? We concluded that an informed position would need to recognize the economic progress of college-educated, professional women willing to forego childbearing, while at the same time pointing out the injustice of persistently low wages for women in working class jobs. Our goal would be to find ways to connect the pay equity problem to issues of family and poverty.

When you try to synthesize points from conflicting positions, as we did here, you tap into the dialectical nature of argument, questioning and modifying positions in response to new perspectives. We cannot claim that the position we are tentatively formulating on the pay equity issue is the right one. We can claim only that it is a reasonable and responsible one in light of the available facts and our own values. We have tried to show how the process of responding to disagreement—coping with ambiguity, pursuing researched answers to questions about fact and value, articulating your own values, and seeking possible syntheses—launches you on the path to becoming a responsible writer of arguments.

CONCLUSION

This chapter has explained why reading arguments is crucially important to writers of argument and has offered suggestions for improving your own reading process. We have suggested four main strategies for deep reading: (1) Read as a believer. (2) Read as a doubter. (3) Consider alternative views and analyze sources of disagreement. (4) Use disagreement productively to prompt further investigation. This chapter has also shown you how to summarize an article and incorporate summaries into your own writing through the use of attributive tags.

In the next chapter we turn from the reading of arguments to the writing of arguments, suggesting ways that you can generate ideas for arguments, structure your arguments, and improve your own writing processes.

3 Writing Arguments

As the opening chapters suggest, when you write an argument, you try to achieve two goals: (1) to persuade your audience toward your stance on an issue and (2) to see the issue complexly enough so that your stance reflects an ethical consideration of conflicting views. Because managing these tasks takes time, the quality of any argument depends on the quality of the thinking and writing processes that produced it. In this chapter, we suggest ways that you can improve these processes. We begin by looking at the social contexts that produce arguments, asking who writes arguments and why. We then present some writing tips based on the composing practices of experienced writers. Finally, we describe nuts-and-bolts strategies for generating ideas and organizing an argument for an intended audience, concluding with two sets of exploratory exercises that can be adapted to any kind of argumentative task.

WHO WRITES ARGUMENTS AND WHY?

To help you see how writers operate in a social context—how they are spurred to write by a motivating occasion and by a desire to change the views of particular audiences—we begin by asking you to consider more fully why someone would produce an argument.

In the classical period of ancient Greece and Rome, when the discipline of rhetoric was born, arguers usually made speeches before deliberative bodies. Arguers today, however, can present their views in a wide range of media and genres: speeches at public hearings, at committee meetings, or on talk radio; letters to legislators, bosses, or newspaper editors; professional proposals, marketing plans, or workplace memos; posters and pamphlets advocating a cause; e-mail letters or posts to chat rooms or personal Web sites; paid advertisements—even T-shirts and bumper stickers. Experienced writers and media specialists have even more options: freelance articles, books, syndicated columns, TV documentaries, and so forth.

To illustrate these multiple contexts for persuasion, let's return to the issue of gender pay equity that we used in Chapter 2. Who in our culture actually writes arguments on pay equity? To whom are they writing and why? Here is a partial list of these writers and their contexts:

- *Lobbyists and advocacy groups.* Advocacy groups commit themselves to a cause, often with passion, and produce avidly partisan arguments aimed at persuading voters, legislators, or other targeted decision makers. Well-financed groups such as the American Civil Liberties Union or the National Rifle Association hire professional researchers, writers, media specialists, and lobbyists. Smaller advocacy groups might create their own Web sites, produce low-budget documents such as pamphlets and newsletters, and orchestrate letter-writing campaigns to legislators and newspapers. Numerous advocacy groups have coalesced around the pay equity issue. The organizations mentioned in Chapter 2 are all advocacy groups arguing for or against pay equity legislation.

- *Legislators.* Whenever new laws are proposed in legislatures, staffers do research for elected representatives and write "white papers" recommending positions for their bosses to take on an issue. Because pay equity is a hot issue, numerous staff researchers have produced white papers on the subject in both state legislatures and Congress.

- *Business professionals.* Businesses and corporations produce numerous internal documents aimed at researching data and recommending policy. Whenever pay equity issues arise in a business or corporation, managers and executives (accountants, comptrollers, planners, labor/management negotiators) analyze pay equity data, debate courses of action, and produce position papers.

- *Employment and corporate lawyers and judges.* Employment lawyers, representing clients with pay equity grievances, write briefs supporting their client's case. Meanwhile, corporate lawyers defend the corporation's interests against pay equity lawsuits. When the decisions of lower courts are appealed to higher judicial courts, arguments become increasingly philosophical. Often other lawyers, particularly law professors, file "friends of the court" briefs aimed at influencing the decision of judges. Finally, judges write court opinions explaining their decisions on a case.

- *Media commentators.* Whenever pay equity issues get in the news, media commentators (journalists, editorial writers, syndicated columnists) write on the issue, filtering it through the perspective of their own political views. The Will and Goodman editorials analyzed in Chapter 2 fall into this category.

- *Professional freelance or staff writers.* Some of the most thoughtful analyses of public issues are composed by freelance or staff writers for public forum magazines such as *Atlantic Monthly,* the *Nation, Ms.,* the *National Review,* and *Utne Reader.* Arguments on pay equity surface whenever the topic seems timely to magazine editors.

- *Scholars and academics.* A key public role played by college professors comes from their scholarly research. Almost all public debates on social policy derive at least some data and analysis from the scholarship of college professors. Although no research can be purely objective—unshaped by the biases of the researcher—scholarly research differs substantially from advocacy argument in its systematic attempt to arrive at the best answers to questions based on the full examination of all relevant data. Much scholarship has been devoted to the pay equity issue—primarily by economists and sociologists. Scholarly research is usually published in refereed academic journals rather than popular magazines. (Of course, scholars can also take personal positions on social issues and use their research for advocacy arguments.)

- *Citizens.* Average citizens influence social policy through letters, contributions to advocacy Web sites, guest editorials for newspapers, or pieces in professional newsletters or other media. The pay equity issue reaches national consciousness when enough individuals make their views heard.

Where do student writers fit on this list? As a student you are already a member of both the "citizen" group and the "scholars and academics" group. Moreover, you may often be given opportunities to role-play membership in other groups as well. As a professional-in-training, you can practice both advocacy arguments and inquiry-based research pieces. Some students taking argument courses in college publish their work as letters to the editor or guest editorials (in the case of advocacy pieces) or present their work at undergraduate research conferences (in the case of scholarly pieces). Others try to influence public opinion by writing persuasive letters to legislators, submitting proposals to decision makers in the workplace, or posting their arguments on Web sites.

What all these writers have in common is a deep engagement with their issues. They share a strong belief that an issue matters, that decisions have consequences, and that the stakes are often high. You can engage an issue either by having a strong position to advocate or by seeking to clarify your stand on a complex problem. What is important to note is how fluid a writer's position can be along this continuum from advocate to inquirer (analogous to the continuum between "persuasion" and "truth seeking" discussed in Chapter 1, pp. 10–12). An advocate, while writing an argument, might discover an issue's complexity and be drawn into inquiry. Likewise, an inquirer, in the course of studying an issue, might clarify her thinking, establish a strong claim, and become an advocate. It is also possible to write arguments from any position on the continuum: You can be a tentative advocate as well as an avidly committed one, or you can be a cautious skeptic. You can even remain an inquirer by arguing that no proposed solution to a problem is yet adequate.

So how do you become engaged? We suggest that you immerse yourself in the arguments of the communities to which you belong—your classroom community, your dorm or apartment community, your work community, your civic community—and look for points of entry into these conversations: either places where you can take a stand or places where you are puzzled and uncertain. By opening yourself to the conversations of your culture, and by initiating these conversations when you encounter situations you would like to change, you will be ready to write arguments.

LEARNING FROM EXPERTS: TIPS FOR IMPROVING YOUR WRITING PROCESS

Once you are motivated to write, you can improve your arguing ability if you know something about the writing processes of experienced writers. Too often inexperienced writers cut this process short, producing undeveloped arguments that don't speak effectively to the needs of the intended audience. Although no two writers follow the same process, we can describe the evolution of an argument in a loose way and offer tips for making your writing processes more effective. You should regard the writing process we are about to describe as *recursive*, meaning that writers often loop back to earlier phases by changing their minds on an issue, by throwing out a draft and starting over, or by going back to do more research late in the process.

Starting point: Most writers of arguments start with an issue about which they are undecided or a claim they want to assert. At the outset, they may pose questions such as these: Who are the interested parties in this conversation? What are the causes of disagreement? What is the best way to solve the problem being debated? Who is the audience that must be persuaded? What is the best means of persuading members of that audience? What are the subtleties and complexities of this issue? Often a specific occasion spurs them to write. They feel hooked.

Tips for Starting the Process

- In many cases arguers are motivated to write because they find situations in their lives that they want to change. You can often focus on argument by asking yourself who has the power to make the changes you desire. How can you craft an argument that connects your desired changes to this audience's beliefs and values? What obstacles in your audience's environment might constrain individuals in that audience from action? How can these obstacles be overcome? This rhetorical focus—identifying the decision makers who have the power to change a situation and looking at the constraints that keep them from action—can give you a concrete sense of audience and clarify how your argument might proceed.

- In a college context you sometimes may have only a secondary occasion for writing—an assignment due date rather than an issue that hooks you. In such cases you can use some of the exploratory exercises described later in this chapter. These exercises help you inventory issues within the communities to which you belong, find points of engagement, and articulate the values and consequences that are at stake for you. Knowing why an issue matters to you can help you make it matter to others.

- Discuss issues with friends and classmates. Talking about ideas in small groups may help you discover claims that you want to make or issues that you find significant yet perplexing. By questioning claims and presenting multiple points of view, groups can help you understand points of disagreement on an issue.

Exploration, research, and rehearsal: To discover, refine, and support their claims, writers typically research their issues carefully, trying to understand arguments on all sides, to resolve disagreements about facts or reality, to clarify their own values, and to identify the beliefs and values of their audience. While researching their issues, writers often discover that their own views evolve. During research, writers often do exploratory writing in online chat rooms, e-mail exchanges, or a writer's journal, sometimes drafting whole pieces of an argument.

Tips for Exploring, Researching, and Rehearsing

- When you research an issue, focus on your rhetorical context. You need to research the issue itself, but also the values and beliefs of your targeted audience, and obstacles in your audience's social environment that might prevent individuals from acting on your claim or adopting your beliefs. The exploratory writing strategies and idea-generating procedures described later in this chapter will help you establish and maintain this focus.

- As you explore divergent views on your issue through library or Internet research or through interviews and field research, pay particular attention to why your views may be threatening to others. Later chapters in this text explain strategies for overcoming audience resistance.

- As you take notes on your research and imagine ways of shaping an argument for an intended audience, try some of the visual techniques suggested later in this chapter. Many writers find that idea maps and tree diagrams help them brainstorm for ideas and visualize structure.

■ Stay in conversation with others. Active discussion of your issue—especially with persons who don't agree with you—is a powerful way to explore an argument and find the best means of persuasion. As you talk through your argument, note where listeners look confused or skeptical and where they question your points. Skeptics may find holes in your reasoning, argue from different values, surprise you by conceding points you thought had to be developed at length, and challenge you by demanding more justification of your claim.

Writing a first draft: At some point in the process, a writer's attention begins to shift away from gathering data and probing an issue to composing a first draft. The act of writing a draft forces deep and focused thinking, which may then send the writer back to do more research and exploration. Effective first drafts are likely to be jumbled, messy, and full of gaps. Ideas appear at the point the writer thought of them rather than where readers need them. The writer's tone and style may be inappropriate, needed evidence may be entirely missing, the audience's beliefs and values may not be adequately addressed, and the whole draft may be confusing to an outside reader. Moreover, writers may discover that their own views are still shifting and unstable. Nevertheless, such drafts are a crucial first step. They get your ideas onto paper and give you material to work with.

Tips for Writing a First Draft

■ Try lowering your expectations. Writers can quickly create writer's block if they aim for perfection on the first draft. If you get blocked, keep writing. Don't worry about grammar, correctness, or polish. Just get ideas on paper.

■ Rehearse your ideas orally. Working in pairs with another student, talk through your argument orally before you write it down. Make a scratch outline first to prompt you as you talk. Then let your partner question you to help you flesh out your argument with more details.

■ For a first draft, try following the template for a "classical argument" described on pages 63–65. This strategy will help you consider and respond to opposing views as well as clarify the reasons and evidence that support your own claim.

■ Do the exploration tasks entitled "Set 2: Exploration and Rehearsal" (pp. 70–71) prior to writing a first draft. These exercises will help you brainstorm most of the ideas you'll need for an initial draft.

Revising through multiple drafts: After completing a first draft, you have materials out on the table to work with. Most writers need multiple drafts to convert an early draft into a persuasive finished product. Sometimes writers revise their claims significantly during revision, having discovered hidden complexities in the issue while composing the first draft.

Tips for Revising

- Don't manicure your drafts; rebuild them. Cross out whole paragraphs and rewrite them from scratch. Move blocks of text to new locations. Make a mess. Inexperienced writers often think of revision as polishing and correcting rather than as making substantial changes (what writing teachers call "global revision"). Revising means to rethink your whole argument. Some writers even throw away the first draft and start fresh.

- Improve your mechanical procedures. We recommend that you revise off double-spaced hard copy rather than off the computer screen. Leave lots of space between lines and in the margins on your drafts so that you have room to draw arrows and make pencil or pen deletions and inserts. When your draft becomes too messy, keyboard your changes back into the computer. If you manage all your drafts on computer, you may find that copying to a new file for each new draft gives you more freedom to experiment with changes (since you can always recover an earlier draft).

- As you revise, think of your audience. Many first drafts show why the writer believes the claim but not why the intended audience should believe it or act on it. As we explain later in this text (especially Chapters 7 and 8), first drafts often contain "writer-based reasons" rather than "audience-based reasons." How can you hook into your audience's beliefs and values? Look also at the obstacles or constraints that keep your audience from adopting your beliefs or acting on your claim. How can you address those constraints in your revision?

- As you revise, also consider the image of yourself conveyed in your tone and style. Do you want to come across as angry? As sarcastic? As conciliatory and sympathetic? Also, to what extent do you want to appeal to readers' emotions and imagination as well as to their logical intellects? These concerns are discussed in Chapter 7 under the headings *ethos* and *pathos.*

- Exchange drafts with classmates. Ask classmates where your argument is not persuasive, where your tone is offensive, where they have doubts, where your writing is unclear or undeveloped. Ask your classmates to role-play your intended audience. Explain the values and beliefs of this audience and the constraints members face. Let them give you their reactions and advice. Classmates can also help you meet your readers' needs for effective organization, development, and style.

- Loop back to do more exploration and research. Writing is a recursive process during which writers frequently loop back to earlier stages. Revising your first draft may involve considerably more research and exploration.

Editing for style, impact, and correctness: Writers now polish their drafts, rephrasing sentences, finding the precise word, and establishing links between sentences. At this point, you should turn to surface features such as spelling, punctuation, and grammar as well as to the appearance and form of the final manuscript.

Tips for Editing

- Read your draft out loud. Your ear can often pick up problems missed by the eye.

- Use your computer's spell check program. Remember, however, that spell checkers won't pick up mistakes with homonyms like *to/two/too, here/hear,* or *affect/effect.* Be skeptical of computerized grammar checkers, which cannot "read" with human intelligence but can only mechanically count, sort, and match. Your instructor can guide you on what grammar checkers can and cannot do.

- Use a good handbook for up-to-date advice on usage, punctuation, style, and manuscript form.

- Ask a classmate or friend to proofread your paper.

- Be prepared to loop back again to earlier stages. Sometimes thinking of a better way to word a sentence uncovers larger problems of clarity and meaning requiring you to rewrite a whole section of your argument.

USING EXPLORATORY WRITING TO DISCOVER IDEAS AND DEEPEN THINKING

What follows is a compendium of strategies to help you discover and explore ideas. None of these strategies works for every writer. But all of them are worth trying. Each requires practice, so don't give up on the strategy if it doesn't work at first. We recommend that you keep your exploratory writing in a journal or in easily identified files in your word processor so you can review it later and test the "staying power" of ideas produced by the different strategies.

Freewriting or Blind Writing

Freewriting is useful at any stage of the writing process. When you freewrite, you put pen to paper and write rapidly *nonstop,* usually ten to fifteen minutes at a stretch. The object is to think of as many ideas as possible without stopping to edit your work. On a computer, freewriters often turn off the monitor so that they can't see the text being produced. Such "blind writing" frees the writer from the urge to edit or correct the text and simply to let ideas roll forth. Some freewriters or blind writers achieve a stream-of-consciousness style, recording their ideas at the very moment they bubble into consciousness, stutters and stammers and all. Others produce more focused chunks, though without clear connections among them. You will probably find your initial reservoir of ideas running out in three to five minutes. If so, force yourself to keep writing or typing. If you can't think of anything to say, write "relax" or "I'm stuck" over and over until new ideas emerge.

Here is an example of a freewrite from a student named Stephen, exploring his thoughts on the question "What can be done about the homeless?" (Stephen eventually wrote the proposal argument found on pages 334–42.)

> Let's take a minute and talk about the homeless. Homeless homeless. Today on my way to work I passed a homeless guy who smiled at me and I smiled back though he smelled bad. What are the reasons he was out on the street? Perhaps an extraordinary string of bad luck. Perhaps he was pushed out onto the street. Not a background of work ethic, no place to go, no way to get someplace to live that could be afforded, alcoholism. To what extent do government assistance, social spending, etc, keep people off the street? What benefits could a person get that stops "the cycle"? How does welfare affect homelessness, drug abuse programs, family planning? To what extent does the individual have control over homelessness? This question of course goes to the depth of the question of how community affects the individual. Relax, relax. What about the signs that I see on the way to work posted on the windows of businesses that read, "please don't give to panhandlers it only promotes drug abuse etc" a cheap way of getting homeless out of the way of business? Are homeless the natural end of unrestricted capitalism? What about the homeless people who are mentally ill? How can you maintain a living when haunted by paranoia? How do you decide if someone is mentally ill or just laughs at society? If one can't function obviously. How many mentally ill are out on the street? If you are mentally ill and have lost the connections to others who might take care of you I can see how you might end up on the street. What would it take to get treatment? To what extent can mentally ill be treated? When I see a homeless person I want to ask, How do you feel about the rest of society? When you see "us" walk by how do you think of us? Do you possibly care how we avoid you.

FOR CLASS DISCUSSION

Individual task: Choose one of the following controversial claims (or another chosen by your instructor) and freewrite your response to it for five or ten minutes. **Group task:** Working in pairs, in small groups, or as a whole class, share your freewrite with classmates. Don't feel embarrassed if your freewrite is fragmentary or disjointed. Freewrites are not supposed to be finished products; their sole purpose is to generate a flow of thought. The more you practice the technique, the better you will become.

1. A student should report a fellow student who is cheating on an exam or plagiarizing an essay.

2. States should legalize marriages between homosexuals.

3. Companies should not be allowed to enforce English-only policies in the workplace.

4. Spanking children should be considered child abuse.

5. State and federal governments should legalize hard drugs.

6. For grades 1 through 12, the school year should be extended to eleven months.

7. Taxpayer money should not be used to fund professional sports stadiums.

8. Violent video games such as Mortal Kombat should be made illegal.

9. Rich people are morally obligated to give part of their wealth to the poor.

10. Women should be assigned to combat duty equally with men.

Idea Mapping

Another good technique for exploring ideas is *idea mapping.* When you make an idea map, draw a circle in the center of the page and write some trigger idea (a broad topic, a question, or working thesis statement) in the center of the circle. Then record your ideas on branches and subbranches extending from the center circle. As long as you pursue one train of thought, keep recording your ideas on the branch. But when that line of thinking gives out, start a new branch. Often your thoughts jump back and forth between branches. That's a major advantage of "picturing" your thoughts; you can see them as part of an emerging design rather than as strings of unrelated ideas.

Idea maps usually generate more ideas, though less well-developed ones, than freewrites. Writers who practice both techniques report that each strategy causes them to think about their ideas very differently. When Stephen, the free-writer on homelessness, created an idea map (see Figure 3.1), he was well into an argument disagreeing with a proposal by columnist Charles Krauthammer advocating the confinement of the homeless mentally ill in state mental hospitals. Stephen's idea map helped him find some order in his evolving thoughts on homelessness and his reasons for disagreeing with Krauthammer.

❦ FOR CLASS DISCUSSION

Choose a controversial issue—national, local, or campus—that's interesting to the class. The instructor will lead a class discussion on the issue, recording ideas on an idea map as they emerge. Your goal is to appreciate the fluidity of idea maps as a visual form of idea generation halfway between an outline and a list.

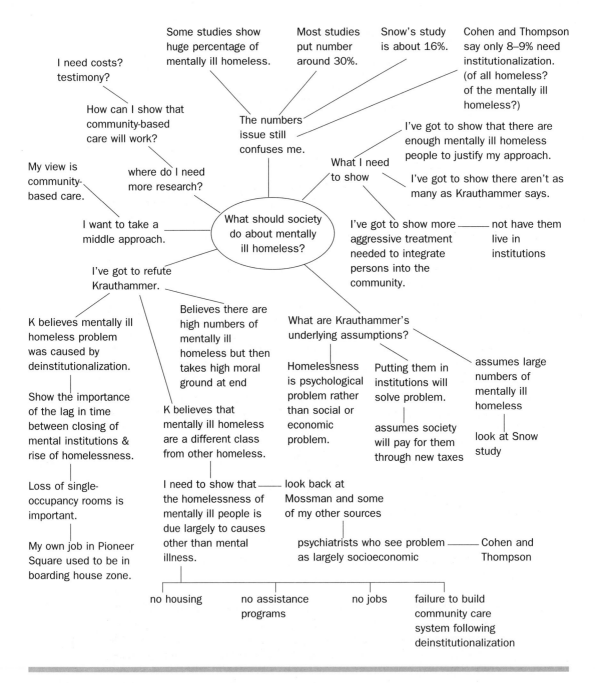

FIGURE 3.1   Stephen's initial idea map on the issue "What should society do about the mentally ill homeless?"

Playing the Believing and Doubting Game

The believing/doubting game* is an excellent way to imagine views different from your own and to anticipate responses to those views.

As a believer, your role is to be wholly sympathetic to an idea, to listen carefully to it, and to suspend all disbelief. You must identify all the ways in which the idea might appeal to different audiences and all the reasons for believing the idea. The believing game is easy so long as you already accept an idea. But in dealing with ideas that strike you as shaky, false, or threatening, you will find that the believing game can be difficult, even frightening.

The doubting game is the opposite of the believing game. As a doubter, your role is to be judgmental and critical, to find faults with an idea. You do your best to find counterexamples and inconsistencies that undermine it. Again, it is easy to play the doubting game with ideas you reject, but doubting those you've invested in can be threatening.

When you play the believing and doubting game with an assertion, simply write two different chunks, one chunk arguing for the assertion (the believing game) and one chunk opposing it (the doubting game). Freewrite both chunks, letting your ideas flow without censoring. Or, alternatively, make an idea map with believing and doubting branches.

Here is how one student played the believing and doubting game as part of a class discussion about the following classified ad seeking young college women to be egg donors for an infertile couple.

> Infertile professional couple seeks egg-donor for artificial insemination. Donor should be slim, athletic, blue-eyed with 1400 SAT's or better. $50,000 and all medical expenses. Must be discrete and willing to sign documents giving up all legal rights to a baby that might be produced.

This student is responding to the assertion "Recent advances in reproductive technology, including the use of egg donors, are good for society."

BELIEVING EXAMPLE

The latest advances in reproductive technology are good for society. Up until now, infertile couples had only adoption to turn to if they wanted a child. Using egg donation enables the parents to feel like real parents because the mother does carry the child. The parents can be a bit more selective about the child they get because egg donors are carefully screened. I think egg donors are more stable and safe than women who carelessly or accidentally get pregnant and give up their babies for adoption. Egg donors can be smart, healthy young women, such as college

---

*A term coined by Peter Elbow, *Writing without Teachers* (New York: Oxford UP, 1973), 147–90.

students. These young women also get an opportunity to make some money. Another point is that women can preserve some of their own eggs from their youth and actually have a child much later in life when they are ready for such a commitment. I can see how egg donation can help infertile couples, young women, and older women.

DOUBTING EXAMPLE

While egg donation sounds promising, I think the supporters of it often leave out the dark side and the moral implications. The process is changing having babies from a natural experience to a completely commercial one. Eggs are bought and judged like any other product. The high prices reaching even tens of thousands of dollars mean that only rich couples will be able to afford the process. The fact that the preferred egg donors have common traits (are Ivy League students, are tall, blonde, and blue eyed) only serves to increase a certain elitism. The donor part has pitfalls too. I can understand the attraction of the large sums of money, but the medical process is not easy. The young women must take fertility drugs and injections to boost their egg production. These drugs may have side effects and long-term complications. I wouldn't want my girlfriend to undergo this process.

Although this writer condemns these medical advances in reproductive technology, he does a good job of trying to sympathize with women who are involved in them. Playing the believing and doubting game has helped him see the issue more complexly.

FOR CLASS DISCUSSION

Return to the ten controversial claims in the For Class Discussion on pages 56–57. **Individual task:** Choose one of the claims and play the believing and doubting game with it by freewriting for five minutes trying to believe the claim and then for five minutes trying to doubt the claim. Or, if you prefer, make an idea map by creating a believing spoke and a doubting spoke off the main hub. Instead of freewriting, enter ideas onto your idea map, moving back and forth between believing and doubting. **Group task:** Share what you produced with members of your group or with the class as a whole.

Repeat the exercise with another claim.

Brainstorming for Pro and Con
Because Clauses

This activity is similar to the believing and doubting game in that it asks you to brainstorm ideas for and against a controversial assertion. In the believing and doubting game, however, you simply freewrite or make an idea map on both sides of the issue. In this activity, you try to state your reasons for and against the proposition as *because* clauses. The value of doing so is discussed in depth in Chapter 4, which shows how a claim with *because* clauses can form the core of an argument.

Here is an example of how you might create *because* clauses for and against the claim "The recent advances in reproductive technology, including the use of egg donors, are good for society."

PRO

The recent advances in reproductive technology, including the use of egg donors, are good for society.

- because children born using this technology are really wanted and will be given loving homes
- because infertility is a medical disorder that can destroy marriages
- because curing this disorder will support marriages and create loving families
- because this technology restores to parents some measure of control over their reproductive capabilities

CON

The recent advances in reproductive technology, including the use of egg donors, are dangerous to society.

- because this technology could lead to situations in which persons have no idea to whom they are genetically related
- because the technology might harm persons such as the egg donors who do not know what the long-term consequences of tampering with their reproductive systems through the use of fertility drugs might be
- because using donor eggs is equivalent to "special ordering" children who may not live up to the parents' expectations (to be smart, tall)
- because the expense of reproductive technology (especially when it results in multiple births) is too large for individuals, insurance companies, or the state to bear

FOR CLASS DISCUSSION

Generating *because* clauses like these is an especially productive discussion activity for groups. Once again return to the ten controversial claims in the For Class Discussion exercise on pages 56–57. Select one or more of these claims (or others provided by your instructor) and, working in small groups, generate pro and con *because* clauses supporting and attacking the claim. Share your group's *because* clauses with those of other groups.

Brainstorming a Network of Related Issues

The previous exercise helps you see how certain issues can provoke strong pro-con stances. Occasionally in civic life, an issue is presented to the public in such a pro-con form, as when voters are asked to approve or disapprove a referendum or when a jury must decide the guilt or innocence of a defendant.

But in most contexts, the argumentative situation is more open-ended and fluid. You can easily oversimplify an issue by reducing it to two opposing sides. Because most issues are embedded in a network of subissues, side issues, and larger issues, seeing an issue in pro-con terms can often blind you to other ways to join a conversation. For example, a writer might propose a middle ground between adversarial positions, examine a subissue in more depth, connect an issue to a related side issue, or redefine an issue to place it in a new context.

Consider, for example, the assertion about reproductive technology. Rather than arguing for or against this claim, a writer might focus on reproductive technology in a variety of other ways:

- Who should determine the ethics of reproductive technology? Families? Doctors? Government?
- How can risky physical outcomes such as multiple births (mothers carrying seven and eight babies) be avoided?
- What effect will the new reproductive technologies have on our concepts of motherhood and family?
- In case of divorce, who has legal rights to frozen embryos and other genetic material?
- Will reproductive technology lead to control over the sex and genetic makeup of children? Should it?
- What is the difference between paying someone to donate a kidney (which is illegal) and paying a woman to donate her eggs (which is currently legal)?
- Currently many adopted children want to seek out their birth mothers. Would children born from donated eggs want to seek out their genetic mothers?
- Who should pay for reproductive technology?

FOR CLASS DISCUSSION

Working as a whole class or in small groups, choose one or more of the controversial assertions on pages 56–57. Instead of arguing for or against them, brainstorm a number of related issues (subissues, side issues, or larger issues) on the same general subject. For example, brainstorm a number of issues related to the general topics of cheating, gay marriage, women in combat, and so forth.

SHAPING YOUR ARGUMENT
FOR YOUR INTENDED AUDIENCE

We turn now from discovery strategies to organizing strategies. As you begin drafting, you need some sort of plan. How elaborate that plan is varies considerably from writer to writer. Some writers plan extensively before writing; others write extensively before planning. But somewhere along the way, all writers must decide on a structure. This section offers two basic organizing strategies: (1) using the conventional structure of "classical argument" as an initial guide and (2) using a tree diagram instead of a traditional outline.

Classical Argument as an Initial Guide

In drafting, writers of argument often rely on knowledge of typical argument structures to guide their thinking. One of the oldest models is the *classical argument*—so called because it follows a pattern recommended by ancient rhetoricians. In traditional Latin terminology, classical argument has the following parts: the *exordium* (which gets the audience's attention); the *narratio* (which provides needed background); the *propositio* (which introduces the speaker's proposition or thesis); the *partitio* (which forecasts the main parts of the speech); the *confirmatio* (which presents arguments supporting the proposition); the *confutatio* (which refutes opposing views); and the *peroratio* (which sums up the argument, calls for action, and leaves a strong last impression). Classical arguments are often best suited for undecided or neutral audiences (see Chapter 8).

In slightly homelier terms (see Figure 3.2), writers of classical argument typically begin with a dramatic story or a startling statistic that commands attention. Then they focus the issue, often by stating it directly as a question and perhaps by briefly summarizing opposing views. Next, they contextualize the issue by providing needed background, explaining the immediate context, or defining key terms. They conclude the introduction by presenting the thesis and forecasting the argument's structure.

Next, in usually the longest part of the classical argument, writers present the major reasons and evidence supporting their thesis, typically trying to develop reasons that appeal to their audience's values and beliefs. Often, each reason is developed in its own section. Each section opens with a statement of the reason, which is then supported with evidence or chains of other reasons. Along the way, writers guide their readers with appropriate transitions.

Subsequently, alternative views are summarized and critiqued. (Some writers put this section *before* the presentation of their own argument.) If opposing arguments consist of several parts, writers may either (1) summarize all opposing arguments before responding or (2) summarize and respond one part at a time. Writers may respond to opposing views either by refuting them or by conceding their strengths but shifting to a different field of values where these strengths are less decisive.

Finally, in their conclusion, writers will sum up their argument, often calling for some kind of action, thereby creating a sense of closure and leaving a strong final impression.

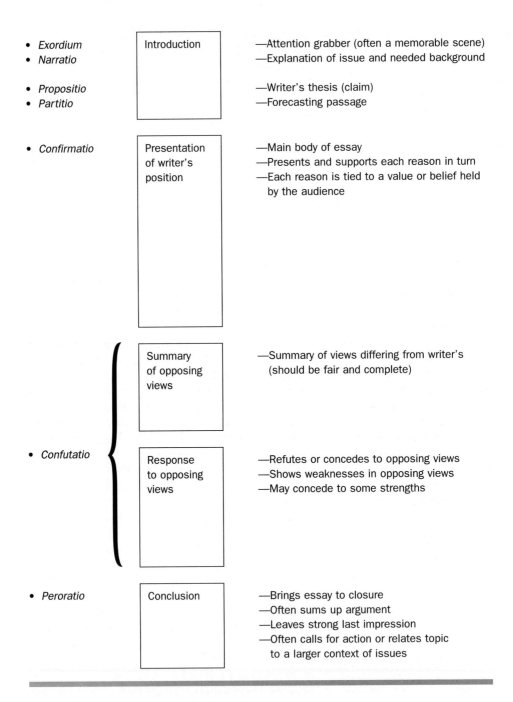

- *Exordium*
- *Narratio*

- *Propositio*
- *Partitio*

Introduction

—Attention grabber (often a memorable scene)
—Explanation of issue and needed background

—Writer's thesis (claim)
—Forecasting passage

- *Confirmatio*

Presentation
of writer's
position

—Main body of essay
—Presents and supports each reason in turn
—Each reason is tied to a value or belief held
   by the audience

Summary
of opposing
views

—Summary of views differing from writer's
   (should be fair and complete)

- *Confutatio*

Response
to opposing
views

—Refutes or concedes to opposing views
—Shows weaknesses in opposing views
—May concede to some strengths

- *Peroratio*

Conclusion

—Brings essay to closure
—Often sums up argument
—Leaves strong last impression
—Often calls for action or relates topic
   to a larger context of issues

FIGURE 3.2   Diagram of a classical argument

For all its strengths, the classical argument may not always be your best model. In some cases, for example, delaying your thesis or ignoring alternative views may be justified (see Chapter 8). Even in these cases, however, the classical argument is a useful planning tool. Its call for a thesis statement and a forecasting statement in the introduction helps you see the whole of your argument in miniature. And by requiring you to summarize and consider opposing views, classical argument alerts you to the limits of your position and to the need for further reasons and evidence. Moreover, the classical argument is a particularly persuasive mode of argument when you address a neutral or undecided audience.

The Power of Tree Diagrams

The classical argument offers a general guide for shaping arguments, but it doesn't help you wrestle with particular ideas. It is one thing to know that you need one or more reasons to support your thesis, but quite another to figure out what those reasons are, to articulate them clearly, and to decide what evidence supports them. Traditionally, writers have used outlines to help them flesh out a structure. For some writers, however, a visual strategy called *tree diagramming* may be more effective.

A *tree diagram* differs from an outline in that headings and subheadings are indicated by spatial relationships rather than by a system of letters and numerals. Figure 3.3 reveals the plan for a classical argument opposing a campus ban on hate speech. The writer envisions the argument as a guest editorial in the campus newspaper aimed at persuading campus opinion away from a proposed ban. The inverted triangle at the top of the tree represents the writer's introduction. The main reasons appear on branches beneath the claim, and the supporting evidence and arguments for each reason are displayed beneath each reason.

The same argument displayed in outline form would look like this:

THESIS: Colleges should not try to ban hate speech.

  I. A ban on hate speech violates the First Amendment.

  II. A ban on hate speech doesn't solve the problem of hate.
    A. It doesn't allow people to understand and hear each other's anger.
    B. It disguises hatred instead of bringing it out in the open where it can be dealt with.
    C. The ability to see both sides of an issue would be compromised.

  III. Of course, there are good arguments in support of a ban on hate speech.
    A. Banning hate speech creates a safer environment for minorities.
    B. It helps eliminate occasions for violence.
    C. It teaches good manners and people skills.
    D. It shows that ignorant hate speech is not the same as intelligent discussion.

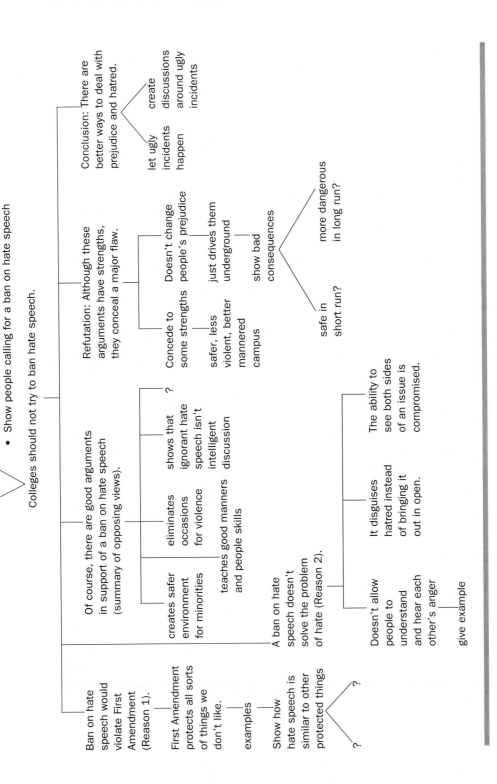

FIGURE 3.3 Tree diagram of an argument opposing a ban on hate speech

IV. Although these arguments have strengths, they conceal a major flaw.
  A. I concede that a hate speech ban might make a safer, less violent campus and might help teach good manners.
  B. But in the long run, it doesn't change people's prejudices; it just drives them underground.

V. CONCLUSION: There are better ways to deal with prejudice and hatred.
  A. Instead of repressing hate, let ugly incidents happen.
  B. Create discussions around the ugly incidents.

In our experience, tree diagrams often lead to fuller, more detailed, and more logical arguments than do traditional outlines. Their strength results from their several advantages. First, they are visual. The main points are laid out horizontally and support is displayed vertically. Writers can literally "see" where they need more support and can move freely between dimensions as they construct their argument.

Second, they are flexible. While traditional outlines require a division of each whole into two or more parts (every A must have a B—based on the principle that no whole can logically have just one part), tree diagrams can represent additional relationships. For example, a tree diagram can logically show a single line descending vertically from a higher-level point to represent, say, a generalization illustrated by a single example. Additionally, the descending lines on a tree diagram function as an informal flowchart, letting you plan out a chain of reasons. (This flexibility explains why the tree diagram in Figure 3.3 contains so much more information than the outline for the same argument.)

Finally, tree diagrams are powerful aids to invention because they invite you to insert question marks as placeholders for information you know you need but haven't yet found. For instance, if you know you need more data to support a point, you can write out your point on the tree diagram and place one or more question marks on descending lines below the point. (See the writer's use of question marks in Figure 3.3.)

DISCOVERING IDEAS: TWO SETS OF EXPLORATORY WRITING TASKS

The following tasks use exploratory writing to help you generate ideas. The first set of tasks helps you gather ideas early in a writing project either by helping you think of issues to write about or by deepening and complicating your response to readings. The second set of tasks helps you think about your ideas systematically before you compose a first draft.

Set 1: Starting Points

Task 1: Make an Inventory of the Communities to Which You Belong. What Issues Arise in Those Communities?

All of us belong to a variety of communities. For example, you have a classroom community for each course you are taking. Each club or organization has its own community, as does the community where you live (dorm, apartment, your family). Beyond these small communities, you have your campus community and beyond that your city, state, region, nation, and world communities. You may also belong to a work or job community, to a church/mosque/synagogue community, or to communities related to your hobbies or avocations.

The occasion for argument grows out of your life in these communities—your desire to make a difference on some issue that divides or troubles the community. As an arguer, you might tackle a big issue in your world community (What is the best way to prevent destruction of rain forests?) or a small issue in your dorm (Should quiet hours be enforced?). In your classroom community, you might tackle a practical problem (What should the instructor do about persons coming in late?) or intellectual issues in the discipline itself (Is Frankenstein's monster good or evil? Is gender socially constructed?).

For this task make a list of the communities to which you belong. Then brainstorm controversies in these communities—issues that are being debated or that you would like to see debated. You might find one or more of the following "trigger questions" helpful:

- Persons in my dorm (at work, in the state legislature, at the United Nations) disagree about . . . .
- Our campus (this dorm, my hometown, my worksite, our state, our country) would be a better place if . . . .
- Something that really makes me mad about this campus (my apartment life, city government, our society) is . . . .
- In the career I hope to pursue, X is a serious problem that needs to be addressed.
- Person X believes . . . ; however, I believe . . . .

Task 2: Make an Inventory of Issues That Interest You

The previous task can overwhelm students with the sheer number of issues that surround them. Once you broaden out to the large communities of city, state, nation, and world, the numbers of issues multiply rapidly. Moreover, each large issue has numerous subissues. For this task make an inventory of ten to fifteen possible issues that you would like to explore more deeply and possibly write about. Share your list with classmates, adding their ideas to yours.

Task 3: Choose Several Areas of Controversy for Exploration

For this task choose two or three possible controversies from the list above and explore them through freewriting or idea mapping. Try responding to the following questions: (a) What is my position on this issue and why? (b) What are opposing or alternative positions on this issue? (c) Why do people disagree about this issue? (Do they disagree about the facts of the case? About underlying values, assumptions, and beliefs?) (d) To argue a position on this issue, what evidence do I need to find and what further research will be required?

Task 4: Choose a Local Issue and Explore Its Rhetorical Context

For this task choose a local issue (some situation that you would like to see changed on your campus, in your place of work, or in your town or city) and explore its rhetorical context: (a) What is the situation you would like to change? (b) Who has the power to change that situation? (c) What are the values and beliefs of these decision makers? (d) What obstacles or constraints may prevent these decision makers from acting on your desires? (e) What reasons and evidence would exert the most pressure on these decision makers? (How can you make acting on your proposal a good thing for them?)

Task 5: Identify and Explore Issues That Are Problematic for You

A major assignment often given in argument courses is to write a research-based argument on an issue or problem initially puzzling to you. Perhaps you don't know enough about the issue (for example, establishing international controls on pesticides), or perhaps the issue draws you into an uncomfortable conflict of values (for example, assisted suicide, legalization of drugs, noncriminal incarceration of sexual predators). Your goal for this task is to identify several issues about which you are undecided, to choose one, and to explore your current uncertainty. Why can't you make up your mind on this issue?

Task 6: Deepen Your Response to Readings

This task requires you to read a collection of arguments on an issue and to explore them thoughtfully. As you read the arguments assigned by your instructor, annotate the margins with believing and doubting notes as explained in Chapter 2. Then respond to one or more of the following prompts, using freewriting or idea mapping:

- Why do the writers disagree? Are there disagreements about facts? About underlying values, beliefs, and assumptions?

- Identify "hot spots" in the readings—passages that evoke strong agreement or disagreement, anger, confusion, or any other memorable response—and explore your reaction to these passages.

- Explore the evolution of your thinking as you read and later review the essays. What new questions have they raised? How did your thinking change? Where do you stand now and why?

- If you were to meet one of the authors on a plane or at a ball game, what would you say to him or her?

Set 2: Exploration and Rehearsal

The following tasks are designed to help you once you have chosen a topic and begun to clarify your thesis. While these tasks may take two or more hours to complete, the effort pays off by helping you produce a full set of ideas for your rough draft. We recommend using these tasks each time you write an argument for this course.

Task 1

What issue do you plan to address in this argument? Try wording the issue as a one-sentence question. Reword your question in several different ways because each version will frame the issue somewhat differently. Then put a box around your best version of the question.

Task 2

Now write out your tentative answer to the question. This will be your beginning thesis statement or claim. Put a box around this answer. Next write out one or more different answers to your question. These will be alternative claims that a neutral audience might consider.

Task 3

Why is this a controversial issue? Is there insufficient evidence to resolve the issue, or is the evidence ambiguous or contradictory? Are definitions in dispute? Do the parties disagree about basic values, assumptions, or beliefs?

Task 4

What personal interest do you have in this issue? What are the consequences for you if your argument succeeds or doesn't succeed? How does the issue affect you? Why do you care about it? (Knowing why you care about it might help you get your audience to care about it.)

Task 5

Who is the audience that you need to persuade? If your argument calls for an action, who has the power to act on your claim? Can you address these persons of power directly? Or do you need to sway others (such as voters) to exert pressure on persons in power? With regard to your issue, what are the values and beliefs of the audience you are trying to sway?

Task 6

What obstacles or constraints in the social or physical environment prevent your audience from acting on your claim or accepting your beliefs? What are some ways these obstacles can be overcome? If these obstacles cannot be overcome, should you change your claim?

Task 7

In this task you will rehearse the main body of your paper. Using freewriting or idea mapping, think of the main reasons and evidence you could use to sway your intended audience. Brainstorm everything that comes to mind that might help you support your case. Because this section will eventually provide the bulk of your argument, proceed rapidly without worrying whether your argument makes sense. Just get ideas on paper. As you generate reasons and evidence, you are likely to discover gaps in your knowledge. Where could your argument be bolstered by additional data such as statistics, examples, and expert testimony? Where and how will you do the research to fill these gaps?

Task 8

Now reread what you wrote for Tasks 5 and 6, in which you examined your audience's perspective. Role-playing that audience, imagine all the counterarguments members might make. Where does your claim threaten them or oppose their values? What obstacles or constraints in their environment are individuals likely to point to? ("I'd love to act on your claim, but we just don't have the money" or "If we grant your request, it will set a bad precedent.") Brainstorm all the objections your audience might raise to your argument.

Task 9

How can you respond to those objections? Take them one by one and brainstorm possible responses.

Task 10

Finally, explore again why this issue is important. What are its broader implications and consequences? What other issues does it relate to? Thinking of possible answers to these questions may prove useful when you write your introduction or conclusion.

WRITING ASSIGNMENTS FOR CHAPTERS 1–3

OPTION 1: *An Argument Summary*   Write a 250-word summary of an argument selected by your instructor. Then write a one-sentence summary of the same argument. Use as models the summaries of George Will's argument on pay equity in Chapter 2.

OPTION 2: *An Analysis of Sources of Disagreement in a Controversy*   Using as a model the analysis of the controversy between Will and Goodman on pay equity in Chapter 2, write an analysis of the sources of disagreement in any two arguments that take differing views on the same issue.

OPTION 3: *Evaluating Your Use of Exploratory Writing*   For this option your instructor will assign one or more of the exploratory exercises in Chapter 3 for you to do as homework. Do the tasks as well as you can, submitting your exploratory writing as an exhibit for evidence. Then write a reflective evaluation of how well the assignment worked for you. In your evaluation address questions such as these:

  a. Did the exercise help you develop ideas? (Why or why not?)
  b. What are examples of some of the ideas you developed?
  c. What did the exercise teach you about the demands of good arguments?
  d. What did the exercise teach you about your own writing and thinking process?

OPTION 4: *Propose a Problem for a Major Course Project*   An excellent major project for an argument course is to research an issue about which you are initially undecided. Your final essay for the course could be an argument in which you take a stand on this issue. Choose one of the issues you listed in "Set 1: Starting Points," Task 5—"I am unable to take a stand on the issue of . . ."—and make this issue a major research project for the course. During the term keep a log of your research activities and be ready, in class discussion or in writing, to explain what kinds of arguments or evidence turned out to be most persuasive in helping you take a stand.

   For this assignment, write a short letter to your instructor identifying the issue you have chosen, and explain why you are interested in it and why you can't make up your mind at this time.

Principles of Argument

4 The Core of an Argument

A Claim with Reasons

THE RHETORICAL TRIANGLE

Before we examine the structure of arguments, we should explain briefly their social context, which can be visualized as a triangle with interrelated points labeled *message, writer/speaker,* and *audience* (see Figure 4.1). Effective arguments consider all three points on this *rhetorical triangle.* As we will see in later chapters, when you alter one point of the triangle (for example, when you change the audience for whom you are writing), you often need to alter the other points (by restructuring the message itself and perhaps by changing the tone or image you project as writer/speaker). We have created a series of questions based on the "rhetorical triangle" to help you plan, draft, and revise your argument.

Each point on the triangle in turn corresponds to one of the three kinds of persuasive appeals that ancient rhetoricians named *logos, ethos,* and *pathos. Logos* (Greek for "word") refers primarily to the internal consistency and clarity of the message and to the logic of its reasons and support. The impact of *logos* on an audience is referred to as its *logical appeal.*

Ethos (Greek for "character") refers to the credibility of the writer/speaker. *Ethos* is often conveyed through the tone and style of the message, through the care with which the writer considers alternative views, and through the writer's investment in his or her claim. In some cases, it's also a function of the writer's reputation for honesty and expertise independent of the message. The impact of *ethos* on an audience is referred to as its *ethical appeal* or *appeal from credibility.*

Our third term, *pathos* (Greek for "suffering" or "experience"), is often associated with emotional appeal. But *pathos* appeals more specifically to an audience's imaginative sympathies—their capacity to feel and see what the writer feels and

Message
(LOGOS: *How can I make the argument*
internally consistent and logical?
How can I find the best reasons and
support them with the best evidence?)

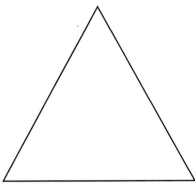

Audience
(PATHOS: *How can I make the reader*
open to my message? How can I best
appeal to my reader's values and
interests? How can I engage my
reader emotionally and imaginatively?)

Writer or Speaker
(ETHOS: *How can I present myself*
effectively? How can I enhance my
credibility and trustworthiness?)

FIGURE 4.1   The rhetorical triangle

sees. Thus, when we turn the abstractions of logical discourse into a palpable and immediate story, we are making a pathetic appeal. While appeals to *logos* and *ethos* can further an audience's intellectual assent to our claim, appeals to *pathos* engage the imagination and feelings, moving the audience to deeper appreciation of the argument's significance.

In Part Two, we treat all three elements of the rhetorical triangle in detail. Although all three terms overlap, Chapters 4–6 focus primarily on *logos*, and Chapters 7 and 8 focus primarily on *ethos* and *pathos*.

Given this background on the rhetorical triangle, let's turn now to *logos*—the logic and structure of arguments.

ISSUE QUESTIONS AS THE ORIGINS OF ARGUMENT

At the heart of any argument is an issue, which we can define as a controversial topic area such as "criminal rights" or "the minimum wage," that gives rise to differing points of view and conflicting claims. A writer can usually focus an issue by asking an issue question that invites at least two alternative answers. Within any complex issue—for example, the issue of abortion—there are usually a number of separate issue questions: Should abortions be legal? Should the federal government authorize Medicaid payments for abortions? When does a fetus become a human being (at conception? at three months? at quickening? at birth?)? What are the effects of legalizing abortion? (One person might stress that legalized abortion leads to greater freedom for women. Another person might respond that it lessens a society's respect for human life.)

Difference between an Issue Question and an Information Question

Of course, not all questions are issue questions that can be answered reasonably in two or more differing ways; thus not all questions can lead to effective argument essays. Rhetoricians have traditionally distinguished between *explication*, which is writing that sets out to inform or explain, and *argumentation*, which sets out to change a reader's mind. On the surface, at least, this seems like a useful distinction. If a reader is interested in a writer's question mainly to gain new knowledge about a subject, then the writer's essay could be considered explication rather than argument. According to this view, the following questions about abortion might be called information questions rather than issue questions:

How does the abortion rate in the United States compare with the rate in Sweden?

If the rates are different, why?

Although both questions seem to call for information rather than for argument, we believe the latter one would be an issue question if reasonable people disagreed on the answer. Thus, two writers might agree that abortion rates in the United States and Sweden differ significantly, but they might disagree in their explanations of why. One might say that Sweden has a higher abortion rate because of the absence of a large Catholic or conservative Protestant population in the country. The other might attribute the higher rate to Sweden's generous national health coverage or to differences in sex education in the schools. Thus, underneath the surface of what looks like a simple explication of the "truth" is really a controversy.

You can generally tell whether a question is an issue question or an information question by examining your purpose in relationship to your audience. If your relationship to your audience is that of teacher to learner, so that your audience hopes to gain new information, knowledge, or understanding that you possess, then your question is probably an information question. But if your relationship to your audience is that of advocate to decision maker or jury, so that your audience needs to make up its mind on something and is weighing different points of view, then the question you address is an issue question.

Often the same question can be an information question in one context and an issue question in another. Let's look at the following examples:

- How does a diesel engine work? (This is probably an information question since reasonable people who know about diesel engines will probably agree on how they work. This question would be posed by an audience of new learners.)

- Why is a diesel engine more fuel-efficient than a gasoline engine? (This also seems to be an information question since all experts will probably agree on the answer. Once again, the audience seems to be new learners, perhaps students in an automotive class.)

- What is the most cost-effective way to produce diesel fuel from crude oil? (This could be an information question if experts agree and you are addressing new learners. But if you are addressing engineers and one engineer says process X is the most cost-effective and another argues for process Y, then the question is an issue question.)

- Should the present highway tax on diesel fuel be increased? (This is certainly an issue question. One person says yes; another says no; another offers a compromise.)

FOR CLASS DISCUSSION

Working as a class or in small groups, try to decide which of the following questions are information questions and which are issue questions. Many of them could be either, depending on the rhetorical context. For such questions, create hypothetical contexts to show your reasoning.

1. What percentage of single-parent families receive welfare support?

2. What is the cause of the large number of out-of-wedlock births in the United States?

3. Should the United States eliminate welfare support for unwed mothers?

4. What percentage of TV shows during prime-time hours depict violence?

5. What is the effect of violent TV shows on children?

6. Are chiropractors legitimate health professionals?

7. How does chiropractic treatment of illness differ from a medical doctor's treatment?

8. Are caffeinated sodas harmful to children?

9. Should a woman with a newly detected breast cancer opt for a radical mastectomy (complete removal of the breast and surrounding lymph tissue) or a lumpectomy (removal of the malignant lump without removal of the whole breast)?

10. Is Simone de Beauvoir correct in calling marriage an outdated, oppressive, capitalist institution?

DIFFERENCE BETWEEN A GENUINE ARGUMENT AND A PSEUDO-ARGUMENT

While every argument features an issue question with alternative answers, not every dispute over answers is a rational argument. Rational arguments require two additional factors: (1) reasonable participants who operate within the conventions of reasonable behavior and (2) potentially sharable assumptions that can serve as a starting place or foundation for the argument. Lacking one or both of these conditions, disagreements remain stalled at the level of pseudo-arguments.

Pseudo-Arguments: Fanatical Believers and Fanatical Skeptics

A reasonable argument assumes the possibility of growth and change; disputants may modify their views as they acknowledge strengths in an alternative view or weaknesses in their own. Such growth becomes impossible—and argument degenerates to pseudo-argument—when disputants are fanatically committed to their positions. Consider the case of the fanatical believer or the fanatical skeptic.

Fanatical believers believe their claims are true because they say so, period. They may cite some authoritative text—the Bible, the *Communist Manifesto*, or *The Road Less Traveled*—but in the end it's their narrow and quirky reading of the text or their faith in the author (which others might not share) that underlies their argument. Disagreeing with a fanatical believer is like ordering the surf to quiet down. The only response is another crashing wave.

The fanatical skeptic, in contrast, dismisses the possibility of proving anything. So what if the sun has risen every day of recorded history? That's no proof that it will rise tomorrow. Short of absolute proof, which never exists, fanatical skeptics accept nothing. In a world where the most we can hope for is increased audience adherence to our ideas, the fanatical skeptic demands an ironclad logical demonstration of our claim's rightness. In the presence of fanatical believers or skeptics, then, genuine argument is impossible.

Another Source of Pseudo-Arguments: Lack of Shared Assumptions

A reasonable argument is difficult to conduct unless the participants share common assumptions on which the argument can be grounded. Like axioms in geometry, these shared assumptions serve as the starting point for the argument. Consider the following conversation, in which Randall refuses to accept Rhonda's assumptions:

RHONDA: Smoking should be banned because it causes cancer.

RANDALL: So it causes cancer. What's so bad about that?

RHONDA: Don't be perverse, Randy. Cancer causes suffering and death.

RANDALL: Rhonda, my dear girl, don't be such a twinkie. Suffering and death are just part of the human condition.

RHONDA: But that doesn't make them desirable, especially when they can be avoided.

RANDALL: Perhaps in particular cases they're avoidable for a while, but in the long run, we all suffer and we all die, so who cares if smoking causes what's inevitable anyway?

This, we would suggest, is a doomed argument. Without any shared assumptions (for example, that cancer is bad, that suffering should be minimized and death delayed), there's no "bottom" to this argument, just an endless regress of reasons based on more reasons. While calling assumptions into question is a legitimate way to deepen and complicate our understanding of an issue, the unwillingness to accept any assumption makes argument impossible.

Our smoking example may be a bit heavy handed, but less obvious variants of this debate happen all the time. Whenever we argue about purely personal opinions—opera is boring, soccer is better than baseball, pizza is tastier than nachos—we're condemned to a bottomless dispute. Because there are no common criteria for "boring" or "better" or "tastier," we can't put our claims to any common test. We can only reassert them.

Of course, reasonable arguments about these disputes become possible once common assumptions are established. For example, a nutritionist could argue that pizza is better than nachos because it provides a better balance of nutrients per calorie. Such an argument can succeed if the disputants accept the nutritionist's assumption that "a better balance of nutrients per calorie" is a criterion for "better." But if one of the disputants responds, "Nah, nachos are better than pizza because nachos taste better," then he makes a different assumption—"My sense of taste is better than your sense of taste." This is a wholly personal standard, an assumption that others are unable to share.

FOR CLASS DISCUSSION

The following questions can all be answered in alternative ways. However, not all of them will lead to reasonable arguments. Try to decide which questions will lead to reasonable arguments and which will lead only to pseudo-arguments.

1. Is Spike Lee a good film director?

2. Is postmodern architecture beautiful?

3. Should cities subsidize professional sports venues?

4. Is this abstract oil painting by a monkey smearing paint on a canvas a true work of art?

5. Are nose rings and tongue studs attractive?

FRAME OF AN ARGUMENT: A CLAIM SUPPORTED BY REASONS

We have said earlier that an argument originates in an *issue question*, which by definition is any question that provokes disagreement about the best answer. When you write an argument, your task is to take a position on the issue and to support it with reasons and evidence. The *claim* of your essay is the position you want your audience to accept. To put it another way, your claim is your essay's thesis statement, a one-sentence summary answer to your issue question. Your task, then, is to make a claim and support it with reasons.

What Is a Reason?

A *reason* (also called a *premise*) is a claim used to support another claim. In speaking or writing, a reason is usually linked to the claim with connecting words such as *because, since, for, so, thus, consequently,* and *therefore,* indicating that the claim follows logically from the reason.

Let's take an example. In one of our recent classes a woman naval ROTC student surprised her classmates by remarking that women should not be allowed to serve on submarines. A heated discussion quickly followed, expanding into the more general issue of whether women should be allowed to join military combat units. Here are frameworks the class developed for two alternative positions on that issue:

One View

CLAIM:　Women should be barred from joining military combat units.

REASON 1:   Women for the most part don't have the strength or endurance for combat roles.

REASON 2:   Serving in combat isn't necessary for women's career advancement in the military.

REASON 3:   Women in close-knit combat units would hurt unit morale by introducing sexual jealousies.

REASON 4:   Pregnancy or need to care for infants and small children would make women less reliable to a unit.

REASON 5:   Women haven't been socialized into fighters and wouldn't have the "Kill them with a bayonet!" spirit that men can get.

Alternative View

CLAIM: Women should be allowed to join combat units in the military.

REASON 1:   Millions of women are stronger and more physically fit than most men; women selected for combat duty would have the strength and endurance to do the job.

REASON 2:   The image of women as combat soldiers would help society overcome harmful gender stereotyping.

REASON 3:   Serving in combat units would open up many more opportunities for women's career advancement in the military.

REASON 4:   The justice of equal rights for women demands that women be allowed to serve in combat units.

Formulating a list of reasons in this way breaks your argumentative task into a series of subtasks. It gives you a frame for building your argument in parts. In the previous example, the frame for the argument opposing women in combat suggests five different lines of reasoning a writer might pursue. A writer might use all five reasons or select only two or three, depending on which reasons would most persuade the intended audience. Each line of reasoning would be developed in its own separate section of the argument.

For example, one section of an argument opposing women in combat might open with the following sentence: "Women shouldn't be allowed to join combat units because they don't have the strength or endurance for combat roles." In this section, the writer would describe the levels of strength and endurance currently required for combat service and provide evidence that these requirements would have to be lowered if women were to join combat units. In this section the writer might also need to support the unstated assumption that underlies this reason—that a high level of physical strength and endurance is a necessary criterion for combat effectiveness. (How one articulates and supports the underlying assumptions of an argument will be developed in Chapter 5 in our discussion of warrants and backing.)

The writer would proceed the same way for each separate section of the argument. Each section would open with a clear statement of the reason to be developed. The writer would then support each reason with evidence or chains of other reasons. In addition, if needed for the intended audience, the writer would support any underlying assumptions on which the reason depends.

To summarize our point in this section, the frame of an argument consists of a claim (the thesis statement of the essay), which is supported by one or more reasons, which are in turn supported by evidence or sequences of further reasons.

Advantages of Expressing Reasons in *Because* Clauses

Chances are that when you were a child the word *because* contained magical explanatory powers:

DOROTHY: I want to go home now.

TOMMY: Why?

DOROTHY: Because.

TOMMY: Because why?

DOROTHY: Just because.

Somehow *because* seemed decisive. It persuaded people to accept your view of the world; it changed people's minds. Later, as you got older, you discovered that *because* only introduced your arguments and that it was the reasons following *because* that made the difference. Still, *because* introduced you to the powers potentially residing in the adult world of logic.

Of course, there are many other ways to express the logical connection between a reason and a claim. Our language is rich in ways of stating *because* relationships:

- Women shouldn't be allowed to join combat units because they don't have the strength or endurance for combat roles.
- Women don't have the strength or endurance for combat roles. Therefore women should not be allowed to join combat units.
- Women don't have the strength or endurance for combat roles, so they should not be allowed to join combat units.
- One reason why women should not be allowed to join combat units is that they don't have the strength or endurance for combat roles.
- My argument that women should not be allowed to join combat units is based mainly on evidence that women don't have the strength or endurance for combat roles.

Even though logical relationships can be stated in various ways, writing out one or more *because* clauses seems to be the most succinct and manageable way to clarify an argument for oneself. We therefore suggest that sometime in the writing process you create a *working thesis statement* that summarizes your main reasons as *because* clauses attached to your claim.* Just when you compose your own working thesis statement depends largely on your writing process. Some writers like to plan out their whole argument from the start and often compose their working thesis statements with *because* clauses before they write their rough drafts. Others discover their arguments as they write. And sometimes it is a combination of both. For these writers, an extended working thesis statement is something they might write halfway through the composing process as a way of ordering their argument when various branches seem to be growing out of control. Or they might compose a working thesis statement at the very end as a way of checking the unity of the final product.

Whenever you write your extended thesis statement, the act of doing so can be simultaneously frustrating and thought provoking. Composing *because* clauses can be a powerful discovery tool, causing you to think of many different kinds of arguments to support your claim. But it is often difficult to wrestle your ideas into the *because* clause shape, which sometimes seems to be overly tidy for the complex network of ideas you are trying to work with. Nevertheless, trying to summarize your argument as a single claim with reasons should help you see more clearly what you have to do.

FOR CLASS DISCUSSION

Try this group exercise to help you see how writing *because* clauses can be a discovery procedure. Divide into small groups. Each group member should contribute an issue that he or she might like to explore. Discussing one person's issue at a time, help each member develop a claim supported by several reasons. Express each reason as a *because* clause. Then write out the working thesis statement for each person's argument by attaching the *because* clauses to the claim. Finally, try to create *because* clauses in support of an alternative claim for each issue. Recorders should select two or three working thesis statements from the group to present to the class as a whole.

---

*A working thesis statement for an argument opposing women in combat units might look like this: *Women should not be allowed to join combat units because they lack the strength, endurance, and "fighting spirit" needed in combat; because being pregnant or having small children would make them unreliable for combat at a moment's notice; and because women's presence would hurt morale of tight-knit combat units.* (A working thesis statement for an argument supporting women in combat is found on page 86.)

You might not put a bulky thesis statement like this into your essay itself; rather, a working thesis statement is a behind-the-scenes way of summarizing your argument for yourself so that you can see it whole and clear.

APPLICATION OF THIS CHAPTER'S
PRINCIPLES TO YOUR OWN WRITING

In Chapter 2 we discussed the difficulties of summarizing various types of arguments. Generally, an argument is easiest to summarize when the writer places her thesis in the introduction and uses explicit transitions to highlight the argument's reasons and structural frame. Such arguments are said to have a *self-announcing structure* because they announce their thesis (and sometimes supporting reasons) and forecast their shape at the outset. Such self-announcing arguments typically follow the conventional format of classical argument discussed in Chapter 3. The invention strategies set forth in this chapter—generating parallel *because* clauses and nutshelling them in a working thesis statement—lead naturally to a classical argument with a self-announcing structure. Each *because* clause, together with its supporting evidence, becomes a separate section of the argument.

An argument with an *unfolding structure*, in contrast, is considerably harder to summarize. In an unfolding structure, the thesis is delayed until the end or is unstated and left to be inferred by the reader from a narrative that may be both complex and subtle. As we explain in Chapter 8, unfolding structures can be especially effective for dealing with hostile audiences or with troubling or tangled issues. In contrast, classical arguments are often best for neutral or undecided audiences weighing alternative views on a clearcut issue.*

In our own classes, we ask students initially to write arguments with self-announcing structures, thereby forcing them to articulate their arguments clearly to themselves and helping them to master the art of organizing complex ideas. Later on in the course, we invite students to experiment with structures that unfold their meanings in subtler, more flexible ways.

In writing classical arguments, students often ask how much of the argument to summarize in the introduction. Consider the following options. You might announce only your claim:

Women should be allowed to join combat units.

Or you could also forecast a series of parallel reasons:

Women should be allowed to join combat units for several reasons.

Or you could forecast the actual number of reasons:

Women should be allowed to join combat units for four reasons.

---

*Instead of the terms *self-announcing* and *unfolding*, rhetoricians sometimes use the terms *closed form* and *open form*. *Closed-form* structures tell the reader in advance where the argument is headed. In choosing to use a closed form, which forecasts the structure in the introduction, the writer also chooses to follow through with that structure in a straightforward, undeviating way. In contrast, *open-form* structures are like stories or narratives, keeping the reader in suspense about the argument's final destination.

Or you could forecast the whole argument:

> Women should be allowed to join combat units because they are physically capable of doing the job; because the presence of women in combat units would weaken gender stereotypes; because opening combat units to women would expand their military career opportunities; and because it would advance the cause of civil rights.

Those, of course, are not your only options. If you choose to delay your thesis until the end (a typical kind of unfolding argument), you might place the issue question in the introduction without giving away your own position:

> Is the nation well served by allowing women to join combat units?

No formula can tell you how much of your argument to forecast in the introduction. In Chapters 7 and 8 we discuss how forecasting or withholding your thesis affects your *ethos*. We also show how a delayed thesis argument may be a better option for hostile audiences. It is clear at this point, though, that the more you forecast, the clearer your argument is to your reader, whereas the less you forecast, the more surprising your argument will be. The only general rule is this: Readers sometimes feel insulted by too much forecasting. In writing a self-announcing argument, forecast only what is needed for clarity. In short arguments readers often need only your claim. In longer arguments, however, or in especially complex ones, readers appreciate your forecasting the complete structure of the argument (claim with reasons).

APPLICATION OF THIS CHAPTER'S PRINCIPLES TO THE READING OF ARGUMENTS

When you read a complex argument that lacks explicit forecasting, it is often hard to discern its structural core, to identify its claim, and to sort out its reasons and evidence. The more "unfolding" its structure, the harder it is to see exactly how the writer makes his or her case. Moreover, extended arguments often contain digressions and subarguments. Thus there may be dozens of small interlinked arguments going on inside a slowly unfolding main argument.

When you feel yourself getting lost in an unfolding structure, try converting it to a self-announcing structure. (It might help to imagine that the argument's author must state the argument as a claim with *because* clauses. What working thesis statement might the writer construct?) Begin by identifying the writer's claim. Then ask yourself: What are the one, two, three, or four main lines of argument this writer puts forward to support that claim? State those arguments as *because* clauses attached to the claim. Then compare your *because* clauses with your class-mates'. You can expect disagreement—indeed, disagreement can enrich your understanding of a text—because the writer has left it to you to infer her intent. You should, however, find considerable overlap in your responses.

Once you have converted the support for the claim to *because* clauses and reached consensus on them, you will find it much easier to analyze the writer's reasoning, underlying assumptions, and use of evidence.

CONCLUSION

This chapter has introduced you to the rhetorical triangle with its key concepts of *logos, ethos,* and *pathos.* It has also shown how arguments originate in issue questions, how issue questions differ from information questions, and how arguments differ from pseudo-arguments. At the heart of this chapter we explained that the frame of an argument is a claim supported by reasons. As you generate reasons to support your own arguments, it is often helpful to articulate them as *because* clauses attached to the claim. Finally, we explained how you can apply the principles of this chapter to your own writing and reading of arguments.

In the next chapter we will see how to support a reason by examining its logical structure, uncovering its unstated assumptions, and planning a strategy of development.

5 The Logical Structure of Arguments

In Chapter 4 you learned that the core of an argument is a claim supported by reasons and that these reasons can often be stated as *because* clauses attached to a claim. In the present chapter we examine the logical structure of arguments in more depth.

AN OVERVIEW OF *LOGOS:* WHAT DO WE MEAN BY THE "LOGICAL STRUCTURE" OF AN ARGUMENT?

As you will recall from our discussion of the rhetorical triangle, *logos* refers to the strength of an argument's support and its internal consistency. *Logos* is the argument's logical structure. But what do we mean by "logical structure"?

First of all, what we *don't* mean by logical structure is the kind of precise certainty you get in a philosophy class in formal logic. Logic classes deal with symbolic assertions that are universal and unchanging, such as "If all ps are qs and if r is a p, then r is a q." This statement is logically certain so long as p, q, and r are pure abstractions. But in the real world, p, q, and r turn into actual things, and the relationships among them suddenly become fuzzy. For example, p might be a class of actions called "Sexual Harassment," while q could be the class called "Actions That Justify Dismissal from a Job." If r is the class "Telling Off-Color Stories," then the logic of our p–q–r statement suggests that telling off-color stories (r) is an instance of sexual harassment (p), which in turn is an action justifying dismissal from one's job (q).

Now, most of us would agree that sexual harassment is a serious offense that might well justify dismissal from a job. In turn, we might agree that telling off-color stories, if the jokes are sufficiently raunchy and are inflicted on an unwilling audience, constitutes sexual harassment. But few of us would want to say categorically that all people who tell off-color stories are harassing their listeners and ought to be fired. Most of us would want to know the particulars of the case before making a final judgment.

In the real world, then, it is difficult to say that *r*s are always *p*s or that every instance of a *p* results in *q*. That is why we discourage students from using the word *prove* in claims they write for arguments (as in "This paper will prove that euthanasia is wrong"). Real-world arguments seldom *prove* anything. They can only make a good case for something, a case that is more or less strong, more or less probable. Often the best you can hope for is to strengthen the resolve of those who agree with you or weaken the resistance of those who oppose you. If your audience believes *x* and you are arguing for *y*, you cannot expect your audience suddenly, as the result of your argument, to start believing *y*. If your argument causes an audience to experience a flicker of doubt or an instant of open-mindedness, if you win some small measure of agreement, you've done well. So proofs and dramatic shifts in position are not what real-world arguments are about.

A key difference, then, between formal logic and real-world argument is that real-world arguments are not grounded in abstract, universal statements. Rather, as we shall see, they must be grounded in beliefs, assumptions, or values granted by the audience. A second important difference is that in real-world arguments these beliefs, assumptions, or values are often unstated. So long as writer and audience share the same assumptions, it's fine to leave them unstated. But if these underlying assumptions aren't shared, the writer has a problem.

To illustrate the nature of this problem, consider one of the arguments we introduced in the last chapter.

> Women should be allowed to join combat units because the image of women in combat would help eliminate gender stereotypes.

On the face of it, this is a plausible argument. But the argument is persuasive only if the audience agrees with the writer's assumption that it is a good thing to eliminate gender stereotyping. The writer assumes that gender stereotyping (for example, seeing men as the fighters who are protecting the women and children back home) is harmful and that society would be better off without such fixed gender roles. But what if you believed that some gender roles are biologically based, divinely intended, or otherwise culturally essential and that society should strive to maintain these gender roles rather than dismiss them as "stereotypes"? If such were the case, you might believe as a consequence that our culture should socialize women to be nurturers, not fighters, and that some essential trait of "womanhood" would be at risk if women served in combat. If these were your beliefs, the argument wouldn't work for you because you would reject its underlying assumption. To persuade you with this line of reasoning, the writer would have to show not only how women in combat would help eliminate gender stereotypes but also why these stereotypes are harmful and why society would be better off without them.

The previous core argument ("Women should be allowed to join combat units because the image of women in combat would help eliminate gender stereotypes") is what the Greek philosopher Aristotle would call an enthymeme. An *enthymeme* is an incomplete logical structure that depends, for its completeness, on one or more unstated assumptions (values, beliefs, principles) that serve as the starting point of the argument. The successful arguer, said Aristotle, is the person who knows how to formulate and develop enthymemes so that the argument is rooted in the audience's values and beliefs.

To clarify the concept of "enthymeme," let's go over this same territory again more slowly, examining what we mean by "incomplete logical structure." The sentence "Women should be allowed to join combat units because the image of women in combat would help eliminate gender stereotypes" is an enthymeme. It combines a claim (women should be allowed to join combat units) with a reason expressed as a *because* clause (because the image of women in combat would help eliminate gender stereotypes). To render this enthymeme logically complete, you must supply an unstated assumption—that gender stereotypes are harmful and should be eliminated. If your audience accepts this assumption, then you have a starting place on which to build an effective argument. If your audience doesn't accept this assumption, then you must supply another argument to support it, and so on until you find common ground with your audience.

To sum up:

1. Claims are supported with reasons. You can usually state a reason as a *because* clause attached to a claim (see Chapter 4).

2. A *because* clause attached to a claim is an incomplete logical structure called an enthymeme. To create a complete logical structure from an enthymeme, the unstated assumption (or assumptions) must be articulated.

3. To serve as an effective starting point for the argument, this unstated assumption should be a belief, value, or principle that the audience grants.

Let's illustrate this structure by putting the previous example—plus a new one— into schematic form.

INITIAL ENTHYMEME:	Women should be allowed to join combat units because the image of women in combat would help eliminate gender stereotypes.
CLAIM:	Women should be allowed to join combat units.
STATED REASON:	because the image of women in combat would help eliminate gender stereotypes

UNSTATED ASSUMPTION:	Gender stereotypes are harmful and should be eliminated.
INITIAL ENTHYMEME:	Cocaine and heroin should be legalized because legalization would eliminate the black market in drugs.
CLAIM:	Cocaine and heroin should be legalized.
STATED REASON:	because legalization would eliminate the black market in drugs
UNSTATED ASSUMPTION:	An action that eliminates the black market in drugs is good. (Or, to state the assumption more fully, the benefits to society of eliminating the black market in drugs outweigh the negative effects to society of legalizing drugs.)

FOR CLASS DISCUSSION

Working individually or in small groups, identify the claim, stated reason, and unstated assumption that completes each of the following enthymemic arguments.

EXAMPLE:

Rabbits make good pets because they are gentle.

CLAIM:	Rabbits make good pets.
STATED REASON:	because they are gentle
UNSTATED ASSUMPTION:	Gentle animals make good pets.

1. We shouldn't elect Joe as committee chair because he is too bossy.

2. Buy this stereo system because it has a powerful amplifier.

3. Drugs should not be legalized because legalization would greatly increase the number of drug addicts.

4. Practicing the piano is good for kids because it teaches discipline.

5. Welfare benefits for unwed mothers should be eliminated because doing so will greatly reduce the nation's illegitimacy rate.

6. Welfare benefits for unwed mothers should not be eliminated because these benefits are needed to prevent unbearable poverty among our nation's most helpless citizens.

7. We should strengthen the Endangered Species Act because doing so will preserve genetic diversity on the planet.

8. The Endangered Species Act is too stringent because it severely damages the economy.

9. The doctor should not perform an abortion in this case because the mother's life is not in danger.

10. Abortion should be legal because a woman has the right to control her own body. (This enthymeme has several unstated assumptions behind it; see if you can recreate all the missing premises.)

ADOPTING A LANGUAGE FOR DESCRIBING ARGUMENTS: THE TOULMIN SYSTEM

Understanding a new field usually requires us to learn a new vocabulary. For example, if you were taking biology for the first time, you'd spend days memorizing dozens and dozens of new terms. Luckily, the field of argument requires us to learn a mere handful of new terms. A particularly useful set of argument terms, one we'll be using occasionally throughout the rest of this text, comes from philosopher Stephen Toulmin. In the 1950s, Toulmin rejected the prevailing models of argument based on formal logic in favor of a very audience-based courtroom model.

Toulmin's courtroom model differs from formal logic in that it assumes that (1) all assertions and assumptions are contestable by "opposing counsel" and that (2) all final "verdicts" about the persuasiveness of the opposing arguments will be rendered by a neutral third party, a judge or jury. Keeping in mind the "opposing counsel" forces us to anticipate counterarguments and to question our assumptions. Keeping in mind the judge and jury reminds us to answer opposing arguments fully, without rancor, and to present positive reasons for supporting our case as well as negative reasons for disbelieving the opposing case. Above all else, Toulmin's model reminds us not to construct an argument that appeals only to those who already agree with us. In short, it helps arguers tailor arguments to their audiences.

The system we use for analyzing arguments combines Toulmin's system with Aristotle's concept of the enthymeme. The purpose of this system is to provide writers with an economical language for articulating the structure of argument and, in the process, to help them anticipate their audience's needs. More particularly, it helps writers see enthymemes—in the form of a claim with because clauses—as the core of their argument and the other structural elements from Toulmin as strategies for elaborating and supporting that core.

This system builds on the one you have already been practicing. We simply need to add a few more key terms from Toulmin. The first key term is Toulmin's *warrant*, the name we will now use for the unstated assumption that turns an enthymeme into a complete logical structure. For example:

INITIAL ENTHYMEME:	Women should be allowed to join combat units because the image of women in combat would help eliminate gender stereotypes.
CLAIM:	Women should be allowed to join combat units.
STATED REASON:	because the image of women in combat would help eliminate gender stereotypes
WARRANT:	Gender stereotypes are harmful and should be eliminated.
INITIAL ENTHYMEME:	Cocaine and heroin should be legalized because legalization would eliminate the black market in drugs.
CLAIM:	Cocaine and heroin should be legalized.
STATED REASON:	because legalization would eliminate the black market in drugs
WARRANT:	An action that eliminates the black market in drugs is good.

Toulmin derives his term *warrant* from the concept of "warranty" or "guarantee." The warrant is the value, belief, or principle that the audience has to hold if the soundness of the argument is to be guaranteed or warranted. We sometimes make similar use of this word in ordinary language when we say, "That is an unwarranted conclusion," meaning one has leapt from information about a situation to a conclusion about that situation without any sort of general principle to justify or "warrant" that move. Thus if we claim that cocaine and heroin ought to be legalized because legalization would end the black market, we must be able to cite a general principle or belief that links our prediction that legalization would end the black market to our claim that legalization ought to occur. In this case the warrant is the statement "An action that eliminates the black market for drugs is good." It is this underlying belief that warrants or guarantees the argument. Just as automobile manufacturers must provide warranties for their cars if they want skeptical customers to buy them, we must provide warrants linking our reasons to our claims if we expect skeptical audiences to "buy" our arguments.

But arguments need more than claims, reasons, and warrants. These are simply one-sentence statements—the frame of an argument, not a developed argument. To flesh out our arguments and make them convincing, we need what Toulmin calls *grounds* and *backing*. Grounds are the supporting evidence—facts, data, statistics, testimony, or examples—that cause you to make a claim in the first place or that you produce to justify a claim in response to audience skepticism. Toulmin suggests that grounds are "what you have to go on" in an argument. In short, they are collectively all the evidence you use to support a reason. It sometimes helps to think of grounds as the answer to a "How do you know that . . . ?" question preceding a reason. (How do you know that letting women into combat units would help eliminate gender stereotypes? How do you know that legalizing drugs will end the black market?) Here is how grounds fit into our emerging argument schema.

CLAIM:	Women should be allowed to join combat units.
STATED REASON:	because the image of women in combat would help eliminate gender stereotypes
GROUNDS:	data and evidence showing that a chief stereotype of women is that they are soft and nurturing whereas men are tough and aggressive. The image of women in combat gear packing a rifle, driving a tank, firing a machine gun from a foxhole, or radioing for artillery support would shock people into seeing women not as "soft and nurturing" but as equal to men.

CLAIM:	Cocaine and heroin should be legalized.
STATED REASON:	because legalization would eliminate the black market in drugs
GROUNDS:	data and evidence showing how legalizing cocaine and heroin would eliminate the black market (statistics, data, and examples describing the size and effect of current black market, followed by arguments showing how selling cocaine and heroin legally in state-controlled stores would lower the price and eliminate the need to buy them from drug dealers)

In many cases, successful arguments require just these three components: a claim, a reason, and grounds. If the audience already accepts the unstated assumption behind the reason (the warrant), then the warrant can safely remain in the background unstated and unexamined. But if there is a chance that the audience will question or doubt the warrant, then the writer needs to back it up by providing an argument in its support. *Backing* is the argument that supports the warrant. Backing answers the question "How do you know that . . . ?" or "Why do you believe that . . . ?" prefixed to the warrant. (Why do you believe that gender stereotyping is harmful? Why do you believe that the benefits of ending the black market outweigh the costs of legalizing cocaine and heroin?) Here is how *backing* is added to our schema:

WARRANT: Gender stereotypes are harmful and should be eliminated.

BACKING: arguments showing how the existing stereotype of soft and nurturing women and tough and aggressive men is harmful to both men and women (examples of how the stereotype keeps men from developing their nurturing sides and women from developing autonomy and power; examples of other benefits that come from eliminating gender stereotypes include more egalitarian society, no limits on what persons can pursue, deeper respect for both sexes)

WARRANT: An action that eliminates the black market in drugs is good.

BACKING: an argument supporting the warrant by showing why eliminating the black market in drugs is good (statistics and examples about the ill effects of the black market, data on crime and profiteering, evidence that huge profits make drug dealing more attractive than ordinary jobs, the high cost of crime created by the black market, the cost to taxpayers of waging the war against drugs, the high cost of prisons to house incarcerated drug dealers.)

Finally, Toulmin's system asks us to imagine how a resistant audience would try to refute our argument. Specifically, the adversarial audience might challenge our reason and grounds by showing how letting women become combat soldiers wouldn't do much to end gender stereotyping or how legalizing drugs would *not* end the black market. Or the adversary might attack our warrant and backing by showing how some gender stereotypes are worth keeping, or how the negative consequences of legalizing drugs might outweigh the benefit of ending the black market.

In the case of the argument supporting women in combat, an adversary might offer one or more of the following rebuttals:

CONDITIONS OF REBUTTAL

Rebutting the reasons and grounds: Evidence that letting women join combat units wouldn't overcome gender stereotyping (very few women would want to join combat units; those that did would be considered freaks; most girls would still identify with Barbie doll models, not with female infantry)

Rebutting the warrant and backing: Arguments showing that it is important to maintain gender role differences because they are biologically based, divinely inspired, or otherwise important culturally; women should be nurturers and mothers, not fighters; essential nature of "womanhood" sullied by putting women in combat

As this example shows, adversaries can question an argument's reasons and grounds or its warrant and backing or sometimes both. Conditions of rebuttal remind writers to look at their arguments from the perspective of skeptical readers. To help writers imagine how skeptics might see weaknesses in an argument, conditions of rebuttal are often stated as conditionals using the word *unless,* as in, "It is good to overcome gender stereotyping *unless* those stereotypes are biologically based or otherwise essential for society." Conditions of rebuttal name the exceptions to the rule, the circumstances under which your reason or warrant might not hold. Stated in this manner, the conditions of rebuttal for the legalization-of-drugs argument might look like this:

CONDITIONS OF REBUTTAL

Rebutting the reason and grounds: Legalizing cocaine and heroin would eliminate the black market in drugs unless taxes on legal drugs kept the price high enough that a black market would still exist; unless new kinds of illegal designer drugs were developed and sold on the black market.

Rebutting the warrant and backing: Ending the black market is good unless the increased numbers of drug users and addicts were unacceptably high; unless harmful changes in social structure due to acceptance of drugs were too severe; unless the health and economic consequences of increased number of drug users were catastrophic; unless social costs to families and communities associated with addiction or erratic behavior during drug-induced "highs" were too great.

Toulmin's final term, used to limit the force of a claim and indicate the degree of its probable truth, is *qualifier.* The qualifier reminds us that real-world arguments almost never prove a claim. We may say things like "very likely," "probably," or "maybe" to indicate the strength of the claim we are willing to draw from our grounds and warrant. Thus if there are exceptions to your warrant or if your grounds are not very strong, you will have to qualify your claim. For example, you might say, "Except in rare cases, women should not be allowed in combat units," or "With full awareness of the potential dangers, I suggest we consider the option of legalizing drugs as a way of ending the ill effects of the black market."

Although the system just described might at first seem complicated, it is actually fairly easy to use after you've had some opportunity to practice. The following chart will help you review the terms:

ORIGINAL ENTHYMEME: your claim with *because* clause

CLAIM: the point or position you are trying to get your audience to accept

STATED REASON: your *because* clause*; your reasons are the subordinate claims you make in support of your main claim

GROUNDS: the evidence (data, facts, testimony, statistics, examples) supporting your stated reason

WARRANT: the unstated assumption behind your enthymeme, the statement of belief, value, principle, and so on, that, when accepted by an audience, warrants or underwrites your argument

BACKING: evidence or other argumentation supporting the warrant (if the audience already accepts the warrant, then backing is usually not needed, but if the audience doubts the warrant, then backing is essential)

CONDITIONS OF REBUTTAL: your acknowledgment of the limits of your claim—those conditions under which it does not hold true, in anticipation of an adversary's counterargument against your reason and grounds or against your warrant and backing

QUALIFIER: words or phrases limiting the force of your claim

To help you practice using these terms, on pages 98–99 are two more examples, displayed this time so that the conditions of rebuttal are set in an opposing column next to the reason/grounds and the warrant/backing.

---

*Most arguments have more than one *because* clause or reason in support of a claim. Each enthymeme thus develops only one line of reasoning, one piece of your whole argument.

INITIAL ENTHYMEME: Women should be barred from combat duty because the presence of women would harm unit morale.

CLAIM: Women should be barred from combat duty.

STATED REASON: because the presence of women would harm unit morale

GROUNDS: evidence and examples of how presence of women would lead to romantic or sexual relationships and create sexual competition and jealousy; evidence that male bonding is difficult when women are present; fear that a woman wouldn't be strong enough to carry a wounded buddy off a battlefield, etc.; fear that men couldn't endure watching a woman with her legs blown off in a minefield

WARRANT: Combat units need high morale to function effectively.

BACKING: arguments supporting the warrant by showing that combat soldiers have to have an utmost faith in buddies to do their job; anything that disrupts male bonding will make the unit less likely to stick together in extreme danger or endure being prisoners of war; examples of how unit cohesion is what makes a fighting unit able to withstand battle

CONDITIONS OF REBUTTAL:
Rebutting the reason and grounds: arguments that letting women join combat units would *not* harm unit morale (times are changing rapidly; men are used to working professionally with women; examples of successful mixed-gender sports teams and mountain-climbing teams; example of women astronauts working in close quarters with men; arguments that sexual and romantic liaisons would be forbidden and sexual activity punished; after a period of initial discomfort, men and women would overcome modesty about personal hygiene, etc.)

Rebutting the warrant and backing: arguments that unit morale is not as important for combat efficiency as are training and discipline; unit morale is not as important as promoting women's rights; men will have to learn to deal with the presence of women and treat them as fellow soldiers; men can learn to act professionally even if their morale is lower

QUALIFIER: In many cases the presence of women would hurt morale.

ORIGINAL ENTHYMEME: The exclusionary rule is a bad law because it allows drug dealers to escape prosecution.*

CLAIM: The exclusionary rule is a bad law.

STATED REASON: because it allows drug dealers to escape prosecution

GROUNDS: numerous cases wherein the exclusionary rule prevented police from presenting evidence in court; examples of nitpicking rules and regulations that allowed drug dealers to go free; testimony from prosecutors and police about how the exclusionary rule hampers their effectiveness

WARRANT: It is beneficial to our country to prosecute drug dealers.

BACKING: arguments showing the extent and danger of the drug problem; arguments showing that prosecuting and imprisoning drug dealers will reduce the drug problem

CONDITIONS OF REBUTTAL:
Rebuttal of reason and grounds: evidence that the exclusionary rule does not allow many drug dealers to escape prosecution (counter-evidence showing numerous times when police and prosecutors followed the exclusionary rule and still obtained convictions; statistical analysis showing that the percentage of cases in which exclusionary rule threw evidence out of court is very low)

Rebuttal of warrant and backing: arguments that reversing the exclusionary rule would have serious costs that outweigh benefits; arguments that softening the exclusionary rule would have serious costs (arguments showing that the value of protecting individual liberties outweighs the value of prosecuting drug dealers)

QUALIFIER: perhaps, tentatively

---

*The exclusionary rule is a court-mandated set of regulations specifying when evidence can and cannot be introduced into a trial. It excludes all evidence that police obtain through irregular means. In actual practice, it demands that police follow strict procedures. Opponents of the exclusionary rule claim that its "narrow technicalities" handcuff police.

FOR CLASS DISCUSSION

Working individually or in small groups, imagine that you have to write arguments developing the ten enthymemes listed in the For Class Discussion exercise on pages 91–92. Use the Toulmin schema to help you determine what you need to consider when developing each enthymeme. As an example, we have applied the Toulmin schema to the first enthymeme.

ORIGINAL ENTHYMEME: We shouldn't elect Joe as committee chair because he is too bossy.

CLAIM: We shouldn't elect Joe as committee chair.

STATED REASON: because he is too bossy

GROUNDS: various examples of Joe's bossiness; testimony about his bossiness from people who have worked with him

WARRANT: Bossy people make bad committee chairs.

BACKING: arguments showing that other things being equal, bossy people tend to bring out the worst rather than the best in those around them; bossy people tend not to ask advice, make bad decisions; etc.

CONDITIONS OF REBUTTAL: *Rebuttal of reason and grounds:* perhaps Joe isn't really bossy (counterevidence of Joe's cooperativeness and kindness; testimony that Joe is easy to work with; etc.)

Rebuttal of the warrant and backing: perhaps bossy people sometimes make good chairpersons (arguments showing that at times a group needs a bossy person who can make decisions and get things done); perhaps Joe has other traits of good leadership that outweigh his bossiness (evidence that, despite his bossiness, Joe has many other good leadership traits such as high energy, intelligence, charisma, etc.)

QUALIFIER: In most circumstances, bossy people make bad committee chairs.

USING TOULMIN'S SCHEMA TO DETERMINE A STRATEGY OF SUPPORT

Having introduced you to Toulmin's terminology for describing the logical structure of arguments, we can turn directly to a discussion of how to use these concepts for developing your own arguments. As we have seen, the claim, supporting reasons, and warrant form the frame for a line of reasoning. The majority of words in an argument, however, are devoted to grounds and backing—the supporting sections that develop the argument frame. Generally these supporting sections take one of two forms: either (1) *evidence* such as facts, examples, case studies, statistics, and testimony from experts or (2) a *sequence of reasons*—that is, further conceptual argument. The Toulmin schema can help you determine what kind of support your argument needs. Let's look at each kind of support separately.

Evidence as Support

It's often easier for writers to use evidence rather than chains of reasons for support because using evidence entails moving from generalizations to specific details—a basic organizational strategy that most writers practice regularly. Consider the following hypothetical case. A student, Ramona, wants to write a complaint letter to the head of the philosophy department about a philosophy professor, Dr. Choplogic, whom Ramona considers incompetent. Ramona plans to develop two different lines of reasoning: (1) Choplogic's courses are disorganized. (2) Choplogic is unconcerned about students. Let's look briefly at how she can develop her first main line of reasoning, which is based on the following enthymeme:

Dr. Choplogic is an ineffective teacher because his courses are disorganized.

The grounds for this argument will be all the evidence Ramona can muster showing that Choplogic's courses are disorganized. Figure 5.1 shows her initial brainstorming notes based on the Toulmin schema. The information Ramona lists under "grounds" is what she sees as the facts of the case—the hard data she will use as evidence to support her reason. Here is how this argument might look when placed into written form:

FIRST PART OF RAMONA'S ARGUMENT

Claim and reason	One reason that Dr. Choplogic is ineffective is that his courses are poorly organized. I have had him for two courses—Introduction to Philosophy and Ethics—and both were disorganized. He
Grounds (evidence in support of reason)	never gave us a syllabus or explained his grading system. At the beginning of the course he wouldn't tell us how many papers he would require, and he never seemed to know how much of the textbook material he planned to cover. For Intro he told us to read the whole text, but he covered only half of it in class. A week before the final I asked him how much of the text would be on the exam and he said he hadn't decided. The Ethics class was even more disorganized. Dr. Choplogic told us to read the text, which provided one set of terms for ethical arguments, and then he told us he didn't like the text and presented us in lecture with a wholly different set of terms. The result was a whole class of confused, angry students.

Claim: Dr. Choplogic is an ineffective teacher.
Stated reason: because his courses are disorganized
Grounds: What evidence is there that his courses are disorganized?
   —no syllabus in either Intro or Ethics
   —never announced how many papers we would have
   —didn't know what would be on tests
   —didn't like the textbook he had chosen; gave us different terms
   —didn't follow any logical sequence in his lectures

FIGURE 5.1   Ramona's initial planning notes

As you can see, Ramona has plenty of evidence to support her contention that Choplogic is disorganized. But how effective is this argument as it stands? Is this all she needs? The Toulmin schema also encourages Ramona to examine the warrant, backing, and conditions of rebuttal for this argument. Figure 5.2 shows how her planning notes continue.

This section of her planning notes helps her see her argument more fully from the audience's perspective. She believes that no one can challenge her reason and grounds—Choplogic is indeed a disorganized teacher. But she recognizes that some people might challenge her warrant ("Disorganized teachers are ineffective"). A supporter of Dr. Choplogic might say that some teachers, even though they are hopelessly disorganized, might nevertheless do an excellent job of stimulating thought and discussion. Moreover, such teachers might possess other valuable traits that outweigh their disorganization. Ramona therefore decides to address these concerns by adding another section to this portion of her argument.

CONTINUATION OF RAMONA'S ARGUMENT

Backing for warrant (shows why disorganization is bad)

Dr. Choplogic's lack of organization makes it difficult for students to take notes, to know what to study, or to relate one part of the course to another. Moreover, students lose confidence in the teacher because he doesn't seem to care enough to prepare for class.

Response to conditions of rebuttal

In Dr. Choplogic's defense, it might be thought that his primary concern is involving students in class discussions or other activities to teach us thinking skills or get us involved in philosophical discussions. But this isn't the case. Students rarely get a chance to speak in class. We just sit there listening to rambling, disorganized lectures.

Claim: Dr. Choplogic is an ineffective
teacher.
Stated reason: because his
courses are disorganized
Grounds: What evidence is there
that his courses are disorganized?
—no syllabus in either Intro or
Ethics
—never announced how many
papers we would have
—didn't know what would be on
tests
—didn't like the textbook he had
chosen; gave us different terms
—didn't follow any logical
sequence in his lectures
Warrant: Disorganized teachers
are ineffective.
Backing:
—organization helps you learn
—gets material organized in a
logical way
—helps you know what to study
—helps you take notes and relate
one part of course to another
—when teacher is disorganized,
you think he hasn't prepared for
class; makes you lose confidence

Conditions of rebuttal: Would
anybody doubt my reasons and
grounds?
—No. Every student I have ever
talked to agrees that these
are the facts about Choplogic's
courses. Everyone agrees that
he is disorganized. Of course,
the department chair might
not know this, so I will have
to provide evidence.
Would anybody doubt my warrant
and backing? Maybe they would.
—Is it possible that in some cases
disorganized teachers are good
teachers? Have I ever had a
disorganized teacher who was
good? My freshman sociology
teacher was disorganized, but
she really made you think. You
never knew where the course was
going but we had some great
discussions. Choplogic isn't like
that. He isn't using classtime to
get us involved in philosophical
thinking or discussions.
—Is it possible that Choplogic
has other good traits that
outweigh his disorganization?
I don't think he does, but I will
have to make a case for this.

FIGURE 5.2   Ramona's planning notes, continued

As the marginal notations show, this section of her argument backs the
warrant that disorganized teachers are ineffective and anticipates some of the
conditions for rebuttal that an audience might raise to defend Dr. Choplogic.
Throughout her draft, Ramona has supported her argument with effective use of
evidence. The Toulmin schema has shown her that she needed evidence primarily to support her stated reason ("Choplogic is disorganized"). But she also needed

some evidence to support her warrant ("Disorganization is bad") and to respond to possible conditions of rebuttal ("Perhaps Choplogic is teaching thinking skills").

In general, the evidence you use for support can come either from your own personal experiences and observations or from reading and research. Although many arguments depend on your skill at research, many can be supported wholly or in part from your own personal experiences, so don't neglect the wealth of evidence from your own life when searching for data. Chapter 6 is devoted to a more detailed discussion of evidence in arguments.

Sequence of Reasons as Support

So far we have been discussing how reasons can be supported with evidence. Often, however, reasons require for their support further conceptual arguing rather than empirical data. Reasons of this kind must be supported with a sequence of other reasons. Consider, for example, a writer proposing a mandatory death penalty for convicted serial killers. Let's assume that this writer, living in a state where the death penalty is legal but seldom used, is angry that a recently convicted serial killer was sentenced to life imprisonment. His claim, along with his main supporting reason, is as follows:

CLAIM:	The law should mandate capital punishment for serial killers.
STATED REASON:	Serial killings belong in a class of their own, that of exceptionally heinous crimes.
WARRANT:	Crimes that are exceptionally heinous deserve a more severe punishment than other crimes.

To make this argument, the writer can use empirical evidence to show that serial killing is heinous (data about the grisliness of the crimes). But the main thrust of the argument requires something more. The writer must show that serial killing is *exceptionally* heinous, an argument requiring a sequence of further reasons. So why should the law single out serial killers for a mandatory death sentence but not other murderers? Since all murders are heinous, what is unique about those committed by serial killers that justifies executing them while letting other murderers get by with lesser sentences? To support his stated reason and gain acceptance for his warrant that a different order of crime deserves a different order of punishment, the writer must establish the peculiarity of serial killings. To distinguish serial killings from other murders, the writer develops the following list of potential reasons:

- Serial killers have murdered more than one person, usually many; the crime is multiple.
- Serial murders are calculated crimes, often requiring extensive planning that goes far beyond the mere "intent" required in first-degree murder cases.

- Serial murders typically involve torture of at least some of the victims in order to satisfy the serial killer's deep need not just to kill but to dominate his victims.

- The repetitious nature of the crime indicates that serial killers cannot be rehabilitated.

- The repetitious nature of the crime also means that the chances of mistakenly executing a defendant, which are minuscule to begin with, are virtually nonexistent with serial killers.

Having developed a list of reasons for singling out serial killers, the writer is ready to draft this part of his argument. Here is a portion of the argument, picking up after the writer has used evidence (in the form of gruesome narratives) to demonstrate the heinous nature of serial murders.

A LINE OF ARGUMENT DEVELOPED WITH A SEQUENCE OF REASONS

These stories show the heinous nature of serial murders. "But aren't all murders heinous?" someone might ask. What makes serial murders exceptionally heinous? Why single these criminals out for a mandatory death sentence while leaving the fate of other murderers to the discretion of judges and juries?

Serial murders represent a different order of crime from other murders and belong in a class of exceptionally heinous crimes. First, serial murderers have killed more than one person, sometimes as many as twenty or thirty. Moreover, these killings are ruthless and brutal. Typically they involve torture of at least some of the victims to satisfy the serial killer's deep need not just to kill but also to humiliate and dominate his victims. Whereas most killers kill for a motive such as greed, jealousy, or momentary rage, the serial killer derives pleasure from killing. Serial killers are particularly frightening because they use their rational intelligence to plot their attack on their next victim. Their crimes are calculated, often involving extensive planning that goes beyond the mere "intent" required for other first-degree murder convictions. The very repetition of this crime indicates that serial killers cannot be rehabilitated. Lastly, when the serial killer is finally caught, he has left behind so many signature marks that it is virtually impossible to execute the wrong person. This frequent objection to capital punishment—that an innocent person may be executed—isn't an issue with serial killers, who differ substantially from other criminals.

As you can tell, this section is considerably more complex than one that simply cites data as evidence in support of a reason. Here the writer must use a sequence of reasons to make his point, showing all the ways that serial killers' crimes belong in a class of their own and thus should be punished differently. Certainly, this argument is not definitive and rests on the cumulative persuasiveness of the reasons themselves, but such an argument is considerably more compelling than simply asserting a claim without elaboration. Although developing a line of argument with a sequence of reasons is harder than using empirical evidence, many arguments will require this kind of support.

CONCLUSION

Chapters 4 and 5 have provided an anatomy of argument. They have shown that the core of an argument is a claim with reasons that usually can be summarized in one or more *because* clauses attached to the claim. Often, it is as important to support the unstated premises in your argument as it is to support the stated ones. In order to plan out an argument strategy, arguers can use the Toulmin schema, which helps writers discover grounds, warrants, and backings for their arguments and to test them through conditions for rebuttal. Finally, we saw how stated reasons and warrants are supported through the use of evidence or through sequences of other reasons. In the next chapter we will look more closely at the uses of evidence in argumentation.

 FOR CLASS DISCUSSION

1. Working individually or in small groups, consider ways you could use evidence from personal experience to support the stated reason in each of the following partial arguments:
   a. Another reason to oppose a state sales tax is that it is so annoying.
   b. Professor X should be rated down on his (her) teaching because he (she) doesn't design homework effectively to promote real learning.
   c. Professor X is an outstanding teacher because he (she) generously spends so much time outside of class counseling students with personal problems.

2. Now try to create a sequence-of-reasons argument to support the warrants in each of the partial arguments in exercise 1. The warrants for each of the arguments are stated below.
   a. Support this warrant: We should oppose taxes that are annoying.
   b. Support this warrant: The effective design of homework to promote real learning is an important criterion for rating teachers.
   c. Support this warrant: Time spent counseling students with personal problems is an important criterion for rating teachers.

3. Using Toulmin's conditions of rebuttal, work out a strategy for refuting either the stated reasons or the warrants or both in each of the arguments above.

6 Evidence in Arguments

In the previous chapter, we examined two basic ways to support arguments: through reasons supported by evidence and through reasons supported by a sequence of other reasons. In this chapter we return to a discussion of evidence—how to find, use, and evaluate it. We focus on four categories of evidence: (1) data from personal experience—either from memory or from observation; (2) data from interviews, surveys, and questionnaires; (3) data from reading, especially library research; and (4) numerical or statistical data. At the end of the chapter, we discuss how to evaluate evidence in order to use it fairly, responsibly, and persuasively.

USING EVIDENCE FROM PERSONAL EXPERIENCE

Your own life can be the source of supporting evidence in many arguments. You can draw examples from your own experience or tell your experiences as narratives to illustrate important points. Personal examples and narratives can build bridges to readers who often find personal experience more engaging and immediate than dry lists of facts or statistics. Moreover, when readers sense a writer's personal connection to and investment in an issue, they are more likely to find the writer's position creditable.

Using Personal Experience Data Collected from Memory

Many arguments can be supported extensively, sometimes even exclusively, by information gathered from personal experience or recalled from memory. Here, for example, is how a student used personal experience to help support her argument that foreign language instruction in the United States should be started in elementary school. In the following passage she supports one of her reasons: Young children can learn foreign languages faster than adults.

> We need to start foreign language training early because young children can pick up a language much faster than adults. This truth is exemplified by the experience of several of my family members. In 1993, my uncle was transferred to Switzerland by his employer. A small village named Ruthi in northeastern Switzerland became the new home of my uncle, his wife, and their two young boys, ages six and nine. To add to the difficulty of the move, no one in the family spoke German. Their experience with language acquisition ended up being a textbook case. The youngest child was able to learn German the fastest; the older child also picked it up, but not as quickly. By contrast, my uncle and aunt, who were in their early forties, could not learn the language at all. This same pattern was repeated several years later when they were transferred again, this time to Japan.

The personal examples in this paragraph support the writer's point that foreign language instruction should begin as early as possible in a child's schooling.

Using Personal Experience Data Collected from Observations

For other arguments you can gather evidence through personal observations, as in the following example:

> The intersection at 5th and Montgomery is particularly dangerous. Traffic volume on Montgomery is so heavy that pedestrians almost never find a comfortable break in the flow of cars. On April 29, I watched fifty-seven pedestrians cross this intersection. Not once did cars stop in both directions before the pedestrian stepped off the sidewalk onto the street. Typically, the pedestrian had to move into the street, start tentatively to cross, and wait until a car finally stopped. On fifteen occasions, pedestrians had to stop halfway across the street, with cars speeding by in both directions, waiting for cars in the far lanes to stop before they could complete their crossing.

USING EVIDENCE FROM INTERVIEWS, SURVEYS, AND QUESTIONNAIRES

In addition to direct observations, you can gather evidence by conducting interviews, taking surveys, or passing out questionnaires.

Conducting Interviews

Interviewing people is a useful way not only to gather expert testimony and important data but also to learn about alternative views. To conduct an effective interview, you must first have a clear sense of purpose: Why are you interviewing the person, and what information is he or she uniquely able to provide? In turn, you need to be professional and courteous.

It's crucial that you write out all questions you intend to ask beforehand, making sure that every question is related to the purpose of your interview. (Of course, be ready to move in unexpected directions if the interview opens up new territory.) Find out as much as possible about the interviewee before the interview. Your knowledge of his or her background will help establish your credibility and build a bridge between you and your source. Be punctual and respectful of your interviewee's time.

In most cases, it is best to present yourself as a listener seeking clarity on an issue rather than as an advocate of a particular position. Except in rare cases, it is a mistake to enter into argument with your interviewee, or to indicate through body language or tone of voice an antagonism toward his or her position. During the interview, play the believing role. Save the doubting role for later, when you are looking over your notes. While conducting the interview, plan either to tape it (in which case you must ask the interviewee's permission) or to take good notes. Immediately after the interview, while your memory is fresh, rewrite your notes more fully and completely.

When you use interview data in your own writing, put quotation marks around any direct quotations. Except when unusual circumstances might require anonymity, identify your source by name and indicate his or her title or credentials—whatever will convince the reader that this person's remarks are to be taken seriously. Here is how one student used interview data to support an argument against carpeting dorm rooms:

> Finally, university-provided carpets will be too expensive. According to Robert Bothell, Assistant Director of Housing Services, the cost will be $300 per room for the carpet and installation. The university would also have to purchase more vacuum cleaners for the students to use. Altogether, Bothell estimated the cost of carpets to be close to $100,000 for the whole campus.

Using Surveys or Questionnaires

Still another form of field research data can come from surveys or questionnaires. Sometimes an informal poll of your classmates can supply evidence persuasive to a reader. One of our students, in an argument supporting public transportation, asked every rider on her bus one morning the following two questions:

> Do you enjoy riding the bus more than commuting by car? If so, why?

She was able to use her data in the following paragraph:

> Last week I polled forty-eight people riding the bus between Bellevue and Seattle. Eighty percent said they enjoyed riding the bus more than commuting by car, while 20 percent preferred the car. Those who enjoyed the bus cited the following reasons in this order of preference: It saved them the hassle of driving in traffic; it gave them time to relax and unwind; it was cheaper than paying for gas and parking; it saved them time.

More formal research can be done through developing and distributing questionnaires. Developing a good questionnaire is a task of sufficient complexity that some academic disciplines devote whole courses to the topic. In general, problems with questionnaires arise when the questions are confusing or when response categories don't allow the respondent enough flexibility of choices. If you are writing an argument that depends on an elaborate questionnaire, consider checking out a book from your library on questionnaire design. A simple questionnaire, however, can be designed without formal training. Type it neatly so that it looks clean, uncluttered, and easy to complete. At the head of the questionnaire you should explain its purpose. Your tone should be courteous and, if possible, you should offer the reader some motivation to complete the questionnaire.

INEFFECTIVE EXPLANATION FOR QUESTIONNAIRE

The following questionnaire is very important for my research. I need it back by Tuesday, January 19, so please fill it out as soon as you get it. Thanks. [doesn't explain purpose; reasons for questionnaire are stated in terms of writer's needs, not audience's need]

MORE EFFECTIVE EXPLANATION

This questionnaire is aimed at improving the quality of Dickenson Library for students and staff. It should take no more than three or four minutes of your time and gives you an opportunity to say what you presently like and don't like about the library. Of course, your responses will be kept anonymous. To enable a timely report to the library staff, please return the questionnaire by Tuesday, January 19. Thank you very much. [purpose is clear; respondents see how filling out questionnaire may benefit them]

When you pass out questionnaires, you should seek a random distribution so that any person in your target population has an equal chance of being selected. Surveys lose their persuasiveness if the respondents are unrepresentative of the total population you intended to survey. For example, if your library questionnaire went only to dorm residents, then you wouldn't know how commuting students feel about the library.

USING EVIDENCE FROM READING

Although you can base some arguments on evidence from personal experience or from questionnaires and interviews, most arguments require research evidence gleaned from reading: books, magazines, journals, newspapers, government documents, computerized data banks, Internet sources, chat groups, specialized encyclopedias and almanacs, corporate bulletins, and so forth. How to find such data; how to incorporate it into your own writing through summary, paraphrase, and quotation; and how to cite it and document it are treated in detail in Part Four of this text (Chapters 16 and 17).

When you use research data from reading, it often takes one or more of the following forms: facts and examples, summaries of research studies, and testimony.

Facts and Examples

A common way to incorporate evidence from reading is to cite facts and examples. Here is how one student writer argues that plastic food packaging and Styrofoam cups aren't necessarily damaging to the environment.

> It's politically correct today to scorn plastic food wrapping and Styrofoam cups. But in the long run these containers may actually help the environment. According to environmentalist writer John Tierney, a typical household in countries that don't use plastic food wrapping produces one-third more garbage from food spoilage than do U.S. households. Those plastic wrappers on foods allow us to buy foods in small quantities and keep them sterile until use. Tierney also claims that plastic packaging requires far less energy to produce than does paper or cardboard and is lighter to transport (27). Similarly, he claims that the energy costs of producing a ceramic coffee mug and of washing it after each use make it less environmentally friendly than throwaway Styrofoam cups (44).*

Knowing that experts can disagree about what is a "fact," this writer attributes her evidence to Tierney ("Tierney claims . . . ") rather than stating Tierney's claims baldly as facts and simply citing him in parentheses.

Summaries of Research

An argument can often be supported by summarizing or quoting summary statements from research studies. Here is how a student writer used a summary statement to support his opposition to mandatory helmet laws for motorcycle riders:

---

*Here the writer is using the MLA (Modern Language Association) system for citing sources. The reader would look under "Tierney" in the Works Cited list at the end of the paper for complete bibliographic information. The numbers in parentheses are page numbers in the Tierney article. See Chapter 17.

However, a helmet won't protect against head injury when one is traveling at normal traffic speeds. According to a U.S. Department of Transportation study, "There is no evidence that any helmet thus far, regardless of cost or design, is capable of rejecting impact stress above 13 mph" ("Head Injuries" 8).*

Testimony

Research data can also take the form of *testimony,* an expert's opinion that you cite to help bolster your case. Testimony, which we might call secondhand evidence, is often blended with other kinds of data. Using testimony is particularly common wherever laypersons cannot be expected to be experts. Thus you might cite an authority on the technical feasibility of cold fusion, the effects of alcohol on fetal tissue development, or the causes of a recent airplane crash. Here is how a student writer used testimony to bolster an argument on global warming:

We can't afford to wait any longer before taking action against global warming. At a recent Senate hearing of the Subcommittee on Environmental Pollution, Senator Chafee warned: "There is a very real possibility that man—through ignorance or indifference or both—is irreversibly altering the ability of our atmosphere to [support] life" (qtd. in Begley 64). At this same hearing, Robert Watson of the National Aeronautics and Space Administration (which monitors the upper atmosphere) claimed: "Global warming is inevitable—it's only a question of magnitude and time" (qtd. in Begley 66).**

Here the writer uses no factual or statistical data that indicate that global warming is occurring; rather, she cites the testimony of experts.

USING NUMERICAL DATA AND STATISTICS

Among the most pervasive kinds of evidence in modern arguments are numerical data and statistics. Many of us, however, are understandably mistrustful of numerical data. "There are three kinds of lies," we have all heard: "lies, damned lies, and statistics."

Those who gather, use, and analyze numerical data have their own language for degrees of data manipulation. *Teasing* and *tweaking* data are usually legitimate attempts to portray data in a better light; *massaging* data may involve a bit of subterfuge but is still within acceptable limits. When the line is crossed and ma-

---

*Here the writer cites a government document listed under "Head Injuries" in the Works Cited list. The quotation is from page 8.

**In this passage the quotations come from an article listed under "Begley" in the Works Cited list. The pages, respectively, are 64 and 66. Again the citation system being used is MLA.

nipulation turns into outright, conscious misrepresentation, however, we say the data have been *cooked*—an unsavory fate for data and people alike. If we are to use data responsibly and protect ourselves from others' abuses of them, it's important for us to understand how to analyze them.

In this section, we explain basic forms of graphic representations—tables, line graphs, bar graphs, and pie charts—and then examine ways to use numerical data both responsibly and persuasively.

Representing Numbers in Tables, Graphs, and Charts

One of the simplest means for presenting numerical data to your audience is in a table. Halfway between a picture and a list, a *table* presents numerical data in columns (vertical groupings) and rows (horizontal groupings), thereby allowing us to see relationships relatively quickly.

The table presented as Figure 6.1 is intended to help people perceive how much progress a large southwestern university has made toward diversifying its faculty during a given decade. It offers snapshots of the faculty's ethnic composition in 1984 and again in 1994, followed by a summary of the changes that took place in between.

You read tables in two directions: from the top down and from left to right. The title of the table is usually at the top. In this case, the title "Southwest State University: A historical review of minority students, faculty, and staff" tells us the most general content of the table—the change over time in the ethnic makeup of the university community. Directly below, we encounter the subtitle "Full-Time faculty by tenure status, fall 1984 and fall 1994." This subtitle tells us which of the three components of the university community identified in the title—SSU faculty—is the subject of the table and the principle means—tenure status and time—used to organize the table's contents.

Continuing down the table, in the first row of categories beneath the labels we find a breakdown of the major ethnic groups ("Native American," "Asian American," etc.) composing SSU's faculty. We then move to the top of the far left column, where we find "Tenure Status." There are three variations of tenure status: "Tenured," "On track" ("on track" faculty typically are eligible to become tenured after six years of successful teaching and scholarship at the institution), and "Not on track"—a category that includes adjunct faculty who were hired with no expectation of a long-term contractual commitment from the university.

Immediately below "Tenure Status" we find the data broken down into "1984 Total," "1994 Total," and "10-Year % Change." Reading across each row, we see a series of numbers telling us the number of people in each category and the percentage of the whole that number represents. In this case, the whole is the number in the "Total" column on the right. Thus, in 1984 there were six tenured Native American faculty, representing 0.6 percent of the 937 tenured faculty in the university.

Southwest State University: A historical review of minority students, faculty, and staff

Full-Time faculty by tenure status, fall 1984 and fall 1994

Tenure status	Native American		Asian American		African American		Hispanic		White		Total		Minority	
	No.	%	No.	%	No.	%	No.	%	No.	%	No.	%	No.	%
1984 Total	9	0.6	64	4.2	21	1.4	44	2.9	1,371	90.9	1,509	100.0	138	9.1
Tenured	6	0.6	30	3.2	10	1.1	24	2.6	867	92.5	937	100.0	70	7.5
On track	2	0.7	15	5.5	5	1.8	13	4.7	240	87.3	275	100.0	35	12.7
Not on track	1	0.3	19	6.4	6	2.0	7	2.4	264	88.9	297	100.0	33	11.1
1994 Total	15	0.8	137	7.5	37	2.0	102	5.6	1,533	84.0	1,824	100.0	291	16.0
Tenured	6	0.5	54	4.9	15	1.4	49	4.5	973	88.7	1,097	100.0	124	11.3
On track	8	2.5	32	9.9	11	3.4	39	12.1	232	72.0	322	100.0	90	28.0
Not on track	1	0.2	51	12.6	11	2.7	14	3.5	328	81.0	405	100.0	77	19.0
10-Year % Change	6	66.7	73	114.1	16	76.2	58	131.8	162	11.8	315	20.9	153	110.9
Tenured	0	0.0	24	80.0	5	50.0	25	104.2	106	12.2	160	17.1	54	77.1
On track	6	300.0	17	113.3	6	120.0	26	200.0	-8	-3.3	47	17.1	55	157.1
Not on track	0	0.0	32	168.4	5	83.3	7	100.0	64	24.2	108	36.4	44	133.3

Source: SSU Office of Institutional Analysis.

FIGURE 6.1 A table showing relationships among numerical data

When you read a table, avoid the temptation simply to plunge into all the numbers. After you've read the title and headings to make basic sense of what the table is telling you, try randomly selecting several numbers in the table and saying aloud what those numbers "mean" to be sure you understand what the table is really about.

Line Graphs

At first glance, line graphs seem significantly simpler to read than tables. Sometimes we literally see the significance of a line graph at a glance. A *line graph* achieves this simplicity by converting numerical data into a series of points on an imaginary grid created by horizontal and vertical axes, and then by connecting those points. The resulting line gives us a picture of the relationship between whatever is represented on the horizontal *x*-axis and whatever is represented on the vertical *y*-axis. Although they are extremely economical, graphs can't convey the same richness of information that tables can. They are most useful when your focus is on a single relationship.

To illustrate how graphs work, consider Figure 6.2, which contains a graphic representation of a learning curve for assembly-line workers. To determine what this graph is telling you, you must first clarify what's represented on the two axes. In this case, the *x*-axis represents "Units produced," and the *y*-axis represents

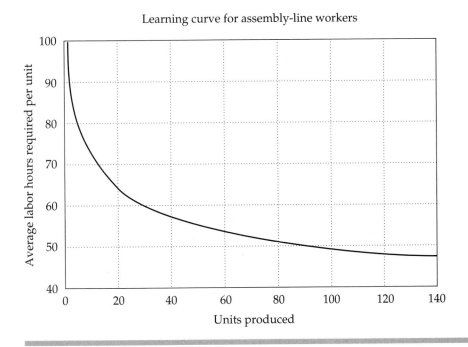

FIGURE 6.2 A line graph depicting a dynamic relationship between two variables

"Average labor hours required." The first point on the x-axis indicates that the number of hours a worker requires to produce the first unit is 100. By the time a worker gets to the 20th unit, however, the number of hours required is down to 63. By the 140th unit, production time is down to only 48 hours.

So what does this graph tell us? How would we generally characterize the nature of the relationship between the variables on the x-axis and the y-axis? Generally, we could say that they are "inversely related": As the number of units produced gets larger, the average number of hours required per unit gets smaller. That general description will hold for all line graphs that look like this one, sloping downward from left to right.

In simple English, we might translate this relationship to something like the following: "As you produce more units of anything, you learn how to produce those units more efficiently and thus spend less time producing each one." But note that the line's slope (its angle of ascent or descent) flattens out as it moves to the right, suggesting that over time the *rate* at which efficiency improves slows down. In the language of data analysis, the flattened slope indicates that changes in the y-axis variable are less and less "sensitive" to changes in the x-axis variable. At some point, presumably, you would see no further increases in efficiency, and the learning curve would be perfectly parallel to the x-axis, meaning that the y-variable is no longer sensitive to the x-variable.

Bar Graphs

Bar graphs use bars of varying length and width, extending either horizontally or vertically, to contrast two or more quantities. As with any graphic presentation, you should read from the top down, being especially careful to note the graph's title. Most bar graphs also have *legends,* or explanations of how to read the graph. Bars are typically shaded in various hues, crosshatched, left clear, or filled in with slanting lines, to differentiate among the quantities or items being compared. The legend identifies what quantity or item each bar represents.

The bar graph in Figure 6.3 is from the national newspaper, *USA Today,* well known for its extensive use of graphics as a means of simplifying complex concepts for a broad audience. The title tells us that the purpose of the graph is to illustrate "How Congress could solve the deficit problem in seven years by holding spending to the projected 3% inflation rate" instead of spending at the rate projected by the Congressional Budget Office (CBO). The legend, in turn, shows us which quantity each of the bars in the graph represents: The lightest bar represents revenues, the darkest bar represents the CBO's projected spending, and the medium-colored bar represents spending at the 3 percent inflation rate.

Reading across the x-axis, we find the *independent variable,* time—in this case a year-by-year comparison of the three quantities from 1995 to 2002. On the y-axis, we find the *dependent variable,* dollars received and expended. As we move from left to right, the revenue bar and the 3 percent growth bar gradually inch closer together, until by 2002 they are exactly equal, meaning that revenue and spending would be balanced. The black middle bar, the CBO's estimated spending, inches

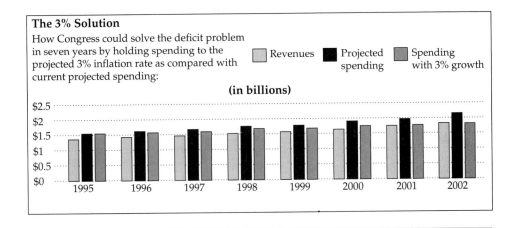

FIGURE 6.3   A bar graph that simplifies a complex concept

Source: Congressional Budget Office.

past the other two bars until finally it represents a significant imbalance between revenue and spending.

The power of this visual is that it takes a particularly dodgy set of figures and gives them the certitude of an accomplished fact. National revenue and spending figures are notoriously difficult to project. Both can be markedly affected by a number of economic factors over which we have very limited control. And the further out we make those projections, the more problematic they become. Seven years, in the world of macroeconomics, is an extraordinarily long time to project into the future. But cast into a series of bars, each one only slightly different from the previous one, the change seems not only plausible but almost inevitable. Hey, that 3 percent solution is a great idea!

Pie Charts

Pie charts, as the name suggests, depict different percentages of a total (the pie) in the form of slices. At tax time, pie charts are a favorite way of depicting all the different places that your tax dollars go. If your main point is to demonstrate that a particular portion of a whole is disproportionately large—perhaps you're arguing that too many of our tax dollars are spent on Medicaid or defense—the pie chart can demonstrate that at a glance. (Conversely, of course, it can also demonstrate that some other part of the whole is undersized relative to other shares.) The effectiveness of pie charts diminishes as we add too many slices. In most cases, you'll begin to confuse readers if you include more than five or six.

Figure 6.4 shows a pie chart from *USA Today* that, in combination with a line graph, effectively illustrates the size of three parts relative to one another. Note how the editors of *USA Today* chose to use a line graph to plot the growth in

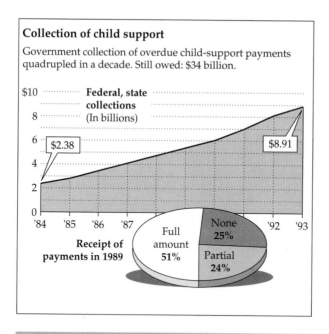

Collection of child support

Government collection of overdue child-support payments quadrupled in a decade. Still owed: $34 billion.

FIGURE 6.4   Pie chart showing relative sizes of three parts

Source: Office of Child Support Enforcement; Census Bureau. By Cliff Vancura, *USA Today.*

collections of child-support payments from 1984 to 1993. The impressive upward slope of the line nicely underscores the editors' point that child-support collections nearly quadrupled during that time period. They use a line graph to do what line graphs do best—illustrate change over time for a given dependent variable. But when they wanted to depict a static relationship, the editors naturally chose a pie chart to show that a great deal of support is still owed: In 1989, only 51 percent of children granted child support in a divorce settlement received their full amount, while 25 percent received nothing. (In place of a legend, the editors simply identify what each slice of the pie represents within the graph itself.)

Using Graphics for Effect

Any time we present numerical data pictorially, the potential for enhancing the rhetorical presence of our argument, or of manipulating our audience outright, increases substantially. By *presence*, we mean the immediacy and impact of our material. For example, raw numbers and statistics, in large doses, are likely to dull people's minds and perplex an audience. But numbers turned into pictures are very immediate. Graphs, charts, and tables help an audience see at a glance what long strings of statistics can only hint at.

We can have markedly different effects on our audience according to how we design and construct a graphic. For example, by coloring one variable prominently and enlarging it slightly, a graphic artist can greatly distort the importance of that variable. Although such depictions may carry warnings that they are "not to scale," the visual impact is often more memorable than the warning.

One of the subtlest ways of controlling an audience's perception of a numerical relationship is the way you assign values to the horizontal *x*-axis and vertical *y*-axis of a line graph. Consider, for example, the graph in Figure 6.5 depicting the monthly net profits of an ice-cream sandwich retailer. When you look at this graph, you may think that Bite O' Heaven's net profits are shooting heavenward. But if you were considering investing in an ice-cream sandwich franchise, you would want to consider how the graph was constructed. One can easily distort or overstate a rate of change on a graph.

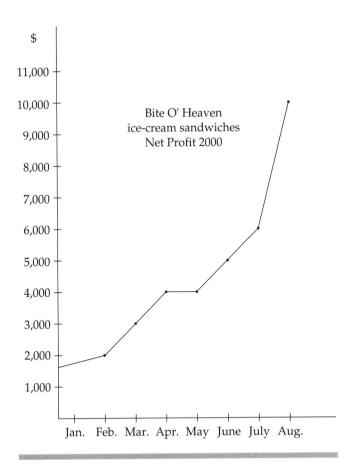

FIGURE 6.5 A line graph that distorts the data

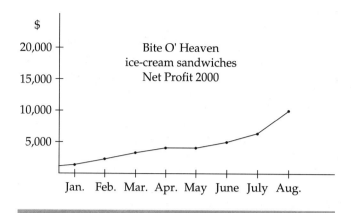

FIGURE 6.6   A line graph that more accurately depicts data

Although Figure 6.5 does represent the correct quantities, the designer's choice of increments on the *x*-axis leads to a wildly exaggerated depiction of success. If the Bite O' Heaven folks had chosen a larger increment—say, $5,000 instead of $1,000—the company's rise in profitability would look like the graph in Figure 6.6.

Another way to create a rhetorical effect with a line graph is to vary the scope of time it covers. Note that Figures 6.5 and 6.6 cover net sales from January through August. What do you think the sales figures for this company might typically be from September through December?

FOR CLASS DISCUSSION

In small groups, create a line graph for Bite O' Heaven's net profits for a whole year based on your best estimates of when people are most likely to buy ice-cream sandwiches. Then draw graphs showing net profits, quarter by quarter, over a three-year period to represent the following conditions:

1. Bite O' Heaven maintains a stable market share with no increase or decrease in the rate of profits over the three years.

2. Bite O' Heaven increases its market share, and each year is more profitable than the preceding one.

3. Bite O' Heaven loses market share, and each year is leaner than the previous one.

Using Numbers Strategically

As we have suggested, your choice and design of a graphic can markedly affect your audience's perception of your subject. But you can also influence your audience through the kinds of numbers you use: raw numbers versus percentages; or raw numbers versus "adjusted" numbers (for example, wages "adjusted for inflation"); or a statistical presentation versus a narrative one. The choice always depends on the audience you're addressing and the purpose you want to achieve.

One of the most common choices writers have to make is between citing raw numbers or citing percentages or rates. In some cases, a raw number will be more persuasive than a percentage. If you were to say that the cost of attending a state college will increase at a rate 15 percent greater than the Consumer Price Index over the next decade, most audiences would be lost—few would know how to translate that number into terms they could understand. But if you were to say that in the year 2007 the cost of attending a state college for one year will be about $21,000, you would surely grab your audience's attention. So, if you were a financial planner trying to talk a young couple into saving money for their children's college education, you would be inclined to use the raw number rather than the percentage increase. But if you were a college administrator trying to play down the increasing costs of college to a hostile legislator, you might well use the percentage increase rather than the raw number.

In turn, how you state raw numbers can markedly increase or decrease their impact on an audience. For example, to say that newspapers consume huge amounts of wood pulp is mildly interesting. To say that publication of the *New York Times* requires 248 million tons of pulp each year is even more impressive. To say that publication of just one Sunday edition of the *New York Times* requires the cutting of 75,000 trees is mind-boggling. Again, translate the number into what is most meaningful to your audience and the impact you wish to have on that audience.

Finally, in using numbers you often have a choice of presenting *indexed* or *adjusted* numbers as opposed to simple raw numbers. In the case of economic data, this difference can be particularly important. For example, in the 1996 presidential debates, Republican supporters suggested that President Clinton had signed the "largest tax increase in history" into law. Clinton supporters retorted that if adjustments were made for inflation, the tax increase was in fact smaller than one signed into law by Republican President Bush. Because of the extremely high rates of inflation during the 1980s, any economic data from that decade or prior to it should be adjusted for inflation in making comparisons to present-day dollar values.

▼ FOR CLASS DISCUSSION

A proposal to build a new ballpark in Seattle, Washington, yielded a wide range of statistical arguments. All of the following statements are reasonably faithful to the same facts:

- The ballpark would be paid for by raising the sales tax from 8.2 percent to 8.3 percent over a twenty-year period.
- The sales tax increase is one-tenth of 1 percent.
- This increase represents an average of $7.50 per person per year—about the price of a movie ticket.
- This increase represents $750 per five-person family over the twenty-year period of the tax.
- For a family building a new home in the Seattle area, this tax will increase building costs by $200.
- This is a $250 million tax increase for the residents of the Seattle area.

How would you describe the costs of the proposed ballpark if you opposed the proposal? How would you describe the costs if you supported the proposal?

WRITING YOUR OWN ARGUMENT: USING EVIDENCE PERSUASIVELY

Once you have arrived at a position on an issue, often after having written a draft that enables you to explore and clarify your own views, you need to select the best evidence possible and to use it persuasively. Whether your evidence comes from research or from personal experience, the following guidelines may be helpful.

When Possible, Select Your Data from Sources Your Reader Trusts

Other things being equal, choose data from sources you think your reader will trust. After immersing yourself in an issue, you will get a sense of who the participants in a conversation are and what their reputations tend to be. One needs to know the political biases of sources and the extent to which a source has a financial or personal investment in the outcome of a controversy. When the global-warming controversy first struck the national consciousness, two prolific writers on the subject were Carl Sagan and Dixie Lee Ray. Both writers held Ph.D. degrees in science, and both had national reputations for speaking out in the popular press on technical and scientific issues. Carl Sagan, however, was an environmentalist, and Dixie Lee Ray tended to support business and industry. To some audiences, neither of these writers was as persuasive as more cautious and less visible scientists who publish primarily in scientific journals. Similarly, citing a conservative magazine such as *Reader's Digest* is likely to be ineffective to liberal audiences, just as citing a Sierra Club publication would be ineffective to conservatives.

Increase Persuasiveness of Factual Data
by Ensuring Recency, Representativeness,
and Sufficiency

Other things being equal, choose data that are recent, representative, and sufficient. The more your data meet these criteria, the more persuasive they are.

Recency: Although some timeless issues don't depend on recent evidence, most issues, especially those related to science and technology or to current political and economic issues, depend on up-to-date information. Make sure your supporting evidence is the most recent you can find.

Representativeness: Supporting examples are more persuasive when the audience believes they are typical examples instead of extreme cases or rare occurrences. Ensuring representativeness is an especially important concern of statisticians, who seek random samples to avoid bias toward one point of view. Seeking representative examples helps you guard against selective use of data—starting with a claim and then choosing only those data that support it, instead of letting the claim grow out of a careful consideration of all the data.

Sufficiency: One of the most common reasoning fallacies, called *hasty generalization* (see pp. 441–42), occurs when a person leaps to a sweeping generalization based on only one or two instances. The criterion of sufficiency (which means having enough examples to justify your point) helps you guard against hasty generalization.

In Citing Evidence, Distinguish Fact
from Inference or Opinion

In citing research data, you should be careful to distinguish facts from inferences or opinions. A *fact* is a noncontroversial piece of data that is verifiable through observation or through appeal to communally accepted authorities. Although the distinction between a fact and an inference is a fuzzy one philosophically, at a pragmatic level all of the following can loosely be classified as facts:

The Declaration of Independence was signed in 1776.

An earthquake took place in San Francisco on the opening day of the World Series in 1989.

The amount of carbon dioxide in the atmosphere has increased by 7 percent since 1955.

An *inference*, in contrast, is an interpretation or explanation of the facts that may be reasonably doubted. This distinction is important because, when reading as a doubter, you often call into question a writer's inferences. If you treat these inferences as facts, you are likely to cite them as facts in your own arguments, thereby opening yourself up to easy rebuttal. For the most part, inferences should be handled as testimony rather than as fact.

> WEAK: Flohn informs us that the warming of the atmosphere will lead to damaging droughts by the year 2035. [treats Flohn's inference as a fact about global warming]

> BETTER: Flohn interprets the data pessimistically. He believes that the warming of the atmosphere will lead to damaging droughts by the year 2035. [makes it clear that Flohn's view is an inference, not a fact]

FOR CLASS DISCUSSION

Suppose that you developed a questionnaire to ascertain students' satisfaction with your college library as a place to study. Suppose further that you got the following responses to one of your questions (numbers in parentheses indicate percentage of total respondents who checked each response):

The library provides a quiet place to study.

Strongly agree (10%)

Agree (40%)

Undecided (5%)

Disagree (35%)

Strongly disagree (10%)

Without distorting any facts, you can report these data so that they place the current library atmosphere in either favorable or unfavorable light. Working individually or in small groups, use the data provided to complete the following sentences:

There seemed to be considerable satisfaction with the library as a quiet place to study. In response to our questionnaire . . . [complete this sentence by selecting data from the above responses].

Students seem dissatisfied with the noise level of the library. In response to our questionnaire . . . [complete this sentence by selecting data from the above responses].

CONCLUSION

Good arguers use evidence effectively. As we have seen, evidence includes facts, examples, statistics, testimony, and other forms of data, and it can come from personal experience as well as from reading and research. It is important to select data from sources that your reader will trust, to ensure the recency, representativeness, and sufficiency of your evidence, and to distinguish between facts and inferences.

WRITING ASSIGNMENTS FOR CHAPTERS 4–6

OPTION 1: *A Microtheme That Supports a Reason with Personal Experience Data* Write a one- or two-paragraph argument in which you support one of the following enthymemes, using evidence from personal experience. Most of your microtheme should support the stated reason with personal experience data. However, also include a brief passage supporting the implied warrant. The opening sentence of your microtheme should be the enthymeme itself, which serves as the thesis statement for your argument.

1. Reading fashion magazines can be detrimental to teenage girls because such magazines can lower a girl's self-esteem.
2. Learning to surf the Web might harm your studying because it causes you to waste time.
3. Getting a part-time job in college might improve your grades because the job will teach you time management.
4. X (a teacher/professor of your choosing) is an outstanding teacher because she (he) generously spends time counseling students with personal problems.
5. Any enthymeme (a claim with *because* clause) of your choice that can be supported through personal experience. Clear your enthymeme with your instructor.

OPTION 2: *A Microtheme That Uses Evidence from Research* The purpose of this microtheme is to help you learn how to support reasons with evidence gathered from research. The following presentation of data attempts to simulate the kinds of research evidence one might typically gather on note cards during a research project. (See Chapters 16 and 17 for further advice on incorporating research data into your own writing. For this assignment, assume you are writing for a popular magazine so that you do not need to use academic citations.)

The situation: By means of startling "before and after" photographs of formerly obese people, the commercial diet industry heavily advertises rapid weight loss diets that use liquids and powders or special low-calorie frozen dinners. **Your**

task: Drawing on the following data, write a short argument warning people of the hazards of these diets.

Source: Representative Ron Wyden (D–Oregon), chairman of a congressional subcommittee investigating the diet industry.

- Wyden fears that diet programs now include many shoddy companies that use misleading advertisements and provide inadequate medical supervision of their clients.
- "This industry has been built almost overnight on a very shaky foundation."
- "All the evidence says that losing large amounts of weight very fast does more harm than good."
- Wyden believes that the diet industry may need to be federally regulated.

Source: Theodore B. VanItallie, M.D., a founder of the Obesity Research Center at St. Luke's Roosevelt Hospital Center in New York.

- Rapid weight loss systems (such as liquid diets) were originally designed for morbidly obese individuals.
- For people who are only slightly overweight, rapid weight loss can be hazardous.
- When weight loss is too rapid, the body begins using lean muscle mass for fuel instead of excess fat. The result is a serious protein deficiency that can bring on heart irregularities.
- "If more than 25 percent of lost weight is lean body mass, the stage is set not only for early regain of lost weight but for a higher incidence of fatigue, hair loss, skin changes, depression and other undesirable side effects."

Source: Bonnie Blodgett, freelance writer on medical/health issues.

- Rapid weight loss may accelerate formation of gallstones. 179 people are currently suing a major diet company because of gallstone complications while pursuing the company's diet. The company denies responsibility.
- For every five people who start a commercial weight-loss program, only one stays with it long enough to lose a significant amount of weight.
- Up to 90 percent of dieters who lose more than 25 pounds gain it all back within two years.
- Only one in fifty maintains the weight loss for seven years.
- The best way to lose weight is through increased exercise, moderate reduction of calories, and a lifelong change in eating habits.

- Unless one is grossly obese and dieting under a physician's supervision, one should strive to lose no more than 1 or 2 pounds per week.

Source: Philip Kern, M.D., in a study appearing in *The New England Journal of Medicine*.

- Rapid weight loss programs result in the "yo-yo" syndrome—a pattern of compulsive fasting followed by compulsive bingeing.
- This pattern may upset the body's metabolism by producing an enzyme called lipoprotein lipase.
- This protein helps restore fat cells shrunken by dieting.
- It apparently causes formerly fat people to crave fatty foods, thereby promoting regain of lost weight.*

OPTION 3: *A Microtheme That Uses Statistical Data to Support a Point*   Defend one of the following theses:

Thesis A—"Women (blacks) made only negligible progress toward job equality between 1972 and 1981."

Thesis B—"Women (blacks) made significant progress toward job equality between 1972 and 1981."

Support your thesis with evidence drawn from the table on page 128. You can write your microtheme about the job progress of either women or blacks.

OPTION 4: *A Classical Argument*   Write a classical argument that uses at least two reasons to support your claim. Classical argument is explained in detail in Chapter 3. As we explain further in Chapter 8, classical argument is particularly effective when you are addressing neutral or undecided audiences. It has a self-announcing or closed-form structure in which you state your claim at the end of the introduction, begin body paragraphs with clearly stated reasons, and use effective transitions throughout to keep your reader on track. In developing your own argument, place your most important reason last, where it will have the greatest impact on your readers. Typically, a classical argument also summarizes anticipated objections to the writer's argument and responds to them briefly. You can place this section either before or after you develop your main argument. (Chapter 8, pages 156–65, gives a detailed explanation of how to respond to objections and alternative views.) See page 64 for a diagram of a classical argument.

The student essay on pages 129–31 illustrates a classical argument.

---

*Source of these data is Bonnie Blodgett, "The Diet Biz," *Glamour* Jan. 1991: 136ff.

TABLE FOR OPTION 3   Employed persons, by sex, race, and occupation, 1972 and 1981

| | 1972 | | | 1981 | | |
| | | Percentage | | | Percentage | |
Occupation	Total Employed (1,000)	Female	Black and Other	Total Employed (1,000)	Female	Black and Other
Professional, Technical	11,538	39.3	7.2	16,420	44.6	9.9
Accountants	720	21.7	4.3	1,126	38.5	9.9
Dentists	108	1.9	5.6	130	4.6	6.2
Engineers	1,111	0.8	3.4	1,537	4.4	7.3
Lawyers	322	3.8	1.9	581	14.1	4.6
Librarians	158	81.6	7.0	192	82.8	5.7
Physicians	332	10.1	8.2	454	13.7	14.5
Registered nurses	807	97.6	8.2	1,654	96.8	12.3
College teachers	464	28.0	9.2	585	35.2	9.2
Administrators	8,081	17.6	4.0	11,540	27.5	5.8
Bank officers	430	19.0	2.6	696	37.5	5.5
Office managers	317	41.9	1.0	504	70.6	4.0
Sales managers	574	15.7	1.6	720	26.5	4.6
Clerical Workers	14,329	75.6	8.7	18,564	80.5	11.6
Bank tellers	290	87.5	4.9	569	93.5	7.6
File clerks	274	84.9	18.0	315	83.8	22.9
Secretaries	2,964	99.1	5.2	3,917	99.1	7.2
Skilled Crafts	10,867	3.6	6.9	12,662	6.3	8.5
Carpenters	1,052	0.5	5.9	1,122	1.9	5.8
Construction	2,261	0.6	9.0	2,593	1.9	10.2
Mechanics	1,040	0.5	8.5	1,249	0.6	8.7
Transportation	3,233	4.2	14.8	3,476	8.9	15.5
Bus drivers	253	34.1	17.1	360	47.2	21.1
Truck drivers	1,449	0.6	14.4	1,878	2.7	13.9
Unskilled Labor	4,242	6.0	20.2	4,583	11.5	16.5
Service Workers	9,584	57.0	18.5	12,391	59.2	18.4
Food service	3,286	69.8	13.9	4,682	66.2	14.0
Nurses' aides	1,513	87.0	24.6	1,995	89.2	24.3
Domestic cleaners	715	97.2	64.2	468	95.1	51.5

"Half-Criminals" or Urban Athletes?
A Plea for Fair Treatment of Skateboarders
David Langley (Student)

For skateboarders, the campus of the University of California at San Diego is a wide-open, huge, geometric, obstacle-filled, stair-scattered cement paradise. The signs posted all over campus read, "No skateboarding, biking, or rollerblading on campus except on Saturday, Sunday, and Holidays." I have always respected these signs at my local skateboarding spot. On the first day of 1999, I was skateboarding here with my hometown skate buddies and had just landed a trick when a police officer rushed out from behind a pillar, grabbed me, and yanked me off my board. Because I didn't have my I.D. (I had emptied my pockets so I wouldn't bruise my legs if I fell—a little trick of the trade), the officer started treating me like a criminal. She told me to spread my legs and put my hands on my head. She frisked me and then called in my name to police headquarters.   1

"What's the deal?" I asked. "The sign said skateboarding was legal on holidays."   2

"The sign means that you can only *roll* on campus," she said.   3

But that's *not* what the sign said. The police officer gave one friend and me a warning.   4
Our third friend received a fifty-dollar ticket because it was his second citation in the last twelve months.

Like other skateboarders throughout cities, we have been bombarded with unfair treatment. We have been forced out of known skate spots in the city by storeowners and police, kicked out of every parking garage in downtown, compelled to skate at strange times of day and night, and herded into crowded skateboard parks. However, after I was searched by the police and detained for over twenty minutes in my own skating sanctuary, the unreasonableness of the treatment of skateboarders struck me. Where are skateboarders supposed to go? Cities need to change their unfair treatment of skateboarders because skateboarders are not antisocial misfits as popularly believed, because the laws regulating skateboarding are ambiguous, and because skateboarders are not given enough legitimate space to practice their sport.   5

Possibly because to the average eye most skateboarders look like misfits or delinquents, adults think of us as criminal types and associate our skateboards with antisocial behavior. But this view is unfair. City dwellers should recognize that skateboards are a natural reaction to the urban environment. If people are surrounded by cement, they are going to figure out a way to ride it. People's different environments have always produced transportation and sports to suit the conditions: bikes, cars, skis, ice skates, boats, canoes, surfboards. If we live on snow, we are going to develop skis or snowshoes to move around. If we live in an environment that has flat panels of cement for ground with lots of curbs and stairs, we are going to invent an ingeniously designed flat board with wheels. Skateboards are as natural to cement as surfboards are to water or skis to snow. Moreover, the resulting sport is as healthful, graceful, and athletic. A fair assessment of skateboarders should respect our elegant, nonpolluting means of transportation and sport, and not consider us hoodlums.   6

7   A second way that skateboarders are treated unfairly is that the laws that regulate skateboarding in public places are highly restrictive, ambiguous, and open to abusive application
by police officers. My being frisked on the UCSD campus is just one example. When I
moved to Seattle to go to college, I found the laws in Washington to be equally unclear.
When a sign says "No Skateboarding," that generally means you will get ticketed if you are
caught skateboarding in the area. But most areas aren't posted. The general rule then is that
you can skateboard so long as you do so safely without being reckless. But the definition of
"reckless" is up to the whim of the police officer. I visited the front desk of the Seattle East
Precinct and asked them exactly what the laws against reckless skateboarding meant. They
said that skaters are allowed on the sidewalk as long as they travel at reasonable speed and
the sidewalks aren't crowded. One of the officers explained that if he saw a skater sliding
down a handrail with people all around, he would definitely arrest the skater. What if there
were no people around, I asked? The officer admitted that he might arrest the lone skater
anyway and not be questioned by his superiors. No wonder skateboarders feel unfairly
treated.

8   One way that cities have tried to treat skateboarders fairly is to build skateboard parks.
Unfortunately, for the most part these parks are no solution at all. Most parks were designed
by nonskaters who don't understand the momentum or gravity pull associated with the
movement of skateboards. For example, City Skate, a park below the Space Needle in Seattle, is very appealing to the eye, but once you start to ride it you realize that the transitions
and the verticals are all off, making it unpleasant and even dangerous to skate there. The
Skate Park in Issaquah, Washington, hosts about thirty to fifty skaters at a time. Collisions
are frequent and close calls, many. There are simply too many people in a small area. The
people who built the park in Redmond, Washington, decided to make a huge wall in it for
graffiti artists "to tag on" legally. They apparently thought they ought to throw all us teenage
"half criminals" in together. At this park, young teens are nervous about skating near a gangster "throwing up his piece," and skaters become dizzy as they take deep breaths from their
workouts right next to four or five cans of spray paint expelling toxins in the air.

9   Of course, many adults probably don't think skateboarders deserve to be treated fairly.
I have heard the arguments against skateboarders for years from parents, storeowners,
friends, police officers, and security guards. For one thing, skateboarding tears up public
and private property, people say. I can't deny that skating leaves marks on handrails and
benches, and it does chip cement and granite. But in general skateboarders help the environment more than they hurt it. Skateboarding places are not littered or tagged up by
skaters. Because skaters need smooth surfaces and because any small object of litter can
lead to painful accidents, skaters actually keep the environment cleaner than the average
citizen does. As for the population as a whole, skateboarders are keeping the air a lot cleaner
than many other commuters and athletes such as boat drivers, car drivers, and skiers on ski
lifts. In the bigger picture, infrequent repair of curbs and benches is cheaper than attempts
to heal the ozone.

10   We skateboarders aren't going away, so cities are going to have to make room for us
somewhere. Here is how cities can treat us fairly. We should be allowed to skate when others are present as long as we skate safely on the sidewalks. The rules and laws should be
clearer so that skaters don't get put into vulnerable positions that make them easy targets

for tickets. I do support the opening of skate parks, but cities need to build more of them, need to situate them closer to where skateboarders live, and need to make them relatively wholesome environments. They should also be designed by skateboarders so that they are skater-friendly and safe to ride. Instead of being treated as "half criminals," skaters should be accepted as urban citizens and admired as athletes; we are a clean population, and we are executing a challenging and graceful sport. As human beings grow, we go from crawling to walking; some of us grow from strollers to skateboards.

7

Moving Your Audience

Audience-Based Reasons, *Ethos,* and *Pathos*

In Chapters 5 and 6 we discussed *logos*—the logical structure of reasons and evidence in an argument. When writers focus on *logos,* they are often trying to clarify their own thinking as much as to persuade. In this chapter and the next, we shift our attention increasingly toward persuasion, in which our goal is to move our audience as much as possible toward our own position on an issue. In this chapter we examine strategies for connecting our argument to our audience's values and beliefs (audience-based reasons), for ensuring that we are credible and trustworthy in their eyes (*ethos*), and for ensuring that our presentation affects their sympathies (*pathos*). In Chapter 8 we explain strategies for varying the tone and structure of an argument to accommodate different kinds of audiences.

Although all these strategies could be misused—that is, they could be exploited to manipulate or mislead an audience—our discussion of them presupposes a responsible arguer whose position is based on a reasoned investigation of evidence and a sincere commitment to consistent values and beliefs that can be articulated. When these strategies are employed responsibly, they can help you create arguments that are not only rationally sound but also effective for a given audience.

STARTING FROM YOUR READERS' BELIEFS: THE POWER OF AUDIENCE-BASED REASONS

Whenever you ask whether a given piece of writing is persuasive, the immediate rejoinder should always be, "Persuasive to whom?" What seems a good reason to you may not be a good reason to others. The force of a logical argument, as Aristotle showed in his explanation of enthymemes, depends on the audience's acceptance of underlying assumptions, values, or beliefs (see pp. 90–92). Finding audience-based reasons means discovering enthymemes that are effectively rooted in your audience's values.

Difference between Writer- and Audience-Based Reasons

To illustrate the difference between writer- and audience-based reasons, consider the following hypothetical case. Suppose you believed that the government should build a dam on the nearby Rapid River—a project bitterly opposed by several environmental groups. Which of the following two arguments might you use to address environmentalists?

1. The government should build a dam on the Rapid River because the only alternative power sources are coal-fired or nuclear plants, both of which pose greater risk to the environment than a hydroelectric dam.
2. The government should build a hydroelectric dam on the Rapid River because this area needs cheap power to attract heavy industry.

Clearly, the warrant of Argument 1 ("Choose the source of power that poses least risk to the environment") is rooted in the values and beliefs of environmentalists, whereas the warrant of Argument 2 ("Growth of industry is good") is likely to make them wince. To environmentalists, new industry means more congestion, more smokestacks, and more pollution. However, Argument 2 may appeal to out-of-work laborers or to the business community, to whom new industry means more jobs and a booming economy.

From the perspective of *logos* alone, Arguments 1 and 2 are both sound. They are internally consistent and proceed from reasonable premises. But they will affect different audiences very differently. Neither argument proves that the government should build the dam; both are open to objection. Passionate environmentalists, for example, might counter Argument 1 by asking why the government needs to build any power plant at all. They could argue that energy conservation would obviate the need for a new power plant. Or they might argue that building a dam hurts the environment in ways unforeseen by dam supporters. Our point, then, isn't that Argument 1 will persuade environmentalists. Rather, our point is that Argument 1 will be more persuasive than Argument 2 because it is rooted in beliefs and values that the intended audience shares.

Let's consider a second example by returning to Chapter 1 and student Gordon Adams's petition to waive his math requirement. Gordon's central argument, as you will recall, was that as a lawyer he would have no need for algebra. In Toulmin's terms, Gordon's argument looks like this:

CLAIM:	I should be exempted from the algebra requirement.
STATED REASON:	because in my chosen field of law I will have no need for algebra
GROUNDS:	testimony from lawyers and others that lawyers never use algebra
WARRANT:	(largely implicit in Gordon's argument) General education requirements should be based on career utility (that is, if a course isn't needed for a particular student's career, it shouldn't be required).
BACKING:	(not provided) arguments that career utility should be the chief criterion for requiring general education courses

In our discussions of this case with students and faculty, students generally vote to support Gordon's request, whereas faculty generally vote against it. And in fact, the University Standards Committee rejected Gordon's petition, thus delaying his entry into law school.

Why do faculty and students differ on this issue? Mainly they differ because faculty reject Gordon's warrant that general education requirements should serve students' individual career interests. Most faculty believe that general education courses, including math, provide a base of common learning that links us to the past and teaches us modes of understanding useful throughout life.

Gordon's argument thus challenges one of college professors' most cherished beliefs—that the liberal arts are innately valuable. Further, it threatens his immediate audience, the committee, with a possible flood of student requests to waive other general education requirements on the grounds of their irrelevance to a particular career choice.

How might Gordon have created a more persuasive argument? In our view, Gordon might have prevailed had he accepted the faculty's belief in the value of the math requirement and argued that he had fulfilled the "spirit" of that requirement through alternative means. He could have based his argument on an enthymeme like this:

> I should be exempted from the algebra requirement because my experience as a contractor and inventor has already provided me with equivalent mathematical knowledge.

Following this audience-based approach, he would drop all references to algebra's uselessness for lawyers and expand his discussion of the mathematical savvy he acquired on the job. This argument would honor faculty values and reduce the faculty's fear of setting a bad precedent. Few students are likely to have Gordon's background, and those who do could apply for a similar exemption without threatening the system. Again, this argument might not have won, but it would have gotten a more sympathetic hearing.

Arguments like Gordon's that call fundamental assumptions into doubt may have a long-range effect even though they lose in the short range. Although he probably would have greatly improved his chances of getting a waiver by appealing to his audience's values and beliefs, his challenge of those beliefs might in the long run contribute to the systemic change he desires. By arguing that he's a special case, Gordon would have left the rule unchallenged. By challenging the rule itself, he followed a high-risk/high-gain strategy that, even if unsuccessful, might force reexamination of the faculty's basic beliefs. If successful, meanwhile, it could affect thousands of students.

FOR CLASS DISCUSSION

Working in groups, decide which of the two reasons offered in each instance would be more persuasive to the specified audience. Be prepared to explain your reasoning to the class. Write out the implied warrant for each *because* clause and decide whether the specific audience would likely grant it.

1. Audience: a beleaguered parent
   a. I should be allowed to stay out until 2 A.M. because all my friends do.
   b. I should be allowed to stay out until 2 A.M. because only if I'm free to make my own decisions will I mature.

2. Audience: a prospective employer
   a. I would be a good candidate for a summer job at the Happy Trails Dude Ranch because I have always wanted to spend a summer in the mountains and because I like to ride horses.
   b. I would be a good candidate for a summer job at the Happy Trails Dude Ranch because I am a hard worker, because I have had considerable experience serving others in my volunteer work, and because I know how to make guests feel welcome and relaxed.

3. Audience: people who oppose the present grading system on the grounds that it is too competitive
   a. We should keep the present grading system because it prepares people for the dog-eat-dog pressures of the business world.
   b. We should keep the present grading system because it tells students that certain standards of excellence must be met if individuals are to reach their full potential.

4. Audience: young people ages fifteen to twenty-five
   a. You should become a vegetarian because an all-vegetable diet is better for your heart than a meaty diet.
   b. You should become a vegetarian because that will help eliminate the suffering of animals raised in factory farms.

   5. Audience: conservative proponents of "family values"
      a. Same-sex marriages should be legalized because doing so will promote public acceptance of homosexuality.
      b. Same-sex marriages should be legalized because doing so will make it easier for gay people to establish and sustain long-term stable relationships.

Finding Audience-Based Reasons: Asking Questions about Your Audience

As the preceding exercise makes clear, reasons are most persuasive when linked to your audience's values. This principle seems simple enough, yet it is easy to forget. For example, employers frequently complain about job interviewees whose first concern is what the company will do for them, not what they might do for the company. Conversely, job search experts agree that most successful job candidates do extensive background research on a prospective company so that in an interview they can relate their own skills to the company's problems and needs. Successful arguments typically grow out of similar attention to audience needs.

To find out all you can about an audience, we recommend that you explore the following questions:

1. *Who is your audience?* Your audience might be a single, identifiable person. For example, you might write a letter to your student body president arguing for a change in intramural policies or to a vice president for research proposing a new research and development project for your company. Or your audience might be a decision-making body such as the University Standards Committee or a philanthropic organization to which you're writing a grant proposal. At other times your audience might be the general readership of a newspaper, church bulletin, magazine, or journal, or you might produce a flier to be handed out on street corners.

2. *How much does your audience know or care about your issue?* Are members of this audience currently part of the conversation on this issue, or do they need considerable background information? If you are writing to specific decision makers (for example, the administration at your college about restructuring the student orientation program), are they currently aware of the problem or issue you are addressing, and do they care about it? If not, how can you get their attention? Your answers to these questions will especially affect your introduction and conclusion.

3. *What is your audience's current attitude toward your issue?* Are members of this audience supportive of your position on the issue? Neutral or undecided? Skeptical? Strongly opposed? What other points of view besides your own will your audience be weighing? In Chapter 8, we will explain how your answers to these questions can help you decide the structure and tone of your argument.

4. *What will be your audience's likely objections to your argument?*   What weaknesses will audience members find? What aspects of your position will be most threatening to them and why? How are your basic assumptions, values, or beliefs different from your audience's? Your answers here will help determine the content of your argument and will alert you to extra research you may need to do to bolster your response to audience objections.

5. *Finally, what values, beliefs, or assumptions about the world do you and your audience share?*   Despite differences of view on this issue, where can you find common links with your audience? How might you use these links to build bridges to your audience?

Suppose, for example, that you support universal mandatory testing for the HIV virus. It's important from the start that you understand and acknowledge the interests of those opposed to your position. Who are they, and what are their concerns? Gays and others in high-risk categories may fear finding out whether they are infected; certainly they will fear discrimination from being publicly identified as HIV carriers. Moreover, gays may see mandatory AIDS testing as part of an ongoing attempt by homophobes to stigmatize the gay community. Liberals, meanwhile, will question the necessity of invading people's privacy and compromising their civil liberties in the name of public health.

What shared values might you use to build bridges to those opposed to mandatory testing? At a minimum, you share a desire to find a cure for AIDS and a fear of the horrors of an epidemic. Moreover, you also share a respect for the dignity and humanity of those afflicted with AIDS and do not see yourself as part of a backlash against gays.

Given all that, you begin to develop a strategy to reduce your audience's fears and to link your reasons to their values. Your thinking might go something like this:

PROBLEM:	How can I create an argument rooted in shared values?
POSSIBLE SOLUTIONS:	I can try to reduce the audience's fear that mandatory AIDS testing implies a criticism of gays. I must assure that my plan ensures confidentiality. I must make clear that my first priority is stopping the spread of the disease and that this concern is shared by the gay community.
PROBLEM:	How can I reduce fear that mandatory HIV-testing will violate civil liberties?
POSSIBLE SOLUTIONS:	I must show that the enemy here is the HIV virus, not victims of the disease. Also, I might cite precedents for how we fight other infectious diseases. For example, many states require marriage license applicants to take a test for sexually transmitted diseases,

and many communities have imposed quarantines to halt the spread of epidemics. I could also argue that the right of everyone to be free from this disease outweighs the right to privacy, especially when confidentiality is assured.

The preceding example shows how a writer's focus on audience can shape the actual invention of the argument.

FOR CLASS DISCUSSION

Working individually or in small groups, plan an audience-based argumentative strategy for one or more of the following cases. Follow the thinking process used by the writer of the mandatory HIV-testing argument: (1) State several problems that the writer must solve to reach the audience, and (2) develop possible solutions to those problems.

1. An argument for the right of software companies to continue making and selling violent video games: Aim the argument at parents who oppose their children's playing these games.

2. An argument to reverse grade inflation by limiting the number of A's and B's a professor can give in a course. Aim the argument at students who fear the results of getting lower grades.

3. An argument supporting a $1-per-gallon increase in gasoline taxes as an energy conservation measure: Aim your argument at business leaders who oppose the tax for fear it will raise the cost of consumer goods.

4. An argument supporting the legalization of cocaine: Aim your argument at readers of *Reader's Digest*, a conservative magazine that supports the current war on drugs.

ETHOS AND *PATHOS* AS PERSUASIVE APPEALS: AN OVERVIEW

The previous section focused on audience-based reasons as a means of moving an audience. In terms of the rhetorical triangle introduced in Chapter 4 (see Figure 4.1), searching for audience-based reasons can be seen primarily as a function of *logos*—finding the best structure of reasons and evidence to sway an audience—although, as we shall see, it also affects the other points of the triangle. In what follows, we turn to the power of *ethos* (the appeal to credibility) and *pathos* (the appeal to an audience's sympathies) as further means of making your arguments more effective.

It's tempting to think of these three kinds of appeals as "ingredients" in an essay, like spices you add to a casserole. Succumbing to this metaphor, you might say to yourself something like this: "Just enough *logos* to give the dish body; but for more piquancy it needs a pinch of *pathos*. And for the back of the palate, a tad more *ethos*."

But this metaphor is misleading because *logos, ethos,* and *pathos* are not substances; they are ways of seeing rather than objects of sight. A better metaphor might be that of different lamps and filters used on theater spotlights to vary lighting effects on a stage. Thus, if you switch on a *pathos* lamp (possibly through using more concrete language or vivid examples), the resulting image will engage the audience's sympathy and emotions more deeply. If you overlay an *ethos* filter (perhaps by adopting a different tone toward your audience), the projected image of the writer as a person will be subtly altered. If you switch on a *logos* lamp (by adding, say, more data for evidence), you will draw the reader's attention to the logical appeal of the argument. Depending on how you modulate the lamps and filters, you shape and color your readers' perception of the issue.

Our metaphor is imperfect, of course, but our point is that *logos, ethos,* and *pathos* work together to create an impact on the reader. Consider, for example, the different impacts of the following arguments, all having roughly the same logical appeal:

1. People should adopt a vegetarian diet because only through vegetarianism can we prevent the cruelty to animals that results from factory farming.

2. I hope you enjoyed your fried chicken this evening. You know, of course, how much that chicken suffered just so you could have a tender and juicy meal. Commercial growers cram the chickens so tightly together into cages that their beaks must be cut off to keep them from pecking each other's eyes out. The only way to end the torture is to adopt a vegetarian diet.

3. People who eat meat are no better than sadists who torture other sentient creatures to enhance their own pleasure. Unless you enjoy sadistic tyranny over others, you have only one choice: Become a vegetarian.

4. People committed to justice might consider the extent to which our love of eating meat requires the agony of animals. A visit to a modern chicken factory—where chickens live their entire lives in tiny darkened coops without room to spread their wings—might raise doubts about our right to inflict such suffering on sentient creatures. Indeed, such a visit might persuade us that vegetarianism is a more just alternative.

Each argument has roughly the same logical core:

CLAIM:	People should adopt a vegetarian diet.
STATED REASON:	because only vegetarianism will end the suffering of animals subjected to factory farming
GROUNDS:	the evidence of suffering in commercial chicken farms, where chickens are crammed together, and lash out at

	each other; evidence that only widespread adoption of vegetarianism will end factory farming
WARRANT:	If we have an alternative to making animals suffer, we should adopt it.

But the impact of each argument varies. The difference between Arguments 1 and 2, most of our students report, is the greater emotional power of Argument 2. Whereas Argument 1 refers only to the abstraction "cruelty to animals," Argument 2 paints a vivid picture of chickens with their beaks cut off to prevent their pecking each other blind. Argument 2 makes a stronger appeal to *pathos* (not necessarily a stronger argument), stirring feelings by appealing simultaneously to the heart and to the head.

The difference between Arguments 1 and 3 concerns both *ethos* and *pathos.* Argument 3 appeals to the emotions through highly charged words like *torture, sadist,* and *tyranny.* But Argument 3 also draws attention to its writer, and most of our students report not liking that writer very much. His stance is self-righteous and insulting. In contrast, Argument 4's author establishes a more positive *ethos.* He establishes rapport by assuming his audience is committed to justice and by qualifying his argument with conditional terms such as *might* and *perhaps.* He also invites sympathy for his problem—an appeal to *pathos*—by offering a specific description of chickens crammed into tiny coops.

Which of these arguments is best? They all have appropriate uses. Arguments 1 and 4 seem aimed at receptive audiences reasonably open to exploration of the issue, whereas Arguments 2 and 3 seem designed to shock complacent audiences or to rally a group of True Believers. Even Argument 3, which is too abusive to be effective in most instances, might work as a rallying speech at a convention of animal liberation activists.

Our point thus far is that *logos, ethos,* and *pathos* are different aspects of the same whole, different lenses for intensifying or softening the light beam you project onto the screen. Every choice you make as a writer affects in some way each of the three appeals. The rest of this chapter examines these choices in more detail.

HOW TO CREATE AN EFFECTIVE *ETHOS:* THE APPEAL TO CREDIBILITY

The ancient Greek and Roman rhetoricians recognized that an argument would be more persuasive if the audience trusted the speaker. Aristotle argued that such trust resides within the speech itself, not in the prior reputation of the speaker. In the speaker's manner and delivery, in the speaker's tone, word choice, and arrangement of reasons, in the sympathy with which he or she treats alternative views, the speaker creates a trustworthy persona. Aristotle called the impact of the speaker's credibility the appeal from *ethos.* How does a writer create credibility? We will suggest three ways.

Be Knowledgeable about Your Issue

The first way to gain credibility is to *be* credible—that is, to argue from a strong base of knowledge, to have at hand the examples, personal experiences, statistics, and other empirical data needed to make a sound case. If you have done your homework, you will command the attention of most audiences.

Be Fair

Besides being knowledgeable about your issue, you need to demonstrate fairness and courtesy to alternative views. Because true argument can occur only where persons may reasonably disagree with one another, your *ethos* will be strengthened if you demonstrate that you understand and empathize with other points of view. There are times, of course, when you may appropriately scorn an opposing view. But these times are rare, and they mostly occur when you address audiences predisposed to your view. Demonstrating empathy to alternative views is generally the best strategy.

Build a Bridge to Your Audience

A third means of establishing credibility—building a bridge to your audience—has been treated at length in our earlier discussion of audience-based reasons. By grounding your argument in shared values and assumptions, you demonstrate your goodwill and enhance your image as a trustworthy person respectful of your audience's views. We mention audience-based reasons here to show how this aspect of *logos*—finding the reasons that are most rooted in the audience's values—also affects your *ethos* as a person respectful of your readers' views.

HOW TO CREATE *PATHOS:* THE APPEAL TO BELIEFS AND EMOTIONS

At the height of the Vietnam protest movement, a group of demonstrators "napalmed" a puppy by dousing it with gasoline and setting it on fire, thereby outraging people all across the country. Many sent indignant letters to their local newspapers, provoking the following response from the demonstrators: "Why are you outraged by the napalming of a single puppy when you are not outraged by the daily napalming of human babies in Vietnam?"

From the demonstrators' view, napalming the puppy constituted an appeal from *pathos*. *Logos*-centered arguments, the protesters felt, numbed the mind to human suffering; in napalming the puppy, they intended to reawaken in their audience a capacity for gut-level revulsion that had been dulled by too many statistics, too many abstract moral appeals, and too much superficial TV coverage of the war.

Of course, the napalmed puppy was a real-life event, a street theater protest, not a written argument. But writers often use a similar strategy. Anti-abortion proponents use it whenever they graphically describe the dismemberment of a fetus during abortion; euthanasia proponents use it when they describe the prolonged suffering of a terminally ill patient hooked hopelessly to machines. And a student uses it when he argues that a professor ought to raise his grade from a C to a B, lest he lose his scholarship and leave college, shattering the dreams of his dear old grandmother.

Are such appeals legitimate? Our answer is yes, if they intensify our response to an issue rather than divert our attention from it. Because understanding is a matter of feeling as well as perceiving, *pathos* can give access to nonlogical, but not necessarily nonrational, ways of knowing. Used effectively, pathetic appeals reveal the fullest human meaning of an issue, helping us walk in the writer's shoes. That is why arguments are often improved through the use of sensory details that allow us to see the reality of a problem or through stories that make specific cases and instances come alive.

Appeals to *pathos* become illegitimate, we believe, when they confuse an issue rather than clarify it. To the extent that students' grades should be based on performance or effort, the student's image of the dear old grandmother is an illegitimate appeal to *pathos* because it diverts the reader from rational to irrational criteria. The weeping grandmother may provide a legitimate motive for the student to study harder but not for the professor to change a grade.

Although it is difficult to classify all the ways that writers can create appeals from *pathos*, we will focus on four strategies: concrete language; specific examples and illustrations; narratives; and connotations of words, metaphors, and analogies. Each of these strategies lends "presence" to an argument by creating immediacy and emotional impact.

Use Concrete Language

Concrete language—one of the chief ways that writers achieve voice—can increase the liveliness, interest level, and personality of a writer's prose. When used in argument, concrete language typically heightens *pathos*. For example, consider the differences between the first and second drafts of the following student argument:

> *First draft:* People who prefer driving a car to taking a bus think that taking the bus will increase the stress of the daily commute. Just the opposite is true. Not being able to find a parking spot when in a hurry to work or school can cause a person stress. Taking the bus gives a person time to read or sleep, etc. It could be used as a mental break.

> *Second draft:* Taking the bus can be more relaxing than driving a car. Having someone else behind the wheel gives people time to chat with friends or cram for an exam. They can balance their checkbooks, do homework, doze off, read the daily newspaper, or get lost in a novel rather than foaming at the mouth looking for a parking space.

In this revision, specific details enliven the prose by creating images that trigger positive feelings. Who wouldn't want some free time to doze off or to get lost in a novel?

Use Specific Examples and Illustrations

Specific examples and illustrations serve two purposes in an argument: They provide evidence that supports your reasons; simultaneously, they give your argument presence and emotional resonance. Note the flatness of the following draft arguing for the value of multicultural studies in a university core curriculum:

> *Early draft:* Another advantage of a multicultural education is that it will help us see our own culture in a broader perspective. If all we know is our own heritage, we might not be inclined to see anything bad about this heritage because we won't know anything else. But if we study other heritages, we can see the costs and benefits of our own heritage.

Now note the increase in "presence" when the writer adds a specific example:

> *Revised draft:* Another advantage of multicultural education is that it raises questions about traditional Western values. For example, owning private property (such as buying your own home) is part of the American dream and is a basic right guaranteed in our Constitution. However, in studying the beliefs of American Indians, students are confronted with a very different view of private property. When the U.S. government sought to buy land in the Pacific Northwest from Chief Sealth, he replied:
>
>> The president in Washington sends words that he wishes to buy our land. But how can you buy or sell the sky? The land? The idea is strange to us. If we do not own the freshness of the air and the sparkle of the water, how can you buy them? [. . .] We are part of the earth and it is part of us. [. . .] This we know: The earth does not belong to man, man belongs to the earth.
>
> Our class was shocked by the contrast between traditional Western views of property and Chief Sealth's views. One of our best class discussions was initiated by this quotation from Chief Sealth. Had we not been exposed to a view from another culture, we would have never been led to question the "rightness" of Western values.

The writer begins his revision by evoking a traditional Western view of private property, which he then questions by shifting to Chief Sealth's vision of land as open, endless, and unobtainable as the sky. Through the use of a specific example, the writer brings to life his previously abstract point about the benefit of multicultural education.

Use Narratives

A particularly powerful way to evoke *pathos* is to tell a story that either leads into your claim or embodies it implicitly and that appeals to your readers' feelings and imagination. Brief narratives—whether true or hypothetical—are particularly effective as opening attention grabbers for an argument. To illustrate how an introductory narrative (either a story or a brief scene) can create pathetic appeals, consider the following first paragraph to an argument opposing jet skis:

> I dove off the dock into the lake, and as I approached the surface I could see the sun shining through the water. As my head popped out, I located my cousin a few feet away in a rowboat waiting to escort me as I, a twelve-year-old girl, attempted to swim across the mile-wide, pristine lake and back to our dock. I made it, and that glorious summer day is one of my most precious memories. Today, however, no one would dare attempt that swim. Jet skis have taken over this small lake where I spent many summers with my grandparents. Dozens of whining jet skis crisscross the lake, ruining it for swimming, fishing, canoeing, row-boating, and even water-skiing. More stringent state laws are needed to control jet-skiing because it interferes with other uses of lakes and is currently very dangerous.

This narrative makes a case for a particular point of view toward jet skis by winning our identification with the writer's experience. She invites us to relive that experience with her while she also taps into our own treasured memories of summer experiences that have been destroyed by change.

Opening narratives to evoke *pathos* can be powerfully effective, but they are also risky. If they are too private, too self-indulgent, too sentimental, or even too dramatic and forceful, they can backfire on you. If you have doubts about an opening narrative, read it to a sample audience before using it in your final draft.

FOR CLASS DISCUSSION

Suppose that you want to write arguments on the following issues. Working individually or in groups, think of an introductory scene or brief story that would create a pathetic appeal favorable to your argument.

1. a. an argument supporting the use of animals for biomedical research
   b. an argument opposing the use of animals for biomedical research
   (Note that the purpose of the first narrative is to create sympathy for the use of animals in medical research; perhaps you could describe the happy homecoming of a child cured by a medical procedure developed through testing on animals. The second narrative, aimed at evoking sympathy for abolishing animal research, might describe a lab rabbit's suffering.)

2. a. an argument for a program to restore a national park to its natural condition

    b. an argument for creating more camping places and overnight sites for recreational vehicles in national parks

3. a. an argument favoring legalization of drugs
   b. an argument opposing legalization of drugs

In addition to their use as opening scenes or as examples and illustrations, narratives can sometimes inform a whole argument. If the argument is conveyed entirely through narrative, then it is an *implicit* rather than *explicit* argument (see Chapter 1, pp. 4–9). But explicit arguments can sometimes contain an extensive narrative component. One source of the powerful appeal of Gordon Adams's petition to waive his math requirement (Chapter 1, pp. 19–22) is that the argument embodies aspects of his personal story.

In his appeal to the Standards Committee, Gordon Adams uses numerous standard argument devices (for example, testimony from legal practitioners that knowledge of algebra is not required in the study or practice of law). But he also makes a strong pathetic appeal by narrating the story of how he assembled his case. By foregrounding his encounters with all the people from whom he seeks information, he makes himself an actor in a story that might be called "Gordon's Quest for Truth."

The story of Gordon's construction of his argument, meanwhile, is situated inside a larger story that lends weight to the points he makes in the smaller story. The larger story, the story of Gordon's "awakening" to injustice and his fierce commitment to overcoming injustice for his people, links Gordon's desire to waive his algebra requirement to a larger, more significant story about overcoming oppression. And beyond Gordon's story lies an even larger, richer story, the history of Native American peoples in the United States over the past century, which lends an even greater resonance and clarity to his personal story. By telling his story, Gordon makes himself more human and familiar, more understandable and less threatening. This is why whenever we want to break down difference, overcome estrangement, grow closer to people we don't know well, we tell them our stories. Telling his story allowed Gordon to negotiate some considerable differences between himself and his audience of mostly white, middle-class faculty members. Even though he lost his case, he made a powerful argument that was taken seriously.

Choose Words, Metaphors, and Analogies with Appropriate Connotations

Another way of appealing to *pathos* is to select words, metaphors, or analogies with connotations that match your aim. A rapidly made decision by a city council might be called "haughty and autocratic" or "bold and decisive," depending on whether you oppose or support the council. Similarly, writers can use favorable or unfavorable metaphors and analogies to evoke different imaginative or emotional responses. A tax bill might be viewed as a "potentially fatal poison pill" or as "unpleasant but necessary economic medicine."

The writer's control over word selection raises the problem of slant or bias. Some contemporary philosophers argue that bias-free, perfectly transparent language is impossible because all language is a lens. Thus, when we choose word A rather than word B, when we put this sentence in the passive voice rather than the active, when we select this detail and omit that detail, we create bias.

Let's illustrate. When you see an unshaven man sitting on a city sidewalk with his back up against a doorway, wearing old, slovenly clothes, and drinking from a bottle hidden in a sack, what is the objective, "true" word for this person?

a person on welfare?	a welfare leech?	a beggar?
a panhandler?	a bum?	a hobo?
a wino?	a drunk?	an alcoholic?
a crazy guy?	a homeless person?	a transient?

None of these words can be called "true" or perfectly objective because each creates its own slant. Each word causes us to view the person through that word's lens. If we call the person a beggar, for example, we evoke connotations of helpless poverty and of the biblical call to give alms to the poor. *Beggar,* then, is slightly more favorable than *panhandler,* which conjures up the image of someone pestering you for money. Calling the person *homeless* shifts the focus away from the person's behavior and onto a faulty economic system that fails to provide sufficient housing. The word *wino* identifies a different cause for the person's condition— alcoholism rather than economics.

Our point, then, is that purely objective language may be impossible. But the absence of pure objectivity doesn't mean that all language is equally slanted or that truth can never be discerned. Readers can recognize degrees of bias in someone's language and distinguish between a reasonably trustworthy passage and a highly distortive one. By being on the lookout for slanted language—without claiming that any language can be totally objective—we can defend ourselves from distortive appeals to *pathos* while recognizing that responsible use of connotation can give powerful presence to an argument.

▼ FOR CLASS DISCUSSION

Outside class rewrite the introduction to one of your previous papers (or a current draft) to include more appeals to *pathos.* Use any of the strategies for giving your argument presence: concrete language, specific examples, narratives, metaphors, analogies, and connotative words. Bring both your original and your rewritten introductions to class. In pairs or in groups, discuss the comparative effectiveness of these introductions in trying to reach your intended audience.

USING VISUAL ARGUMENTS FOR EMOTIONAL APPEAL

One of the most powerful ways to engage an audience emotionally is to use photos or other visual images. If you think of any news event that has captured wide media attention, you will probably recall memorable photos. Think of the famous photograph of three-year-old John F. Kennedy Jr. saluting his father's coffin. Or think of the image most frequently used to accompany stories of the U.S. women's soccer team winning the world championship in 1999—not the great goal-keeping photo of African American Briana Scurry blocking the last penalty kick, but the photo of Brandi Chastain removing her jersey to reveal a black sports bra. Sometimes we are only partially aware of how the specific subject matter selected for a photo, its angle and cropping, the arrangement and posing of figures, and other details can encode an argument. Many analysts, for example, observed that the famous Brandi Chastain photograph linked women's sports with stereotypical views of women as sex objects rather than with athletic prowess.

Because of the power of visual images, professional writers often try to use photographs or drawings to enhance their arguments. Visual images accompanying an argument can be particularly effective at grabbing viewers' attention, conveying the seriousness of an issue, and evoking strong emotions ranging from compassion to revulsion.

One especially charged kind of visual argument is the political cartoon. Political cartoons are often mininarratives that can portray an issue dramatically, compactly, and humorously. They may illustrate the cartoonist's perspective on an issue by exaggerating and exposing the absurdity of those who take the other side or by humorously illustrating the consequences of pursuing a course of action. Political cartoons have a long history. For example, consider a cartoon on one of the most controversial issues of mid-nineteenth-century America: women's rights. The cartoon shown in Figure 7.1, from an 1868 issue of *Harper's Weekly*, depicts the cartoonist's vision of a society gone awry. It shows gender roles confused and reversed—men knitting, sewing, and struggling with babies in a crowded room while the women lounge and smoke in a saloon. The disagreeable "unnaturalness" of this gender reversal supports the cartoonist's argument that women's attempts to gain more rights threaten to undo the social order. The cartoon appealed to its nineteenth-century audience by arousing anxiety while inspiring a mocking rejection of the women's rights cause.

Although many written arguments do not lend themselves to visual illustrations, we suggest that when you construct arguments you consider the potential of visual support. Imagine that your argument is to appear in a newspaper or

FIGURE 7.1   Mid-nineteenth-century political cartoon

magazine where space will be provided for one or two visuals. What photographs or drawings might help persuade your audience toward your perspective? When visual images work well, they are analogous to the verbal strategies of concrete language, specific illustrations, narratives, and connotative words. The challenge in using visuals is to find material that is straightforward enough not to require elaborate explanations, that is timely and relevant, and that clearly adds impact to a specific part of your argument.

FOR CLASS DISCUSSION

In the following exercise, we ask you to consider the effect of visual images on a recent event that pitted cultural values against the interests of environmentalists and animal rights activists, as well as raising numerous issues related to world trade and international fisheries. This conflict centered on the Makah people's desire to resume their traditional practice of hunting gray whales—a right guaranteed them by treaty. When a U.S. federal court granted the tribe permission to resume whaling (the tribe was allotted four whales), an extended conflict broke out between the tribe and antiwhaling protesters. Both sides hired public relations firms to help sway the general public toward their views and interests. On the day that the Makah killed their first whale, the media filmed the event, creating photographs that were a public relations disaster for the tribe.

For this exercise, we ask you to read the following excerpt from an op-ed newspaper article and then answer the questions that follow. The purpose of the whole article is to give a balanced description of the killing from the viewpoints of both the Makah themselves and the antiwhaling protesters. This excerpt focuses on the power of visual images.

From "Tradition vs. a Full-Blown PR Problem: Now Come Reactions to a Very Public Death"
Eric Sorensen

You are a big public-relations firm and your client, the Makah Tribe, has just killed a whale. 1

Live. On television. And the hunt is now being replayed on screens across the nation. 2

The harpoon going in. The whale taking off. The speedboat pulling alongside and firing several shots that explode in the sea. The whale rolling. The towline going slack. 3

In Neah Bay, this is cause for celebration, a triumphant embrace of tradition and heritage, a culture's central symbol giving itself up for the kill. 4

But in living rooms across the country, unaccustomed to hunting or the ways of an obscure Northwest tribe, it's a tough moment. 5

If you're doing PR for the tribe, you're in a tough spot. 6

"The pictures are brutal," said David Margulies, president of a Dallas-based public-relations firm specializing in crisis communications. "As one of the reporters said, 'It's a brutal killing.' The average person is going to say, 'I don't see the point of doing that.'" 7

ABC anchor Peter Jennings called it "a bad chapter" in the battle over protecting whales and protecting tradition. NBC's Tom Brokaw called it "a day of ritual, death and protest." CBS referred to the "death of a beautiful titan of the sea." 8

All three showed ample footage of the whale being killed. 9

And the Makahs saw their long-simmering public-relations difficulties grow into what some experts call a full-blown PR problem. 10

Where before they juggled interview requests and stressed that whale hunting helps preserve their heritage, they now must deal with the more visceral reaction that comes from watching a big animal die a nine-minute public death. 11

Video is that powerful. It's why the U.S. military has clamped down on media access since television turned public opinion against the Vietnam War. 12

"The picture is always the most powerful element of the story," said Margulies, who advises clients on how to deal with hard-hitting programs such as *60 Minutes.* 13

"One of the first things you want to do in public relations is control the picture. Whichever side has the better picture very often controls the argument," Margulies said. 14

Moreover, he said, the picture of a dying whale now stands to be replayed over the coming months and years, whenever a television producer needs images to go with an update of the Makahs whaling controversy. 15

Jim McCarthy, a Washington, D.C.–based public-relations consultant who has advised the Makahs, suggested last year they hunt in the early morning darkness to avoid being photographed. The tribe refused. 16

17   "The bottom line is they have nothing to hide," said McCarthy, a frequent adviser of tribal groups. "They're proud of what they're doing."

18   The task for the tribe now is to appeal to the public's intellect, asking it to apply to non-Indian culture the same standard it might be asking of the Makahs, he said.

19   "There's a kind of schizophrenia going on here," McCarthy said. "More than 50,000 animals are killed for the mainstream public every day. That is often done in a more graphic way than what the Makahs are doing."

20   The killing underscores the cultural gap between tribal customs that condone killing a whale and nontribal values that cherish the imagery of *Free Willy.*

Working in small groups or as a whole class, respond to the following questions:

1. Figures 7.2 and 7.3 show two photographs taken during the day of the whale killing. Freewrite your response to these photos. How would you describe their emotional impact on the viewer? Then share your freewrites with classmates.

FIGURE 7.2 Media photograph of a scene from a whale killing

FIGURE 7.3   Another photograph of a scene from a whale killing

2. In the preceding extract, the author quotes a public relations officer who says, "One of the first things you want to do in public relations is control the picture. Whichever side has the better picture very often controls the argument." If you were a public relations consultant for the Makah, which of the two photos would you select to support the tribe's view of whale hunting as noble action—an ancient tribal custom in harmony with the tribe's traditional values? Why?

3. Which picture would best support the protesters' anti-whaling views? Why?

4. Find several different photos of a historical event or a recent news event and explain how these photos have been used to present different perspectives on the event. What emotions do the photos appeal to?

CONCLUSION

In this chapter, we have explored ways that writers can strengthen the persuasiveness of their arguments by using audience-based reasons and by creating appeals to *ethos* and *pathos*. Arguments are more persuasive if they are rooted in underlying assumptions, beliefs, and values of the intended audience. Similarly, arguments are more persuasive if readers trust the credibility of the writer and if the argument appeals to readers' hearts and imaginations as well as their intellects. Sometimes visual images may reinforce the argument by evoking strong emotional responses, thus enhancing *pathos*.

8

Accommodating Your Audience

Treating Differing Views

In the previous chapter we discussed ways of moving an audience. In this chapter we discuss a writer's options for accommodating differing views on an issue—whether to omit them, refute them, concede to them, or incorporate them through compromise and conciliation. In particular, we show you how your choices about structure, content, and tone may differ depending on whether your audience is sympathetic, neutral, or strongly resistant to your views. The strategies explained in this chapter will increase your flexibility as an arguer and enhance your chance of persuading a wide variety of audiences.

ONE-SIDED VERSUS MULTISIDED ARGUMENTS

Arguments are sometimes said to be one-sided or multisided. A *one-sided* argument presents only the writer's position on the issue without summarizing and responding to alternative viewpoints. A *multisided* argument presents the writer's position but also summarizes and responds to possible objections that an audience might raise. Which kind of argument is more persuasive to an audience?

According to some researchers, if people already agree with a writer's thesis, they usually find one-sided arguments more persuasive. A multisided argument appears wishy-washy, making the writer seem less decisive. But if people initially disagree with a writer's thesis, a multisided argument often seems more persuasive because it shows that the writer has listened to other views and thus seems more open-minded and fair. An especially interesting effect has been documented for neutral audiences. In the short run, one-sided arguments seem more persuasive to neutral audiences, but in the long run multisided arguments seem to have more staying power. Neutral audiences who've heard only one side of an issue tend to change their minds when they hear alternative arguments. By anticipating and in some cases refuting opposing views, the multisided argument diminishes the surprise and force of subsequent counterarguments and also exposes their weaknesses.

In the rest of this chapter we will show you how your choice of writing one-sided or multisided arguments is a function of how you perceive your audience's resistance to your views.

DETERMINING YOUR AUDIENCE'S RESISTANCE TO YOUR VIEWS

When you write an argument, you must always consider your audience's point of view. One way to imagine your relationship to your audience is to place it on a scale of resistance ranging from strong support of your position to strong opposition (see Figure 8.1). At the "Accord" end of this scale are like-minded people who basically agree with your position on the issue. At the "Resistance" end are those who strongly disagree with you, perhaps unconditionally, because their values, beliefs, or assumptions sharply differ from your own. Between "Accord" and "Resistance" lies a range of opinions. Close to your position will be those leaning in your direction but with less conviction than you have. Close to the resistance position will be those basically opposed to your view but willing to listen to your argument and perhaps willing to acknowledge some of its strengths. In the middle are those undecided people who are still sorting out their feelings, seeking additional information, and weighing the strengths and weaknesses of alternative views.

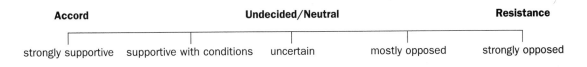

FIGURE 8.1   Scale of resistance

Seldom, however, will you encounter an issue in which the range of disagreement follows a simple line from accord to resistance. Often resistant views fall into different categories so that no single line of argument appeals to all those whose views are different from your own. You have to identify not only your audience's resistance to your ideas but also the causes of that resistance.

Consider, for example, an issue that divided the state of Washington when the Seattle Mariners baseball team demanded a new stadium. A ballot initiative asked citizens to raise taxes to build a new retractable-roof stadium for the Mariners.

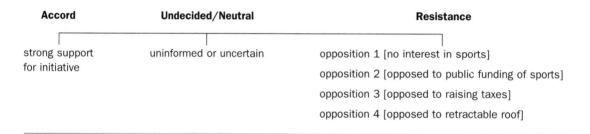

FIGURE 8.2   Scale of resistance, baseball stadium issue

Supporters of the initiative faced a complex array of resisting views (see Figure 8.2). Opponents of the initiative could be placed into four categories. Some simply had no interest in sports, cared nothing about baseball, and saw no benefit in building a huge sports facility in downtown Seattle. Another group loved baseball, perhaps followed the Mariners passionately, but was philosophically opposed to subsidizing rich players and owners with taxpayer money. This group argued that the whole sports industry needed to be restructured so that stadiums were paid for out of sports revenues. Still another group was opposed to tax hikes in general. It focused on the principle of reducing the size of government and of using tax revenues only for essential services. Finally, another powerful group supported baseball and supported the notion of public funding of a new stadium but opposed the kind of retractable-roof stadium specified in the initiative. This group wanted an old-fashioned, open-air stadium like Baltimore's Camden Yards or Cleveland's Jacobs Field.

Writers supporting the initiative found it impossible to address all these resisting audiences at once. If a supporter of the initiative wanted to aim an argument at sports haters, he or she could stress the spinoff benefits of a new ballpark (for example, the new ballpark would attract tourist revenue, renovate the deteriorating Pioneer Square neighborhood, create jobs, make sports lovers more likely to vote for public subsidies of the arts, and so forth). But these arguments were irrelevant to those who wanted an open-air stadium, who opposed tax hikes categorically, or who objected to public subsidy of millionaires.

Another kind of complexity occurs when a writer is positioned between two kinds of resisting views. Consider the position of student writer Sam, a gay man who wished to argue that gay and lesbian people should actively support legislation to legalize same-sex marriage (see Figure 8.3). Most arguments that support same-sex marriage are aimed at conservative heterosexual audiences who tend to disapprove of homosexuality and stress traditional family values. But Sam imagined writing for a gay magazine such as the *Harvard Gay and Lesbian Review* or *The Advocate,* and he wished to aim his argument at liberal gay and lesbian activists who opposed traditional marriage on different grounds. These thinkers, critiquing traditional marriage for the way it stereotypes gender roles and limits the freedom

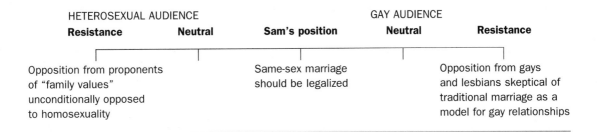

FIGURE 8.3   Scale of resistance for same-sex marriage issue

of partners, argued that heterosexual marriage wasn't a good model for relationships in the gay community. These persons constituted an audience 180 degrees removed from the conservative proponents of family values who oppose same-sex marriage on moral and religious grounds.

In writing his early drafts, Sam was stymied by his attempt to address both audiences at once. Only after he blocked out the conservative "family values" audience and imagined an audience of what he called "liberationist" gays and lesbians was he able to develop a consistent argument. (You can read Sam's essay on pages 294–96.)

The Mariners example and the same-sex marriage example illustrate the difficulty of adapting your argument to your audience's position on the scale of resistance. Yet doing so is important because you need a stable vision of your audience before you can determine an effective content, structure, and tone for your argument. As we showed in Chapter 7, an effective content derives from your choosing audience-based reasons that appeal to your audience's values, assumptions, and beliefs. As we show in the rest of this chapter, an effective structure and tone are often a function of where your audience falls on the scale of resistance. The next sections show how you can adjust your arguing strategy depending on whether your audience is supportive, neutral, or hostile.

APPEALING TO A SUPPORTIVE AUDIENCE: ONE-SIDED ARGUMENT

Although arguing to a supportive audience might seem like preaching to the choir, such arguments are common. Usually, the arguer's goal is to convert belief into action—to inspire a party member to contribute to a senator's campaign or a bored office worker to sign up for a change-your-life weekend seminar.

Typically, appeals to a supportive audience are structured as one-sided arguments that either ignore opposing views or reduce them to "enemy" stereotypes. Filled with motivational language, these arguments list the benefits that will ensue from your donations to the cause and the horrors just around the corner if the other side wins. One of the authors of this text recently received a fundraising letter from an environmental lobbying group declaring, "It's crunch time for the polluters and their pals on Capitol Hill." The "corporate polluters" and "anti-environment politicians," the letter continues, have "stepped up efforts to roll back our environmental protections—relying on large campaign contributions, slick PR firms and well-heeled lobbyists to get the job done before November's election." This letter makes the reader feel part of an in-group of good guys fighting the big business "polluters." Nothing in the letter examines environmental issues from business's perspective or attempts to examine alternative views fairly. Since the intended audience already believes in the cause, nothing in the letter invites readers to consider the issues more complexly. Rather, the goal is to solidify support, increase the fervor of belief, and inspire action. Most appeal arguments make it easy to act, ending with an 800 phone number to call, a tear-out postcard to send in, or a congressperson's address to write to.

APPEALING TO A NEUTRAL OR UNDECIDED AUDIENCE: CLASSICAL ARGUMENT

The in-group appeals that motivate an already supportive audience can repel a neutral or undecided audience. Because undecided audiences are like jurors weighing all sides of an issue, they distrust one-sided arguments that caricature other views. Generally the best strategy for appealing to undecided audiences is the classical argument described in Chapter 3 (pp. 63–65).

What characterizes the classical argument is the writer's willingness to summarize opposing views fairly and to respond to them openly—either by trying to refute them or by conceding to their strengths and then shifting to a different field of values. Let's look at these strategies in more depth.

Summarizing Opposing Views

The first step toward responding to opposing views in a classical argument is to summarize them fairly. Follow the *principle of charity*, which obliges you to avoid loaded, biased, or "straw man" summaries that oversimplify or distort opposing arguments, making them easy to knock over.

Consider the differences between an unfair and a fair summary of George Will's "Lies, Damned Lies, and . . ." (pp. 28–30), which we examined in Chapter 2.

UNFAIR SUMMARY

In a recent *Newsweek* editorial, right-wing columnist George Will parrots the capitalist party line about the virtues and successes of the free enterprise system. He mocks women who complain about the gender pay gap, labeling them whiny feminists. Citing biased statistics gathered by two ultra-conservative, antifeminist women authors, Will claims that women are not discriminated against in the workplace even though they make only 74 cents to a man's dollar and even though only a tiny percentage of top executives in Fortune 500 companies are women. He insults women by claiming that women's unequal pay is the result of their "cheerful" acceptance of their natural roles as mothers that lead them to desire flexible jobs rather than well-paying ones. He blindly dismisses the need for government action. Normal women, he claims, should be able to see that women have the best of all possible worlds because our wonderful economy lets them combine family with jobs.

This summary both distorts and oversimplifies Will's position. By adopting a sarcastic tone ("our wonderful economy") and by using loaded phrases ("right-wing," "parrots the capitalist party line," and so forth), the writer reveals a bias against Will that neutral readers will distrust. In failing to summarize Will's statistical explanations for both the current pay gap and the absence of women in top executive positions, the writer oversimplifies Will's argument, preventing the reader from understanding Will's reasoning. The writer thus sets up a straw man that is easier to knock over than is Will's original argument.

For an example of fair summaries of Will, see the versions we have written in Chapter 2 (pp. 34–35). In those examples we follow the principle of charity by summarizing Will's views as justly and accurately as possible.

FOR CLASS DISCUSSION

Suppose that you believe that ROTC courses ought to receive academic credit and thus you oppose the views of the student writer of "ROTC Courses Should Not Get College Credit" on pp. 458–60. Working individually or in groups, prepare two different summaries of this writer's views, as follows:

1. Unfair summary using loaded language or straw man oversimplification or distortion

2. Fair summary following the principle of charity

When you are finished, be prepared to read your summaries aloud to the class as a whole.

Refuting Opposing Views

Once you have summarized opposing views, you can either refute them or concede to their strengths. In refuting an opposing view, you attempt to convince readers that its argument is logically flawed, inadequately supported, or based on erroneous assumptions. In refuting an argument, you can rebut (1) the writer's stated reason and grounds, (2) the writer's warrant and backing, or (3) both. Put in less specialized language, you can rebut a writer's reasons and evidence or the writer's underlying assumptions. Let's begin with a simple example. Suppose you wanted to refute this argument:

We shouldn't elect Joe as committee chair because he is too bossy.

Displayed in Toulmin's terms, the argument looks like this:

CLAIM:	We shouldn't elect Joe as committee chair.
STATED REASON:	because he is too bossy
GROUNDS:	evidence that Joe is bossy
WARRANT:	Bossy people make bad committee chairs.

One way to refute this argument is to rebut the stated reason and grounds:

REBUTTAL OF REASON AND GROUNDS

I disagree with you that Joe is bossy. In fact, Joe is very unbossy. He's a good listener who's willing to compromise, and he involves others in decisions. The example you cite for his being bossy wasn't typical. It was a one-time circumstance that doesn't represent his normal behavior. [The writer could then provide examples of Joe's cooperative nature.]

Or you could concede that Joe is bossy but rebut the argument's warrant that bossiness is a bad trait:

REBUTTAL OF WARRANT

I agree that Joe is bossy, but in this circumstance bossiness is just the trait we need. This committee hasn't gotten anything done for six months and time is running out. We need a decisive person who can come in, get the committee organized, assign tasks, and get the job done.

Let's now illustrate these strategies in a more complex situation. For an example, we'll look at the issue of whether recycling is an effective strategy for saving the environment. A controversial subissue of recycling is whether the United States is running out of space for sanitary landfills. Here is how one environmental writer argues that there are no places left to dump our garbage:

Because the United States is running out of landfill space, Americans will simply not be able to put the 180 million tons of solid waste they generate each year into landfills, where 70 percent of it now goes. Since 1979, the United States has exhausted more than two-thirds of its landfills; projections indicate that another one-fifth will close over the next five years. Between 1983 and 1987, for example, New York closed 200 of its 500 landfills; this year Connecticut will exhaust its landfill capacity. If the problem seemed abstract to Americans, it became odiously real in the summer of 1989 as most of the nation watched the notorious garbage barge from Islip, New York, wander 6,000 miles, searching for a place to dump its rancid 3,100-ton load.*

This passage tries to persuade us that the United States is running out of landfill space. Now watch how writer John Tierney attempts to refute this argument in an influential 1996 *New York Times Magazine* article entitled "Recycling Is Garbage:"

REBUTTAL OF ARGUMENT THAT AMERICA IS RUNNING OUT OF LANDFILL SPACE

[Proponents of recycling believe that] our garbage will bury us. The *Mobro's*[†] saga was presented as a grim harbinger of future landfill scarcity, but it actually represented a short-lived scare caused by new environmental regulations. As old municipal dumps were forced to close in the 1980's, towns had to send their garbage elsewhere and pay higher prices for scarce landfill space. But the higher prices predictably encouraged companies to open huge new landfills, in some regions creating a glut that set off price-cutting wars. Over the past few years, landfills in the South and Middle West have been vying for garbage from the New York area, and it has become cheaper to ship garbage there than to bury it locally.

America has a good deal more landfill space available than it did 10 years ago. [. . .] A. Clark Wiseman, an economist at Gonzaga University in Spokane, Wash., has calculated that if Americans keep generating garbage at current rates for 1,000 years, and if all their garbage is put in a landfill 100 yards deep, by the year 3000 this national garbage heap will fill a square piece of land 35 miles on each side.

This doesn't seem a huge imposition in a country the size of America. The garbage would occupy only 5 percent of the area needed for the national array of solar panels proposed by environmentalists. The millennial landfill would fit on one-tenth of 1 percent of the range land now available for grazing in the continental United States.[‡]

In this case, Tierney uses counterevidence to rebut the reason and grounds of the original enthymeme: "Recycling is needed because the United States is running out of landfill space." Tierney attacks this argument by disagreeing with the stated reason that the United States is running out of landfill space.

Writers are also likely to question the underlying assumptions (warrants) of an opposing view. For an example, consider another recycling controversy: From

---

*George C. Lodge and Jeffrey F. Rayport, "Knee-Deep and Rising: America's Recycling Crisis," *Harvard Business Review* Sept–Oct. 1991, 132.

[†]*Mobro* is the name of the notorious garbage barge from Islip, New York, referred to at the end of the previous quotation.

[‡]John Tierney, "Recycling Is Garbage," *New York Times Magazine* 30 June 1996, 28.

an economic perspective, is recycling cost-effective? In criticizing recycling, Tierney argues that recycling wastes money; he provides evidence that "every time a sanitation department crew picks up a load of bottles and cans from the curb, New York City loses money." In Toulmin's terms, Tierney's line of reasoning is structured as follows:

TIERNEY'S ENTHYMEME:	Promoting recycling is bad policy because it costs more to recycle material than to bury the same material in a landfill.
CLAIM:	Promoting recycling is bad policy.
STATED REASON:	because it costs more to recycle material than to bury the same material in a landfill
GROUNDS:	evidence of the high cost of recycling [Tierney cites evidence that it costs New York City $200 more per ton to collect and dispose of recyclables than to bury them]
WARRANT:	We should dispose of garbage in the least expensive way.

In rebutting Tierney's argument, proponents of recycling typically accepted Tierney's figures on recycling costs in New York City (that is, they agreed that in New York City recycling was more expensive than burying garbage). But in various ways they attacked his warrant. Typically, proponents of recycling said that even if the costs of recycling were higher than burying wastes in a landfill, recycling still benefited the environment by reducing the amount of virgin materials taken from nature. This argument says, in effect, that saving virgin resources takes precedence over economic costs.

These examples show how a refutation can focus either on the stated reasons and grounds of an argument or on the warrants and backing.

FOR CLASS DISCUSSION

Imagine how each of the following arguments might be fleshed out with grounds and backing. Then attempt to refute each argument by suggesting ways to rebut the reason and grounds, or the warrant and backing, or both.

1. Writing courses should be pass/fail because the pass/fail system would encourage more creativity.

2. The government should make cigarettes illegal because cigarettes cause cancer and heart disease.

3. Majoring in engineering is better than majoring in music because engineers make more money than musicians.

4. People should not eat meat because doing so causes needless pain and suffering to animals.

5. The endangered species law is too stringent because it seriously hampers the economy.

Strategies for Rebutting Evidence

Whether you are rebutting an argument's reasons and grounds or its warrant and backing, you will frequently need to question a writer's use of evidence. Here are some strategies that you can use.

Deny the Truth of the Data

What one writer considers a fact another may consider a case of wrong information. If you have reason to doubt a writer's facts, then call them into question.

Cite Counterexamples or Countertestimony

One of the most effective ways to counter an argument based on examples is to cite a counterexample. The effect of counterexamples is to deny the conclusiveness of the original data. Similarly, citing an authority whose testimony counters other expert testimony is a good way to begin refuting an argument based on testimony.

Cast Doubt on the Representativeness or Sufficiency of Examples

Examples are powerful only if the audience feels them to be representative and sufficient. Many environmentalists complained that John Tierney's attack on recycling was based too largely on data from New York City and that it didn't accurately take into account the more positive experiences of other cities and states. When data from outside New York City were examined, the cost-effectiveness and positive environmental impact of recycling seemed more apparent.

Cast Doubt on the Relevance or Recency of the Examples, Statistics, or Testimony

The best evidence is up-to-date. In a rapidly changing universe, data that are even a few years out-of-date are often ineffective. For example, as the demand for recycled goods increases, the cost of recycling will be reduced. Out-of-date statistics will skew any argument about the cost of recycling. Another problem with data is their occasional lack of relevance. For example, in arguing that an adequate ozone layer is necessary for preventing skin cancers, it is not relevant to cite statistics on the alarming rise of lung cancers.

Call into Question the Credibility of an Authority

If an opposing argument is based on testimony, you can undermine its persuasiveness if you show that a person being cited lacks up-to-date or relevant expertise in the field. (This procedure is different from the *ad hominem* fallacy discussed in Appendix 1 because it doesn't attack the personal character of the authority but only the authority's expertise on a specific matter.)

Question the Accuracy or Context of Quotations

Evidence based on testimony is frequently distorted by being either misquoted or taken out of context. Often scientists qualify their findings heavily, but these qualifications are omitted by the popular media. You can thus attack the use of a quotation by putting it in its original context or by restoring the qualifications accompanying the quotation in its original source.

Question the Way Statistical Data Were Produced or Interpreted

Chapter 6 provides fuller treatment of how to question statistics. In general, you can rebut statistical evidence by calling into account how the data were gathered, treated mathematically, or interpreted. It can make a big difference, for example, whether you cite raw numbers or percentages or whether you choose large or small increments for the axes of graphs.

Example of a Student Essay Using Refutation Strategy

The following extract from a student essay is the refutation section of a classical argument appealing to a neutral or undecided audience. In this essay, student writer Marybeth Hamilton argues the claim that First Place, an alternative public school for homeless children that also provides support services for their families, should continue to be publicly funded because it provides the emotional and educational support homeless children need to become mainstreamed. In the beginning of her essay, Marybeth explains that First Place provides not only a nurturing, supportive educational environment for its homeless students but also services such as counseling and therapy for the students' families. At least 80 percent of the children at First Place have witnessed domestic violence or have experienced physical, sexual, or emotional abuse. Lacking permanent housing, many of these children have moved from school to school. Because running First Place is costly and can accommodate only 4 percent of her city's homeless children who need help, Marybeth recognizes that her audience may object to First Place. Consequently, to reach the neutral and resistant members of her audience, she devotes the following portion of her argument to summarizing and refuting opposing views.

From "First Place: A Healing School for Homeless Children"

Marybeth Hamilton (Student)

... As stated earlier, the goal of First Place is to prepare students for returning to main- 1
stream public schools. Although there are many reasons to continue operating an agency
like First Place, there are some who would argue against it. One argument is that the school
is too expensive, costing many more taxpayer dollars per child than a mainstream school.
I can understand this objection to cost, but one way to look at First Place is as a preventa-
tive action by the city to reduce the future costs of crime and welfare. Because all the students at First Place are at-risk for educational failure, drug and alcohol abuse, or numerous
other long-term problems, a program like First Place attempts to stop the problems before
they start. In the long run, the city could be saving money in areas such as drug rehabili-
tation, welfare payments, or jail costs.

Others might criticize First Place for spending some of its funding on social services 2
for the students and their families instead of spending it all on educational needs. When
the city is already making welfare payments and providing a shelter for the families, why
do they deserve anything more? Basically, the job of any school is to help a child become
educated and have social skills. At First Place, students' needs run deep, and their entire
families are in crisis. What good is it to help just the child when the rest of the family is
still suffering? The education of only the child will not help the family out of poverty. Therefore, First Place helps parents look for jobs by providing job search help including assistance
with résumés. They even supply clothes to wear to an interview. First Place also provides
a parent support group for expressing anxieties and learning coping skills. This therapy
helps parents deal with their struggles in a productive way, reducing the chance that they
will take out their frustration on their child. All these "extras" are an attempt to help the
family get back on its feet and become self-supporting.

Another objection to an agency like First Place is that the short-term stay at First Place 3
does no long-term good for the student. However, in talking with Michael Siptroth, a
teacher at First Place, I learned that the individual attention the students receive helps
many of them catch up in school quite quickly. He reported that some students actually
made a three-grade-level improvement in one year. This improvement definitely contributes
to the long-term good of the student, especially in the area of self-esteem. Also, the students
at First Place are in desperate situations. For most, any help is better than no help. Thus
First Place provides extended day care for the children so they won't have to be unsuper-
vised at home while their parents are working or looking for work. For example, some
homeless children live in motels on Aurora Avenue, a major highway that is overrun with
fast cars, prostitutes, and drugs. Aurora Avenue is not a safe place for children to play, so
the extended day care is important for many of First Place's students.

Finally, opponents might question the value of removing students from mainstream 4
classrooms. Some might argue that separating children from regular classrooms is not good
because it further highlights their differences from the mainstream children. Also, the separation period might cause additional alienation when the First Place child does return to

a mainstream school. In reality, though, the effects are quite different. Children at First Place are sympathetic to each other. Perhaps for the first time in their lives, they do not have to be on the defensive because no one is going to make fun of them for being homeless; they are all homeless. The time spent at First Place is usually a time for catching up to the students in mainstream schools. When students catch up, they have one fewer reason to be seen as different from mainstream students. If the students stayed in the mainstream school and continued to fall behind, they would only get teased more.

5   First Place is a program that merits the community's ongoing moral and financial support. With more funding, First Place could help many more homeless children and their families along the path toward self-sufficiency. While this school is not the ultimate answer to the problem of homelessness, it is a beginning. These children deserve a chance to build their own lives, free from the stigma of homelessness, and I, as a responsible citizen, feel a civic and moral duty to do all I can to help them.

FOR CLASS DISCUSSION

Having worked as a teacher's aide at First Place school, Marybeth Hamilton is familiar with the public criticism that the school receives. Individually or in groups, analyze the refutation strategies she employs in her argument.

1. Summarize each of the opposing reasons that Marybeth anticipates from her audience.

2. How does she attempt to refute each line of reasoning in the opposing argument? In each case does she refute her audience's reason and grounds, the warrant, or both?

3. Which of her counterexamples and counter-reasons do you think is her strongest? After reading her argument, would you as a city resident vote for the allotment of more public money for this school? Why or why not?

Conceding to Opposing Views

In writing a classical argument, a writer must sometimes concede to an opposing argument rather than refute it. Sometimes you encounter portions of an argument that you simply can't refute. For example, suppose you support the legalization of hard drugs such as cocaine and heroin. Adversaries argue that legalizing hard drugs will increase the number of drug users and addicts. You might dispute the size of their numbers, but you reluctantly agree that they are right. Your strategy in this case is not to refute the opposing argument but to concede to it by admitting that legalization of hard drugs will promote heroin and cocaine addiction. Having made that concession, your task is then to show that the benefits of drug legalization still outweigh the costs you've just conceded.

As this example shows, the strategy of a concession argument is to switch from the field of values employed by the writer you disagree with to a different field of values more favorable to your position. You don't try to refute the writer's stated reason and grounds (by arguing that legalization will *not* lead to increased drug usage and addiction) or the writer's warrant (by arguing that increased drug use and addiction is not a problem). Rather, you shift the argument to a new field of values by introducing a new warrant, one that you think your audience can share (that the benefits of legalization—eliminating the black market and ending the crime and violence associated with procurement of drugs—outweigh the costs of increased addiction). To the extent that opponents of legalization share your desire to stop drug-related crime, shifting to this new field of values is a good strategy. Although it may seem that you weaken your own position by conceding to an opposing argument, you may actually strengthen it by increasing your credibility and gaining your audience's goodwill. Moreover, conceding to one part of an opposing argument doesn't mean that you won't refute other parts of that argument.

APPEALING TO A RESISTANT AUDIENCE: DELAYED THESIS OR ROGERIAN ARGUMENT

Whereas classical argument is effective for neutral or undecided audiences, it is often less effective for audiences strongly opposed to the writer's position. Because resisting audiences often hold values, assumptions, or beliefs widely different from the writer's, they are unswayed by classical argument, which attacks their worldview too directly. On many values-laden issues such as abortion, gun control, gay rights, and welfare reform, the distance between a writer and a resisting audience can be so great that dialogue hardly seems possible.

Because of these wide differences in basic beliefs and values, a writer's goal is seldom to convert resistant readers to the writer's position. The best that the writer can hope for is to reduce somewhat the level of resistance, perhaps by opening a channel of conversation, increasing the reader's willingness to listen, and preparing the way for future dialogue. If you can get a resistant audience to say, "Well, I still don't agree with you, but I now understand you better and respect your views more," you will have been highly successful.

Delayed-Thesis Argument

In many cases you can reach a resistant audience by using a *delayed-thesis* structure in which you wait until the end of your argument to reveal your thesis. Classical argument asks you to state your thesis in the introduction, support it with reasons and evidence, and then summarize and refute opposing views. Rhetorically, however, it is not always advantageous to tell your readers where you stand at the start of your argument or to separate yourself so definitively from alternative views. For resistant audiences, it may be better to keep the issue open, delaying the revelation of your own position until the end of the essay.

To illustrate the different effects of classical versus delayed-thesis arguments, we invite you to read a delayed-thesis argument by nationally syndicated columnist Ellen Goodman. The article appeared shortly after the nation was shocked by a brutal gang rape in New Bedford, Massachusetts, in which a woman was raped on a pool table by patrons of a local bar.*

Minneapolis Pornography Ordinance
Ellen Goodman

1   Just a couple of months before the pool-table gang rape in New Bedford, Mass., *Hustler* magazine printed a photo feature that reads like a blueprint for the actual crime. There were just two differences between *Hustler* and real life. In *Hustler,* the woman enjoyed it. In real life, the woman charged rape.

2   There is no evidence that the four men charged with this crime had actually read the magazine. Nor is there evidence that the spectators who yelled encouragement for two hours had held previous ringside seats at pornographic events. But there is a growing sense that the violent pornography being peddled in this country helps to create an atmosphere in which such events occur.

3   As recently as last month, a study done by two University of Wisconsin researchers suggested that even "normal" men, prescreened college students, were changed by their exposure to violent pornography. After just ten hours of viewing, reported researcher Edward Donnerstein, "the men were less likely to convict in a rape trial, less likely to see injury to a victim, more likely to see the victim as responsible." Pornography may not cause rape directly, he said, "but it maintains a lot of very callous attitudes. It justifies aggression. It even says you are doing a favor to the victim."

4   If we can prove that pornography is harmful, then shouldn't the victims have legal rights? This, in any case, is the theory behind a city ordinance that recently passed the Minneapolis City Council. Vetoed by the mayor last week, it is likely to be back before the Council for an overriding vote, likely to appear in other cities, other towns. What is unique about the Minneapolis approach is that for the first time it attacks pornography, not because of nudity or sexual explicitness, but because it degrades and harms women. It opposes pornography on the basis of sex discrimination.

5   University of Minnesota Law Professor Catherine MacKinnon, who co-authored the ordinance with feminist writer Andrea Dworkin, says that they chose this tactic because they believe that pornography is central to "creating and maintaining the inequality of the sexes. . . . Just being a woman means you are injured by pornography."

---

*The rape occurred in 1985 and was later made the subject of an Academy Award–winning movie, *The Accused,* starring Jodie Foster.

They defined pornography carefully as, "the sexually explicit subordination of women, graphically depicted, whether in pictures or in words." To fit their legal definition it must also include one of nine conditions that show this subordination, like presenting women who "experience sexual pleasure in being raped or . . . mutilated. . . ." Under this law, it would be possible for a pool-table rape victim to sue *Hustler.* It would be possible for a woman to sue if she were forced to act in a pornographic movie. Indeed, since the law describes pornography as oppressive to all women, it would be possible for any woman to sue those who traffic in the stuff for violating her civil rights.   6

In many ways, the Minneapolis ordinance is an appealing attack on an appalling problem. The authors have tried to resolve a long and bubbling conflict among those who have both a deep aversion to pornography and a deep loyalty to the value of free speech. "To date," says Professor MacKinnon, "people have identified the pornographer's freedom with everybody's freedom. But we're saying that the freedom of the pornographer is the subordination of women. It means one has to take a side."   7

But the sides are not quite as clear as Professor MacKinnon describes them. Nor is the ordinance.   8

Even if we accept the argument that pornography is harmful to women—and I do—then we must also recognize that anti-Semitic literature is harmful to Jews and racist literature is harmful to blacks. For that matter, Marxist literature may be harmful to government policy. It isn't just women versus pornographers. If women win the right to sue publishers and producers, then so could Jews, blacks, and a long list of people who may be able to prove they have been harmed by books, movies, speeches or even records. The Manson murders, you may recall, were reportedly inspired by the Beatles.   9

We might prefer a library or book store or lecture hall without *Mein Kampf* or the Grand Whoever of the Ku Klux Klan. But a growing list of harmful expressions would inevitably strangle freedom of speech.   10

This ordinance was carefully written to avoid problems of banning and prior restraint, but the right of any woman to claim damages from pornography is just too broad. It seems destined to lead to censorship.   11

What the Minneapolis City Council has before it is a very attractive theory. What MacKinnon and Dworkin have written is a very persuasive and useful definition of pornography. But they haven't yet resolved the conflict between the harm of pornography and the value of free speech. In its present form, this is still a shaky piece of law.   12

Consider now how this argument's rhetorical effect would be different if Ellen Goodman had revealed her thesis in the introduction using the classical argument form. Here is how this introduction might have looked:

GOODMAN'S INTRODUCTION REWRITTEN IN CLASSICAL FORM

Just a couple of months before the pool-table gang rape in New Bedford, Mass., *Hustler* magazine printed a photo feature that reads like a blueprint for the actual crime. There were just two differences between *Hustler* and real life. In *Hustler,* the woman enjoyed it. In real life, the woman charged rape. Of course, there is no evidence that the four men charged with this crime had actually read the magazine. Nor is there evidence that the spectators who yelled encouragement for two hours had held previous ringside seats at pornographic events.

But there is a growing sense that the violent pornography being peddled in this country helps to create an atmosphere in which such events occur. One city is taking a unique approach to attack this problem. An ordinance recently passed by the Minneapolis City Council outlaws pornography not because it contains nudity or sexually explicit acts, but because it degrades and harms women. Unfortunately, despite the proponents' good intentions, the Minneapolis ordinance is a bad law because it has potentially dangerous consequences.

Even though Goodman's position can be grasped more quickly in this classical form, our students generally find the original-delayed thesis version more effective. Why is this?

Most people point to the greater sense of complexity and surprise in the delayed-thesis version, a sense that comes largely from the delayed discovery of the writer's position. Whereas the classical version immediately labels the ordinance a "bad law," the original version withholds judgment, inviting the reader to examine the law more sympathetically and to identify with the position of those who drafted it. Rather than distancing herself from those who see pornography as a violation of women's rights, Goodman shares with her readers her own struggles to think through these issues, thereby persuading us of her genuine sympathy for the ordinance and for its feminist proponents. In the end, her delayed thesis renders her final rejection of the ordinance not only more surprising but more convincing.

Clearly, then, a writer's decision about when to reveal her thesis is critical. Revealing the thesis early makes the writer seem more hardnosed, more sure of her position, more confident about how to divide the ground into friendly and hostile camps, more in control. Delaying the thesis, in contrast, complicates the issues, increases reader sympathy for more than one view, and heightens interest in the tension among alternative views and in the writer's struggle for clarity.

Rogerian Argument

An even more powerful strategy for addressing resistant audiences is a conciliatory strategy often called *Rogerian argument*, named after psychologist Carl Rogers, who used this strategy to help people resolve differences.* Rogerian argument emphasizes "empathic listening," which Rogers defined as the ability to see an issue sympathetically from another person's perspective. He trained people to withhold judgment of another person's ideas until after they listened attentively to the other person, understood that person's reasoning, appreciated that

---

*See Carl Rogers's essay "Communication: Its Blocking and Its Facilitation" in his book *On Becoming a Person* (Boston: Houghton Mifflin, 1961), 329–37. For a fuller discussion of Rogerian argument, see Richard Young, Alton Becker, and Kenneth Pike, *Rhetoric: Discovery and Change* (New York: Harcourt Brace, 1972).

person's values, respected that person's humanity—in short, walked in that person's shoes. Before disagreeing with another person, Rogers would tell his clients, you must be able to summarize that person's argument so accurately that he or she will say, "Yes, you understand my position."

What Carl Rogers understood is that traditional methods of argumentation are threatening. When you try to persuade people to change their minds on an issue, Rogers claimed, you are actually demanding a change in their worldview—to get other people, in a sense, to quit being their kind of person and start being your kind of person. Research psychologists have shown that persons are often not swayed by a logical argument if it somehow threatens their own view of the world. Carl Rogers was therefore interested in finding ways to make arguments less threatening. In Rogerian argument the writer typically waits until the end of the essay to present his position, and that position is often a compromise between the writer's original views and those of the resisting audience. Because Rogerian argument stresses the psychological as well as logical dimensions of argument, and because it emphasizes reducing threat and building bridges rather than winning an argument, it is particularly effective when dealing with emotionally laden issues.

Under Rogerian strategy, the writer reduces the sense of threat in her argument by showing that *both writer and resistant audience share many basic values.* Instead of attacking the audience as wrongheaded, the Rogerian writer respects the audience's intelligence and humanity and demonstrates an understanding of the audience's position before presenting her own position. Finally, the Rogerian writer never asks the audience to capitulate entirely to the writer's side—just to shift somewhat toward the writer's views. By acknowledging that she has already shifted toward the audience's views, the writer makes it easier for the audience to accept compromise. All of this negotiation ideally leads to a compromise between—or better, a synthesis of—the opposing positions.

The key to successful Rogerian argument, besides the art of listening, is the ability to point out areas of agreement between the writer's and reader's positions. For example, if you support a woman's right to choose abortion and you are arguing with someone completely opposed to abortion, you're unlikely to convert your reader, but you might reduce the level of resistance. You begin this process by summarizing your reader's position sympathetically, stressing your shared values. You might say, for example, that you also value babies; that you also are appalled by people who treat abortion as a form of birth control; that you also worry that the easy acceptance of abortion diminishes the value society places on human life; and that you also agree that accepting abortion lightly can lead to lack of sexual responsibility. Building bridges like these between you and your readers makes it more likely that they will listen to you when you present your own position.

In its emphasis on establishing common ground, Rogerian argument has much in common with recent feminist theories of argument. Many feminists criticize classical argument as rooted in a male value system and tainted by metaphors of war and combat. Thus, classical arguments, with their emphasis on assertion and refutation, are typically praised for being "powerful" or "forceful." The writer "defends" his position and "attacks" his "opponent's" position using facts and data as "ammunition" and reasons as "big guns" to "blow away" his opponent's claim. According to some theorists, viewing argument as war can lead to inauthenticity, posturing, and game playing. The traditional pro-con debate—defined in one of our desk dictionaries as "a formal contest of argumentation in which two opposing teams defend and attack a given proposition"—treats argument as verbal jousting, more concerned to determine a winner than to clarify an issue.

One of our female students, who excelled as a debater in high school and received straight A's in argument classes, recently explained in an essay her growing alienation from male rhetoric: "Although women students are just as likely to excel in 'male' writing [. . .] we are less likely to feel as if we were saying something authentic and true." Later the student elaborated on her distrust of "persuasion":

> What many writing teachers have told me is that "the most important writing/ speaking you will ever do will be to persuade someone." My experience as a person who has great difficulty naming and expressing emotions is that the most important communication in my life is far more likely to be simply telling someone how I feel. To say "I love you," or "I'm angry with you," will be far more valuable in most relationship contexts than to say "These are the three reasons why you shouldn't have done what you did [. . .] ."*

Writers who share this woman's distrust of classical argumentation often find Rogerian argument appealing because it stresses self-examination, clarification, and accommodation rather than refutation. Rogerian argument is more in tune with win-win negotiation than with win-lose debate.

To illustrate a conciliatory or Rogerian approach to an issue, here is how one student wrote a letter to her boss recommending a change in the kind of merchandise stocked in a small-town music store.

Letter to Beth Downey

Ms. Beth Downey, Owner/Manager
Downey's Music
Grayfish

Dear Ms. Downey:

1   I would just like to comment on the success of "Downey's Music" in Grayfish and say that, as owner and manager, you have done a wonderful job. I'm sure that you have the most ex-

---

*Our thanks to Catherine Brown for this paragraph from an unpublished paper written at Seattle University.

tensive classical music, music teaching books, piano and acoustic guitar inventory of any store in a 100-square-mile area. After working for you for three years, I have encountered music teachers and classical music lovers coming as far as 70 miles to buy their music from Downey's. All have had nothing but compliments for you and for the store. However, I would once again like to bring up the subject of introducing an inventory of electronic music equipment to the store. Since Grayfish is mainly a tourist town, many times a week I have people from touring bands, visiting Canadians, and also locals coming into the store looking for such things as electronic keyboards, electric guitars, and amplifiers. I know that you have qualms about this idea, but I believe that I have a suggestion that we could both agree on.

First, let me restate your reasons for objecting to such a move. You have already stated   2
that if a change will benefit the store, the initial investment is well worth the expense in the long run (e.g., when pianos were added to the inventory). Therefore, I assume that cost is not a factor at this time. However, you feel that the "kind of people" that electronics may draw could possibly offend our present clientele. You feel, as well as others, that the people who are drawn by electronics are often long-haired, dirty, and give a bad impression. This would in effect change the store's image. Also, you are afraid that the noise caused by these instruments could turn classical music lovers away from the store. The sounds of electronic instruments are not always pleasing, and since most of our clientele are older, more refined persons, you feel that these sounds will force some to go to other stores. Mainly, however, you are worried about the result that the change in the store's image could have upon a community the size of Grayfish. Many people in this area, I realize, feel that electronic music means heavy rock music, while this in turn means alcohol and drugs.

Basically, I agree with you that Grayfish needs a "classical" music store and that the   3
culture that your store brings to Grayfish greatly enhances the area. I also love classical music and want to see it growing and alive. I also have some of the same fears about adding electronic music to the inventory. I enjoy the atmosphere of Downey's, and I have always enjoyed working there, so I don't want to see anything adverse happen to it, either. On the other hand, I feel that if a large electronic music section were added to the store with sound-proof rooms, a "sit and try it" atmosphere, and a catalog inventory large enough to special-order anything that a customer might want that is not in the store, it would help immensely in the success of the store. With the way that Downey's is built, on two levels, it would be very easy to accommodate the needs of both departments. Even now we are only using about half the floor space available, while the rest is empty storage area. By building sound-proof rooms on the lower level, we could easily double the in-use floor area, increase our tourist clientele, have the music business in *all* areas cornered for approximately 60 square miles, and also add practice rooms for our present customers to use when they are choosing music.

I know that you are wrestling with this idea of such a drastic changeover, so I would   4
like to propose a nonthreatening, easy-to-reverse first step. My solution is to start slowly, on a trial basis, and see how it works. I suggest that we start with a few small electronic keyboards, a few electric guitars, and one or two amps. In this way, we could begin to collect the information and literature on other electronic equipment that may be added later on, see how the community responds to such a move, find out how our present clientele

reacts, get a feel for the demand in this field, and yet still be a small hometown music store without a great investment in this electronic area. I still feel that a large addition would be more successful, but I also believe that this little test may help prove to you, or disprove to me, that electronic music instruments in this area are in high demand. I honestly feel that electronics could produce fantastic profits for the people who get into the business first. I would love it if these "people" could be the owners and workers at Downey's Music.

Sincerely,

Mary Doe

FOR CLASS DISCUSSION

1. In this letter, what shared values between writer and audience does the writer stress?

2. Imagine the letter rewritten as a classical argument. How would it be different?

APPEALING TO A RESISTANT AUDIENCE: USING HUMOR

Another strategy that can sometimes appeal to a resistant audience is humor. Anyone who has experienced moments of hilarity with others—friends, a lover, family members, coworkers—knows how powerful laughing together can be in building relationships. Humor can also relieve stress and open up fresh perspectives, even momentarily turn the world upside down to show us what we couldn't see before. In arguments, humor can strengthen the bonds among people who already agree by solidifying their common ground. It can also be used in arguments to win over resistant audiences, often by neutralizing their objections through entertaining amusement. Humor, especially when it evokes laughter, is disarming; it melts opposition, sometimes winning our assent to ideas we might reject if they were presented seriously. Humor can also be a way for you, the arguer, to express your concern, exasperation, or anger about an issue more productively than through direct or serious confrontation with your audience. When and how you use humor in your arguments has to be your call, based on context. Despite our fondness for humorous writing, we have to offer this caveat: Using humor in arguments is risky business that may backfire on you, especially if a resistant audience feels ridiculed. But humor may be powerfully persuasive.

Although we can't give you simple rules to determine when to use humor in your arguments, we can briefly explain some of the tools you can employ to construct an argument using humor. Some of the humorist's main tools are these imaginative uses of language: hyperbole (or exaggeration), understatement, repetition, and witty, memorable lines. *Hyperbole* refers to a writer's exaggeration of an idea. Often, inflating or blowing up an idea to enormous proportions compels an audience to see that idea as ridiculous and to laugh with you about it. *Understatement* works in an opposite manner: A writer leaves unsaid, but strongly implies, an idea, drawing the audience into a "shared" joke by asking the audience to see beyond the words. When you use understatement, you express an idea so far below the intensity it deserves that you push readers to supply the unsaid meaning in their own minds. *Repetition* of an idea builds up momentum (that "on a roll now" feeling) and collaborates with exaggeration by piling up details or ideas to ridiculous levels, conveying an idea through the sheer weight and rhythm of the language. *Witty, memorable lines* are funny flashes of insight expressed in well-placed colorful images or surprisingly suitable words; they can be those zingers or punch lines that drive home a point and leave the audience amazed and amused.

To show you how these tools of humor can operate in argument, we present below excerpts from the transcript of a public hearing in New York City on the possible relocation of Richard Serra's *Tilted Arc*, a sculpture placed in the plaza of the Jacob Javits Federal Building in lower Manhattan.* Some members of the community found this gigantic piece of metal offensive. In this hearing, the artist and his sympathizers argued that art should resist easy comprehension and challenge, even disturb, our perceptions. Other people at the hearing condemned and rejected this notion of art.

In the following passage, Phil La Basi, a federal employee who worked in a building on the plaza, protests the artist's definition of art and uses hyperbole, repetition, and witty lines to try to make the audience see his vision of this sculpture.

USING HYPERBOLE, WIT, AND REPETITION TO ARGUE A POSITION

Hyperbole

What I see there is something that looks like a tank trap to prevent an armed attack from Chinatown in case of a Soviet invasion. In my mind it probably wouldn't even do that well, because one good Russian tank could probably take it out.

Witty lines playing on "tilted arc"

To be very serious, I wouldn't call it *Tilted Arc*. To me it looks like crooked metal or bent metal. I think we can call anything art if we call that art. I think any one of those people here

Hyperbole

Repetition

could come along with an old broken bicycle that perhaps got run over by a car, or some other piece of material, and put it up and call it art and name it something. I think that is what was done here. [. . .]

---

*A more complete version of the transcripts of the public hearing in New York City on *Tilted Arc* is printed in Margaret P. Battin, John Fisher, Ronald Moore, and Anita Silvers, *Puzzles about Art* (New York: St. Martin's Press, 1989). Phil La Basi's remarks appear on pages 186–87; Peter Hirsh's testimony is on pages 183–84.

Another speaker at the hearing, Peter Hirsh, the research director and legal counsel for the Association of Immigration Attorneys, used understatement to denounce the sculpture. Notice the low-key way in which Hirsh basically says he thinks the sculpture is garbage.

USING UNDERSTATEMENT TO MAKE A POINT

Understatement leaving unsaid the writer's full dislike and disgust

My membership has authorized me to say that we are entirely opposed to *Tilted Arc.* My own personal view is that a good place to put *Tilted Arc* would be in the Hudson River. [. . .] I am told that they are going to have to put artificial things in the river to provide shelter for the striped bass. I think *Tilted Arc* would make a very fine shelter.

Humorous arguments can often take the form of satire or parody. In *satire,* a writer adopts an ironic point of view and appears to praise the very thing he or she is holding up for criticism. Often by exaggerating the weaknesses, foolishness, wrongness, or evils of some issue while seeming to support the issue (saying the opposite of what is really thought or meant), the writer can expose those weaknesses to ridicule. In this indirect and disruptive way, satire seeks to win the audience's acceptance of the writer's perspective. On a continuum ranging from "playfully critical and funny" to "harshly condemning and biting," satire often leans toward the latter.

Humorous argument can also be written as parody. A *parody* imitates a serious piece of work or even an event but seeks to ridicule it. It takes the familiar but changes it into something new that reminds readers of the original, plays off it, and in some way criticizes the original.

As a reaction to the recent volatile discussions of government regulation of guns in the House of Representatives, an article entitled "The Gun Commandments" appeared in the magazine *The Economist.** In the passages from this article that follow, you can see that the piece employs both satire and parody. The article satirizes the House's ineffective approach to gun control by appearing to side with the anti–gun control position and by exaggerating that position to absurd proportions. It also parodies the House's stance toward gun control and its decision to post the Ten Commandments in schools by rewriting the Ten Commandments as Gun Commandments.

USING SATIRE AND PARODY TO ARGUE A POSITION

Satire

It is in the spirit of Mr. DeLay that the House decided, rather than controlling guns, to allow the Ten Commandments to be posted on the walls of every public school in America. That will teach them.

---

*"The Gun Commandments," *Economist* 26 June 1999, 22. The article is anonymous.

Satire

It is, of course, possible that the Supreme Court (a Godless institution) will decide that this offends against the separation of church and state. If this happens, Congress has an alternative set of commandments ready. They will do just as well.

Parody

1. Honour the National Rifle Association, and remember that it doth contribute $4m to congressional campaigns. [. . .]
3. Honour the Sabbath day and keep it holy. Six days shalt thou labour and do all thy work, and on the seventh thou shalt do target practice. [. . .]
5. Thou shalt not kill, except when provoked. But if thou dost, remember that thy *gun* had nothing to do with it. [. . .]

In this example of satire and parody, the writer manages to express harsh criticism of and anger at Congress and the anti–gun control faction but does so in a clever, surprising way that makes even a resistant audience listen before turning off. The piece lures readers into its perspective, couching its real view of gun control in irony. If nothing else, the writer makes the audience think of the gun control issue in a wacky, distorted way that exposes the flaws in the anti–gun control position and the weaknesses in Congress's response.

As you contemplate both your investment in your claim and the level of resistance of your intended audience, determine whether humor as a main approach or as a way to make a point here and there might be an effective means to diminish your audience's resistance and perhaps even warm the audience up to your argument.

FOR CLASS DISCUSSION

George F. Will's article "The Perils of Brushing" appeared in the May 10, 1999, issue of *Newsweek* as a "The Last Word" column. After reading this piece, work individually or in groups to answer the questions that follow.

The Perils of Brushing

George F. Will

All of us have seen lots of them, those words of warning or instruction that appear on products we buy. "Do not eat this sled." "For best results do not apply this floor wax to your teeth." "This antifreeze is not intended for pouring on breakfast cereal." We hardly notice them, let alone consider what they say about the times in which we live. The sled, wax and antifreeze warnings are apocryphal. But you could not know that. After all, *The American Enterprise* magazine offers these from real life:

2   On a bag of Fritos: "You could be a winner! No purchase necessary. Details inside." On a bread pudding: "Product will be hot after heating." On a bar of Dial soap: "Use like regular soap." On a hotel shower cap: "Fits one head." On a package of Nytol sleeping aid: "May cause drowsiness." On a string of Christmas lights: "For indoor or outdoor use only." On the packaging of a Rowenta iron. "Do not iron clothes on body."

3   The warning about a product's being hot after heating may be a response to the famous case wherein a woman successfully sued McDonald's because she was burned when she spilled—she was a passenger in a stationary car at the time, with the cup between her legs— the hot McDonald's coffee she had just bought. (If the coffee had been cool, a complaint about that could have been packaged as a lawsuit.) But try to picture in your mind the event involving two or more heads that the manufacturer of the shower cap was worried about.

4   Give up? Well, then, answer this: If there are people who press their pants while in their pants, are they the sort of people whose behavior will be changed by a warning on the packaging the iron comes in? If there are people who have done that once, are there any who have done it twice? If not, does that demonstrate that even the dimmest among us has a learning curve that actually curves?

5   Such questions are stirred by the great toothbrush litigation just getting underway in Chicago. What Charles Dickens did with *Jarndyce v. Jarndyce* in *Bleak House* as an index of cultural conditions, perhaps some modern novelist will do with *Trimarco v. Colgate Palmolive et al.*

6   The et al.'s include some other manufacturers of toothbrushes, and the American Dental Association. All are to be hauled before the bar of justice by Mark Trimarco, speaking for himself and—this is a class-action suit—"all others similarly situated." The others are suffering from what Trimarco's complaint calls "a disease known as 'toothbrush abrasion'." Abrasion a disease? The plaintiff's materials also call it "an injury." And "a distinct clinical entity caused by toothbrushes of the following bristle types: firm, medium and soft, both natural and synthetic."

7   The complaint says people suffering from this self-inflicted injury are consumers who were not "informed or warned about the danger of toothbrush abrasion." And: "It was the duty of the defendant manufacturers to furnish a product, i.e., toothbrush, which was in reasonably safe condition when put to a use in a manner that was reasonably foreseeable considering the nature and intended function of the product."

8   But the toothbrushes "were unsafe and unreasonably dangerous for their intended use in that the packaging contained no warning as to the risks of toothbrush abrasion or instructions on how to brush to avoid toothbrush abrasion." The American Dental Association is a defendant because it gave its seal of approval to the toothbrushes.

9   The complaint charges negligence because the manufacturers knew or should have known about the disease/injury/clinical entity since "at least 1949" but continued to manufacture toothbrushes that were "likely" to cause abrasion. *Likely?* If the result is "likely," you would think that the class of plaintiffs would be a majority of all who brush their teeth.

10   If toothbrushes are, as charged, "unreasonably dangerous" because of the absence of warnings and instructions, try to imagine the words which, if printed on toothbrush packages, would immunize manufacturers against such a complaint. "Warning: In brushing, too

much is too much." "Instructions: Hold brush in hand. Insert the end with the bristles into your mouth. Move brush up and down. Stop before you wear out your teeth." Or perhaps: "Look, this toothbrush is not normally a dangerous implement, but neither is it intended for ninnies who can't figure out how to brush their teeth without doing them irreparable harm."

This suit is just part of a great American growth industry—litigation that expresses the belief that everyone has an entitlement to compensation for any unpleasantness; litigation that displaces responsibility from individuals to corporations with money. This industry was, of course, up and running before the tobacco litigation, but that taught lawyers just how lucrative it could be to blame individuals' foolishness on, say, Joe Camel. 11

Now many cities are suing gun manufacturers for the "costs"—the numbers are guesses—of shootings. In a new wrinkle in tort law—a move that would make a trial lawyer blush, if that were possible—individuals who have been shot are suing groups of manufacturers without claiming to have been injured by a product made by any of the targeted manufacturers. 12

If you—your teeth *are* suddenly feeling a bit abraded, are they not?—want to climb aboard the latest gravy train pulling out of the station, log on to www.toothbrushlawsuit.com. You will be greeted warmly: "Welcome to the Toothbrush Lawsuit Web Site." Illinois residents can dial 1-877-SORE GUMS. From the Web site you will learn that the disease is "progressive." That means not that Al Gore likes it, but that it gets worse if you keep making it worse. You also will learn that toothbrush abrasion "is most prevalent in those with good oral hygiene, i.e., people who brush their teeth." And "there are studies that show that people who do not brush their teeth, never develop" symptoms of toothbrush abrasion. Consider yourself warned. 13

1. What examples of hyperbole, understatement, repetition, and witty lines can you find in this article?

2. Do you see elements of satire and parody in this article? If so, where?

3. What is Will's main claim in this argument? In other words, what is the position he is arguing?

4. As you think about rhetorical context—Will's purpose, audience, genre, and style—speculate why humor is an effective approach to convey this argument. What audiences does Will reach that might not have listened to him had he written a more serious, straightforward argument? Do you agree or disagree with Will's argument? Has his humor moved you or changed your perspective in any way?

CONCLUSION

This chapter has shown you the difference between one-sided and multisided arguments and explained why multisided arguments are likely to be more persuasive to neutral or resisting audiences. A multisided argument generally includes a fair summary of differing views, followed by either refutation, concession, or

Rogerian synthesis. The strategies you use for treating resistant views depend on the audience you are trying to reach and your purpose. We explained how audiences can be placed on a scale of resistance ranging from "strongly supportive" to "strongly resistant." In addressing supportive audiences, writers typically compose one-sided arguments with strong motivational appeals to action. Neutral or undecided audiences generally respond most favorably to classical arguments that set out strong reasons in support of the writer's position yet openly address alternative views, which are first summarized and then either rebutted or conceded to. When the audience is strongly resistant, a delayed thesis or Rogerian strategy is most effective at reducing resistance and helping move the audience slightly toward the writer's views. Sometimes humor is also effective at winning consideration from a resistant audience.

WRITING ASSIGNMENT FOR CHAPTERS 7 AND 8

The assignment for Chapters 7 and 8 has two parts. Part One is an actual argument you will write. Part Two is your own self-reflective analysis on how you chose to appeal to and accommodate your audience.

PART ONE: For this assignment, argue against a popular cultural practice or belief that you think is wrong, or argue for an action or belief that you think is right even though it will be highly unpopular. Your claim, in other words, must be controversial—going against the grain of popular actions, values, and beliefs—so that you can anticipate considerable resistance to your views. This essay invites you to stand up for something you believe in even though your view will be highly contested. Your goal is to persuade your audience toward your position.

In writing and revising your argument, draw upon appropriate strategies from Chapters 7 and 8. From Chapter 7 consider the concept of audience-based reasons and strategies for increasing your appeals to *ethos* and *pathos*. From Chapter 8 consider strategies for appealing to audiences according to their level of resistance. Choose the most resistant audience that you think you can sway to your point of view. Whether you use a refutation strategy, a delayed-thesis strategy, a Rogerian strategy, a humorous strategy, or some combination of these approaches is up to you.

PART TWO: Attach to your argument a self-reflective letter to your instructor and classmates explaining and justifying the choices you made for appealing to your audience and accommodating their views. In your letter address questions such as the following:

1. At the most resistant end of the spectrum, why are people opposed to your claim? How does your claim challenge their views and perhaps threaten their own value system?

2. Whom did you picture as the audience you were trying to sway? Where on the spectrum from "accord" to "resistance" did you address your argument? Why?

3. What strategies did you use for appealing to that audience?

4. What choices did you make in trying to accommodate differing views?

5. What challenges did this assignment present for you? How successful do you think you were in meeting those challenges?

Arguments in Depth

Six Types of Claims

9

An Introduction to the Types of Claims

In Part One of this text, we discussed the reading and writing of arguments, linking argument to both persuasion and inquiry. In Part Two we examined the internal structure of arguments and showed how persuasive writers link their arguments to the beliefs and values of their audience. We also showed how writers can vary their content, structure, and style to reach audiences with varying degrees of resistance to the writer's views.

Now in Part Three we examine arguments in depth by explaining six types of claims and by showing how each type has its own characteristic patterns of development and support. Because almost all arguments use one or more of these types of claims as basic argumentative "moves" or building blocks, knowing how to develop each claim type will advance your skills in argument. The types of claims to be examined in Part Three are related to an ancient rhetorical concept called *stasis* from a Greek term meaning "stand" as in "to take a *stand* on something." There are many competing theories of stasis, so no two rhetoricians discuss stasis in exactly the same way. But all the theories have valuable components in common.

In Part Three we present our own version of stasis theory, or, to use more ordinary language, our own approach to argument based on the types of claims. The payoff for you will be twofold. First, understanding the types of claims will help you focus an argument and generate ideas for it. Second, a study of claim types teaches you characteristic patterns of support for each type, thereby helping you organize and develop your arguments.

AN OVERVIEW OF THE TYPES
OF CLAIMS

To appreciate what a study of claim types can do, imagine one of those heated but frustrating arguments—let's suppose it's about gun control—where the question at issue keeps shifting. Everyone talks at cross-purposes, each speaker's point unconnected to the previous speaker's. The disputants start gesticulating at each other, faces contorted, voice levels rising. Sometimes you can get such a discussion back on track if one person says, "Hold it for a moment. What are we actually disagreeing about here? Are we debating whether the government should enact gun control? Whether gun ownership prevents crime? Whether getting a gun license is like getting a car license? Let's figure out what we agree on and where we disagree because we can't debate all these questions at once." Whether she recognizes it or not, this person is applying the concept of claim types to get the argument focused.

To understand how claim types work, let's return to the concept of stasis. A *stasis* is an issue or question that focuses a point of disagreement. You and your audience might agree on the answer to Question A and so have nothing to argue about. Likewise you might agree on the answer to Question B. But on Question C you disagree. Question C constitutes a *stasis* where you and your audience diverge. It is the place where disagreement begins, where as an arguer you take a *stand* against another view. Thus you and your audience might agree that handgun ownership is legal. You might agree further that widespread ownership of handguns reduces crime. But if you ask the question "Is widespread handgun ownership a good thing?" you and your audience might disagree. This last question constitutes a *stasis*, the point where you and your audience part company.

Rhetoricians have discovered that the kinds of questions that divide people have classifiable patterns. In this text we identify six broad types of claims—each type originating in a different kind of question. To emphasize the structural pattern of each type, we will first use an X and a Y to represent slots so that you can focus on the structure rather than the content of the claim type. Then we'll move quickly to actual examples. Here is a brief overview of the six claim types.

Type 1: Simple Categorical Arguments
(Is X a Y? [Where You and Your Audience
Agree on the Meaning of Y])

A *categorical argument* occurs when persons disagree about the category (Y) that a given thing (X) belongs to. A categorical question is said to be simple if there is no dispute about the meaning of the Y term. Examples of questions leading to simple categorical arguments are the following:

Was Richard Nixon a workaholic?

Is surfing the Internet a new kind of addiction?

Was Senator Weasel's vote for increased military spending politically motivated?

In these examples, we assume that writer and audience agree on the meaning of "workaholic," "addiction," and "politically motivated." At issue is whether Nixon, surfing the Internet, and Senator Weasel belong to these categories.

The strategy for conducting a simple categorical argument is to provide examples or other evidence to show that X does or does not belong to category Y. Yes, Nixon was a workaholic (provide examples). Yes, surfing the Internet is a new kind of addiction (provide examples, testimony from psychologists). No, Senator Weasel's support for new weapons funding was not politically motivated (provide evidence that Weasel has a long record of pro-military spending). Simple categorical arguments are discussed in the first part of Chapter 10.

Type 2: Definitional Arguments (Is X a Y? [Where the Definition of Y Is Contested])

A categorical argument becomes more complex if you and your audience disagree about the meaning of the Y term. In this second type of claim, you have to define the Y term and defend your definition against objections and alternative definitions. Suppose, for example, you want to argue that using animals for medical research constitutes cruelty to animals. Here you would have to define what you mean by "cruelty to animals" and show how using animals for medical research fits your definition. Almost all legal disputes require definitional arguing because courts must determine whether an action meets or does not meet the criteria for a crime or civil tort as defined by a law, statute, or series of previous court rulings. Examples of questions leading to definitional arguments are the following:

Is occasional telling of off-color jokes in the workplace an instance of sexual harassment?

Is flag burning constitutionally protected free speech?

Is Pluto a planet or an asteroid?

The general strategy for conducting a definitional argument is to define the second term and then argue whether the first term meets or does not meet the definition. We call this strategy *criteria-match arguing* because to define the second term you must specify the criteria that something must meet to fit the category. Then you must argue that your first term does or does not match these criteria. Definitional arguments are treated in depth in Chapter 10.

Type 3: Cause/Consequence Arguments (Does X Cause Y? Is Y a Consequence of X?)

Another major argument type entails cause and effect reasoning. Often such arguments arise from disagreements about the cause of an event or a trend: "What caused the crash of American Airlines Flight 800?" or "What causes teenage males to become violent?" Just as frequently, causal arguments arise from speculations about the possible consequences of an action: "What will be the consequences of changing from a progressive to a flat income tax?" "Will gun control legislation reduce violence in the schools?"

The general strategy for conducting causal arguments is to describe the chain of events that lead from X to Y. If a causal chain cannot be directly established, you can argue indirectly, using inductive methods, statistical analyses, or analogies. Causal arguments are treated in detail in Chapter 11.

Type 4: Resemblance Arguments (Is X like Y?)

A fourth argument type involves disputes about appropriate analogies or precedents. Suppose you disapproved of investing in the stock market and wanted to argue that stock market investing is like gambling. In showing the similarities between investing and gambling, you would be making a resemblance argument. Examples of questions that lead to resemblance arguing are the following:

> Was Slobodan Milosovic's policy of "ethnic cleansing" in Kosovo like Hitler's "final solution" against the Jews?

> Is killing starlings in your attic like killing rats in your attic? (Are starlings like rats?)

> Does pornography disparage women the way neo-Nazi propaganda disparages people of color? (Is pornography like racist propaganda?)

The general strategy for resemblance arguments is to compare the first term to the second, pointing out similarities between them (if your goal is to make X like Y) or differences between them (if your goal is to make X unlike Y). Resemblance arguments are covered in Chapter 12.

Type 5: Evaluation Arguments (Is X Good or Bad? Is X a Good or Bad Y?)

Categorical, causal, and resemblance arguments (types 1–4) are often called reality or truth arguments. In such arguments, people question the way things are, were, or will be; they are disagreeing about the nature of reality. In contrast, evaluation and proposal arguments (types 5 and 6) deal with values, what people consider important, good, or worth doing. Although a person's values often begin as feelings founded on personal experience, they can nevertheless form the basis of reasonable argument in the public sphere if they are articulated and justified. When you articulate your values, explain their source (if necessary), and apply them consistently to specific cases, you make your values transpersonal and shareable and can use them to build coherent and reasonable arguments.

Evaluation arguments (type 5) ask questions about whether X is good or bad. Examples of evaluation questions are the following:

Is a European-style, single-payer health insurance system a good policy for the United States to enact?

Is acquiring job experience between college and graduate school a good career plan?

Is a sports utility vehicle a good urban vehicle?

The general strategy for evaluation arguments uses criteria-match arguing similar to that used for definitional arguments: You first establish your criteria for "good" in the specific case and then show how your first term does or does not meet the criteria. Evaluation arguments are covered in Chapter 13. A special category of evaluation arguments—dealing with ethical or moral issues (for example, "Is it morally justifiable to spank children?" or "Are cloning experiments ethical?")—is treated in Chapter 15.

Type 6: Proposal Arguments (Should We Do X?)

Whereas argument types 1–5 all involve changing your audience's beliefs about something—whether about reality (types 1–4) or about the value of something (type 5)—proposal arguments call for action. Proposals ask your audience to *do* something, to act in some way. Typically, proposals use words like *should, ought,* or *must* followed by an action of some kind. The following questions all lead to proposal arguments:

Should the United States shift from a progressive to a flat income tax?

Should teens who commit crimes receive the same sentences as adult criminals?

Should gay marriages be legalized?

The most typical strategy for making proposal arguments is to follow a problem-solution-justification structure whereby the opening section convinces the audience that a problem exists, the second section proposes a solution to solve the problem, and the last section justifies the solution by demonstrating that the benefits of acting on the proposal outweigh the costs or that the inherent "rightness" of the solution (on moral grounds) compels action. Proposal arguments are covered in Chapter 14.

▼ FOR CLASS DISCUSSION

Working as a whole class or in small groups, decide which claim type is represented by each of the following questions. Sometimes the argument categories overlap or blend together. For example, the question "Is airline travel safe?" might be considered either a simple categorical question or an evaluation question.

1. Should violent video games be made illegal?

2. How effective is aspirin in reducing the risk for heart attacks and stroke?

3. Why is anorexia nervosa primarily a white, middle-class female disease?

4. Is depression in the elderly common in Asian cultures?

5. Will military intervention in Country X be like U.S. intervention in Vietnam or like U.S. intervention in Iraq?

6. Should professional baseball impose a salary cap on its superstar players?

7. Is this Web site racist?

8. Is tobacco a drug?

9. Are Nike's Asian shoe factories sweatshops?

10. What causes American girls to lose self-esteem when they reach puberty?

WHAT IS THE VALUE OF STUDYING CLAIM TYPES?

Having provided an overview of the types of claims, we conclude this chapter by showing you two substantial benefits you will derive from knowing about each type: help in focusing and generating ideas for an argument and help in organizing and developing an argument.

Help in Focusing an Argument and Generating Ideas

Knowing the different types of claims can help you focus an argument and generate ideas for it. Understanding claim types helps you focus by asking you to determine what's at stake between you and your audience. Where do you and your audience agree and disagree? What are the questions at issue? It helps you generate ideas by guiding you to pose questions that suggest lines of development.

To illustrate, let's take a hypothetical case—one Isaac Charles Little (affectionately known as I. C. Little), who desires to chuck his contact lenses and undergo the new lasik procedure to cure his near-sightedness. ("Lasik" is the common name for laser in-situ keratomileusis, a recent advance in surgical treatments for myopia. Sometimes known as "flap and zap" surgery, it involves using a laser to cut a layer of the corneal tissue thinner than a human hair and then flattening the cornea. It's usually not covered by insurance and is quite expensive.) I. C. has two different arguments he'd like to make: (1) He'd like to talk his parents into helping him pay for the procedure, and (2) he'd like to convince insurance companies that the lasik procedure should be covered under standard medical insurance policies. In the discussions that follow, note how the six types of claims can help I. C. identify points of disagreement for each audience and simultaneously suggest lines of argument for persuading each one. Note, too, how the questions at issue vary for each audience.

First imagine what might be at stake in I. C.'s discussions with his parents.

Claim Type Analysis: Parents as Audience

- *Simple categorical argument:* I. C.'s parents will be concerned about the safety and effectiveness of this procedure. Is lasik safe? Is it effective? (These are the first questions at issue. I. C.'s mom has heard a horror story about an earlier surgical procedure for myopia, so I. C. knows he will have to persuade her that lasik is safe and effective.)

- *Definitional argument:* With parents as audience, I. C. will have to define what lasik surgery is so they won't have misconceptions about what is involved. However, he can't think of any arguments that would ensue over this definition, so he proceeds to the next claim type.

- *Causal argument:* Both parents will question I. C.'s underlying motivation for seeking this surgery. "What causes you to want this lasik procedure?" they will ask. (I. C.'s dad, who has worn eyeglasses all his adult life, will not be swayed by cosmetic desires. "If you don't like contacts," he will say, "just wear glasses.") Here I. C. needs to argue that permanently correcting his near sightedness will improve his quality of life. I. C. decides to emphasize his desire for an active, outdoor life, and especially his passion for water sports including swimming and scuba diving, where his need for contacts or glasses is a serious handicap. Also, I. C. says that if he doesn't have to wear contacts he can get a summer job as a lifeguard.

- *Resemblance argument:* I. C. can't think of any resemblance questions at issue.

- *Evaluation argument:* When the pluses and minuses are weighed, is lasik a good thing? Would the results of the surgery be beneficial enough to justify the cost and the risks? In terms of costs, I. C. might argue that even though the procedure is initially expensive (from $1,000 to $4,000), over the years he will save money by not needing contacts or glasses. The pleasure of seeing well in the water and not being bothered by contacts or glasses while hiking and camping constitutes a major psychological benefit. (The cosmetic benefits—I. C. thinks he'll look cooler without glasses—he decides to leave out, since his dad thinks wearing glasses is fine.)

- *Proposal:* Should I. C. (or a person in general) get this operation for treatment of myopia? (All the previous points of disagreement are subissues related to this overarching proposal issue.)

What this example should help you see is that the values arguments in the last two claim types (evaluation and proposal) depend on the writer's resolving related reality/truth questions in one or more of the first four types (simple categorical, definition, cause, resemblance). In this particular case, before convincing his parents that they should help him pay for the lasik procedure (I. C.'s proposal claim), I. C. would need to convince them that the procedure is safe and effective (simple categorical arguments), that there are significant recreational and professional reasons for this surgery (causal argument), and that the benefits outweigh the costs (evaluation argument). Almost all arguments combine subarguments in this way so that lower-order claims provide supporting materials for addressing higher-order claims.

The previous illustration focused on parents as audience. If we now switch audiences, we can use our theory of claim types to identify different questions at issue. Let's suppose I. C. wants to persuade insurance companies to cover the lasik procedure. He imagines insurance company decision makers as his primary audience, along with the general public and state legislators who may be able to influence them.

Claim Type Analysis: Insurance Decision Makers as Audience

- *Simple categorical argument:* No disagreements come immediately to mind (This audience shares I. C.'s belief that lasik is safe and effective.)

- *Definitional argument:* Should lasik be considered "cosmetic surgery" (as insurance companies contend) or as "medically justifiable surgery" (as I. C. contends)? This definitional question constitutes a major stasis. I. C. wants to convince his audience that lasik belongs in the category of "medically justifiable surgery" rather than "cosmetic surgery." He will need to define "medically justifiable surgery" in such a way that lasik can be included.

- *Causal argument:* What will be the consequences to insurance companies and to the general public of making insurance companies pay for lasik? For this audience, consequence issues are crucial. Will insurance companies be overloaded with claims? What will happen to insurance rates? Will optometrists and eyeglass manufacturers go out of business?

- *Resemblance argument:* Does lasik more resemble a facelift (not covered by insurance) or plastic surgery to repair a cleft palate (covered by insurance)?

- *Evaluation argument:* Would it be good for society as a whole if insurance companies had to pay for lasik?

- *Proposal argument:* Should insurance companies be required to cover lasik?

As this analysis shows, the questions at issue change when you consider a different audience. Now the chief question at issue is definition: Is lasik cosmetic surgery or medically justifiable surgery? I. C. needs to spend no time arguing that the surgery is safe and effective (major concerns for his parents); instead he must establish criteria for "medically justifiable surgery" and then argue that lasik meets these criteria. Again note how the higher-order issues of value depend on resolving one or more lower-order issues of truth/reality.

So what can a study of claim types teach you about focusing an argument and generating ideas? First, it teaches you to analyze what's at stake between you and your audience by determining major points of disagreement. Second, it shows that you can make any of the claim types your argument's major focus. Rather than tackle a values issue, you might tackle only a reality/truth issue. You could, for example, focus an entire argument on the simple categorical question "Is lasik safe?" (an argument requiring you to research the medical literature). Likewise you could write a causal argument focusing on what might happen to optometrists and eyeglass manufacturers if the insurance industry decided to cover lasik. Often arguers jump too quickly to issues of value without first resolving issues of reality/truth. Finally, a study of claim types helps you pose questions that generate ideas and suggest lines of reasoning. Later in Part Three, we will show you a particularly powerful way of using lower-order questions about reality/truth to generate supporting ideas for a proposal argument (see Chapter 14, pp. 313–17).

FOR CLASS DISCUSSION

Select an issue familiar to most members of the class—perhaps a current campus issue, an issue prominent in the local or national news, or an issue that the class has recently discussed—and analyze it using our sequence of claim types. Consider how a writer or speaker might address two different audiences on this issue. Hypothesizing the writer/speaker's perspective and claim, make a list of points of agreement and disagreement for both audiences, using as a pattern our claim types analyses for lasik.

Help in Organizing and Developing an Argument

The second main benefit of studying claim types will become clearer as you read the chapters in Part Three. Because each type of claim has its own characteristic pattern of development, learning these patterns will help you organize and develop your arguments. Studying claim types shows you how different arguments are typically structured, teaching you generic moves needed in many different kinds of argumentative situations. If, for example, you make a proposal claim, a study of claim types will show you the generic moves typically needed in proposal arguments. If one of your supporting reasons is a definition claim or an evaluation claim, study of claim types will show you how to do the criteria-match arguing typical of such claims. Likewise such a study shows you how to develop each of the other claim types to help you construct arguments that tap into your audience's values and that include strong support to overcome your audience's resistance.

In the following chapters in Part Three, we discuss each of the claim types in depth.

10

Categorical and Definitional Arguments

X Is (Is Not) a Y

CASE 1

The impeachment trial of President Bill Clinton, following his affair with Monica Lewinsky, involved a number of definitional issues: Did Clinton's behavior with Lewinsky and his evasions of the truth while testifying to a grand jury in the Paula Jones lawsuit constitute "Treason, Bribery, or other high Crimes and Misdemeanors"—the constitutional phrase that describes an impeachable offense? More narrowly, did Clinton's testimony in the Paula Jones lawsuit, when he denied having sexual relations with Monica Lewinsky, constitute "perjury"? More narrowly still, did Clinton's behavior with Monica Lewinsky meet the legal definition of "sexual relations"? At each of these levels of debate, lawyers and pundits put forth competing definitions of these disputed terms and argued that Clinton's actions did or did not meet the definitions.

CASE 2

Recent developments in reproductive technology are spurring mind-numbing ethical and legal questions. For example, suppose an infertile couple conceives several embryos in a test tube and then freezes the fertilized embryos for future use. What happens when the couple divorces and disagrees about the disposition of the frozen embryos? (In one actual case, the woman wanted to use the frozen embryos to try to get pregnant, and the man wanted to destroy the embryos.) What should be done with the embryos and who decides? Should frozen embryos be treated as "persons," thus becoming analogous to children in custody arguments? Or should they be divided up as "property" with the man getting one half of the frozen embryos and the woman getting the other half? Or should a new legal category be created for them that regards them as more than property but less than actual persons? In one court case, the judge decided that frozen embryos "are not, strictly speaking, either 'persons' or 'property,' but occupy an interim category that entitles them to special respect because of their potential for human life."*

AN OVERVIEW OF CATEGORICAL ARGUMENTS

Categorical arguments are among the most common argument types you will encounter. They can occur whenever you claim that any given X belongs in category Y. Did NATO bombing of Serbia during the Kosovo crisis belong in the category "a just war"? Does skateboarding belong in the category "a true sport"? Does my swerving across the center lane while trying to slap a bee on my windshield belong in the category "reckless driving"?

We place items in categories all the time, and the categories we choose can have subtle but powerful rhetorical effects, creating implicit mini-arguments. Consider, for example, how a review of the film *American Pie* categorizes first-time sex for teens: "In what must be the raunchiest coming-of-age film ever, 'American Pie' tackles the most hallowed rite of teenage passage: losing one's virginity."† Here loss of virginity is placed in the category "hallowed rite of teenage passage." By placing teenage sexuality in this category, the reviewer urges readers to view first-time sex for teens as a humorous coming-of-age moment like getting a driver's license or chugging your first beer. Later in the review, those who might object to the movie's depersonalized, comic, amoral depiction of sexuality are categorized as "Victorians." The review implicitly divides readers into two categories: prudish Victorians and normal people who enjoy raunchy movies and see teenage sex as a rite of passage. But there are other categories into which teenage sex can be placed. Some commentators see teenage sex as a national disaster leading to out-of-wedlock pregnancy, a frightening rise in STDs, and the decline of the stable, two-parent family. Often, the categories we create rhetorically have real-life consequences: They can shape legislation, influence court decisions, even determine our personal values and behavior.

Similar examples of implicit categorical claims can be found in almost any kind of text. Consider the competing categories proposed for whales in an international whaling controversy accelerated in the late 1990s by the Makahs' pursuit of their U.S. treaty rights to hunt whales. What category does a whale belong to? Some arguers placed whales in the category "sacred animals" that should never be killed because of their intelligence, beauty, grace, and power. Others categorized

---

*See Vincent F. Stempel, "Procreative Rights in Assisted Reproductive Technology: Why the Angst?" *Albany Law Review* 62 (1999), 1187.

†*Review* (1999). Sharon Pian Chan, " 'American Pie' Sweet but Raunchy," rev. of *American Pie*, *Seattle Times* 9 July 1999, F1, F3.

whales as a "renewable food resource" like tuna, crabs, cattle, and chickens. Others worried whether the specific kinds of whales being hunted were an "endangered species"—a concept that argues for the preservation of whale stocks but not necessarily for a ban on controlled hunting of individual whales once population numbers rise sufficiently. Each of these whaling arguments places whales within a different category that implicitly urges the reader to adopt that category's perspective on whaling.

Categorical claims shift from implicit to explicit arguments whenever the arguer supplies reasons and evidence to persuade us that X does (or does not) belong in category Y. In the rest of this chapter we discuss two kinds of categorical arguments: (1) simple categorical arguments in which the writer and an audience agree on the meaning of the Y term and (2) definitional arguments in which the meaning of the Y term is itself controversial.

SIMPLE CATEGORICAL ARGUMENTS

A categorical argument can be said to be "simple" if there is no disagreement about the meaning of the Y term. For example, suppose you are discussing with fellow committee members whom to select as committee chairperson. You want to make the case that "David won't make a good committee chair because he is too bossy." Your supporting reason ("David is too bossy") is a simple categorical claim. You assume that everyone agrees what *bossy* means; the point of contention is whether David is or is not bossy. To support your claim, you would supply examples of David's bossiness. To refute it, someone else might supply counterexamples of David's cooperative and kind nature. As this example suggests, the basic procedural rule for developing a simple categorical claim is to supply examples and other data that show how X is (or is not) a member of category Y.

Difference between Facts and Simple Categorical Claims

Simple categorical claims are interpretive statements about reality. They claim that something does (or does not) exist or that something does (or does not) possess the qualities of a certain category. Often simple categorical claims look like facts, so it is important to distinguish between a fact and a simple categorical claim.

A *fact* is a statement that can be verified in some way, either by empirical observation or by reference to a reliable source (say, an encyclopedia) trusted by you and your audience. Here are some facts: Water freezes at 32 degrees. Boise is in Idaho, not Montana. The bald eagle is no longer on the EPA's endangered species list. These are all facts because they can be verified; no supporting arguments are needed or called for.

In contrast, a *simple categorical claim* is a contestable interpretation of facts. Consider the difference between these two sentences:

Fact: The bald eagle is no longer on the EPA's endangered species list.

Simple categorical claim: The bald eagle is no longer an endangered species.

The factual statement can be verified by looking at the list of endangered species published by the Environmental Protection Agency. We can see the date the bald eagle was placed on the list and the date it was removed. The second statement is a claim. Imagine all the debates and arguments the EPA must have had as it poured over statistical data about eagle population numbers and over field reports from observers of eagles before deciding to remove the bald eagle from the list.

Often, it is difficult to draw the line between a fact and a claim. The acceptance or skepticism of a given audience can determine what passes as a fact or what becomes a claim that the arguer needs to support. Consider the statement "John F. Kennedy was killed by Lee Harvey Oswald." Most people call this statement a fact; to them, the report of the Warren Commission appointed to investigate the assassination is a reliable document that settles the issue. But conspiracy theorists, many of whom regard the Warren report as an unreliable rush to judgment, consider the statement above a highly contestable claim.

FOR CLASS DISCUSSION

Working individually or in small groups, determine which of the following statements are facts and which are categorical claims. If you think a statement could be a "fact" for some audiences and a "claim" for others, explain your reasoning.

1. State sales taxes are not deductible on your federal income tax form.

2. State sales taxes are annoying to both buyers and sellers.

3. State sales taxes are a hardship on low-income families.

4. *The Phantom Menace* is a George Lucas film.

5. *The Phantom Menace* was not well received by movie critics.

6. *The Phantom Menace* is a racist movie.

7. Eleanor Roosevelt was a very unconventional woman.

8. Eleanor Roosevelt was the most influential first lady ever to inhabit the White House.

9. Eleanor Roosevelt sometimes seemed anti-Semitic.

10. Eleanor Roosevelt was one of the drafters of the United Nations' Universal Declaration of Human Rights.

Variations in the Wording
of Simple Categorical Claims

Simple categorical claims typically take the grammatical structure "X is a Y." Grammarians describe this structure as a subject followed by a linking verb (such as *to be* or *to seem*) followed by a predicate noun or adjective:

> David is bossy.
>
> State sales taxes are annoying.
>
> Eleanor Roosevelt sometimes seemed anti-Semitic.

But other grammatical constructions can be used to make the same categorical claims:

> David frequently bosses people around. (He belongs to the category "people who are bossy.")
>
> Sales taxes really annoy people. (Sales taxes belong to the category "things that are annoying.")
>
> On occasion, Eleanor Roosevelt made anti-Semitic remarks. (Eleanor Roosevelt belongs to the category "people who occasionally seem anti-Semitic.")

Almost any kind of interpretive statement about reality (other than causal statements, which are covered in Chapter 11) is a categorical claim of some kind. Here are a couple more examples of different kinds of categorical claims that can be translated into an "X is Y" format:

> The Kosovo Liberation Army waged terrorism against the Serbs. (The Kosovo Liberation Army was in part an anti-Serb terrorist organization.)
>
> Corporations often exaggerate the money they give to charities. (Corporate claims about their charitable giving are often exaggerated.)

Our point is to demonstrate that categorical claims are very common. Whether they are worded directly as "X is Y" statements or disguised in different grammatical structures, they assert that item X belongs in category Y or possesses the features of category Y.

Supporting Simple Categorical Claims:
Supply Examples

The basic strategy for supporting a simple categorical claim is to give examples or other data showing how X belongs in category Y. If you want to argue that Sam is a party animal, provide examples of his partying behavior. If you want to argue that Eleanor Roosevelt sometimes seemed anti-Semitic, quote excerpts of anti-Semitic statements from her personal correspondence.* Because simple categorical arguments are common building blocks for longer, more complex arguments, they often take no more than one or two paragraphs inside a longer piece.

For an example of a simple categorical argument, consider the following paragraph from an article supporting regulated hunting of whales. In this article, the writer explains that many countries oppose whaling because they are no longer dependent on whale oil, having found synthetic substitutes. Whaling was never a deep part of the culture of these industrialized countries. As part of his argument, the writer wants to contrast these countries with traditional whaling countries. He makes the categorical claim that in Norway and Japan whaling was an "ancient occupation" worthy of respect. The following paragraph supports that categorical claim:

> Things were different in other nations, especially Norway and Japan, where whaling is an ancient occupation worthy of the respect and support that Americans award to, say, the running of a farm. Norwegians view whaling as part of the hard, honorable life of a fisherman—a reliable slow-season activity that helps fishing communities to make it through the year. The Japanese who come from a long line of whalers have deeply held moral beliefs about maintaining their family tradition. To be prevented from honoring their ancestors in this manner is a source of shame. After the 1982 moratorium [on whaling] some Norwegian fishers went bankrupt. The same thing happened in Iceland. Given the abundance of the whale stocks, these nations ask, why can't such people be free to practice their traditional livelihood? Anthropologists have long observed the primary role played by traditional foods in the social structure and moral norms of a community—a role that is captured in the widely repeated aphorism "you are what you eat." Asking people to give up their customary diet is in many ways like asking them to give up part of their identity.†

Of course, a simple categorical claim can also be the thesis for a whole argument. We provide such an example on pages 218–19, where columnist John Leo cites numerous examples from the Star Wars movie *Episode I: The Phantom Menace* to argue that this film "is packed with awful stereotypes."

---

*Roosevelt's biographer Blanche Wiesen Cook deals sensitively with this complex issue, largely exonerating Roosevelt from the charge of anti-Semitism. See *Eleanor Roosevelt*, vol. 2, *1933–38* (New York: Viking, 1999).

†William Aron, William Burke, and Milton Freeman. "Flouting the Convention." *Atlantic*, May, 1999, p. 26.

Refuting Simple Categorical Claims

If you wish to challenge or question someone else's simple categorical claim, you have three common strategies at your disposal:

- *Deny the accuracy or truth of the examples and data.* "You say that David is bossy. But you are remembering incorrectly. That wasn't David who did those bossy things; that was Paul."

- *Provide counterexamples that place X in a different category.* "Well, maybe David acted bossy on a few occasions. But more often he is kind and highly cooperative. For example . . ."

- *Raise definitional questions about the Y term.* "Well, that depends on what you mean by 'bossy.' What you call bossiness, I call decisiveness."

The last of these strategies shows how easily a simple categorical claim can slip into a definitional dispute. In the rest of this chapter we turn our attention to definitional arguments.

FOR CLASS DISCUSSION

Working as a whole class or in small groups, prepare brief arguments in support of each of the following categorical claims. Then discuss ways that you might call these claims into question.

1. Americans today are obsessed with their appearance.

2. Professional athletes are overpaid.

3. The video games most enjoyed by children are extremely violent.

AN OVERVIEW OF DEFINITIONAL ARGUMENTS

As we turn now to definitional arguments, it is important to distinguish between cases where definitions are needed and cases where definitions are *disputed*. Many arguments require a definition of key terms. If you are arguing, for example, that after-school jobs are harmful to teenagers because they promote materialism, you will probably need to define *materialism* somewhere in your argument. Writers regularly define key words for their readers by providing synonyms, by citing a dictionary definition, by stipulating a definition, or by some other means. In the rest of this chapter, we focus on arguments in which the meaning of a key term is disputed. Consider, for example, the environmental controversy over the definition of *wetlands*. Section 404 of the federal Clean Water Act provides for federal protection of wetlands, but it leaves the task of defining wetlands to administrative agencies and the courts. Currently about 5 percent of the land surface of the contiguous forty-eight states is potentially affected by the wetlands provision, and 75 percent of this land is privately owned. Efforts to define wetlands have created a battleground between pro-environment and pro-development (or pro–private property rights) groups. Farmers, homeowners, and developers often want a narrow definition of wetlands so that more property is available for commercial or private use. Environmentalists favor a broad definition in order to protect different habitat types and maintain the environmental safeguards that wetlands provide (control of water pollution, spawning grounds for aquatic species, floodwater containment, and so forth). The problem is that defining wetlands is tricky. For example, one federal regulation defines a wetland as any area that has a saturated ground surface for twenty-one consecutive days during the year. But how would you apply this law to a pine flatwood ecosystem that was wet for ten days this year but thirty days last year? And how should the courts react to lawsuits claiming that the regulation itself is either too broad or too narrow? One can see why the wetlands controversy provides hefty incomes for lawyers and congressional lobbyists.

THE CRITERIA-MATCH STRUCTURE OF DEFINITIONAL ARGUMENTS

As the wetlands example suggests, definitional arguments usually have a two-part structure—a definition part that tries to establish the meaning of the Y term (What do we mean by *wetland?*) and a match part that argues whether a given X meets that definition (Does this 30-acre parcel of land near Swan Lake meet the criteria for a wetland?) We use the term *criteria-match* to describe this structure, which occurs regularly not only in definitional arguments but also, as we shall see in Chapter 13, in evaluation arguments of the type "X is (is not) a good Y." The *criteria* part of the structure defines the Y term by setting forth the criteria that must be met for something to be considered a Y. The *match* part examines whether the X term meets these criteria. Here are some examples:

- *Definitional issue:* In a divorce proceeding, is a frozen embryo a "person" rather than "property"?

  Criteria part: What legal criteria must be met for something to be a "person"?

  Match part: Does a frozen embryo meet these criteria?

- *Definitional issue:* For purposes of my feeling good about buying my next pair of running shoes, is the Hercules Shoe Company a socially responsible company?

  Criteria part: What criteria must be met for a company to be deemed "socially responsible"?

  Match part: Does the Hercules Shoe Company meet these criteria?

To show how a definitional issue can be developed into a claim with supporting reasons, let's look more closely at this second example. Let's suppose you work for a consumer information group that wishes to encourage patronage of socially responsible companies while boycotting irresponsible ones. Your group's first task is to define *socially responsible company*. After much discussion and research, your group establishes three criteria that a company must meet to be considered socially responsible:

> *Your definition:* A company is socially responsible if it (1) avoids polluting the environment, (2) sells goods or services that contribute to the well-being of the community, and (3) treats its workers justly.

The criteria section of your argument would explain and illustrate these criteria.

The match part of the argument would then try to persuade readers that a specific company does or does not meet the criteria. A typical thesis statement might be as follows:

> *Your thesis statement:* Although the Hercules Shoe Company is nonpolluting and provides a socially useful product, it is *not* a socially responsible company because it treats workers unjustly.

Here is how the core of the argument could be displayed in Toulmin terms (note how the criteria established in your definition serve as warrants for your argument):

INITIAL ENTHYMEME:	The Hercules Shoe Company is not a socially responsible company because it treats workers unjustly.
CLAIM:	The Hercules Shoe Company is *not* a socially responsible company.
STATED REASON:	because it treats workers unjustly
GROUNDS:	evidence that the company manufactures its shoes in East Asian sweatshops; evidence of the inhumane conditions in these shops; evidence of hardships imposed on displaced American workers
WARRANT:	Socially responsible companies treat workers justly.
BACKING:	arguments showing that just treatment of workers is right in principle and also benefits society; arguments that capitalism helps society as a whole only if workers achieve a reasonable standard of living, have time for leisure, and are not exploited
POSSIBLE CONDITIONS OF REBUTTAL	Opponents of this thesis might argue that justice needs to be considered from an emerging nation's

standpoint: The wages paid workers are low by American standards but are above average by East Asian standards. Displacement of American workers is part of the necessary adjustment of adapting to a global economy and does not mean that a company is unjust.

As this Toulmin frame illustrates, the writer's argument needs to contain a criteria section (warrant and backing) showing that just treatment of workers is a criterion for social responsibility and a match section (stated reason and grounds) showing that the Hercules Shoe Company does not treat its workers justly. Your audience's initial beliefs determine how much emphasis you need to place on justifying each criterion and supporting each match. The conditions of rebuttal help the writer imagine alternative views and see places where opposing views need to be acknowledged and rebutted.

FOR CLASS DISCUSSION

Consider the following definitional claims. Working as individuals or in small groups, identify the criteria issue and the match issue for each of the following claims.

EXAMPLE: A Honda assembled in Ohio is (is not) an American-made car.

CRITERIA PART: What criteria have to be met before a car can be called "American made"?

MATCH PART: Does a Honda assembled in Ohio meet these criteria?

1. Computer programming is (is not) a creative profession.
2. Writing graffiti on subways is (is not) vandalism.
3. American Sign Language is (is not) a "foreign language" for purposes of a college graduation requirement.
4. Beauty contests are (are not) sexist events.
5. Bungee jumping from a crane is (is not) a "carnival amusement ride" subject to state safety inspections.

CONCEPTUAL PROBLEMS OF DEFINITION

Before moving on to discuss ways of defining the Y term in a definitional argument, we should explore briefly some of the conceptual difficulties of definition. Language, for all its wonderful powers, is an arbitrary system that requires agreement among its users before it can work. And it's not always easy to get that agreement. In fact, the task of defining something can be devilishly complex.

Why Can't We Just Look in the Dictionary?

What's so hard about defining? you might ask. Why not just look in a dictionary? To get a sense of the complexity of defining something, consider again the word *wetland*. A dictionary can tell us the ordinary meaning of a word (the way it is commonly used), but it can't resolve a debate between competing definitions when different parties have interests in defining the word in different ways. For example, the *Webster's Seventh New Collegiate Dictionary* defines *wetland* as "land containing much soil moisture"—a definition that is hardly helpful in determining whether the federal government can prevent the development of a beach resort on some landowner's private property. Moreover, dictionary definitions rarely tell us such things as *to what degree* a given condition must be met before it qualifies for class membership. How wet does a wetland have to be before it is *legally* a wetland? How long does this wetness have to last? When is a wetland a mere swamp that ought to be drained rather than protected?

Definitions and the Rule of Justice: At What Point Does X Quit Being a Y?

For some people, all this concern about definition may seem misplaced. How often, after all, have you heard people accuse each other of getting bogged down in "mere semantics"? But how we define a given word can have significant implications for people who must either use the word or have the word used on them. Take, for example, what some philosophers refer to as the *rule of justice*. According to this rule, "Beings in the same essential category should be treated in the same way." Should an insurance company, for example, treat anorexia nervosa as a physical illness like diabetes (in which case treatment is paid for by the insurance company) or as a mental illness like paranoia (in which case insurance payments are minimal)? Or, to take another example, if a company gives "new baby" leave to a mother, should it also give "new baby" leave to a father? In other words, is this kind of leave "new mother" leave, or is it "new parent" leave? And what if a couple adopts an infant? Should "new mother" or "new parent" leave be available to adoptive parents also? These questions are all definitional issues involving arguments about what class of beings an individual belongs to and about what actions to take to comply with the rule of justice, which demands that all members of that class be treated equally.

The rule of justice becomes even harder to apply when we consider Xs that grow, evolve, or otherwise change through time. When Young Person back in Chapter 1 argued that she could set her own curfew because she was mature, she raised the question "What are the attributes or criteria of a 'mature' person?" In this case, a categorical distinction between two separate kinds of things ("mature" versus "not mature") evolves into a distinction of degree ("mature enough"). So perhaps we should ask not whether Young Person is mature but whether she is "mature enough." At what point does a child become an adult? (When does a fetus become a human person? When does a social drinker become an alcoholic?)

Although we may be able arbitrarily to choose a particular point and declare, through stipulation, that "mature" means eighteen years old or that "human person" includes a fetus at conception, or at three months, or at birth, in the everyday world the distinction between child and adult, between egg and person, between social drinking and alcoholism seems an evolution, not a sudden and definitive step. Nevertheless, our language requires an abrupt shift between classes. In short, applying the rule of justice often requires us to adopt a digital approach to reality (switches are either on or off, either a fetus is a human person or it is not), whereas our sense of life is more analogical (there are numerous gradations between on and off, there are countless shades of gray between black and white).

As we can see by the preceding examples, the promise of language to fix what psychologist William James called "the buzz and confusion of the world" into an orderly set of categories turns out to be elusive. In most definitional debates, an argument, not a quick trip to the dictionary, is required to settle the matter.

FOR CLASS DISCUSSION

Suppose your landlord decides to institute a "no pets" rule. The rule of justice requires that all pets have to go—not just your neighbor's barking dog, but also Mrs. Brown's cat, the kids' hamster downstairs, and your own pet tarantula. That is, all these animals have to go unless you can argue that some of them are not "pets" for purposes of a landlord's "no pets" rule.

1. Working in small groups or as a whole class, define *pets* by establishing the criteria an animal would have to meet to be included in the category "pets." Consider your landlord's "no pets" rule as the rhetorical context for your definition.

2. Based on your criteria, which of the following animals is definitely a pet that would have to be removed from the apartment? Based on your criteria, which animals could you exclude from the "no pets" rule? How would you make your argument to your landlord?
   - a German shepherd dog
   - a small housecat
   - a tiny, well-trained lapdog
   - a gerbil in a cage
   - a canary
   - a tank of tropical fish
   - a tarantula

KINDS OF DEFINITIONS

In this section we discuss two methods of definition commonly used in definitional arguments: Aristotelian and operational.

Aristotelian Definition

Aristotelian definitions, regularly used in dictionaries, define a term by placing it within the next larger class or category and then showing the specific attributes that distinguish the term from other terms within the same category. For example, a *pencil* is a "writing implement" (next larger category) that differs from other writing implements in that it makes marks with lead or graphite rather than ink. You could elaborate this definition by saying, "Usually the lead or graphite is a long, thin column embedded in a slightly thicker column of wood with an eraser on one end and a sharpened point, exposing the graphite, on the other." You could even distinguish a wooden pencil from a mechanical pencil, thereby indicating again that the crucial identifying attribute is the graphite, not the wooden column.

As you can see, an Aristotelian definition of a term identifies specific attributes or criteria that enable you to distinguish it from other members of the next larger class. We created an Aristotelian definition in our example about socially responsible companies. A socially responsible company, we said, is any company (next larger class) that meets three criteria: (1) It doesn't pollute the environment; (2) it creates goods or services that promote the well-being of the community; and (3) it treats its workers justly.

In constructing Aristotelian definitions, you may find it useful to employ the concepts of accidental, necessary, and sufficient criteria. An *accidental criterion* is a usual but not essential feature of a concept. For example, "made out of wood" is an accidental feature of a pencil. Most pencils are made out of wood, but something can still be a pencil even if it isn't made out of wood (a mechanical pencil). In our example about socially responsible companies, "makes regular contributions to charities" might be an accidental criterion; most socially responsible companies contribute to charities, but some do not. And many socially irresponsible companies also contribute to charities—often as a public relations ploy.

A *necessary criterion* is an attribute that *must* be present for something to belong to the category being defined. For example, the property of "being a writing implement" is a necessary criterion for an object to be a pencil. The property of "marking with graphite or lead" is also a necessary criterion. However, neither of these criteria is a sufficient criterion for an object to be a pencil because many writing implements are not pencils (for example, pens), and many things that mark with graphite or lead aren't pencils (for example, a lead paperweight can make lead marks). Because an object that possesses both of these criteria together must be a pencil, we say that these two qualities together form a *sufficient criterion* for an object to be a pencil.

To show you how these concepts can help you carry on a definitional argument with more precision, let's apply them to a few examples. Suppose Felix

Ungar and Oscar Madison are arguing whether an original Dodge Stealth is a true sports car. At issue are the criteria for "true sports car." Felix might argue that a Stealth is not a true sports car because it has rear seats. (To Felix, having seating for only two people is thus a necessary criterion for a true sports car.) Oscar Madison might argue, however, that having two seats is only an accidental feature of sports cars and that a Stealth is indeed a true sports car because it has a racy appearance and is designed to handle superbly on narrow curving roads. (For Oscar, racy appearance and superb handling are together sufficient criteria for a true sports car.)

As another example, consider again our defining criteria for a "socially responsible" company: (1) The company must avoid polluting the environment; (2) the company must create goods or services that contribute to the well-being of the community; and (3) the company must treat its workers justly. In this definition, each criterion is necessary, but none of the criteria alone is sufficient. In other words, to be defined as socially responsible, a company must meet all three criteria at once. It is not enough for a company to be nonpolluting (a necessary but not sufficient criterion); if that company makes a shoddy product or treats its workers unjustly, it fails to meet the other necessary criteria and can't be deemed socially responsible. Because no one criterion by itself is sufficient, all three criteria together must be met before a company can be deemed socially responsible.

In contrast, consider the following definition of *sexual harassment* as established by the U.S. Equal Employment Opportunity Commission in its 1980 guidelines:

> Unwelcome sexual advances, requests for sexual favors, and other verbal or physical conduct of a sexual nature constitute sexual harassment when (1) submission to such conduct is made either explicitly or implicitly a term or condition of an individual's employment, (2) submission to or rejection of such conduct by an individual is used as the basis for employment decisions affecting such individual, or (3) such conduct has the purpose or effect of unreasonably interfering with an individual's work performance or creating an intimidating, hostile, or offensive working environment.*

Here each of these criteria is sufficient but none is necessary. In other words, an act constitutes sexual harassment if any one of the three criteria is satisfied.

FOR CLASS DISCUSSION

Working individually or in small groups, try to determine whether each of the following is a necessary criterion, a sufficient criterion, an accidental criterion, or

---

*Quoted by Stephanie Riger, "Gender Dilemmas in Sexual Harassment Policies and Procedures," *American Psychologist* 46 (May 1991), 497–505.

no criterion for defining the indicated concept. Be prepared to explain your reasoning and to account for differences in points of view.

CRITERION	CONCEPT TO BE DEFINED
presence of gills	fish
profane and obscene language	R-rated movie
birthplace inside the United States	American citizen
age of 65 or older	senior citizen
line endings that form a rhyming pattern	poem
spanking a child for discipline	child abuse
diet that excludes meat	vegetarian
killing another human being	murder
good sex life	happy marriage

Effect of Rhetorical Context on Aristotelian Definitions

It is important to appreciate how the context of a given argument can affect your definition of a term. The question "Is a tarantula kept in the house a pet?" may actually have opposing answers, depending on the rhetorical situation. You may argue that your tarantula is or is not a pet, depending on whether you are trying to exclude it from your landlord's "no pet" rule or include it in your local talk show's "weird pet contest." Within one context you will want to argue that what your landlord really means by *pet* is an animal (next larger class) capable of disturbing neighbors or harming the landlord's property (criteria that distinguish it from other members of the class). Thus you could argue that your tarantula isn't a pet in your landlord's sense because it is incapable of harming property or disturbing the peace (assuming you don't let it loose!). In the other context you would argue that a pet is "any living thing" (note that in this context the "next larger class" is much larger) with which a human being forms a caring attachment and which shares its owner's domicile. In this case you might say, "Tommy Tarantula here is one of my dearest friends and if you don't think Tommy is weird enough, wait 'til I show you Vanessa, my pet Venus's-flytrap."

To apply the same principle to a different field of debate, consider whether obscene language in a student newspaper should be protected by the First Amendment. The purpose of school officials' suspending editors responsible for such language is to maintain order and decency in the school. The school officials thus hope to narrow the category of acts that are protected under the free-speech amendment in order to meet their purposes. In contrast, the American Civil Liberties Union (which has long defended student newspaper editors) is intent on avoiding any precedent that will restrict freedom of speech any more than is absolutely necessary. The different definitions of *free speech* that are likely to emerge thus reflect the different purposes of the disputants.

The problem of purpose shows why it is so hard to define a word out of context. Some people try to escape this dilemma by returning to the "original intent" of the authors of precedent-setting documents such as the Constitution. But if we try to determine the original intent of the writers of the Constitution on such matters as "free speech," "cruel and unusual punishment," or the "right to bear arms," we must still ask what their original purposes were in framing the constitutional language. If we can show that those original purposes are no longer relevant to present concerns, we have begun to undermine what would otherwise appear to be a static and universal definition to which we could turn.

Operational Definitions

In some rhetorical situations, particularly those arising in the physical and social sciences, writers need precise definitions that can be measured empirically and are not subject to problems of context and disputed criteria. Consider, for example, an argument involving the concept "aggression": "Do violent television programs increase the incidence of aggression in children?" To do research on this issue, a scientist needs a precise, measurable definition of *aggression.* Typically, a scientist might measure "aggression" by counting the number of blows or kicks a child gives to an inflatable bozo doll over a fifteen-minute period when other play options are available. The scientist might then define *aggressive behavior* as six or more blows to the bozo doll. In our wetlands example, a federal authority created an operational definition of *wetland:* A wetland is a parcel of land that has a saturated ground surface for twenty-one consecutive days during the year. Such definitions are useful because they are precisely measurable, but they are also limited because they omit criteria that may be unmeasurable but important. Many scientists, for example, object to definitions of *wetland* based on consecutive days of wetness. What is more relevant, they argue, is not the duration of wetness in any parcel of land but the kind of plants and animals that depend on the wetland as a habitat. As another example, we might ask whether it is adequate to define a *superior student* as someone with a 3.5 GPA or higher or a *successful sex education program* as one that results in a 25 percent reduction in teenage pregnancies. What important aspects of a superior student or a successful sex education program are not considered in these operational definitions?

STRATEGIES FOR DEFINING THE CONTESTED TERM IN A DEFINITIONAL ARGUMENT

In constructing criteria to define your contested term, you can take two basic approaches—what rhetoricians call reportive and stipulative definitions. A *reportive definition* cites how others have used the term. A *stipulative definition* cites how you define the term. To put it another way, you can take a reportive approach by turning to standard or specialized dictionaries, judicial opinions, or expert testimony to establish a definition based on the authority of others. A lawyer defining a wetland based on twenty-one consecutive days of saturated ground surface would be using a reportive definition with a federal regulation as her source. The other approach is to use your own critical thinking to stipulate a definition, thereby defining the contested term yourself. Our definition of a socially responsible company, specifying three criteria, is an example of a stipulative definition. This section explains these approaches in more detail.

Reportive Approach: Research How Others Have Used the Term

When you take a reportive approach, you research how others have used the term, searching for authoritative definitions acceptable to your audience yet favorable to your case. Student writer Kathy Sullivan uses this approach in her argument that photographs displayed at the Oncore Bar are not obscene (see pp. 220–22). To define *obscenity*, she turns to *Black's Law Dictionary* and Pember's *Mass Media Laws*. (Specialized dictionaries are a standard part of the reference section of any library. See your reference librarian for assistance.) Other sources of specialized definitions are state and federal appellate court decisions, legislative and administrative statutes, and scholarly articles examining a given definitional conflict. Lawyers use this research strategy exhaustively in preparing court briefs. They begin by looking at the actual text of laws as passed by legislatures or written by administrative authorities. Then they look at all the court cases in which the laws have been tested and examine the ways courts have refined legal definitions and applied them to specific cases. Using these refined and elaborated definitions, lawyers then apply them to their own case at hand.

When research fails to uncover a definition favorable to the arguer's case, the arguer can sometimes adopt an *original intentions strategy*. For example, if a scientist is dissatisfied with definitions of *wetland* based on consecutive days of saturated ground surface, she might proceed as follows: "The original intention of the Congress in passing the Clean Water Act was to preserve the environment." What Congress intended, she could then claim, was to prevent development of those wetland areas that provide crucial habitat for wildlife or that inhibit water pollution. She could then propose an alternative definition (either a stipulative one that she develops herself or a reportive one that she uncovers in research) based on criteria other than consecutive days of ground saturation. (Of course, original intentions arguments can often be refuted by a "times have changed" strategy or by a "we can't know what they originally intended; we can only know what they wrote" strategy.)

Another way to make a reportive definition is to employ a strategy based on etymology, or *earlier meaning strategy*. Using an etymological dictionary or the *Oxford English Dictionary* (which traces the historical evolution of a word's meaning), an arguer can often unveil insights favorable to the writer's case. For example, if you wanted to argue that portrayal of violence in films is *obscene,* you could point to the etymology of the word, which literally means "offstage." The word derives from the practice of classical Greek tragedy, where violent acts occurred offstage and were only reported by a messenger. This strategy allows you to show how the word originally applied to violence rather than to sexual explicitness.

Stipulative Approach: Create Your Own Definition Based on Positive, Contrastive, and Borderline Cases*

Often, however, you need to create your own definition of the contested term. An effective strategy for developing your own definition is to brainstorm examples of positive, contrastive, and borderline cases. Suppose, for example, you wanted to argue the claim that "Computer programming is (is not) a creative activity." Your first goal is to establish criteria for creativity. You could begin by thinking of examples of obvious creative behaviors, then of contrastive behaviors that seem similar to the previous behaviors but yet are clearly not creative, and then finally of borderline behaviors that may or may not be creative. Your list might look like this:

EXAMPLES OF CREATIVE BEHAVIORS

Beethoven composes a violin concerto.

An architect designs a house.

Edison invents the lightbulb.

An engineer designs a machine that will make widgets in a new way.

A poet writes a poem. (Later revised to "A poet writes a poem that poetry experts say is beautiful"—see following discussion.)

CONTRASTIVE EXAMPLES OF NONCREATIVE BEHAVIORS

A conductor transposes Beethoven's concerto into a different key.

A carpenter builds a house from the architect's plan.

I change a lightbulb in my house.

A factory worker uses the new machine to stamp out widgets.

A graduate student writes sentimental "lovey/dovey" verses for greeting cards.

---

*The defining strategies and collaborative exercises in this section are based on the work of George Hillocks and his research associates at the University of Chicago. See George Hillocks Jr., Elizabeth A. Kahn, and Larry R. Johannessen, "Teaching Defining Strategies as a Mode of Inquiry: Some Effects on Student Writing," *Research in the Teaching of English 17* (October 1983), 275–84. See also Larry R. Johannessen, Elizabeth A. Kahn, and Carolyn Calhoun Walter, *Designing and Sequencing Prewriting Activities* (Urbana, IL: NCTE, 1982).

EXAMPLES OF BORDERLINE CASES

A woman gives birth to a child.

An accountant figures out your income tax.

A musician arranges a rock song for a marching band.

A monkey paints an oil painting by smearing paint on canvas; a group of art critics, not knowing a monkey was the artist, call the painting beautiful.

Next you can begin developing your criteria by determining what features the "clearly creative" examples have in common and what features the "clearly non-creative" examples lack. Then refine your criteria by deciding on what grounds you might include or eliminate your borderline cases from the category "creative." For example, you might begin with the following criterion:

DEFINITION: FIRST TRY

For an act to be creative, it must result in an end product that is significantly different from other products.

But then, by looking at some of the examples in your creative and noncreative columns, you decide that just producing a different end product isn't enough. A bad poem might be different from other poems, but you don't want to call a bad poet creative. So you refine your criteria:

DEFINITION: SECOND TRY

For an act to be creative, it must result in an end product that is significantly different from other products and is useful or beautiful.

This definition would allow you to include all the acts in your creative column but eliminate the acts in the noncreative column.

Your next step is to refine your criteria by deciding whether to include or reject items in your borderline list. You decide to reject the childbirth case by arguing that creativity must be a mental or intellectual activity, not a natural process. You reject the monkey as painter example on similar grounds, arguing that although the end product may be both original and beautiful, it is not creative because it is not a product of the monkey's intellect. However, when you consider the example of the musician who arranges a rock song for a marching band, you encounter disagreement. One member of your group says that arranging music is not creative. This person says that the musician, like a carpenter who makes a few alterations in the blueprint of a house, isn't designing a new product but rather is adapting an already existing one.

A musician in the group reacts angrily, arguing that musicians—in their arrangements of music and in their renditions of musical pieces—"interpret" music. She contends that different renditions of music are actually significantly different pieces that are experienced differently by audiences, and therefore both arranging music and playing a piece in a different musical style are creative acts. The group hesitantly acknowledges that arranging a rock song in marching-band style is different from the example of a carpenter who adds a door between the kitchen and the dining room in a new house. The group concedes to the music major and includes the example of arranging a musical piece in a different musical style.

Your group's final definition, then, looks like this:

DEFINITION: THIRD TRY

> For an act to be creative, it must be produced by intellectual design, and it must result in an end project that is significantly different from the other products and is useful or beautiful.

Having established these criteria, you are ready to apply them to your controversial case of computer programming. Based on your criteria, you decide to argue that computer programming exists on a continuum ranging from "noncreative activity" to "highly creative activity." At the "noncreative" end of the continuum, computer programmers churn out lines of code following algorithmic procedures requiring intelligence, knowledge, problem-solving skills, and a high level of craftsmanship, but not creative thought. Such programmers apply established procedures to new situations; although the applications are new, the programs themselves are not significantly different or innovative. At the other end of the continuum, computer programmers are highly creative. The original Macintosh computer, with its icon-based operating system (later imitated by Microsoft in its Windows© programs), has been heralded as one of the twentieth century's most creative inventions. Programmers who develop ideas for new products, who solve old problems in new ways, or who do research in artificial intelligence, computer simulation, or other interdisciplinary fields requiring synthetic thought are all meeting the criteria of significant newness, usefulness (or beauty), and intellectual design required by our stipulated definition of *creativity*.

This strategy using positive examples, contrastive examples, and borderline cases produces a systematic procedure for developing a definitional argument. Moreover, it provides the examples you will need to explain and illustrate your criteria.

FOR CLASS DISCUSSION

1. Suppose you wanted to define the concept "courage." Working in groups, try to decide whether each of the following cases is an example of courage:
   a. A neighbor rushes into a burning house to rescue a child from certain death and emerges, coughing and choking, with the child in his arms. Is the neighbor courageous?

b. A firefighter rushes into a burning house to rescue a child from certain death and emerges with the child in her arms. The firefighter is wearing protective clothing and a gas mask. When a newspaper reporter calls her courageous, she says, "Hey, this is my job." Is the firefighter courageous?

c. A teenager rushes into a burning house to recover a memento given to him by his girlfriend, the first love of his life. Is the teenager courageous?

d. A parent rushes into a burning house to save a trapped child. The fire marshal tells the parent to wait because there is no chance that the child can be reached from the first floor. The fire marshal wants to try cutting a hole in the roof to reach the child. The parent rushes into the house anyway and is burned to death. Was the parent courageous?

2. As you make your decisions on each of these cases, create and refine the criteria you use.

3. Make up your own series of controversial cases, like those above for "courage," for one or more of the following concepts:
   a. cruelty to animals
   b. child abuse
   c. true athlete
   d. sexual harassment
   e. free speech protected by the First Amendment

Then, using the strategy of positive, contrastive, and borderline cases, construct a definition of your chosen concept.

CONDUCTING THE MATCH PART OF A DEFINITIONAL ARGUMENT

In conducting a match argument, you need to supply examples and other evidence showing that your contested case does (does not) meet the criteria you established in your definition. In essence, you support the match part of your argument in much the same way you would support a simple categorical claim.

For example, if you were developing the argument that the Hercules Shoe Company is not socially responsible because it treats its workers unjustly, your match section would provide evidence of this injustice. You might supply data about the percentage of shoes produced in East Asia, about the low wages paid these workers, and about the working conditions in these factories. You might also describe the suffering of displaced American workers when Hercules closed its American factories and moved operations to Asia, where the labor was nonunion and cheap. The match section should also summarize and respond to opposing views.

WRITING A DEFINITIONAL ARGUMENT

WRITING ASSIGNMENT FOR CHAPTER 10

Write an argument that develops a definitional claim of the form "X is (is not) a Y," where Y is a controversial term with a disputed definition. Typically your argument will have a criteria section in which you develop an extended definition of your Y term and a match section in which you argue that your X does (does not) meet the criteria for Y.

Exploring Ideas

Ideally, in writing this argument you will join an ongoing conversation about a definitional issue that interests you. What cultural and social issues that concern you involve disputed definitions? In the public area, you are likely to find numerous examples simply by looking through a newspaper—the strategy used by student writer Kathy Sullivan, who became interested in the controversy over allegedly obscene photographs in a gay bar (see pp. 220–22). Others of our students have addressed definitional issues such as these: Is Dr. Kevorkian a murderer (because he administered a lethal dosage to a paralyzed patient on national TV)? Are skateboarders punks or athletes? Is spanking a form of child abuse? Is flag burning protected free speech? Are today's maximum security prisons "cruel and unusual punishment"? Is tobacco a drug for purposes of federal regulation? Are chiropractors "real doctors"?

If you have trouble discovering a local or national issue that interests you, you can create fascinating definitional controversies among your classmates by asking whether certain borderline cases are "true" examples of some category: Are highly skilled video game players (race car drivers, synchronized swimmers, marbles players) true athletes? Is a gourmet chef a true artist? Is rap music truly misogynist? Is the novel (or film) *Sophie's Choice* a true tragedy? Working as a whole class or in small groups inside or out of class, create an argumentative discussion on one or more of these issues. Listen to the various voices in the controversy, and then write out your own argument.

You can also stimulate definitional controversies by brainstorming borderline cases for such terms as *courage* (Is mountain climbing an act of courage?), *cruelty to animals* (Are rodeos [zoos, catch-and-release trout fishing, use of animals for medical research] cruelty to animals?), or *police brutality* (Is use of a stun gun an example of police brutality?).

As you explore your definitional issue, try to determine how others have defined your Y term (a reportive procedure). If no stable definition emerges from your search, stipulate your own definition by deciding what criteria must be met for any X to be deemed a Y. Try using the strategy of positive examples, negative examples, and borderline cases that we discussed on pages 209–12 with reference to creativity. Once you have determined your criteria for your Y term, freewrite for five or ten minutes, exploring whether your X term meets each of the criteria. Before writing your first draft, you might also explore your ideas further by doing the ten freewriting tasks on pages 70–71 in Chapter 3.

Organizing a Definitional Argument

As you compose a first draft of your essay, you may find it helpful to know a prototypical structure for definitional arguments. Here are several possible plans.

Plan 1 (Criteria and Match in Separate Sections)

- Introduce the issue by showing disagreements about the definition of a key term or about its application to a problematic case.
- State your claim.
- Present your definition of the key term.

    State and develop criterion 1.

    State and develop criterion 2.

    Continue with rest of criteria.

- Summarize and respond to possible objections to your definition.
- Restate your claim about the contested case (it does [does not] meet your definition).

    Apply criterion 1 to your case.

    Apply criterion 2 to your case.

    Continue the match argument.

- Summarize and respond to possible objections to your match argument.
- Conclude your argument.

Plan 2 (Criteria and Match Interwoven)

- Introduce the issue by showing disagreements about the definition of a key term or about its application to a problematic case.
- Present your claim.

    State criterion 1 and argue that contested case meets (does not meet) criterion.

State criterion 2 and argue that contested case meets (does not meet) criterion.

Continue with criteria-match sections for additional criteria.

- Summarize opposing views.
- Refute or concede to opposing views.
- Conclude your argument.

Revising Your Draft

Once you have written a discovery draft, your goal should be to make your argument more clear and persuasive to your audience. Where might your audience call your claim, reasons, or evidence into question? Reengage with your audience to better appreciate the complexity of your issue. One way to strengthen your appeal to your readers is to use a Toulmin analysis to determine where your reasoning needs to be bolstered for your particular audience. In a definitional argument, the criteria established in your definition of the Y term are the warrants for your match argument. You might find it helpful at this time to summarize your argument as a claim with *because* clauses and to test it with Toulmin's schema. Here is how student writer Kathy Sullivan used Toulmin to analyze a draft of her essay examining the possible obscenity of photographs displayed in a gay bar in Seattle. The final version of this essay is printed on pages 220–22.

ENTHYMEME:	The photographs displayed in the Oncore bar are not obscene because they do not violate the community standards of the patrons of the bar, because they do not appeal to prurient interest, because children are not likely to be exposed to them, and because they promote an important social value, safe sex, in order to prevent AIDS.
CLAIM:	The photographs are not obscene.
STATED REASONS:	(1) They don't violate community standards. (2) They do not appeal to prurient interests. (3) Children are not exposed to them. (4) They promote an important social purpose of preventing AIDS through safe sex.
GROUNDS:	(1) evidence that most Oncore patrons are homosexual and that these photographs don't offend them (no complaints, etc.); (2) purpose of photographs is not prurient sexuality, they don't depict explicit sexual acts, the only thing complained about by the

	liquor board is visible body parts; (3) because this is a bar, children aren't allowed; (4) evidence that the purpose of these photographs is to promote safe sex, thus they have a redeeming social value
WARRANT:	Things that don't violate community standards, do not appeal to prurient interests, don't come in view of children, and promote an important purpose are not obscene.
BACKING:	These criteria come from the definition of *obscenity* in *Black's Law Dictionary,* which in turn is based on recent court cases. This is a very credible source. In addition, arguments showing why the community standard here should be that of the homosexual community rather than the community at large; arguments showing that the social importance of safe sex overrides other considerations.
CONDITIONS OF REBUTTAL:	An opponent might say that the community standards should be those of the Seattle community at large, not those of the gay community. An opponent might say that photographs of male genitalia in a gay bar appeal to prurient interest.
QUALIFIER:	Those photographs would be obscene if displayed anywhere but in a gay bar.

As a result of this analysis, Kathy revised her final draft considerably. By imagining where her arguments were weak ("conditions of rebuttal"), she realized that she needed to include more backing by arguing that the community standards to be applied in this case should be those of the homosexual community rather than the community at large. She also added a section arguing that visible genitalia in the photographs didn't make the photos obscene. By imagining how your readers might rebut your argument, you will see ways to strengthen your draft. Consequently, we close out this chapter by looking more carefully at the ways a definitional argument can be rebutted.

QUESTIONING AND CRITIQUING A DEFINITIONAL ARGUMENT

Another powerful way to stimulate revision of a draft is to role-play a skeptical audience. The following means of questioning a definitional argument can be applied to your own draft to help you strengthen it or to someone else's definitional argument as a means of critiquing it closely. In critiquing a definitional argument, you need to appreciate its criteria-match structure. Your critique can question the argument's criteria, the match, or both.

Questioning the Criteria

Might a skeptic claim that your criteria are not the right ones? This is the most common way to attack a definitional argument. Skeptics might say that one or more of your argument's criteria are only accidental criteria, not necessary or sufficient ones. Or they might argue for different criteria or point out crucial missing criteria.

Might a skeptic point out possible bad consequences of accepting your argument's criteria? Here a skeptic could raise doubts about your definition by showing how it would lead to unintended bad consequences.

Might a skeptic cite extraordinary circumstances that weaken your argument's criteria? Skeptics might argue that your criteria are perfectly acceptable in ordinary circumstances but are rendered unacceptable by extraordinary circumstances.

Might a skeptic point out a bias or slant in your definition? Writers create definitions favorable to their case. By making this slant visible, a skeptic may be able to weaken the persuasiveness of your definition.

Questioning the Match

A match argument usually uses examples and other evidence to show that the contested case meets (does not meet) the criteria in the definition. The standard methods of refuting evidence apply (see pp. 161–62). Thus skeptics might ask one or more of the following questions:

Are your examples out-of-date or too narrow and unrepresentative?

Are your examples inaccurate?

Are your examples too extreme?

Are there existing counterexamples that alter the case?

By using these questions to test your own argument, you can reshape and develop your argument to make it thought provoking and persuasive for your audience.

READINGS

Our first reading makes a simple categorical claim about the *Star Wars* movie *Episode I: The Phantom Menace.* The movie's appearance in May 1999 was a media event generating much discussion in the newspapers. In this op-ed piece, syndicated columnist John Leo argues that this film recirculates and perpetuates old racist stereotypes.

*Stereotypes No Phantom
in New* Star Wars *Movie*

John Leo

1   Everyone's a victim these days, so America's touchiness industry is dedicated to seeing group slights everywhere. But sometimes even touchy people are right. Complaints about the new *Star Wars* movie, for instance, are correct. *Episode I: The Phantom Menace* is packed with awful stereotypes.

2   Consider the evil Neimodians. They are stock Oriental villains out of black-and-white B movies of the 1930s and 1940s, complete with Hollywood Asian accents, sinister speech patterns, and a space-age version of stock Fu Manchu clothing.

3   Watto, the fat, greedy junk dealer with wings, is a conventional, crooked Middle Eastern merchant. This is a generic and anti-Semitic image, Jewish if you want him to be, or Arab if you don't.

4   Law Professor Patricia Williams says Watto looks strikingly like an anti-Jewish caricature published in Vienna at the turn of the century—round-bellied, big-nosed, with spindly arms, wings sprouting from his shoulders, and a scroll that says "anything for money."

5   Perhaps Watto isn't supposed to be Jewish. Some people thought he sounded Italian. But by presenting the character as an unprincipled, hook-nosed merchant (and a slave-owner, to boot), the movie is at least playing around with traditional anti-Semitic imagery. It shouldn't.

6   The loudest criticism has been directed at Jar Jar Binks, the annoying, computer-generated amphibian who looks like a cross between a frog and a camel and acts, as one critic put it, like a cross between Butterfly McQueen and Stepin Fetchit. His voice, the work of a black actor, is a sort of slurred, pidgin Caribbean English, much of it impossible to understand.

7   "Me berry, berry scay-yud," says Jar Jar, in one of his modestly successful attempts at English. For some reason, he keeps saying "yousa" and "meesa," instead of "you" and "me." He is the first character in the four *Star Wars* movies to mess up Galactic Basic (the English language) on a regular basis.

8   Trouble with English in one of the key traits of a racist caricature, from all the 19th-century characters named Snowball down to the sophisticated wit of Amos 'n' Andy. Whether endearing or pathetic, this trouble with language is supposed to demonstrate the intellectual inferiority of blacks.

9   Childlike confusion is another familiar way of stereotyping blacks, and Jar Jar shows that trait too. He steps in alien-creature doo-doo, gets his tongue caught in a racing engine and panics during the big battle scene. He is, in fact, a standard-issue black caricature.

10   A stereotype on this level is more than insult. It is a teaching instrument and a powerful, non-verbal argument saying that racial equality is a hopeless cause. If blacks talk and act like this movie says they do, how can they possibly expect equal treatment?

11   What is going on in this movie? George Lucas, director of the *Star Wars* movies, says media talk about stereotypes is creating "a controversy out of nothing."

But many visual cues support the charge that stereotypes are indeed built into the film. Jar Jar has head flaps drawn to look like dreadlocks. The ruler of his tribe, Boss Nass, wears what looks to be an African robe and African headdress. (Nass, fat and slobbering, seems to come right out of an old movie about the Zulu.)   12

A Neimodian senator named Lott (Trent Lott?), representing the evil viceroy Nute Gunray (Newt Gingrich?), wears a version of a Catholic bishop's miter and a Catholic priest's stole over a dark robe. This can't be an accident. It duplicates, almost exactly, the appearance of a real bishop. It's a small reference, but an unmistakable one. So Catholics, along with Asians and Republicans, are at least vaguely associated with Neimodian treachery.   13

Lucas is a visually sophisticated and careful moviemaker. In a TV interview, he said that he researched imagery of Satan in every known culture before deciding on how evil warrior Darth Maul should look in the film (tattooed, with horns). A *Star Wars* book that came out with the movie, *The Visual Dictionary,* describes in detail almost every image used in the film. So it's hard to believe that all the stereotyped imagery just happened.   14

One of the keys to Lucas' success is that his movies are made up of brilliantly reimagined themes and scenes from earlier films (World War II aerial dogfights, cowboys and Indians, swashbuckling sword fights, a *Ben Hur* chariot race, etc.). After three very inventive *Star Wars* movies, the not-so-inventive fourth seems to have fallen back on some tired Hollywood ethnic themes and characters he mostly avoided in the first three.   15

So *The Phantom Menace* offers us revived versions of some famous stereotypes. Jar Jar Binks as the dithery Butterfly McQueen; Watto, a devious, child-owning wheeler-dealer, as the new Fagin; the two reptilian Neimodian leaders as the inscrutably evil Fu Manchu and Dr. No. What's next—an interplanetary version of the Frito Bandito?   16

The *Star Wars* films deserve better than this. Let's put all these characters to sleep and start over in the next movie.   17

Critiquing "Stereotypes No Phantom in New 'Star Wars' Movie"

1. Simple categorical arguments are typically developed by the use of examples to support the claim. What examples does Leo use to demonstrate that stereotypes are common in *The Phantom Menace?*

2. Leo assumes his audience is familiar with Butterfly McQueen (who played the maid Prissy in *Gone with the Wind*), Fagin (the hook-nosed Jewish stereotype in Charles Dickens's *Oliver Twist*), Stepin Fetchit (the stereotype of the black sidekick/servant), Fu Manchu (the stereotype of the threatening, inscrutable Asian), Dr. No (the ethnically "other" villain), and the Frito Bandito (a Mexican stereotype used in Frito advertisements)—famous stereotypes from an earlier era. Share any knowledge you have of these stereotypes. Does *The Phantom Menace* deserve to be classified with earlier films that are now justly castigated for perpetuating racial and ethnic stereotypes?

3. Leo's article is a simple categorical argument rather than a definitional argument because there is no controversy over the meaning of the Y term "stereotype."

However, Lucas claims that critics' complaints about stereotyping in the film are "a controversy over nothing." How does Leo argue that the stereotypes are both intentional and damaging? What is the larger conversation about the influence of art on society that Leo's article is joining? Do you agree with Leo's implicit claim in this larger conversation—namely, that films have a powerful influence on society?

The second reading, by student Kathy Sullivan, was written for the definition assignment on page 213. The definitional issue that she addresses—"Are the Menasee photographs obscene?"—became a local controversy in the state of Washington when the state liquor control board threatened to revoke the liquor license of a Seattle gay bar, the Oncore, unless it removed a series of photographs that the board deemed obscene.

Oncore, Obscenity, and the Liquor Control Board

Kathy Sullivan (student)

1   In early May, Geoff Menasee, a Seattle artist, exhibited a series of photographs with the theme of "safe sex" on the walls of an inner city, predominantly homosexual restaurant and lounge called the Oncore. Before hanging the photographs, Menasee had to consult with the Washington State Liquor Control Board because, under the current state law, art work containing material that may be considered indecent has to be approved by the board before it can be exhibited. Of the almost thirty photographs, six were rejected by the board because they partially exposed "private parts" of the male anatomy. Menasee went ahead and displayed the entire series of photographs, placing Band-Aids over the "indecent" areas, but the customers continually removed the Band-Aids.

2   The liquor control board's ruling on this issue has caused controversy in the Seattle community. The *Seattle Times* has provided news coverage, and a "Town Meeting" segment was filmed at the restaurant. The central question is this: Should an establishment that caters to a predominantly homosexual clientele be enjoined from displaying pictures promoting "safe sex" on the grounds that the photographs are obscene?

3   Before I can answer this question, I must first determine whether the art work should truly be classified as obscene. To make that determination, I will use the definition of obscenity in *Black's Law Dictionary:*

Material is "obscene" if to the average person, applying contemporary community standards, the dominant theme of material taken as a whole appeals to prurient interest, if it is utterly without redeeming social importance, if it goes substantially beyond customary limits of candor in description or representation, if it is characterized by patent offensiveness, and if it is hard core pornography.

An additional criterion is provided by Pember's *Mass Media Laws:* "A work is obscene if it has a tendency to deprave and corrupt those whose minds are open to such immoral influences (children for example) and into whose hands it might happen to fall" (394). The art work in question should not be prohibited from display at predominantly homosexual establishments like the Oncore because it does not meet the above criteria for obscenity.

First of all, to the average person applying contemporary community standards, the predominant theme of Menasee's photographs is not an appeal to prurient interests. The first element in this criterion is "average person." According to Rocky Breckner, manager of the Oncore, 90 percent of the clientele at the Oncore is made up of young white homosexual males. This group therefore constitutes the "average person" viewing the exhibit. "Contemporary community standards" would ordinarily be the standards of the Seattle community. However, this art work is aimed at a particular group of people—the homosexual community. Therefore, the "community standards" involved here are those of the gay community rather than the city at large. Since the Oncore is not an art museum or gallery, which attracts a broad spectrum of people, it is appropriate to restrict the scope of "community standards" to that group who voluntarily patronize the Oncore.   4

Second, the predominant theme of the photographs is not "prurient interest" nor do the photographs go "substantially beyond public limits of candor." There are no explicit sexual acts found in the photographs; instead, their theme is the prevention of AIDS through the practice of safe sex. Homosexual displays of affection could be viewed as "prurient interest" by the larger community, but same-sex relationships are the norm for the group at whom the exhibit is aimed. If the exhibit were displayed at McDonald's or even the Red Robin it might go "substantially beyond customary limits of candor," but it is unlikely that the clientele of the Oncore would find the art work offensive. The manager stated that he received very few complaints about the exhibit and its contents.   5

Nor is the material pornographic. The liquor control board prohibited the six photographs based on their visible display of body parts such as pubic hair and naked buttocks, not on the basis of sexual acts or homosexual orientation. The board admitted that the photographs depicted no explicit sexual acts. Hence, it can be concluded that they did not consider the suggestion of same-sex affection to be hard-core pornography. Their sole objection was that body parts were visible. But visible genitalia in art work are not necessarily pornographic. Since other art work, such as Michelangelo's sculptures, explicitly depict both male and female genitalia, it is arguable that pubic hair and buttocks are not patently offensive.   6

It must be conceded that the art work has the potential of being viewed by children, which would violate Pember's criterion. But once again the incidence of minors frequenting this establishment is very small.   7

But the most important reason for saying these photographs are not obscene is that they serve an important social purpose. One of Black's criteria is that obscene material is "utterly without redeeming social importance." But these photographs have the explicit purpose of promoting safe sex as a defense against AIDS. Recent statistics reported in the *Seattle Times* show that AIDS is now the leading cause of death of men under forty in the Seattle area. Any methods that can promote the message of safe sex in today's society have strong redeeming social significance.   8

9   Those who believe that all art containing "indecent" material should be banned or covered from public view would most likely believe that Menasee's work is obscene. They would disagree that the environment and the clientele should be the major determining factor when using criteria to evaluate art. However, in the case of this exhibit I feel that the audience and the environment of the display are factors of overriding importance. Therefore, the exhibit should have been allowed to be displayed because it is not obscene.

Critiquing "Oncore, Obscenity, and the Liquor Control Board"

1. Kathy Sullivan here uses a reportive approach for defining her Y term "obscenity." Based on the definitions of *obscenity* in *Black's Law Dictionary* and Pember's *Mass Media Laws,* what criteria for obscenity does Kathy use?

2. How does she argue that the Menasee photographs do *not* meet the criteria?

3. Working as a whole class or in small groups, share your responses to the following questions: (a) If you find Kathy's argument persuasive, which parts were particularly influential or effective? (b) If you are not persuaded, which parts of her argument do you find weak or ineffective? (c) How does Kathy shape her argument to meet the concerns and objections of her audience? (d) How might a lawyer for the liquor control board rebut Kathy's argument?

Our last reading concerns sexual harassment, which continues to be a hotly debated legal, economic, and social issue. Vicki Schultz, a Yale law professor, first wrote a version of the article "Sex Is the Least of It: Let's Focus Harassment Law on Work, Not Sex," for the *Yale Law Journal.* She then rewrote this article for a more general audience, and this is the version we are printing here. It appeared in the May 25, 1998, issue of the *Nation,* a moderately liberal magazine devoted to politics and public issues. Here she addresses the complex issue of how sexual harassment should be defined. She looks at current definitions, shows the bad social consequences of following these definitions, and poses a new definition based on new criteria.

As background for reading this article, you should understand some of the context that it addresses. In the controversy over sexual harassment, most parties agree on the *quid pro quo* criterion (Latin for "something for something"—something given for something received), which covers those direct incidents of sexual harassment where a superior demands sexual favors in exchange for job benefits (or threatens demotion or firing if the favors are not granted). But the standard definition of *sexual harassment* (see the definition from the Equal Employment Opportunity Commission that we reprinted on p. 205) also includes a "hostile workplace" criterion, which has led to extensive confusion and debate. It is worded as follows in the EEOC guidelines: Sexual harassment occurs if someone's "conduct has the purpose or effect of unreasonably interfering with an individual's work performance or creating an intimidating, hostile, or offensive working environment." In this article, Schultz argues that limiting the defining features of a hostile environment to sexual conditions (such as telling off-color jokes) has unfortunate consequences.

Sex Is the Least of It: Let's Focus Harassment Law on Work, Not Sex

Vicki Schultz

The Clarence Thomas hearings, the Tailhook incident, the Gene McKinney trial, the Clinton scandals—if these events spring to mind when you hear the words "sexual harassment," you are not alone. That such images of powerful men making sexual come-ons toward female subordinates should be the defining ones simply proves the power of the popular perception that harassment is first and foremost about sex. It's easy to see why: The media, the courts and some feminists have emphasized this to the exclusion of all else. But the real issue isn't sex, it's sexism on the job. The fact is, most harassment isn't about satisfying sexual desires. It's about protecting work—especially the most favored lines of work—as preserves of male competence and authority.

This term the Supreme Court heard three cases involving sex harassment in the workplace. Along with media coverage of current events, the Court's decisions will shape our understanding of this issue into the next century, for all these controversies raise the same fundamental question: Does sex harassment require a special body of law having to do with sexual relations, or should it be treated just like any other form of workplace discrimination?

If the Court decides that harassment is primarily a problem of sexual relations, it will be following the same misguided path some courts have taken since they first accepted that such behavior falls under the prohibitions of Title VII of the Civil Rights Act, the major federal statute forbidding sex discrimination in employment. Early decisions outlawed what is known as quid pro quo harassment—typically, a situation where a supervisor penalizes a subordinate who refuses to grant sexual favors. It was crucial for the courts to acknowledge that sexual advances and other interactions *can* be used in the service of discrimination. Yet their reasoning spelled trouble. The courts said harassment was sex bias because the advances were rooted in a sexual attraction that the harasser felt for a woman but would not have felt for another man. By locating the problem in the sexual character of the advances rather than in the workplace dynamics of which they were a part—for instance, the paternalistic prerogative of a male boss to punish an employee on the job for daring to step out of her "place" as a woman—the decisions threatened to equate sex harassment with sexual pursuits. From there it was a short step to the proposition that sex in the workplace, or at least sexual interactions between men and women in unequal jobs, is inherently suspect.

Yet the problem we should be addressing isn't sex, it's the sexist failure to take women seriously as workers. Sex harassment is a means for men to claim work as masculine turf.

By driving women away or branding them inferior, men can insure the sex segregation of the work force. We know that women who work in jobs traditionally held by men are more likely than other women to experience hostility and harassment at work. Much of the harassment they experience isn't "sexual" in content or design. Even where sexually explicit harassment occurs, it is typically part of a broader pattern of conduct intended to reinforce gender difference and to claim work as a domain of masculine mastery. As one experienced electrician put it in Molly Martin's *Hard-Hatted Women,* "[We] . . . face another pervasive and sinister kind of harassment which is gender-based, but may have nothing to do with sex. It is harassment aimed at us simply because we are women in a 'man's' job, and its function is to discourage us from staying in our trades."

5   This harassment can take a variety of forms, most of which involve undermining a woman on the job. In one case, male electricians stopped working rather than submit to the authority of a female subforeman. In another, Philadelphia policemen welcomed their new female colleagues by stealing their case files and lacing their uniforms with lime that burned their skin. Even more commonly, men withhold the training and assignments women need to learn to do the job well, or relegate them to menial duties that signal they are incompetent to perform the simplest tasks. Work sabotage is all too common.

6   Nor is this a purely blue-collar phenomenon. About one-third of female physicians recently surveyed said they had experienced sexual harassment, but almost half said they'd been subjected to harassment that had no sexual or physical component but was related simply to their being female in a traditionally male field. In one 1988 court case, a group of male surgical residents went so far as to falsify a patient's medical records to make it appear as though their female colleague had made an error.

7   Men do, of course, resort to sexualized forms of harassment Sexual overtures may intimidate a woman or label her incompetent in settings where female sexuality is considered incompatible with professionalism. In one 1993 Supreme Court case, a company president suggested that a female manager must have had sex with a client to land an important account. Whether or not the harassment assumes a sexual form, however, what unites all these actions is that they create occupational environments that define womanhood as the opposite of what it takes to be a good worker.

8   From this starting point, it becomes clear that the popular view of harassment is both too narrow and too broad. Too narrow, because that focus on rooting out unwanted sexual activity has allowed us to feel good about protecting women from sexual abuse while leading us to overlook equally pernicious forms of gender-based mistreatment. Too broad because the emphasis on sexual conduct has encouraged some companies to ban all forms of sexual interaction, even when these do not threaten women's equality on the job.

9   How has the law become too narrow? The picture of harassment-as-sex that developed out of the quid pro quo cases has overwhelmed the conception of the hostile work environment, leading most courts to exonerate seriously sexist misconduct if it does not resemble a sexual come-on. In *Turley v. Union Carbide Corp.,* a court dismissed the harassment claim of a woman whose foreman "pick[ed] on [her] all the time" and treated her worse than the men. Citing Catharine MacKinnon's definition of sexual harassment as "the unwanted imposition of sexual requirements in the context of a relationship of unequal power," the court concluded that the case did not involve actionable harassment

because "the foreman did not demand sexual relations, he did not touch her or make sexual jokes."

By the same reasoning, in *Reynolds v. Atlantic City Convention Center,* the court ruled   10
against a female electrical subforeman, Reynolds, whose men refused to work for her, made obscene gestures and stood around laughing while she unloaded heavy boxes. Not long before, the union's business agent had proclaimed, "[Now] is not the time, the place or the year, [nor] will it ever be the year for a woman foreman." When the Miss America pageant came to town, an exhibitor asked that Reynolds be removed from the floor—apparently, the incongruity between the beauty contestants and the tradeswoman was too much to take—and Reynolds's boss replaced and eventually fired her. Yet the court concluded that none of this amounted to a hostile work environment: The obscene gestures that the court considered "sexual" were too trivial, and the rest of the conduct wasn't sufficiently sexual to characterize as gender-based.

These are not isolated occurrences. I recently surveyed hundreds of Title VII hostile   11
work environment cases and found that the courts' disregard of nonsexual forms of harassment is an overwhelming trend. This definitely works against women in male-dominated job settings, but it has also hurt women in traditionally female jobs, who share the experience of harassment that denigrates their competence or intelligence as workers. They are often subjected to sexist forms of authority, humiliation and abuse—objectified not only as sexual commodities but as creatures too stupid or worthless to deserve respect, fit only to be controlled by others ("stupid women who have kids," "too fat to clean rooms," "dumb females who [can't] read or write").

Just as our obsession with sexual misconduct obscures many debilitating forms of   12
harassment facing women, it also leads us to overlook some pernicious harassment confronting men on the job. If the legal cases provide any indication, the most common form of harassment men experience is not, as the film *Disclosure* suggests, a proposition from a female boss. It is, instead, hostility from male co-workers seeking to denigrate or drive away men who threaten the work's masculine image. If a job is to confer manliness, it must be held by those who project the desired sense of manhood. It isn't only women who can detract from that image. In some work settings, men are threatened by the presence of any man perceived to be gay—for homosexuality is often seen as gender deviance—or any other man perceived to lack the manly competence considered suitable for those who hold the job. The case logs are filled with harassment against men who are not married, men who are not attractive to women, men who are seen as weak or slow, men who are openly supportive of women, men who wear earrings and even young men or boys. Some men have taunted and tormented, battered and beaten other men in the name of purging the brotherhood of wimps and fags—not suitable to stand alongside them as workers.

We have been slow to name this problem sex-based harassment because it doesn't fit   13
our top-down, male-female, sexual come-on image of harassment. In *Goluszek v. Smith,* the court ruled against an electronic maintenance mechanic who was disparaged and driven out by his fellow workers. They mocked him for not having a wife, saying a man had to be married to be a machinist. They used gender-based images to assault his competence, saying that if he couldn't fix a machine they'd send in his "daddy"—the supervisor—to do it. They drove jeeps at him and threatened to knock him off his ladder, and when he filed a

grievance, his supervisor wrote him up for carelessness and eventually fired him. Not only did the court dismiss Goluszek's claim, the judge simply couldn't conceive that what happened to him was sexual harassment. "The 'sexual harassment' that is actionable under Title VII 'is the exploitation of a powerful position to impose sexual demands or pressures on an unwilling but less powerful person,' " the judge wrote. Perhaps lower courts will adopt a broader view now that the Supreme Court has ruled, in the recent *Oncale v. Sundowner Offshore Services* decision, that male-on-male harassment may be actionable even when it is not sexual in design.

14   Meanwhile, the traditional overemphasis on sex can lead to a repressive impulse to eliminate all hints of sexual expression from the workplace, however benign. Instead of envisioning harassment law as a tool to promote women's equality as workers, the popular understanding of harassment encourages courts and companies to "protect" women's sexual sensibilities. In *Fair v. Guiding Eyes for the Blind,* a heterosexual woman who was the associate director of a nonprofit organization claimed her gay male supervisor had created an offensive environment by making gossipy conversation and political remarks involving homosexuality. It is disturbing that current law inspired such a claim, even though the court correctly ruled that the supervisor's conduct was not sexual harassment.

15   Other men haven't fared so well. In *Pierce v. Commonwealth Life Insurance Co.,* a manager was disciplined for participating in an exchange of sexually explicit cards with a female office administrator. One of the cards Pierce had sent read, "Sex is a misdemeanor. De more I miss, de meanor I get." After thirty years with the company, he was summarily demoted and transferred to another office, with his pay slashed and his personal belongings dumped at a roadside Hardee's. True, Pierce was a manager and he was responsible for enforcing the company's harassment policy. Still, the reasoning that led to his ouster is unsound—and dangerous. According to his superiors, he might as well have been a "murderer, rapist or child molester; that wouldn't be any worse [than what he had done]." This sort of thing gives feminism a bad name. If companies want to fire men like Pierce, let them do it without the pretense of protecting women from sexual abuse.

16   Equally alarming are reports that, in the name of preventing sexual harassment, some companies are adopting policies that prohibit a man and woman from traveling or staying at the same hotel together on business, or prevent a male supervisor from giving a performance evaluation to a female underling behind closed doors without a lawyer present. One firm has declared that its construction workers can't even look at a woman for more than five seconds. With such work rules, who will want to hire women? How will women obtain the training they need if their male bosses and colleagues can't interact with them as equals?

17   It's a mistake to try to outlaw sexual interaction in the workplace. The old Taylorist project of purging organizations of all sexual and other emotional dynamics was deeply flawed. Sexuality is part of the human experience, and so long as organizations still employ people rather than robots, it will continue to flourish in one form or another. And sexuality is not simply a tool of gender domination; it is also a potential source of empowerment and even pleasure for women on the job. Indeed, some research suggests that where men and women work as equals in integrated settings, sex harassment isn't a problem. Sexual talk and joking continues, but it isn't experienced as harassment. It's not impossible to imag-

ine sexual banter as a form of playfulness, even solidarity, in a work world that is increasingly competitive and stressful.

Once we realize that the problem isn't sex but sexism, we can re-establish our concept   18
of harassment on firmer ground. Title VII was never meant to police sexuality. It was meant to provide people the chance to pursue their life's work on equal terms—free of pressure to conform to prescribed notions of how women and men are supposed to behave in their work roles. Properly conceived, quid pro quo harassment is a form of discrimination because it involves men exercising the power to punish women, as workers, who have the temerity to say no, as women. Firing women who won't have sex on the job is no different from firing black women who refuse to perform cleaning work, or female technicians who refuse to do clerical work, that isn't part of their job descriptions.

So, too, hostile-work-environment harassment isn't about sexual relations; it's about   19
how work relations engender inequality. The legal concept was created in the context of early race discrimination cases, when judges recognized that Jim Crow systems could be kept alive not just through company acts (such as hiring and firing) but also through company atmospheres that made African-American workers feel different and inferior. That discriminatory environments are sometimes created by "sexual" conduct is not the point. Sex should be treated just like anything else in the workplace: Where it furthers sex discrimination, it should go. Where it doesn't, it's not the business of our civil rights laws.

It's too easy to allow corporate America to get away with banning sexual interaction   20
without forcing it to attend to the larger structures of workplace gender discrimination in which both sexual and not-so-sexual forms of harassment flourish. Let's revitalize our understanding of harassment to demand a world in which all women and even the least powerful men can work together as equals in whatever endeavors their hearts and minds desire.

Critiquing "Sex Is the Least of It: Let's Focus Harassment Law on Work, Not Sex"

1. Try to restate Schultz's main argument in your own words. What does she mean when she says, "Yet the problem we should be addressing isn't sex, it's the sexist failure to take women seriously as workers. Sex harassment is a means for men to claim work as masculine turf"? What definition of *sexual harassment* is she advocating?

2. Give a typical example of what the courts currently mean by a "hostile workplace" based on prevailing sexual criteria. Then give a typical example of a "hostile workplace" as Schultz would define it. How do the two examples differ?

3. What does Schultz mean when she says that the "popular view of harassment is both too narrow and too broad"?

4. What contribution does Schultz make to the conflicted conversation about sexual harassment in the workplace? What would be the consequences of adopting her enlarged definition of *sexual harassment?* Are there any drawbacks to her definition?

11

Causal Arguments

X Causes (Does Not Cause) Y

CASE 1

In the Spring of 1999 two male students of Columbine High School in Littleton, Colorado, opened fire on their classmates. Twelve students and a teacher were killed, and the two boys killed themselves; twenty-three were wounded. For months following the killings, social scientists and media commentators analyzed the massacre, trying to determine what caused it and what solutions might be enacted to reduce teen violence. Among the causes proposed were the following: violent movies, violent video games, violent TV, the music of Marilyn Manson, easy access to guns, breakdown of the traditional family, absence of parental involvement in teen lives, erosion of school discipline, inadequate school counseling, Internet neo-Nazi chat rooms, Internet lessons on how to make bombs, and the irresponsible prescribing of antidepressants to teenagers (one of the assailants was taking Prozac). For each proposed cause, the arguer suggested a different approach for reducing teen violence.

CASE 2

Four years ago, the Fiji Islands got satellite television, and Fijians began watching such American television shows as *Beverly Hills 90210* and *Melrose Place*. In the next four years, the number of teens at risk for eating disorders doubled. According to columnist Ellen Goodman, "74 percent of the Fiji teens in a study said they felt 'too big or fat' at least some of the time and 62 percent said they had dieted in the past month." Emphasizing eating as pleasure and a rite of hospitality, Fiji culture has traditionally valued ample flesh and a robust shape for women, an image very opposite from that of thin American television stars. A Harvard anthropologist and psychiatrist has been studying this connection between television and eating disorders. Although "a direct causal link" may not be easy to support, there does seem to be a connection between projected television images of women and illness. Goodman poses the question of what harm television images can cause to women.*

AN OVERVIEW OF CAUSAL ARGUMENTS

We encounter causal issues all the time. What caused the Columbine High School massacre? What caused young women in Fiji to start feeling fat? What would be the consequences of legalizing drugs? What are the causes of illegal immigration into the United States and of the federal government's failure to stem it? (One proposed answer to the last question: Many powerful U.S. businesses want illegal immigration to continue because they rely on illegal immigrants as a source of cheap labor.)

Sometimes an argument can be devoted entirely to a causal issue. Just as frequently, causal arguments support proposal arguments in which the writer argues that we should (should not) do X *because doing X will lead to good (bad) consequences.* Convincing readers how X will lead to these consequences—a causal argument— thus bears on the success of many proposal arguments.

Because causal arguments require close analysis of phenomena, effective causal arguing is closely linked to critical thinking. Studies of critical thinking show that good problem solvers systematically explore the causes of a problem before proposing a solution. Equally important, before making a decision, good problem solvers predict and weigh the consequences of alternative solutions to a problem, trying to determine a solution that produces the greatest benefits with the least cost. Adding to the complexity of causal arguing is the way a given event can have multiple causes and multiple consequences. In an effort to save salmon, for example, environmentalists have proposed the elimination of several dams on the Snake River above Lewiston, Idaho. Will the removal of these dams save the salmon? Nobody knows for sure, but three universally agreed-upon consequences of removing the dams will be the loss of several thousand jobs in the Lewiston area, loss of some hydroelectric power, and the shift in wheat transportation from river barges to overland trucks and trains. So the initial focus on consequences to salmon soon widens to include consequences to jobs, to power generation, and to agricultural transportation.

THE NATURE OF CAUSAL ARGUING

Typically, causal arguments try to show how one event brings about another. On the surface, causal arguments may seem a fairly straightforward matter—more

---

*Ellen Goodman, "The Skinny on Fiji's Loss of a Robust Cultural Identity," *Seattle Times* 28 June 1999, B3.

concrete, to be sure, than the larger moral issues in which they are often embedded. But consider for a moment the classic illustration of causality—one billiard ball striking another on a pool table. Surely we are safe in saying that the movement of the second ball was "caused" by a transfer of energy from the first ball at the moment of contact. Well, yes and no. British philosopher David Hume (among others) argued long ago that we don't really perceive "causality"; what we perceive is one ball moving and then another ball moving. We infer the notion of causality, which is a human construct, not a property of billiard balls.

When humans become the focus of a causal argument, the very definition of causality is immediately vexed. When we say that a given factor X "caused" a person to do Y, what do we mean? On the one hand, we might mean that X "forced her to do Y," thereby negating her free will (for example, the presence of a brain tumor caused my erratic behavior, which caused me to lose my job). On the other hand, we might simply mean that factor X "motivated" her to do Y, in such a way that doing Y is still an expression of freedom (for example, my love of the ocean caused me to give up my job as a Wal-Mart greeter and become a California surf bum).

When we argue about causality in human beings, we must guard against confusing these two senses of "cause" or assuming that human behavior can be predicted or controlled in the same way that nonhuman behavior can. A rock dropped from a roof will always fall to the ground at 32 feet per second squared, and a rat zapped for making left turns in a maze will always quit making left turns. But if we raise interest rates, will consumers save more? If so, how much? This is the sort of question we debate endlessly.

Fortunately, most causal arguments can avoid the worst of these scientific and philosophical quagmires. As human beings, we share a number of assumptions about what causes events in the observable world, and we can depend on the goodwill of our audiences to grant us most of these assumptions. Most of us, for example, would be satisfied with the following explanation for why a car went into a skid: "In a panic the driver locked the brakes of his car, causing the car to go into a skid."

panic → slamming brake pedal → locking brakes → skid

We probably do not need to defend this simple causal chain because the audience will grant the causal connections between events A, B, C, and D. The sequence seems reasonable according to our shared assumptions about psychological causality (panic leads to slamming brake pedal) and physical causality (locked brakes lead to skid).

But if you are an attorney defending a client whose skidding car caused considerable damage to an upscale boutique, you might see all sorts of additional causal factors. ("Because the stop sign at that corner was obscured by an untrimmed willow tree, my client innocently entered what he assumed was an open intersection only to find a speeding beer truck bearing down on him. When my client took immediate decelerating corrective action, the improperly maintained, oil-slicked roadway sent his car into its near-fatal skid and into the boutique's bow windows—windows that extrude into the walkway 11 full inches beyond the limit allowed by city code.") Okay, now what's the cause of the crash, and who's at fault?

As the previous example shows, explaining causality entails creating a plausible chain of events linking a cause to its effect. Let's take another example—this time a real rather than hypothetical one. Consider an argument put forward by syndicated columnist John Leo as an explanation for the Columbine High School massacre.* Leo attributes part of the cause to the desensitizing effects of violent video games. After suggesting that the Littleton killings were partly choreographed on video game models, Leo suggests the following causal chain:

> Many youngsters are left alone for long periods of time → they play violent video games obsessively → their feelings of resentment and powerlessness "pour into the killing games" → the video games break down a natural aversion to killing, analogous to psychological techniques employed by the military → realistic touches in modern video games blur the "boundary between fantasy and reality" → youngsters begin identifying not with conventional heroes but with sociopaths who get their kicks from blowing away ordinary people ("pedestrians, marching bands, an elderly woman with a walker") → having enjoyed random violence in the video games, vulnerable youngsters act out the same adrenaline rush in real life.

DESCRIBING A CAUSAL ARGUMENT IN TOULMIN TERMS

Because causal arguments can involve lengthy or complex causal chains, they are often harder to summarize in *because* clauses than are other kinds of arguments. Likewise, they are not as likely to yield quick analysis through the Toulmin schema. Nevertheless, a causal argument can usually be stated as a claim with *because* clauses. Typically, a *because* clause for a causal argument pinpoints one or two key elements in the causal chain rather than trying to summarize every link. Leo's argument could be summarized in the following claim with *because* clause:

> Violent video games may have been a contributing cause to the Littleton massacre because playing these games can make random, sociopathic violence seem pleasurable.

---

*John Leo, "Kill-for-Kicks Video Games Desensitizing Our Children," *Seattle Times* 27 Apr. 1999, B4.

Once stated as an enthymeme, the argument can be analyzed using Toulmin's schema. (It is easiest to apply Toulmin's schema to causal arguments if you think of the grounds as the observable phenomena at any point in the causal chain and the warrants as the shareable assumptions about causality that join links together.)

CLAIM:	Violent video games may have been a contributing cause to the Littleton massacre
STATED REASON:	because playing these games can make random, sociopathic violence seem pleasurable
GROUNDS:	evidence that the killers, like many young people, played violent video games; evidence that the games are violent; evidence that the games involve random, sociopathic violence (not heroic cops against aliens or gangsters, but a killer blowing away ordinary people— marching bands, little old ladies, and so forth); evidence that young people derive pleasure from these games
WARRANT:	If youngsters derive pleasure from random, sociopathic killing in video games, then they can transfer this pleasure to real life, thus leading to the Littleton massacre.
BACKING:	testimony from psychologists; evidence that violent video games desensitize persons to violence; analogy to military training where video game strategies are used to "make killing a reflex action"; evidence that the distinction between fantasy and reality becomes especially blurred for unstable children.
CONDITIONS OF REBUTTAL:	*Questioning the reason and grounds:* Perhaps the killers didn't play video games; perhaps the video games are no more violent than traditional kids' games (such as cops and robbers); perhaps the video games do not feature sociopathic killing.
	Questioning the warrant and backing: Perhaps kids are fully capable of distinguishing fantasy from reality; perhaps the games are just fun with no transference to real life; perhaps these video games are substantially different from military training strategies.

QUALIFIER: (Claim is already qualified by *may* and *con-
                                tributing cause*)

❖ FOR CLASS DISCUSSION

1. Working individually or in small groups, create a causal chain to show how
    the item mentioned in the first column could help lead to the item mentioned
    in the second.

    a. invention of the automobile   redesign of cities

    b. invention of the automobile   changes in sexual mores

    c. invention of the telephone   loss of sense of community in
                                           neighborhoods

    e. development of the "pill"   rise in the divorce rate

    f. development of way to prevent   liberalization of euthanasia laws
        rejections in transplant operations

2. For each of your causal chains, compose a claim with an attached *because*
    clause summarizing one or two key links in the causal chain. For example,
    "The invention of the automobile helped cause the redesign of cities because
    automobiles made it possible for people to live farther away from their places
    of work."

THREE METHODS FOR ARGUING THAT ONE EVENT CAUSES ANOTHER

One of the first things you need to do when preparing a causal argument is to
note exactly what sort of causal relationship you're dealing with. Are you concerned with the causes of a specific event or phenomenon such as NATO's decision to bomb Serbia or the crash of John F. Kennedy Jr.'s private airplane? Or are
you planning to write about the cause of some recurring phenomenon such as eating disorders or the economic forces behind global warming? Or are you writing
about a puzzling trend such as the decline of salmon runs on the Columbia River
or the rising popularity of extreme sports?

With recurring phenomena or with trends, you have the luxury of being able
to study multiple cases over long periods of time and establishing correlations between suspected causal factors and effects. In some cases you can even intervene
in the process and test for yourself whether diminishing a suspected causal factor
results in a lessening of the effect or whether increasing the causal factor results in
a corresponding increase in the effect. Additionally, you can spend a good deal of
time exploring just how the mechanics of causation might work.

But with a one-time occurrence your focus is on the details of the event and specific causal chains that may have contributed to the event. Sometimes evidence has disappeared or changed its nature. You often end up in the position more of a detective than of a scientific researcher, and your conclusion will have to be more tentative as a result.

Having briefly stated these words of caution, let's turn now to the various ways you can argue that one event causes another.

First Method: Explain the Causal Mechanism Directly

The most convincing kind of causal argument identifies every link in the causal chain, showing how X causes A, which causes B, which in turn causes C, which finally causes Y. In some cases, all you have to do is fill in the missing links. In other cases—when your assumptions about causality may seem questionable to your audience—you have to argue for the causal connection with more vigor.

A careful spelling out of each step in the causal chain is the technique used by science writer Robert S. Devine in the following passage from his article "The Trouble with Dams."* Although the benefits of dams are widely understood (cheap, pollution-free electricity; flood control; irrigation; barge transportation), the negative effects are less commonly known and understood. In this article, Devine tries to persuade readers that dams have serious negative consequences. In the following passage, he explains how dams reduce salmon flows by slowing the migration of smolts (newly hatched young salmon) to the sea.

CAUSAL ARGUMENT DESCRIBING A CAUSAL CHAIN

Such transformations lie at the heart of the ongoing environmental harm done by dams. Rivers are rivers because they flow, and the nature of their flows defines much of their character. When dams alter flows, they alter the essence of rivers.

Consider the erstwhile river behind Lower Granite [a dam on Idaho's Snake River]. Although I was there in the springtime, when I looked at the water it was moving too slowly to merit the word "flow"—and Lower Granite Lake isn't even one of the region's enormous storage reservoirs, which bring currents to a virtual halt. In the past, spring snowmelt sent powerful currents down the Snake during April and May. Nowadays hydropower operators of the Columbia and Snake systems store the runoff behind the dams and release it during the winter, when demand—and the price—for electricity rises. Over the ages, however, many populations of salmon have adapted to the spring surge. The smolts used the strong flows to migrate, drifting downstream with the current. During the journey smolts' bodies undergo physiological changes that require them to reach salt

---

*Robert S. Devine, "The Trouble with Dams," *Atlantic* Aug. 1995, 64–75. The example quotation is from page 70.

water quickly. Before dams backed up the Snake, smolts coming down from Idaho got to the sea in six to twenty days; now it takes from sixty to ninety days, and few of the young salmon reach salt water in time. The emasculated current is the single largest reason that the number of wild adult salmon migrating up the Snake each year has crashed from predevelopment runs of 100,000–200,000 to what was projected to be 150–75 this year.

This tightly constructed passage connects various causal chains to explain the decline of salmon runs:

Smolts use river flow to reach the sea → dams restrict flow of river → a trip that before development took 6–20 days now takes 60–90 days → migrating smolts undergo physiological changes that demand quick access to salt water → delayed migration time kills the smolts.

Describing each link in the causal chain—and making each link seem as plausible as possible—is the most persuasive means of convincing readers that X causes Y.

Second Method: Use Various Inductive Methods to Establish a High Probability of a Causal Link

If we can't explain a causal link directly, we often employ a reasoning strategy called *induction.* Through induction we infer a general conclusion based on a limited number of specific cases. For example, if on several occasions you got a headache after drinking red wine but not after drinking white wine, you would be likely to conclude inductively that red wine causes you to get headaches. However, because there are almost always numerous variables involved, because there are exceptions to most principles arrived at inductively, and because we can't be certain that the future will always be like the past, inductive reasoning gives only probable truths, not certain ones.

When your brain thinks inductively, it sorts through data looking for patterns of similarity and difference. But the inductive process does not explain the causal mechanism itself. Thus, through induction you know that red wine gives you a headache, but you don't know how the wine actually works on your nervous system—the causal chain itself.

In this section we explain three kinds of inductive reasoning: informal induction, scientific experimentation, and correlation.

Informal Induction

Informal induction is our term for the habitual kind of inductive reasoning we do all the time. Toddlers think inductively when they learn the connection between flipping a wall switch and watching the ceiling light come on. They hold all variables constant except the position of the switch and infer inductively a causal connection between the switch and the light. Typical ways that the mind infers causality described by the nineteeth-century philosopher John Stuart Mill include looking for a common element that can explain a repeated circumstance. For example, psychologists attempting to understand the causes of anorexia have discovered that many anorexics (but not all) come from perfectionist, highly work-oriented homes that emphasize duty and responsibility. This common element is thus a suspected causal factor leading to anorexia. Another of Mill's methods is to look for a single difference. When infant death rates in the state of Washington shot up in July and August 1986, one event stood out making these two months different: increased radioactive fallout from the Chernobyl nuclear meltdown in the Ukraine. This single difference led some researchers to suspect radiation as a possible cause of infant deaths. Informal induction typically proceeds from this kind of "common element" or "single difference" reasoning.

Largely because of its power, informal induction can often lead you to wrong conclusions. You should be aware of two common fallacies of inductive reasoning that can tempt you into erroneous assumptions about causality. (Both fallacies are treated more fully in Appendix 1.)

The *post hoc, ergo propter hoc* fallacy ("after this, therefore because of this") mistakes precedence for cause. Just because event A regularly precedes event B doesn't mean that event A causes event B. The same reasoning that tells us that flipping a switch causes the light to go on can make us believe that low levels of radioactive fallout from the Chernobyl nuclear disaster caused a sudden rise in infant death rates in the state of Washington. The nuclear disaster clearly preceded the rise in death rates. But did it clearly *cause* it? Our point is that precedence alone is no proof of causality and that we are guilty of this fallacy whenever we are swayed to believe that X causes Y primarily because X precedes Y. We can guard against this fallacy by seeking plausible link-by-link connections showing how X causes Y.

The *hasty generalization* fallacy occurs when you make a generalization based on too few cases or too little consideration of alternative explanations: You flip the switch, but the lightbulb doesn't go on. You conclude—too hastily—that the power has gone off. (Perhaps the lightbulb has burned out or the switch is broken.) How many trials does it take before you can make a justified generalization rather than a hasty generalization? It is difficult to say for sure. Both the *post hoc* fallacy and the hasty generalization fallacy remind us that induction requires a leap from individual cases to a general principle and that it is always possible to leap too soon.

Scientific Experimentation

One way to avoid inductive fallacies is to examine our causal hypotheses as carefully as possible. When we deal with a recurring phenomenon such as cancer, we can create scientific experiments that give us inductive evidence of causality with a fairly high degree of certainty. If, for example, we were concerned that a particular food source such as spinach might contain cancer-causing chemicals, we could test our hypothesis experimentally. We could take two groups of rats and control their environment carefully so that the only difference between them (in theory, anyway) was that one group ate large quantities of spinach and the other group ate none. Spinach eating, then, would be the one variable between the two groups that we are testing. After a specified period of time, we would check to see what percentage of rats in each group developed cancer. If twice as many spinach-eating rats contracted cancer, we could probably conclude that our hypothesis held up.

Correlation

Still another method of induction is *correlation*, which expresses a statistical relationship between X and Y. A correlation between X and Y means that when X occurs, Y is likely to occur also, and vice versa. To put it another way, correlation establishes a possibility that an observed link between an X and a Y is a causal one rather than a mere coincidence. The existence of a correlation, however, does not tell us whether X causes Y, whether Y causes X, or whether both are caused by some third phenomenon. For example, there is a fairly strong correlation between near-sightedness and intelligence. (That is, in a given sample of nearsighted people and people with normal eyesight, a higher percentage of the nearsighted people will be highly intelligent. Similarly, in a sample of high-intelligence people and people with normal intelligence, a higher percentage of the high-intelligence group will be nearsighted.) But the direction of causality isn't clear. It could be that high intelligence causes people to read more, thus ruining their eyes (high intelligence causes nearsightedness). Or it could be that near-sightedness causes people to read more, thus raising their intelligence (near-sightedness causes high intelligence). Or it could be that some unknown phenomenon inside the brain causes both near-sightedness and high intelligence.

In recent years, correlation studies have been made stunningly sophisticated through the power of computerized analyses. For example, we could attempt to do the spinach-cancer study without resorting to a scientific experiment. If we identified a given group that ate lots of spinach (for example, vegetarians) and another group that ate little if any spinach (Inuits) and then checked to see if their rates of cancer correlated to their rates of spinach consumption, we would have the beginnings of a correlation study. But it would have no scientific validity until we factored out all the other variables between vegetarians and Inuits that might skew the findings—variables such as lifestyle, climate, genetic inheritance, and differences in diet other than spinach. Factoring out such variables is one of the complex feats that modern statistical analyses attempt to accomplish. But the fact remains that the most sophisticated correlation studies still cannot tell us the direction of causality or even for certain that there is causality.

Conclusion about Inductive Methods

Induction, then, can tell us within varying degrees of certainty whether X causes Y. It does not, however, explain the causal mechanism itself. Typically, the *because* clause structure of an inductive argument would take one of the following three shapes: (1) "Although we cannot explain the causal mechanism directly, we believe that X and Y are very probably causally linked because we have repeatedly observed their conjunction"; (2) "... because we have demonstrated the linkage through controlled scientific experiments"; or (3) "... because we have shown that they are statistically correlated and have provided a plausible hypothesis concerning the causal direction."

FOR CLASS DISCUSSION

Working individually or in small groups, develop plausible causal chains that might explain the correlations between the following pairs of phenomena:

a. A person who registers a low stress level on an electrochemical stress meter   Does daily meditation

b. A person who regularly consumes frozen dinners   Is likely to vote for improved rapid transit

c. A person who is a high achiever   Is a first-born child

d. A person who is a member of the National Rifle Association   Favors tough treatment of criminals

Third Method: Argue by Analogy or Precedent

Another common method of causal arguing is through analogy or precedent. (See also Chapter 12, which deals in more depth with the strengths and weaknesses of this kind of arguing.) When you argue through resemblance, you try to find a case that is similar to the one you are arguing about but is better known and less controversial to the reader. If the reader agrees with your view of causality in the similar case, you then try to transfer this understanding to the case at issue. In the following example, the writer tries to explain the link between environmental and biological factors in the creation of teen violence. In this analogy, the biological predisposition for violent behavior is compared to some children's biological predisposition for asthma. Cultural and media violence is then compared to air pollution.

CAUSAL ARGUMENT BY ANALOGY

To deny the role of these influences [bad parenting, easy access to guns, violence in the media] is like denying that air pollution triggers childhood asthma. Yes, to develop asthma a child needs a specific, biological vulnerability. But as long as some children have this respiratory vulnerability—and some always will—then allowing pollution to fill our air will make some children wheeze, and cough, and die. And as long as some children have a neurological vulnerability [to violent behavior]—and some always will—then turning a blind eye to bad parenting, bullying, and the gun culture will make other children seethe, and withdraw, and kill.*

Causal arguments by analogy and precedent are logically weaker than arguments based on causal chains or scientific induction. Although they can be powerfully persuasive, you should be aware of their limits. If any two things are alike in some ways (analogous), they are different in others (disanalogous), and these differences shouldn't be ignored. Consider the following example:

> A huckster markets a book called *30 Days to a More Powerful Brain.* The book contains logical puzzles and other brain-teasing exercises that he calls "weight training for the mind."

This argument depends on the warrant that the brain is like a muscle. Because the audience accepts the causal belief that weight training strengthens muscles, the marketers hope to transfer that same belief to the field of mental activity (mind exercises strengthen the brain). However, cognitive psychologists have shown that the brain does *not* work like a muscle, so the analogy is false. Although the argument seems powerful, you should realize that the warrant that says X is like Y is almost always vulnerable.

All resemblance arguments, therefore, are in some sense "false analogies." But some analogies are so misleading that logicians have labeled them "fallacious"—the fallacy of *false analogy.* The false analogy fallacy covers those truly blatant cases where the differences between X and Y are too great for the analogy to hold. An example might be the following: "Putting red marks all over students' papers causes great emotional distress just as putting knife marks over their palms would cause great physical distress." It is impossible to draw a precise line, however, between an analogy that has true clarifying and persuasive power and one that is fallacious. Whether the analogy works in any situation depends on the audience's shared assumptions with the arguer.

GLOSSARY OF TERMS ENCOUNTERED IN CAUSAL ARGUMENTS

Because causal arguments are often easier to conduct if writer and reader share a few specialized terms, we offer the following glossary for your convenience.

Fallacy of Oversimplified Cause: One of the greatest temptations when establishing causal relationships is to fall into the habit of looking for *the* cause

---

*Sharon Begley, "Why the Young Kill," *Newsweek* 3 May 1999, 35.

of something. Most phenomena, especially the ones we argue about, have multiple causes. For example, scientists know that a number of different causes must work together to create a complex disease such as cancer. But though we know all this, we still long to make the world less complex by looking for *the* cause of cancer, thus attributing a single cause to puzzling effects.

Universal/Existential Quantifiers: Closely related to the fallacy of the single clause is the tendency to confuse what logicians call the universal quantifier *(all)* with the existential quantifier *(some)*. The mixing up of universal and existential quantifiers can falsify an argument. For example, to argue that *all* the blame for recent school shootings comes from the shooters' playing violent video games is to claim that playing violent video games is the sole cause—a universal statement. An argument will be stronger and more accurate if the arguer makes an existential statement: *Some* of the blame for this violent behavior can be attributed to playing violent video games. Arguers sometimes deliberately mix up these quantifiers to misrepresent and dismiss opposing views. For example, someone might argue that because the violent video games are not totally and exclusively responsible for the students' violent behavior, they are not an influential factor at all. In this instance, arguers are attempting to dismiss potential causes by framing them as universal statements that can be rejected because they are too extreme and indefensible. Because something is not a sole or total cause does not mean that it could not be a partial cause.

Immediate/Remote Causes: Every causal chain links backward indefinitely into the past. An immediate cause is the closest in time to the event being examined. When John F. Kennedy Jr.'s plane crashed into the Atlantic Ocean south of Martha's Vineyard in July 1999, experts speculated that the *immediate cause* was Kennedy's becoming disoriented in the night haze, losing visual control of the plane, and sending the plane into a fatal dive. A slightly less immediate cause was his decision to make an over-water flight at night without being licensed for instrument flying. The cause of that decision was the need to get to Hyannis Port quickly to attend a wedding. Farther back in time were all the factors that made Kennedy the kind of risk taker who took chances with his own life. For example, several months earlier he had broken an ankle in a hang-gliding accident. Many commentators said that the numerous tragedies that befell the Kennedy family helped shape his risk-taking personality. Such causes going back into the past are considered *remote causes*. It is sometimes difficult to determine the relative significance of remote causes. Immediate causes are obviously linked to an event, but remote causes often have to be dug out or inferred. It's difficult to know, for example, just how seriously to take Hillary Clinton's explanation for her husband's extramarital affairs with Monica Lewinsky and other women. Clinton's womanizing tendencies, she claimed, were caused by "a terrible conflict between his mother and grandmother" when Clinton was four years old. During this period, she said, he "was scarred by abuse."*

Precipitating/Contributing Causes: These terms are similar to *immediate* and *remote* causes but don't designate a temporal linking going into the past. Rather, they refer to a main cause emerging out of a background of subsidiary causes. The *contributing causes* are a set of conditions that give rise to the *precipitating cause,* which triggers the effect. If, for example, a husband and wife decide to separate, the precipitating cause may be a stormy fight over money, which itself is a symptom of their inability to communicate with each other any longer. All the factors that contribute to that inability to communicate— preoccupation with their respective careers, anxieties about money, in-law problems—may be considered contributing causes. Note that the contributing causes and precipitating cause all coexist simultaneously in time—none is temporally more remote than another. But the marriage might have continued had the contributing causes not finally resulted in frequent angry fighting, which doomed the marriage.

Constraints: Sometimes an effect occurs not because X happened but because another factor—a *constraint*—was removed. At other times a possible effect will not occur because a given constraint prevents it from happening. A constraint is a kind of negative cause that limits choices and possibilities. As soon as the constraint is removed, a given effect may occur. For example, in the marriage we have been discussing, the presence of children in the home might have been a constraint against divorce; as soon as the children graduate from high school and leave home, the marriage may well dissolve.

Necessary/Sufficient Causes: A *necessary cause* is one that has to be present for a given effect to occur. For example, fertility drugs are necessary to cause the conception of septuplets. Every couple who has septuplets must have used fertility drugs. In contrast, a *sufficient cause* is one that always produces or guarantees a given effect. Smoking more than a pack of cigarettes per day is sufficient to raise the cost of one's life insurance policy. This statement means that if you are a smoker life insurance companies will always place you in a higher risk bracket and charge you more for life insurance. In some cases, a single cause can be both necessary and sufficient. For example, lack of ascorbic acid is both a necessary and a sufficient cause of scurvy. (Think of all those old sailors who didn't eat fruit for months.) It is a necessary cause because you can't get scurvy any other way except through absence of ascorbic acid; it is a sufficient cause because the absence of ascorbic acid always causes scurvy.

---

*"First Lady's Remarks Take White House by Surprise," *Seattle Times* 2 Aug. 1999, A1.

FOR CLASS DISCUSSION

The terms in the preceding glossary can be effective brainstorming tools for thinking of possible causes of an event. For the following events, try to think of as many causes as possible by brainstorming possible *immediate causes, remote causes, precipitating causes, contributing causes,* and *constraints:*

1. Working individually, make a list of different kinds of causes/constraints for one of the following:
   a. your decision to attend your present college
   b. an important event in your life or your family (a job change, a major move, etc.)
   c. a personal opinion you hold that is not widely shared

2. Working as a group, make a list of different kinds of causes/constraints for one of the following:
   a. why women's fashion and beauty magazines are the most frequently purchased magazines in college bookstores
   b. why the majority of teenagers don't listen to classical music
   c. why the number of babies born out of wedlock has increased dramatically in the last thirty years

WRITING YOUR CAUSAL ARGUMENT

WRITING ASSIGNMENT
FOR CHAPTER 11

Choose an issue about the causes or consequences of a trend, event, or other phenomenon. Write an argument that persuades an audience to accept your explanation of the causes or consequences of your chosen phenomenon. Within your essay you should examine alternative hypotheses or opposing views and explain your reasons for rejecting them. You can imagine your issue either as a puzzle or as a disagreement. If a puzzle, your task will be to create a convincing case for an audience that doesn't have an answer to your causal question already in mind. If a disagreement, your task will be more overtly persuasive since your goal will be to change your audience's views.

Exploring Ideas

Arguments about causes and consequences abound in public, professional, or personal life, so you shouldn't have difficulty finding a causal issue worth investigating and arguing. Angered by media explanations for the Columbine High School massacre, student writer Daeha Ko contributed his own argument to the conversation by blaming popular cliques and the school establishment that supports them (see pp. 247–49). Others of our students have focused on causal issues such as these: What causes promiscuous teen sex? What effect does TV violence have on children? What would be the consequences of breaching dams on the Snake River? What causes anorexia? What will be the consequences of allowing the Makah to hunt whales? What are the chief causes of the destruction of tropical rain forests? Why does it take so long to approve experimental drugs in the United States? What would be the consequences of raising the retirement age as a means of saving Social Security? What are the causes of different sexual orientations?

If you find yourself uninterested in major public issues involving cause or consequence, you can often create provocative controversies among your classmates through the following strategies:

- *Make a list of unusual likes and dislikes.* Think about unusual things that people like or dislike. We find it really strange, for example, that so many people like professional wrestling or dislike bats. You could summarize the conventional explanations that persons give for an unusual pleasure or aversion and then argue for a surprising or unexpected cause. Why do people like playing the lottery? What attracts people to extreme sports? What causes math phobia? How do you explain the popularity of the new VW Beetle?

- *Make a list of puzzling events or trends.* Another strategy is to make a list of puzzling phenomena and try to explain their causes. Start with one-time events (the sudden appearance of deformed frogs in Minnesota lakes; the Senate acquittal of Bill Clinton in his impeachment trial). Then list puzzling repeatable events (infant sudden death syndrome; failure of many children to become good readers). Finally, list some recent trends (growth of naturopathic medicine; teen interest in the gothic; hatred of women in much gangsta rap). Engage classmates in discussions of one or more of the items on your list. Look for places of disagreement as entry points into the conversation.

- *Brainstorm consequences of a recent or proposed action.* Arguments about consequences are among the most interesting and important of causal disputes. If you can argue for an unanticipated consequence of a real, hypothetical, or proposed action—for example, a bad consequence of an apparently positive event or a good consequence of an apparently negative event—you can make an important contribution to the conversation. What might be the consequences, for example, of some of the following: a cure for cancer; total prevention of illegal immigration; the legalization of same-sex marriage; a heavy tax on families having more than two children; replacement of federal income tax with a federal sales tax; ending "social promotion" in the schools; depletion of the world's oil supply; any similar recent, hypothetical, or proposed event or action?

Organizing a Causal Argument

At the outset, it is useful to know some of the standard ways that a causal argument can be organized. Later, you may decide on a different organizational pattern, but these standard ways will help you get started.

Plan 1

When your purpose is to describe and explain all the links in a causal chain:

- Introduce phenomenon to be explained and show why it is problematical.
- Present your thesis in summary form.
- Describe and explain each link in the causal chain.

Plan 2

When your purpose is to explore the relative contribution of a number of causes to a phenomenon or to explore multiple consequences of a phenomenon:

- Introduce the phenomenon to be explained and suggest how or why it is controversial.
- Devote one section to each possible cause/consequence and decide whether it is necessary, sufficient, contributory, remote, and so forth. (Arrange sections so that those causes most familiar to the audience come first and the most surprising ones come last.)

Plan 3

When your purpose is to argue for a cause or consequence that is surprising or unexpected to your audience:

- Introduce a phenomenon to be explained and show why it is controversial.
- One by one, examine and reject the causes or consequences your audience would normally assume or expect.
- Introduce your unexpected or surprising cause or consequence and argue for it.

Plans 2 and 3 are similar in that they examine numerous possible causes or consequences. Plan 2, however, tries to establish the relative importance of each cause or consequence, whereas plan 3 aims at rejecting the causes or consequences normally assumed by the audience and argues for an unexpected surprising cause or consequence.

Plan 4

When your purpose is to change your audience's mind about a cause or consequence:

- Introduce the issue and show why it is controversial.
- Summarize your opponent's causal argument and then refute it.
- Present your own causal argument.

Plan 4 is a standard structure for all kinds of arguments. This is the structure you would use if you were the attorney for the person whose car skidded into the boutique (pp. 230–31). The opposing attorney would blame your client's reckless driving. You would lay blame on a poorly signed intersection, a speeding beer truck, and violation of building codes.

QUESTIONING AND CRITIQUING A CAUSAL ARGUMENT

Because of the strenuous conditions that must be met before causality can be proven, causal arguments are vulnerable at many points. The following strategies will generally be helpful.

If you described every link in a causal chain, would skeptics point out weaknesses in any of the links? Describing a causal chain can be a complex business. A skeptic can raise doubts about an entire argument simply by questioning one of the links. Your best defense is to make a diagram of the linkages and role-play a skeptic trying to refute each link in turn. Whenever you find possible arguments against your position, see how you can strengthen your own argument at that point.

If your argument is based on a scientific experiment, could skeptics question the validity of the experiment? The scientific method attempts to demonstrate causality experimentally. If the experiment isn't well designed, however, the demonstration is less likely to be acceptable to skeptical audiences. Here are ways to question and critique a scientific argument:

- *Question the findings.* Skeptics may have reason to believe that the data collected were not accurate or representative. They might provide alternative data or simply point out flaws in the way the data were collected.

- *Question the interpretation of the data.* Many research studies are divided into "findings" and "discussion" sections. In the discussion section the researcher analyzes and interprets the data. A skeptic might provide an alternative interpretation of the data or otherwise argue that the data don't support what the original writer claims.

- *Question the design of the experiment.* A detailed explanation of research design is beyond the scope of this text, but we can give a brief example of how a typical experiment did go wrong. When home computers were first developed in the 1980s, a group of graduate students conducted an experiment to test the effect of word processors on students' writing in junior high school. They reported that students who used the word processors for revising all their essays did significantly better on a final essay than a control group of students who didn't use word processors. It turned out, however, that there were at least two major design flaws in the experiment. First, the researchers allowed students to volunteer for the experimental group. Perhaps these students were already better writers than the control group from the start. (Can you think of a causal explanation of why the better students might volunteer to use the computers?) Second, when the teachers graded essays from both the computer group and the control group, the essays were not retyped uniformly. Thus the computer group's essays were typed with "computer perfection," whereas the control group's essays were handwritten or typed on ordinary typewriters. Perhaps the readers were affected by the pleasing appearance of the computer-typed essays. More significantly, perhaps the graders were biased in favor of the computer project and unconsciously scored the computer-typed papers higher.

If you have used correlation data, could skeptics argue that the correlation is much weaker than you claim or that you haven't sufficiently demonstrated causality? As we discussed earlier, correlation data tell us only that two or more phenomena are likely to occur together. They don't tell us that one phenomenon caused the other. Thus correlation arguments are usually accompanied by hypotheses about causal connections between the phenomena. Correlation arguments can often be refuted as follows:

- Find problems in the statistical methods used to determine the correlation.
- Weaken the correlation by pointing out exceptions.
- Provide an alternative hypothesis about causality.

If you have used an analogy argument, could skeptics point out disanalogies? Although among the most persuasive of argumentative strategies, analogy arguments are also among the easiest to refute. The standard procedure is to counter your argument that X is like Y by pointing out all the ways that X is *not* like Y. Once again, by role-playing an opposing view, you may be able to strengthen your own analogy argument.

Could a skeptic cast doubt on your argument by reordering your priority of causes? Up to this point we've focused on refuting the claim that X causes Y. However, another approach is to concede that X helps cause Y but that X is only one of several contributing causes and not the most significant one at that.

READINGS

The following essay, by student writer Daeha Ko, appeared as an op-ed piece in the *University of Washington Daily* on 9 May 1999, several weeks after the Columbine High School massacre in Littleton, Colorado. Daeha's motivation for writing is his anger at media attempts to explain the massacre—none of which focuses on the cliquish social structure of high school itself.

The Monster That Is High School

Daeha Ko (student)

In the past weeks, intensive media coverage has surrounded the shooting incident in Littleton, Colorado, where 12 students and a teacher died, along with 23 wounded. Yet people forget the real victims of the Littleton massacre are Dylan Klebold and Eric Harris. 1

What they did was against the law, but let's face it—the incident was waiting to happen. And there's nothing surprising about it. 2

The social priorities of high school are to blame. In truth, high school is a place where jocks, cheerleaders and anyone associated with them can do whatever they want and get away with it. Their exploits are celebrated in pep rallies, printed in school papers and shown off in trophy cases. The popular cliques have the most clout, and are—in a sense—local celebrities. If they ever run into disciplinary problems with the school or police, they get let off the hook under the guise that they are just kids. 3

Public schools claim to support all students, but in reality choose to invest their priorities in activities associated with popular cliques. Schools are willing to go to any means necessary to support the sports teams, for example. They care less about students who don't belong to popular cliques, leaving them almost nothing. School becomes less about getting a good education, instead priding itself on the celebration of elite cliques. 4

The popular cliques are nice to their own but spit out extremely cruel insults to those who don't fit in. As noted in *Time,* jocks admitted they like to pick on unpopular kids 5 "because it's just fun to do." Their insulting words create deep emotional wounds, while school authorities ignore the cruelty of the corrupt high-school social system.

6   Schools refuse to accept any accountability and point to parents instead. While it is the job of parents to condition their kids, it is impossible for them to supervise their kids 24 hours a day.

7   As an outcast, I was harrassed on an everyday basis by jocks, and received no help from school authorities. It got so bad that I attempted suicide.

8   Yes, I did (and still do) wear all black, play Doom and listen to raucous heavy metal, punk and Goth music. I was into the occult and had extensive knowledge on guns and how to build bombs.

9   I got into several fights, including one where I kicked the shit out of a basketball player. The only reason why I didn't shoot him and his jock cronies is because I lacked access to guns. I would've blown every single one of them away and not cared.

10   To defend myself, I carried around a 7-inch blade. If anyone continued to mess with me, I sent them anonymous notes with a big swastika drawn on them. I responded to harassment with "Yeah, heil Hitler," while saluting.

11   They got the hint. Eventually, I found some friends who were also outcasts. We banded together and didn't judge each other by the way we looked or what we liked. But I still held contempt for jocks whom I believed should be shot and fed to the sharks.

12   Even in their deaths, Klebold and Harris are still treated like outcasts. How dare *Time* call them "The Monsters Next Door." News analysis poured over the "abnormal" world of "Goth" culture, Marilyn Manson, violent computer games and gun control. It also targeted other outcast students as trenchcoat-goth, submerged, socially challenged kids who fail to fit the "correct" image of American teens.

13   The popular cliques have their likeness reinforced through the images of trashy teen media as seen on MTV, *90210,* and *Dawson's Creek.* It's heard in the bubble-gum pop of Britney Spears and Backstreet Boys, along with their imitators. Magazines like *YM* and *Seventeen* feature pretty-looking girls, offering advice on the latest trends in dress, makeup and dating.

14   Media coverage was saturated with memorials and funeral services of the deceased. Friends and family remembered them as "good kids." Not all those killed knew or made fun of Klebold or Harris. Obviously there were members of the popular cliques who made fun of them and escaped harm. But innocent people had to die in order to bring injustices to light that exist in our society.

15   It's tragic, but perhaps that's the price that had to be paid. Perhaps they are shocked by the fact that some "nerds" have actually defeated them for once because teasing isn't fun and games anymore.

16   With the last of the coffins being laid to rest, people are looking for retribution, someone to prosecute. Why? The two kids are dead—there is no sense in pursuing this problem any further. But lawyers are trying to go after those who they believe influenced Harris and

Klebold: namely their parents, gun dealers, and the Trenchcoat Mafia. Police heavily questioned Harris' girlfriend about the guns she gave them and arrested one person.

The families of the deceased, lawyers and the police need to get a clue and leave the 17 two kids' families and friends alone. They are dealing with just as much grief and do not need to be punished for someone else's choices. Filing lawsuits will drag on for years, burdening everyone and achieving little.

It's not like you can bring your loved ones back to life after you've won your case. 18

What we need is bigger emphasis on academic discipline and more financing toward 19 academic programs. Counselors and psychiatrists need to be hired to attend to student needs. People need practical skills, not the pep-rally fluff of popular cliques.

The people of Littleton need to be at peace with the fate of their town and heal wounds 20 instead of prying them open with lawsuits.

Critiquing "The Monster That Is High School"

1. Summarize Daeha Ko's argument by creating a plausible causal chain leading from popular high school cliques to the Littleton massacre. How persuasive is Daeha's argument?

2. Daeha is angered at *Time* magazine for characterizing Klebold and Harris as "the monsters next door." How would you characterize Daeha's *ethos* in this piece? Do you see him as "monstrous" himself? Or does his *ethos* help create sympathy for social outcasts in high school culture?

3. Daeha presents his causal argument as a contribution to the frantic, contentious social conflict that raged among social scientists, columnists, and other media commentators after the shootings at Columbine High School in Littleton, Colorado (see a summary of this discussion in Case 1, p. 228). Which alternative explanations for the shooting does Daeha address? What strategy does he use to rebut alternative causal arguments? Do you regard Daeha's argument as a valuable contribution to the controversy? Why or why not?

Our second reading, by a professor of psychology at the University of Alaska, appeared in the journal *Academic Questions*, a publication of the National Association of Scholars. This philosophically conservative organization tries to preserve traditional humanistic values, believes the academic curriculum has been debased by educational fads, and actively opposes postmodernism and the "political correctness" movement associated with liberal politics. In this article, Judith Kleinfeld attacks the Morella Bill, a federal funding program aimed at attracting women into scientific and technical fields. Her article explores the puzzling causal question "Why do so few women go into science?" and provides an answer contrary to the causal explanations espoused by most liberals.

―――――――――――

The Morella Bill, My Daughter Rachel, and the Advancement of Women in Science
Judith Kleinfeld

1   The advancement of women in science and mathematics has become something of a cottage industry fueled by federal dollars. The Morella Bill, passed in the fall of 1998 by the 105th Congress, is the latest effort. This bill established yet another commission to figure out why women are underrepresented in scientific and technical fields. The commission, in turn, is apt to recommend more of the same science programs for young women that we already have. Many of these special programs, as a practical matter, are closed to boys. Leaving aside the questions of the ethics and the legality of such sex-segregated federal programs, let us ask if these kinds of programs are even in the interests of women themselves? My own experience in trying to get my daughter Rachel interested in mathematics and science suggests the risks of such social engineering.

2   The Program for Women and Girls in the National Science Foundation's Directorate for Human Resources and Education is a good example of what is likely to emerge from the Morella Bill. The NSF Program for Women and Girls spends close to $10 million a year on a potpourri of educational initiatives. Many are designed to get young girls, especially those from low-income families, interested in science, mathematics, and technology. The program "Creating After School Science" is a typical example:

> *Creating After School Science Opportunities for Girls in NYC Settlement Houses: A Model Project.* Supports the piloting of a hands-on science/gender equity model for girls 6 to 11 in after school programs at four New York City settlement houses. Builds on the Educational Equity Concept's "Playtime is Science" program. Start date August 1, 1996, NSF Award #9633332241, $119,053 (Estimated).[1]

3   The NSF Program for Women and Girls also funds a multitude of programs designed to make sure that teachers are up to date on the cooperative, rather than competitive, methods of teaching that are supposedly more congruent with the fragile female psyche. While most of these programs are funded in the $100,000 range, Arizona State University managed to pick up this plum:

> *Guiding Math/Science Talented Girls and Women.* Supports one-week summer and winter seminars where counselors, administrators, and science educators will be taught the knowledge and skills for guiding career development of math/science talented girls and especially at-risk girls. Start Date May 1, 1997, NSF Award #9619121, $730,382 (Estimated).

Such summer camps and after-school programs should be interesting and enjoyable, with their emphasis on field trips, cooperative projects, and hands-on science activities. But boys do not get to participate in these stimulating activities. The "Frequently Asked Questions and Answers" page of the NSF Program for Women and Girls website indeed gives potential grantees this counsel:

Question #2. Do you have any information about Title IX? Can a federally funded education program exclude boys?

> NSF programs for girls may not exclude boys. However, projects can be proposed and conducted by organizations which serve girls primarily, can actively recruit girls, and can study girls as their focus. They do not have to make an effort to include boys; they just can't categorically keep them out.

After clarifying the law, the potential grantee is shown, as a practical matter, how to flout it:

> It is rare that, for example, boys want to come to an after-school Girls Club event, or "Girls in Science Day" or such. (There is a natural disinterest, for example—boys wanting to be Girl Scouts.)

The author of these questions and answers evidently believes there can be a "natural disinterest" on the part of boys, although suggesting any natural disinterest on the part of girls would not be acceptable.

Do such programs succeed in increasing the number of women in mathematics, the physical sciences, engineering, and computer science? When I posed this question to an NSF administrator, she responded with admirable candor.[2] These programs provide interesting activities for girls, especially low-income girls, who might otherwise not have another way to go to summer camp, she told me. But she doubted they did much to advance women in science.

The Morella Bill—The Wisdom of WISETECH

Effective or not, more such programs are on their way. On 9 November 1997, Representative Connie Morella (R–Maryland) with sixteen cosponsors introduced H.R. 3007, "a bill to establish the Commission on the Advancement of Women and Minorities in Science, Engineering, and Technology Development" (dubbed WISETECH). The commission is charged with such tasks as reviewing the research on the number of women in science, engineering, and technology and identifying barriers to their advancement. It is required to report its findings and recommendations in one year.

As the Congressional Budget Office points out, in estimating the cost of WISETECH at $1 million, such a short time span means that the commission would have to "rely heavily on available information."[3] A great deal of information indeed is available. To take just one example, the National Research Council established in 1991 a Committee on Women in Science and Engineering, which compiled a list of organizations working to increase the participation of women in science and engineering. They located 290 organizations.

The White House indeed opposed the Morella Bill on the grounds of expensive duplication.[4] The actual basis for White House opposition was probably political—Congresswoman Morella is a Republican who stood for reelection in 1998.[5] Needed or not, WISETECH made it through the legislative process. The bill sailed through committee hearings with barely an objection.

Women and the Physical Sciences—The Puzzle

8   Since the 1960s, women have vastly increased their numbers in the professions and the biological sciences.[6] In 1994, women attained more than 40 percent of all professional degrees, up from less than 3 percent in 1961. In such professional fields as veterinary medicine, women now receive the majority of professional degrees (65 percent). The gender gap in the biological sciences is also closing. Indeed, American women in 1994 received 43 percent of the doctorates in biology and 63 percent of the doctorates in health.[7] Still, only 24 percent of the doctorates in mathematics, 22 percent of the doctorates in the physical sciences, 18 percent of the doctorates in computer sciences, and 15 percent of the doctorates in engineering went to American women.

9   In noting this gender gap, it is also important to note that the careers and prospects of very few women are affected. An important point, constantly forgotten, is how few people, men or women, choose scientific and technical careers. The number of doctorates awarded to American men in the physical sciences, mathematics, engineering, and the computer sciences in 1994 totaled only 5,532; the number awarded to American women totaled 1,291. But almost 17,000 women got law degrees that year.

10   Still, success in science is an important cultural symbol. Men like Albert Einstein, Richard Feynman, and Stephen Hawking create our popular images of spectacular intellectual achievement. Most undergraduates, in my experience, can name no famous female scientist other than Marie Curie.

Cultural and Biological Explanations for the Gender Gap

11   So what is a program to do? Can the Morella Bill, the Program for Women and Girls at the National Science Foundation, the Committee on Women in Science and Engineering of the National Research Council, or any of the other 290 organizations fighting on the ramparts make a difference?

12   Attempts to explain the gender gap in science and mathematics are not wanting. In a paper reviewing the literature on what causes gender differences, for example, Gita Wilder cites so many studies that her references take up eighteen pages.[8] Virtually every serious effort to understand the gender gap, as Wilder points out, acknowledges the importance of both biological and cultural influences.

13   **Cultural Influences—The Negative Stereotype Effect.**   Cultural stereotypes are one prominent explanation for the gender gap in science and mathematics. Some of the most convincing research on the effect of negative cultural stereotypes has been done by Claude Steele, a psychologist at Stanford University.[9] Steele and his colleagues recruited male and female college students with talent in mathematics, who saw themselves as strong math students. He gave them a difficult mathematics test taken from the Graduate Record Examinations. In one condition, the students were told that the test typically showed gender differences in favor of males. In the other condition, students were told this test showed no gender differences.

When threatened with the negative stereotype about female abilities in mathematics, women indeed performed significantly worse than men. When told that the test showed no gender differences, men and women got approximately equal scores. Steele sees this result as evidence of the negative influence of female stereotypes, and he is right. What he does not point out is that the scores became equal not only because women's mathematics scores went up but also because men's scores went down. Steele also neglects to point out that the women in this study never achieved mathematics scores as high as men reached, even when the threat of cultural stereotypes was removed.

14

Biological Explanations—The Testosterone Effect.   While Steele's studies and similar research do demonstrate the negative effects of cultural stereotypes on women, this research does not succeed in dismissing biological explanations. Strong spatial-rotational abilities, for example, are important to advanced mathematical reasoning and to scientific achievement in physics. Reviewing the research literature, psychologist Diane Halpern emphasizes that testosterone is clearly linked to such skills:

15

> The spatial-skills performance of normal males fluctuates in concert with daily variations in testosterone and seasonal variations. . . . When normal, aging men were given testosterone to enhance sexual functioning, they also showed improved performance on visual-spatial tests.
> Additionally, when female-to-male transsexuals were given high doses of testosterone in preparation for sex change therapy, their visual spatial skills improved dramatically and their verbal fluency skills declined dramatically within three months. The results of these studies and others provide a strong causal link between levels of adult hormones and sex-typical patterns of performance.[10]

Cultural influences reinforce and amplify these biological patterns. Women tend to excel in verbal skills while men tend to excel in spatial reasoning.[11] This is the distribution of abilities that such policy initiatives as the Morella Bill are fighting.

16

What My Daughter Rachel and (Many) Women Want

Still, some women have strong spatial abilities and talent in mathematics and science. Would these women be helped by the kinds of programs apt to come out of the Morella Bill?

17

The voluminous research literature on gender offers surprisingly few case studies that would give us some insight into why women with talent in science and mathematics do not choose these fields. For this reason, I offer here, in the spirit of a case study, my experience with my own daughter, Rachel. She is just the kind of young woman who would be the target of the program efforts likely to emerge from the Morella Bill. Indeed, she was the target of my own extensive efforts to interest her in science and mathematics, efforts far more determined than any likely to come from a federal program. But Rachel, like so many other young women, insisted that she was "not interested" in science and wanted "to work with people." Why?

18

19   I first realized Rachel was gifted in mathematics when she entered junior high school. She had scored high on a mathematics test that her school gave to choose students for "MathCounts," a national mathematics competition. MathCounts winners are overwhelmingly male.[12] Rachel was hardly a victim of cultural stereotypes about women. She was the only one of our three children (the other two are boys) who learned to use tools. For her birthdays, she asked for building sets. On her sixth birthday, I found her packing up the new Barbie doll her grandmother had sent her. "If grandma likes dolls so much," she said with disgust, "she can have all of mine."

20   The more I thought about Rachel's interests and skills, the more it all fell into place. I had a mathematically and technically inclined daughter whose talents I should develop. Rachel was already getting tutored in advanced mathematics twice a week to prepare her for the statewide MathCounts meet. Her school had arranged private tutoring for her and another high-scoring student, a boy. But there was more I could do! I got her to enroll in a science course sponsored by the Center for Talented Youth. She had qualified for both the writing and science courses but had always chosen the writing courses.

21   To give her practical experience in a scientific career and let her meet female role models, I arranged for her to work after school with a doctoral student (female, of course) at the University of Alaska's Institute for Arctic Biology. Rachel got to look at samples of Bering Sea water using an electron microscope. I was thrilled. Rachel was not. She told me to lay off.

22   "I am not part of your agenda for the advancement of women in science," she informed me in a tone that left no room for further discussion. "I want to work with people. I want to help people."

23   These are the standard reasons women give when they explain why they are not interested in scientific careers. As I thought more about Rachel's experience, I realized that there was a lot more to her decision than her preference for working with people. This reason masked other reasons, good reasons, for not choosing science as a career.

24   Let us take a closer look at Rachel's actual skills from the viewpoint of where she has the greatest "comparative advantage." Yes, Rachel did score about as high as the male student in the local MathCounts competition. But the tutoring sessions revealed great differences in their mathematical gifts. The young boy could solve problems in a flash while she had to struggle. I asked him how he did it, but he wasn't very verbal. "I don't know," he said. "The solutions just come to me." The solutions did not "just come" to Rachel. In the pressure of the statewide MathCounts competition, the boy did much better. Rachel's reaction was again typical of what girls say—she did not like the "competitiveness" of the math contest. But the issue was not male versus female competitiveness. Rachel was an avid competitor when her chances of winning were high.

25   The science course also gave Rachel valuable information about her areas of comparative advantage. In her writing courses with the Center for Talented Youth, she had always been at the top. In the CTY science course, she found herself stuck in the middle. Her reaction—she was "not interested" in science.

26   Like most of us, Rachel finds most interesting the areas she is best at. But Rachel was able to discover her relative strengths and weaknesses only because she was in mathematics and science settings where both males and females were present. Had she been in sex-segregated programs, like the ones likely to come out of the Morella Bill, she would have

been deprived of valuable information about her abilities. In an all-girls program, she would most likely have been a star.

Lop-Sided Males and Balanced Females

Many females with talent in science and mathematics, in my experience, resemble my daughter Rachel. They are "balanced," apt to be bright in both verbal skills and mathematics skills. These young women have a wide range of choices—to go into a scientific field or to go into another field where their verbal skills are valuable.   27

Many males with talent in science and mathematics, in my experience, resemble the young boy who was also competing in MathCounts. These males are "lop-sided," strong in mathematical skills but far weaker in verbal skills. These young men, playing to their strengths, are apt to choose scientific and technical fields. Of course, some young men will have strength in both the verbal and mathematical areas. But I suspect a larger number of young men, compared to young women, will have this "lop-sided" pattern. I am currently testing this theory through an analysis of SAT scores, in order to see what proportions of females and males who have high scores on the mathematics section of the SAT also have high scores on the verbal section of the test. My bet is that women who have high mathematical skills will also tend to have high verbal skills, while men who have high mathematical skills are more apt to be "lop-sided."   28

In a free society, where people can make their own career choices, it should not be surprising that males and females choose somewhat different careers.[13] A 1996 survey of college freshmen, for example, shows that 20 percent of females but less than 10 percent of males are choosing professional careers. Women are indeed seeking high-status and high-paying careers but they prefer the professions. This survey also showed that over 20 percent of male college freshmen compared to 6 percent of females are choosing careers in physical sciences, engineering, and the computer sciences. Despite all the efforts of federal agencies, females and males seek out work they enjoy and work at which they excel.   29

Is there anything really wrong with this picture? I think not. The danger of the Morella Bill and the sex-segregated programs this legislation is likely to spawn is that young women will be pressured, or seduced by scholarships, into scientific and technical careers which do not fit them well and which they will not find satisfying. Science may need women in order to meet current demands for political correctness, but women have many other satisfying career choices.   30

Notes

1. These examples are drawn from the web page of the Program for Women and Girls at the National Science Foundation. On the web, go to http://www.nsf.gov/verity/srchawd.htm and type 1544 in the dialog window.
2. I deliberately leave the identity of this NSF administrator vague because I do not wish to embarrass her. We were speaking on the record, but she may have been too open.
3. This Congressional Budget Office Cost Estimate was prepared on 21 May 1998 and can be found on this web site: http://www.thomas.loc.gov by following the queries.

4. Letter from Kerri-Ann Jones, Acting Director, Office of Science and Technology Policy, Executive Office of the President, sent to The Honorable William F. Goodling, Chairman of the Committee on Education and the Workforce, 11 May 1998.

5. These points come from a source in the Committee on Education and the Workforce.

6. Precise documentation for these statistics and others in this essay may be found in *The Myth That Schools Shortchange Girls* (Washington, DC: Women's Freedom Network, 1998).

7. These statistics track the proportion of American women who receive doctorates in the sciences, compared to American men. Reports on gender equity often underestimate the progress of American women, because they ignore the preponderance of foreign students who are receiving doctorates from American universities. These foreign students are overwhelmingly (in a ratio of 3 to 1) male.

8. See Gita Wilder, "Antecedents of Gender Differences," in *Supplement to Gender and Fair Assessment* (Princeton, NJ: Educational Testing Service, 1997).

9. See Claude M. Steele, "A Threat in the Air: How Stereotypes Shape Intellectual Identity and Performance," *American Psychologist* 52, 6 (1997): 613–629.

10. See Diane Halpern, "Sex Differences in Intelligence: Implications for Education," *American Psychologist* 52, 20, 1091–1102.

11. For a review of the specific evidence, using both grades and standardized test scores, see W. W. Willingham and N. S. Cole, *Gender and Fair Assessment* (Mahwah, NJ: Lawrence Erlbaum, 1997).

12. For a discussion of MathCounts, see C. A. Dwyer and L. M. Johnson, "Grades, Accomplishments, and Correlates," in Willingham and Cole, *Gender and Fair Assessment,* 127–156.

13. See the survey conducted by Alexander Austin, reported in Y. Bae and T. M. Smith, "Women in Mathematics and Science," in National Center for Educational Statistics, *The Condition of Education 1997* (Washington, DC: U.S. Department of Education, 1997), 13–21.

Critiquing "The Morella Bill, My Daughter Rachel, and the Advancement of Women in Science"

1. The central puzzle Kleinfeld addresses is why a significantly smaller percentage of women than men pursue careers in mathematics, science, and engineering. What are the usual causes cited for this phenomenon? What is Kleinfeld's explanation?

2. In wrestling with the question of scientific careers for women, Kleinfeld joins a larger social controversy about girls and education. For example, education professors Myra and David Sadker in their book *Failing at Fairness: How American Schools Cheat Girls* (1994) and groups such as the American Association of University Women argue that girls are still being short-changed intellectually and that many gaps in girls' education still persist. What contribution does Kleinfeld make to this larger conversation?

3. It is unusual (and often dangerous) to base a causal argument on a single case study. How persuasive do you find Kleinfeld's use of her daughter Rachel?

What rhetorical strategies does Kleinfeld use to increase the persuasiveness of the material based on Rachel?

4. Role-play a debate on the Senate floor preceding a vote on the Morella Bill. Have one group of students represent Kleinfeld's view in the debate. Have another group support the Morella Bill.

Our final causal argument, by student writer Holly Miller, examines the causes of teen sexual behavior. It uses the documentation form of the American Psychological Association (APA).

The Causes of Teen Sexual Behavior
Holly M. Miller (Student)

Teen sex, leading all too frequently to casual promiscuity, abortion, single motherhood, or STDs including AIDS, is a widely discussed problem in our culture. According to a recent survey conducted by the Kaiser Family Foundation, whereas only 35 percent of girls and 55 percent of boys had had sex by their eighteenth birthdays in the early 1970s, 56 percent of teenage girls and 73 percent of boys had had sex by age eighteen in 1996. The same study revealed that only "one in five teenagers do not have intercourse during their teenage years." Fifty-five percent of the teens cite readiness as the reason they have sex. Simply, "they think they are ready" (Survey, 1996).

However, there should be little doubt that most teens are not ready for sexual activity. High rates of pregnancy and STDs indicate that teens do not properly protect themselves, and high numbers of abortions suggest that they are not ready for parenthood. Moreover, much sexual behavior seems attributable to emotional immaturity, which may contribute to the particularly disturbing statistic that many girls are pressured to have sex or do so involuntarily. Seventy percent of the girls who had sex before age fourteen, and 60 percent of the girls who had sex prior to their fifteenth birthday claimed that the sexual intercourse was involuntary. Additionally, "six out of ten teenage girls say another reason why teen girls may have sex is because a boyfriend is pressuring them" (Survey, 1996).

There can be no question that teen sexual behavior is a growing problem, but the explanation for this increase in sexual activity is controversial. This paper's focus is on the causes of teen sexual behavior. Why are teens having sex? Who or what is the greatest influence on teen sexual behavior? How can we slow the rate of teen sexual activity?

Although many causes work together to influence teen sex, one of the most significant contributing causes is the media. Victor C. Strasburger (1997), an expert on adolescence, notes, "Teenagers watch an average of three hours of TV per day" (p. 18). A study cited by the Kaiser Foundation examined TV shows most popular with teenagers in 1992–1993. This study "found that one in four interactions among characters per episode conveyed a sexual message. . . . Only two of the ten shows included messages about sexual responsibility" (Entertainment, 1996). Popular shows in 1992–1993, such as *90210* and *Melrose*

Place, were just the trailblazers for the prime-time dramas now aimed at teens, such as *Dawson's Creek, Party of Five,* and *Felicity.* Beyond the sexually explicit story lines of programs, commercials use sex appeal to sell everything from cars to potato chips, and teens see twenty thousand commercials per year (Strasburger, 1997, p. 18). Another multimedia influence on teens is pornography. While statistics are hard to find because selling pornography to children is illegal, it is obvious that teens have access to pornography. One fifteen-year-old boy interviewed by *Life* magazine claimed, "No one tells you how to [have sex]. You learn it from watching pornos" (Adato, 1999, p. 38).

5   The effect of the media on teenage sexuality is probably subtle rather than direct. The media don't encourage teenagers to have sex, at least explicitly. But the influence is still there. Hollywood has long been blamed for desensitizing our culture to violence; it is entirely plausible that they have also desensitized our culture, and youth, to sex. According to Drew Altman, president of the Kaiser Family Foundation, "With the problems facing adolescents today, how sex is shown on TV is just as important as how much sex is shown on TV" (Entertainment, 1996). The frequent and graphic depictions of sex normalize the behavior for teenagers. Watching stars play characters their own age—characters with whom they can identify, characters who, just like them, have part-time jobs, too much homework, and problems with their parents—encourages teens to emulate the sexual behaviors of Bailey, Sara, Dawson, or Joey.

6   Teenagers themselves, however, will usually deny that they emulate TV characters, so we need to look also at other factors. Another contributing cause of teen sexual activity is peer pressure. The problem comes from teens' willingness to say and do things to impress others. The tendency to brag about sexual exploits was egregiously illustrated by the Spur Posse scandal of 1993. A group of popular high school "jocks" from a suburban California community formed a clique with the purpose of sleeping with girls. In fact, they competed with each other to see who could sleep with the most girls, going so far as to pressure girls as young as ten to have sex. Once exposed, several members were charged with lewd conduct, felony intercourse, and rape. The Posse members themselves say they learned about sex "the old-fashioned way": from older brothers and friends (Gelman, 1993, p. 29). Few, if any, of the guys would probably have gone to such extremes to sleep with girls had their friends not been competing in the same contest.

7   Another contributing cause is schools. According to many critics, sex education programs in the schools do little to promote safe sexual behavior, and they are often criticized by conservatives as promoting the message that it is good and normal to be sexually active (so long as you use a condom). Why are sex education programs so ineffective? One critic notes that sex education classes focus on the mechanics of sex and avoid issues of emotions, love, and morality. "They talk about zygotes," according to one fourteen-year-old boy (Adato, 1999, p. 38). Another critic, NYU psychology professor Paul C. Vitz (1999), reviewed leading high school health textbooks and is troubled by their lack of focus on "the meaning and possibility of true love and its relationship to sexual union and marriage." Vitz claims that textbooks encourage students to evaluate behavior in terms of their own needs rather than the needs of their partners or of a relationship. He claims that "[o]ur growing

tolerance of the adult 'do your own thing' morality runs smack up against the need to socialize and protect the young" (p. 547). In short, Vitz desires a sex education program that emphasizes love and morality. Yet schools avoid creating such programs because while parents are generally comfortable with their kids learning about sex from school, they are not as complacent when it comes to schools teaching morality.

The schools are criticized from another direction by some feminist scholars who have   8
blamed conventional schooling for the vulnerability of girls. Nancy J. Perry (1992), citing an American Association of University Women study showing that teachers pay less attention to girls than to boys, charges that "girls come out of school ill-prepared to get ahead in society" (p. 83). Though the AAUW did not address the sexual behavior of girls, their hypothesis that schools marginalize girls, making them vulnerable, may contribute to the fact that between 60 and 70 percent of teenage girls feel pressured into sex.

In explaining why adolescence is so difficult for girls, however, Perry puts primary re-   9
sponsibility not on the schools but on parents. Although she acknowledges that peer pressure and the media's portrayal of women as sex objects are contributing factors to sexual activity among teenage girls, she identifies parental involvement as the critical factor in the development of young girls.

In fact, differences in parenting styles might be the chief variable that influences   10
teenage sexual behavior. Drs. Sharon D. White and Richard R. DeBlassie, writing in the journal *Adolescence,* point out that "parents are the earliest and most important influence on sexuality" (1992, p. 184). According to their research, different parenting styles have a measurable influence on teenagers' sexual behavior. The highest rates of sexual activity come from teenagers with permissive parents who set no rules. The next highest rates, ironically, come from teenagers whose parents are unduly strict and controlling, a parenting style that often fosters rebellion. The lowest rates of sexual activity come from teenagers whose parents set firm but reasonable and moderate rules. White and DeBlassie show that parents who insist on reasonable curfews, and who supervise their teens' dating by knowing whom they are with and where they are going, produce teens with the most responsible attitudes toward sex. They suggest also that parents' implicit values—for example, abstinence until marriage or at least sex linked to love and commitment—are most likely to be transmitted to teens when the teens feel connected to their parents in a safe environment with rules.

So what can be done to reduce the problems of teen sexuality? Research suggests that   11
parents have the most direct and strongest influence over teens' sexual behavior, but by no means are they the only influences. Thus, television producers ought to provide role models of teens with less promiscuous views of sex. Teachers need to pay better attention to the needs of their students, whether the teens need to hear about emotional sides of sex or the advantages of waiting until marriage to have intercourse. Parents need to turn off the TV and open dialogue with their children. Parents need to set moderate and reasonable rules for their teens and carefully supervise their behavior. Only when parents take the lead in responsibly educating their children about sex, and in pressuring the media and the schools to create a holistic view of sex in the context of love and commitment, can we curb the trend of teen sex and its unhealthy consequences.

References

Adato, A. (1999, March 1). The secret lives of teens. *Life,* p. 38.

Entertainment media as "sex educators?" and other ways teens learn about sex, contraception, STDs, and AIDS. (1996). Kaiser Family Foundation. Retrieved May 16, 1999 from the World Wide Web: http://www.kff.org (Scroll "Reproductive and Sexual Health." Then choose "surveys.")

Gelman, D. (1993, April 12). Mixed messages. *Newsweek,* p. 29.

Perry, N. (1992, August 10). Why it's so tough to be a girl. *Fortune,* pp. 82–84.

Strasburger, V. (1997, May 19). Tuning in to teenagers. *Newsweek,* pp. 18–19.

Survey on teens and sex: What they say teens today need to know, and who they listen to. (1996). Kaiser Family Foundation. Retrieved May 16, 1999, from the World Wide Web: http://www.kff.org (Scroll "Reproductive and Sexual Health." Then choose "surveys.")

Vitz, P. (1999, March). Cupid's broken arrow. *Phi Delta Kappan,* p. 547.

White, S., & DeBlassie, R. (1992). Adolescent sexual behavior. *Adolescence, 27,* 183–191.

Critiquing "The Causes of Teen Sexual Behavior"

1. How does Holly Miller establish the issue of teen sexuality and suggest the controversy surrounding it?

2. What kind of causal links does Holly employ to explain why teenagers have sex? What data does she use to support those links? Are these data persuasive? What would make her interpretations more persuasive?

3. What features of causal argument contribute to the strength of her argument? What insights does this argument add to the ongoing social conflict and confusion over teen sexuality?

12 Resemblance Arguments

X Is (Is Not) like Y

CASE 1

When NATO began bombing Serbia during the Kosovo crisis, the Clinton administration, along with the U.S. media, likened Yugoslavian president Slobodan Milosovic to Adolf Hitler and compared the "ethnic cleansing" of Kosovo to the Nazis' "final solution" against the Jews. When justifying the bombing, Clinton frequently evoked the Holocaust and the lessons of World War II. "Never again," he said. Meanwhile, the Serbian community in the United States (and many Balkan scholars) criticized the Holocaust analogy. The Serbian community likened the Kosovo crisis not to the Nazi annihilation of the Jews but to a civil war in which Serbs were protecting their homeland against Albanian terrorists. They pointed to explanatory precedents when the Serbs themselves were victims, especially the "ethnic cleansing" of Serbs from Croatia in 1995.

CASE 2

When the voting age was reduced from twenty-one to eighteen, many people argued for the lower voting age by saying, "If you are old enough to fight for your country in a war, you are old enough to vote." But author Richard Weaver claimed that this analogy was true "only if you believe that fighting and voting are the same kind of thing which I, for one, do not. Fighting requires strength, muscular coordination and, in a modern army, instant and automatic response to orders. Voting requires knowledge of men, history, reasoning power; it is essentially a deliberative activity. Army mules and police dogs are used to fight; nobody is

261

interested in giving them the right to vote. This argument rests on a false analogy."* Someone else might argue that Weaver's counteranalogy is also weak.

AN OVERVIEW OF
RESEMBLANCE ARGUMENTS

Resemblance arguments support a claim by comparing one thing to another with the intention of transferring the audience's understanding of (or feelings about) the second thing back to the first. Sometimes an entire argument can be devoted to a resemblance claim. More commonly, brief resemblance arguments are pieces of larger arguments devoted to a different stasis. Thus lawyer Charles Rembard, in attacking the American Civil Liberties Union for its opposition to mandatory reporting of AIDS at the start of the AIDS crisis, compared the ACLU's desire to protect the privacy of individuals to out-of-date war tactics:

> [The ACLU] clings to once useful concepts that are inappropriate to current problems. Like the French military, which prepared for World War II by building the Maginot Line, which was nicely adapted to the trench warfare of World War I, the ACLU sometimes hauls up legal arguments effective to old libertarian battles but irrelevant to those at hand.†

The strategy of resemblance arguments is to take the audience's understanding of the point made in the comparison (you shouldn't fight World War II with out-of-date strategies from World War I) and transfer it to the issue being debated (you shouldn't fight the battle against AIDS with an out-of-date libertarian philosophy).

In some cases it may seem that a resemblance argument (X is like Y) is not very different from a definitional argument (X is Y). For example, if you were to say that Slobodan Milosovic is "like" Adolf Hitler, you might simply be making a definitional argument, claiming that both men belong to the same class—say, the class "fascist dictators" or "racial supremacists." Their similarities would be restricted to the traits of whatever class they are put into. In effect, the *like* statement is a definitional claim in which both X and Y are said to belong to class Z.

But a resemblance argument doesn't work in quite this way. For one thing, in a resemblance argument the overarching class Z is usually not mentioned but left to the audience's imagination; the focus stays on Y—that is, on the specific case to which X is being compared. Often, in fact, there is no single overarching category Z that effectively sums up all the points of comparison between X and Y. (What common category do the ACLU's position on AIDS testing and France's building of the Maginot Line belong to?) This definitional blurring moves resemblance

---

*Richard M. Weaver, "A Responsible Rhetoric," *The Intercollegiate Review,* Winter 1976–77: 86–87.

†Charles Rembar, *New York Times,* 15 May 1987: I, 31:2.

arguments away from strict logic and toward a kind of metaphoric or imaginative persuasiveness.

The persuasive power of resemblance arguments comes from their ability to clarify an audience's conception of contested issues while conveying powerful emotions. Resemblance arguments typically take the form X is (is not) like Y. Resemblance arguments work best when the audience has a clear (and sometimes emotionally charged) understanding of the Y term. The writer then hopes to transfer this understanding, along with accompanying emotions, to the X term. The danger of resemblance arguments, as we shall see, is that the differences between the X and Y terms are often so significant that the resemblance argument collapses under close examination.

Like most other argument types, resemblance arguments can be analyzed using the Toulmin schema. Suppose, for example, that you wanted to write an argument favoring a balanced federal budget. In one section of your argument you might develop the following claim of resemblance: "Just as a family will go bankrupt if it continually spends more than it makes, so the federal government will go bankrupt if its expenses exceed its revenues." This claim depends on the resemblance between the fiscal problems of the federal government and the fiscal problems of a private family. The argument can be displayed in Toulmin terms as follows:

ENTHYMEME:	If the federal government doesn't balance its budget, it will go bankrupt because the federal government is like a family that goes bankrupt when it fails to balance its budget.
CLAIM:	If the federal government doesn't balance its debt, it will go bankrupt.
STATED REASON:	because the federal government is like a family that goes bankrupt when it fails to balance its budget
GROUNDS:	evidence showing that families that overspend their budgets go bankrupt
WARRANT:	The economic laws that apply to families apply also to governments.
BACKING:	evidence that when governments and families behave in economically similar ways, they suffer similar consequences
CONDITIONS OF REBUTTAL:	all cases in which governments and families behaved in similar ways and did not suffer similar consequences; all the ways that families and governments differ
QUALIFIER:	The claim is supported by the analogy only to the extent that family and government economics resemble each other.

For many audiences, this comparison of the government to a family might be persuasive: It uses an area of experience familiar to almost everyone (the problem of balancing the family budget) to help make sense of a more complex area of experience (the problem of balancing the federal budget). At its root is the warrant that what works for the family will work for the federal government.

But this example also illustrates the dangers of resemblance arguments, which often ignore important differences or *disanalogies* between the terms of comparison. One can think, for instance, of many differences between the economics of a family and that of the federal government. For example, unlike a private family, the federal government prints its own money and does most of its borrowing from its own members. Perhaps these differences negate the claim that family debt and federal debt are similar in their effects. Thus an argument based on resemblance is usually open to refutation if a skeptic points out important disanalogies.

We turn now to the two types of resemblance arguments: analogy and precedent.

ARGUMENTS BY ANALOGY

The use of *analogies* can constitute the most imaginative form of argument. If you don't like your new boss, you can say that she's like a marine drill sergeant, the cowardly captain of a sinking ship, or a mother hen. Each of these analogies suggests a different management style, clarifying the nature of your dislike while conveying an emotional charge. The ubiquity of analogies undoubtedly stems from their power to clarify the writer's understanding of an issue through comparisons that grip the audience.

Of course, this power to make things clear comes at a price. Analogies often clarify one aspect of a relationship at the expense of other aspects. Thus, for example, in nineteenth-century America many commentators were fond of justifying certain negative effects of capitalism (for example, the squalor of the poor) by comparing social and economic processes to Darwinian evolution—the survival of the fittest. In particular, they fastened on one aspect of evolution, competition, and spoke darkly of life as a cutthroat struggle for survival. Clearly the analogy clarified one aspect of human interaction: People and institutions do indeed compete for limited resources, markets, and territory. Moreover, the consequences of failure are often dire (the weak get eaten by the strong).

But competition is only one aspect of evolution—albeit a particularly dramatic one. The ability to dominate an environment is less important to long-term survival of a species than the ability to adapt to that environment. Thus the mighty dinosaur disappeared, but the lowly cockroach continues to flourish because of the latter's uncanny ability to adjust to circumstance.

The use of the evolutionary analogies to stress the competitive nature of human existence fit the worldview (and served the interests) of those who were most fond of invoking them, in particular the so-called robber barons and conservative Social Darwinists. But in overlooking other dimensions of evolution, especially the importance of adaptation and cooperation to survival, the analogy created a great deal of mischief.

So analogies have the power to get an audience's attention like virtually no other persuasive strategy. But seldom are they sufficient in themselves to provide full understanding. At some point with every analogy you need to ask yourself, "How far can I legitimately go with this? At what point are the similarities between the two things I am comparing going to be overwhelmed by their dissimilarities?" They are useful attention-getting devices; used carefully and cautiously, they can be extended to shape an audience's understanding of a complex situation. But they can conceal and distort as well as clarify.

With this caveat, let's look at the uses of both undeveloped and extended analogies.

Using Undeveloped Analogies

Typically, writers will use short, *undeveloped analogies* to drive home a point (and evoke an accompanying emotion) and then quickly abandon the analogy before the reader's awareness of disanalogies begins to set in. Thus conservative columnist James Kilpatrick, in arguing that it is not unconstitutional to require drug testing of federal employees, compares giving a urine specimen when applying for a federal job to going through an airport metal detector when flying:

> The Constitution does not prohibit all searches and seizures. It makes the people secure in their persons only from "unreasonable" searches and seizures. [. . .] A parallel situation may be observed at every airport in the land. Individuals may have a right to fly, but they have no right to fly without having their persons and baggage inspected for weapons. By the same token, the federal worker who refuses a urine specimen [has no right to a federal job].*

Kilpatrick wants to transfer his audience's general approval of weapons searches as a condition for airplane travel to drug testing as a condition for federal employment. But he doesn't want his audience to linger too long on the analogy. (Is a urine specimen for employment really analogous to a weapons search before an airplane trip?)

Using Extended Analogies

Sometimes writers elaborate an analogy so that it takes on a major role in the argument. As an example of a claim based on an *extended analogy,* consider the following excerpt from a professor's argument opposing a proposal to require a writing proficiency exam for graduation. In the following portion of his argument,

---

*From "A Conservative View" by James J. Kilpatrick. ©Universal Press Syndicate. Reprinted with permission. All rights reserved.

the professor compares development of writing skills to the development of physical fitness.

> A writing proficiency exam gives the wrong symbolic messages about writing. It suggests that writing is simply a skill, rather than an active way of thinking and learning. It suggests that once a student demonstrates proficiency then he or she doesn't need to do any more writing.
>
> Imagine two universities concerned with the physical fitness of their students. One university requires a junior-level physical fitness exam in which students must run a mile in less than 10 minutes, a fitness level it considers minimally competent. Students at this university see the physical fitness exam as a one-time hurdle. As many as 70 percent of them can pass the exam with no practice; another 10–20 percent need a few months' training; and a few hopeless couch potatoes must go through exhaustive remediation. After passing the exam, any student can settle back into a routine of TV and potato chips having been certified as "physically fit."
>
> The second university, however, believing in true physical fitness for its students, is not interested in minimal competency. Consequently, it creates programs in which its students exercise 30 minutes every day for the entire four years of the undergraduate curriculum. There is little doubt which university will have the most physically fit students. At the second university, fitness becomes a way of life with everyone developing his or her full potential. Similarly, if we want to improve our students' writing abilities, we should require writing in every course throughout the curriculum.

If you choose to write an extended analogy such as this, you will focus on the points of comparison that serve your purposes. The writer's purpose in the preceding case is to support the achievement of mastery rather than minimalist standards as the goal of the university's writing program. Whatever other disanalogous elements are involved (for example, writing requires the use of intellect, which may or may not be strengthened by repetition), the comparison reveals vividly that a commitment to mastery involves more than a minimalist test. The analogy serves primarily to underscore this one crucial point. In reviewing the different groups of students as they "prepare" for the fitness exam, the author makes clear just how irrelevant such an exam is to the whole question of mastery. Typically, then, in developing your analogy, you are not developing all possible points of comparison so much as you are bringing out those similarities consistent with the point you are trying to make.

FOR CLASS DISCUSSION

The following is a two-part exercise to help you clarify for yourself how analogies function in the context of arguments. Part 1 is to be done outside class; part 2 is to be done in class.

PART 1   Think of an analogy that accurately expresses your feeling toward each of the following topics. Then write your analogy in the following one-sentence format:

> X is like Y: A, B, C . . . (where X is the main topic being discussed; Y is the analogy; and A, B, and C are the points of comparison).

EXAMPLES:

Cramming for an exam to get better grades is like pumping iron for 10 hours straight to prepare for a weightlifting contest: exhausting and counterproductive.

A right-to-lifer bombing an abortion clinic is like a vegetarian bombing a cattle barn: futile and contradictory.

a. Spanking a child to teach obedience is like . . .

b. Building low-cost housing for poor people is like . . .

c. The use of steroids by college athletes is like . . .

d. Mandatory AIDS testing for all U.S. residents is like . . .

e. A legislative proposal to eliminate all federally subsidized student loans is like . . .

f. The effect of American fast food on our health is like . . .

g. The personal gain realized by people who have committed questionable or even illegal acts and then made money by selling book and movie rights is like . . .

In each case, begin by asking yourself how you feel about the subject. If you have negative feelings about a topic, then begin by calling up negative pictures that express those feelings (or if you have positive feelings, call up positive comparisons). As they emerge, test each one to see if it will work as an analogy. An effective analogy will convey both the feeling you have toward your topic and your understanding of the topic. For instance, the writer in the "cramming for an exam" example obviously believes that pumping iron for 10 hours before a weightlifting match is stupid. This feeling of stupidity is then transferred to the original topic—cramming for an exam. But the analogy also clarifies understanding. The writer imagines the mind as a muscle (which gets exhausted after too much exercise and which is better developed through some exercise every day rather than a lot all at once) rather than as a large container (into which lots of stuff can be "crammed").

PART 2   Bring your analogies to class and compare them to those of your classmates. Select the best analogies for each of the topics and be ready to say why you think they are good.

ARGUMENTS BY PRECEDENT

Precedent arguments are like analogy arguments in that they make comparisons between an X and a Y. In precedent arguments, however, the Y term is usually a past event where some sort of decision was reached, often a moral, legal, or political decision. An argument by precedent tries to show that a similar decision should be (should not be) reached for the present issue X because the situation of X is (is not) like the situation of Y. For example, if you wanted to argue that your college or university could increase retention by offering seminars for first-year students, you could point to the good results at other colleges that have instituted first-year seminars. If you wanted to argue that antidrug laws will never eradicate drug use, you could point to the failure of alcohol prohibition in the United States in the 1920s.

A good example of a precedent argument is the following excerpt from a speech by President Lyndon Johnson in the early years of the Vietnam War:

> Nor would surrender in Vietnam bring peace because we learned from Hitler at Munich that success only feeds the appetite of aggression. The battle would be renewed in one country and then another country, bringing with it perhaps even larger and crueler conflict, as we have learned from the lessons of history.*

Here the audience knows what happened at Munich: France and Britain tried to appease Hitler by yielding to his demand for a large part of Czechoslovakia, but Hitler's armies continued their aggression anyway, using Czechoslovakia as a staging area to invade Poland. By arguing that surrender in Vietnam would lead to the same consequences, Johnson brings to his argument about Vietnam the whole weight of his audience's unhappy knowledge of World War II. Administration white papers developed Johnson's precedent argument by pointing toward the similarity of Hitler's promises with those of the Viet Cong: You give us this and we will ask for no more. But Hitler didn't keep his promise. Why should the Viet Cong?

Johnson's Munich precedent persuaded many Americans during the early years of the war and helps explain U.S. involvement in Southeast Asia. Yet many scholars attacked Johnson's reasoning. Let's analyze the Munich argument, using Toulmin's schema:

ENTHYMEME: The United States should not withdraw its troops from Vietnam because conceding to the Viet Cong will have the same disastrous consequences as did conceding to Hitler in Munich.

---

*From *Public Papers of the Presidents of the United States*, vol. 2, *Lyndon B. Johnson* (Washington, DC: GPO, 1965), 794.

CLAIM:	The United States should not withdraw its troops from Vietnam.
STATED REASON:	because conceding to the Viet Cong will have the same disastrous consequences as did conceding to Hitler in Munich
GROUNDS:	evidence of the disastrous consequences of conceding to Hitler at Munich: Hitler's continued aggression; his using of Czechoslovakia as a staging area to invade Poland
WARRANT:	What happened in Europe will happen in Southeast Asia.
BACKING:	evidence of similarities between 1939 Europe and 1965 Southeast Asia (for example, similarities in political philosophy, goals, and military strength of the enemy; similarities in the nature of the conflict between the disputants)
CONDITIONS OF REBUTTAL:	acknowledged differences between 1939 Europe and 1965 Southeast Asia that might make the outcomes different

Laid out like this, we see that the persuasiveness of the comparison depends on the audience's acceptance of the warrant, which posits close similarity between 1939 Europe and 1965 Southeast Asia. But many critics of the Vietnam War attacked this warrant.

During the Vietnam era, historian Howard Zinn attacked Johnson's argument by claiming three crucial differences between Europe in 1939 and Southeast Asia in 1965: First, Zinn argued, the Czechs were being attacked from outside by an external aggressor (Germany), whereas Vietnam was being attacked from within by rebels as part of a civil war. Second, Czechoslovakia was a prosperous, effective democracy, whereas the official Vietnam government was corrupt and unpopular. Third, Hitler wanted Czechoslovakia as a base for attacking Poland, whereas the Viet Cong and North Vietnamese aimed at reunification of their country as an end in itself.*

The Munich example shows again how arguments of resemblance depend on emphasizing the similarities between X and Y and playing down the dissimilarities. One could try to refute the counterargument made by Zinn by arguing first that the Saigon government was more stable than Zinn thinks and second that the Viet Cong and North Vietnamese were driven by goals larger than reunification of

---

*Based on the summary of Zinn's argument in J. Michael Sproule, *Argument: Language and Its Influence* (New York: McGraw-Hill, 1980), 149–50.

Vietnam, namely, communist domination of Asia. Such an argument would once again highlight the similarities between Vietnam and prewar Europe.

 FOR CLASS DISCUSSION

1. Consider the following claims of precedent, and evaluate how effective you think each precedent might be in establishing the claim. How would you develop the argument? How would you cast doubt on it?
   a. Don't vote for Governor Frick for president because governors have not proven to be effective presidents.
   b. Gays should be allowed to serve openly in the U.S. military because they are allowed to serve openly in the militaries of most other Western countries.
   c. Gun control will reduce violent crime in the United States because many countries that have strong gun control laws (such as Japan and England) have low rates of violent crime.

2. Advocates for "right to die" legislation legalizing active euthanasia under certain conditions often point to the Netherlands as a country where acceptance of euthanasia works effectively. Assume for the moment that your state has a ballot initiative legalizing euthanasia. Assume further that you are being hired as a lobbyist for (against) the measure and have been assigned to do research on euthanasia in the Netherlands. Working in small groups, make a list of research questions you would want to ask. Your long-range rhetorical goal is to use your research to support (attack) the ballot initiative by making a precedence argument focusing on the Netherlands.

WRITING A RESEMBLANCE ARGUMENT

 ## WRITING ASSIGNMENT FOR CHAPTER 12

Write a letter to the editor of your campus or local newspaper or a slightly longer guest editorial in which you try to influence public opinion on some issue through the use of a persuasive analogy or precedent. T. D. Hylton's argument against using sirens in radio commercials is a student piece written for this assignment (see p. 273).

Exploring Ideas

Because letters to the editor and guest editorials are typically short, writers often lack space to develop full arguments. Because of their clarifying and emotional power, arguments from analogy or precedent are often effective in these situations.

Newspaper editors usually print letters or guest editorials only on current issues or on some current problem to which you can draw attention. For this assignment look through the most recent back issues of your campus or local newspaper, paying particular attention to issues being debated on the op-ed pages. Join one of the ongoing conversations about an existing issue, or draw attention to a current problem or situation that annoys you. In your letter or guest editorial, air your views. As part of your argument, include a persuasive analogy or precedent.

Organizing a Resemblance Argument

The most typical way to develop a resemblance argument is as follows:

- Introduce the issue and state your claim.
- Develop your analogy or precedent.
- Draw the explicit parallels you want to highlight between your claim and the analogy or precedent.
- Anticipate and respond to objections (optional depending on space and context).

Of course, this structure can be varied in many ways, depending on your issue and rhetorical context. Sometimes writers open an argument with the analogy, which serves as an attention grabber.

QUESTIONING AND CRITIQUING A RESEMBLANCE ARGUMENT

Once you have written a draft of your letter or guest editorial, you can test its effectiveness by role-playing a skeptical audience. What follows are some typical questions audiences will raise about arguments of resemblance.

Will a skeptic say I am trying to prove too much with my analogy or precedent? The most common mistake people make with resemblance arguments is to ask them to prove more than they're capable of proving. Too often, an analogy is treated as if it were a syllogism or algebraic ratio wherein necessary truths are deduced (*a* is to *b* as *c* is to *d*) rather than as a useful but basically playful figure that suggests uncertain but significant insight. The best way to guard against this charge is to qualify your argument and to find other means of persuasion to supplement an analogy or precedent argument.

For a good example of an analogy that tries to do too much, consider President Ronald Reagan's attempt to prevent the United States from imposing economic sanctions on South Africa. Ronald Reagan wanted to argue that harming South Africa's economy would do as much damage to blacks as to whites. In making this argument, he compared South Africa to a zebra and concluded that one couldn't hurt the white portions of the zebra without also hurting the black.

The zebra analogy might work quite well to point up the interrelatedness of whites and blacks in South Africa. But it has no force whatsoever in supporting Reagan's assertion that economic sanctions would hurt blacks as well as whites. To refute this analogy, one need only point out the disanalogies between the zebra stripes and racial groups. (There are, for example, no differences in income, education, and employment between black and white stripes on a zebra.)

Will a skeptic point out disanalogies in my resemblance argument?   Although it is easy to show that a country is not like a zebra, finding disanalogies is sometimes quite tricky. As one example, we have already shown you how Howard Zinn identified disanalogies between Europe in 1939 and Southeast Asia in 1965. To take another similar example, during the Kosovo conflict critics of NATO policy questioned the NATO claim that Milosovic's "ethnic cleansing" of ethnic Albanians in Kosovo was analogous to Hitler's extermination of the Jews (see Case 1, p. 261). Although acknowledging the horror of Serbian atrocities, critics pointed out several disanalogies between the Serbs and the Nazis: (1) Jews in Germany and Poland were not engaged in a land dispute with the Germans, unlike ethnic Albanians, who wanted political control over Kosovo. (2) There was no Jewish equivalent of the Kosovo Liberation Army, which was committing terrorist acts against Serbs in Kosovo. (3) Although Germany was traumatized by its defeat in World War I, the Germans themselves were not recent victims of "ethnic cleansing," as were the Serbs in Croatia. (4) The Serbs were not motivated by a centralized philosophy of racial superiority supposedly grounded in evolutionary theory. (5) The Serbs' goal was to drive ethnic Albanians out of Kosovo, not to systematically exterminate an "inferior" race. Critics were not denying the evil of the Serbs' actions. But they held the Holocaust as a darker and "purer" form of evil, something of unique malignance not to be lumped in the same category as the ethnic wars in the Balkans or even the horrors of Pol Pot's killing fields in Cambodia or Stalin's massacre of the Russian peasants.*

---

*NATO's comparison of Kosovo to the Holocaust came during a decade when many scholars were reexamining the historical significance of the Holocaust. For an overview of these debates, see Karen Winkler, "German Scholars Sharply Divided over Place of Holocaust in History," *Chronicle of Higher Education* 27 May 1987, 4–5.

READINGS

Our first reading is a student argument written in response to the assignment on page 270. Notice how this student uses an analogy to analyze and protest an experience that has troubled her.

Don't Fake Sirens!

T. D. Hylton (Student)

As I drove down I-5 slightly over the 65-mph speed limit, I heard the scream of a siren. Naturally my adrenaline started to flow as I transferred attention from the road ahead to searching for the source of the howling siren. Then I realized my mistake: I had not heard a real emergency vehicle; I had heard a radio commercial. Distracted by the sound of the siren, I had put my fellow drivers at risk. The use of sirens in commercials has potentially dangerous consequences. We should not wait for a fatal car accident to ban such commercials. 1

Compare this type of commercial to a prank call. Pretend that your sister called you up, told you that a loved one had just died unexpectedly, and said that she would get back to you about details as soon as she heard. You would be upset, right? Your attention would no longer be focused on what you had been doing before the phone call. Then, after getting all worked up, pretend that your sister called you back and said it was all a joke. During the time you were distracted, something bad might have happened: You might have left the stove on high or failed to meet an important deadline at work. 2

While this case is more extreme than a radio commercial siren, hearing a siren while driving does release in us a flood of fears and anxieties. I suspect my reaction is typical: I start to think I did something wrong. Am I speeding? I instinctively look at my speedometer and begin braking. Then I start scanning the road, searching my rear-view mirror for flashing lights, and even pulling into the right lane. Flustered and distracted, I become momentarily a less safe driver. Then I realize that the commercial has played a joke on me. 3

Just as we would get mad at our sisters for a stupid prank, we should get mad at the commercial writers for fooling us with a siren. It is currently a crime to impersonate a police officer; it ought to be a crime to fake an emergency vehicle. Let's ban these distracting commercials. 4

Critiquing "Don't Fake Sirens"

1. What is the analogy in this piece?

2. How effective is this analogy? How does T. D. Hylton attempt to draw readers into her perspective?

The second and third readings were published respectively as a guest editorial and a letter to the editor in the *Seattle Times*. They are responses to proposals for stronger gun control laws following the Columbine High School massacre in Littleton, Colorado.

Creeping Loopholism Threatens Our Rights

Michael D. Lubrecht

1   Imagine for a moment that ethanol is recognized as a primary root of crime and social dysfunction in America. Not alcoholism, not drunken driving, not teen drinking, but ethanol, grain alcohol, booze.

2   To address the serious issues arising from the presence of ethanol in society, Congress passes "reasonable" legislation to ban malt liquor, reduce six-packs of beer to four-packs, and prohibit the import of fine French Bordeaux. When these "reasonable" efforts don't stop the problems, the search expands to find "loopholes" in the previous legislation and plug them. We limit the alcohol content in microbrews, require labeling changes on wine coolers, and ban the particularly evil double-malt Scotches. That doesn't work either.

3   The process goes on until there is no legal way left to purchase alcohol. The end result is functionally equivalent to Prohibition, and guess what—it didn't work. Alcohol abuse was rampant, crime soared and a new black market was created.

4   At least the misguided congressmen who engineered the original Prohibition had the courage to stand up and lay their principles on the line. Our current crop of gun-control proponents know that guns in the hands of law-abiding citizens do not increase criminal activity; in many demonstrated ways, they actually reduce crime. The current examples of gun prohibition in countries like Australia show astounding increases in violent crime when guns are removed from the citizenry.

5   But still, these proponents keep chipping away incrementally at, not criminal behavior, but the guns themselves—guns with bayonet lugs, guns that are inexpensive, guns that are painted black, guns that hold too many bullets, guns from other countries, guns that look too evil.

6   Before the Youth Violence Bill—with its "loophole filling" background checks, gunsmith licensing, and other misdirected contents—was even voted Yea or Nay, Rep. Rod Blagojevich (D–Ill.) introduced a new bill to restrict access to rifles in .50 caliber. These rifles, of course, are designed only for killing people.

7   Now, I could write a treatise advancing a plausible hunting sporting or self-defense justification for individual ownership of each and every weapon on the gun-banners' list, despite the fact that we "know" they are all really just death-dealing instruments of destruction. But I won't, for the simple fact is that the gun-control lobby's ultimate goal is the total prohibition of firearms. No matter what "reasonable" law is compromised on, there is another waiting in the wings, to add to the stack of restrictions.

8   It is time to stop defending the functionality, "sporting use" or other arbitrarily selected evil qualities of particular classes of firearms, stand fast, and say, "No More!"

Congress? If guns are the root of all evil, then let's see the House resolution to ban 'em all, right here, right now. If you really think restricting law-abiding citizens' access to particular types of guns will reduce crime in America, then banning them all should halt crime entirely. If you believe that restricting firearms possession by citizens who are too young or too poor will make the streets safer, then getting rid of all the guns will restore our streets to perfect safety. If restricting magazine capacity to 10 rounds will reduce homicides by some arbitrary number, then reducing their capacity to zero should result in a null homicide rate. 9

History will not agree with you, but let's try your social experiment. Summon up some backbone and ban them already. Show the character to reveal your agenda in one courageous piece of legislation and be done with it. 10

Or, come to your senses, address the real issues, leave guns and gun owners alone and stop this endless, senseless, pointless trend of creeping loopholism. 11

Violence Is a Symptom
(Letter to the Editor)
Rev. Marilyn Redmond

Editor, The Times:

Letters to the Editor and television shows discussing the shootings such as in Littleton, Colo., miss the point. *Guns don't kill people, people kill people.* 1

Violence is a symptom, like alcoholism is a symptom, of something deeper. We need to grow out of the denial and see the reality of pain and misery. These people have a medical condition called addiction. It needs medical treatment and therapy. 2

I speak from my 50 years of a violent childhood and marriage. Unless appropriate help is available from therapists and counselors who understand the imbalance—physically, mentally, emotionally and spiritually—recovery is not possible. 3

All the talk, laws and programs in the world will not heal an illness. A genetic, hereditary condition aggravated by generational conditioning needs analysis for the root causes, not superficial bandages of laws and blame from feeling powerless. 4

Without appropriate solutions, the epidemic will still erupt with other destructive substitutions, because the illness—a chronic and progressive condition—is not healed. Proactive responsible decisions create resolution and health. 5

Critiquing "Creeping Loopholism Threatens Our Rights" and "Violence Is a Symptom"

1. What analogy does each writer use in these pieces?

2. These pieces join the social controversy over gun control reinvigorated by the Columbine school shootings. What beliefs, assumptions, and values would an audience have to hold to accept the analogies of each writer? Do these arguments consider alternative views and speak to them? Do any disanalogies come to mind? How effective are these arguments for you?

Our last reading is from feminist writer Susan Brownmiller's *Against Our Will: Men, Women, and Rape.* First published in 1975, Brownmiller's book was chosen by the *New York Times Book Review* as one of the outstanding books of the year. In the following excerpt, Brownmiller makes an argument from resemblance, claiming that pornography is "anti-female propaganda."

From Against Our Will

Men, Women, and Rape

Susan Brownmiller

1   Pornography has been so thickly glossed over with the patina of chic these days in the name of verbal freedom and sophistication that important distinctions between freedom of political expression (a democratic necessity), honest sex education for children (a societal good) and ugly smut (the deliberate devaluation of the role of women through obscene, distorted depictions) have been hopelessly confused. Part of the problem is that those who traditionally have been the most vigorous opponents of porn are often those same people who shudder at the explicit mention of any sexual subject. Under their watchful, vigilante eyes, frank and free dissemination of educational materials relating to abortion, contraception, the act of birth, the female biology in general is also dangerous, subversive and dirty. (I am not unmindful that frank and free discussion of rape, "the unspeakable crime," might well give these righteous vigilantes further cause to shudder.) Because the battle lines were falsely drawn a long time ago, before there was a vocal women's movement, the anti-pornography forces appear to be, for the most part, religious, Southern, conservative and right-wing, while the pro-porn forces are identified as Eastern, atheistic and liberal.

2   But a woman's perspective demands a totally new alignment, or at least a fresh appraisal. The majority report of the President's Commission on Obscenity and Pornography (1970), a report that argued strongly for the removal of all legal restrictions on pornography, soft and hard, made plain that 90 percent of all pornographic material is geared to the male heterosexual market (the other 10 percent is geared to the male homosexual taste), that buyers of porn are "predominantly white, middle-class, middle-aged married males" and that the graphic depictions, the meat and potatoes of porn, are of the naked female body and of the multiplicity of acts done to that body.

3   Discussing the content of stag films, "a familiar and firmly established part of the American scene," the commission report dutifully, if foggily, explained, "Because pornography historically has been thought to be primarily a masculine interest, the emphasis in stag films seems to represent the preferences of the middle-class American male. Thus male homosexuality and bestiality are relatively rare, while lesbianism is rather common."

The commissioners in this instance had merely verified what purveyors of porn have always known: hard-core pornography is not a celebration of sexual freedom; it is a cynical exploitation of female sexual activity through the device of making all such activity, and consequently all females, "dirty." Heterosexual male consumers of pornography are frankly turned on by watching lesbians in action (although never in the final scenes, but always as a curtain raiser); they are turned off with a sudden swiftness of a water faucet by watching naked men act upon each other. One study quoted in the commission report came to the unastounding conclusion that "seeing a stag film in the presence of male peers bolsters masculine esteem." Indeed. The men in groups who watch the films, it is important to note, are *not* naked.   4

When male response to pornography is compared to female response, a pronounced difference in attitude emerges. According to the commission, "Males report being more highly aroused by depictions of nude females, and show more interest in depictions of nude females than [do] females." Quoting the figures of Alfred Kinsey, the commission noted that a majority of males (77 percent) were "aroused" by visual depictions of explicit sex while a majority of females (68 percent) were not aroused. Further, "females more often than males reported 'disgust' and 'offense.' "   5

From whence comes this female disgust and offense? Are females sexually backward or more conservative by nature? The gut distaste that a majority of women feel when we look at pornography, a distaste that, incredibly, it is no longer fashionable to admit, comes, I think, from the gut knowledge that we and our bodies are being stripped, exposed and contorted for the purpose of ridicule to bolster that "masculine esteem" which gets its kick and sense of power from viewing females as anonymous, panting playthings, adult toys, dehumanized objects to be used, abused, broken and discarded.   6

This, of course, is also the philosophy of rape. It is no accident (for what else could be its purpose?) that females in the pornographic genre are depicted in two cleanly delineated roles: as virgins who are caught and "banged" or as nymphomaniacs who are never sated. The most popular and prevalent pornographic fantasy combines the two: an innocent, untutored female is raped and "subjected to unnatural practices" that turn her into a raving, slobbering nymphomaniac, a dependent sexual slave who can never get enough of the big, male cock.   7

There can be no "equality" in porn, no female equivalent, no turning of the tables in the name of bawdy fun. Pornography, like rape, is a male invention, designed to dehumanize women, to reduce the female to an object of sexual access, not to free sensuality from moralistic or parental inhibition. The staple of porn will always be the naked female body, breasts and genitals exposed, because as man devised it, her naked body is the female's "shame," her private parts the private property of man, while his are the ancient, holy, universal, patriarchal instrument of his power, his rule by force over *her.*   8

Pornography is the undiluted essence of anti-female propaganda. Yet the very same liberals who were so quick to understand the method and purpose behind the mighty propaganda machine of Hitler's Third Reich, the consciously spewed-out anti-Semitic caricatures and obscenities that gave an ideological base to the Holocaust and the Final Solution, the very same liberals who, enlightened by blacks, searched their own conscience and came to understand that their tolerance of "nigger" jokes and portrayals of shuffling, rolling-eyed   9 servants in movies perpetuated the degrading myths of black inferiority and gave an ideological base to the continuation of black oppression—these very same liberals now fervidly maintain that the hatred and contempt for women that find expression in four-letter words used as expletives and in what are quaintly called "adult" or "erotic" books and movies are a valid extension of freedom of speech that must be preserved as a Constitutional right.

10   To defend the right of a lone, crazed American Nazi to grind out propaganda calling for the extermination of all Jews, as the ACLU has done in the name of free speech, is, after all, a self-righteous and not particularly courageous stand, for American Jewry is not currently threatened by storm troopers, concentration camps and imminent extermination, but I wonder if the ACLU's position might change if, come tomorrow morning, the bookstores and movie theaters lining Forty-second Street in New York City were devoted not to the humiliation of women by rape and torture, as they currently are, but to a systematized commercially successful propaganda machine depicting the sadistic pleasures of gassing Jews or lynching blacks?

11   Is this analogy extreme? Not if you are a woman who is conscious of the ever-present threat of rape and the proliferation of a cultural ideology that makes it sound like "liberated" fun. The majority report of the President's Commission on Obscenity and Pornography tried to pooh-pooh the opinion of law enforcement agencies around the country that claimed their own concrete experience with offenders who were caught with the stuff led them to conclude that pornographic material is a causative factor in crimes of sexual violence. The commission maintained that it was not possible at this time to scientifically prove or disprove such a connection.

12   But does one need scientific methodology in order to conclude that the antifemale propaganda that permeates our nation's cultural output promotes a climate in which acts of sexual hostility directed against women are not only tolerated but ideologically encouraged? A similar debate has raged for many years over whether or not the extensive glorification of violence (the gangster as hero; the loving treatment accorded bloody shoot-'em-ups in movies, books and on TV) has a causal effect, a direct relationship to the rising rate of crime, particularly among youth. Interestingly enough, in this area—nonsexual and not specifically related to abuses against women—public opinion seems to be swinging to the position that explicit violence in the entertainment media does have a deleterious effect; it makes violence commonplace, numbingly routine and no longer morally shocking.

13   More to the point, those who call for a curtailment of scenes of violence in movies and on television in the name of sensitivity, good taste and what's best for our children are not accused of being pro-censorship or against freedom of speech. Similarly, minority group organizations, black, Hispanic, Japanese, Italian, Jewish, or American Indian, that campaign against ethnic slurs and demeaning portrayals in movies, on television shows and in commercials are perceived as waging a just political fight, for if a minority group claims to be offended by a specific portrayal, be it Little Black Sambo or the Frito Bandito, and relates it to a history of ridicule and oppression, few liberals would dare to trot out a Constitutional argument in theoretical opposition, not if they wish to maintain their liberal credentials. Yet when it comes to the treatment of women, the liberal consciousness remains fiercely obdurate, refusing to be budged, for the sin of appearing square or prissy in the age of the so-called sexual revolution has become the worst offense of all.

Critiquing the Passage from *Against Our Will: Men, Women, and Rape*

1. Summarize Brownmiller's argument in your own words.

2. Brownmiller states that pornography degrades and humiliates women the same way that anti-Semitic literature degrades and humiliates Jews or that myths of black inferiority degrade and humiliate blacks. According to Brownmiller, how does pornography degrade and humiliate women?

3. What disanalogies might a skeptic point out between pornography and anti-Semitic or other racist propaganda?

4. One reviewer of Brownmiller's book said, "Get into this book and hardly a single thought to do with sex will come out the way it was." How does this passage from Brownmiller contribute to a public conversation about sexuality? What is thought provoking about this passage? How does it cause you to view sex differently?

13 Evaluation Arguments

X Is (Is Not) a Good Y

CASE 1

A young engineer has advanced to the level of a design group leader. She is now being considered for promotion to a management position. Her present supervisor is asked to write a report evaluating her as a prospective manager. He is asked to pay particular attention to four criteria: technical competence, leadership, interpersonal skills, and communication skills.

CASE 2

The federal government has long contemplated reforming the federal tax system. Many competing models have been proposed, each with characteristic strengths and weaknesses. How can one evaluate a tax system? What criteria should be applied? Murray Weidenbaum, an economic analyst for the *Christian Science Monitor,* proposed six criteria. The tax system, he said, should (1) be fair to the average taxpayer, (2) be understandable to the average tax payer, (3) eliminate costly loopholes, (4) promote savings and investment, (5) make it easier to start a new business, and (6) foster a strong, sustainable economy. According to Weidenbaum, any tax system that meets these criteria would be vastly superior to our present system.*

---

*Murray Weidenbaum, "How to Reform the Federal Tax System: Just the Basics, Please," *Christian Science Monitor* 18 July 1996.

AN OVERVIEW OF EVALUATION ARGUMENTS

In our roles as citizens and professionals we are continually expected to make difficult evaluations, to defend them, and even to persuade others to accept them. Often we will defend our judgments orally—in committees making hiring and promotion decisions, in management groups deciding which of several marketing plans to adopt, or at parent advisory meetings evaluating the success of school policies. Sometimes, too, we will be expected to put our arguments in writing.

Practice in thinking systematically about the process of evaluation, then, is valuable experience. In this chapter we focus on evaluation arguments of the type "X is (is not) a good Y" or "X is good (bad)" and on the strategy needed for conducting such arguments.* In Chapter 15, we will return to evaluation arguments to examine in more detail some special problems raised by ethical issues.

CRITERIA-MATCH STRUCTURE OF EVALUATION ARGUMENTS

An "X is (is not) a good Y" argument follows the same criteria-match structure that we examined in definitional arguments (see Chapter 10). A typical claim for such an argument has the following form:

X is (is not) a good Y because it meets (fails to meet) criteria A, B, and C.

The main structural difference between an evaluation argument and a definition argument involves the Y term. In a definition argument, one argues whether a particular Y term is the correct class in which to place X. (Does this swampy area qualify as a *wetland*?) In an evaluation argument, we know the Y term—that is, what class to put X into (Dr. Choplogic is a *teacher*)—but we don't know whether X is a good or bad instance of that class. (Is Dr. Choplogic a *good* teacher?) As in definition arguments, warrants specify the criteria to be used for the evaluation, whereas the stated reasons and grounds assert that X meets these criteria.

Let's look at an example that, for the sake of illustration, asserts just one criterion for "good" or "bad." (Most arguments will, of course, develop several criteria.)

ENTHYMEME: Computer-aided instruction (CAI) is an effective teaching method because it encourages self-paced learning. (The complete argument would develop other reasons also.)

---

*In addition to the contrasting words *good/bad*, a number of other evaluative terms involve the same kinds of thinking: *effective/ineffective, successful/unsuccessful, workable/unworkable,* and so forth. Throughout this chapter, terms such as these can be substituted for *good/bad.*

CLAIM:	Computer-aided instruction is an effective teaching method.
STATED REASON:	Computer-aided instruction encourages self-paced learning.
GROUNDS:	evidence that CAI encourages self-paced learning; examples of different learners working at different paces
WARRANT (CRITERION):	Self-paced learning is an effective teaching method.
BACKING:	explanations of why self-paced learning is effective; research studies or testimonials showing effectiveness of self-pacing
CONDITIONS OF REBUTTAL:	*Attacking stated reason and grounds:* Perhaps students don't really pace themselves in CAI.
	Attacking the warrant and backing: Perhaps self-paced learning isn't any more effective than other methods; perhaps the disadvantages of other features of CAI outweigh the value of self-pacing.

As this Toulmin schema shows, the writer needs to show that self-paced learning is an effective teaching method (the warrant or criterion) and that computer-aided instruction meets this criterion (the stated reason and grounds—the match argument).

GENERAL STRATEGY FOR EVALUATION ARGUMENTS

The general strategy for evaluation arguments is to establish criteria and then to argue that X meets or does not meet the criteria. In writing your argument, you have to decide whether your audience is likely to accept your criteria. If you want to argue, for example, that pit bulls do not make good pets because they are potentially vicious, you can assume that most readers will share your assumption that viciousness is bad. Likewise, if you want to praise the new tax bill because it cuts out tax cheating, you can probably assume readers agree that tax cheating is bad.

Often, however, selecting and defending your criteria are the most difficult parts of a criteria-match argument. For example, people who own pit bulls because they *want* a vicious dog for protection may not agree that viciousness is bad. In this case, you would need to argue that another kind of dog, such as a German shepherd or a Doberman pinscher would make a better choice than a pit bull or that the bad consequences of owning a vicious dog outweigh the benefits. Several kinds of difficulties in establishing criteria are worth discussing in more detail.

The Problem of Standards:
What's Commonplace or What's Ideal?

To get a sense of this problem, consider again Young Person's archetypal argument with Parent about her curfew (see Chapter 1). She originally argued that staying out until 2 A.M. is fair "because all the other kids' parents let their kids stay out late," to which Parent might respond: "Well, *ideally*, all the other parents should not let their kids stay out that late." Young Person based her criterion for fairness on what is *commonplace*; her standards arose from common practices of a social group. Parent, however, argued from what is *ideal*, basing her or his criteria on some external standard that transcends social groups.

We experience this dilemma in various forms throughout our lives. It is the conflict between absolutes and cultural relativism, between written law and customary practice. There is hardly an area of human experience that escapes the dilemma: Is it fair to get a ticket for going 70 mph on a 65-mph freeway when most of the drivers go 70 mph or higher? Is it better for high schools to pass out free contraceptives to students because the students are having sex anyway (what's *commonplace*), or is it better not to pass them out in order to support abstinence (what's *ideal*)? When you select criteria for an evaluation argument, you may well have to choose one side or the other of this dilemma, arguing for what is ideal or for what is commonplace. Neither position should be seen as necessarily better than the other; common practice may be corrupt just as surely as ideal behavior may be impossible.

The Problem of Mitigating Circumstances

When confronting the dilemma raised by the "commonplace" versus the "ideal," we sometimes have to take into account circumstances as well as behavior. In particular, we have the notion of *mitigating* circumstances, or circumstances that are extraordinary or unusual enough to cause us to change our standard measure of judgment. Ordinarily it is wrong to be late for work or to miss an exam. But what if your car had a flat tire?

When you argue for mitigating circumstances as a reason for modifying judgment in a particular case, you are arguing against the conditions of both common behavior and ideal behavior as the proper criterion for judgment. Thus, when you make such an argument, you will likely assume an especially heavy burden of proof. People assume the rightness of usual standards of judgment unless there are compelling arguments for abnormal circumstances.

The Problem of Choosing
between Two Goods or Two Bads

Not all arguments of value, of course, clearly deal with bad and good. Some deal with choosing between two bads or two goods. Often we are caught between a rock and a hard place. Should we cut pay or cut people? Put our parents in a nursing home or let them stay at home where they have become a danger to themselves? In such cases one has to weigh conflicting criteria, knowing that the choices are too much alike—either both bad or both good.

The Problem of Seductive Empirical Measures

The need to make distinctions among relative goods or relative bads has led many persons to seek quantifiable criteria that can be weighed mathematically. Thus we use grade point averages to select scholarship winners, MCAT scores to decide who gets into medical school, and student evaluation scores to decide which professor gets the University Teaching Award.

In some cases, such empirical measures can be quite acceptable. But they can be dangerous if they don't adequately measure the value of the people or things they purportedly evaluate. (Some people would argue that they *never* adequately measure anything significant.) To illustrate the problem further, consider the problems of relying on grade point average as a criterion for employment. Many employers rely heavily on grades when hiring college graduates. But according to every major study of the relationship between grades and work achievement, grades are about as reliable as palm reading when it comes to predicting life success. Why do employers continue to rely so heavily on grades? Clearly because it is so easy to classify job applicants according to a single empirical measure that appears to rank order everyone along the same scale.

The problem with empirical measures, then, is that they seduce us into believing that complex judgments can be made mathematically, thus rescuing us from the messiness of alternative points of view and conflicting criteria. Empirical measures seem extremely persuasive next to written arguments that try to qualify and hedge and raise questions. We suggest, however, that a fair evaluation of any X might require such hedging.

The Problem of Cost

A final problem that can crop up in evaluations is cost. In comparing an X to others of its kind, we may find that on all the criteria we can develop, X comes out on top. X is the best of all possible Ys. But if X costs too much, we have to rethink our evaluation.*

If we're looking to hire a new department head at Median State University, and the greatest scholar in the field, a magnificent teacher, a regular dynamo of diplomacy, says she'll come—for a hundred Gs a year—we'll probably have to withdraw our offer. Whether the costs are expressed in dollars or personal dis-

---

*We can avoid this problem somewhat by placing items into different classes on the basis of cost. For example, a Mercedes may come out far ahead of a Hyundai, but the more relevant evaluative question to ask is "How does a Mercedes compare to a Cadillac?"

comfort or moral repugnance or some other terms, our final evaluation of X must take cost into account, however elusive that cost might be.

HOW TO DETERMINE CRITERIA FOR YOUR ARGUMENT

Now that we have explored some of the difficulties you may encounter in establishing and defending criteria for your evaluation of X, let's turn to the practical problem of trying to determine criteria themselves. How do you go about finding the criteria you'll need for distinguishing a good teacher from a poor teacher, a good movie from a bad movie, a successful manager from an unsuccessful manager, a healthy diet from an unhealthy diet, and so forth?

Step 1: Determine the Category in Which the Object Being Evaluated Belongs

In determining the quality or value of any given X, you must first figure out what your standard of comparison is. If, for example, you asked one of your professors to write you a letter of recommendation for a summer job, what class of things should the professor put you into? Is he or she supposed to evaluate you as a student? a leader? a worker? a storyteller? a party animal? or what? This is an important question because the criteria for excellence in one class (student) may be very different from criteria for excellence in another class (party animal).

To write a useful letter, your professor should consider you first as a member of the general class "summer job holder" and base her evaluation of you on criteria relevant to that class. To write a truly effective letter, however, your professor needs to consider your qualifications in the context of the smallest applicable class of candidates: not "summer job holder," but "law office intern" or "highway department flagperson" or "golf course groundsperson." Clearly, each of these subclasses has very different criteria for excellence that your professor needs to address.

We thus recommend placing X into the smallest relevant class because of the apples-and-oranges law. That is, to avoid giving a mistaken rating to a perfectly good apple, you need to make sure you are judging an apple under the class "apple" and not under the next larger class "fruit" or a neighboring class "orange." And to be even more precise, you may wish to evaluate your apple in the class "eating apple" as opposed to "pie apple" because the latter class is supposed to be tarter and the former class juicier and sweeter.

Obviously, there are limits to this law. For example, the smallest possible class of apples would contain only one member—the one being evaluated. At that point, your apple is both the best and the worst member of its class, and evaluation of it is meaningless. Also, we sometimes can't avoid apples-and-oranges comparisons because they are thrust on us by circumstances, tradition, or some other factor. Thus the Academy Award judges selecting "best movie" aren't allowed to distinguish between "great big box office hits" and "serious little films that make socially significant points."

Step 2: Determine the Purpose
or Function of This Class

Once you have located X in its appropriate class, you should next determine what the purpose or function of this class is. Let's suppose that the summer job you are applying for is tour guide at the city zoo. The function of a tour guide is to make people feel welcome, to give them interesting information about the zoo, to make their visit pleasant, and so forth. Consequently, you wouldn't want your professor's evaluation to praise your term paper on Napoleon Bonaparte or your successful synthesis of some compound in your chemistry lab. Rather, the professor should highlight your dependability, your neat appearance, your good speaking skills, and your ability to work with groups. But if you were applying for graduate school, then your term paper on Bonaparte or your chem lab wizardry would be relevant. In other words, the professor has to evaluate you according to the class "tour guide," not "graduate student," and the criteria for each class derive from the purpose or function of the class.

Let's take another example. Suppose that you are the chair of a committee charged with evaluating the job performance of Lillian Jones, director of the admissions office at Clambake College. Ms. Jones has been a controversial manager because several members of her staff have filed complaints about her management style. In making your evaluation, your first step is to place Ms. Jones into an appropriate class, in this case, the general class "manager," and then the more specific class "manager of an admissions office at a small, private college." You then need to identify the purpose or function of these classes. You might say that the function of the general class "managers" is to "oversee actual operations of an organization so that the organization meets its goals as harmoniously and efficiently as possible," whereas the function of the specific class "manager of an admissions office at a small, private college" is "the successful recruitment of the best students possible."

Step 3: Determine Criteria Based
on the Purposes or Function
of the Class to Which X Belongs

Once you've worked out the purposes of the class, you are ready to work out the criteria by which you judge all members of the class. Criteria for judgment will be based on those features of Y that help it achieve the purposes of its class. For example, once you determine the purpose and function of the position filled by Lillian Jones, you can develop a list of criteria for managerial success:

1. Criteria related to "efficient operation"
   - articulates priorities and goals for the organization
   - is aggressive in achieving goals
   - motivates fellow employees
   - is well organized, efficient, and punctual
   - is articulate and communicates well

2. Criteria related to "harmonious operation"
   - creates job satisfaction for subordinates
   - is well groomed, sets good example of professionalism
   - is honest, diplomatic in dealing with subordinates
   - is flexible in responding to problems and special concerns of staff members

3. Criteria related to meeting specific goals of a college admissions office
   - creates a comprehensive recruiting program
   - demonstrates that recruiting program works

Step 4: Give Relative Weightings to the Criteria

Even though you have established criteria, you must still decide which of the criteria are most important. In the case of Lillian Jones, is it more important that she bring in lots of students to Clambake College or that she create a harmonious, happy office? These sorts of questions are at the heart of many evaluative controversies. Thus a justification for your weighting of criteria may well be an important part of your argument.

DETERMINING WHETHER X MEETS THE CRITERIA

Once you've established your criteria, you've got to figure out how well X meets them. You proceed by gathering evidence and examples. The success of the recruiting program at Clambake College can probably be measured empirically, so you gather statistics about applications to the college, SAT scores of applicants, number of acceptances, academic profiles of entering freshmen, and so forth. You might then compare those statistics to those compiled by Ms. Jones's predecessor or to her competitors at other, comparable institutions.

You can also look at what the recruiting program actually does—the number of recruiters, the number of high school visitations, the quality of admissions brochures and other publications. You can also look at Ms. Jones in action, searching for specific incidents or examples that illustrate her management style. For example, you can't measure a trait such as diplomacy empirically, but you can find specific instances where the presence or absence of this trait was demonstrated. You could turn to examples where Ms. Jones may or may not have prevented a potentially divisive situation from occurring or where she offered or failed to offer encouragement at psychologically the right moment to keep someone from getting demoralized. As with criteria-match arguments in definition, one must provide examples of how the X in question meets each of the criteria that have been set up.

Your final evaluation of Ms. Jones, then, might include an overview of her strengths and weaknesses along the various criteria you have established. You might say that Ms. Jones has done an excellent job with recruitment (an assertion you can support with data on student enrollments over the last five years) but was relatively poor at keeping the office staff happy (as evidenced by employee complaints, high turnover, and your own observations of her rather abrasive management style). Nevertheless, your final recommendation might be to retain Ms. Jones for another three-year contract because you believe that an excellent recruiting record is the most important criterion for her position at Clambake. You might justify this heavy weighting of recruiting on the grounds that the institution's survival depends on its ability to attract adequate numbers of good students.

FOR CLASS DISCUSSION

The following small-group exercise can be accomplished in one or two class hours. It gives you a good model of the process you will need to go through in order to write your own evaluation essay. Working in small groups, suppose that you are going to evaluate a controversial member of one of the following classes:

    a. a teacher
    b. a political figure
    c. an athlete
    d. a school newspaper or school policy
    e. a play or film or Web site
    f. a recent Supreme Court decision
    g. a rock singer or group or MTV video
    h. a dorm or living group
    i. a restaurant or college hangout
    j. an X of your choice

1. Choose a controversial member within one of these classes as the specific person, thing, or event you are going to evaluate (Professor Choplogic, the Wild Dog Bar, Eminem, and so forth).

2. Narrow the general class by determining the smallest relevant class to which your X belongs (from "athlete" to "basketball guard"; from "college hangout" to "college hangout for people who want to hold late-night bull sessions").

3. Make a list of the purposes or functions of that class, and then list the criteria that a good member of that class would have to have in order to accomplish the purposes.

4. If necessary, rank-order your criteria.

5. Evaluate your X by matching X to each of the criteria.

WRITING AN EVALUATION ARGUMENT

WRITING ASSIGNMENT FOR CHAPTER 13

Write an argument in which you try to change someone's mind about the value of X. The X you choose should be controversial or at least problematic. While you would be safe in arguing that a Mercedes is a good car or that smoking is bad for your health, your claim would be unlikely to surprise anyone. By *controversial* or *problematic*, we mean that people are likely to disagree with your evaluation or X, that they are surprised at your evaluation, or that you are somehow opposing the common or expected view of X. By choosing a controversial or problematic X, you will be able to focus on a clear issue. Somewhere in your essay you should summarize alternative views and either refute them or concede to them (see Chapter 8).

Note that this assignment asks you to do something different from a typical movie review, restaurant review, or product review in a consumer magazine. Many reviews are simply informational or analytical; the writer's purpose is to describe the object or event being reviewed and explain its strengths and weaknesses. In contrast, your purpose here is persuasive. You must change someone's mind about the evaluation of X.

Exploring Ideas

Evaluation issues are all around us, sometimes in subtle forms. The most frequent evaluation arguments occur when we place an X in its most common or expected class: Was Bill Clinton a good president? Is *Ally McBeal* a good TV drama? But more interesting and provocative evaluation issues can sometimes arise if we place X in a different class: Was Bill Clinton a good liberal? Is *Ally McBeal* a good feminist drama? Does *Ally McBeal* portray legal issues effectively? If you think again of the various communities to which you belong, chances are each community has disagreements over the evaluation of many Xs.

If no ideas come immediately to mind, try creating idea maps with spokes chosen from among the following categories: *people* (athletes, political leaders, musicians, clergypeople, entertainers, businesspeople); *science and technology* (weapons systems, word-processing programs, spreadsheets, automotive advancements, treatments for diseases); *media* (a newspaper, a magazine or journal, a TV program, a radio station, an advertisement); *government and world affairs* (an economic policy, a Supreme Court decision, a law or legal practice, a government custom or practice, a foreign policy); *the arts* (a movie, a book, a building, a painting, a piece of music); *your college or university* (a course, a teacher, a textbook, a curriculum, an administrative policy, the financial aid system); *world of work* (a job, a company operation, a dress policy, a merit pay system, a hiring policy, a supervisor); or any other categories of your choice.

Then brainstorm possibilities for controversial Xs that might fit into the categories on your map. As long as you can imagine disagreement about how to evaluate X, you have a potentially good topic for this assignment.

Once you have found an issue and have taken a tentative position on it, explore your ideas by freewriting your responses to the ten guided tasks in Chapter 3, (pp. 70–71).

Organizing an Evaluation Argument

As you write a draft, you might find useful the following prototypical structures for evaluation arguments. Of course, you can always alter these plans if another structure better fits your material.

Plan 1 (Criteria and Match in Separate Sections)

- Introduce the issue by showing disagreements about how to evaluate a problematic X (Is X a good Y?).
- State your claim.
- Present your criteria for evaluating members of class Y.
  State and develop criterion 1.
  State and develop criterion 2.
  Continue with the rest of your criteria.
- Summarize and respond to possible objections to your criteria.
- Restate your claim, asserting that X is (is not) a good member of class Y.
  Apply criterion 1 to your case.
  Apply criterion 2 to your case.
  Continue the match argument.

- Summarize and respond to possible objections to your match argument.
- Conclude your argument.

Plan 2 (Criteria and Match Interwoven)

- Introduce the issue by showing disagreements about how to evaluate a problematic X (Is X a good Y?).
- Present your claim.
  State criterion 1 and argue that your X meets (does not meet) this criterion.
  State criterion 2 and argue that your X meets (does not meet) this criterion.
  Continue with criteria-match sections for additional criteria.
- Summarize opposing views.
- Refute or concede to opposing views.
- Conclude your argument.

Revising Your Draft

Once you have written a rough draft, your goal is to make it clearer and more persuasive to your audience. Where might your audience question your claim, demand more evidence, or ask for further clarification and support of your criteria? One way to evaluate your draft's persuasiveness is to analyze it using the Toulmin schema.

Imagine that you are on a committee to determine whether to retain or fire Ms. Lillian Jones, the director of admissions at Clambake College (see details about Ms. Jones in our example on pages 286–88). You have been asked to submit a written argument to the committee. Here is how you might use Toulmin to suggest revision strategies for making your argument more persuasive (your thinking processes are indicated in italics):

ENTHYMEME:	Despite some weaknesses, Ms. Jones has been a good manager of the admissions office at Clambake College because her office's recruiting record is excellent.
CLAIM:	Ms. Jones has been a good manager of the admissions office at Clambake College.
STATED REASON:	Her office's recruitment record is excellent.
GROUNDS:	*My draft has statistical data showing the good results of Ms. Jones's recruiting efforts. Can I get more data? Do I need more data? Would other grounds be useful such as testimony from other college officials or comparison with other schools?*

WARRANT:	Successful recruitment is the most important criterion for rating job performance of the director of admissions.
BACKING:	*In my draft I don't have any backing. I am just assuming that everyone will agree that recruiting is the most important factor. But a lot of people are angry at Ms. Jones for personnel problems in her office. How can I argue that her recruitment record is the most important criterion? I could mention that maintaining a happy, harmonious staff serves no purpose if we have no students. I could remind people of how much tuition dollars drive our budget; if enrollments go down, we're in big trouble.*
CONDITIONS OF REBUTTAL:	*How could committee members who don't like Ms. Jones question my reason and grounds? Could they show that her recruitment record isn't that good? Might they argue that plenty of people in the office could do the same good job of recruitment—after all, Clambake sells itself— without stirring up any of the personnel problems that Ms. Jones has caused? Maybe I should add to the draft the specific things that Ms. Jones has done to improve recruiting.* *Will anyone attack my warrant by arguing that staff problems in Ms. Jones's office are severe enough that we ought to search for a new director? How can I counter that argument?*
QUALIFIER:	*I will need to qualify my general rating of an excellent record by acknowledging Ms. Jones's weaknesses in staff relations. But I want to be definite in saying that recruitment is the most important criterion and that she should definitely keep her job because she meets this criterion fully.*

QUESTIONING AND CRITIQUING AN EVALUATION ARGUMENT

To strengthen your draft of an evaluation argument, you can role-play a skeptic by asking the following questions:

Will a skeptic accept my criteria?   Many evaluative arguments are weak because the writers have simply assumed that readers will accept their criteria. Whenever your audience's acceptance of your criteria is in doubt, you will need to make your warrants clear and provide backing in their support.

Are my criteria based on the "smallest applicable class" for X?   For example, the film *The Blair Witch Project* will certainly be a failure if you evaluate it in the general class "movies," in which it would have to compete with *Citizen Kane* and other great classics. But if you evaluated it as a "horror film" or a "low-budget film," it would have a greater chance for success and hence of yielding an arguable evaluation.

Will a skeptic accept my general weighting of criteria?   Another vulnerable spot in an evaluation argument is the relative weight of the criteria. How much anyone weights a given criterion is usually a function of his or her own interests relative to the X in question. You should always ask whether some particular group affected by the quality of X might not have good reasons for weighting the criteria differently.

Will a skeptic question my standard of reference?   In questioning the criteria for judging X, we can also focus on the standard of reference used—what's commonplace versus what's ideal. If you have argued that X is bad because it doesn't live up to what's ideal, you can expect some readers to defend X on the basis of what's common. Similarly, if you argue that X is good because it is better than its competitors, you can expect some readers to point out how short it falls from what is ideal.

Will a skeptic criticize my use of empirical measures?   The tendency to mistake empirical measures for criteria is a common one that any critic of an argument should be aware of. As we have discussed earlier, what's most measurable isn't always significant when it comes to assessing the essential traits needed to fulfill whatever function X is supposed to fulfill. A 95-mph fastball is certainly an impressive empirical measure of a pitcher's ability—but if the pitcher doesn't get batters out, that measure is a misleading gauge of performance.

Will a skeptic accept my criteria but reject my match argument?   The other major way of testing an evaluation argument is to anticipate how readers might object to your stated reasons and grounds. Will readers challenge you by finding sampling errors in your data or otherwise find that you used evidence selectively? For example, if you think your opponents will emphasize Lillian Jones's abrasive management style much more heavily than you did, you may be able to undercut their arguments by finding counterexamples that show Ms. Jones acting diplomatically. Be prepared to counter objections to your grounds.

READINGS

Our first reading, by student writer Sam Isaacson, was written for the assignment on page 289.

Would Legalization of Gay Marriage
Be Good for the Gay Community?

Sam Isaacson (student)

1   For those of us who have been out for a while, nothing seems shocking about a gay pride parade. Yet at this year's parade, I was struck by the contrast between two groups—the float for the Toys in Babeland store (with swooning drag queens and leather-clad, whip-wielding, topless dykes) and the Northwest chapters of Integrity and Dignity (Episcopal and Catholic organizations for lesbians and gays), whose marchers looked as conservative as the congregation of any American church.

2   These stark differences in dress are representative of larger philosophical differences in the gay community. At stake is whether or not we gays and lesbians should act "normal." Labeled as deviants by many in straight society, we're faced with various opposing methods of response. One option is to insist that we are normal and work to integrate gays into the cultural mainstream. Another response is to form an alternative gay culture with its own customs and values; this culture would honor deviancy in response to a society which seeks to label some as "normal" and some as "abnormal." For the purposes of this paper I will refer to those who favor the first response as "integrationists" and those who favor the second response as "liberationists." Politically, this ideological clash is most evident in the issue of whether legalization of same-sex marriage would be good for the gay community. Nearly all integrationists would say yes, but many liberationists would say no. My belief is that while we must take the objections of the liberationists seriously, legalization of same-sex marriage would benefit both gays and society in general.

3   Let us first look at what is so threatening about gay marriage to many liberationists. Many liberationists fear that legalizing gay marriage will reinforce current social pressures that say monogamous marriage is the normal and right way to live. In straight society, those who choose not to marry are often viewed as self-indulgent, likely promiscuous, and shallow—and it is no coincidence these are some of the same stereotypes gays struggle against. If gays begin to marry, married life will be all the more the norm and subject those outside of marriage to even greater marginalization. As homosexuals, liberationists argue, we should be particularly sensitive to the tyranny of the majority. Our sympathies should lie with the deviants—the transsexual, the fetishist, the drag queen, and the leather-dyke. By choosing marriage, gays take the easy route into "normal" society; we not only abandon the sexual minorities of our community, we strengthen society's narrow notions of what is "normal" and thereby further confine both straights and gays.

4   Additionally, liberationists worry that by winning the right to marry gays and lesbians will lose the distinctive and positive characteristics of gay culture. Many gay writers have commented on how as a marginalized group gays have been forced to create different forms of relationships that often allow for a greater and often more fulfilling range of life experiences. Writer Edmund White, for instance, has observed that there is a greater fluidity in the relationships of gays than straights. Gays, he says, are more likely than straights to stay friends with old lovers, are more likely to form close friendships outside the romantic relationship, and are generally less likely to become compartmentalized into isolated

couples. It has also been noted that gay relationships are often characterized by more equality and better communication than are straight relationships. Liberationists make the reasonable assumption that if gays win the right to marry they will be subject to the same social pressure to marry that straights are subject to. As more gays are pressured into traditional life patterns, liberationists fear the gay sensibility will be swallowed up by the established attitudes of the broader culture. All of society would be the poorer if this were to happen.

I must admit that I concur with many of the arguments of the liberationists that I have outlined above. I do think if given the right, gays would feel social pressure to marry; I agree that gays should be especially sensitive to the most marginalized elements of society; and I also agree that the unique perspectives on human relationships that the gay community offers should not be sacrificed. However, despite these beliefs, I feel that legalizing gay marriage would bring valuable benefits to gays and society as a whole.   5

First of all, I think it is important to put the attacks the liberationists make on marriage into perspective. The liberationist critique of marriage claims that marriage in itself is a harmful institution (for straights as well as gays) because it needlessly limits and normalizes personal freedom. But it seems clear to me that marriage in some form is necessary for the well-being of society. Children need a stable environment in which to be raised. Studies have shown that children whose parents divorce often suffer long-term effects from the trauma. Studies have also shown that people tend to be happier in stable long-term relationships. We need to have someone to look over us when we're old, when we become depressed, when we fall ill. All people, gay or straight, parents or nonparents, benefit from the stabilizing force of marriage.   6

Second, we in the gay community should not be too quick to overlook the real benefits that legalizing gay marriage will bring. We are currently denied numerous legal rights of marriage that the straight community enjoys: tax benefits, insurance benefits, inheritance rights, and the right to have a voice in medical treatment or funeral arrangements for a dying partner.   7

Further, just as important as the legal impacts of being denied the right to marriage is the socially symbolic weight this denial carries. We are sent the message that while gay sex in the privacy of one's home will be tolerated, gay love will not be respected. We are told that it is not important to society whether we form long-term relationships or not. We are told that we are not worthy of forming families of our own. By gaining the same recognitions by the state of our relationships and all the legal and social weight that recognition carries, the new message will be that gay love is just as meaningful as straight love.   8

Finally, let me address what I think is at the heart of the liberationist argument against marriage—the fear of losing social diversity and our unique gay voice. The liberationists are wary of society's normalizing forces. They fear that if gays win the right to marry gay relationships will simply become imitations of straight relationships—the richness gained through the gay experience will be lost. I feel, however, this argument unintentionally plays into the hands of conservatives. Conservatives argue that marriage is, by definition, the union between man and woman. As a consequence, to the broad culture gay marriage can only be a mockery of marriage. As gays and lesbians we need to argue that conservatives are imposing arbitrary standards on what is normal and not normal in society. To fight the conservative agenda, we must suggest instead that marriage is, in essence, a contract of love and commitment between two people. The liberationists, I think, unwittingly feed into   9 conservative identification and classification by pigeonholing gays as outsiders. Reacting against social norms is simply another way of being held hostage by them.

10   We need to understand that the gay experience and voice will not be lost by gaining the right to marry. Gays will always be the minority by simple biological fact and this will always color the identity of any gay person. But we can only make our voice heard if we are seen as full-fledged members of society. Otherwise we will remain an isolated and marginalized group. And only when we have the right to marry will we have any say in the nature and significance of marriage as an institution. This is not being apologetic to the straight culture, but is a demand that we not be excluded from the central institutions of Western culture. We can help merge the fluidity of gay relationships with the traditionally more compartmentalized married relationship. Further, liberationists should realize that the decision *not* to marry makes a statement only if one has the ability to choose marriage. What would be most radical, most transforming, is two women or two men joined together in the eyes of society.

Critiquing "Would Legalization of Gay Marriage Be Good for the Gay Community?"

1. Who is the audience that Sam Isaacson addresses in this argument?

2. Ordinarily when we think of persons opposing gay marriage, we imagine socially conservative heterosexuals. However, Sam spends little time addressing the anti-gay marriage arguments of straight society. Rather, he addresses the anti-marriage arguments made by "liberationist" gay people. What are these arguments? How well does Sam respond to them?

3. What are the criteria Sam uses to argue that legalizing gay marriage would be good for the gay community?

4. How persuasive do you think Sam's argument is to the various audiences he addresses?

Our second reading, another student essay also written for the assignment on page 289, evaluates the Spice Girl phenomenon of the late 1990s. At the time this essay was written, Ginger Spice had just left the band. Critics predicted a quick decline of Spice Girl popularity.

The Spice Girls: Good at Marketing but Not Good for Their Market

Pat Inglenook (student)

1   When my eight-year-old sister asked for a Baby Spice talking doll (It plays Baby Spice's voice saying "In my bed I've got two teddies, a rabbit, two dollies," and "Fantastic. I love it."), and my eleven-year-old sister and her friends seemed to be dancing to Spice Girl CDs

all the time, I started to wonder about this strange relationship between capitalism and culture in the late 1990s. What is it about the Spice Girls—Ginger Spice, Posh Spice, Baby Spice, Scary Spice, and Sporty Spice—that has attracted mobs of screaming, hysterical girls, aged 7–14, and created for the Spice Girls a multi-million-dollar industry almost overnight? Clearly, my two sisters and their friends with their three-inch Spice Girl figurines ($3.99 each) and their seven-inch Spice Girl dolls ($7.99 each) and their Spice Girl Hair Play set, Nail Salon set, and Tattoo Graphix set ($9.97 each), to say nothing of the CDs ($16.85 each), have helped to support this industry. But why? As I have watched my sisters I have wondered, What is the fascination here? The Spice Girls do wear hip, hot-looking outfits, but the group's music is bubblegum for the brain. One critic says that the Spice Girl music is an "ideal hollow-commodity for a world increasingly obsessed with 'low': low-fat, low-sodium, low-calorie, low-IQ" (Crumley). Neither do they fare well in the category "actresses," where they won the anti-Oscar "Golden Raspberry Award" as "Worst Actress" for 1998. According to the judge, "They have the talent of one bad actress between them" ("Shiteworld").

So if we place the Spice Girls in the categories "musician" or "actress," they fail miserably. But if we evaluate them in the category "marketers," they obviously excel. They are excellent marketers because, in targeting a specific audience of preteen girls, they have shrewdly created an image that appeals to that audience's interests and psychological desires. 2

Their first mark of excellence is that they understand girl psychology, which wants sexy fashion without sex. As any good marketer knows, the younger part of the Spice Girls' target audience values Barbie dolls, and so the Spice Girls created a Barbie image of décolletage and fashion without any Madonna-like interest in real sex. In their film *Spice World,* the girls look music-video sexy, but they aren't seeking sex. When one of the directors tries to put some buff male dancers on the stage, the girls do an "Ick, Boys" routine and mock them. No real boy friends intrude on this Barbie doll world. 3

Instead of sex, the Spice Girls value an endless slumber party where giggling girls share secrets. In *Spice World,* they bond together like fun-seeking little girls on vacation from the grown-up world of responsibility represented by their manager. In this intimate little girl world, they look out for each other like Care Bears. They are even willing to miss their concert date to stay with their friend who is having a baby. 4

Another example of their marketing shrewdness is the way that the Spice Girls appeal to individualism and the belief that any self has many sides. Just as it was a calculatingly clever marketing move for the Barbie people to create an astronaut Barbie, a teacher Barbie, and a doctor Barbie, so was it brilliant to give each Spice Girl a different personality type and a different style of hot, sexy clothes. On any given day, your typical ten-year-old girl can live out her baby side, her posh side, her sporty side, her scary side, and her fun-loving Ginger side. 5

But their shrewdest marketing move is to create an illusion that a girl can be both a sex object and a liberated woman. Popular culture today pummels young girls with two contradictory messages. First, it tells girls to make themselves objects of sexual desire by being consumers of beauty and glamour products and purchasers of fashion magazines. Conversely, it tells girls to be liberated women, fully equal to men, with men's freedom and power and array of career choices. The Spice Girls, with their "girl power" logos on midriff 6

T's worn over micro-skirts, send both messages simultaneously. Their girl power side is acted out in *Spice World* by their defiance of the male authority figures. For instance, they "steal" a boat and go for a frolicking excursion on a speedboat. Later in the movie, their "heroic" bus ride (a parody of James Bond pursuit scenes) shows the girls having another adventure and taking control of their lives. Even their rise from poverty to fame in a music culture dominated by men demonstrates girl power. Their object-of-sexual-desire side is portrayed constantly by their sexy clothes and dance routines. The effect is to urge young girls to become capitalist consumers of beauty products while believing they possess power as girls. Girls get the same illusion when they comb the hair of their astronaut Barbies.

7   Despite the overwhelming marketing success of the Spice Girls, I question whether monetary gain should be the main measure of this cultural product. Furthermore, although the Spice Girls sell themselves as models for young girls and appear to succeed, are they promoting models that can and should be imitated?

8   Some people would say that combining sexuality and girl power is good and beneficial. Critics of feminism often complain that hard-line feminists want women to give up beauty and sex appeal. These critics don't like that de-sexed view of women. They think a truly liberated woman should be able to use *all* her powers, and some of this power comes from her being a sex object. This view would say that beauty pageant contestants, topless dancers, and even prostitutes could be liberated women if they use their sexuality to get what they want and if they feel good about themselves. From this perspective, the Spice Girls use their sexuality in the name of liberation. This view perhaps led the United Nations to send Geri Halliwell (the former Ginger Spice) to be an ambassador of goodwill for the United Nations Population Fund to promote contraceptives in Third World countries ("Church Attacks" A18).

9   But to me this argument doesn't work. I think the Spice Girls are confusing, even bad, models for helping young girls integrate sexuality and liberation. The sex is voyeuristic only. The Spice Girls flaunt their sexuality but don't show any signs of establishing healthy adult relationships. The projected scene of married life in *Spice World* shows fat or pregnant housewives bored out of their skulls—no love, no husbands, no families. Equally strange is the childbirth scene where the Spice Girls seem to know nothing about female bodies. It is closer to a stork delivery than to the real thing: no messy water, blood, and umbilical cords. The cherubic, powdered baby pops out like toast from a toaster.

10   The Spice Girl image sends all kinds of mixed messages, urging preteens to become sex objects while remaining little girls. I'm surprised that parents aren't up in arms (but they are the ones, of course, who supply the money that drives the Spice enterprise). In a review of *Spice World* from *Screen It: Entertainment Reviews for Parents,* the reviewers rated the movie "mild" for sex/nudity (parents were concerned primarily about naked male butts in one scene), and under the criteria "topics to talk about" they found almost nothing in the movie that needs discussion with one's children. On the lookout for things like visible nipples, sex scenes, and violence, parents have failed to see the unhealthy, fragmented, and warped view of womanhood the Spice Girls project to their young audience. Their strange clashing mixture of sexuality and liberation promotes confusion, not health.

Near the end of *Spice World* the girls are stopped by a cop who aims to give them a   11
ticket for reckless driving. Undaunted, they turn to Baby Spice, who gives Daddy Policeman
her best I'm-a-sorry-little-girl smile, and his heart melts. Rather than face the consequences
of choice making in an adult world, Baby Spice knows just the right daddy-pleasing gesture
to make all their troubles go away. I grant that the Spice Girls are great at marketing themselves, but I don't think their product is good for their market. Maybe soon all the Spice
Girl dolls and CDs in my house will be given away like other outgrown, faddish toys. I hope
the next pop cultural sensation aimed at preteen girls has more wholesome substance than
this mixture of illusory independence, sexiness, and lollipops.

Works Cited

"Church Attacks Ex-Spice Girl's Sex-Education Tour." *Seattle Times* 15 June 1999: A18.

Crumley, Bruce. "Spice Invaders." *Culture* Kiosque 12 June 1997. Paris. 23 Aug. 1999 <http://www.
  culturekiosque.com/nouveau/comment/rhespice.htm>.

Rev. of *Spice World,* dir. Bob Spiers. *Screen It! Entertainment Reviews for Parents.* 12 Jan. 1998.
  24 Aug. 1999 <http://www.screenit.com/movies/1998/spice_world.html>.

"Shiteworld: The Movies." *New Musical Express Online.* 23 Aug. 1999 <http://nme.com/newsdesk/
  19990222143334news.html>.

Critiquing "The Spice Girls: Good at Marketing but Not Good for Their Market"

1. Inglenook evaluates the Spice Girls in four different categories: musician,
actress, marketer, and role model. Explain how each category requires different
criteria for excellence.

2. What criteria does Inglenook use to argue that the Spice Girls are excellent
marketers? What criteria does she use to argue that the Spice Girls are not good
role models for preteen girls?

3. Why do you suppose that many parents have no objections to the Spice
Girls and in fact encourage Spice Girl adoration by doling out the money for Spice
Girls products? Similarly, why did the parents reviewing *Spice World* find it so
mild and nonobjectionable? Do you think Inglenook does a good job of persuading her audience that the Spice Girls are a bad influence on preteen girls?

4. How effectively does Inglenook summarize and respond to alternative
assessments of the Spice Girls?

Our third reading evaluates the B-2 stealth bomber, a highly controversial, incredibly expensive Air Force plane that made its military debut in the air war
against Yugoslavia during the Kosovo crisis. Carrying a crew of two persons, each
plane costs $2.1 billion. With its radar-absorbing black paint and its flat sawtooth
shape that deflects radar signals, the plane is nearly undetectable by enemy sur-
veillance. In an introductory sidebar, the author, Paul Richter, writing for the *Los*

Angeles Times, states: "Once mocked as the Pentagon's ultimate boondoggle, the B-2 is suddenly looking like the answer to the kind of conflict the U.S. has faced in the Balkans and the Persian Gulf."

Stealth Bomber Proves Its Mettle

Paul Richter

1   KNOB KNOSTER, Mo.—Two years ago, an Air Force ground crew rolled a B-2 stealth bomber from a hanger here and hosed it down before a skeptical civilian audience to settle a question: Would an afternoon cloudburst melt the bomber's delicate skin and knock the plane out of the sky?

2   These days when the B-2 emerges from its shelter at Whitman Air Force Base, onlookers ponder a far different question: Is a plane once mocked by critics as the Pentagon's ultimate boondoggle about to become America's weapon of choice in the early 21st century?

3   The most expensive and controversial warplane ever built, the B-2 has undergone a stunning reversal of fortune with its combat debut in the air war against Yugoslavia. With its radar-evading capacity and huge payload, the bat-winged bomber is suddenly looking like the answer to the kind of military emergencies that the U.S. has encountered in the Balkans, the Persian Gulf and the terrorist training camps of Afghanistan.

4   With only 24 hours' notice and apparently minimal risk to its crew, the B-2 can accurately drop as many as 16 2,000-pound bombs on heavily guarded targets in any corner of the world. The B-1 bomber is faster, and the 37-year-old B-52 can carry more bombs, but the B-2's stealth qualities give the Air Force the ability to strike anywhere before the enemy knows an attack is underway.

Technological Success Story

5   Although some technical questions remain, the B-2 in many circumstances can strike with more speed and punch than the cruise missiles that have become the hallmark of the Clinton administration's approach to warfare.

6   Some military officers, including Air Force Lt. Gen. Michael Short, U.S. air commander in the Kosovo campaign, have called the B-2 and its all-weather, satellite-guided bombing system the greatest technology success story of Operation Allied Force. They are predicting that America's regional military commanders, who are cautious about using unproved systems and who delayed the B-2's debut for months, will now turn to it regularly.

7   Development of the B-2 began in 1981 in the early days of President Reagan's arms buildup. The Pentagon's objective was to acquire a heavy nuclear bomber that, barely visible to radar, could penetrate Soviet air defenses to destroy elusive mobile nuclear missiles.

8   The sleek plane, shaped like a boomerang, has a wingspan of 172 feet and a length of only 69 feet. Its tailless, horizontal design, radar-absorbing plastic composite skin and other features make it very hard to track with radar. It is also tough to find with sensors that pick up heat, sound or electromagnetic impulses.

The Toughest Targets

The B-2 was used from the first night of the airstrikes on Yugoslavia to smash well-protected and fixed targets, including air defenses that put other NATO planes at risk.   9

Flying in pairs on a 30-hour round-trip mission from Whitman Air Force Base 60 miles   10
southeast of Kansas City, the B-2s smashed Yugoslav command bunkers, radar installations, communications sites, bridges, arms factories and other heavily defended targets. The B-2s were refueled in the air twice each way.

The B-2's mission was to "go in after the highest threat and the hardest targets," said   11
Air Force Brig. Gen. Leroy Barnidge Jr., commander of the 509th Bomber Wing, which includes all the B-2s.

A major ingredient in the B-2's successful combat debut is a new technology that uses   12
satellite guidance to direct bombs to their targets. Unlike laser munitions, which are disabled by clouds, these Joint Direct Attack Munitions can be dropped under any weather conditions.

As a result, the B-2s were sometimes the only bombers on the attack during frequent   13
bouts of bad weather that hampered the air campaign through much of April.

Overall, the six B-2s used in the war flew about 50 missions, less than 1 percent of the   14
total. But they dropped about 11 percent of the bombs used, nearly 700.

Stealth and Accuracy

Defense officials have declined to release a full list of the plane's targets. But they have   15
disclosed that it was a B-2 that dropped three bombs on the Chinese Embassy in Belgrade, killing three people.

The blunder was not a mistake by the air crew but rather by NATO strike planners,   16
who mistakenly thought they were striking a military supply center nearby.

The mission illustrates that the airplane was considered stealthy enough and accurate   17
enough to be sent against sites in congested downtown Belgrade, where air defenses were formidable and the risk of unintended damage was high.

Andrew Krepinevitch, executive director of the Center for Strategic and Budgetary Assessments, a nonpartisan defense think tank, praises the B-2's performance in the Balkans   18
but says the "jury is still out" on some key technological issues.

Also, some senior military officials say the Pentagon's regional commanders will be cautious in calling the B-2 into service because the cost of the plane is so high it is considered   19
a "national asset."

"No one wants to be the first to lose a B-2," said one Pentagon planner.   20

The Bomber's Assets

Nevertheless, even some longtime critics acknowledge that the B-2's debut proved the   21
plane has a combination of assets that will make it highly attractive to military leaders:

- It can be flown from the U.S. heartland, at a time when it is increasingly difficult to find forward bases for U.S. aircraft.

- With a turnaround time of 24 or more hours, it often can reach faraway targets faster than Tomahawk cruise missiles, which are carried on ships that sometimes take days to steam into position.

- And its radar-evading capacity, although not conclusively proved in the Kosovo air war, is doubted by few. Experts predict that the B-2's stealthiness will be valued more and more as politicians' tolerance for casualties declines.

22   The advent of the B-2, said William Arkin, an air-power expert, has now "really eclipsed the era of the cruise missile."

23   A key ingredient is the B-2's sophisticated radar targeting system, considered the best of its kind, that gives the pilots nearly photo-quality pictures of the targets they are about to hit. The pilots compare this information to spy-satellite images and correct the targeting data loaded into their bombs.

24   "The real capability is the fliers, and all the people who plan the mission," said Gen. Ronald Marcotte, the 8th Air Force commander who oversees all U.S. heavy bombers.

Pilots as Problem-Solvers

25   The 51 B-2 pilots are picked in a competitive selection process somewhat like the one used to choose astronauts. The Air Force does not want hot-dog fighter jocks piloting its B-2s; it is looking instead for sober fliers in their 30s.

26   Their most important skill is not what they can do with the joystick—there is little need to manually steer the highly automated B-2, even in combat, pilots said. Rather, the Air Force wants pilots with good judgment and analytical problem-solving skills.

27   During the airstrikes against Yugoslavia, the pilots often used their judgment to calibrate bomb fuses to destroy the intended targets without causing excessive collateral damage. Instead of setting the fuse to detonate the bomb several feet above ground, which would cause maximum destruction, pilots often delayed detonation for several milliseconds, to put off the explosion until the bomb's nose was buried in the ground.

28   The B-2's capabilities send a clear and powerful message to adversaries, said one B-2 pilot: "If the United States is angry enough, they can go anywhere in the world—you won't even know they're coming—to strike you."

Critiquing "Stealth Bomber Proves Its Mettle"

1. Critics of the military often attack the Pentagon's penchant for expensive weapons and runaway costs (jokes about thousand-dollar toilet seats and five-hundred-dollar hammers abound). The B-2 stealth bomber was bitterly opposed by critics because of its cost. Yet Richter argues that the plane may be worth it. What criteria does Richter use for his evaluation of the B-2? In your own words, summarize his argument.

2. How does Richter justify and defend these criteria? How do these criteria relate specifically to war in a post-Cold War era?

3. Theologians and philosophers raised questions about whether the war in Kosovo was a "just war." One of the questions raised was whether it was just that no NATO or U.S. soldiers were killed in the war. Two pilots, reasonably safe in a two-billion-dollar plane, could drop tons of explosives on the enemy. Such air-power meant that NATO could wage war without using ground troops, even though many critics of the war argued that early use of ground troops might have prevented much of the suffering of the Kosovo refugees. Why do you suppose that, in Richter's words, "politicians' tolerance for casualties" has declined? How might the presence of the B-2 bomber have contributed to the way the war was fought?

Our final reading, "Eight Is Too Many: The Case against the Octuplets," is by Dr. Ezekiel Emanuel, the chair of the department of clinical bioethics at the National Institute of Health. The public, he observes, is always fascinated by multiple births, praising the miracle of life and the heroism of the parents. Dr. Emanuel, writing for the *New Republic,* attempts to reverse that evaluation.

Eight Is Too Many: The Case against Octuplets

Dr. Ezekiel J. Emanuel

Just like the McCaughey septuplets of Iowa, whose first birthday recently made head-lines in *People* magazine, the Chukwu octuplets of Texas have become a media spectacle. Daily bulletins detailing each child's respiratory status, ultrasound results, and other devel-opments fill the papers—not just the tabloids, but respectable outlets like the *New York Times* and the *Washington Post,* as well. Inevitably, writers describe the eight live births in glowing terms—amazing, wonderful, even a miracle; they describe the mother as the brave survivor of adversity; they portray the hard-battling physicians as heroes and champions.

But what are we all celebrating? Modern reproductive technologies have brought the miracle of children to many infertile couples, thereby producing enormous good. The McCaughey septuplets and Chukwu octuplets, however, represent too much of that good thing. They are the product of fertility technology misused—an error, not a wonder, and one that even the few public voices of skepticism seem not fully to appreciate.

First and most obvious, large multiple births lead to all sorts of medical problems, for mothers and children alike. Nkem Chukwu had to stay in the hospital for months prior to delivery, on a bed that tilted her nearly upside down. It's too early to know how well her surviving children will fare (one died seven days after birth), but the odds do not favor them. Among children born prematurely and weighing just two pounds or less—the largest of the Chukwu infants weighed one pound, eleven ounces at birth—breathing difficulties, brain damage, and fluid imbalances are not rare.

The result is a comparatively high level of infant mortality and, in the survivors, long-term complications. Studies of low-birth-weight children (not from multifetal pregnancies

1

2

3

4

but from premature births) have shown that approximately 20 percent have severe disabilities; among those weighing less than 750 grams (1.7 pounds) at birth, 50 percent have functional impairments. A recent study that followed these very small infants to school showed that up to 50 percent of them scored low on standardized intelligence tests, including 21 percent who were mentally retarded. In addition, nine percent had cerebral palsy, and 25 percent had severe vision problems. As a result, 45 percent ended up enrolling in special-education programs.

5   Equally important, but rarely articulated, are the emotional health risks children in multiple births face. Loving and raising children through the normal developmental milestones is enormously wonderful and rewarding. But it is also hard work. Raising children is not a sprint to a healthy birth but a marathon through variable terrain until the goal of independent adulthood. The real way to assess these miraculous pregnancies—indeed, any pregnancy—is whether they are ultimately good for children. Quite clearly, they are not.

6   Attending to the physical, emotional, intellectual, and social needs of children for 18 years is hard and demanding. For infants and toddlers there are the simple physical demands—feeding, changing diapers, bathing, chasing after them to prevent injuries. Then there are the emotional and intellectual demands—cuddling them, talking to them, responding meaningfully to their smiles and first words, reading books to them, playing with them and their toys, handling the tantrums, and so on. And, while the physical demands may lessen once children grow (although parents who often feel like chefs, maids, chauffeurs, and all-around gofers may disagree with that), the emotional and intellectual demands become more complex with time. Older children need help with homework, mediation of sibling rivalry, constructive discipline, support in the trials and tribulations of friendships, encouragement in their participation in sports and other activities, help in coping with losses and defeats, and guidance through the many pitfalls of adolescence.

7   It is challenging enough to balance the demands of one or two children of different ages and attend to their needs; it is simply not physically possible for two parents to do this successfully for seven children of the same age, even if one of the parents is a full-time caregiver. Regardless of the motivation, dedication, love, or stamina of these parents, the sheer limitations of time make it impossible for each of seven identically aged children to receive appropriate parental attention and affection.

8   Just ask yourself: Would you trade being born a healthy single or twin for being born one of the "miraculous" septuplets, even a healthy one? Most of us would probably say "no" because of parental attention we would have lost. And we would be right to think that way.

9   The McCaugheys' experience proves the point. They have been able to raise their septuplets for one year only because they can fall back on a veritable army of volunteers—scores of people with tightly coordinated schedules who assist in the food preparation, feeding, diapering, and care of the seven babies. Few families with quintuplets or more children can expect or rely on such community effort. (Indeed, a Washington, D.C., couple who recently bore quintuplets, had hardly any community help at all until some belated publicity highlighted the family's plight.) And, while the McCaugheys' community-wide effort appears to have worked for the first year of life, it's hardly a sure thing that the assistance will always be there. The first is the year when, despite the demands on time, parents are most

interchangeable and caregiving has the greatest, most unmitigated emotional rewards. The terrible twos and threes will try the patience and dedication of volunteers.

What's more, having multiple caregivers cannot fully substitute for parental time. 10 While it's true that many children do just fine spending large amounts of time in paid day care, where multiple providers care for them, these children at least have the chance to go home and have one-on-one parental time spread among just a few siblings, of different ages. (Having multiple caregivers also becomes more problematic as the children grow, because of child-rearing styles that may differ from those of the parents, particularly on issues like discipline.) This is not possible in the McCaughey or Chukwu families, and it never will be. Spending just 20 minutes a day focusing on each individual child—hardly a lavish amount—will take nearly two and a half hours each day. When competing with sleep, meals, shopping, and all the other demands of basic existence for a family with septuplets, this focused time is likely to disappear.

Remember, too, that, while the McCaughey septuplets seem to have brought together 11 a community to support their care, such children also impose significant costs on the community. It is now estimated that the hospital costs from birth to discharge (or death) for the Chukwu infants will exceed $2 million. And the health care costs don't stop after birth. Any complications—neurological, vision, or other problems—can drive the medical care costs sky-high. Plus, no one knows how much will be required for permanent problems that require ongoing special-education and other accommodations. Yes, there's health insurance. But health insurance exists to cover ill health and problems such as cancer, genetic defects, and accidents that are the result of random chance. The birth of octuplets, by contrast, is not a chance event; it is the result of deliberate actions (or inactions) by physicians, patients, and society. Remember, too, that financial resources are limited; money spent on octuplets is money not spent on other children with special health care and educational needs.

For these reasons, the standard of medical care is not to proceed with such large mul- 12 tiple births. But this raises legitimate ethical problems for many couples. The most common method for interrupting multiple pregnancies is "selective reduction"—that is, doctors abort some of the fetuses for the sake of the mother's health. Many people believe couples who agree to infertility treatments must not only be informed about—but should consent to—the potential need for selective reduction even before beginning the treatments. Yet this is clearly not an option for families like the McCaugheys and the Chukwus, who oppose abortion on religious grounds.

Fortunately, this issue doesn't have to be so morally knotty. In the usual treatment for 13 problems with egg maturation and release (this is what both the McCaughey and Chukwu families were treated for), doctors prescribe drugs such as human menopausal gonadotropin (hMG) or Clomiphene (commonly known as Clomid) to stimulate egg development. Then they administer an additional drug, human chorionic gonadatropin (hCG), to induce ovulation. Using measurements of estrogen and ultrasound monitoring, physicians can assess the number of egg follicles developing in the ovaries. If they observe too many developing follicles, making the likelihood of multiple fertilizations high, physicians can withhold the drugs necessary to stimulate ovulation and advise against intercourse or withhold sperm injection until the next cycle, when they can go through the process again. To be sure, that treatment process can be a little more frustrating for aspiring parents. And many couples are reluctant to skip a cycle because it wastes thousands of dollars on the drugs and treatments, usually out of their own pockets. But carrying septuplets to term has costs, too.

14   In the end, new laws or regulations won't fix this problem. The real solution is leadership by the medical profession and by the media. Reproductive specialists who care for infertile couples are not simply passive technicians following the orders of the parents. They are engaged professionals guiding important technology that can create great joy—but also great pain. Professionalism requires deliberating with the parents about the goals and purposes of the treatments; doctors should draw upon their experience to advise and strongly recommend the best course to the parents, which is to avoid large multiple pregnancies.

15   And the media must stop glorifying the septuplets and octuplets. We live in an era that measures success in terms of quantity, that thinks bigger is necessarily better, where the best is defined by size. The best movie is the one that makes the most money; the best law firm is the one with the highest billings; the best painting is auctioned for the highest price; and the best book is the best-selling book. But, in this case, bigger may not be better— indeed, it may actually be worse. The true miracle of birth is the mysterious process by which the fusing of an egg and a sperm can create in just nine months the complex organism that is an infant with the potential to become an independent, thinking, feeling, socially responsible adult. In this way, the millions of babies born each year are miraculous whether born of singleton, twin, triplet, or octuplet pregnancies. It is the wonder of each infant that we should celebrate.

Critiquing "Eight Is Too Many: The Case against Octuplets"

1. What criteria does Emanuel use in making his case against octuplets? In your own words, summarize his argument.

2. Emanuel's article raises numerous questions of value of the kind we treat in more depth in Chapter 15, "Ethical Arguments." What broad contemporary criteria for value is Emanuel objecting to in this argument? Specifically, what are the popular criteria for "best" (as in "best fertility treatment" or "best professional ethics"), and how does Emanuel hope to change these criteria?

3. Emanuel argues that octuplets are an "error," not a wonder—"the product of fertility technology misused." How convincing is Emanuel's argument? At what points does Emanuel summarize and respond to opposing views? How might defenders of the McCaugheys or the Chukwus and their doctors respond?

14 Proposal Arguments

We Should (Should Not) Do X

CASE 1

Many cultural commentators are alarmed by a new social disease brought on by addictive spending. Dubbed "affluenza" and "credititis," this disease is spreading through aggressive promotion of credit cards. Economic analysts are particularly concerned at the way credit card companies are deluging teenagers with credit card offers. Some argue that encouraging credit card debt among the young is highly irresponsible corporate behavior. In order to raise public awareness of the problem, a group of legislators proposes that the following warning label be placed prominently on all credit cards: "WARNING: Failure to research interest rates and credit cards may result in personal financial loss or possible bankruptcy."*

CASE 2

In response to the lack of African American, Latino, Asian American, American Indian, and other ethnic characters in new prime-time TV shows, Kweisi Mfume, president and CEO of the National Association for the Advancement of Colored People (NAACP), lobbies Congress and the Federal Communications Commission to correct this racial imbalance. Specifically, he proposes that the NAACP call for congressional hearings on "network ownership, licensing, and programming" to ensure that the four major broadcast networks include a fair representation of minorities in their prime-time TV shows. Mfume asserts that "The airwaves belong to the public. . . . African Americans make up 13 percent of the population; we feel that our presence should be appropriately reflected during prime time."†

---

*"Credit Cards: Wealth Hazard," *Seattle Times* 4 Feb. 1999, B2.

†"NAACP Attacks Four Major Networks," *Seattle Times* 12 July 1999, A3.

AN OVERVIEW OF
PROPOSAL ARGUMENTS

Although proposal arguments are the last type we examine, they are among the most common arguments that you will encounter or be called on to write. Their essence is that they call for action. In reading a proposal, the audience is enjoined to make a decision and then to act on it—to *do* something. Proposal arguments are sometimes called *should* or *ought* arguments because those helping verbs express the obligation to act: "We *should* do X" or "We *ought* to do X."

For instructional purposes, we will distinguish between two kinds of proposal arguments, even though they are closely related and involve the same basic arguing strategies. The first kind we will call *practical proposals,* which propose an action to solve some kind of local or immediate problem. A student's proposal to change the billing procedures for scholarship students would be an example of a practical proposal, as would an engineering firm's proposal for the design of a new bridge being planned by a city government. The second kind we will call *policy proposals,* in which the writer offers a broad plan of action to solve major social, economic, or political problems affecting the common good. An argument that the United States should adopt a national health insurance plan or that the terms for senators and representatives should be limited to twelve years would be examples of policy proposals.

The primary difference is the narrowness versus breadth of the concern. *Practical* proposals are narrow, local, and concrete; they focus on the nuts and bolts of getting something done in the here and now. They are often concerned with the exact size of a piece of steel, the precise duties of a new person to be hired, or a close estimate of the cost of paint or computers to be purchased. *Policy* proposals, in contrast, are concerned with the broad outline and shape of a course of action, often on a regional, national, or even international issue. What government should do about overcrowding of prisons would be a problem addressed by policy proposals. How to improve the security alarm system for the county jail would be addressed by a practical proposal.

Learning to write both kinds of proposals is valuable. Researching and writing a *policy* proposal is an excellent way to practice the responsibilities of citizenship. By researching a complex issue, by attempting to weigh the positive and negative consequences of any policy decision, and then by committing yourself to a course of action, you will be doing the kind of thinking necessary for the survival of a democratic society. Writing *practical* proposals may well be among your most important duties on the job. Writing persuasive practical proposals is the lifeblood of engineering companies and construction firms because through such proposals a company wins bids and creates work. In many companies, employees can initiate improvements in company operations through practical proposals, and it is through grant proposals that innovative people gain funding for research or carry on the work of volunteer and nonprofit organizations throughout our society.

THE GENERAL STRUCTURE AND STRATEGY OF PROPOSAL ARGUMENTS

Proposal arguments, whether practical proposals or policy proposals, generally have a three-part structure: (1) description of a problem, (2) proposed solution, and (3) justification for the proposed solution. In the justification section of your proposal argument, you develop *because* clauses of the kinds you have practiced throughout this text.

SPECIAL CONCERNS FOR PROPOSAL ARGUMENTS

In their call for action, proposal arguments entail certain emphases and audience concerns that you don't generally face with other kinds of arguments. Let's look briefly at some of these special concerns.

The Need for Presence

It's one thing for a person to assent to a value judgment, but it's another thing to act on that judgment. The personal cost of acting may be high for members of your audience. That means that you have to engage not only your audience's intellects but their emotions as well. Thus proposal arguments often require more attention to *pathos* than do other kinds of arguments (see pp. 141–51).

In most cases, convincing people to act means that an argument must have presence as well as intellectual force. An argument is said to have *presence* when the reader senses the immediacy of the writer's words. The reader not only recognizes the truth and consistency of the argument but experiences its very life. An argument with presence includes the reader in the writer's point of view—the writer's emotions, the force of the writer's personal engagement with the issue. It promotes the reader's assent to the writer's conclusions.

How do you achieve presence in an argument? There are a number of ways. For one, you can appeal directly to the reader's emotions through the effective use of details, brief scenes, and compelling examples that show the reader the seriousness of the problem you are addressing or the consequences of not acting on your proposal.

Additionally, writers can use figurative language such as metaphor and analogy to make the problem being addressed more vivid or real to the audience, or they can shift from abstract language to descriptions, dialogs, statistics, and illustrative narratives. Here is how one student used personal experience in the problem section of her proposal calling for redesign of the mathematics department's introductory calculus curriculum:

My own experience in the Calculus 134 and 135 sequence last year showed me that it was not the learning of calculus that was difficult for me. I was able to catch on to the new concepts. The problem for me was in the fast pace. Just as I was assimilating new concepts and feeling the need to reinforce them, the class was on to a new topic before I had full mastery of the old concept. [. . .] Part of the reason for the fast pace is that calculus is a feeder course for computer science and engineering. If prospective engineering students can't learn the calculus rapidly, they drop out of the program. The high dropout rate benefits the Engineering School because they use the math course to weed out an overabundance of engineering applicants. Thus the pace of the calculus course is geared to the needs of the engineering curriculum, not to the needs of someone like me who wants to be a high school mathematics teacher and who believes that my own difficulties with math—combined with my love for it—might make me an excellent math teacher.

By describing the fast pace of the math curriculum from the perspective of a future math teacher rather than an engineering student, this writer turned a non-problem into a problem. What before didn't look like a problem (it is good to weed out weak engineering majors) suddenly became a problem (it is bad to weed out future math teachers). Establishing herself as a serious student genuinely interested in learning calculus, she gave presence to the problem by calling attention to it in a new way.

The Need to Overcome People's Natural Conservatism

Another difficulty faced by a proposal maker is the innate conservatism of all human beings, whatever their political persuasion. One philosopher refers to this conservatism as the *law of inertia*, the tendency of all things in the universe, including human beings, to remain at rest if possible. The popular adage "If it ain't broke, don't fix it" is one expression of this tendency. Proposers of change face an extraordinary burden of proof. They have to prove that something needs fixing, that it can be fixed, and that the cost of fixing it will be outweighed by the benefits of fixing it.

The difficulty of proving that something needs fixing is compounded by the fact that frequently the status quo appears to be working. So sometimes when writing a proposal, you can't argue that what we have is bad, but only that what we could have would be better. Often, then, a proposal argument will be based not on present evils but on the evils of lost potential. And getting an audience to accept lost potential may be difficult indeed, given the inherently abstract nature of potentiality.

The Difficulty of Predicting Future Consequences

Further, most proposal makers will be forced to predict consequences of a given act. As we've seen in our earlier discussions of causality, it is difficult enough to argue backward from event Y in order to establish that X caused Y. Think how much harder it is to establish that X will, in the future, cause certain things to occur. We all know enough of history to realize that few major decisions have led neatly to their anticipated results. This knowledge indeed accounts for much of our conservatism. All the things that can go wrong in a causal argument can go wrong in a proposal argument as well; the major difference is that in a proposal argument we typically have less evidence for our conjectures.

The Problem of Evaluating Consequences

A final difficulty faced by all proposal arguments concerns the difficulty of evaluating the consequences of the proposal. In government and industry, managers often turn to a tool known as *cost-benefit analysis* to calculate the potential consequences of a given proposal. As much as possible, a cost-benefit analysis tries to reduce all consequences to a single scale for purposes of comparison. Most often, the scale will be money. Although this scale may work well in some circumstances, it can lead to grotesquely inappropriate conclusions in other situations.

Just how does one balance the money saved by cutting Medicare benefits against the suffering of the people denied benefits? How does one translate the beauty of a wilderness area into a dollar amount? On this score, cost-benefit analyses often run into a problem discussed in the previous chapter: the seductiveness of empirical measures. Because something can't be readily measured doesn't mean it can be safely ignored. And finally, what will be a cost for one group will often be a benefit for others. For example, if Social Security benefits are cut, those on Social Security will suffer, but current workers who pay for it with taxes will take home a larger paycheck.

These, then, are some of the general difficulties facing someone who sets out to argue in favor of a proposal. Although not insurmountable, they are at least daunting.

DEVELOPING A PROPOSAL ARGUMENT

Writers of proposal arguments must focus in turn on three main phases or stages of the argument: showing that a problem exists, explaining the proposed solution, and offering a justification.

Convincing Your Readers That a Problem Exists

There is one argumentative strategy generic to all proposal arguments: awakening in the reader a sense of a problem. Typically, the development of a problem occurs in one of two places in a proposal argument—either in the introduction prior to the presentation of the arguer's proposal claim or in the body of the paper as the first main reason justifying the proposal claim. In the second instance the writer's first *because* clause has the following structure: "We should do X *because* we are facing a serious problem that needs a solution."

At this stage of your argument, it's important to give your problem presence. You must get people to see how the problem affects people, perhaps through examples of suffering or other loss or through persuasive statistics and so forth. Your goal is to awaken your readers to the existence of a problem, a problem they may well not have recognized before.

Besides giving presence to the problem, a writer must also gain the readers' intellectual assent to the depth, range, and potential seriousness of the problem. Suppose, for illustration, that you wanted to propose a special tax to increase funding for higher education in your state. In trying to convince taxpayers in your state that a problem exists, what obstacles might you face? First of all, many taxpayers never went to college and feel that they get along just fine without it. They tend to worry more about the quality of roads, social services, elementary and secondary schools, police and fire protection, and so forth. They are not too convinced that they need to worry about professors' salaries or better-equipped research labs. Thus it's not enough to talk about the importance of education in general or to cite figures showing how paltry your state's funding of higher education is.

To convince your audience of the need for your proposal, you'll have to describe the consequences of low funding levels in terms they can relate to. You'll have to show them that potential benefits to the state are lost because of inadequate funding. Perhaps you can show the cost in terms of inadequately skilled graduates, disgruntled teachers, high turnover, brain drain to other states, inadequate educational services to farmers and businesspeople, lost productivity, and so forth. Or perhaps you can show your audience examples of benefits realized from better college funding in other states. Such examples give life to the abstract notion of lost potential.

All of this is not to say that you can't or shouldn't argue that higher education is inherently good. But until your reader can see low funding levels as "problematic" rather than "simply the way things are," your proposal stands little chance of being enacted.

Showing the Specifics of Your Proposal

Having decided that there is a problem to be solved, you should lay out your thesis, which is a proposal for solving the problem. Your goal now is to stress the feasibility of your solution, including costs. The art of proposal making is the art of the possible. To be sure, not all proposals require elaborate descriptions of the implementation process. If you are proposing, for example, that a local PTA chapter should buy new tumbling mats for the junior high gym classes, the procedures for buying the mats will probably be irrelevant. But in many arguments the specifics of your proposal—the actual step-by-step methods of implementing it—may be instrumental in winning your audience's support.

You will also need to show how your proposal will solve the problem either partially or wholly. Sometimes you may first need to convince your reader that the problem is solvable, not something intractably rooted in "the way things are," such as earthquakes or jealousy. In other words, expect that some members of your audience will be skeptical about the ability of any proposal to solve the problem you are addressing. You may well need, therefore, to "listen" to this point of view in your refutation section and to argue that your problem is at least partially solvable.

In order to persuade your audience that your proposal can work, you can follow any one of several approaches. A typical approach is to lay out a causal argument showing how one consequence will lead to another until your solution is effected. Another approach is to turn to resemblance arguments, either analogy or precedent. You try to show how similar proposals have been successful elsewhere. Or, if similar things have failed in the past, you try to show how the present situation is different.

The Justification: Convincing Your Readers That Your Proposal Should Be Enacted

The justification phase of a proposal argument will need extensive development in some arguments and minimal development in others, again depending on your particular problem and the rhetorical context of your proposal. If your audience already acknowledges the seriousness of the problem you are addressing and has simply been waiting for the right solution to come along, then your argument will be successful so long as you can convince your audience that your solution will work and that it won't cost too much. Such arguments depend on the clarity of your proposal and the feasibility of its being implemented.

But what if the costs are high? What if your readers don't think the problem is serious? What if they don't appreciate the benefits of solving the problem or the bad consequences of not solving it? In such cases you have to develop persuasive reasons for enacting your proposal. You may also have to determine who has the power to act on your proposal and apply arguments directly to that person's or agency's immediate interests. You need to know to whom or to what your power source is beholden or responsive and what values your power source holds that can be appealed to. You're looking, in short, for the best pressure points.

In the next two sections, we explain invention strategies you can use to generate persuasive reasons for proposal arguments and to anticipate your audience's doubts and reservations. We call these the "claim-type strategy" and the "stock issues strategy."

USING THE CLAIM-TYPE STRATEGY TO DEVELOP A PROPOSAL ARGUMENT

In Chapter 9 we explained how claim-type theory can help you generate ideas for an argument. Specifically, we explained how values claims often depend for their supporting reasons on the reality claims of category, cause, or resemblance. This principle leads to a powerful idea-generating strategy that can be schematized as follows:

Overview of Claim-Type Strategy

We should do X (proposal claim)

- because X is a Y (categorical claim)
- because X will lead to good consequences (causal claim)
- because X is like Y (resemblance claim)

With each of those *because* clauses, the arguer's goal is to link X to one or more goods the audience already values. For a specific example, suppose that you wanted insurance companies to pay for long-term psychological counseling for anorexia. The claim-type strategy could help you develop arguments such as these:

Insurance companies should pay for long-term psychological counseling for anorexia (proposal claim)

- because paying for such counseling is a demonstration of commitment to women's health (categorical claim)
- because paying for such counseling might save insurance companies from much more extensive medical costs at a later date (causal claim)
- because paying for anorexia counseling is like paying for alcoholism or drug counseling, which is already covered by insurance (resemblance claim)

Proposal arguments using reality claims as reasons are very common. Here is another example, this time from a famous art exhibit controversy in the early 1990s when conservatives protested government funding for an exhibition of homo-erotic photographs by artist Robert Mapplethorpe:

Taxpayer funding for the Mapplethorpe exhibits should be withdrawn (proposal claim)

- because the photographs are pornographic (a categorical claim linking the photographs to pornography, which the intended audience opposes)
- because the exhibit promotes community acceptance of homosexuality (a causal claim linking the exhibit to acceptance of homosexuality, which the intended audience opposes)
- because the photographs are more like political statements than art (a resemblance claim linking the exhibit to politics rather than art, a situation that the intended audience would consider unsuitable for arts funding)

Whatever you might think of this argument, it shows how the supporting reasons for a proposal claim can be drawn from claims of category, cause, and resemblance. Each of these arguments attempts to appeal to the value system of the audience. Each tries to show how the proposed action is within the class of things that the audience already values, will lead to consequences desired by the audience, or is similar to something the audience already values. The invention procedure can be summarized in the following way.

Argument from Category

To discover reasons by using this strategy, conduct the following kind of search:

> We should (should not) do X because X is _____.

Try to fill in the blank with an appropriate adjective (for example, *good, just, ethical, criminal, ugly, violent, peaceful, wrong, inflationary,* or *healing)* or noun (such as *an act of kindness, terrorism, murder, true art,* or *political suicide).* The point is to try to fill in the blank with a noun or adjective that appeals in some way to your audience's values. Your goal is to show that X belongs to the chosen class or category.

Here are examples:

Using a "Category" Search to Generate Reasons

- Our university should abolish fraternities and sororities *because they are elitist* (or "racist" or "sexist" or "an outdated institution" or whatever).

- Our church should start an active ministry to AIDS patients *because doing so would be an act of love* (or "justice" or "an example of spiritual courage" or whatever).

Argument from Consequence

To discover reasons by using this category, conduct the following kind of search:

> We should (should not) do X because X leads to these good (bad) consequences: _____, _____, _____, _____.

Then think of consequences that your audience will agree are good (bad) as your argument requires.

Here are examples, using the same claims as before:

Using a "Consequence" Search to Generate Reasons

- Our university should abolish fraternities and sororities *because eliminating the Greek system will improve our school's academic reputation* (or "fill our dormitories," "allow us to experiment with new living arrangements," "replace rush with a better first-year orientation," "reduce the campus drinking problem," and so forth).

- Our church should start an active ministry to AIDS patients *because doing so will help increase community understanding of the disease* (or "reduce fear and prejudice," or "bring comfort to the suffering," and so forth).

Argument from Resemblance

To discover supporting reasons by using this strategy, conduct the following kind of search:

We should (should not) do X because doing X is like _____.

Then think of analogies or precedents that are similar to doing X but currently have greater appeal to your audience. Your task is then to transfer to X your audience's favorable (unfavorable) feelings toward the analogy/precedent.

Here are examples:

Using a "Resemblance" Search to Generate Reasons

- Our university should abolish fraternities and sororities *because other universities that have eliminated the Greek system have reported good results* (or "because eliminating the Greek system is like leveling social classes to promote more democracy and individualism," and so forth).

- Our church should start an active ministry to AIDS patients *because doing so is like Jesus' ministering to the lepers, who were outcasts in their society in the way that AIDS victims are outcasts in ours.*

These three kinds of searches—supporting a proposal claim from the perspectives of category, consequence, and resemblance—are powerful means of invention. In selecting among these reasons, choose those most likely to appeal to your audience's assumptions, beliefs, and values.

FOR CLASS DISCUSSION

1. Working individually or in small groups, use the strategies of principle, consequence, and resemblance to create *because* clauses that support each of the following claims. Try to have at least one *because* clause from each of the categories, but generate as many reasons as possible. Don't worry about whether any individual reason exactly fits the category. The purpose is to stimulate thinking, not fill in the slots.

EXAMPLE

CLAIM:	Pit bulls make bad pets.
REASON FROM CATEGORY:	because they are vicious
REASON FROM CONSEQUENCE:	because owning a pit bull leads to conflicts with neighbors
REASON FROM RESEMBLANCE:	because owning a pit bull is like having a shell-shocked roommate—mostly they're lovely companions but they can turn violent if startled

a. Marijuana should be legalized.
b. Division I college athletes should receive salaries.
c. High schools should pass out free contraceptives.
d. Violent video games should be made illegal.
e. Parents should be heavily taxed for having more than two children.

2. Repeat the first exercise, taking a different position on each issue.

USING THE "STOCK ISSUES" STRATEGY TO DEVELOP A PROPOSAL ARGUMENT

An effective way to generate ideas for a proposal argument is to ask yourself a series of questions based on the "stock issues" strategy. Suppose, for example, you wanted to develop the following argument: "In order to solve the problem of students who won't take risks with their writing, the faculty at Weasel College should adopt a pass/fail method of grading in all writing courses." The stock issues strategy invites the writer to consider "stock" ways (that is, common, usual, frequently repeated ways) that such arguments can be conducted.

Stock issue 1: *Is there really a problem here that needs to be solved?* Is it really true that a large number of student writers won't take risks in their writing?

Is this problem more serious than other writing problems such as undeveloped ideas, lack of organization, and poor sentence structure? This stock issue invites the writer to convince her audience that a true problem exists. Conversely, an opponent to the proposal might argue that a true problem does not exist.

Stock issue 2: *Will the proposed solution really solve this problem?* Is it true that a pass/fail grading system will cause students to take more risks with their writing? Will more interesting, surprising, and creative essays result from pass/fail grading? Or will students simply put less effort into their writing? This stock issue prompts a supporter to demonstrate that the proposal will solve the problem; in contrast, it prompts the opponent to show that the proposal won't work.

Stock issue 3: *Can the problem be solved more simply without disturbing the status quo?* An opponent of the proposal might agree that a problem exists and that the proposed solution might solve it. However, the opponent might say, "Are there not less radical ways to solve this problem? If we want more creative and risk-taking student essays, can't we just change our grading criteria so that we reward risky papers and penalize conventional ones?" This stock issue prompts supporters to show that *only* the proposed solution will solve the problem and that no minor tinkering with the status quo will be adequate. Conversely, opponents will argue that the problem can be solved without acting on the proposal.

Stock issue 4: *Is the proposed solution really practical? Does it stand a chance of actually being enacted?* Here an opponent to the proposal might agree that the proposal would work but that it involves pie-in-the-sky idealism. Nobody will vote to change the existing system so radically; therefore, it is a waste of our time to debate it. Following this prompt, supporters would have to argue that pass/fail grading is workable and that enough faculty members are disposed to it that the proposal is worth debating. Opponents might argue that the faculty at Weasel College is so traditional that pass/fail has utterly no chance of being accepted, despite its merits.

Stock issue 5: *What will be the unforeseen positive and negative consequences of the proposal?* Suppose we do adopt a pass/fail system. What positive or negative consequences might occur that are different from what we at first predicted? Using this prompt, an opponent might argue that pass/fail grading will reduce the effort put forth by students and that the long-range effect will be writing of even lower quality than we have now. Supporters would try to find positive consequences—perhaps a new love of writing for its own sake rather than the sake of a grade.

FOR CLASS DISCUSSION

The following collaborative task takes approximately two class days to complete. The exercise takes you through the process of creating a proposal argument.

1. In small groups, identify and list several major problems facing students in your college or university.

2. Decide among yourselves which are the most important of these problems and rank them in order of importance.

3. Take your group's number one problem and explore answers to the following questions. Group recorders should be prepared to present your group's answers to the class as a whole:
   a. Why is the problem a problem?
   b. For whom is the problem a problem?
   c. How will these people suffer if the problem is not solved? (Give specific examples.)
   d. Who has the power to solve the problem?
   e. Why hasn't the problem been solved up to this point?
   f. How can the problem be solved? (That is, create a proposal.)
   g. What are the probable benefits of acting on your proposal?
   h. What costs are associated with your proposal?
   i. Who will bear those costs?
   j. Why should this proposal be enacted?
   k. Why is it better than alternative proposals?

4. As a group, draft an outline for a proposal argument in which you
   a. describe the problem and its significance.
   b. propose your solution to the problem.
   c. justify your proposal by showing how the benefits of adopting that proposal outweigh the costs.

5. Recorders for each group should write their group's outline on the board and be prepared to explain it to the class.

WRITING A PROPOSAL ARGUMENT

WRITING ASSIGNMENT
FOR CHAPTER 14

OPTION 1: *A Practical Proposal Addressing a Local Problem* Write a practical proposal offering a solution to a local problem. Your proposal should have three main sections: (1) description of the problem, (2) proposed solution, and (3) justification. You may include additional sections or subsections as needed. Longer proposals often include an *abstract* at the beginning of the proposal to provide a summary overview of the whole argument. (Sometimes called the *executive summary*, this abstract may be the only portion of the proposal read by high-level managers.) Sometimes proposals are accompanied by a *letter of transmittal*—a one-page business letter that introduces the proposal to its intended audience and provides some needed background about the writer.

Document design is important in practical proposals, which are aimed at busy people who have to make many decisions under time constraints. Because the writer of a practical proposal usually produces the finished document (practical proposals are seldom submitted to newspapers or magazines for publication), the writer must pay particular attention to the attractive design of the document. An effective design helps establish the writer's *ethos* as a quality-oriented professional and helps make the reading of the proposal as easy as possible. Document design includes effective use of heading and subheadings, attractive typeface and layout, flawless editing, and other features enhancing the visual appearance of the document.

OPTION 2: *A Policy Proposal as a Guest Editorial* Write a two- to three-page policy proposal suitable for publication as a feature editorial in a college or city newspaper or in some publication associated with a particular group or activity such as a church newsletter or employee bulletin. The voice and style of your argument should be aimed at general readers of your chosen publication. Your editorial should have the following features:

1. The identification of a problem (Persuade your audience that this is a genuine problem that needs solving; give it presence.)

2. A proposal for action that will help alleviate the problem

3. A justification of your solution (the reasons why your audience should accept your proposal and act on it)

OPTION 3: *A Researched Argument Proposing Public Policy* Write an eight- to twelve-page proposal argument as a formal research paper, using research data for support. Your argument should include all the features of the shorter argument in Option 2 and also a summary and refutation of opposing views (in the form of alternative proposals and/or differing cost-benefit analyses of your proposal.) An example of a researched policy proposal is student writer Stephen Bean's "What Should Be Done about the Mentally Ill Homeless?" on pages 334–42.

Exploring Ideas

Since *should* or *ought* issues are among the most common sources of arguments, you may already have ideas for proposal issues. To think of ideas for practical proposals, try making an idea map of local problems you would like to see solved. For initial spokes, try trigger words such as the following:

- problems at my university (dorms, parking, registration system, financial aid, campus appearance, clubs, curriculum, intramural program, athletic teams)

- problems in my city or town (dangerous intersections, ugly areas, inadequate lighting, parks, police policy, public transportation, schools)

- problems at my place of work (office design, flow of customer traffic, merchandise display, company policies)

- problems related to my future careers, hobbies, recreational time, life as a consumer, life as a homeowner

If you can offer a solution to the problem you identify, you may make a valuable contribution to some phase of public life.

To find a topic for policy proposals, stay in touch with the news, which will keep you aware of current debates on regional and national issues. Also, visit the Web sites of your congressional representatives to see what issues they are currently investigating and debating. You might think of your policy proposal as a white paper for one of your legislators.

Once you have decided on a proposal issue, we recommend you explore it by trying one or more of the following activities:

- *Explore ideas by using the claim-type strategy.* Briefly this strategy invites you to find supporting reasons for your proposal by arguing that (1) X is a Y that the audience values; (2) doing X will lead to good consequences; and (3) doing X has been tried with good results elsewhere, or doing X is like doing Y, which the audience values.

- *Explore ideas by using the "stock issues" strategy.* You will raise vital ideas for your argument by asking the stock questions: (1) Is there really a problem here that has to be solved? (2) Will the proposed solution really solve this problem? (3) Can the problem be solved in a simpler way without disturbing the status quo? (4) Is the proposed solution practical enough that it really stands a chance of being acted on? (5) What will be the positive and negative consequences of the proposal? A fuller version of the stock questions is the eleven questions (a–k) in the third For Class Discussion exercise on page 319.

- *Explore ideas for your argument by completing the ten exploratory tasks in Chapter 3 (pp. 70–71).* These tasks help you generate enough material for a rudimentary rough draft.

Organizing a Proposal Argument

When you write your draft, you may find it helpful to have at hand some plans for typical ways of organizing a proposal argument. What follows are two common methods of organization. Option 1 is the plan most typical for practical proposals. Either Option 1 or Option 2 is effective for a policy proposal.

Option 1

- Presentation of a problem that needs solving:
    Description of problem
    Background, including previous attempts to solve problem
    Argument that the problem is solvable (optional)
- Presentation of writer's proposal:
    Succinct statement of the proposed solution serves as thesis statement
    Explain specifics of proposed solution
- Summary and rebuttal of opposing views (in practical proposals, this section is often a summary and rejection of alternative ways of solving the problem)
- Justification persuading reader that proposal should be enacted:
    Reason 1 presented and developed
    Reason 2 presented and developed
    Additional reasons presented and developed
- Conclusion that exhorts audience to act
    Give presence to final sentences.

Option 2

- Presentation of issue, including background
- Presentation of writer's proposal
- Justification
    Reason 1: Show that proposal addresses a serious problem.

323 / Proposal Arguments

Reason 2: Show that proposal will solve problem.
Reason 3: Give additional reasons for enacting proposal.
- Summary and refutation of opposing views
- Conclusion that exhorts audience to act

Revising Your Draft

As you revise your draft based on peer reviews and on your own assessment of its problems and strengths, consider using a Toulmin analysis to test your argument's persuasiveness. Recall that Toulmin is particularly useful for helping you link each of your reasons to your audience's beliefs, assumptions, and values.

Suppose that there is a debate at Clambake College about whether to banish fraternities and sororities. Suppose further that you are in favor of banishing the Greek system. One of your arguments is that eliminating the Greek system will improve your college's academic reputation. Here is how you might use the Toulmin system to make this line of reasoning as persuasive as possible.

CLAIM:	Clambake College should eliminate the Greek system.
STATED REASON:	because doing so will improve Clambake College's academic reputation
GROUNDS:	*I've got to provide evidence that eliminating the Greek system will improve Clambake's academic reputation. I have shown that last year the GPA of students in fraternities and sororities was 20 percent lower than the GPA of non-Greek students. What else can I add? I can talk about the excessive party atmosphere of some Greek houses, about the emphasis placed on social life rather than studying, about how new pledges have so many house duties that their studies suffer, about how new students think about rush more than about the academic life.*
WARRANT:	It is good for Clambake College to achieve a better academic reputation.
BACKING:	*I see that my draft doesn't have any backing for this warrant. How can I argue that it would be good to have a better academic reputation? Clambake would attract more serious students; its prestige would rise; it might attract and retain better faculty; the college would be a more intellectually interesting place; the long-range careers of our students might improve with a better education.*

CONDITIONS FOR REBUTTAL: *How would skeptics doubt my reason and grounds? Might they say that I am stereotyping Greeks? Might they argue that some of the brightest and best students on campus are in fraternities and sororities? Might they argue that only a few rowdy houses are at fault? Might they point to very prestigious institutions that have fraternities and sororities? Might they say that the cause of a poor academic reputation has nothing to do with fraternities and sororities and point instead to other causes? How can I respond to these arguments?*

How could they raise doubts about my warrant and backing? They probably wouldn't argue that it is bad to have a good academic reputation. They will probably argue instead that eliminating sororities and fraternities won't improve the academic reputation of Clambake but will hurt its social life and its wide range of living options. To respond to these arguments, maybe I should do some research into what happened at other colleges when they eliminated the Greek system.

QUALIFIER: *Should I add a "may" by saying that eliminating the Greek system* may *help improve the academic reputation of Clambake?*

As this example shows, thinking systematically about the grounds, warrant, backing, and conditions of rebuttal for each of your reasons can help you generate additional ideas to strengthen your first draft.

QUESTIONING AND CRITIQUING A PROPOSAL ARGUMENT

As we've suggested, proposal arguments need to overcome the innate conservatism of people, the difficulty of anticipating all the consequences of a proposal, and so forth. What questions, then, can we ask about proposal arguments to help us anticipate these problems?

Will a skeptic deny that my problem is really a problem? The first question to ask of your proposal is "What's so wrong with the status quo that change is necessary?" The second question is "Who loses if the status quo is changed?" Be certain not to overlook this second question. Most proposal makers can demonstrate that some sort of problem exists, but often it is a problem only for certain groups of people. Solving the problem will thus prove a benefit to some people but a cost to others. If audience members examine the problem from the perspective of the potential losers rather than the winners, they can often raise doubts about your proposal.

For example, one state recently held an initiative on a proposed "bottle bill" that would fight litter by permitting the sale of soda and beer only in returnable bottles. Sales outlets would be required to charge a substantial deposit on the bottles in order to encourage people to return them. Proponents of the proposal emphasized citizens as "winners" sharing in the new cleanliness of a landscape no longer littered with cans. To refute this argument, opponents showed consumers as "losers" burdened with the high cost of deposits and the hassle of collecting and returning bottles to grocery stores.

Will a skeptic doubt the effectiveness of my solution? Assuming that you've satisfied yourself that a significant problem exists for a significant number of people, a number of questions remain to be asked about the quality of the proposed solution to solve the problem. First, "Does the problem exist for the reasons cited, or might there be alternative explanations?" Here we return to the familiar ground of causal arguments. A proposal supposedly strikes at the cause of a problem. But perhaps striking at that "cause" won't solve the problem. Perhaps you've mistaken a symptom for a cause, or confused two commonly associated but essentially unlinked phenomena for a cause-effect relationship. For example, will paying teachers higher salaries improve the quality of teaching or merely attract greedier rather than brighter people? Maybe more good teachers would be attracted and retained if they were given some other benefit (fewer students? smaller classes? more sabbaticals? more autonomy? more prestige?).

Another way to test your solution is to list all the uncertainties involved. This might be referred to as "The Devil you know is better than the Devil you don't know" strategy. Remind yourself of all the unanticipated consequences of past changes. Who, for example, would have thought back in the days when aerosol shaving cans were being developed that they might lead to diminished ozone layers, which might lead to more ultraviolet rays getting through the atmosphere from the sun, which would lead to higher incidences of skin cancer? The history of technology is full of such cautionary tales that can be invoked to remind you of the uncertain course that progress can sometimes take.

Will a skeptic think my proposal costs too much? The most commonly asked question of any proposal is simply, "Do the benefits of enacting the proposal outweigh the costs?" As we saw above, you can't foresee all the consequences of any proposal. It's easy, before the fact, to exaggerate both the costs and the benefits of a proposal. So, in asking how much your proposal will cost, we urge you to make an honest estimate. Will your audience discover costs you hadn't anticipated— extra financial costs or unexpected psychological or environmental or aesthetic costs? As much as you can, anticipate these objections.

Will a skeptic suggest counterproposals? Related to all that's been said so far is the counterproposal. Can you imagine an appealing alternative to both the status quo and the proposal that you're making? The more clearly your proposal shows that a significant problem exists, the more important it is that you be able to identify possible counterproposals. Any potential critic of a proposal to remedy an acknowledged problem will either have to make such a counterproposal or have to argue that the problem is simply in the nature of things. So, given the likelihood that you'll be faced with a counterproposal, it only makes sense to anticipate it and to work out a refutation of it before you have it thrown at you. And who knows, you may end up liking the counterproposal better and changing your mind about what to propose!

READINGS

Our first reading, by student writer Jeffrey Cain, is a practical proposal for saving a neighborhood Jewish restaurant in Seattle, Washington. As a practical proposal, it uses headings and subheadings and other elements of document design aimed to give it a finished and professional appearance. When sent to the intended audience, it is accompanied by a single-spaced letter of transmittal following the conventional format of a business letter.

515 West Olympic Pl.
Seattle, Washington 98119

Martin _____
Owner, Bernie's Blintzes Restaurant
1201 10th Avenue
Seattle, Washington 98185

Dear Mr. _____:

Enclosed is a proposal that addresses Bernie's Blintzes' present economic trouble. It provides an inexpensive alternative to the $60,000 "makeover" plan proposed by the recently hired restaurant consultant. Having been an employee of Bernie's Blintzes for over three years, and having previously been an employee of a catering business, I hope that my observations will be of some interest and help to you.

In brief, my proposal suggests that investing $60,000 into a complete restaurant upgrade not only exposes you to unnecessary economic risk, but also fails to
build on Bernie's Blintzes' strengths and sixteen-year legacy. Instead, I propose that through the production and distribution of Bernie's Blintzes' chocolate chip cookies to area espresso stands and coffee shops, Bernie's Blintzes Restaurant can reestablish itself as a viable money-making business. Unlike the consultant's proposal, this plan recommends that Bernie's Blintzes build on what it has done well for sixteen years, preserving an important part of Seattle's Jewish culture—something I know that is important to you.

As a member of the Bernie's Blintzes staff, I share your interest in keeping the restaurant economically viable. I hope my thoughts are of some benefit. Thank you for your consideration.

Sincerely,

Jeffrey Cain

A Proposal to Save
Bernie's Blintzes Restaurant
Submitted to the Owner, Mr. Martin _____
Jeffrey Cain

Summary

This proposal argues that investing $60,000 in a complete restaurant upgrade   1
not only exposes the owners of Bernie's Blintzes to unnecessary economic risk, it
also fails to build on Bernie's Blintzes' strengths and sixteen-year legacy. Instead, I
propose that through the production and distribution of Bernie's Blintzes' chocolate
chip cookies to area espresso stands and coffee shops, Bernie's Blintzes Restaurant
can reestablish itself as a viable money-making business.

Problem

Bernie's Blintzes Restaurant is currently in financial crisis and must either   2
close its doors or substantially increase its sales and profits.

Background on Bernie's Blintzes Restaurant

For over sixteen years Bernie's Blintzes Restaurant has been serving   3
traditional kosher-style food in a family dining atmosphere in Seattle's Queen Anne
district. Known for its excellent matzoh ball soup, blintzes, potato latkes, pastrami
sandwiches, and giant chocolate chip cookies, Bernie's Blintzes remains one of
Seattle's only family-operated ethnic Jewish restaurants. In addition to providing
sit-down and take-out dining, Bernie's Blintzes also offers an extensive catering
service that has steadily grown since its inception five years ago.

During the past two years, however, a slow but constant decrease in   4
restaurant patronage has led to a decline in Bernie's Blintzes' sales and profits. In
an effort to reestablish their restaurant as a money-making business, the owners of
Bernie's Blintzes have employed the professional services of a restaurant
consultant. After three months of observation and study, the consultant identified
three areas that have led to Bernie's Blintzes' decline in patronage: (1) increased
competition with the addition of seven new restaurants in the neighborhood over
the past three years; (2) menu items that are out of fashion with health-conscious
consumers; (3) a lack of marketing and name familiarity—although Bernie's Blintzes
is well known around the neighborhood, few in the greater Seattle area would
recognize its name. As a remedy, the consultant has recommended a $60,000
restaurant upgrade, including a complete interior remodel, new menu, and an
advertising and marketing plan that would include changing the Bernie's Blintzes
name and logo. In short, the consultant envisions an entirely new restaurant:
rebuilding Bernie's Blintzes from the ground up.

Problems with the Consultant's Proposal

5   A continued loss of patronage would certainly force the owners of Bernie's Blintzes to discontinue their sixteen-year-old labor; yet the prospect of investing $60,000 into a completely "new" restaurant brings economic risk and great uncertainty. A $60,000 investment would require the owners to assume a second home mortgage, and there are certainly no guarantees that their investment would pay off. The owners are rightfully apprehensive. But putting economic considerations aside for the moment, the consultant's "ground-up" proposal also brings great uncertainty because it fails to build on Bernie's Blintzes' strengths in three significant ways.

6   First, increased competition is not necessarily a bad thing. Paragon consultants are correct in observing that new restaurants have brought more competition to Bernie's Blintzes' neighborhood, but these same new restaurants have also brought more potential customers. Bernie's Blintzes' sixteen-year tenure in the neighborhood is a strength that could lure some of the neighborhood's new visitors. A well-established restaurant is a welcome respite from today's ever-changing fast-food culture.

7   Second, a dated menu can be advantageous. While it may be true that consumers have become more health conscious, it is also the case that consumers have become more aware of ethnic cuisine—consider the popularity of Thai food. Bernie's Blintzes' traditional kosher-style menu is a rarity in Seattle and may be a welcome alternative to other more familiar ethnic foods, like Chinese or Mexican.

8   Finally, new isn't always better. The consultant rightfully recognizes that Bernie's Blintzes has poor name familiarity throughout the city; however, it does have strong name familiarity within its neighborhood. Changing Bernie's Blintzes' name, as the consultant's proposal calls for, would take away whatever name familiarity already exists, obscuring what for some is a local landmark.

9   A proposal that builds on Bernie's Blintzes' existing strengths could be less risky and certainly less expensive than the consultant's plan.

Proposal

10   This proposal is offered as a cost-effective, low-risk alternative to the consultant's plan that would utilize Bernie's Blintzes' existing facilities, build on its time-tested strengths, and maintain its traditional ethnic cuisine and character. The nucleus of this proposal involves the production and distribution of Bernie's Blintzes' chocolate chip cookies to area espresso carts and coffee shops. This plan

capitalizes on the popularity of Bernie's Blintzes' cookies and the booming espresso cart and coffee shop industry in Seattle.

Bernie's Blintzes' chocolate chip cookies are well known to customers as "the best coffee cookies in the world." This is because unlike other cookies, Bernie's Blintzes' cookies are a little harder than most, making them excellent for dipping into a hot cup of coffee. It is not unusual for customers to special-order a dozen cookies to have with their coffee at home, and at catering events the cookies quickly disappear when coffee is served.   11

Bernie's Blintzes' chocolate chip cookies are a perfect match for the booming coffee industry in the greater Seattle area. Espresso stands and coffee shops decorate nearly every public place in Seattle, from schools and gas stations to shopping malls and street corners. In addition to selling coffee products, these coffee vendors also sell pastries and sweets. Some carts sell in excess of 200 cookies a week. With very few companies currently distributing quality pastries to espresso carts, the potential for the owners of Bernie's Blintzes to tap into this new and growing market is excellent.   12

Because Bernie's Blintzes already has the means for cookie production, this plan could begin almost immediately. Presently, the restaurant experiences slow hours during the evening and in between lunches when restaurant employees, particularly kitchen staff, have little to do. During this slow time, employees could assist in the production of the chocolate chip cookies, particularly kitchen personnel. Orders for the cookies would be taken via phone or fax by employees who are already being paid. If cookie production exceeded the amount of time that employees who were already on the clock were available, then extended working hours could be offered to existing employees without having to hire new help, at least initially. Delivery would be made the following morning, within twenty-four hours. (The cookies would be delivered, until it became necessary to hire a new employee, by the owner—reducing costs and ensuring positive customer relations.)   13

At least initially, then, the labor cost involved in producing the cookies would be minimal. Therefore, the cookies could continue to sell at their present retail price of $.75, maintaining a $.45 net profit on each cookie. With this scenario, it may be possible to lower the wholesale price of the cookie to $.50. However, it is recommended that Bernie's Blintzes increase the retail price of its cookies to $1.00 instead, with a wholesale price of $.75. A random sampling of area espresso carts reveals that most carts market their cookies for $1.00 to $1.50, some as high as $1.75. In raising the retail cost of the cookie to $1.00 and the wholesale cost to $.75,   14

Bernie's Blintzes would be announcing its cookie as a "high-end" cookie that is competitively priced. Cookies at a wholesale price of $1.00 would realize a $.70 net profit.

15   Distribution to ten coffee carts that each sold 100 cookies a week would yield $700.00, weekly. Given the hundreds of coffee carts in the greater Seattle area, it is likely that Bernie's Blintzes' distribution would far exceed ten coffee carts. Thus, there is a genuine opportunity to make a substantial amount of money from a product that Bernie's Blintzes is already producing. Yet the benefits from such a simple endeavor would far exceed the monetary profit from each cookie.

Justification

16   In several important ways, the production and distribution of Bernie's Blintzes' chocolate chip cookies would help restore Bernie's Blintzes to financial prosperity.

17   First, this proposal builds on existing strengths. Bernie's Blintzes' chocolate chip cookies have already been market-tested—sixteen years of experience shows that Bernie's Blintzes' cookies sell. Moreover, establishing a cookie distribution system would open the door for Bernie's Blintzes to distribute more of its other time-tested items, like its famous matzoh ball soup. Also, distribution need not be limited to Seattle; in time, Bernie's Blintzes' cookies could be distributed throughout the region.

18   Second, initial costs and risks are very low. Because producing chocolate chip cookies takes advantage of existing facilities and labor, the cookies could be distributed and marketed at a very competitive rate, allowing Bernie's Blintzes to establish itself in a citywide market at a nominal cost—producing and distributing cookies would not require a second mortgage.

19   Third, cookie distribution would increase name familiarity. Each cookie would carry a label on one side that would include the Bernie's Blintzes logo, phone number, and address. Coffee drinkers across town will want to visit Bernie's Blintzes Restaurant after they come to appreciate these fine cookies. Curious new visitors to the neighborhood will match the restaurant sign to the label on the cookie they purchased at the espresso cart near their home. Another label on the other side of the cookie could promote Bernie's Blintzes' catering and specialty menu items.

20   Finally, Bernie's Blintzes could continue to do what it does best: serve traditional kosher-style food. Unlike the consultant's proposal, this plan allows Bernie's Blintzes to build on what it has done well for sixteen years, preserving an important part of Seattle's Jewish culture.

Skeptics may criticize a plan such as this because it is simplistic in appearance.   21
After all, it does seem somewhat "starry-eyed" to think that chocolate chip cookies could be the source of economic prosperity. Yet one might consider the millions of dollars made today by Famous Amos Cookies, a company that began on nothing more than a dream and a kitchen in a garage. Sometimes the most effective plans are the simplest ones.

Conclusion

By building on existing strengths and doing what Bernie's Blintzes has   22
been doing well for sixteen years, the owners of Bernie's Blintzes Restaurant can reestablish it as a profitable business. Producing and distributing chocolate chip cookies addresses Bernie's Blintzes' shortcomings while building on its strengths, and in contrast to the Paragon plan, this proposal can be executed immediately with a nominal investment.

Critiquing "A Proposal to Save Bernie's Blintzes Restaurant"

1. Bernie's Blintzes Restaurant (not its real name) was in a state of decline at the time this proposal was written. As a quirky, family-operated business, it seemed out-of-step with new upscale trends in the restaurant business. The owner hired a consultant for advice. What was the consultant's analysis of the problem and recommended solution?

2. Jeffrey Cain's proposal grows out of his personal experience and practical knowledge of a restaurant business. What is Jeffrey's analysis and proposed solution?

3. How does Jeffrey use his experiential knowledge to rebut the consultant's report and support his own ideas? What rhetorical strategies does he use?

4. How effective do you find Jeffrey's proposal argument?

Our second reading, by student writer Stephen Bean, is a policy proposal written for the assignment on pages 320–21. Bean's paper joins a heated social debate about what to do about the mentally ill homeless. In 1988, conservative columnist Charles Krauthammer published an influential article arguing that states should confine the mentally ill homeless—involuntarily if necessary—in state mental hospitals. Krauthammer argued that the huge rise of homeless people in the 1970s and 1980s was the result of the closing of state mental hospitals following court rulings that persons could not be involuntarily committed. In this researched policy argument, Bean aims to refute Krauthammer's argument and offer a counter-proposal. Bean's argument is formatted as a formal research paper using the documentation system of the Modern Language Association (MLA). A full explanation of this format is given in Chapter 17.

Stephen Bean

Professor Arness

English 110

June 1, 200–

What Should Be Done about the Mentally Ill Homeless?

1   Winter paints Seattle's streets gray with misting rain that drops lightly but steadily into pools. Walking to work through one of Seattle's oldest districts, Pioneer Square, I see an incongruous mixture of people: both successful business types and a large population of homeless. Some walk to offices or lunches grasping cups of fresh ground coffee; others slowly push wobbling carts containing their earthly possessions wrapped carefully in black plastic. These scenes of homelessness have become common throughout America's urban centers—so common, perhaps, that despite our feelings of guilt and pity, we accept the presence of the homeless as permanent. The empty-stomach feeling of confronting a ragged panhandler has become an often accepted fact of living in the city. What can we do besides giving a few cents of spare change?

2   Recently, a growing number of commentators have been focusing on the mentally ill homeless. In response to the violent murder of an elderly person by a homeless mentally ill man, New York City recently increased its efforts to locate and hospitalize dangerous homeless mentally ill individuals. New York's plan will include aggressive outreach—actively going out into the streets and shelters to locate mentally ill individuals and then involuntarily hospitalizing those deemed dangerous either to others or to themselves (Dugger, "Danger" B1). Although the New York Civil Liberties Union has objected to this action on the grounds that involuntary hospitalization may violate the rights of the mentally ill, many applaud the city's action as a first step in dealing with a problem which the nation has grossly ignored. One highly influential commentator, Charles Krauthammer, has recently called for widescale involuntary reinstitutionalization of the mentally ill homeless—a seemingly persuasive proposal until one begins to do research on the mentally ill homeless. Adopting Krauthammer's proposal would be a dangerous and wrong-headed policy for America. Rather, research shows that community-based care in which psychiatrists and social workers provide coordinated services in the community itself is a more

effective solution to the problems of the mentally ill homeless than widescale institutionalization.

In his article "How to Save the Homeless Mentally Ill," Charles Krauthammer argues that the federal government should assist the states in rebuilding a national system of asylums. He proposes that the criteria for involuntary institutionalization be broadened: The state should be permitted to institutionalize mentally ill persons involuntarily not only if they are deemed dangerous to others or themselves (the current criterion for institutionalization) but also if they are "degraded" or made helpless by their illness. He points to the large number of patients released from state institutions in the 1960s and 1970s who, finding no support in communities, ended up on the streets. Arguing that the mentally ill need the stability and supervision that only an institution can provide, Krauthammer proposes substantial increases in federal taxes to fund rebuilding of asylums. He argues that the mentally ill need unique solutions because of their unique problems; their homelessness, he claims, stems from mental illness not poverty. Finally, Krauthammer rebuts the argument that involuntary hospitalization violates civil liberties. He argues that "liberty" has no meaning to someone suffering from severe psychosis. To let people suffer the pains of mental illness and the pains of the street when they could be treated and recover is a cruel right indeed. He points to the project HELP program where less than a fifth of those involuntarily hospitalized protested their commitment; most are glad, he claims, for a warm bed, nutritious food, and a safe environment.

Krauthammer's argument, while persuasive on first reading, is based on four seriously flawed assumptions. His first assumption is the widely accepted notion that deinstitutionalization of state mental hospitals in the 1960s and 1970s is a primary cause of the current homelessness problem in America. Krauthammer talks about the hundreds of thousands released from the hospitals who have become "an army of grate-dwellers" (24). However, recent research has shown that the relationship of deinstitutionalization to homelessness is vastly overstated. Ethnologist Kim Hopper argues that while deinstitutionalization has partly contributed to increased numbers of mentally ill homeless its influence is far smaller than popularly believed. She argues that the data many used to support this claim were methodologically flawed and that researchers who found symptoms of mental illness in homeless people didn't try to ascertain whether these symptoms were the cause or effect of living on the street. Finally, she points out that a lag time of five years existed between the major release of state hospital patients and the rise of mentally ill individuals in shelters. This time lag suggests that other social and economic factors might have come into play to account for the rise of homelessness (156–57). Carl Cohen and Kenneth Thompson also point to this time lag as evidence to reject deinstitutionalization as the major cause of mentally ill homelessness (817). Jonathan Kozol argues that patients released from state hospitals in the late sixties and early seventies didn't go directly to the streets but went to single-room occupancy housing, such as cheap hotels or boarding houses. Many of these ex-patients became homeless, he argues, when almost half of single-room occupancy housing was replaced by more expensive housing between 1970 and 1980 (18). The effects of this housing shortage might account for the lag time that Hopper and Cohen and Thompson cite.

5   Krauthammer's focus on mental illness as a cause of much of the homelessness problem leads to another of the implicit assumptions in his argument: that the mentally ill comprise a large percentage of the homeless population. Krauthammer avoids mentioning specific numbers until the end of his article when he writes:

> The argument over how many of the homeless are mentally ill is endless. The estimates, which range from one-quarter to three-quarters, vary with method, definition, and ideology. But so what if even the lowest estimates are right? Even if treating the mentally ill does not end homelessness, how can that possibly justify not treating the tens, perhaps hundreds of thousands who would benefit from a partial solution? (25)

This paragraph is rhetorically shrewd. It downplays the numbers issue and takes the moral high road. But by citing estimates between one-quarter and three-quarters, Krauthammer effectively suggests that a neutral estimate might place the number around fifty percent—a high estimate reinforced by his leap from "tens" to "perhaps hundreds of thousands" in the last sentence.

6   Close examination of the research, however, reveals that the percentage of mentally ill people on the streets may be even lower than Krauthammer's lowest figure of 25%. In an extensive study conducted by David Snow and colleagues, a team member lived among the homeless for 12 months to collect data on mental

illness. Additionally, the researchers tracked the institutional histories of a random sample of homeless. The study found that only 10% of the street sample and 16% of the tracking sample showed mental illness. The researchers pointed to a number of reasons why some previous estimates and studies may have inflated the numbers of mentally ill homeless. They suggest that the visibility of the mentally ill homeless (their odd behaviors make them stand out) combined with the widespread belief that deinstitutionalization poured vast numbers of mentally ill onto the streets caused researchers to bias their data. Thus researchers would often interpret behavior such as socially inappropriate actions, depression, and sleeping disorders as indications of mental illness, when in fact these actions may simply be the natural response to living in the harsh environment of the street. Additionally, the Snow study points to the medicalization of homelessness. This phenomenon means that when doctors and psychiatrists treat the homeless they focus on their medical and psychological problems while ignoring their social and economic ones. Because studies of the mentally ill homeless have been dominated by doctors and psychologists, these studies tend to inflate the numbers of mentally ill on the streets (419–21).

Another persuasive study showing low percentages of mentally ill homeless— although not as low as Snow's estimates—comes from Deborah Dennis and colleagues, who surveyed the past decade of research on mentally ill homeless. The combined findings of all these research studies suggest that the mentally ill comprise between 28% and 37% of the homeless population (Dennis et al. 1130). Thus we see that while the mentally ill make up a significant proportion of the homeless population they do not approach a majority as Krauthammer and others would have us believe.

Krauthammer's third assumption is that the causes of homelessness among the mentally ill are largely psychological rather than socioeconomic. By this thinking, the solutions to their problems involve the treatment of their illnesses rather than the alleviation of poverty. Krauthammer writes, "Moreover, whatever solutions are eventually offered the non-mentally ill homeless, they will have little relevance to those who are mentally ill" (25). Closer examination, however, shows that other factors play a greater role in causing homelessness among the mentally ill than mental illness. Jonathan Kozol argues that housing and the economy played the largest role in causing homelessness among the mentally ill. He points to two million jobs lost every year since 1980, an increase in poverty, a massive shortage in low-income housing, and a drop from 500,000 subsidized private housing units to 25,000 during the Reagan era (17–18). Cohen and Thompson also place primary emphasis on poverty and housing shortages:

> Data suggest that most homeless mentally ill persons lost their rooms in single-room-occupancy hotels or low-priced apartments not because of psychoticism but because they 1) were evicted because of renewal projects and fires, 2) were victimized by unscrupulous landlords or by other residents, or 3) could no longer afford the rent. (818)

Douglas Mossman and Michael Perlin cite numerous studies which show that mental illness itself is not the primary factor causing homelessness among the mentally ill; additionally, they point out that the severity of mental illness itself is closely linked to poverty. They argue that lack of private health care increases poor health and the frequency of severe mental illness. They conclude, "Homelessness is, if nothing else, a condition of poverty, and poor individuals in general are at increased risk for episodes of psychiatric illness" (952). Krauthammer's article conveniently ignores the role of poverty, suggesting that much of the homeless problem could be solved by moving the mentally ill back into institutions. But the evidence suggests that symptoms of mental illness are often the <u>results</u> of being homeless and that any efforts to treat the psychological problems of the mentally ill must also address the socioeconomic problems.

9   Krauthammer's belief that the causes of mentally ill homelessness are psychological rather than social and economic leads to a fourth assumption that the mentally ill homeless are a distinct subgroup who need different treatment from the other homeless groups. Krauthammer thus divides the homeless into three primary groups: (1) the mentally ill; (2) those who choose to live on the street; and (3) "the victims of economic calamity, such as family breakup or job loss" (25). By believing that the mentally ill homeless are not also victims of "economic calamity," Krauthammer greatly oversimplifies their problems. As Cohen and Thompson show, it is difficult to separate the mentally ill homeless and the non–mentally ill homeless. "On closer examination, 'not mentally ill' homeless people have many mental health problems; similarly, the 'mentally ill' homeless have numerous nonpsychiatric problems that arise from the sociopolitical elements affecting all homeless people" (817). Because the two groups are so similar, it is counterproductive to insist on entirely different solutions for both groups.

Krauthammer's proposal thus fails on a number of points. It won't solve nearly   10
as much of the homelessness problem as he leads us to believe. It would commit
valuable taxpayer dollars to building asylums rather than attacking the underlying
causes of homelessness in general. And perhaps most importantly, its emphasis on
involuntary confinement in asylums is not the best long-range method to treat the
mentally ill homeless. Instead of moving the mentally ill homeless away from
society into asylums, we would meet their needs far more effectively through
monitored community-based care. Instead of building expensive institutions, we
should focus on finding alternative low-cost housing for the mentally ill homeless
and meet their needs through teams of psychiatrists and social workers who could
oversee a number of patients' treatments, monitoring such things as taking
medications and receiving appropriate counseling. Involuntary hospitalization may
still be needed for the most severely deranged, but the majority of mentally ill
homeless people can be better treated in their communities.

From a purely financial perspective, perhaps the most compelling reason to   11
prefer community-based care is that it offers a more efficient use of taxpayer
dollars. In a letter to the New York Times on behalf of the Project for Psychiatric
Outreach to the Homeless, Drs. Katherine Falk and Gail Albert give us the following
statistics:

> It costs $105,000 to keep someone in a state hospital for a year. But it
> costs only $15,000 to $35,000 (depending on the intensity of services) to
> operate supported residences in the community with the necessary
> onsite psychiatrists, case workers, case managers, drug counselors, and
> other rehabilitation services. (A30)

It can be argued, in fact, that the cost of maintaining state hospitals for the
mentally ill actually prevents large numbers of mentally ill from receiving
treatment. When large numbers of mentally ill persons were released from state
hospitals during the deinstitutionalization movement of the 1960s and 1970s, the
original plan was to convert resources to community-based care. Even though the
number of patients in state institutions has dramatically decreased over the past
two decades, institutions have continued to receive large shares of state funding.
According to David Rothman of Columbia University, "Historically, the dollars have
remained locked in the institutions and did not go into community mental health"
(qtd. in Dugger, "Debate" B2). In fact, cutting New York's state hospital budget

would provide enough money for over 20,000 units in supported community residences (Falk and Albert A30). Furthermore, Linda Chafetz points out that having the money to pay for such resources as clothes, bathing facilities, meals, and housing is the most urgent concern among caregivers in treating the mentally ill homeless. According to Chafetz, "The immediate and urgent nature of the resource dilemma can make other issues appear almost frivolous by comparison" (451). With such an obvious shortage of resources, pouring what money we have into the high-cost institutional system would be a grave disservice to the majority of the mentally ill homeless population and to the homeless population as a whole.

12   A second reason to adopt community-based care over widescale institutionalization is that the vast majority of the homeless mentally ill do not need the tight control of the hospital system. Cohen and Thompson cite a number of studies which show "that only 5%–7% of single adult homeless persons are in need of acute inpatient care" (820). Involuntarily hospitalizing a large number of homeless who don't demand institutionalized care is not only a waste of resources but also an unnecessary assault on individual freedom for many.

13   Finally, the community-based care system is preferable to institutionalization because it most often gives the best treatment to its patients. Although Krauthammer claims that less than a fifth of involuntarily hospitalized patients have legally challenged their confinement (25), numerous studies indicate there is widespread resistance to institutional care by the homeless mentally ill. Mossman and Perlin cite multiple sources indicating that many mentally ill have legitimate reasons to fear state hospitals. Moreover, they provide evidence that many would rather suffer the streets and their mental illness than suffer the conditions of state hospitals and the side effects of medications. The horrible track record of conditions of state hospitals supports the logic of this thinking. Mossman and Perlin also point out that many mentally ill homeless persons will accept treatment from the type of alternative settings community-based care offers (953). Powerful evidence showing the success of community-based care comes from early evaluation reports of ACCESS (Access to Community Care and Effective Services), a community-based program of the Center for Mental Health. More than 11,000 mentally ill homeless have received services through this program, which reports "significant

improvements in almost all outcome measures," such as "a 66 percent decrease in minor criminal activity" and "a 46 percent decrease in reported psychotic symptoms" ("Articles"). Given that institutionalization can leave mentally ill persons feeling humiliated and disempowered (Cohen and Thompson 819), community-based solutions such as ACCESS seem the best approach.

Given the advantages of community-based care, what is the appeal of Krauthammer's proposal? Involuntary institutionalization appeals to our common impulse to lock our problems out of sight. As crime increases, we want to build more prisons; when we see ragged men and women mumbling in the street, we want to shut them up in institutions. But the simple solutions are not often the most effective ones. Institutionalization is tempting, but alternative methods have shown themselves to be more effective. Community-based care works better because it's based on a better understanding of the problem. Community-based care, by allowing the psychiatrist and social worker to work together, attacks both the mental and social dimensions of the problem: The client receives not only psychological counseling and medication but also help on how to find affordable housing, how to manage money and shop effectively, and how to live in a community. Without roots in a community, a patient released from a mental asylum will quickly return to the streets. To pour scarce resources into the expensive project of rebuilding asylums—helping the few while ignoring the many—would be a terrible misuse of taxpayer dollars.

Krauthammer's argument appeals in another way also. By viewing the homeless as mentally ill, we see them as inherently different from ourselves. We needn't see any connection to those mumbling bag ladies and those ragged men lying on the grates. When we regard them as mentally ill, we see ourselves as largely unresponsible for the conditions that led them to the streets. Those professional men and women carrying their espresso Starbuck's coffees to their upscale offices in Seattle's Pioneer Square don't have to be reminded that this historic district used to contain a number of single-occupancy boarding houses. The professionals work where the homeless used to live. The rich and the poor are thus interconnected, reminding us that homelessness is primarily a social and economic problem, not a mental health problem. And even the most deranged of the mentally ill homeless are messengers of a nationwide scourge of poverty.

Works Cited

"Articles to Focus on National Effort to Help People Who Are Homeless and
Have Mental Illness." Press release. National Mental Health Services
Knowledge Exchange Network (KEN) 3 Mar. 1997. 23 Apr. 1998
<http://www.mentalhealth.org./resource/praccess.htm>.

Chafetz, Linda. "Withdrawal from the Homeless Mentally Ill." Community Mental
Health Journal 26 (1990): 449–61.

Cohen, Carl I., and Kenneth S. Thompson. "Homeless Mentally Ill or Mentally Ill
Homeless?" American Journal of Psychiatry 149 (1992): 816–23.

Dennis, Deborah L., et al. "A Decade of Research and Services for Homeless
Mentally Ill Persons: Where Do We Stand?" American Psychologist 46 (1991):
1129–38.

Dugger, Celia W. "A Danger to Themselves and Others." New York Times 24
Jan. 1993: B1+.

---. "A Debate Unstilled: New Plan for Homeless Mentally Ill Does Not Address
Larger Questions." New York Times 22 Jan. 1993: B2.

Falk, Katherine, and Gail Albert. Letter. New York Times 11 Feb. 1993: A30.

Hopper, Kim. "More Than Passing Strangers: Homelessness and Mental Illness in
New York City." American Ethnologist 15 (1988): 155–57.

Kozol, Jonathan. "Are the Homeless Crazy?" Harper's Sept. 1988: 17–19.

Krauthammer, Charles. "How to Save the Homeless Mentally Ill." New Republic 8
Feb. 1988: 22–25.

Mossman, Douglas, and Michael L. Perlin. "Psychiatry and the Homeless Mentally
Ill: A Reply to Dr. Lamb." American Journal of Psychiatry 149 (1992): 951–56.

Snow, David A., et al. "The Myth of Pervasive Mental Illness among the Homeless."
Social Problems 33 (1986): 407–23.

Critiquing "What Should Be Done about the Mentally Ill Homeless?"

1. In your own words, summarize Charles Krauthammer's argument for reopening mental hospitals and reinstitutionalizing the mentally ill homeless. How does Stephen Bean attempt to refute Krauthammer's argument? What is Stephen's own proposal for solving the problem of the mentally ill homeless? What reasons does Stephen give in support of his proposal?

2. What rhetorical strategies does Stephen use to make his argument as compelling as possible? How does he try to create presence? How does he appeal to *ethos* and *pathos* as well as *logos*?

3. How effective do you find Stephen's argument?

Our last reading is an op-ed piece by professional columnist E. J. Dionne Jr. Dionne joins an ongoing public conversation about how to improve the academic performance of public schools. Many politicians advocate strengthening standards and ending the social promotion of poorly performing students. (Social promotion is the practice of letting a student advance to the next grade even if he or she flunked the previous grade.) In his 1999 State of the Union speech, President Clinton proposed ending all social promotion in the schools. Dionne's purpose in this argument is to raise doubts about Clinton's proposal.

Ending Social Promotion
Means Fixing Failing Schools

E. J. Dionne Jr.

WASHINGTON—If a politician wants applause for a speech on improving the schools, all it takes are a few magic words. President Clinton knows this. In his State of the Union address, he declared: "All schools must end social promotion." On cue, members of Congress stood up and cheered. 1

The craze to end social promotion—the practice of moving children on to the next grade whether or not they've passed the previous grade—is national in scope and as bipartisan as you can get. Last Thursday, the Texas State Senate unanimously approved Gov. George W. Bush's plan to end social promotion. 2

Bush, the undeclared front-runner for the Republican presidential nomination, pronounced the bill "a strong message that no child will be left behind in our state—that when a child is identified with reading deficiency, we'll correct it early, before it's too late." 3

Hartford, Conn., welcomed a new school superintendent last Wednesday. "We will be relentless on literacy," Anthony Amato declared. Part of that relentlessness, reported *The Hartford Courant,* includes an end to social promotion. 4

5   On the same day, across the country in Escondido, Calif., school administrators announced a summer-school program for 360 students who were not making the grade.

6   Interim superintendent David Jenkins told the *San Diego Union-Tribune* reporter Anna
Cearley that remedial help was part of his effort to end social promotion. "Each year that
goes by makes it more difficult for these students to be successful in high school," he
said. California's new Democratic governor, Gray Davis, has made a statewide campaign
against—you guessed it—social promotion, a key part of his education reform package.

7   Now it's hard to defend social promotion, which is one reason why politicians have
latched onto the war against it. When Clinton declares "we do our children no favors when
we allow them to pass from grade to grade without mastering the material," everybody
nods.

8   But you needn't be a cynic to see that this cause has a certain advantage for those who
run schools: It moves the burden of failing systems from the adults who run them to the
children who aren't making it.

9   "Simply pounding the kids on the head is not going to get the result we need," says
Kati Haycock, president of The Education Trust, a group that battles for better teachers and
more accountability. If students fail "there are already serious consequences for the kids,
but not for the adults."

10   Writing last year in the American Association of School Administrators magazine, Linda
Darling-Hammond pointed to "dozens of studies" showing that holding kids back "actually
contributes to greater academic failure, higher levels of dropping out, and greater behav-
ioral difficulties."

11   "Instead of looking carefully at classroom or school practices when students are
not achieving, schools typically send students back to repeat the same experience," said
Darling-Hammond, executive director of the National Commission on Teaching and America's Future. "Little is done to ensure that the experience will be either more appropriate
for the individual needs of the child, or higher quality."

12   It's true, of course, that those who advocate an end to social promotion know that by
itself, it's not a solution. Both Clinton and Bush would link its abolition to a variety of remedial and summer-school programs—and, in Bush's case, to teacher training and to a
broader program to demand results from teachers and administrators.

13   In Texas, state Sen. Royce West, a Dallas Democrat, insisted on an amendment under
which the ban on social promotion would stay in effect only if the state put up the money
for the remedial programs. West's worry—a sensible one—is that the current eagerness to
hold kids back when they fail tests might be just a "legislative fad."

14   If you want to be an optimist (and I certainly do), you might see the campaign against
social promotion as part of a larger effort to ensure accountability by schools, teachers and
students alike. It holding kids back focuses attention on how and why schools are failing,
if kids get the help they need to move forward and if the practice leads to the hiring of better teachers—if all these things happen, it might work.

15   What the schools don't need is another gimmick, something that sounds tough in a
politician's speech but doesn't produce reform. "The federal government's job is to help
educate poor kids, not to add more pain," says Haycock of Clinton's program. "The way for
the federal government to do that is to help poor kids have the best teachers not the worst."

Critiquing "Ending Social Promotion
Means Fixing Failing Schools"

1. Dionne's argument is not itself a proposal but instead a critique of a proposal. Explain in your own words, why the cry to "end social promotion" has become so popular among politicians.

2. What is Dionne's chief concern about social promotion? What motivates him to write this op-ed piece? In your own words, summarize Dionne's argument.

3. Which of the strategies for questioning and challenging a proposal argument (see pp. 324–26) does Dionne employ to raise doubts about social promotion?

4. How effective is Dionne's argument?

5. If you were to join this argumentative conversation by developing a proposal of your own, what specific aspects of the problem, costs, and consequences would you need to explore first?

Ethical Arguments

The line between ethical arguments ("Is X morally good?") and other kinds of values disputes is often pretty thin. Many apparently straightforward practical values issues can turn out to have an ethical dimension. For example, in deciding what kind of car to buy, most people would base their judgments on criteria such as cost, reliability, safety, comfort, and stylishness. But some people might feel morally obligated to buy the most fuel-efficient car, or not to buy a car from a manufacturer whose investment or labor policies they found morally repugnant. Depending on how large a role ethical considerations played in the evaluation, we might choose to call this an *ethical argument* as opposed to a simpler kind of values argument. In any case, we here devote a separate chapter to ethical arguments because we believe they represent special difficulties to the student of argumentation. Let's take a look now at some of those special difficulties.

SPECIAL DIFFICULTIES OF ETHICAL ARGUMENTS

One crucial difficulty with ethical arguments concerns the role of purpose in defining criteria for judgment. In Chapter 13, we assumed that every class of beings has a purpose, that the purpose should be defined as narrowly as possible, and that the criteria for judgment derive directly from that purpose. For example, the purpose of a computer repairperson is to analyze the problem with my computer, to fix it, and to do so in a timely and cost-efficient manner. Once I formulate this purpose, it is easy for me to define criteria for a good computer repairperson.

In ethics, however, the place of purpose is much fuzzier. Just what is the purpose of human beings? Before I can begin to determine what ethical duties I have to myself and to others, I'm going to have to address this question; and because the chance of reaching agreement on that question remains remote, many ethical arguments are probably unresolvable. In ethical discussions we don't ask what a "manager" or a "judge" or a "point guard" is supposed to do in situations relevant to the respective classes; we're asking what John Doe is supposed to be or what Jane Doe is supposed to do with her life. Who they are or what their social function is makes no difference to our ethical assessment of their actions or traits of character. A morally bad person may be a good judge and a morally good person may be a bad manager.

As the discussion so far has suggested, disagreements about ethical issues often stem from different systems of belief. We might call this problem the problem of warrants. That is, people disagree because they do not share common assumptions on which to ground their arguments.

If, for example, you say that good manners are necessary for keeping us from reverting to a state of raw nature, your implied warrant is that raw nature is bad. But if you say that good manners are a political tool by which a ruling class tries to suppress the natural vitality of the working class, then your warrant is that liberation of the working classes from the corrupt habits of the ruling class is good. It would be difficult, therefore, for people representing these opposing belief systems to carry on a reasonable discussion of etiquette—their assumptions about value, about the role of the natural self, and about political progress are different. This is why ethical arguments are often so acrimonious—they frequently lack shared warrants to serve as starting places for argument.

It is precisely because of the problem of warrants, however, that you should try to confront issues of ethics with rational deliberation. The arguments you produce may not persuade others to your view, but they should lay out more clearly the grounds and warrants of your own beliefs. Such arguments serve the purpose of clarification. By drafting essays on ethical issues, you begin to see more clearly what you believe and why you believe it. Although the arguments demanded by ethical issues require rigorous thought, they force us to articulate our most deeply held beliefs and our richest feelings.

AN OVERVIEW OF MAJOR ETHICAL SYSTEMS

When we are faced with an ethical issue, such as the issue of whether terrorism can be justified, we must move from arguments of good or bad to arguments of right or wrong. The terms *right* and *wrong* are clearly different from the terms *good* and *bad* when the latter terms mean simply "effective" (meets purposes of class, as in "This is a good stereo system") or "ineffective" (fails to meet purposes of class, as in "This is a bad cookbook"). But *right* and *wrong* often also differ from what seems to be a moral use of the terms *good* and *bad*. We might say, for example, that sunshine is good because it brings pleasure and that cancer is bad because it brings pain and death, but that is not quite the same thing as saying that sunshine is "right" and cancer is "wrong." It is the problem of "right" and "wrong" that ethical arguments confront.

Thus it is not enough to say that terrorism is "bad"; obviously everyone, including most terrorists, would agree that terrorism is "bad" because it causes suffering and anguish. If we want to condemn terrorism on ethical grounds, we have to say that it's also "wrong" as well as "bad." In saying that something's wrong, we're saying that all people ought to refrain from doing it. We're also saying that acts that are morally "wrong" are in some way blameworthy and deserve censure, a conclusion that doesn't necessarily follow a negative nonethical judgment, which might lead simply to our not buying something or not hiring someone. From a nonethical standpoint, you may even say that someone is a "good" terrorist in that he fully realizes the purposes of the class "terrorist": He causes great damage with a minimum of resources, brings a good deal of attention to his cause, and doesn't get caught. The ethical question here, however, is not whether this person is a good member of the class, but whether it is wrong for such a class to exist.

In asking the question "Ought the class 'terrorist' to exist?" or, to put it more colloquially, "Are there ever cases where terrorism is justified?" we need to seek some consistent approach or principle. In the phrase used by some philosophers, ethical judgments are typically "universalizable" statements. That is, when we oppose a terrorist act, our ethical argument (assuming it's a coherent one) should be capable of being generalized into an ethical principle that will hold for all similar cases. Ethical disputes usually involve clashes between such principles. For example, a pro-terrorist might say, "My ends justify my means," whereas an anti-terrorist might say, "The sanctity of human life is not to be violated for any reason." The differences in principles such as these account for different schools of ethical thought.

There are many different schools of ethical thought—too many to present in this chapter. But to help you think your way through ethical issues, we'll look at some of the most prevalent methods of resolving ethical questions. The first of these methods, "naive egoism," is really less a method than a retreat from method. It doesn't represent a coherent ethical view, but it is a position that many people lapse into on given issues. It represents, in short, the most seductive alternative to rigorous ethical thought.

Naive Egoism

Back in Chapter 1, we touched on the morality of the Sophists and suggested that their underlying maxim was something like "Might makes right." That is, in ethical terms, they were essentially egoists who used other people with impunity to realize their own ends. The appeal of this position, however repugnant it may sound when laid out like this, is that it rationalizes self-promotion and pleasure seeking: If we all follow the bidding of our egos, we'll be happy.

On examination, this philosophy proves to be incoherent. It should be noted, however, that philosophers don't reject naive egoism simply because they believe "selfishness is bad." Rather, philosophers tend to assess ethical systems according to such factors as their scope (how often will this system provide principles to guide our moral action?) and their precision (how clearly can we analyze a given situation using the tools of the system?) rather than their intuition about whether the system is right or wrong. Although naive egoism has great scope (you can always ask, "What's in it for me?"), it is far from precise, as we'll try to show.

Take the case of young Ollie Unger, who has decided that he wants to quit living irrationally and to join some official school of ethical thought. The most appealing school at the moment—recommended to him by a philosophy major over at the Phi Upsilon Nu house—is the "I'm Number One!" school of scruples. He heads downtown to the school's opulent headquarters and meets with the school's guru, Dr. Pheelgood.

"What's involved in becoming a member of your school?" Ollie inquires.

"Ahhh, my apple-cheeked chum, that's the beauty of it. It's so simple. You just give me all your worldly possessions and do whatever I tell you to do."

Ollie is puzzled. He had in mind something a bit more, well, gratifying. He was hoping for something closer to the philosophy of eat, drink, and make merry—all justified through rational thought.

"You seem disappointed," Pheelgood observes. "What's the matter?"

"Well, gee, it just doesn't sound like I'm going to be number one here. I thought that was the idea. To look out for *numero uno.*"

"Of course not, silly boy. This is after all the "I'm Number One School of Scruples." And I, *moi*, am the I who's number one.

"But I thought the idea of your school was for everyone to have the maximum amount of enjoyment in life."

Peevishness clouds Pheelgood's face. "Look here, Unger, if I arrange things for you to have a good time, it's going to cost me. Next you'll be asking me to open soup kitchens. If I'm to look out for number one, then you've got to act entirely differently from me. I take, you give. *Capiche?*"

As should be obvious by now, it's very difficult to systematize egoism. You have two sets of demands in constant conflict—the demands of your own personal ego and those of everyone else's. Thus it's impossible to universalize a statement that all members of the school could hold equally without contradicting all other members of the school.

Some egoists try to get around this problem by conceding that we must limit our self-gratification either by entering into contracts or institutional arrangements with others or by sacrificing short-term interests for long-term ones. We might, for example, give to the poor now in order to avoid a revolution of the masses later. But once they've let the camel's nose of concern for others into the tent, it's tough to hang onto egoistic philosophy. Having considered naive egoism, let's turn to a pair of more workable alternatives.

In shifting to the two most common forms of ethical thought, we shift point of view from "I" to "us." Both groups, those who make ethical judgments according to the consequences of any act and those who make ethical judgments according to the conformity of any act with a principle, are guided by their concern for the whole of humanity rather than simply the self.

Consequences as the Base of Ethics

Perhaps the best-known example of evaluating acts according to their ethical consequences is utilitarianism, a down-to-earth philosophy that grew out of nineteenth-century British philosophers' concern to demystify ethics and make it work in the practical world. Jeremy Bentham, the originator of utilitarianism, developed the goal of the greatest good for the greatest number, or "greatest happiness," by which he meant the most pleasure for the least pain. John Stuart Mill, another British philosopher, built on Bentham's utilitarianism, using predicted consequences to determine the morality of a proposed action.

Mill's consequentialist approach allows you readily to assess a wide range of acts. You can apply the principle of utility—which says that an action is morally right if it produces a greater net value (benefits minus costs) than any available alternative action—to virtually any situation and it will help you reach a decision. Obviously, however, it's not always easy to make the calculations called for by the principle, since, like any prediction of the future, an estimate of consequences is conjectural. In particular, it's often very hard to assess the long-term consequences of any action. Too often, utilitarianism seduces us into a short-term analysis of a moral problem simply because long-term consequences are very difficult to predict.

Principles as the Base of Ethics

Any ethical system based on principles will ultimately rest on one or two moral tenets that we are duty bound to uphold, no matter what the consequences. Sometimes the moral tenets come from religious faith—for example, the Ten Commandments. At other times, however, the principles are derived from philosophical reasoning, as in the case of German philosopher Immanuel Kant. Kant held that no one should ever use another person as a means to his own ends and that everyone should always act as if his acts were the basis of universal law. In other words, Kant held that we were duty bound to respect other people's sanctity and to act in the same way that we would want all other people to act. The great advantage of such a system is its clarity and precision. We are never overwhelmed by a multiplicity of contradictory and difficult-to-quantify consequences; we simply make sure we are not violating a principle of our ethical system and proceed accordingly.

The Two Systems Compared

In the eyes of many people, a major advantage of a system such as utilitarianism is that it impels us to seek out the best solution, whereas systems based on principle merely enjoin us not to violate a principle by our action. In turn, applying an ethical principle will not always help us resolve necessarily relativistic moral dilemmas. For instance, what if none of our available choices violates our moral principles? How do we choose among a host of permissible acts? Or what about situations where none of the alternatives is permitted by our principles? How might we choose the least bad alternative?

To further our comparison of the two systems, let's ask what a Mill or a Kant might say about the previously mentioned issue of terrorism. Here the Kantian position is clear: To kill another person to realize your own ends is palpably evil and forbidden.

A follower of Mill will face a less clear choice. A utilitarian could not automatically rule out terrorism or any other means so long as it led ultimately to the greatest good for the greatest number. If a nation is being slowly starved by those around it, if its people are dying, its institutions crumbling, and its future disappearing, who is to say that the aggrieved nation is not justified in taking a few hundred lives to improve the lot of hundreds of thousands? The utilitarian's first concern is to determine whether terrorism will most effectively bring about that end. So long as the desired end represents the best possible net value and the means are effective at bringing about the end, the utilitarian can, in theory anyway, justify almost any action.

Given the shared cultural background and values of most of us, not to mention our own vulnerability to terrorism, the Kantian argument is probably very appealing here. Indeed, Kantian ethical arguments have overwhelming appeal for us when the principle being invoked is already widely held within our culture, and when the violation of that principle will have clear and immediate negative consequences for us. But in a culture that doesn't share that principle and for whom the consequences of violation are positive rather than negative, the argument will undoubtedly appear weaker, a piece of fuzzy-headed idealism.

FOR CLASS DISCUSSION

Working as individuals or in small groups:

1. Try to formulate a utilitarian argument to persuade terrorist leaders in the Mideast, the Balkans, Ireland, or elsewhere to stop terrorist action.

2. Try to formulate an ethical principle or rule that would permit terrorism.

Some Compromise Positions between Consequences and Principles

In the end, most of us would not be entirely happy with an ethic that forced us to ignore either principles or consequences. We all have certain principles that we simply can't violate no matter what the consequences. Thus, for example, some of us would not have dropped the bomb on Hiroshima even if it did mean saving many lives ultimately. And certainly, too, most of us will compromise our principles in certain situations if we think the consequences justify it. For instance, how many of us would not deceive, harm, or even torture a kidnapper to save the life of a stolen child? Indeed, over the years, compromise positions have developed on both sides to accommodate precisely these concerns.

Some "consequentialists" have acknowledged the usefulness of general rules for creating more human happiness over the long run. To go back to our terrorism example, a consequentialist might oppose terrorist action on the grounds that "Thou shalt not kill another person in the name of greater material happiness for the group." This acknowledgment of an inviolable principle will still be based on a concern for consequences—for instance, a fear that terrorist acts may lead to World War III—but having such a principle allows the consequentialist to get away from a case-by-case analysis of acts and to keep more clearly before himself the long-range consequences of acts.

Among latter-day ethics of principle, meanwhile, the distinction between absolute obligation and what philosophers call *prima facie* obligation has been developed to take account of the force of circumstances. An *absolute* obligation would be an obligation to follow a principle at all times, no matter what. A *prima facie* obligation, in contrast, is an obligation to do something "other things being equal," that is, in a normal situation. Hence, to use a classic moral example, you would not, other things being equal, cannibalize an acquaintance. But if there are three of you in a lifeboat, one is dying and the other two will surely die if they don't get food, your *prima facie* obligation not to eat another might be waived. (However, the Royal Commission, which heard the original case, took a more Kantian position and condemned the action of the seamen who cannibalized their mate.)

These, then, in greatly condensed form, are the major alternative ways of thinking about ethical arguments. Let's now briefly summarize the ways you can use your knowledge of ethical thought to develop your arguments and critique those of others.

DEVELOPING AN ETHICAL ARGUMENT

To help you see how familiarity with these systems of ethical thought can help you develop an ethical argument, let's take an example case. How, for example, might we go about developing an argument in favor of abolishing the death penalty?

Our first task is to examine the issue from the two points of view just discussed. How might a utilitarian or a Kantian argue that the death penalty should be abolished? The argument on principle, as is usually the case, would appear to be the simpler of the two. Taking another life is difficult to justify under most ethical principles. For Kant, the sanctity of human life is a central tenet of ethics. Under Judeo-Christian ethics, meanwhile, one is told that "Vengeance is Mine, saith the Lord" and "Thou shalt not kill."

Unfortunately for our hopes of simplicity, Kant argued in favor of capital punishment:

> There is no sameness of kind between death and remaining alive even under the most miserable conditions, and consequently there is no equality between the crime and the retribution unless the criminal is judicially condemned and put to death.*

Kant is here invoking an important principle of justice—that punishments should be proportionate to the crime. Kant appears to be saying that this principle must take precedence over his notion of the supreme worth of the individual. Some philosophers think he was being inconsistent in taking this position. Certainly, in establishing your own position, you could support a case against capital punishment based on Kant's principles, even if Kant himself did not reach the same conclusion. But you'd have to establish for your reader why you are at odds with Kant in this case. Kant's apparent inconsistency here illustrates how powerfully our intuitive judgments can affect our ethical judgment.

Likewise, with the Judeo-Christian position, passages can be found in the Bible that would support capital punishment, notably, the Old Testament injunction to take "an eye for an eye and a tooth for a tooth." The latter principle is simply a more poetic version of "Let the punishment fit the crime." Retribution should be of the same kind as the crime. And the commandment "Thou shalt not kill" is often interpreted as "Thou shalt not commit murder," an interpretation that not only permits just wars or killing in self-defense but is also consistent with other places in the Bible that suggest that people have not only the right but the obligation to punish wrongdoers and not leave their fate to God.

So, there appears to be no clearcut argument in support of abolishing capital punishment on the basis of principle. What about an argument based on consequences? How might abolishing capital punishment result in a net good that is at least as great as allowing it?

A number of possibilities suggest themselves. First, in abolishing capital punishment, we rid ourselves of the possibility that someone may be wrongly executed. To buttress this argument, we might want to search for evidence of how many people have been wrongly convicted of or executed for a capital crime. In making arguments based on consequence, we must, whenever possible, offer

---

*From Immanuel Kant, *The Metaphysical Elements of Justice.*

empirical evidence that the consequences we assert exist—and exist to the degree we've suggested.

There are also other possible consequences that a utilitarian might mention in defending the abolition of capital punishment. These include leaving open the possibility that the person being punished will be reformed, keeping those charged with executing the murderer free from guilt, and putting an end to the costly legal and political process of appealing the conviction.

But in addition to calculating benefits, you will need also to calculate the costs of abolishing the death penalty and to show that the net result favors abolition. Failure to mention such costs is a serious weakness in many arguments of consequence. Moreover, in the issue at hand, the consequences that favor capital punishment—deterrence of further capital crimes, cost of imprisoning murderers, and so forth—are well known to most members of your audience.

In our discussion of capital punishment, then, we employed two alternative ways of thinking about ethical issues. In pursuing an argument from *principle*, we looked for an appropriate rule that permitted or at least did not prohibit our position. In pursuing an argument from *consequence*, we moved from what's permissible to what brings about the most desirable consequences. Most ethical issues, argued thoroughly, should be approached from both perspectives, so long as irreconcilable differences don't present themselves.

Should you choose to adopt one of these perspectives to the exclusion of the other, you will find yourself facing many of the problems mentioned here. This is not to say that you can't ever go to the wall for a principle or focus solely on consequences to the exclusion of principles; it's simply that you will be hard-pressed to convince those of your audience who happen to be of the other persuasion and demand different sorts of proof. For the purpose of developing arguments, we encourage you to consider both the relevant principles and the possible consequences when you evaluate ethical actions.

TESTING ETHICAL ARGUMENTS

Perhaps the first question you should ask in setting out to analyze your draft of an ethical argument is "To what extent is the argument based on consequences or on ethical principles?" If it's based exclusively on one of these two forms of ethical thought, then it's vulnerable to the sorts of criticism discussed here. A strictly principled argument that takes no account of the consequences of its position is vulnerable to a simple cost analysis. What are the costs in the case of adhering to this principle? There will undoubtedly be some, or else there would be no real argument. If the argument is based strictly on consequentialist grounds, we should ask if the position violates any rules or principles, particularly such commandments as the Golden Rule—"Do unto others as you would have others do unto you"—which most members of our audience adhere to. By failing to mention these alternative ways of thinking about ethical issues, we undercut not only our argument but our credibility as well.

Let's now consider a more developed examination of the two positions, starting with some of the more subtle weaknesses in a position based on principle. In practice people will sometimes take rigidly "principled" positions because they live in fear of "slippery slopes"; that is, they fear setting precedents that might lead to ever more dire consequences. Consider, for example, the slippery slope leading from birth control to euthanasia if you have an absolutist commitment to the sanctity of human life. Once we allow birth control in the form of condoms or pills, the principled absolutist would say, then we will be forced to accept birth control "abortions" in the first hours after conception (IUDs, "morning after" pills), then abortions in the first trimester, then in the second or even the third trimester. And once we have violated the sanctity of human life by allowing abortions, it is only a short step to euthanasia and finally to killing off all undesirables.

One way to refute a slippery-slope argument of this sort is to try to dig a foothold into the side of the hill to show that you don't necessarily have to slide all the way to the bottom. You would thus have to argue that allowing birth control does not mean allowing abortions (by arguing for differences between a fetus after conception and sperm and egg before conception), or that allowing abortions does not mean allowing euthanasia (by arguing for differences between a fetus and a person already living in the world).

Consequentialist arguments have different kinds of difficulties. As discussed before, the crucial difficulty facing anyone making a consequentialist argument is to calculate the consequences in a clear and reliable way. Have you considered all significant consequences? If you project your scenario of consequences further into the future (remember, consequentialist arguments are frequently stronger over the short term than over the long term, where many unforeseen consequences can occur), can you identify possibilities that work against the argument?

As also noted, consequentialist arguments carry a heavy burden of empirical proof. What evidence can you offer that the predicted consequences will in fact come to pass? Do you offer any evidence that alternative consequences won't occur? And just how do you prove that the consequences of any given action are a net good or evil?

In addition to the problems unique to each of the two positions, ethical arguments are vulnerable to the more general sorts of criticism, including consistency, recency, and relevance of evidence. Obviously, however, consequentialist arguments will be more vulnerable to weaknesses in evidence, whereas arguments based on principle are more open to questions about consistency of application.

READING

In the following essay, "The Case for Torture," philosopher Michael Levin argues that torture not only can be justified but is positively mandated under certain circumstances.

The Case for Torture

Michael Levin

1   It is generally assumed that torture is impermissible, a throwback to a more brutal age. Enlightened societies reject it outright, and regimes suspected of using it risk the wrath of the United States.

2   I believe this attitude is unwise. There are situations in which torture is not merely permissible but morally mandatory. Moreover, these situations are moving from the realm of imagination to fact.

3   **Death:**   Suppose a terrorist has hidden an atomic bomb on Manhattan Island which will detonate at noon on July 4 unless . . . (here follow the usual demands for money and release of his friends from jail). Suppose, further, that he is caught at 10 A.M. of the fateful day, but—preferring death to failure—won't disclose where the bomb is. What do we do? If we follow due process—wait for his lawyer, arraign him—millions of people will die. If the only way to save those lives is to subject the terrorist to the most excruciating possible pain, what grounds can there be for not doing so? I suggest there are none. In any case, I ask you to face the question with an open mind.

4   Torturing the terrorist is unconstitutional? Probably. But millions of lives surely outweigh constitutionality. Torture is barbaric? Mass murder is far more barbaric. Indeed, letting millions of innocents die in deference to one who flaunts his guilt is moral cowardice, an unwillingness to dirty one's hands. If *you* caught the terrorist, could you sleep nights knowing that millions died because you couldn't bring yourself to apply the electrodes?

5   Once you concede that torture is justified in extreme cases, you have admitted that the decision to use torture is a matter of balancing innocent lives against the means needed to save them. You must now face more realistic cases involving more modest numbers. Someone plants a bomb on a jumbo jet. He alone can disarm it, and his demands cannot be met (or if they can, we refuse to set a precedent by yielding to his threats). Surely we can, we must, do anything to the extortionist to save the passengers. How can we tell 300, or 100, or 10 people who never asked to be put in danger, "I'm sorry, you'll have to die in agony, we just couldn't bring ourselves to . . . ."

6   Here are the results of an informal poll about a third, hypothetical, case. Suppose a terrorist group kidnapped a newborn baby from a hospital. I asked four mothers if they would approve of torturing kidnappers if that were necessary to get their own newborns back. All said yes, the most "liberal" adding that she would like to administer it herself.

7   I am not advocating torture as punishment. Punishment is addressed to deeds irrevocably past. Rather, I am advocating torture as an acceptable measure for preventing future evils. So understood, it is far less objectionable than many extant punishments. Opponents of the death penalty, for example, are forever insisting that executing a murderer will not bring back his victim (as if the purpose of capital punishment were supposed to be resurrection, not deterrence or retribution). But torture, in the cases described, is intended not to bring anyone back but to keep innocents from being dispatched. The most powerful argument against using torture as a punishment or to secure confessions is that such prac-

tices disregard the rights of the individual. Well, if the individual is all that important—and he is—it is correspondingly important to protect the rights of individuals threatened by terrorists. If life is so valuable that it must never be taken, the lives of the innocents must be saved even at the price of hurting the one who endangers them.

Better precedents for torture are assassination and pre-emptive attack. No Allied leader would have flinched at assassinating Hitler, had that been possible. (The Allies did assassinate Heydrich.) Americans would be angered to learn that Roosevelt could have had Hitler killed in 1943—thereby shortening the war and saving millions of lives—but refused on moral grounds. Similarly, if nation A learns that nation B is about to launch an unprovoked attack, A has a right to save itself by destroying B's military capability first. In the same way, if the police can by torture save those who would otherwise die at the hands of kidnappers or terrorists, they must.   8

Idealism: There is an important difference between terrorists and their victims that should mute talk of the terrorists' "rights." The terrorist's victims are at risk unintentionally, not having asked to be endangered. But the terrorist knowingly initiated his actions. Unlike his victims, he volunteered for the risks of his deed. By threatening to kill for profit or idealism, he renounces civilized standards, and he can have no complaint if civilization tries to thwart him by whatever means necessary.   9

Just as torture is justified only to save lives (not extort confessions or recantations), it is justifiably administered only to those *known* to hold innocent lives in their hands. Ah, but how can the authorities ever be sure they have the right malefactor? Isn't there a danger of error and abuse? Won't We turn into Them?   10

Questions like these are disingenuous in a world in which terrorists proclaim themselves and perform for television. The name of their game is public recognition. After all, you can't very well intimidate a government into releasing your freedom fighters unless you announce that it is your group that has seized its embassy. "Clear guilt" is difficult to define, but when 40 million people see a group of masked gunmen seize an airplane on the evening news, there is not much question about who the perpetrators are. There will be hard cases where the situation is murkier. Nonetheless, a line demarcating the legitimate use of torture can be drawn. Torture only the obviously guilty, and only for the sake of saving innocents, and the line between Us and Them will remain clear.   11

There is little danger that the Western democracies will lose their way if they choose to inflict pain as one way of preserving order. Paralysis in the face of evil is the greater danger. Some day soon a terrorist will threaten tens of thousands of lives, and torture will be the only way to save them. We had better start thinking about this.   12

Critiquing "The Case for Torture"

1. Most people think of torture as an abhorrently barbarian practice that civilized society has outgrown. Yet Levin argues that in some cases torture is not only justified but mandated. In your own words, summarize Levin's argument.

2. Analyze Levin's argument in terms of our distinction between arguments from *principle* and arguments from *consequence*.

3. In "The Case for Torture," Levin mentions the possibility of some "murkier" cases in which it is difficult to draw a line demarcating legitimate from illegitimate use of torture. Try to come up with several examples of these "murkier" cases and explain what makes them murky.

part four

Writing from Sources

The Argument as a Formal Research Paper

16 Finding and Selecting Sources

The Library and the Internet

Although the "research paper" is a common writing assignment in college, students are often baffled by their professor's expectations. The problem is that students often think of research writing as presenting information rather than as creating an argument. One of our business school colleagues calls these sorts of research papers "data dumps": The student backs a truckload full of fresh data up to the professor's desk, dumps it, and says: "Here's your load of info on 'world poverty,' Prof. You make sense of it."

But a research paper shouldn't be a data dump. Like any other argument, it should use its information to support a contestable claim. Formal researched arguments have much in common with arguments that freelancers might write in a popular magazine. Consider the following passage from a science writer arguing that male aggression has a strong biological component:

> Preliminary work shows that fetal boys are a little more active than fetal girls. It's pretty difficult to argue socialization at this point. There is a strong suspicion that testosterone may create the difference.
>
> And there are a couple of relevant animal models to emphasize the point. Back in the 1960s, Robert Goy, a psychologist at the University of Wisconsin at Madison, first documented that young male monkeys play much more roughly than young females. Goy went on to show that if you manipulate testosterone level—raising it in females, damping it down in males—you can reverse those effects, creating sweet little male monkeys and rowdy young females. [. . .] Studies have found that girls with congenital adrenal hypoplasia—who run high in testosterone—tend

to be far more fascinated by trucks and weaponry than most little girls are. They lean toward rough-and-tumble play too.*

This article shares many features of a good research paper. It makes a contestable claim ("Testosterone levels account for much of the difference between male and female behavior"), and the author's supporting data come from external sources rather than personal experiences—in this case, scientific research.

However, there is one major difference between this article and a formal academic research paper—absence of citations. Because readers can't track down the author's sources, they have no way to judge the reliability of her information or to see whether the experiments being cited are open to different interpretations. (From our own research on gender identity, we know that many scientists would contest her claim; they would cite studies showing that cultural conditioning is a far greater factor than biology in creating gender differences.) In academic research, the purpose of in-text citations and a complete bibliography is to enable readers to follow the trail of the author's research. The proper formats for citations and bibliographic entries are simply conventions within an academic discipline to facilitate the reader's retrieval of the original sources.

Fortunately, you will find that writing an argument as a formal research paper draws on the same argumentation skills you have been using all along—the ability to pose a good question at issue within a community, to formulate a contestable claim, and to support your claim with audience-based reasons and evidence. What special skills are required? The main ones are these:

- The ability to use your research effectively to frame your issue and to support your claim, revealing your reputable ethos and knowledge of the issue. Sources should be woven seamlessly into your argument, which is written in your own voice throughout. Writers should avoid a pastiche of block quotations.

- The ability to tap the resources of libraries, online databases, Internet forums, and the World Wide Web.

- The ability to evaluate sources for credibility, bias, and accuracy. Special care is needed to evaluate anything retrieved from the "free access" portion of the World Wide Web.

- The ability to summarize, quote, or paraphrase sources and to avoid plagiarism through citations and attributive tags such as "according to Jones" or "Peterson says."

- The ability to cite and document sources according to appropriate conventions.

This chapter and the next should help you to develop these skills. In Chapter 16 we focus on posing a research question and on unlocking the resources of your

---

*Deborah Blum, "The Gender Blur," *Utne Reader* Sept.–Oct. 1998, 47–48.

library and the Internet. In Chapter 17 we explain the more nitty-gritty details of how to incorporate that information into your writing and how to document it properly.

FORMULATING A RESEARCH QUESTION

The best way to avoid writing a data dump is to begin with a good research question—the formulation of a problem or issue that your essay will address. The research question, usually in the form of an issue question, will give you a guiding purpose in doing your library research. Let's say you are interested in how toys affect the development of gender identity in children. You can see that this topic is big and unfocused. Your library research will be much easier if you give yourself a clear direction through a focused research question. For example, you might formulate a specific question like one of these:

- Why have Barbie dolls been so continuously popular?
- Does the Barbie doll reinforce traditional ideas of womanhood or challenge them?
- Is culture or biology the stronger force in making little boys interested in trucks and guns?
- Do boys' toys such as video games, complex models, electronic gadgets, and science sets develop intellectual and physical skills more than girls' toys do?

The sooner you can settle on a research question, the easier it will be to find the source materials you need in a time-saving, efficient manner. The exploration methods we suggested in Chapter 3 can help you find a research topic that interests you.

A good way to begin formulating a research question is to freewrite for ten minutes or so, reflecting on recent readings that have stimulated your interest, on recent events that have sparked arguments, or on personal experiences that might open up onto public issues. If you have no idea for a topic, try starting with the trigger question "What possible topics am I interested in?" If you already have an idea for a topic area, explore why you are interested in it. Search for the personal connections or the particular angles that most intrigue you. Here is how Lynnea, a student writer, began exploring a topic related to police work. She chose this topic because she had a friend who was a patrol officer.

LYNNEA'S FIRST FREEWRITE

Why am I attracted to this issue? What personal connections do I have?

My friend is a police officer and has been telling me about some of the experiences he has had while walking "the beat" downtown. The people he has to deal with are mostly street people: bums, gang members, drug dealers, etc. He tells me how he just harasses them to get them to move on and to leave the area, or he looks for a reason to give them a ticket so that eventually they will accumulate a few unpaid tickets, and they will have to go to jail. My friend told me about an experience where an alcoholic tramp started kicking his feet against the patrol car after he and his partner had walked about a block away to begin their night shift. The man started yelling at them to come back and kept hitting and throwing himself against the car. "OK, what are you doing that for?" they asked. The man stammered that he wanted to go to "detox." They told the guy that they would not take him to detox, so he kept on banging the car. What can be done about these people? Not only the alcoholics and vagrants, but what about the gang members, prostitutes, drug dealers, etc.? The police forces out on the streets at night seem to be doing little more than just ruffling a few feathers, but what else can they do under the circumstances?

On finishing this freewrite, Lynnea was certain that she wanted to write her research argument on something related to police work. The topic interested her, and having a patrol officer as a friend gave her an opportunity for interview data. She decided she was most interested in gangs and called her friend to get some more insights. Several days later, she met her friend at a local restaurant during his lunch break. After that meeting, she again did a freewrite.

LYNNEA'S SECOND FREEWRITE

Today I went with my friend for a cup of coffee to discuss some possible topics for my paper. He took me to a coffee shop where several of the officers in the area meet for lunch. I had wanted to ask Bob specific questions about gangs in the area, but when we joined the rest of the officers, I didn't have the chance. However, something they brought into the discussion *did* interest me. They were talking about a woman who had recently graduated from the academy and was now trying to pass the student officer's phase. This woman, I was informed, was 4'9" and weighed about 90 pounds. Apparently, at the academy she couldn't perform many of the physical exercises that her fellow trainees could. Where most of the men could pull a trigger between 80 and 90 times during the allotted time, she could pull the trigger of her police issue .38 revolver only once. And she was so tiny that they had to make a booster seat for the patrol car. One of the instructors said that her being in the academy was a joke. Well, it does seem that way to me. I can imagine this woman trying to handle a situation. How could she handcuff someone who resisted arrest? It seems dangerous that someone who is so weak should be allowed to be on patrol duty. I wouldn't want her as my back-up.

Lynnea now knew she had a topic that interested her. She wanted to research women patrol officers, especially the success rate of small women. She formulated her initial research question this way: "Can a small, physically weak woman, such as this 4'9" police candidate, make a good patrol officer?" Her initial thesis was that small, physically weak women could not make good patrol officers, but she wanted to keep an open mind, using argument as a means of clarification. As this chapter progresses, we will return occasionally to Lynnea's research project. (Her final argument essay is reproduced in full at the end of Chapter 17.)

EXPLORING ON THE INTERNET

Besides freewriting and sharing ideas with friends, today's researchers have the vast resources of the Internet and the World Wide Web as sources of ideas and help. Throughout a project, many researchers get invaluable assistance from list-serv discussions, Usenet newsgroups, or real-time chat groups.

Listserv Discussions

A potentially productive way to use e-mail is to join a listserv interest group. A listserv compiles any number of e-mail accounts into a mailing list and forwards copies of messages to all people on the list. There are thousands of well-established listservs about a wide variety of topics. You need to know the address of a list in order to join. Specific information about joining various listservs and an index of active lists can be found by entering either the Uniform Resource Locator (URL) address "http://tile.net/lists/" or "http://www.liszt.com" once you are on the World Wide Web in a browser.* Once you have subscribed to a listserv, you receive all messages sent to the list and any message you send to the list address will be forwarded to the other members.

A message sent to a listserv interest group is sure to find a responsive audience because all members on the list have chosen to take part in an ongoing discussion of the list's specific topic. Such lists often archive and periodically post important messages or frequently asked questions (FAQs) for you to study. Most lists are for serious students of the list's topic, so to avoid offending any list members, learn the conventions for posting a message before you jump in.

Although you may find all kinds of interactions on a listserv, many users expect thoughtful, well-organized statements. If you are posting a message that introduces a new thread of discussion, you should clearly state your position (or question) and summarize those of others. Here is a sample posting to a listserv on the environment.

```
To: environL@brahms.usdg.org
From: alanw@armadillo.edu (Alan Whigum)
Subject: Acid Rain and Action

I've been doing research on acid rain and am
troubled by some of the things I've found. For
instance, I've learned that washing coal gases with
```

*Each file on the World Wide Web has a unique address, or URL, that allows writers to link to information on the Web and lets users move to specific sites.

```
limestone before they are released could reduce
sulfur emissions. I know that the government has
the power to mandate such devices, but the real
problem seems to be lack of public pressure on
the government. Why don't people push for better
legislation to help end acid rain? I suppose it's
an economic issue.
```

In turn, you can expect cogent, thoughtful responses from the list members. Here's a possible reply to the preceding message.

```
To: environL@brahms.usdg.org
From: bboston@armadillo.edu
Subject: Re Acid Rain and Action

I think you are right in pointing out that it is
ultimately public pressure that will need to be
applied to reduce acid rain. I've heard the
argument that it is cost that prevents steps from
being taken; people will pay more for goods and
services if these measures are taken, so they
resist. However, judging from the people I've
talked to about the subject, I would say that a
bigger problem may be knowledge. Most of them
said they would be willing to pay a little bit
more for their electricity if it meant a safer
environment. People aren't aware that action
needs to be taken now, because the problem seems
remote.
```

When you join a listserv, you are granted instant access to a discourse community that is committed and knowledgeable about its topic. You can join one of the discussions already taking place on the list or post a request to get information and clarification about your own interests.

Listservs can take your ideas through a productive dialectic process as your message is seconded, refuted, complicated, and reclarified by the various list members. They also afford valuable opportunities to practice your summarizing skills as you respond to messages or provide additional information in a second posting. For example, suppose you take issue with a long message that placed the blame for youth violence on the music industry. Rather than reproducing that entire message, you might provide a brief summary of the main points. The summary not only would give the readers enough background information to appreciate fully your response, it also would help you determine the main points of the original message and pinpoint the issues on which you disagree.

Usenet Newsgroups

Among the most useful sections of the Internet for writers are the bulletin-board-like forums of Usenet newsgroups. Newsgroups are electronic forums that allow you to post or respond to messages about nearly any topic imaginable. Newsgroups can be powerful tools for exploring problems and considering alternative viewpoints. The news server at your school determines the organization and number of groups available to you. Some schools carry groups that provide articles from professional news services, such as AP, Reuters, and UPI. Others provide topic-centered discussion groups. Your campus system may also offer class newsgroups for exchanging messages and drafts with others at your school.

The majority of newsgroups are used by members of the larger Internet community. Although some groups are devoted to subjects that don't lend themselves directly to the work you are probably undertaking in the composition class, many are frequented by regulars who are professionals in their fields or individuals deeply interested in the topic of the newsgroup. One key to successfully interacting on newsgroups, then, is finding a group that is appropriate to your work. Most of the newsreading programs that are built into Web browsers have a search function that can help you select appropriate groups. Another strategy is to spend some time searching through the archives of newsgroup postings at the DejaNews site (http://www.dejanews.com). Using keywords, you can comb through postings either to tap into preexisting conversations or to pinpoint newsgroups that seem to take up the issues that you are interested in.

Once you find an appropriate group, you will need to work through the logistics of accessing the newsgroup, reading messages and, perhaps, posting messages of your own. Check with your instructor or computer center to find out how to access and interact with the groups available to you.

Although you may be tempted to begin participating in a group immediately, you should familiarize yourself with some of the style conventions and the audience for that particular newsgroup before jumping in. Take time to "lurk"— read and listen in to the group's postings. Debate on Usenet can become fairly heated, and a message that ignores previous postings can elicit angry responses ("flames"). In addition, a message that doesn't consider the newsgroup's audience or its favored style will likely be challenged. For example, if you want to post something in the "alt.fan.rush-limbaugh" group, you should be cautious about composing a message that openly contradicts Rush Limbaugh's brand of politics. If you send a message to the newsgroup "soc.history," you might be able to tread less carefully—this list is more politically diverse—although members of this group might take offense if asked an obvious factual question.

Regardless of their makeup, most groups resent being asked questions that have already been answered. Some groups provide an archive of frequently asked questions (FAQs). If your interest is in something practical that is likely to be covered in the FAQ files, refer to them before posting a query. You should use the expertise of the group to find information that you might not be able to uncover otherwise.

When you are ready to post a message, use some of the strategies outlined for composing a message to a listserv: Try to summarize and synthesize your own position as well as the positions of others; highlight what you see as the most problematic or murky aspects of the topic. Carefully constructed messages are most likely to receive useful responses.

When you do receive feedback, evaluate it with special care. The unfiltered nature of all Internet media makes critical reading an essential skill. Because anyone with an Internet connection can take part in a discussion or post a message or article, you need to evaluate this information differently than you would articles from national newsmagazines, which are professionally written, edited for clarity, and checked for accuracy.

Although most postings are thoughtful, you will also find carelessly written messages that misconstrue an argument, personal rants that offer few (if any) stated reasons for their claims, and propaganda and offensive speech of many kinds in certain newsgroups. It is your responsibility, and unique opportunity, to read newsgroup messages critically, looking for their various biases and making decisions about their relative authority.

Of course, printed sources are marked by their own biases. Deadlines and space constraints may limit the depth and accuracy of printed coverage, and firsthand insights may be screened by authors and editors. If you were studying attitudes toward the Middle East peace process, a newsgroup exchange between a conservative Jew in Israel and a Palestinian student in the United States might provide better insight than a news article for your work. As you read through newsgroup messages, take time to evaluate the users' personal investments in the issue. Compare their comments to those in traditional sources, check for accuracy, and look for differing perspectives. Work these perspectives into your own thinking and writing about the topic. Treat information and points of view gathered from the Internet as primary rather than as secondary material; many of the people who contribute such material care passionately about an issue. It is up to you to place this material in context and edit it for your own audience.

Real-Time Discussion or Chat

Real-time discussions, or chat, are *synchronous* exchanges that take place on a network—meaning that messages are transferred instantly back and forth among members taking part in the discussion. We focus on real-time interactions that take place on the Internet, but you can apply many of the strategies outlined here to local chat programs in your writing class. One of the most popular forms of real-time interaction takes place in the various channels of Internet Relay Chat (IRC). Additionally, many course Web sites now incorporate a chat function. As with newsgroup and listserv communications, in chat you compose messages on your own computer and send them through the chat program to other users on the network. Since the specifics for connecting and issuing the various commands vary, you will need to check with your instructor or an experienced user for information about using chat resources at your school.

Like other Internet forums, chat groups are organized around common interests, but real-time sessions are more spontaneous and informal than is communication through newsgroups or listservs because they consist of exchanges from people who are logged on at the same time. In these conversations, typographical and spelling errors are mostly overlooked, and abbreviations are an acceptable part of real-time style. The pace can be extremely fast, so users generally focus on getting their thoughts out rather than on producing highly polished messages.

Chat sessions and many other real-time exchanges also allow users to act as characters and to include scripted actions in the conversations. Imagine three users discussing flag burning:

```
William: I'm studying the constitutionality of
flag-burning amendments. Does anybody have any
opinions?

Pat Buchanan: I think that if you are an American,
you should respect the country enough not to deface
her symbols.

*Thomas Jefferson takes out a match and sets fire
to the corner of an old thirteen star flag. It's
probably more important to respect the underlying
principles of our country than its symbols.
```

The asterisk denotes that the user Thomas Jefferson has issued an "Action" or "Emote" command. By putting his name at the beginning of the message, other users see whatever follows as an action performed by that character. Users can construct a third-person narrative by mixing speech with the actions of their characters. You may use this feature in role-playing exercises or to explore some open-ended thinking about your topic.

Perhaps even more than newsgroup or listserv discussions, chat sessions tend to heat up easily. Many real-time forums on the Internet allow users to take on pseudonyms, and some people use the opportunity to become irresponsible in what they say and write.

Real-time interactions give rise to many ethical issues. In these uncensored forums, you will at times encounter discussions and materials that aren't appropriate for your assignments and classwork. You may be challenged to assess your own feelings about censorship, pornography, hate speech, and free speech. And you will need to consider the impact of your persona and words on others as you take on a character or act out an idea.

Perhaps the most useful function of chat sessions is that they promote brainstorming and freewriting. When you are writing in a real-time environment, treat the activity as an exploratory one. Expect the message that you send to be challenged, seconded, or modified by the other writers in the session. Keep an open mind about the various messages that fly back and forth, and be sure to respond to points that you find particularly useful or problematic. If you are interacting with classmates, you will be talking to people you know, so the conversation will be more predictable. When it's over, you might ask your instructor for a transcript of a chat session; reading it later will help solidify the free thinking that goes into a real-time discussion.

LOCATING SOURCES IN THE LIBRARY OR ONLINE

To be a good researcher, you need to unlock the resources of your college's or university's library. Today, most researchers are also using the vast resources of the Internet and the World Wide Web to find materials.

In addition to books, libraries have a wealth of other resources, such as articles in magazines and journals, statistical reports from government agencies, articles and editorials in newspapers (often on microfilm or microfiche), and congressional records. Books, of course, are important, but they tend to be less current than periodical sources. The key is to become skilled at using all of a library's resources.

Using the Online Catalog

Most libraries have converted their card catalogs to online computer-based systems, making card catalogs obsolete. The library online catalog is now your first source of information about the library's holdings. Indexed by subject, title, and author, the online catalog identifies most of the library's holdings: books, magazines, and journals (but not the titles of articles in them), newspapers, theses and dissertations, major government documents (but not minor ones), and most multimedia items including records, cassettes, and filmstrips.

To find the book, magazine, or journal in the stacks, you will need to know the two major systems for shelving books—the Dewey decimal system, which uses a series of numbers and decimals, and the Library of Congress system, which uses letters followed by numbers. Most college and university libraries use the Library of Congress system, although they may have an older book collection still classified using the Dewey decimal system. The following lists show the major categories in each system:

Dewey Decimal System

000	General Works
100	Philosophy and Related Disciplines
200	Religion

300	Social Sciences
400	Language
500	Pure Science
600	Technology and Applied Science
700	The Arts
800	Literature and Rhetoric
900	General Geography and History

Library of Congress System

A	General Works, Polygraphy
B	Philosophy, Psychology, and Religion
C	Auxiliary Sciences of History
D	General and Old World History (except America)
E–F	American History
G	Geography, Anthropology, Manners and Customs, Folklore, Recreation
H	Social Science, Statistics, Economics, Sociology
J	Political Science
K	Law
L	Education
M	Music
N	Fine Arts
P	Language and Literature
Q	Science
R	Medicine
S	Agriculture, Plant and Animal Industry, Fish Culture, Fisheries, Hunting, Game Protection
T	Technology
U	Military Science
V	Naval Science
Z	Bibliography and Library Science

Each of these headings is further subdivided according to an elaborate system of subclassifications. For example, in the Library of Congress system the book by William C. Grimm called *Familiar Trees of America* is filed under QK481 (Q = Science; K = Botany; 481 = North American trees). Knowing something of the system's logic helps you browse.

Figure 16.1 shows how one library's online catalog presents a book entry. Your library's online catalog will probably look similar.

```
                            ITEM REPORT
        Personal author:  Owings, Chloe.
                  Title:  Women police; a study of the
                          development and status of the
                          women police movement.
      Publication info:   Montclair, N.J., Patterson Smith,
                          1969.
  Physical description:   xxii, 337 p. 22 cm.
                 Series:  (Patterson Smith reprint series
                          in criminology, law enforcement,
                          and social problems, no. 28)
          General note:   Reprint of the 1925 ed.
                Subject:  Policewomen.

                          COPY MATERIAL      LOCATION
  1)363.22 OW3W               1 BOOK          STACKS
```

FIGURE 16.1   Book entry in online catalog

Accessing Online Databases

Often the best sources of information to support a researched argument come from periodicals (magazines, scholarly journals, and newspapers). Today most libraries use major online indexes called "general databases" to catalog such articles. Although the general databases available and the methods for accessing them vary from institution to institution, we offer a few guidelines that are widely applicable. Reference librarians at your institution can show you the specific commands you will need. Note also that online databases can often be accessed from anywhere in the world through your library's World Wide Web site. (Students, faculty, and staff usually have passwords or personal identification numbers for accessing the databases.)*

Most likely your library will have one or more of the following general databases online. Many of these databases indicate that they include not just abstracts of articles but the entire articles (full text).

> *EBSCOhost:* Includes interdisciplinary citations and abstracts as well as the full text of many articles from over 3,000 journals; its *Academic Search Elite* function covers back to the early 1980s.

---

*The general databases discussed in this section are sometimes called "licensed databases" because libraries have to pay a substantial fee to have access to them. The information in these databases is substantially different from that contained in the "free-access" part of the World Wide Web that one surfs with search engines such as Infoseek, Yahoo, or Lycos.

UMI Proquest Direct: Gives access to the full text of articles from journals in a variety of subject areas; includes the full text of articles from newspapers.

Infotrac: Is often called Expanded Academic Index; similar to EBSCOhost and UMI Proquest in its coverage of interdisciplinary subjects.

FirstSearch Databases: Includes multiple specialized databases in many subject areas; includes WorldCat, which contains records of books, periodicals, and multimedia formats in libraries worldwide.

Lexis-Nexis Academic Universe: Is primarily a full-text database covering current events and business and financial news; includes company profiles and legal, medical, and reference information.

Britannica Online: Includes the complete *Encyclopedia Britannica.*

Your first task when using these online resources is to choose which database to search. Sometimes, as with FirstSearch Databases, you will also have to choose from a list of databases contained within the general one. For example, in some libraries, ERIC, an important database that lists articles on education, is found within FirstSearch Databases. The reference librarians in your college or university library will be able to direct you to the most useful General Database for your purpose. For instance, for our purposes we found EBSCOhost and Lexis-Nexis particularly fruitful in helping us find many of the arguments used as readings in this textbook.

To use an online database—or most electronic research technology—effectively, you need to be adept at keyword searching. Figure 16.2 shows a page from a Results List for a search under the keyword "policewomen" in the database EBSCOhost. The page icon in the second left-hand column indicates that the full text of the article is available on the database. The "Note" under each entry indicates whether your particular library subscribes to the magazine. If you click on a specific article in the article listings, you get a full display page showing complete publishing information about that article. Figure 16.3 shows a full display page for the article "A Municipal Mother: Portland's Lola Greene Baldwin, America's First Policewoman." Note that this page provides an abstract of the article—useful for helping you decide whether you want to read the entire text.

When using online databases to find articles, you need to be persistent and flexible in your keyword searches. For example, if you are trying to find information on the economic influence of the timber industry in South America, you might enter the keywords "timber AND economics." If these keywords produce numerous entries on the spotted owl controversy in the Pacific Northwest, you might alter your keywords to "timber AND economics NOT owl" to free your screen of owl references. Most online catalogs allow you to refine keyword searches in a similar way, but you should check the options available before you begin working with an unfamiliar system. Again, your reference librarians can help you narrow down your searches or find other possible keywords to make your searches efficient.

Mark	Full Text	Select Result For More Detail
☐	📄	<u>Who Are the New Beat Poets? Hint: They're Blue.</u>; By: Grace, Julie., Time, 09/13/99, Vol. 154 Issue 11, p20, 1/5p, 1c **Note:** We subscribe to this magazine.
☐		<u>Officer Charged in Sexual Abuse of Ex-Companion.</u>; By: Cooper, Michael., New York Times, 08/31/99, Vol. 148 Issue 51631, pB4, 0p **Note:** We subscribe to this magazine.
☐		<u>Ban on Skirts For Guards Is Challenged.</u>; By: Herszenhorn, David M.., New York Times, 08/26/99, Vol. 148 Issue 51626, pB6, 0p **Note:** We subscribe to this magazine.
☐	📄	<u>Women face 'blue wall' of resistance.</u> (cover story); By: Marks, Alexandra., Christian Science Monitor, 08/18/99, Vol. 91 Issue 184, p1, 0p, 1c **Note:** We subscribe to this magazine.
☐	📄	<u>Affirmative Action, Political Representation, Unions, and Female Police Employment.</u>; By: Sass, Tim R., and Troyer, Jennifer L.., Journal of Labor Research, Fall99, Vol. 20 Issue 4, p571, 17p, 4 charts **Note:** We do not subscribe to this magazine.
☐	📄	<u>Do women make better peacekeepers?</u>; By: DeGroot, Gerard J.., Christian Science Monitor, 07/14/99, Vol. 91 Issue 159, p9, 0p, 1 cartoon **Note:** We subscribe to this magazine.
☐	📄	<u>She goes 'mano a mano' with drug lords.</u> (cover story); By: Marks, Alexandra., Christian Science Monitor, 06/01/99, Vol. 91 Issue 129, p1, 0p, 1c **Note:** We subscribe to this magazine.
☐		<u>Iran to Train *Policewomen.*</u>, New York Times, 05/27/99, Vol. 148 Issue 51535, pA5, 0p **Note:** We subscribe to this magazine.
☐	📄	<u>News Digest.</u>, Workforce, May99, Vol. 78 Issue 5, p18, 1/3p **Note:** We do not subscribe to this magazine.
☐		<u>A municipal mother: Portland's Lola Greene Baldwin, America's first policewoman.</u>; By: Myers, Gloria E., Peace Research Abstracts Journal, 2/1/99, Vol. 36, Issue 1, p0, 0p **Note:** We subscribe to this magazine.

FIGURE 16.2   Sample results list for a search using EBSCOhost

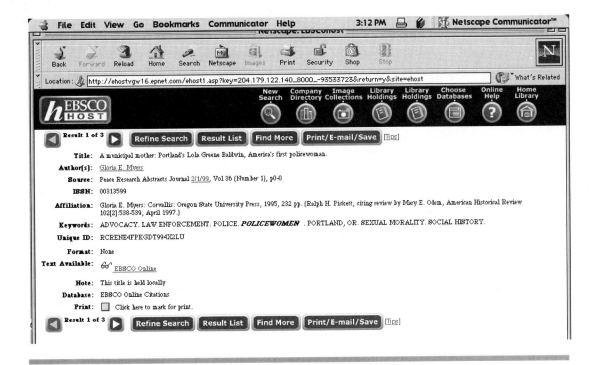

FIGURE 16.3   Sample full display for an article listing on EBSCOhost

Although the full texts of many articles are available online, you should always locate the original magazine or scholarly journal if possible. Articles printed online are decontextualized, giving you no clues about the author, the intended audience, the political bias of the original publication, and so forth. When you look at the original publication—its format, its table of contents, the advertisements it contains, the length and range and style of its articles—you have a rhetorical context for analyzing the article. Therefore if your library has the magazine, newspaper, or scholarly journal—or if it provides quick access to interlibrary loan—jot down all the key information given in the database: name of the magazine or journal, the volume, year, and page numbers. You will need this information to find the article in your library's periodical collection or to order it through interlibrary loan.

Using Specialized Indexes

Depending on the subject area of your research, you may find that specialized indexes can give you more useful information than general databases. Formerly, specialized indexes, which list articles in more narrow and specific areas than do general databases, appeared as hard-copy volumes housed in the reference area of libraries. Today many of these specialized indexes are online as well as in print, and the online versions are substantially easier to use. In the following list, we briefly describe some of the specialized indexes that writers of arguments might find useful. The information given after each index title indicates whether the index exists in both book (noted as "print") and online form:

ABI/Inform. (Online). Includes citations on business and management topics in U.S. and international publications.

America: History and Life. (Print and online). Includes abstracts and scholarly articles on the history of the United States and Canada.

ERIC Database. (Online). Consists of references to thousands of educational topics and includes journal articles, books, theses, curricula, conference papers, and standards and guidelines.

General Science Abstracts. (Print and online). Includes journals and magazines from the United States and Great Britain, covering such subjects as anthropology, astronomy, biology, computers, earth sciences, medicine, and health; includes articles, reviews, biographical sketches, and letters to the editor.

Historical Abstracts. (Print and online). Includes abstracts of scholarly articles on world history (excluding the United States and Canada) from 1775 to 1945.

Humanities Abstracts. (Print and online). Includes periodicals in archaeology, art, classics, film, folklore, journalism, linguistics, music, the performing arts, philosophy, religion, world history, and world literature.

Medline. (Online). Includes journals published internationally covering all areas of medicine.

MLA (Modern Language Association) Bibliography. (Print and online). Indexes scholarly articles on literature, languages, linguistics, and folklore published worldwide.

New York Times Index. (Print and online). Covers international, national, business, and New York regional news as well as sciences, medicine, arts, sports, and lifestyle news; makes the full text of articles available for the last ninety days.

Public Affairs Information Service (PAIS) International. (Print and online). Consists of articles, books, conference proceedings, government documents, book chapters, and statistical directories about public affairs.

Social Sciences Abstracts. (Print and online). Covers international, English-language periodicals in sociology, anthropology, geography, economics, political science, and law; concentrates on articles published in scholarly journals aimed at professional scholars rather than the general audience.

UMI Newspaper Abstracts. (Online). Covers national and regional newspapers; includes the *Wall Street Journal.*

Awareness of these specialized indexes may increase the efficiency of your research as well as expand your skill and power as a researcher.

Using Other Library Sources

Besides being a storehouse for books and periodicals, your library has a wealth of material in the reference section that may be useful to you in finding background information, statistics, and other kinds of evidence. Here are some sources that we have found particularly useful in our own research.

1. *Encyclopedias.* For getting quick background information on a topic, you will often find that a good encyclopedia is your best bet. Besides the well-known general-purpose encyclopedias such as the *Encyclopedia Britannica,* there are excellent specialized encyclopedias devoted to in-depth coverage of specific fields. Among the ones you might find most useful are these:

The International Encyclopedia of the Social Sciences

Dictionary of American History

Encyclopedia of World Art

McGraw-Hill Encyclopedia of Science and Technology

2. *Facts on File.* These interesting volumes give you a year-by-year summary of important news stories. If you wish to assemble a chronological summary of a news event such as Hillary Clinton's task force on national health coverage, ethnic wars in the Balkan countries, or the end of apartheid in South Africa, *Facts on File* gives you a summary of the events along with information about exact dates so that you can find the full stories in newspapers. A special feature is a series of excellent maps in the back of each volume, allowing you to find all geographical place names that occur in the year's news stories. The front cover of each volume explains how to use the series.

3. *Statistical Abstracts of the United States.* Don't even consider picking up one of these volumes if you don't have some spare time. You will get hooked on the fascinating graphs, charts, and tables compiled by the Bureau of Statistics. For statistical data about birth rates and abortions, marriages and divorces, trends in health care, trends in employment and unemployment, nutritional habits, and a host of other topics, these yearly volumes are a primary source of quantitative information about life in the United States.

4. *Congressional Abstracts.* For people working on current or historical events related to politics or any controversy related to the public sector, this index can guide you to all debates about the topic in the Senate or the House of Representatives.

5. *Book Review Digest.* For writers of argument, this series can be a godsend because it provides not only a brief summary of a book but also excerpts from a variety of reviews of the book, allowing the writer to size up quickly the conversation surrounding the book's ideas. To use *Book Review Digest,* you need to know the publishing date of the book for which you want to find reviews. Generally, reviews first appear in the same year the book was published and for several years thereafter. If you want to read reviews, for example, of a book appearing in 1992, you would probably find them in the 1992, 1993, and (if the book was very popular or provocative) 1994 volumes of *Book Review Digest.*

LOCATING AND EVALUATING SOURCES ON THE WORLD WIDE WEB

Another valuable resource for writers of argument is the network of linked computers known broadly as the Internet and more narrowly as the World Wide Web. In this section we begin by explaining briefly the logic of the Internet—the difference between restricted, licensed databases of the kind we discussed in the previous section and the amorphous, ever-changing "free-access" portion of the Internet commonly called the World Wide Web. Then we explain common methods of searching the Web. Finally, we suggest strategies for evaluating Web sites, which can vary enormously in their reliability, accuracy, and usefulness.

The Logic of the Internet

To learn the logic of Internet search engines, you should realize that the Internet is divided into a restricted section open only to those with special access rights (for example, the library online catalogs and general databases discussed in the previous section of this chapter) and a free-access section. Web search engines such as Yahoo or Infoseek search only the free-access portion of the Web; they do not have access to licensed databases or the holdings of libraries. When you search a topic through a licensed database such as EBSCOhost, for example, you retrieve the titles of articles (and often full texts) that originally appeared in magazines, newspapers, and scholarly journals. When you search the same topic through a Web search engine such as Yahoo, you retrieve information posted to the Web by users of the world's networked computers—government agencies, corporations, advocacy groups, information services, individuals with their own Web sites, and hosts of others.

The following example will quickly show you the difference. When we entered the keyword "policewomen" into EBSCOhost, we received 67 "hits"—the titles of 67 recent articles on the subject of policewomen (see Figure 16.2). In contrast, when we entered the same keyword into the Web search engine Infoseek, we received 3,941 "hits"—all the Web sites available to Infoseek that had the word "policewomen" appear somewhere in the site. When we plugged the same word into AltaVista, we received 2,704 hits, and only two of the first ten from AltaVista matched the first ten from Infoseek.

FOR CLASS DISCUSSION

The figures on pages 380 and 381 show the first seven "hits" for the keyword "policewomen" retrieved by the search engine GoTo (Figure 16.4) and the first five hits retrieved by AltaVista (Figure 16.5). Working in small groups or as a whole class, compare these items with those retrieved from a search for "policewomen" in the licensed database EBSCOhost (Figure 16.2).

1. Explain in your own words why the results for the Web searches are different both from each other and from the licensed database search.

2. Which of the Web sites from AltaVista and GoTo might prove useful for Lynnea's research project on whether a physically weak woman can make a good police officer?

Using Search Engines

Although the World Wide Web contains everything from gold to garbage, its resources for writers of argument are breathtaking. At your fingertips you have access to government documents and statistics, legislative white papers, court cases, persuasive appeals of advocacy groups—the list seems endless. Moreover, the hypertext structure of Web sites lets Web designers create links to other sites so that users can read an argument from an advocacy group in one Web site and then have instant links to the argument's sources at other Web sites.

The World Wide Web can be searched with a variety of powerful browsers, which collect and categorize a large number of Internet files and search them for keywords. Most of these search engines will find not only text files but also graphical, audio, and video files. Some look through the titles of files; others scan the entire text of documents. Different search engines can scan different resources, so it is important that you try a variety of searches when you look for information. Although the Web is evolving rapidly, some of the best search engines are fairly stable. For starters, you might try the following:

Hotbot (http://www.hotbot.com)   Webcrawler (http://www.webcrawler.com)

Yahoo (http://www.yahoo.com)   AltaVista (http://www.altavista.com)

Lycos (http://www.lycos.com)   GoTo (http://www.goto.com)

If you are in doubt, your reference librarians can help you choose the most productive search engine for your needs.

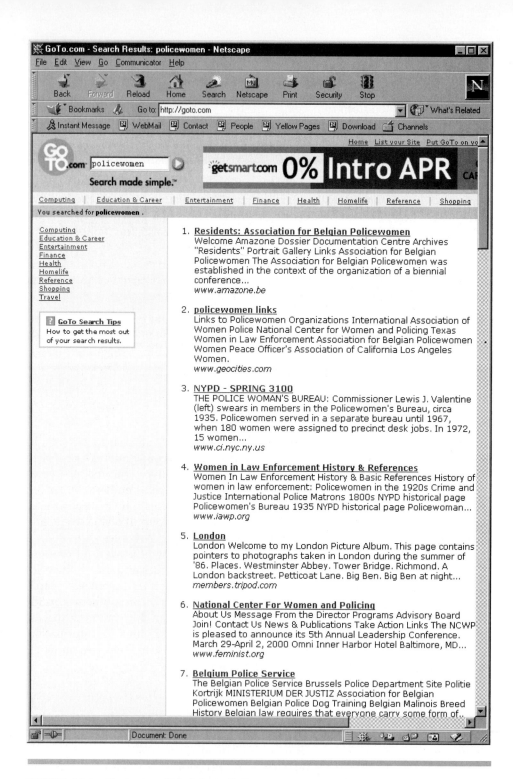

FIGURE 16.4   First seven "hits" from GoTo

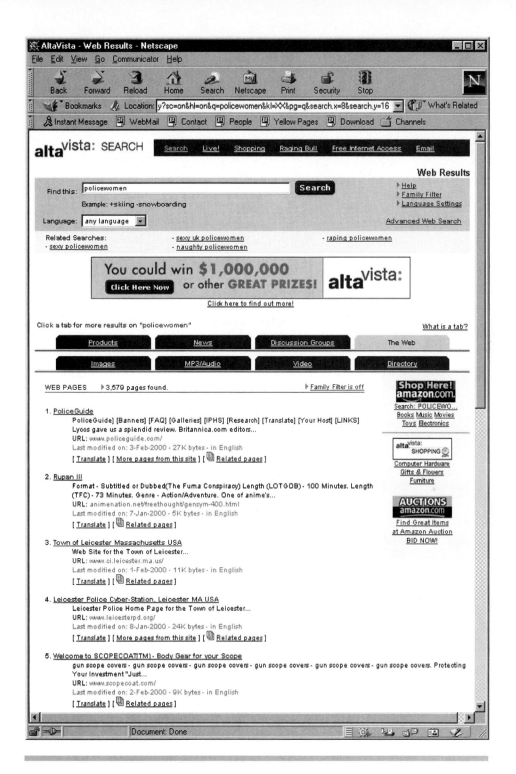

FIGURE 16.5   First five hits from AltaVista

Browsing the Web is an excellent way to help focus your thinking about an issue or topic and scout for resources. Some of the links that you follow will be dead ends; others will lead to new discoveries and useful collections of subject-related sources. Always be aware that anybody can put practically anything on the Web. The next section will help you learn to evaluate Web sites.

Evaluating Web Sites

Although the Web is an exciting, inexhaustible source of information, it also contains lots of junk, and therefore you need to evaluate Web material carefully. Anyone with hypertext skills can put up a Web page that furthers his or her own agenda. Flashy graphics and other design elements can sometimes overwhelm the information that is being presented or lend an air of authority to an otherwise suspect argument or position.

When you look at a Web site, begin by asking the following two questions:

- *What kind of Web site is it?* Web sites can have distinctly different purposes. Business/marketing Web sites are aimed at attracting and serving customers as well as creating a favorable public image. Informational/ government Web sites are aimed at providing basic data ranging from traffic information to bills being debated in Congress. News Web sites supplement coverage in other media. Advocacy Web sites (often indicated by *.org* at the end of their URL address) attempt to influence public opinion on disputed issues. Special interest Web sites are aimed at connecting users with common interests ranging from recent film reviews to kayaking. Personal home pages are created by individuals for their own purposes.
- *What is my purpose in using this Web site?* Am I trying to get an initial understanding of the various points of view on an issue, looking for reliable data, or seeking expert testimony to support my thesis? Joe's Web page— let's say Joe wants California to secede from the United States—may be a terrible source for reliable data about the federal government but an excellent source for helping you understand the views of fringe groups.

One of the most challenging parts of using the Web is determining whether a site offers gold or glitter. Sometimes the case may not be clear-cut. How do you sort out reliable, worthwhile sites from unreliable ones? We offer the following criteria developed by scholars and librarians as points to consider when you are using Web sites.

Criterion 1: Authority

- Is the author or sponsor of the Web site clearly identified?
- Does the site identify the occupation, position, education, experience, and credentials of the site's authors?

- Does the introductory material reveal the author's or sponsor's motivation for publishing this information on the Web?
- Does the site provide contact information for the author or sponsor such as an e-mail or organization address?

Criterion 2: Objectivity or Clear Disclosure of Advocacy

- Is the site's purpose (to inform, explain, or persuade) clear?
- Is the site explicit about declaring its author's or sponsor's point of view?
- Does the site indicate whether authors are affiliated with a specific organization, institution, or association?
- Does the site indicate whether it is directed toward a specific audience?

Criterion 3: Coverage

- Are the topics covered by the site clear?
- Does the site exhibit suitable depth and comprehensiveness for its purpose?
- Is sufficient evidence provided to support the ideas and opinions presented?

Criterion 4: Accuracy

- Are the sources of information stated? Can you tell whether this information is original or taken from someplace else?
- Does the information appear to be accurate? Can you verify this information by comparing this source with other sources in the field?

Criterion 5: Currency

- Are dates included in the Web site?
- Do the dates apply to the material itself or to its placement on the Web? Is the site regularly revised and updated?
- Is the information current, or at least still relevant, for the site's purpose?

To illustrate how these criteria can help you deal with the good points and the deficiencies of Web material, we give an example of how to use the criteria to assess the value of Web information. We wanted to investigate the United States' involvement in exploitation of workers in sweatshops. We specifically wanted to investigate this question: "To what extent are caps and shirts with university logos produced under sweatshop conditions?"

To start our investigation of the link between university-licensed clothing and sweatshops, we entered the keyword "sweatshop" into Yahoo, our selected search engine. We discovered a vast anti-sweatshop movement with a number of promising sites for our first-step initiation into the issues. We decided to investigate the site of "NMASS," which we discovered was the abbreviation for "National Mobilization against Sweatshops" (http://www.nmass.org). Figure 16.6 shows the initial Web page of this site. Using the criteria for evaluating Web sites, we were able to identify the strengths and weaknesses of this site in the light of our question and purpose.

This site does well when measured against the criteria "authority" and "clear disclosure of advocacy." On the home page, the organization's title, "National Mobilization Against Sweatshops," boldly announces its perspective. Information in the bulleted list openly declares its purpose: "Become a sweatshop buster!" The links then provide more detailed information on the goals of the organization. In the "Mission Statement" link, the site forthrightly declares:

> The National Mobilization Against Sweatshops (NMASS) is a grassroots educational effort by and for working people and youth of all backgrounds and communities. NMASS was first started by members and supporters of the Chinese Staff and Workers' Association, an independent workers' center in New York's Chinatown.

Links mentioned on the home page indicate that this site is directed toward both members and prospective members; it seeks to rally the members of the organization and to win new supporters. The site does provide contact information by giving an address for comments and suggestions: nmass@yahoo.com.

We found that this site provides good coverage of material for its purpose, even though it does not specifically address our research question. Particularly, the link called "8 Myths about Sweatshops" introduced us to important sweatshop issues such as the existence of sweatshops in the United States, the exploitation of immigrant workers, the level of government involvement in addressing the problem, and the ineffectiveness of unions. Several of these links identify industries involved with sweatshops, but the site does not give specific information about university-licensed clothing and sweatshops.

The fourth criterion ("accuracy") enabled us to identify some problems with the accuracy of the site's information for our purposes. The links called "Global Sweatshop" and "8 Myths about Sweatshops" offer a number of facts and figures about the origin and history of sweatshops and about current working-conditions, yet no specific sources are cited. These statements are startling and compelling, but are they accurate? And what opposing information should be considered?

Finally, the site seemed satisfactory, but a little vague, with regard to currency. Although the links revealed sources with recent, up-to-date copyright dates, the site itself does not indicate how often it is updated.

In short, we found this site helpful as a first stop to acquaint us with the stakes in the anti-sweatshop movement, but we concluded that this site's information is too broad for our purposes. Furthermore, this site could not stand as a major, unverified source. Using the evaluation criteria helped us recognize our need for more

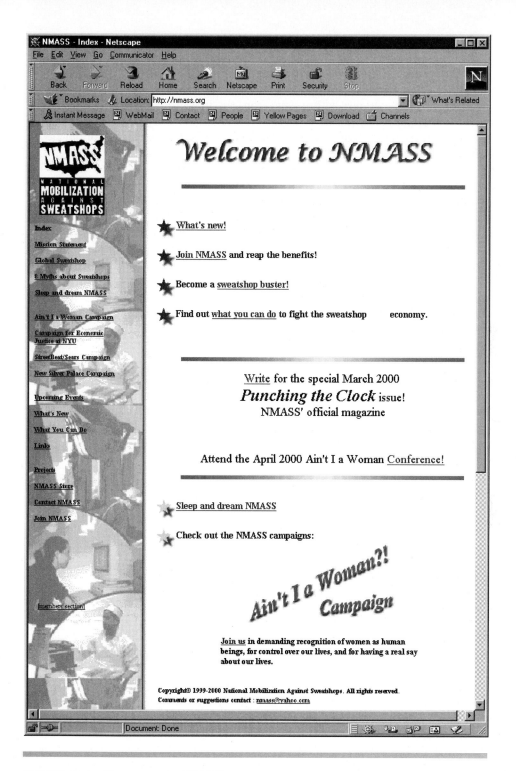

FIGURE 16.6   Home page for NMASS

in-depth research and follow-up investigations. We realized, particularly, that we would need to investigate sweatshops from the perspective of industry (such as the American Apparel Manufacturers Association at www.americanapparel.org) and government regulatory agencies (such as the Bureau of International Labor Affairs at www.dol.gov/dol/ilab).

USING YOUR SOURCES: SITTING DOWN TO READ

Once you have developed a working bibliography of books and articles and have gathered a collection of materials, how do you go about reading and note-taking? There is no easy answer. At times you need to read articles carefully, fully, and empathically—reading as a believer and as a doubter, as discussed in Chapter 2, trying to understand various points of view on your issue, seeing where the disagreements are located, and so forth. Your goal at this time is to clarify your own understanding of the issue in order to join responsibly the ongoing conversation.

At other times you need to read quickly, skimming an article in search of a needed piece of information, an alternative view, or a timely quotation. All these considerations and others—how to get your ideas focused, how to take notes, how to incorporate source material into your own writing, and how to cite and document your sources—are the subjects of the next chapter.

17

Using and Documenting Sources

The previous chapter helped you pose a good research question and begin unlocking some of the resources of your library and the Internet. This chapter helps you see what to do with your sources once you have found them—how to use them to clarify your own thinking and how to incorporate them into your writing through effective use of quotations, paraphrases, and summaries along with appropriate conventional formats for citations and documentation.

CLARIFYING YOUR OWN THINKING: THE CASE OF LYNNEA

In the previous chapter, we followed Lynnea's progress as she posed her research question on the effectiveness of policewomen and began her search for sources. Once Lynnea located several articles on policewomen, she found a quiet spot in the library and began to read. She was guided by two related questions: What physical requirements must someone meet in order to be an effective patrol officer? How successful have policewomen been when assigned to patrol duty? After reading some recent articles, Lynnea noticed that writers often referred to significant earlier studies, particularly a 1984 study called *Policewomen on Patrol, Final Report* by P. B. Bloch and D. Anderson. Lynnea tracked down this study as well as several others referred to in the first articles she read.

Both Lynnea's experience and her research strategy are typical. As a researcher becomes familiar with the ongoing conversation on an issue, she will notice that recent writers frequently refer to the same earlier studies or to the same earlier voices in the conversation. In scientific writing, this background reading is so important that the introductions to scientific studies usually include a "review of the literature" section, wherein writers summarize important research done to date on the question under investigation and identify areas of consensus and disagreement.

Therefore, during the first hours of her research project, Lynnea conducted her own "review of the literature" concerning women on patrol. During an early visit to her university's writing center, she reported that she had found three kinds of studies:

1. *Studies attempting to identify the attitude of the police establishment (overwhelmingly male) toward women entering the police profession and the attitude of the general public toward women patrol officers.* Although the findings weren't entirely consistent, Lynnea reported that male police officers generally distrusted women on patrol and felt that women didn't have the required physical strength or stamina to be patrol officers. The public, however, was more accepting of women patrol officers.

2. *Studies attempting to evaluate the success of women on patrol by examining a variety of data such as arrests made, use of force, firing of weapons, interviews with persons involved in incidents, and evaluation reports by superiors.* Lynnea reported that these studies were generally supportive of women police officers and showed that women cops were as successful as men cops.

3. *Studies examining the legal and political battles fought by women to gain access to successful careers in police work.* Lynnea reported being amazed at how much prejudice against women was evident in the police establishment.

At a writing center conference Lynnea confessed that, as a result of her readings, she was beginning to change her mind: She was now convinced that women could be effective patrol officers. But she wasn't convinced that *all* women could be effective officers any more than *all* men could be. She still felt that minimum size and strength requirements should be necessary. The problem was, she reported, that she couldn't find any information related to size and strength issues. Moreover, the research on women police officers did not mention anything about the size or strength of the women being studied. Were these successful patrol officers "big, husky" women, Lynnea asked, or "petite" women, or both? She left the writing center in pursuit of more data.

Lynnea's dilemma is again typical. As we discussed in Chapter 2, the search for clarification often leads to uncertainty. As you immerse yourself in the conversation surrounding an issue, you find that the experts often disagree and that no easy answers emerge. Your goal under these circumstances is to find the best reasons available and to support them with the best evidence you can muster. But the kind of uncertainty Lynnea felt is both healthy and humbling. If your own research leads to similar feelings, we invite you to reread Strategy 4 in Chapter 2 (pp. 44–47) where, in our discussion of the pay equity controversy, we suggest our own methods for coping with ambiguity.

We'll leave Lynnea at this point to take up the technical side of writing research arguments. Besides using research to clarify your own thinking, you also need to have strategies for note taking and for incorporating the results of your reading into your own writing through proper citations and documentation.

DEVELOPING A GOOD SYSTEM OF NOTE TAKING

There is no one right way to take notes. For short research papers, many students keep all their notes in a spiral notebook; others use a system of 3-by-5 cards (for bibliographic information) and 5-by-8 cards (for actual notes). Increasingly, researchers use database software on their personal computers. Whatever system you use, the key is to take notes that are complete enough so that you don't have to keep going back to the library to reread your sources. Some students try to get around this problem by photocopying all articles they might use in their essays or printing complete texts from online databases, but this is an expensive habit that doesn't help you synthesize information or make it your own.

It is much easier to take good notes for a research project if you have your issue question clearly formulated. When you know your issue question, you can anticipate how information from books and articles is likely to get incorporated into your essay. Sometimes you will need to write an accurate summary of a whole article as part of your research notes. At other times you may want to jot down only some facts or figures from an article. At still other times you may want to copy a passage word for word as a potential quotation. There is no way to know what kind of notes you will need to take on each book or article unless you can predict what kind of thesis you will be supporting. We therefore continue our comments on the art of note taking as we discuss ways information can be used in a research essay.

INCORPORATING SOURCES INTO YOUR ARGUMENT: SOME GENERAL PRINCIPLES

To illustrate different ways that you can use a source, we will use the following brief article from the magazine *Science '86*.

Reading, Writing, and (Ugh!) You Know What

ANN ARBOR, Mich.—Not only are American high school students worse at mathematics than their Japanese and Chinese peers, they start falling behind in kindergarten.   1

That's one conclusion of a five-year study done by psychologist Harold Stevenson and   2
graduate student Shin-ying Lee, both of the University of Michigan, and psychologist James

Stigler of the University of Chicago. The study also shows for the first time that parents must share the blame.

3   More than 2,000 children in kindergarten and the first and fifth grades were tested and interviewed in Minneapolis, in Sendai, Japan, and in Taipei, China. The researchers composed the test for each grade from math problems found in textbooks in all three cities.

4   All the children in each grade performed equally well on reading and general intelligence tests, but math scores differed from the start. While average scores for U.S. and Chinese kindergarten students were the same, Japanese kindergartners scored about 10 percent higher. First graders in the U.S. were surpassed by their peers in both China and Japan by an average of 10 percent. Then the gap widened. The top U.S. fifth-grade class scored below the lowest Japanese class and the second lowest Chinese class. Of the 100 highest scoring fifth graders, one was American.

5   A crucial difference is time: Chinese and Japanese students spend more hours in math class and attend school some 240 days a year, Americans about 180. But another difference, the researchers found, is parental influence. Chinese and Japanese parents give their children more help with math homework than U.S. parents, who tended to believe that "ability" was the premier reason for academic success, according to the researchers' interviews. Chinese and Japanese parents, in contrast, most often said "effort" was most important. And more than 90 percent of U.S. parents believed the schools did an "excellent" job teaching math and other subjects; most Japanese and Chinese parents said the schools did a "fair" job.

6   "American parents are very involved in teaching reading," says Stigler. "But they seem to think that teaching math is the school's job. It's as if it gets them off the hook."

Citing Information

Sometimes the complete argument of an article may not be relevant to your essay. Often you will use only a piece of information from the article. For example, let's suppose you are writing an argument claiming that American society, as a whole, values individual creativity more than does Japanese society. You plan to contrast an open classroom in an American grade school with a more regimented Japanese classroom. At the end of the passage, you might write something like this:

> Not only is education in Japan more regimented than it is in the United States, it continues through a much longer school year. A typical Japanese grade school student attends classes 240 days a year compared with 180 days a year in the United States ("Reading" 7). Although such a system might produce more academic achievement, it provides little time for children to be children, to play and daydream—essential ingredients for nurturing creativity.*

---

*The material in parentheses ("Reading" 7) cites the source of the information in MLA format. This citation directs the reader to look in the Works Cited list at the end of the essay and find the entry listed alphabetically by its title as "Reading, Writing, and (Ugh!) You Know What" for complete bibliographic information. The cited information is found on page 7 of that article. Ordinarily, the author's name rather than the shortened title would be cited in the parenthetical reference, but in this case no author's name was mentioned in the source.

Here the total argument of the *Science '86* article isn't relevant to the writer's essay. He has borrowed only the small detail about the length of the school year (which, of course, the writer documents by means of a citation in parentheses). In his original note cards, the writer would not have had to summarize the whole *Science '86* article. By knowing his research question, he would have known that only this piece of information was relevant.

Summarizing an Argument: Different Contexts Demand Different Summaries

On other occasions, however, you may need to summarize the entire argument of an essay, or at least a major portion of the argument. How you summarize it depends once again on the context of your own essay because your summary must focus on your own thesis. To illustrate how context influences a summary, we will examine passages by two different writers, Cheryl and Jeff, each of whom uses the *Science '86* article, "Reading, Writing, and (Ugh!) You Know What," but in the context of different arguments. Cheryl is writing on the issue of heredity versus environment in the determination of scholastic achievement. She is making the causal claim that environment plays a key role in scholastic high achievement. Jeff is writing on American mathematics education. He is making the evaluation claim that American mathematics education is in a dangerous shambles. Both writers include a summary of the *Science '86* article,* but their summaries are written in different ways in order to emphasize different aspects of the article.

PASSAGE FROM CHERYL'S ESSAY ON HEREDITY VERSUS ENVIRONMENT

Another argument showing the importance of environment on scholastic achievement comes from a research study done by psychologists at the University of Chicago and the University of Michigan ("Reading" 7). These researchers compared the mathematics achievement of 2000 kindergartners, first graders, and fifth graders from the United States, Japan, and China. At the beginning of the study the researchers determined that the comparison groups were equal in terms of reading ability and general intelligence. But the American students were far behind in mathematics achievement. At the first grade level, the researchers reported, American students were 10 percent behind Japanese and Chinese students and considerably further behind by the end of the fifth grade. In fact, only one American student scored in the top 100 of all students.

What is significant about this study is that heredity seems to play no factor in accounting for the differences between American students and their Japanese and Chinese counterparts since the comparison groups were shown to be of equal intelligence at the beginning of the study. The researchers attribute the differences between the groups to the time they spent on math (Japanese students go to class

_____

*The citations follow the MLA format described later in this chapter.

240 days per year while Americans are in class only 180 days per year) and to parental influence. According to the study, American parents believe that native "ability" is the key factor in math achievement and don't seem to push their children as much. Japanese and Chinese parents, however, believe that "effort" is the key factor and spend considerably more time than American parents helping their children with their math homework (8). Thus, it is the particular environment created by Chinese and Japanese societies, not inherited intelligence, that accounts for the greater math achievement of children in those cultures.

PASSAGE FROM JEFF'S ESSAY ON THE FAILURE
OF MATHEMATICS EDUCATION IN THE UNITED STATES

Further evidence of the disgraceful nature of mathematics education in the United States is the dismal performance of American grade school students in mathematics achievement tests as compared to children from other cultures. One study, reported in the magazine *Science '86,* revealed that American kindergarten students scored 10 percent lower on mathematics knowledge than did kindergartners from Japan. This statistic suggests that American parents don't teach arithmetical skills in the home to preschoolers the way Japanese parents do.

But the most frightening part of the study showed what happens by the fifth grade. The best American class in the study scored below the worst Chinese or Japanese class, and of the top 100 students only one was an American ("Reading" 8). The differences between the American students and their Chinese and Japanese counterparts cannot be attributed to intelligence because the article reports that comparison groups were matched for intelligence at the beginning of the study. The difference can be accounted for only by the quality of education and the effort of students. The researchers who did this study attributed the difference first of all to time. According to the study, Chinese and Japanese students spend 240 days per year in school while Americans spend only 180. The second reason for the difference is parental influence, since Japanese and Chinese parents spend much more time than American parents helping their children with mathematics. The study suggests that if we are to do anything about mathematics education in the United States we need a revolution not only in the schools but in the home.

FOR CLASS DISCUSSION

Although both of the preceding passages summarize the *Science '86* article, "Reading, Writing, and (Ugh!) You Know What," they use the article to support somewhat different claims. Working as individuals or in groups, prepare short answers to the following questions. Be ready to elaborate on your answers in class if called on to defend them.

1. What makes each passage different from a data dump?

2. In what ways are the summaries different? (Compare the summaries to each other and to the original article.)

3. How does the difference between the summaries reflect a different purpose in each passage?

Article Summaries as a Note-Taking Tool

Both Cheryl's passage and Jeff's summarize the *Science '86* article accurately. To be able to write summaries such as these when you compose your rough drafts, you need to have the articles at hand (by photocopying them from the library or printing them online), or you need to have written summaries of the articles in your note cards. We strongly recommend the second practice—writing summaries of articles in your note cards when their arguments seem relevant to your research project. Taking notes this way is time-consuming in the short run but time-efficient in the long run. The act of summarizing forces you to read the article carefully and to perceive its whole argument. It also steers you away from the bad habit of noting facts or information from an article without perceiving how the information supports a meaning. Because summary writing is a way of reading as a believer (see Chapter 2), it helps you listen to the various voices in the conversation about your issue.

Paraphrasing Portions of an Argument

Whereas a summary places a whole argument in a nutshell by leaving out supporting details but keeping the main argument, a paraphrase is about the same length as the original but places the ideas of the original in the writer's own words. Paraphrase often includes pieces of quotation worked neatly into the writer's passage. When you are summarizing a short article, such as the *Science '86* article used in the previous section, parts of your summary can blend into paraphrase. The distinction isn't important. What is important is that you avoid plagiarism by making sure you are restating the original argument in your own words. Generally you should avoid paraphrasing a lengthy passage because then you will simply be turning someone else's argument into your own words. A good research argument weaves together supporting material from a variety of sources; it doesn't paraphrase someone else's argument.

Quoting

Inexperienced writers tend to quote too much material and at too great a length. To see a skillful use of quotations, look again at the *Science '86* article we have been using as an illustration. That article is actually a summary of a much longer and more technical research study written by the researchers Stevenson,

Shin-ying Lee, and Stigler. Note that the summary includes only two kinds of quotation: quotation of the single words *ability, effort, excellent,* and *fair;* and a brief quotation from Stigler to conclude the article.

The first kind of quotation—quoting individual words or short phrases—is a matter of accuracy. The writer summarizing the original research study wanted to indicate the exact terms the researchers used at key points in their argument. The second kind of quotation—quoting a brief passage from an article—has a different purpose. Sometimes writers want to give readers a sense of the flavor of their original source, particularly if the source speaks in a lively, interesting style. At other times a writer might wish to quote a source exactly on an especially important point, both to highlight the point and to increase readers' confidence that the writer has elsewhere been summarizing or paraphrasing accurately. The ending quotation in the *Science '86* article serves both purposes.

As a general rule, avoid too much quotation, especially long quotations. Remember that a research essay, like any other essay, should present *your* argument in *your* voice. When you use summary and to a lesser extent paraphrase, you are in command because you are fitting the arguments of your sources to your own purposes. But when you quote, you are lifting material from a different context with a different purpose and plunking it into an alien home, inevitably mixing voices and styles. Too much quotation is the hallmark of a data dump essay; the writer strings together other people's words instead of creating his own argument.

INCORPORATING SOURCES INTO YOUR ARGUMENT: TECHNICAL ADVICE ON SUMMARIZING, PARAPHRASING, AND QUOTING

As a research writer, you need to be able to move back and forth gracefully between conducting your own argument and using material from your research in the form of summary, paraphrase, or quotation. Let's suppose that you are investigating the following question: "Is terrorism ever ethically justifiable?" As part of your research, you encounter a short argument by philosopher Michael Levin entitled "The Case for Torture." Levin's argument, which originally appeared in *Newsweek,* is reprinted in Chapter 15 on ethical arguments (pp. 356–57). We will use Levin's argument to illustrate summary, paraphrase, and quotation, so you should read the argument before proceeding to the explanations that follow.

Once you have read Levin's argument on torture, suppose that you would like to incorporate some of his ideas into your own argument on terrorism. You have a number of options: summary, paraphrase, long block quotation, short quotations inserted into your own sentences, and inserted quotations modified slightly to fit the grammar of your own sentence. Let's look at each in turn.

Summary

When you wish to include a writer's complete argument (or a large sustained portion of it) in your own essay, you will need to summarize it. For a detailed explanation of how to summarize, see Chapter 2. Summaries can be quite long or very short. The following condensation of Levin's essay illustrates a short summary.

> Levin believes that torture can be justifiable if its purpose is to save innocent lives and if it is certain that the person being tortured has the power to save those lives. Torture is not justifiable as punishment. Levin likens the justified use of torture to the justified use of assassination or preemptive strikes in order to preclude or shorten a war.

This short passage summarizes the main points of the Levin argument in a few sentences. As a summary, it condenses the whole down to a small nutshell. For an example of a somewhat longer summary, see Chapter 2, pages 34–35.

Paraphrase

Unlike summary, which is a condensation of an essay, a paraphrase is a "translation" of an essay into the writer's own words. It is approximately the same length as the original but converts the original into the writer's own voice. Be careful when you paraphrase to avoid both the original writer's words and the original writer's grammatical structure and syntax. If you follow the original sentence structure while replacing occasional words with synonyms, you are cheating: That practice is plagiarism, not paraphrase. Here is a paraphrase of paragraph 4 in Levin's essay:

> Levin asks whether it is unconstitutional to torture a terrorist. He believes that it probably is, but he argues that saving the lives of millions of innocent people is a greater good than obeying the Constitution. Although torture is brutal, so is letting innocent people die. In fact, Levin believes that we are moral cowards if we don't torture a guilty individual in order to save millions of lives.

This paraphrase of paragraph 4 is approximately the same length as the original paragraph. The purpose of a paraphrase is not to condense the original, but to turn the original into one's own language. Even though you are not borrowing any language, you will still need to cite the source to indicate that you are borrowing ideas.

Block Quotation

Occasionally, you will wish to quote an author's words directly. You must be meticulous in copying down the words *exactly* so that you make no changes. You must also be fair to your source by not quoting out of context. When the quoted material takes up more than three lines in your original source, use the following block quotation method:

> In his argument supporting torture under certain circumstances, Levin is careful to insist that he doesn't see torture as punishment but solely as a way of preventing loss of innocent lives:
>
>> I am not advocating torture as punishment. Punishment is addressed to deeds irrevocably past. Rather, I am advocating torture as an acceptable measure for preventing future evils. So understood, it is far less objectionable than many extant punishments.

Here the writer wants to quote Levin's words as found in paragraph 7. Because the passage to be quoted is longer than three lines, the writer uses the block quotation method. Note that the quotation is introduced with a colon and is not enclosed in quotation marks. The indented block format takes the place of quotation marks.

Inserted Quotation

If the passage you wish to quote is less than three lines, you can insert it directly into your own paragraph by using quotation marks instead of the block method:

> In his argument favoring torture, Levin is careful to distinguish between torture and punishment. "I am not advocating torture as punishment," Levin asserts. "Punishment is addressed to deeds irrevocably past. Rather, I am advocating torture as an acceptable measure for preventing future evils."

Here the writer breaks the quotation into parts so that no part is longer than three lines. Thus the writer is able to use quotation marks rather than the indented block format.

If the inserted quotation is a complete sentence in your own essay, then it should begin with a capital letter. The quotation is usually separated from preceding explanatory matter by a colon or comma. However, if the quotation is not a complete sentence in your own essay, then you insert it using quotation marks only and begin the quotation with a small letter.

QUOTATION AS INDEPENDENT SENTENCE

According to Levin, "Punishment is addressed to deeds irrevocably past."

QUOTATION AS CLAUSE OR PHRASE THAT IS NOT AN INDEPENDENT SENTENCE

Levin claims that punishment is concerned with "deeds irrevocably past," while torture is aimed at "preventing future evils."

In the first example, the quotation begins with a capital *P* because the quotation comprises an independent sentence. Note that it is separated from the preceding phrase by a comma. In the second example the quotations do not comprise independent sentences. They are inserted directly into the writer's sentence, using quotation marks only.

Shortening or Modifying Quotations

Sometimes you wish to quote the exact words from a source, but in order to make the quotation fit gracefully into your own sentence you need to alter it in some way, either by shortening it, by changing it slightly, or by adding explanatory material to it. There are several ways of doing so: through judicious selection of phrases to be quoted or through use of ellipses and brackets.

SHORTEN A PASSAGE BY SELECTING ONLY KEY PHRASES FOR QUOTING

In his argument favoring torture, Levin is careful to distinguish between torture and punishment. "I am not advocating torture as punishment," Levin asserts, but only "as an acceptable measure for preventing future evils."

Here the writer quotes only selected pieces of the longer passage and weaves them into her own sentences.

USE ELLIPSES TO OMIT MATERIAL FROM A QUOTATION

Levin continues by distinguishing torture from capital punishment:

> Opponents of the death penalty [. . .] are forever insisting that executing a murderer will not bring back his victim. [. . .] But torture [. . .] is intended not to bring anyone back but to keep innocents from being dispatched.

In this block quotation from paragraph 7, the writer uses ellipses in three places. Made with three spaced periods, an ellipsis indicates that words have been omitted. Note that the second ellipsis in this passage seems to contain four periods. The first period ends the sentence; the last three periods are the ellipsis. The square brackets around the ellipses show that they were inserted by you, the writer, rather than being in the original work.

USE SQUARE BRACKETS TO MAKE SLIGHT CHANGES
IN A QUOTATION OR TO ADD EXPLANATORY MATERIAL

According to Levin, "By threatening to kill for profit or idealism, he [the terrorist] renounces civilized standards."

The writer puts "the terrorist" in brackets to indicate the antecedent of the quoted pronoun "he." This passage is from paragraph 9.

According to Levin, "[T]orture [is] an acceptable measure for preventing future evils."

This passage, from paragraph 7, changes the original slightly: a small *t* has been raised to a capital *T*, and the word *as* has been changed to *is*. These changes are indicated by brackets. You don't usually have to indicate when you change a small letter to a capital or vice versa. But it is important to do so here because the writer is actually changing the grammar of the original by converting a phrase into a sentence.

Using Quotations within Quotations

Sometimes you may wish to quote a passage that already has quotation marks within it. If you use the block quotation method, keep the quotation marks exactly as they are in the original. If you use the inserted quotation method, then use single quotation marks (' ') instead of double marks (" ") to indicate the quotation within the quotation.

> Levin is quick to dismiss the notion that a terrorist has rights:
>
> > There is an important difference between terrorists and their victims that should mute talk of the terrorists' "rights." The terrorist's victims are at risk unintentionally, not having asked to be endangered. But the terrorist knowingly initiated his actions.

Because the writer uses the block quotation method, the original quotation marks around *rights* remain. See the original passage in paragraph 9.

> Levin claims that "an important difference between terrorists and their victims . . . should mute talk of the terrorists' 'rights.' "

Here the writer uses the inserted quotation method. Therefore the original double quotation marks (" ") around *rights* have been changed to single quotation marks (' '), which on a keyboard are made with an apostrophe.

An Extended Illustration: Martha's Argument

To help you get a feel for how a writer integrates brief quotations into paraphrases or summaries, consider the following passage written by Martha, a student who was disturbed by a class discussion of Levin's essay. Several classmates argued that Levin's justification of torture could also be used to justify terrorism. Martha did not believe that Levin's argument could be applied to terrorism. Here is the passage from Martha's argument that summarizes Levin. (Page references in Martha's passage refer to the original *Newsweek* source that she used—part of the MLA citation system to be described shortly.)

> Now it may seem that if terrorism is always wrong then torture should always be wrong also since torture, even more so than terrorism, is a barbaric practice

from a pre-civilized age. But philosopher Michael Levin shows a flaw in this reasoning. Torture is justifiable, says Levin, but only in some cases. First of all, he says that torture should be applied only to those "*known* to hold innocent lives in their hands" and only if the person being tortured is clearly guilty and clearly can prevent a horrible act from occurring (13). Levin uses the example of using torture on a captured terrorist to find the location of an atomic bomb set to go off on Manhattan Island. The principle here is that you are saving the lives of millions of innocent bystanders by applying systematic pain to one person who "renounc[ed] civilized standards" (13) when becoming a terrorist. For Levin, saving the lives of innocent bystanders is a higher moral imperative than refusing to torture the person who can prevent the deaths. In fact, Levin claims, refusal to torture the terrorist is "moral cowardice, an unwillingness to dirty one's hands" (13). "If life is [. . .] valuable," Levin argues, then "the lives of the innocents must be saved even at the price of hurting the one who endangers them" (13).

We can now return to the problem I posed earlier. If Levin is able to justify torture under some conditions, why can't we also justify terrorism under some conditions? The answer is that . . . [Martha's argument continues].

FOR CLASS DISCUSSION

Working as individuals or as small groups, prepare brief answers for the following questions:

1. How is Martha's passage different from a data dump?

2. Without being able to read her whole essay, can you determine Martha's purpose for summarizing Levin within her own argument on terrorism? If so, what is her purpose?

3. Why did the writer use square brackets [ ] within one quotation and bracketed ellipses ([. . .]) within another?

4. What effects did Martha achieve by using only short quotations instead of longer block quotations from Levin's argument?

Signaling Directions:
The Use of Attributive Tags

In all of our examples of citing, summarizing, paraphrasing, and quoting, the writers have used attributive tags to signal to readers which ideas are the writer's own and which ideas are being taken from another source. Attributive tags are phrases such as the following: "according to the researchers . . . ," "Levin claims that . . . ," "the author continues . . . ." Such phrases signal to the reader that the material immediately following is from the cited source. Parenthetical citations are used only to give readers follow-up information on where the source can be found, not to indicate that the writer is using a source. The source being cited should always be mentioned in the text. Note how confusing a passage becomes if these attributive tags are omitted.

CONFUSING ATTRIBUTION

Now it may seem that if terrorism is always wrong then torture should always be wrong also since torture, even more so than terrorism, is a barbaric practice from a pre-civilized age. But there is a flaw in this reasoning. Torture should be applied only to those *"known* to hold innocent lives in their hands" (Levin 13) and only if the person being tortured is clearly guilty and clearly can prevent a terrorist act from occurring. A good example is using torture on a captured terrorist to find the location of an atomic bomb set to go off on Manhattan Island.

Although this writer cites Levin as the source of the quotation, it is not clear just when the borrowing from Levin begins or ends. For instance, is the example of the captured terrorist on Manhattan Island the writer's own or does it come from Levin? As the following revision shows, the use of attributive tags within the text makes it clear exactly where the writer's ideas leave off and a borrowed source begins or ends. In the following example of clear attribution, attributive tags are printed in boldface:

CLEAR ATTRIBUTION

Now it may seem that if terrorism is always wrong then torture should always be wrong also since torture, even more so than terrorism, is a barbaric practice from a pre-civilized age. But **philosopher Michael Levin shows** a flaw in this reasoning. Torture is justifiable, **says Levin,** but only in some cases. First, **he says that** torture should be applied only to those *"known* to hold innocent lives in their hands" and only if the person being tortured is clearly guilty and clearly can prevent a horrible act from occurring (13). **Levin uses** the example of using torture on a captured terrorist to find the location of an atomic bomb set to go off on Manhattan Island.

AVOIDING PLAGIARISM

Plagiarism, a form of academic cheating, is always a serious academic offense. You can plagiarize in one of two ways: (1) by borrowing another person's ideas without indicating the borrowing with attributive tags in the text and a proper citation or (2) by borrowing another person's language without putting the borrowed language in quotation marks or using a block indentation. The first kind of plagiarism is usually outright cheating; the writer usually knows he is stealing material and tries to disguise it.

The second kind of plagiarism, however, often begins in a hazy never-never land between paraphrasing and copying. We refer to it in our classes as "lazy cheating" and still consider it a serious offense, like stealing from your neighbor's vegetable garden because you are too lazy to do your own planting, weeding, and harvesting. Anyone who appreciates how hard it is to write and revise even a short passage will appreciate why it is wrong to take someone else's language ready-made. Thus, in our classes, we would fail a paper that included the following passage. (Let's call the writer Lucy.)

> Another argument showing the importance of environment on scholastic achievement comes from a research study done by psychologists at the University of Chicago and the University of Michigan (*Science '86* 7, 8). The study shows that parents must share the blame for the poor math performance of American students. In this study more than 2,000 children in kindergarten and the fifth grade were tested and interviewed in Minneapolis, in Sendai, Japan, and in Taipei, China. The researchers made up a test based on math problems found in textbooks used in all three cities. All the children in each grade performed equally well on reading and general intelligence tests, but their math scores differed from the start. The kindergartners from Japan scored about 10 percent higher than American kindergartners. The gap widened by the fifth grade. The top U.S. fifth-grade class scored below the lowest Japanese class and the second lowest Chinese class. Of the 100 highest scoring fifth graders, one was American (*Science '86* 8).

FOR CLASS DISCUSSION

Do you think it was fair to flunk Lucy's essay? She claimed she wasn't cheating since she gave two different parenthetical citations accurately citing the *Science '86* article as her source. Before answering this question, compare the passage above with the original article on pp. 389–90; also compare the passage above with the opening paragraph from Cheryl's summary (pp. 391–92) of the *Science '86* article. What justification could a professor use for giving an A to Cheryl's essay while flunking Lucy's?

Note Taking to Avoid Plagiarism

When you take notes on books or articles, be extremely careful to put all borrowed language in quotation marks. If you write summaries of arguments, as we strongly recommend you do, take time at the note-taking stage to put the summaries in your own words. If you wish to paraphrase an important passage, make sure you either copy the original into your notes word for word and indicate that you have done so (so that you can paraphrase it later), or paraphrase it entirely in your language when you take the notes. Inadvertent plagiarism can occur if you copy something in your notes word for word and then later assume that what you copied was actually a paraphrase.

DOCUMENTING YOUR SOURCES

To many students, the dreariest aspect of research writing is documenting their sources—that is, getting citations in the proper places and in the correct forms. As we noted at the beginning of the previous chapter, however, documentation of sources is a service to readers who may want to follow up on your research. Documentation in the proper form allows them to find your sources quickly.

There are two questions that you must answer to ensure proper documentation: "When do I cite a source?" and "Which format do I use?"

When to Cite Sources

As a general rule, cite everything you borrow. Some students take this rule to unnecessary extremes, arguing that everything they "know" comes from somewhere. They end up citing lectures, conversations with a friend, notes from an old high school class, and so forth. Use common sense. If you successfully avoid writing a data dump essay, then your research will be used to support a thesis, which will reflect your own individual thinking and synthesis of material. You will know when you are using evidence from your own personal experience as source material and when you are using evidence you got from doing library research. Document all the material you got from the library or from another external source.

Which Format to Use

Formats for citations and bibliographies vary somewhat from discipline to discipline. At the present time, footnotes have almost entirely disappeared from academic writing as a means of citing sources. Rather, citations for quotations or paraphrased material are now usually made in the text itself by putting brief identifying symbols inside parentheses.

AN OVERVIEW OF THE MLA AND APA SYSTEMS OF DOCUMENTATION

The two main systems used today for academic essays aimed at general college audiences are the MLA (Modern Language Association) system, generally favored in the humanities, and the APA (American Psychological Association) system, generally favored in the social sciences. Other general systems are sometimes encountered—for example, the *Chicago Manual of Style*—and many specialized disciplines such as biology or chemistry have their own style manuals. But familiarity with the MLA and APA systems should serve you well throughout college.

The sample research argument written by Stephen Bean (pp. 334–42) follows the MLA style. The sample research argument written by Lynnea Clark (pp. 424–30) follows the APA style.

Neither the MLA nor the APA system uses footnotes to document sources. In both systems a source is cited by means of a brief parenthetical reference following the quotation or the passage in which the source is used. Complete bibliographic information on each source is then included in an alphabetical list at the end of the text. Let us now turn to a more complete discussion of these two features.

Feature 1: Place a Complete Bibliographic List at the End of the Text

In both the MLA and the APA styles, a list of all the sources you have cited is included at the end of the research paper. In the MLA system, this bibliographic list is called Works Cited. In the APA system this list is called References. In both systems, entries are listed alphabetically by author (if no author is given for a particular source, then that source is alphabetized by title).

Let's look at how the two style systems would have you cite the Levin article on torture. The article appears in the June 7, 1982, issue of *Newsweek* on page 13. In the MLA style the complete bibliographic reference would be placed at the end of the paper under Works Cited, where it would appear as follows:

MLA: Levin, Michael. "The Case for Torture." <u>Newsweek</u> 7 June 1982: 13.

In the APA system, the complete bibliographic reference would be placed at the end of the paper under References, where it would appear as follows:

APA: Levin, M. (1982, June 7). The case for torture. <u>Newsweek,</u> p. 13.

When you refer to this article in the text—using either system—you place a brief citation in parentheses.

Feature 2: Cite Sources in the Text by Putting Brief References in Parentheses

Both the MLA and the APA systems cite sources through brief parenthetical references in the text. However, the two systems differ somewhat in the way these citations are structured.

In-Text Citation: MLA System

In the MLA system, you place the author's name and the page number of the cited source in parentheses. (If the author's name is mentioned in a preceding attributive tag, only the page number should be placed in parentheses.)

Torture, claims one philosopher, should be applied only to those "<u>known</u> to hold innocent lives in their hands" and only if the person being tortured is clearly guilty and clearly can prevent a terrorist act from occurring (Levin 13).

or

Torture, claims Michael Levin, should be applied only to those "<u>known</u> to hold innocent lives in their hands" and only if the person being tortured is clearly guilty and clearly can prevent a terrorist act from occurring (13).

If your readers wish to follow up on this source, they will look up the Levin article in the Works Cited list at the end of your essay. If more than one work by Levin has been used as sources in the essay, then you would include in the in-text citation an abbreviated title of the article following Levin's name.

(Levin, "Torture" 13)

Once Levin has been cited the first time and it is clear that you are still quoting from Levin, then you need put only the page number in parentheses and eliminate the author's name.

In-Text Citation: APA System

In the APA system, you place the author's name and the date of the cited source in parentheses. If you are quoting a particular passage or citing a particular table, include the page number where the information is found. Use a comma to separate each element of the citation and use the abbreviation *p.* or *pp.* before the page number. (If the author's name is mentioned in a preceding attributive tag, then only the date needs to be placed in parentheses.)

Torture, claims one philosopher, should be applied only to those "<u>known</u> to hold innocent lives in their hands" and only if the person being tortured is clearly guilty and clearly can prevent a terrorist act from occurring (Levin, 1982, p. 13).

or

Torture, claims Michael Levin, should be applied only to those "<u>known</u> to hold innocent lives in their hands" and only if the person being tortured is clearly guilty and clearly can prevent a terrorist act from occurring (1982, p. 13).

If your readers wish to follow up on this source, they will look for the 1982 Levin article in the References at the end of your essay. If Levin had published more than one article in 1982, the articles would be distinguished by small letters placed alphabetically after the date:

(Levin, 1982a)

or

(Levin, 1982b)

In the APA style, if an article or book has more than one author, the word *and* is used to join them in the text but the ampersand (&) is used to join them in the parenthetical reference:

Smith and Peterson (1983) found that . . .

More recent data (Smith & Peterson, 1983) have shown . . .

Citing a Quotation or Other Data from a Secondary Source

Occasionally, you may wish to use a quotation or other kinds of data from a secondary source. For example, suppose you are writing an argument that the United States should reconsider its trade policies with China. You read an article entitled "China's Gilded Age" by Xiao-huang Yin appearing in the April 1994 issue of the *Atlantic*. This article contains the following passage appearing on page 42:

> Dual ownership has in essence turned this state enterprise into a private business. Asked if such a practice is an example of China's "socialist market economy," a professor of economics at Nanjing University, where I taught in the early 1980's, replied, "Nobody knows what the concept means. It is only rhetoric, and it can mean anything but socialism."

In citing material from a secondary source, it is always best, when possible, to locate the original source and cite your data directly. But in the above case, no other source is likely available. Here is how you would cite it in both the MLA and APA systems.

MLA: According to an economics professor at Nanjing University, the term "socialist market economy" has become confused under capitalistic influence: "Nobody knows what the concept means. It is only rhetoric, and it can mean anything but socialism" (qtd. in Yin 42)

APA: According to an economics professor at Nanjing University, the term "socialist market economy" has become confused under capitalistic influence: "Nobody knows what the concept means. It is only rhetoric, and it can mean anything but socialism" (cited in Yin, 1994, p. 42).

In both systems you would place the Yin article in the end-of-text bibliographic list. What follows is a description of the format for the end-of-text bibliographic entries under Works Cited in the MLA system and under References in the APA System.

BIBLIOGRAPHIC LISTINGS AT THE END OF YOUR PAPER

Both the MLA and the APA systems specify a complete list of all items cited, placed at the end of the paper. The list should comprise all sources from which you gathered information, including articles, books, videos, letters, and electronic sources. The list should not include works you read but did not cite. In both systems, all works are listed alphabetically by author, or by title if there is no author.

In the MLA system, the words *Works Cited*, in uppercase and lowercase letters, are centered one inch from the top of the page. Sources are listed alphabetically, the first line flush with the left margin and succeeding lines indented one-half inch (or five spaces if you are using a typewriter). Here is a typical example of a work cited in MLA form.

> Karnow, Stanley. In Our Image: America's Empire in the Philippines. New York: Random, 1989.

The same information with a slightly different arrangement is used in the APA system. The word *References* is typed in uppercase and lowercase letters at the top of the page. Entries for sources are listed alphabetically. After the first line, which is flush at the left margin, succeeding lines are indented five spaces.

> Karnow, S. (1989). In our image: America's empire in the Philippines. New York: Random House.

The remaining pages in this section show examples of MLA and APA formats for different kinds of sources, including electronic sources. Following these examples are typical pages from a Works Cited list and a References list featuring formats for the most commonly encountered kinds of sources.

General Format for Books

MLA: Author. Title. City of Publication: Publisher, year of publication.

APA: Author. (Year of Publication). Title. City of Publication: Publisher.

Note these important differences between the two systems:

- In MLA style, author entries include first names and middle initials. In APA style, only the initials of the first and middle names are given, unless full names are needed to distinguish persons with the same initials.

- In MLA style, the first word and all important words are capitalized in the title. In APA style, only the first word, proper nouns, and the first word after a dash or a colon are capitalized in the title.

- In MLA style, the year of publication comes last, after the publisher. In APA style, the year of publication follows in parentheses immediately after the author's name.

- In MLA style, names of publishers have standardized abbreviations, listed in section 6.5 of the *MLA Handbook for Writers of Research Papers,* 5th ed. In APA style, names of publishers are not usually abbreviated except for the elimination of unnecessary words such as *Inc., Co.,* and *Publishers.*

- In MLA style, punctuation following the underlined title is not underlined. In APA style, punctuation following the underlined title *is* underlined.

One Author

MLA: Coles, Robert. The Youngest Parents: Teenage Pregnancy As It Shapes Lives. New York: Norton, 1997.

APA: Coles, R. (1997). The youngest parents: Teenage pregnancy as it shapes lives. New York: W. W. Norton.

Two or More Listings for One Author

MLA: Hass, Robert. Human Wishes. New York: Ecco, 1989.

  ---, ed. Rock and Hawk: A Selection of Shorter Poems by Robinson Jeffers. New York: Random, 1987.

  ---. Sun under Wood. New York: Ecco, 1996.

  ---, ed. Tomas Tranströmer: Selected Poems, 1954–1986. New York: Ecco, 1987.

In the MLA style, when two or more works by one author are cited, the works are listed in alphabetical order by title. For the second and all additional entries, type three hyphens and a period in place of the author's name. Then type the title. If the person named edited, translated, or compiled the book, place a comma (not a period) after the three hyphens and write the appropriate abbreviation (*ed., trans.,* or *comp.*) before giving the title.

APA: Hass, R. (Ed.). (1987a). Rock and hawk: A selection of shorter poems
            by Robinson Jeffers. New York: Random House.

Hass, R. (Ed.). (1987b). Tomas Tranströmer: Selected poems,
            1954–1986. New York: Ecco Press.

Hass, R. (1989). Human wishes. New York: Ecco Press.

Hass, R. (1996). Sun under wood. New York: Ecco Press.

In APA style, when an author has more than one entry in the References list, the author's name is repeated and the entries are listed chronologically (oldest to newest) rather than alphabetically. When two entries by the same author have the same date, they are then listed in alphabetical order. Lowercase letters are added after the year of publication to distinguish them from each other when cited by date in the text.

Two or More Authors of a Single Work

MLA: Ciochon, Russell, John Olsen, and Jamie James. The Search for the
            Giant Ape in Human Prehistory. New York: Bantam, 1990.

APA: Ciochon, R., Olsen, J., & James, J. (1990). The search for the giant ape
            in human prehistory. New York: Bantam Books.

Note that APA style uses the ampersand (&) to join the names of multiple authors in the Reference list.

Using et al. for Works with Several Authors

MLA: Maimon, Elaine P., et al. Writing in the Arts and Sciences. Cambridge:
            Winthrop, 1981.

In the MLA system, if there are four or more authors, you have the option of using the form et al. (meaning "and others") after the name of the first author listed on the title page.

APA: Maimon, E. P., Belcher, G. L., Hearn, G. W., Nodine, B. F., & O'Connor,
            F. W. (1981). Writing in the arts and sciences. Cambridge, MA:
            Winthrop.

APA style calls for you to write out the names of all authors for one work in your References list, no matter how many.

Edited Anthology

MLA: Gates, Henry Louis, Jr., and Nellie Y. McKay, eds. The Norton
            Anthology of African American Literature. New York: Norton,
            1997.

APA: Gates, H. L., Jr., & McKay, N. Y. (Eds.). (1997). The Norton anthology
            of African American literature. New York: W. W. Norton.

Essay in an Anthology or Other Collection

MLA: Thomson, Peter. "Playhouses and Players in the Time of Shakespeare."
            The Cambridge Companion to Shakespeare Studies. Ed. Stanley
            Wells. Cambridge, Eng.: Cambridge UP, 1986. 67–83.

In the MLA system, the words *University Press* are always abbreviated as *UP*. If
several cities are listed in the book as the place of publication, list only the first.
For cities outside the United States, add an abbreviation of the country (or
province in Canada) if the name of the city is ambiguous or unfamiliar.

APA: Thomson, P. (1986). Playhouses and players in the time of Shakespeare.
            In S. Wells (Ed.), The Cambridge companion to Shakespeare
            studies (pp. 67–83). Cambridge, England: Cambridge University
            Press.

Book in a Later Edition or Revised Edition

MLA: Burns, E. Bradford. Latin America: A Concise Interpretive History. 6th
            ed. Englewood Cliffs: Prentice, 1994.

            Schmidt, Rick. Feature Filmmaking at Used-Car Prices: How to
            Write, Produce, Direct, Film, Edit, and Promote a Feature-Length
            Film for Less than $10,000. Rev. ed. New York: Penguin,
            1995.

APA: Burns, E. B. (1994). Latin America: A concise interpretive history (6th
            ed.). Englewood Cliffs, NJ: Prentice Hall.

            Schmidt, R. (1995). Feature filmmaking at used-car prices: How to
            write, produce, direct, film, edit, and promote a feature-length
            film for less than $10,000 (Rev. ed.). New York: Penguin Books.

Multivolume Work

Cite the whole work when you have used more than one volume of the work.

MLA: Churchill, Winston S. A History of the English-Speaking Peoples.
4 vols. New York: Dodd, 1956–58.

APA: Churchill, W. S. (1956–1958). A history of the English-speaking
peoples (Vols. 1–4). New York: Dodd, Mead.

Include the volume number when you have used only one volume of a multi-volume work.

MLA: Churchill, Winston S. The Great Democracies. New York: Dodd, 1957.
Vol. 4 of A History of the English-Speaking Peoples. 4 vols.
1956–58.

APA: Churchill, W. S. (1957). A history of the English-speaking peoples:
Vol. 4. The great democracies. New York: Dodd, Mead.

Reference Work with Frequent Editions

MLA: Pei, Mario. "Language." World Book Encyclopedia. 1976 ed.

In citing familiar reference works under the MLA system, you don't need to include all the normal publication information.

APA: Pei, M. (1976). Language. In World book encyclopedia (Vol. 12,
pp. 62–67). Chicago: Field Enterprises.

Less Familiar Reference Work without Frequent Editions

MLA: Ling, Trevor O. "Buddhism in Burma." Dictionary of Comparative
Religion. Ed. S. G. F. Brandon. New York: Scribner's, 1970.

APA: Ling, T. O. (1970). Buddhism in Burma. In S. G. F. Brandon (Ed.),
Dictionary of comparative religion. New York: Scribner's.

Edition in Which Original Author's Work
Is Prepared by an Editor

MLA: Brontë, Emily. Wuthering Heights. 1847. Ed. V. S. Pritchett. Boston:
Houghton, 1956.

> **APA:** Brontë, E. (1956). <u>Wuthering Heights</u> (V. S. Pritchett, Ed.). Boston: Houghton Mifflin. (Original work published 1847)

Translation

> **MLA:** Camus, Albert. <u>The Plague</u>. Trans. Stuart Gilbert. New York: Modern Lib., 1948. Trans. of <u>La Peste</u>. Paris: Gallimard, 1947.

In MLA style, some or all of the original publication information may be added at the end of the entry. Though it is not required, adding the date avoids the suggestion that the original work was written in the same year that it was translated.

> **APA:** Camus, A. (1948). <u>The plague</u> (S. Gilbert, Trans.). New York: Modern Library. (Original work published 1947)

In APA style, the date of the translation is placed after the author's name; the date of original publication of the work is placed in parentheses at the end of the reference. In text, this book would be cited as follows:

(Camus, 1947/1948)

Corporate Author (a Commission, Committee, or Other Group)

> **MLA:** American Red Cross. <u>Standard First Aid</u>. St. Louis: Mosby, 1993.

> **APA:** American Red Cross. (1993). <u>Standard first aid.</u> St. Louis: Mosby Lifeline.

Anonymous Work

> **MLA:** <u>The New Yorker Cartoon Album: 1975–1985</u>. New York: Penguin, 1987.

> **APA:** <u>The New Yorker cartoon album: 1975–1985</u>. (1987). New York: Penguin Books.

Republished Work (For Example, a Newer Paperback Published after the Original Edition)

> **MLA:** Wollstonecraft, Mary. <u>A Vindication of the Rights of Woman, with Strictures on Political and Moral Subjects</u>. 1792. Rutland: Tuttle, 1995.

APA: Wollstonecraft, M. (1792/1995). <u>A vindication of the rights of woman, with strictures on political and moral subjects.</u> Rutland, VT: Tuttle and Company.

General Format for Articles

Scholarly Journals

MLA: Author. "Article Title." <u>Journal Title</u> volume number (year): inclusive page numbers.

APA: Author. (year). Article title. <u>Journal Title, volume number,</u> inclusive page numbers.

Magazines and Newspapers

MLA: Author. "Article Title." <u>Magazine or Newspaper Title</u> day month year: inclusive page numbers.

APA: Author. (year, month day). Article title. <u>Magazine or Newspaper Title,</u> volume number, inclusive page numbers.

Note these important details about the two systems:

- MLA and APA styles change slightly between scholarly and popular media sources. Scholarly journals are cited by volume number with the year given in parentheses, while citations for popular media sources do not use the volume number and give all details of the date without parentheses.

- Titles of articles in MLA style are placed in quotation marks (with the period *inside* the closing quotation mark). APA style does not place quotation marks around titles.

- In MLA style, the date is followed by a colon, followed by the inclusive page numbers. The APA system uses a comma to separate the title and volume number from the inclusive page numbers.

- As in book citations, the two styles differ in underlining. MLA style underlines only the title (not the punctuation or volume number). APA style calls for the title, the volume number (if there is one), and the comma to be underlined, unless there is an issue number. In that case, neither the issue number nor the comma is underlined (see the example that follows).

Scholarly Journal with Continuous Annual Pagination

MLA: Barton, Ellen L. "Evidentials, Argumentation, and Epistemological Stance." <u>College English</u> 55 (1993): 745–69.

APA: Barton, E. L. (1993). Evidentials, argumentation, and epistemological stance. College English, 55, 745–769.

Scholarly Journal with Each Issue Paged Separately

MLA: Pollay, Richard W., Jung S. Lee, and David Carter-Whitney. "Separate, but Not Equal: Racial Segmentation in Cigarette Advertising." Journal of Advertising 21.1 (1992): 45–57.

APA: Pollay, R. W., Lee, J. S., & Carter-Whitney, D. (1992). Separate, but not equal: Racial segmentation in cigarette advertising. Journal of Advertising, 21(1), 45–57.

Note that in both systems when each issue is paged separately, both the volume number (in this case, 21) and the issue number (in this case, 1) are given.

Magazine Article

MLA: Fallows, James. "Vietnam: Low-Class Conclusions." Atlantic Apr. 1993: 38–44.

APA: Fallows, J. (1993, April). Vietnam: Low-class conclusions. Atlantic Monthly, 38–44.

Note that this form is for a magazine published each month. The next entry shows the form for a magazine published each week.

Anonymous Article

MLA: "The Rebellious Archbishop." Newsweek 11 July 1988: 38.

APA: The rebellious archbishop. (1988, July 11). Newsweek, 38.

Review

MLA: Lakey, Jennifer. "Exploring Native American Traditions with Children." Rev. of She Who Watches, by Willa Holmes. Writers NW Winter 1997: 7.

For both movie and book reviews, if the reviewer's name is not given, begin with the title of the reviewed work, preceded by "Rev. of" in the MLA system or "[Review of *title*]" in the APA system. Begin with the title of the review if the review is titled but not signed.

> **APA:**   Lakey, J. (1997, Winter). Exploring Native American traditions with
> children [Review of the book She Who Watches]. Writers NW, 7.

Newspaper Article

> **MLA:**   Henriques, Diana B. "Hero's Fall Teaches Wall Street a Lesson."
> Seattle Times 27 Sept. 1998: A1+.

The *A1+* indicates that the article begins on page 1 but continues later in the newspaper on a later page or pages.

> **APA:**   Henriques, D. B. (1998, September 27). Hero's fall teaches Wall Street
> a lesson. The Seattle Times, pp. A1, A24.

The *pp. A1, A24* indicates that the article begins on section A, page 1, and ends on
section A, page 24. Note that for both systems, the newspaper section is indicated
if each section is paged separately.

Newspaper Editorial

> **MLA:**   Dowd, Maureen. "Legacy of Lust." Editorial. New York Times
> 23 Sept. 1998: A31.

> **APA:**   Dowd, M. (1998, September 23). Legacy of lust [Editorial]. The New
> York Times, p. A31.

Letter to the Editor of a Magazine or Newspaper

> **MLA:**   Tomsovic, Kevin. "Culture Clash." Letter. New Yorker 13 July 1998: 7.

> **APA:**   Tomsovic, K. (1998, July 13). Culture clash [Letter to the editor].
> The New Yorker, p. 7.

Include a title if one is given to the letter in the publication.

Information Service such as ERIC (Educational Resources Information Center) or NTIS (National Technical Information Service)

> **MLA:**   Eddy, P. A. The Effects of Foreign Language Study in High School on
> Verbal Ability as Measured by the Scholastic Aptitude Test—
> Verbal. Washington: Center for Applied Linguistics, 1981. ERIC
> ED 196 312.

APA: Eddy, P. A. (1981). <u>The effects of foreign language study in high school on verbal ability as measured by the Scholastic Aptitude Test—Verbal.</u> Washington, DC: Center for Applied Linguistics. (ERIC Document Reproduction Service No. ED 196 312)

General Format for Electronic Sources

While rules for formatting electronic sources are still being developed, the principle that governs electronic citations is the same as for print sources: *Give enough information so that the reader can find the source you used.* If the reader cannot relocate the Web page, listserv, or other electronic source from your citation, then you haven't given enough details. It is also important to give the date that you accessed the material as part of your citation, since Web sites are fluid—frequently updated, altered, or dropped. The reader will know from the date of your citation whether a cite may be inaccessible because it has not been updated, or whether the information on the page is different from your data because it has been updated.

The MLA and APA have developed general guidelines for citing electronic sources, which are applied here to specific examples. Nevertheless, you have more freedom of judgment in this area than in the area of print media citations, because electronic sources are in constant development and flux. When in doubt, always make entries as clear and informative as possible. Also, when you write an electronic citation, use your own citation to relocate the data just to make sure your address is accurate. If you cannot duplicate your own path to the material, give a simpler citation to the site's home page directory that will lead the reader to the original source. (See the example that follows.)

Books, Pamphlets, or Texts in Online Databases or CD-ROMs That Are Also Available in Print

MLA: Melville, Herman. <u>Moby-Dick, or The White Whale</u>. 1851. Ed. Luther S. Mansfield and Howard P. Vincent. New York: Hendricks, 1952. 27 Sept. 1998 <http://etext.lib.virginia.edu/modeng/modeng0.browse. html>.

MLA style uses the book citation format followed by the date of access and the URL (Uniform Resource Locator) enclosed in angle brackets. In this case, the URL is so long that the reader is directed to the browser at the University of Virginia Electronic Text Center. The reader can easily access *Moby-Dick* from there. If you must divide the URL to go to another line, break after a punctuation mark other than a period.

APA: Melville, H. (1851). <u>Moby-Dick, or the white whale.</u> University of Virginia Electronic Text Center. Retrieved September 27, 1998

from the World Wide Web: http://etext.lib.virginia.edu/modeng/
modeng0.browse.html

APA style calls for the Web site that provides the text, the word *Retrieved* followed by the access date and the phrase *from the World Wide Web,* and the URL. Note that the URL is not followed by a period in APA style.

Journals or Periodicals in Databases or CD-ROMs That Are Also Available in Print

MLA: Kowaleski-Wallace, Beth. "Women, China, and Consumer Culture in Eighteenth-Century England." Eighteenth Century Studies 29.2 (1995–96): 153–67. 1 Feb. 1999 <http://direct.press.jhu.edu/ journals/eighteenth-century_studies/toc/ecsv029.html#v029.2>.

APA: Kowaleski-Wallace, B. (1995–1996). Women, China, and consumer culture in eighteenth-century England. Eighteenth-Century Studies, 29(2), 153–167. Retrieved February 1, 1999 from the World Wide Web: http://direct.press.jhu.edu/journals/ eighteenth-century_studies/toc/ ecsv029.html#v029.2

Books, Journals, or Periodicals in Online Databases or CD-ROMs That Are Not Available in Print

MLA: Lal, Vinay. "Indians and The Guinness Book of World Records: The Political and Cultural Contours of a National Obsession." Suitcase: A Journal of Transcriptural Traffic 3 (1998). 2 Oct. 1998 <http:// www.suitcase.net/lai.html>.

APA: Lal, V. (1998). Indians and The Guinness book of world records: The political and cultural contours of a national obsession. Suitcase: A journal of transcriptural traffic, 3, Retrieved October 2, 1998 from the World Wide Web: http://www.suitcase.net/lai.html

Computer Disks That Are Not Available in Print

MLA: Microsoft Age of Empires. CD-ROM. Redmond: Microsoft, 1998.

APA: Microsoft age of empires [Computer software]. (1998). Redmond, WA: Microsoft Software.

For both MLA and APA, include the medium, city of issue, vendor name, and date of issue. APA style follows the specifications for online books available in print.

Scholarly Project, Web Site, or Database

MLA: Starr, Kenneth W. "Report of the Independent Counsel." <u>Thomas: Legislative Information on the Internet</u>. 9 Sept. 1998. Lib. of Congress, Washington. 2 Oct. 1998 <http://icreport.loc.gov/icreport/1cover.htm>.

For MLA, include the title of the scholarly project, Web site, or database (underlined), the name of the editor of the project if there is one, and the electronic publication information, including date of last update, date of access, and URL.

APA: Starr, K. W. (1998, September 9). Report of the Independent Counsel. Washington, DC: Library of Congress. Retrieved October 2, 1998 from the World Wide Web: http://icreport.loc.gov/icreport/1cover.htm

For APA, omit the name of the project, Web site, or database. The access date and URL follow the same format as in an entry for an online book or article.

E-mail, Listservs, and Other Nonretrievable Sources

MLA: Rushdie, Salman. "My Concern about the Fatwa." E-mail to the author. 1 May 1995.

Note that this format specifies that the document is an e-mail letter, to whom it was addressed, and the date of transmission.

In APA style, this material is not listed in the References. You should, however, acknowledge it in in-text citations.

The novelist has repeated this idea recently (Salman Rushdie, personal communication, May 1, 1995).

Bulletin Board or Newsgroup Posting

MLA: MacDonald, James C. "Suggestions for Promoting Collaborative Writing in College Composition." Online posting. 10 Nov. 1994. NCTE Forum/current topics/bulletin posting. 12 Mar. 1995. America Online.

Include the date of transmission or posting, the medium, network name, location information, an address or path for electronic access, and date of access.

In APA style, this material is acknowledged in in-text citations only. See the specifications for e-mail, listservs, and other nonretrievable sources on page 417.

General Format for Miscellaneous Materials

Films, Filmstrips, Slide Programs, and Videotapes

MLA: Chagall. Dir. Kim Evans. Videocassette. London Weekend Television, 1985.

APA: Evans, K. (Director). (1985). Chagall [Videocassette]. London: London Weekend Television.

Television and Radio Programs

MLA: Korea: The Forgotten War. Narr. Robert Stack. KCPQ, Seattle. 27 June 1988.

APA: Stack, R. (Narrator). (1988, June 27). Korea: The forgotten war. Seattle: KCPQ.

Interview

MLA: Deltete, Robert. Personal interview. 27 Feb. 1994.

APA: Deltete, R. (1994, February 27). [Personal interview].

The APA *Publication Manual* says to omit nonrecoverable material—such as personal correspondence, personal interviews, and lectures—from the References. However, in college research papers, professors usually like to have such information included.

Lecture, Address, or Speech

MLA: North, Oliver. Speech. Washington Policy Council. Seattle. 20 July 1988.

APA: North, O. (1988, July 20). Speech presented to Washington Policy Council, Seattle, WA.

In the MLA system, if the title of the speech is known, give the title in quotation marks instead of the word *Speech*. The APA *Publication Manual* has no provisions for citing lectures, addresses, or speeches because these are nonrecoverable items. However, the manual gives authors leeway to design citations for instances not covered explicitly in the manual. This format is suitable for college research papers.

For more complicated entries, consult the *MLA Handbook for Writers of Research Papers*, fifth edition, or the *Publication Manual of the American Psychological Association*, fourth edition. Both books should be available in your library or bookstore. For additional help in citing online sources, see the Web sites for these organizations, http://www.mla.org and http://www.apa.org.

Quick Check Reference: MLA and APA Bibliographic Entries

As a handy reference to the most commonly encountered kinds of entries in college research papers, see pages 420–21. These two pages illustrate a Works Cited list (MLA format) and a References list (APA format). These lists give you a quick summary of the formats for the most commonly used sources.

FORMATTING A RESEARCH PAPER

College instructors usually ask students to follow standard academic conventions for formatting research papers. Although conventions vary from discipline to discipline, the most common formatting styles are the MLA or the APA. The MLA formatting style is illustrated in Stephen Bean's paper on pages 334–42. The APA formatting style is illustrated in Lynnea Clark's paper on pages 424–30.

Formatting Features Common to Both MLA and APA

- Double-space the text throughout, including quotations and notes.
- Use one-inch margins top and bottom, left and right.
- Indent five spaces at the beginning of every paragraph.
- Number pages consecutively throughout the manuscript including the bibliographic section at the end.
- Begin the bibliographic section (called Works Cited in MLA and References in APA) on a separate page.

Distinctive Formatting Features for MLA

- Do not include a cover page. Type your name, professor's name, course number, and date in the upper left-hand corner of your paper (all double-spaced) beginning one inch from the top of the page; then double-space and type your title, centered, without underlines, boldface, or all caps

Works Cited: MLA Style Sheet for the Most Commonly Used Sources

Ross 27

Works Cited

Adler, Freda. Sisters in Crime. New York: McGraw, 1975.

Andersen, Margaret L. Thinking about Women:
Sociological Perspectives on Sex and Gender.
3rd ed. New York: Macmillan, 1993.

Bart, Pauline, and Patricia O'Brien. Stopping Rape:
Successful Survival Strategies. New York:
Pergamon, 1985.

Durkin, Kevin. "Social Cognition and Social Context
in the Construction of Sex Differences." Sex
Differences in Human Performances. Ed. Mary
Anne Baker. New York: Wiley, 1987. 45–60.

Fairburn, Christopher G., et al. "Predictors of Twelve-
Month Outcome in Bulimia Nervosa and the
Influence of Attitudes to Shape and Weight."
Journal of Consulting and Clinical Psychology 61
(1993): 696–98.

Kantrowitz, Barbara. "Sexism in the Schoolhouse."
Newsweek 24 Feb. 1992: 62.

Langewiesche, William. "The World in Its Extreme."
Atlantic Nov. 1991: 105–40.

National Law Center. "Selected Rights of Homeless
Persons." National Law Center on Homelessness
and Poverty 19 Apr. 1998 <http://www.nlchp.org/
rights2.htm>.

Taylor, Chuck. "After Cobain's Death: Here Come
the Media Ready to Buy Stories." Seattle Times
10 Apr. 1994: A1+.

Writer's last name and page number in upper right corner.

Book entry, one author. Use standard abbreviations for common publishers.

Book entry in a revised edition.

Book by two or three authors. With four or more authors, name only the first and use *et al.,* as in Jones, Peter, et al.

Article in anthology; author heads the entry; editor cited after the book title. Inclusive page numbers come after the period following the year.

Article in scholarly journal paginated consecutively throughout year. This article has four or more authors.

Weekly or biweekly popular magazine; abbreviate all months except May, June, and July.

Monthly, bimonthly, or quarterly magazine.

Online document with corporate author; title in quotation marks; Web site underlined; date of access; Web address in angle brackets.

Newspaper article with identified author; if no author, begin with title.

References: APA Style Sheet for the Most Commonly Used Sources

Women, Health, and Crime   27

References

Adler, F. (1975). Sisters in crime. New York: McGraw-Hill.

Andersen, M. L. (1993). Thinking about women: Sociological perspectives on sex and gender (3rd ed.). New York: Macmillan.

Bart, P., & O'Brien, P. (1985). Stopping rape: Successful survival strategies. New York: Pergamon Press.

Durkin, K. (1987). Social cognition and social context in the construction of sex differences. In M. A. Baker (Ed.), Sex differences in human performances (pp. 45–60). New York: Wiley & Sons.

Fairburn, C. G., Pevaler, R. C., Jones, R., & Hope, R. A. (1993). Predictors of 12-month outcome in bulimia nervosa and the influence of attitudes to shape and weight. Journal of Consulting and Clinical Psychology, 61, 696–698.

Kantrowitz, B. (1992, February 24). Sexism in the schoolhouse. Newsweek, 62.

Langewiesche, W. (1991, November). The world in its extreme. The Atlantic Monthly, 105–140.

National Law Center. Selected rights of homeless persons. (n.d.) Retrieved April 19, 1998 from the World Wide Web: http://www.nlchp.org./rights2.htm

Taylor, C. (1994, April 10). After Cobain's death: Here come the media ready to buy stories. The Seattle Times, pp. A1+.

Running head and page number separated by five spaces.

Book entry, one author. Don't abbreviate publisher but omit unnecessary words.

Book entry in a revised edition.

Book with multiple authors; uses ampersand instead of *and* before last name. Authors' names listed last name first.

Article in anthology; no quotation marks around article title. Name of editor comes before book title.

Article in scholarly journal paginated consecutively throughout year. APA lists all authors in the References rather than using *et al.*

Weekly or biweekly popular magazine; do not abbreviate months.

Monthly, bimonthly, or quarterly magazine.

Online document with corporate author; roman title; access date; no period after Web address. (No date is available for this source.)

Newspaper article with identified author; if no author, begin with title.

(capitalize first word and important words only); then double-space and begin your text (see p. 334 for an example).

- Page numbers go in the upper right-hand corner flush with the right margin and one-half inch from the top of the page. The page number should be preceded by your last name (see pp. 334–42). The text begins one inch from the top of the page.

- Start a new page for your bibliography, which is titled Works Cited (centered, one inch from top of page, without underlining, quotation marks, bold face, or all caps). Format each entry according to the instructions on pages 406–22 (see p. 342 for an example; also see p. 420).

Distinctive Formatting Features for APA

- Has a separate title page, numbered page 1, and a 100-to-150-word abstract, numbered page 2 (the main body of your text begins with page 3). Papers for undergraduate courses often omit the abstract. Approximately one-third from the top of the page, type your title centered and double-spaced, without underlines or all caps (capitalize first word and important words only). Two spaces below the title type your name (centered). Two spaces below your name, type your course number (centered), and two spaces below that type the date (for an example of an APA title page, see p. 424).

- Page numbers go in the upper right-hand corner, flush with the right margin. Five spaces to the left of your page number, type your running head (a short version of your title), capitalizing only the first letters. Note that the first page of the main text is numbered either 2 or 3, depending on whether the paper includes an abstract (see p. 425).

- Start a new page for your bibliography, which is titled References (centered, one inch from top of page, without underlining, quotation marks, bold face, or all caps). Format each entry according to the instructions on pages 406–22 (see p. 430 for an example; also see p. 421).

FOR CLASS DISCUSSION

Now that you have reviewed the formats of the most commonly used kinds of sources, consider the differences between the MLA and the APA systems. The MLA system is used most frequently in the humanities, while the APA system is used in the social sciences. Why do you suppose the MLA system gives complete first names of authors as well as middle initials, while the APA system uses only initials for the first and middle names? Why does the APA system emphasize date of publication by putting dates prominently near the front of an entry just after the author's name? On the basis of the MLA and APA formats, could you make some observations about differences in values between the humanities and the social sciences?

CONCLUSION

This chapter has shown that research writing is a variation on the thesis-governed writing with which you are already familiar. We have discussed how to focus and refine your research question, suggesting that you remain flexible throughout your research process so that your purpose and thesis can evolve as you discover new information. The chapter has explained purposeful strategies for reading, thinking, and note taking to help you avoid random inclusion of data and keep all research information focused on your own thesis. The chapter has also discussed methods of summarizing, paraphrasing, and quoting through the effective use of attributive tags, quotation marks, and block indentation. These methods enable you to work research sources smoothly into your own writing, distinguish your ideas from those of your sources, and avoid plagiarism. Finally, the chapter has explained how to use the MLA and the APA systems to cite and document your sources.

STUDENT EXAMPLE OF A RESEARCHED ARGUMENT PAPER (APA STYLE)

We conclude with a sample of a successful effort: Lynnea Clark's researched argument on policewomen. She uses the APA system for citing and documenting her sources.

Women Police Officers:

Should Size and Strength Be Criteria for Patrol Duty?

Lynnea Clark

English 301

15 November 199X

This research paper follows the APA style for format and documentation.

Women Police Officers:

Should Size and Strength Be Criteria for Patrol Duty?

A marked patrol car turns the corner at 71st and Franklin Avenue and   1
cautiously proceeds into the parking lot of an old shopping center. About a dozen
gang members, dressed in their gang colors, stand alert, looking down the alley
that runs behind the store. As the car moves toward the gathering, they suddenly
scatter in all directions. Within seconds, several shots are fired from the alley.
Switching on the overhead emergency lights, the officer bolts from the car when
he sees two figures running past him. "Freeze! Police!" the officer yells. The men
dart off in opposite directions. Chasing one, the policeman catches up to him, and,
observing no gun, tackles him. After a violent struggle, the officer manages to
handcuff the man, just as the backup unit comes screeching up.

This policeman is my friend. The next day I am with him as he sits at a cafe   2
with three of his fellow officers, discussing the incident. One of the officers
comments, "Well, at least you were stronger than he was. Can you imagine if
Connie Jones was on patrol duty last night?" "What a joke," scoffs another officer.
"How tall is she anyway?" "About 4'10" and 90 pounds," says the third officer. "She
could fit in my backpack." Connie Jones (not her real name) has just completed
police academy training and has been assigned to patrol duty in _____. Because
she is so small, she has to have a booster seat in her patrol car and has been given
a special gun, since she can barely manage to pull the trigger of a standard police-
issue .38 revolver. Although she passed the physical requirements at the academy,
which involved speed and endurance running, situps, and monkey bar tests, most
of the officers in her department doubt her ability to perform competently as a
patrol officer. But nevertheless she is on patrol because men and women receive
equal assignments in most of today's police forces. But is this a good policy? Can a
person who is significantly small and weak make an effective patrol officer?

Because the "small and weak" people in question are almost always women,   3
the issue becomes a woman's issue. Considerable research has been done on
women in the police force, and much of it suggests that women, who are on the
average smaller and weaker than men, can perform competently in law enforcement,
regardless of their size or strength. More specifically, most research concludes that
female police workers in general perform just as well as their fellow officers in
patrolling situations. A major study by Bloch and Anderson (1984), commissioned

by the Urban Institute, revealed that in the handling of violent situations, women performed well. In fact, women and men received equally satisfactory evaluation ratings on their overall performances.

4   In another more recent study (Grennan, 1987) examining the relationship between outcomes of police-citizen confrontations and the gender of the involved officers, female officers were determined to be just as productive as male officers in the handling of violent situations. In his article on female criminal justice employment, Potts (1982) reviews numerous studies on evaluation ratings of policewomen and acknowledges that "the predominant weight of evidence is that women are equally capable of performing police work as are men" (p. 11). Additionally, female officers score higher on necessary traits for leadership (p. 10), and it has been often found that women are better at dealing with rape and abuse victims. Again, a study performed by Grennan (1987), concentrating on male and female police officers' confrontations with citizens, revealed that the inborn or socialized nurturing ability possessed by female police workers makes them "just as productive as male officers in the handling of a violent confrontation" (p. 84).

5   This view has been strengthened further by the recent achievement of Katherine P. Heller, who was honored by receiving the nation's top award in law enforcement for 1990 (Proctor, 1990). Heller, a United States park policewoman, risked her life by stepping in the open to shoot dead an assailant while he leveled his gun to shoot at her fellow police officer. Five feet three inches and 107 pounds, Heller is not only the first woman to be awarded with Police Officer of the Year, but she is also the smallest recipient ever. Maybe Heller's decisiveness will help lay to rest doubts about many women's abilities as police workers.

6   However, despite the evidence provided by the above-cited research, I am not convinced. Although these studies show that women make effective police officers, I believe the studies must be viewed with skepticism. My concern is public safety. In light of that concern, the evidence suggests that police departments should set stringent size and strength requirements for patrol officers, even if these criteria exclude many women.

7   First of all, the research studies documenting the success of women as patrol officers are marred by two major flaws: The amount of evidence gathered is scanty and the way that the data have been gathered doesn't allow us to study factors of size and strength. Because of minimal female participation in patrol work prior to

the past decade, limited amounts of research and reports exist on the issue. And of the research performed, many studies have not been based on representative samples. Garrison, Grant, and McCormick (1988) found that

> [l]iterature on women in patrol or nontraditional police roles tends to be idiosyncratic. . . . Many of the observations written about a relatively small number of women performing successfully in a wider range of police tasks support the assumption that they are exceptions rather than the norm. (p. 32)

Similarly, Bloch and Anderson (1984) note that in the course of their study

> it was not possible to observe enough incidents to be sure that men and women are equally capable in all such situations. It is clear from the incidents which were described that women performed well in the few violent situations which did arise. (p. 61)

Another problem with the available research is that little differentiation has been made within the large group of women being considered; all women officers seem to be grouped and evaluated based on only two criteria: that they are on the police force and that they are female. But like men, women come in all shapes and sizes. To say that women as a class make effective or ineffective police workers is to make too general a claim. The example of women officers such as Katherine Heller proves that some women make excellent patrol cops. But, presumably, some women probably would not make good patrol cops just as some men would not. The available data do not allow us to determine whether size and strength are factors. Because no size differentiation has been made within the groups of women officers under observation in the research studies, it is impossible to conclude whether or not smaller, weaker women performed patrol duties as well as larger, stronger women did. In fact, for Bloch and Anderson's study (which indicates that, from a performance viewpoint, it is appropriate to hire women for patrol assignments on the same basis as men) both men and women had to meet a minimum height requirement of 5'7". Therefore, the performance of smaller, weaker women in handling violent situations remained unevaluated. Thus the data show that many women are great cops; the data do <u>not</u> show that many small women with minimal strength make great cops.

The case of Katherine Heller might seem to demonstrate that smaller women can perform patrol duties successfully. Heller acknowledged in an interview in <u>Parade</u> magazine that ninety percent of her adversaries will be bigger than she

(Proctor, 1990, p. 5). But she is no fluttering fluffball; rather, she has earned the reputation for being an extremely aggressive cop and has compensated for her size by her bearing. But how many women (or men) of Heller's size or smaller could maintain such "officer presence"? How can we be certain that Heller is in fact representative of small women rather than being an exception?

10   This question leads to my second reason for supporting stringent size and strength requirements: Many police officers, both male and female, have real doubts about the abilities of small and physically weak patrol workers, most of whom are women. For example, police officer Elizabeth Demetriou, a six-year veteran of the New York Police Department, said in an interview, "Women on the job still depend on men to help them during confrontations, more so than men do. Male police officers want their partners to be 'tough' or big so that automatically excludes women" (Kennedy, 1996). In a study done by Vega and Silverman (1982), almost 75% of male police officers felt that women were not strong enough to handle the demands of patrol duties, and 42% felt women lacked the needed assertiveness to enforce the law vigorously (p. 32). Unfortunately, however, because of frequent media reports of discrimination and sexism among police personnel and because of pressure from the Equal Employment Opportunity Commission (EEOC) on police agencies and other employers (Vega & Silverman, 1982; Lord, 1986), these reservations and attitudes have not been seriously taken into account.

11   The valid concerns and opinions of police workers who feel that some women officers are not strong enough to deal effectively with violent situations have been asphyxiated by the smoldering accusations of civil rights activists and feminists, who see only layers of chauvinism, conservatism, cynicism, and authoritarianism permeating our law enforcement agencies. These activists view the problem as being only a "women" issue rather than a "size" issue. But the fact remains that both male and female officers think that many patrol workers are incapable of handling violent situations because of small stature and lack of physical strength. Another policewoman belonging to the same department as Connie Jones explained, "She [Jones] doesn't have the authoritarian stance needed to compensate for her size. She's not imposing and is too soft spoken. Once she responded to a call and was literally picked up and thrown out the door" (anonymous personal communication, October 6, 1990).

Finally, patrol duties, unlike other areas of police work, constitute one of the   12
few jobs in our society that may legitimately require above-average strength.
Because the job involves great personal risk and danger, the concern for public
safety overrides the-concern for equal rights in this instance. Patrolling is a
high-visibility position in police departments as opposed to jobs such as radio
dispatching, academy training, or clerical duties. Patrol workers directly face the
challenges presented by the public, and violence is always a threat for officers on
patrol (Vega & Silverman, 1982; Grennan, 1987). Due to the nature of patrol work,
officers many times must cope with violent situations by using physical force, such
as that needed for subduing individuals who resist arrest. However, pressure from
liberal groups has prevented special consideration being given to these factors of
patrol duty. As long as student officers pass the standard academy Physical Ability
Test (in addition to the other academy requirements), then they are eligible for
patrol assignments; in fact, everyone out of the academy <u>must</u> go on patrol. But
the minimum physical requirements are not challenging. According to Lord
(1986), police agencies "struggle to find a nondiscriminatory, empirically valid
entry level physical agility test which does not discriminate against women by
overemphasizing upper body strength" (p. 91). In short, the liberal agenda leading
to women on patrol has forced the lowering of strength requirements.

Without establishing minimum size and strength requirements for patrol   13
workers, police departments are not discharging their duties with maximum
competency or effectiveness. Police training programs stress that police officers
should be able to maintain an authoritarian presence in the face of challenges and
possess the ability to diffuse a situation just by making an appearance. But some
individuals who are able to pass basic training programs still lack the size needed to
maintain an imposing physical stance. And as many citizens obviously do not respect
the uniform, police workers must possess the strength to efficiently handle violent
encounters. Even if size and strength requirements have a disproportionate impact
on women, these physical standards are lawful, so long as they relate to the demands
of the job and "constitute valid predictors of an employee's performance on the job"
(Steel & Lovrich, 1987, p. 53). Patrol duties demand highly capable and effective
workers, and in order to professionalize law-enforcement practices and to maintain
the degree of order necessary for a free society, police agencies must maintain a high
level of competency in their street-patrol forces.

References

Bloch, P., & Anderson, D. (1984). Police women on patrol: Final report. Washington, DC: Police Foundation.

Garrison, C., Grant, N., & McCormick, K. (1988). Utilization of police women. The Police Chief, 55(9), 32–73.

Grennan, S. (1987). Findings on the role of officer gender in violent encounters with citizens. Journal of Police Science and Administration, 15(1), 78–84.

Kennedy, E. A. (1996, Spring). Defensive tactics and the female officer. WomenPolice. Retrieved May 4, 1996 from the World Wide Web; http://www.mwarrior.com/DT-fem2.htm

Lord, L. (1986). A comparison of male and female peace officers' stereotypic perceptions of women and women peace officers. Journal of Police Science and Administration, 14(2), 83–91.

Potts, L. (1981). Equal employment opportunity and female criminal justice employment. Police Studies, 4(3), 9–19.

Proctor, P. (1990, September 30). "I didn't have time to taste the fear." Parade, pp. 4–5.

Steel, B., & Lovrich, N., Jr. (1987). Equality and efficiency tradeoffs in affirmative action--real or imagined? The case of women in policing. The Social Science Journal, 24(1), 53–67.

Vega, M., & Silverman, I. (1982). Female police officers as viewed by their male counterparts. Police Studies, 5(1), 31–39.

appendix one

Informal Fallacies

In this appendix, we look at ways of testing the legitimacy of an argument. Sometimes, there are fatal logical flaws hiding in the heart of a perfectly respectable-looking argument, and if we miss them, we may find ourselves vainly defending the indefensible. Take, for example, the following cases. Do they seem persuasive to you?

Creationism must be a science because hundreds of scientists believe in it.

I am opposed to a multicultural curriculum because it will lead to ethnic separatism similar to what is happening in eastern Europe.

Smoking must cause cancer because a higher percentage of smokers get cancer than do nonsmokers.

Smoking doesn't cause cancer because my grandfather smoked two packs per day for fifty years and died in his sleep at age ninety.

An abnormal percentage of veterans who were marched to ground zero during atomic tests in Nevada died of leukemia and lung cancer. Surely their deaths were caused by the inhalation of radioactive isotopes.

THE PROBLEM OF CONCLUSIVENESS
IN AN ARGUMENT

Although it may distress us to think so, none of the arguments listed above is conclusive. But that doesn't mean they're false, either. So what are they? Well, they are, to various degrees, "persuasive" or "unpersuasive." The problem is that some people will mistake arguments such as those above for "conclusive" or airtight arguments. A person may rest an entire argument on them and then fall right through the holes that observant logicians open in them. Although few people will mistake an airtight case for a fallacious one, lots of people mistake logically unsound arguments for airtight cases. So let's see how to avoid falling into specious reasoning.

Some arguments are flawed because they fail to observe certain formal logical rules. In constructing syllogisms, for example, there are certain formal laws that must be followed if we are to have a valid syllogism. The following argument is beyond doubt invalid and inconclusive:

> No Greeks are bald.
>
> No Lithuanians are Greek.
>
> Therefore, all Lithuanians are bald.

But to say the argument is invalid isn't to say that its conclusion is necessarily untrue. Perhaps all Lithuanians really are bald. The point is, if the conclusion were true, it would be by coincidence, not design, because the argument is invalid. All invalid arguments are inconclusive. And, by the same token, a perfectly valid syllogism may be untrue. Just because the premises follow the formal laws of logic doesn't mean that what they say is true. For a syllogistic argument to be absolutely conclusive, its form must be valid and its premises must be true. A perfectly conclusive argument would therefore yield a noncontroversial truth—a statement that no one would dispute.

This is a long way around to reach one point: The reason we argue about issues is that none of the arguments on any side of an issue is absolutely conclusive; there is always room to doubt the argument, to develop a counterargument. We can only create more or less persuasive arguments, never conclusive ones.

We have examined some of these problems already. In Chapter 11 on causal arguments we discussed the problem of correlation versus causation. We know, for example, that smoking and cancer are correlated but that further arguments are needed in order to increase the conclusiveness of the claim that smoking *causes* cancer.

In this appendix we explore the problem of conclusiveness in various kinds of arguments. In particular, we use the *informal fallacies* of logic to explain how inconclusive arguments can fool us into thinking they are conclusive.

AN OVERVIEW OF INFORMAL FALLACIES

The study of informal fallacies remains the murkiest of all logical endeavors. It's murky because informal fallacies are as unsystematic as formal fallacies are rigid and systematized. Whereas formal fallacies of logic have the force of laws, informal fallacies have little more than explanatory power. Informal fallacies are quirky; they identify classes of less conclusive arguments that recur with some frequency, but they do not contain formal flaws that make their conclusions illegitimate no matter what the terms may say. Informal fallacies require us to look at the meaning of the terms to determine how much we should trust or distrust the conclusion. The most common mistake one can make with informal fallacies is to assume that they have the force of laws like formal fallacies. They don't. In evaluating arguments with informal fallacies, we usually find that arguments are "more or less" fallacious, and determining the degree of fallaciousness is a matter of judgment.

Knowledge of informal fallacies is most useful when we run across arguments that we "know" are wrong, but we can't quite say why. They just don't "sound right." They look reasonable enough, but they remain unacceptable to us. Informal fallacies are a sort of compendium of symptoms for arguments flawed in this way. We must be careful, however, to make sure that the particular case before us "fits" the descriptors for the fallacy that seems to explain its problem. It's much easier, for example, to find informal fallacies in a hostile argument than in a friendly one simply because we are more likely to expand the limits of the fallacy to make the disputed case fit.

Not everyone agrees about what to include under the heading "informal fallacies." In selecting the following set of fallacies, we left out far more candidates than we included. Since Aristotle first developed his list of thirteen *elenchi* (refutations) down to the present day, literally dozens of different systems of informal fallacy have been put forward. Although there is a good deal of overlap among these lists, the terms are invariably different, and the definition of fallacy itself shifts from age to age. In selecting the following set of fallacies, we left out a number of other candidates. We chose the following because they seemed to us to be the most commonly encountered.

In arranging the fallacies, we have, for convenience, put them into three categories derived from classical rhetoric: *pathos, ethos,* and *logos.* Fallacies of *pathos* rest on a flawed relationship between what is argued and the audience for the argument. Fallacies of *ethos* rest on a flawed relationship between the argument and the character of those involved in the argument. Fallacies of *logos* rest on flaws in the relationship among statements of an argument.

Fallacies of *Pathos*

Argument to the People (Appealing to Stirring Symbols)

This is perhaps the most generic example of a *pathos* fallacy. Argument to the people appeals to the fundamental beliefs, biases, and prejudices of the audience in order to sway opinion through a feeling of solidarity among those of the group. For example, when a politician says, "My fellow Americans, I stand here, draped in this flag from head to foot, to indicate my fundamental dedication to the values and principles of these sovereign United States," he's redirecting to his own person our allegiance to nationalistic values by linking himself with the prime symbol of those values, the flag. The linkage is not rational, it's associative. It's also extremely powerful—which is why arguments to the people crop up so frequently.

Appeal to Ignorance (Presenting Evidence the Audience Can't Examine)

Those who commit this fallacy present assumptions, assertions, or evidence that the audience is incapable of judging or examining. If, for example, a critic were to praise the novel *Clarissa* for its dullness on the grounds that this dullness was the intentional effect of the author, we would be unable to respond because we have no idea what was in the author's mind when he created the work.

Appeal to Irrational Premises (Appealing to Reasons That May Have No Basis in Logic)

This mode of short-circuiting reason may take one of three forms:

1. Appeal to common practice. (It's all right to do X because everyone else does it.)

2. Appeal to traditional wisdom. (It's all right because we've always done it this way.)

3. Appeal to popularity—the bandwagon appeal. (It's all right because lots of people like it.)

In all three cases, we've moved from saying something is popular, common, or persistent to saying it is right, good, or necessary. You have a better chance of rocketing across the Grand Canyon on a motorcycle than you have of going from "is" to "ought" on a *because* clause. Some examples of this fallacy would include (1) "Of course I borrowed money from the company slush fund. Everyone on this floor has done the same in the last eighteen months"; (2) "We've got to require everyone to read *Hamlet* because we've always required everyone to read it"; and (3) "You should buy a Ford Escort because it's the best-selling car in the world."

Provincialism (Appealing to the Belief That the Known Is Always Better Than the Unknown)

Here is an example from the 1960s: "You can't sell small cars in America. In American culture, automobiles symbolize prestige and personal freedom. Those cramped little Japanese tin boxes will never win the hearts of American consumers." Although we may inevitably feel more comfortable with familiar things, ideas, and beliefs, we are not necessarily better off for sticking with them.

Red Herring (Shifting the Audience's Attention from a Crucial Issue to an Irrelevant One)

A good example of a red herring showed up in a statement by Secretary of State James Baker that was reported in the November 10, 1990, *New York Times*. In response to a question about the appropriateness of using American soldiers to defend wealthy, insulated (and by implication, corrupt) Kuwaiti royalty, Baker told an anecdote about an isolated encounter he had with four Kuwaitis who had suffered; he then made a lengthy statement on America's interests in the Persian Gulf. Although no one would argue that America is unaffected by events in the Middle

East, the question of why others with even greater interests at stake had not contributed more troops and resources went unanswered.

Fallacies of *Ethos*

Appeal to False Authority (Appealing to the Authority of a Popular Person Rather Than a Knowledgeable One)

Appeals to false authority involve relying on testimony given by a person incompetent in the field from which the claims under question emerge. Most commercial advertisements are based on this fallacy. Cultural heroes are paid generously to associate themselves with a product without demonstrating any real expertise in evaluating that product. In at least one case, consumers who fell victim to such a fallacy made a legal case out of it. People bilked out of their life savings by a Michigan mortgage company sued the actors who represented the company on TV. Are people fooled by such appeals to false authority entitled to recover assets lost as a result?

The court answered no. The judge ruled that people gullible enough to believe that George Hamilton's capped-tooth smile and mahogany tan qualify him as a real estate consultant deserve what they get. Their advice to consumers? "Buyers beware," because even though sellers can't legally lie, they can legally use fallacious arguments—all the more reason to know your fallacies.

Keep in mind, however, that occasionally the distinction between a false authority fallacy and an appeal to legitimate authority can blur. Suppose that Tiger Woods were to praise a particular company's golf club. Because he is an expert on golf, it is possible that Woods actually speaks from authority and that the golf club he praises is superior. But it might also be that he is being paid to advertise the golf club and is endorsing a brand that is no better than its competitors'. The only way we could make even a partial determination of Woods's motives would be if he presented an *ad rem* ("to the thing") argument showing us scientifically why the golf club in question is superior. In short, appeals to authority are legitimate when the authority knows the field and when her motive is to inform others rather than profit herself.

Appeal to the Person/Ad Hominem (Attacking the Character of the Arguer Rather Than the Argument Itself)

Literally, *ad hominem* means "to the man" or "to the person." Any argument that focuses on the character of the person making the argument rather than the quality of the reasoning qualifies as an *ad hominem* argument. Ideally, arguments are supposed to be *ad rem*, or "to the thing," that is, addressed to the specifics of the case itself. Thus an *ad rem* critique of a politician would focus on her voting record, the consistency and cogency of her public statements, her responsiveness to constituents, and so forth. An *ad hominem* argument would shift attention from her record to irrelevant features of her personality or personal life. Perhaps an *ad hominem* argument would suggest that she had a less than stellar undergraduate academic record.

But not all *ad hominem* arguments are *ad hominem* fallacies. It's not always fallacious to address your argument to the arguer. There are indeed times when the credibility of the person making an opposing argument is at issue. Lawyers, for example, when questioning expert witnesses who give damaging testimony, will often make an issue of their credibility, and rightfully so. And certainly it's not that clear, for instance, that an all-male research team of social scientists would observe and interpret data in the same way as a mixed-gender research group. An *ad hominem* attack on an opponent's argument is not fallacious so long as (1) personal authority is what gives the opposing argument much of its weight, and (2) the critique of the person's credibility is fairly presented.

An interesting example of an *ad hominem* argument occurred in the 1980s in context of the Star Wars antiballistic missile system debate. Many important physicists around the country signed a statement in which they declared their opposition to Star Wars research. Another group of physicists supportive of that research condemned them on the grounds that none of the protesting physicists stood to get any Star Wars research funds anyway. This attack shifted attention away from the reasons given by the protesting physicists for their convictions and put it instead on the physicists' motives. To some extent, of course, credibility is an issue here, because many of the key issues raised in the debate required some degree of expertise to resolve. Hence, the charges meet the first test for nonfallacious reasoning directed to the arguer.

But we must also ask ourselves if the charges being made are fair. If you'll recall from earlier discussions of fairness, we said that fairness requires similar treatment of similar classes of things. Applying this rule to this situation, we can simply reverse the charge being levied against the anti–Star Wars group and say of its supporters: "Because you stand to gain a good deal of research money from this project, we can't take your support of the Star Wars initiatives seriously." The Star Wars supporters would thus become victims of their own logic. *Ad hominem* attacks are often of this nature: The charges are perfectly reversible—for example, "Of course you support abortion; all your friends are feminists." "Of course you oppose abortion; you've been a Catholic all your life." *Ad hominem* debates resemble nothing so much as mental quick-draw contests. Whoever shoots first wins because the first accuser puts the burden of proof on the opposition.

It's important to see here that an *ad hominem* argument, even if not fallacious, can never be definitive. Like analogies, they are simply suggestive; they raise doubts and focus our attention. Catholic writers can produce reasonable arguments against abortion, and feminists can produce reasonable ones for it. *Ad hominem* attacks don't allow us to discount arguments; but they do alert us to possible biases, possible ways the reasoned arguments themselves are vulnerable.

Several subcategories of *ad hominem* argument that are almost never persuasive include

1. Name calling (referring to a disputant by unsavory names)
2. Appeal to prejudice (applying ethnic, racial, gender, or religious slurs to an opponent)
3. Guilt by association (linking the opposition to extremely unpopular groups or causes)

Name calling is found far more often in transcripts of oral encounters than in books or essays. In the heat of the moment, speakers are more likely to lapse into verbal abuse than are writers who have time to contemplate their words. The *Congressional Record* is a rich source for name calling. Here, for example, one finds a duly elected representative referring to another duly elected representative as "a pimp for the Eastern establishment environmentalists." One of the biggest problems with such a charge is that it's unlikely to beget much in the way of reasoned response. It's far easier to respond in kind than it is to persuade people rationally that one is not a jackass of *that* particular sort.

When name calling is "elevated" to include slighting reference to the opponent's religion, gender, race, or ethnic background, we have encountered an appeal to prejudice. When it involves lumping an opponent with unsavory, terminally dumb, or extremely unpopular causes and characters, it constitutes guilt by association.

Straw Man (Greatly Oversimplifying an Opponent's Argument to Make It Easier to Refute or Ridicule)

Although typically less inflammatory than the preceding sorts of *ethos* fallacies, the straw man fallacy changes the character of the opposition in order to suit the arguer's own needs. In committing a straw man fallacy, you basically make up the argument you *wish* your opponents had made and attribute it to them because it's so much easier to refute than the argument they actually made. Some political debates consist almost entirely of straw man exchanges such as: "You may think that levying confiscatory taxes on homeless people's cardboard dwellings is the surest way out of recession, but I don't." Or: "While my opponent would like to empty our prisons of serial killers and coddle kidnappers, I hold to the sacred principles of compensatory justice."

Fallacies of *Logos*

Logos fallacies comprise flaws in the relationships among the statements of an argument. Thus, to borrow momentarily from the language of the Toulmin schema discussed earlier, you can think of *logos* fallacies as breakdowns between arguments' warrants and their claims, between their warrants and their backing, or between their claims and their reasons and grounds.

Begging the Question (Supporting a Claim with a Reason That Is Really a Restatement of the Claim in Different Words)

Question begging is probably the most obvious example of a *logos* fallacy in that it involves stating a claim as though it warranted itself. For example, the statement "Abortion is murder because it involves the intentional killing of an unborn human being" is tantamount to saying "Abortion is murder because it's murder." The warrant "If something is the intentional killing of a human life, it is murder" simply repeats the claim; murder is *by definition* the intentional killing of another human being. Logically, the statement is akin to a statement like "That fellow is fat because he's considerably overweight." The crucial issue in the abortion debate is whether a fetus is a human being in the legal sense. This crucial issue is avoided in the argument that begins by assuming that the fetus is a legal human being. That argument goes in an endless circle from claim to warrant and back again.

Or consider the following argument: "How can you say Minnie Minoso belongs in the Hall of Fame? He's been eligible for over a decade, and the Selection Committee turned him down every year. If he belonged in the Hall of Fame, the Committee would already have chosen him." Because the point at issue is whether the Hall of Fame Selection Committee *should* elect Minnie Minoso (it should, we think), the use of the committee's vote as proof of the contention that it should not elect him is wholly circular and begs the question.

In distinguishing valid reasoning from fallacious examples of question begging, some philosophers say that a question has been begged when the premises of an argument are at least as uncertain as the claim. In such cases, we are not making any movement from some known general principle toward some new particular conclusion; we are simply asserting an uncertain premise in order to give the appearance of certainty to a shaky claim.

To illustrate the preceding observation, consider the controversy that arose in the late 1980s over whether to impose economic sanctions against South Africa in order to pressure the South Africans into changing their racial policies. One argument against economic sanctions went like this: "We should not approve economic sanctions against South Africa (claim) because economic sanctions will hurt blacks as much as whites" (premise or stated reason). The claim ("We should not impose economic sanctions") is only as certain as the premise from which it was derived ("because blacks will suffer as much as whites"), but many people argued that that premise was extremely uncertain. They thought that whites would suffer the most under sanctions and that blacks would ultimately benefit. The question would no longer be begged if the person included a documented defense of the premise. But without such a defense, the arguer's claim is grounded on a shaky premise that sounds more certain than it is.

*Complex Question (Confronting the Opponent
with a Question That Will Put Her in a Bad Light
No Matter How She Responds)*

A complex question is one that requires, in legal terms, a self-incriminating response. For example, the question "When did you stop abusing alcohol?" requires the admission of alcohol abuse. Hence the claim that a person has abused alcohol is silently turned into an assumption.

*False Dilemma/Either–Or (Oversimplifying
a Complex Issue So That Only Two Choices
Appear Possible)*

A good extended analysis of this fallacy is found in sociologist Kai Erikson's analysis of President Truman's decision to drop the A-bomb on Hiroshima. His analysis suggests that the Truman administration prematurely reduced numerous options to just two: Either drop the bomb on a major city, or sustain unacceptable losses in a land invasion of Japan. Erikson, however, shows there were other alternatives. Typically, we encounter false dilemma arguments when people are trying to justify a questionable action by creating a false sense of necessity, forcing us to choose between two options, one of which is clearly unacceptable. Hence, when someone orders us to "Do it my way or hit the highway" or to "Love it or leave it," it's probably in response to some criticism we made about the "way" we're supposed to do it or the "it" we're supposed to love.

But of course not all dilemmas are false. People who reject all binary oppositions (that is, thinking in terms of pairs of opposites) are themselves guilty of a false dilemma. There are times when we might determine through a rational process of elimination that only two possible choices exist. Deciding whether a dilemma is truly a dilemma or only an evasion of complexity often requires a difficult judgment. Although we should initially suspect any attempt to convert a complex problem into an either/or choice, we may legitimately arrive at such a choice through thoughtful deliberation.

*Equivocation (Using to Your Advantage
at Least Two Different Definitions of the
Same Term in the Same Argument)*

For example, if we're told that people can't "flourish" unless they are culturally literate, we must know which of the several possible senses of *flourish* are being used before we can test the persuasiveness of the claim. If by *flourishing* the author means acquiring great wealth, we'll look at a different set of grounds than if *flourishing* is synonymous with moral probity, recognition in a profession, or simple contentment. To the extent that we're not told what it means to flourish, the relationship between the claim and the grounds and between the claim and the warrant remains ambiguous and unassailable.

*Confusing Correlation for Cause/*Post Hoc, Ergo
Propter Hoc *(After This, Therefore Because of This)*
(Assuming That Event X Causes Event Y
Because Event X Preceded Event Y)

Here are two examples in which this fallacy may be at work:

Cramming for a test really helps. Last week I crammed for a psychology test and I got an A on it.

I am allergic to the sound of a lawn mower because every time I mow the lawn I start to sneeze.

We've already discussed this fallacy in Chapter 11, particularly in our discussion of the difference between correlation and causation. This fallacy occurs when a sequential relationship is mistaken for a causal relationship. To be sure, when two events occur frequently in conjunction with each other in a particular sequence, we've got a good case for a causal relationship. But until we can show how one causes the other, we cannot be certain that a causal relationship is occurring. The conjunction may simply be a matter of chance, or it may be attributable to some as-yet-unrecognized other factor. For example, your A on the psych test may be caused by something other than your cramming. Maybe the exam was easier, or perhaps you were luckier or more mentally alert.

Just when an erroneous causal argument becomes an example of the *post hoc* fallacy, however, is not cut-and-dried. Many reasonable arguments of causality later turn out to have been mistaken. We are guilty of the *post hoc* fallacy only when our claim of causality seems naively arrived at, without reflection or consideration of alternative hypotheses. Thus in our lawn mower argument, it is probably not the sound that creates the speaker's sneezing but all the pollen stirred up by the spinning blades.

We arrived at this more likely argument by applying a tool known as Occam's Razor—the principle that "What can be explained on fewer principles is explained needlessly by more," or "Between two hypotheses, both of which will account for a given fact, prefer the simpler." If we posit that sound is the cause of our sneezing, all sorts of intermediate causes are going to have to be fetched from afar to make the explanation persuasive. But the blades stirring up the pollen will cause the sneezing more directly. So, until science connects lawn mower noises to human eardrums to sneezing, the simpler explanation is preferred.

Slippery Slope

The slippery slope fallacy is based on the fear that once we take a first step in a direction we don't like we will have to keep going.

We don't dare send weapons to eastern Europe. If we do so, we will next send in military advisers, then a special forces battalion, and then large numbers of troops. Finally, we will be in all-out war.

Look, Blotnik, no one feels worse about your need for open-heart surgery than I do. But I still can't let you turn this paper in late. If I were to let you do it, then I'd have to let everyone turn in papers late.

We run into slippery slope arguments all the time, especially when person A opposes person B's proposal. Those opposed to a particular proposal will often foresee an inevitable and catastrophic chain of events that would follow from taking a first, apparently harmless step. In other words, once we put a foot on that slippery slope, we're doomed to slide right out of sight. Often, such arguments are fallacious insofar as what is seen as an inevitable effect is in fact dependent on some intervening cause or chain of causes to bring it about. Will smoking cigarettes lead inevitably to heroin addiction? Overwhelming statistical evidence would suggest that it doesn't. A slippery slope argument, however, would lovingly trace a teenager's inevitable descent from a clandestine puff on the schoolground through the smoking of various controlled substances to a degenerate end in some Needle Park somewhere. The power of the slippery slope argument lies as much as anything in its compelling narrative structure. It pulls us along irresistibly from one plausible event to the next, making us forget that it's a long jump from plausibility to necessity.

One other common place to find slippery slope arguments is in confrontations between individuals and bureaucracies or other systems of rules and laws. Whenever individuals ask to have some sort of exception made for them, they risk the slippery slope reply. "Sorry, Mr. Jones, if we rush your order, then we will have to rush everyone else's order also."

The problem, of course, is that not every slippery slope argument is an instance of the slippery slope fallacy. We all know that some slopes are slippery and that we sometimes have to draw the line, saying, "To here, but no farther." And it is true also that making exceptions to rules is dangerous; the exceptions soon get established as regular procedures. The slippery slope becomes a fallacy, however, when we forget that some slopes don't *have* to be slippery unless we let them be slippery. Often we do better to imagine a staircase with stopping places all along the way. The assumption that we have no control over our descent once we take the first step makes us unnecessarily rigid.

Hasty Generalization (Making a Broad Generalization on the Basis of Too Little Evidence)

Typically, a hasty generalization occurs when someone reaches a conclusion on the basis of insufficient evidence. But what constitutes "sufficient" evidence? No generalization arrived at through empirical evidence would meet a logician's strict standard of certainty. And generally acceptable standards of proof in any given field are difficult to determine.

The Food and Drug Administration (FDA), for example, generally proceeds very cautiously before certifying a drug as "safe." However, whenever doubts arise about the safety of an FDA-approved drug, critics accuse the FDA of having made a hasty generalization. At the same time, patients eager to have access to a new drug and manufacturers eager to sell a new product may lobby the FDA to "quit dragging its feet" and get the drug to market. Hence, the point at which a hasty generalization about drug safety passes over into the realm of a prudent generalization is nearly always uncertain and contested.

A couple of variants of hasty generalization that deserve mention are

1. Pars pro toto/*Mistaking the part for the whole (assuming that what is true for a part will be true for the whole).* *Pars pro toto* arguments often appear in the critiques of the status quo. If, say, individuals wanted to get rid of the National Endowment for the Arts, they might focus on several controversial grants they've made over the past few years and use them as justification for wiping out all NEA programs.

2. *Suppressed evidence (withholding contradictory or unsupportive evidence so that only favorable evidence is presented to an audience).* The flip side of *pars pro toto* is suppressed evidence. If the administrator of the NEA were to go before Congress seeking more money and conveniently forgot about those controversial grants, he would be suppressing damaging but relevant evidence.

Faulty Analogy (Claiming That Because X Resembles Y in One Regard, X Will Resemble Y in All Regards)

Faulty analogies occur whenever a relationship of resemblance is turned into a relationship of identity. For example, the psychologist Carl Rogers uses a questionable analogy in his argument that political leaders should make use of discoveries about human communication derived from research in the social sciences. "During the war when a test-tube solution was found to the problem of synthetic rubber, millions of dollars and an army of talent was turned loose on the problem of using that finding. [. . .] But in the social science realm, if a way is found of facilitating communication and mutual understanding in small groups, there is no guarantee that the finding will be utilized."

Although Rogers is undoubtedly right that we need to listen more carefully to social scientists, his analogy between the movement from scientific discovery to product development and the movement from insights into small group functioning to political change is strained. The laws of cause and effect at work in a test tube are much more reliable and generalizable than the laws of cause and effect observed in small human groups. Whereas lab results can be readily replicated in different times and places, small group dynamics are altered by a whole host of factors, including the cultural background, gender, and age of participants. The warrant that licenses you to move from grounds to claim in the realm of science runs up against a statute of limitation when it tries to include the realm of social science.

Non Sequitur *(Making a Claim That Doesn't Follow Logically from the Premises, or Supporting a Claim with Irrelevant Premises)*

The *non sequitur* fallacy (literally, "it does not follow") is a miscellaneous category that includes any claim that doesn't follow logically from its premises or that is supported with irrelevant premises. In effect, any fallacy is a kind of *non sequitur* because what makes all fallacies fallacious is the absence of a logical connection between claim and premises. But in practice the term *non sequitur* tends to be restricted to problems like the following:

A completely illogical leap: "Clambake University has one of the best faculties in the United States because a Nobel Prize winner used to teach there." (How does the fact that a Nobel Prize winner used to teach at Clambake University make its present faculty one of the best in the United States?)

A clear gap in the chain of reasoning: "People who wear nose rings are disgusting. There ought to be a law against wearing nose rings in public." (This is a *non sequitur* unless the arguer is willing to state and defend the missing premise: "There ought to be a law against anything that I find disgusting.")

Use of irrelevant reasons to support a claim: "I should not receive a C in this course because I have received B's or A's in all my other courses (here is my transcript for evidence) and because I worked exceptionally hard in this course (here is my log of hours worked)." (Even though the arguer has solid evidence to support each premise, the premises themselves are irrelevant to the claim. Course grades should be based on actual performance in the class, not on performance in other classes or on amount of effort devoted to the material.)

FOR CLASS DISCUSSION

Working individually or in small groups, determine the potential persuasiveness of each argument. If the arguments are nonpersuasive because of one or more of the fallacies discussed in this appendix, identify the fallacies and explain how they render the argument nonpersuasive.

1. a. All wars are not wrong. The people who say so are cowards.
   b. Either we legalize marijuana or we watch a steady increase in the number of our citizens who break the law.
   c. The Bible is true because it is the inspired word of God.
   d. Mandatory registration of handguns will eventually lead to the confiscation of hunting rifles.
   e. All these tornadoes started happening right after they tested the A-bombs. The A-bomb testing has changed our weather.

f. Most other progressive nations have adopted a program of government-provided health care. Therefore, it is time the United States abandoned its outdated practice of private medicine.

g. The number of Hollywood movie stars who support liberal policies convinces me that liberalism is the best policy. After all, they are rich and will not benefit from better social services.

h. Society has an obligation to provide housing for the homeless because people without adequate shelter have a right to the resources of the community.

i. I have observed the way the two renters in our neighborhood take care of their rental houses and have compared that to the way homeowners take care of their houses. I have concluded that people who own their own homes take better care of them than those who rent. [This argument goes on to provide detailed evidence about the house-caring practices of the two renters and of the homeowners in the neighborhood.]

j. Since the universe couldn't have been created out of nothing, it must have been created by a divine being.

2. Consider the following statements. Note places where you think the logic is flawed. If you were asked by writers or speakers to respond to their statements, what advice would you give to those who wrote or said them to rescue them from charges of fallaciousness? What would each of these speakers/writers have to show, in addition to what's given, to render the statement cogent and persuasive?

a. "America has had the luxury throughout its history of not having its national existence directly threatened by a foreign enemy. Yet we have gone to war. Why?

"The United States of America is not a piece of dirt stretching mainly from the Atlantic to the Pacific. More than anything else, America is a set of principles, and the historical fact is that those principles have not only served us well, but have also become a magnet for the rest of the world, a large chunk of which decided to change course last year.

"Those principles are not mere aesthetic ideas. Those principles are in fact the distillation of 10,000 years of human social evolution. We have settled on them not because they are pretty; we settled on them because they are the only things that work. If you have trouble believing that, ask a Pole." (novelist Tom Clancy)

b. "What particularly irritated Mr. Young [Republican congressman from Alaska] was the fact that the measure [to prohibit logging in Alaska's Tongass National Forest] was initiated by . . . Robert Mrazek, a Democrat from Long Island. 'Bob Mrazek never saw a tree in his entire life until he went to Alaska' said Mr. Young." (*New York Times*, November 10, 1990)

c. "When Senator Tim Wirth . . . was in Brazil earlier this year on behalf of an effort to save the tropical rain forest of the Amazon basin, the first thing Brazilian President Jose Sarney asked him was, 'What about the Tongass?' " (*New York Times*, November 10, 1990)

a p p e n d i x   t w o

The Writing Community

Working in Groups

In Chapter 1 we stressed that today truth is typically seen as a product of discussion and persuasion by members of a given community. Instead of seeing "truth" as grounded in some absolute and timeless realm such as Plato's forms or the unchanging laws of logic, many modern thinkers assert that truth is the product of a consensus among a group of knowledgeable peers. Our own belief in the special importance of argumentation in contemporary life follows from our assumption that truth arises out of discussion and debate rather than dogma or pure reason.

In this appendix, we extend that assumption to the classroom itself. We introduce you to a mode of learning often called *collaborative learning*. It involves a combination of learning from an instructor, learning independently, and learning from peers. Mostly it involves a certain spirit—the same sort of inquiring attitude that's required of a good arguer.

FROM CONFLICT TO CONSENSUS: HOW TO GET THE MOST OUT OF THE WRITING COMMUNITY

Behind the notion of the writing community lies the notion that thinking and writing are social acts. At first, this notion may contradict certain widely accepted stereotypes of writers and thinkers as solitary souls who retreat to cork-lined studies where they conjure great thoughts and works. But although we agree that every writer at some point in the process requires solitude, we would point out that most writers and thinkers also require periods of talk and social interchange before they retreat to solitude. Poets, novelists, scientists, philosophers, and technological innovators tend to belong to communities of peers with whom they share their ideas, theories, and work. In this section, we try to provide you with some practical advice on how to get the most out of these sorts of communities in developing your writing skills.

Avoiding Bad Habits of Group Behavior

Over the years, most of us have developed certain bad habits that get in the way of efficient group work. Although we use groups all the time to study and accomplish demanding tasks, we tend to do so spontaneously and unreflectively without asking why some groups work and others don't. Many of us, for example, have worked on committees that just didn't get the job done and wasted our time, or else got the job done because one or two tyrannical people dominated the group. Just a couple of bad committee experiences can give us a healthy skepticism about the utility of groups in general. "A committee," according to some people, "is a sort of centipede. It has too many legs, no brain, and moves very slowly."

At their worst, this is indeed how groups function. In particular, they have a tendency to fail in two opposite directions, failures that can be avoided only by conscious effort. Groups can lapse into "clonethink" and produce a safe, superficial consensus whereby everyone agrees with the first opinion expressed in order to avoid conflict or to get on to something more interesting. At the other extreme is a phenomenon we'll call "egothink." In egothink, all members of the group go their own way and produce a collection of minority views that have nothing to do with each other and would be impossible to act on. Clonethinkers view their task as conformity to a norm; egothinkers see their task as safeguarding the autonomy of individual group members. Both fail to take other people and other ideas seriously.

Successful groups avoid both extremes and achieve unity out of diversity. This means that any successful community of learners must be willing to endure creative conflict. Creative conflict results from an initial agreement to disagree respectfully with each other and to focus that disagreement on ideas, not people. For this reason, we say that the relationship among the members of a learning community is not so much interpersonal or impersonal as *transpersonal,* or "beyond the personal." Each member is personally committed to the development of ideas and does whatever is necessary to achieve that development.

The Value of Group Work for Writers

Because we are basically social animals, we find it natural, pleasurable even, to deal with problems in groups. Proof of this fact can be found on any given morning in any given student union in the country. Around the room you will find many students working in groups. Math, engineering, and business majors will be solving problems together, comparing solutions and their ways of arriving at solutions. Others will be comparing their class notes and testing their understanding of concepts and terms by explaining them to each other and comparing their explanations. To be sure, their discussions will occasionally drift off the topic to encompass pressing social issues such as what they're going to do next weekend, or why they like or dislike the class they're working on, but much of the work of college students seems to get done in convivial conversation over morning coffee or late-night popcorn. Why not ease into the rigors of writing in a similar fashion?

A second major advantage of working on writing in a group is that it provides a real and immediate audience for people's work. Too often, when students write in a school setting, they get caught up in the writing-for-teacher racket, which may distort their notion of audience. Argumentative writing is best aimed either at opponents or at a neutral "jury" that will be weighing both sides of a controversy. A group of peers gives you a better sense of a real-world audience "out there" than does a single teacher.

There's danger, of course, in having several audiences consider your writing. Your peer audience may well respond differently to your writing than your instructor. You may feel misled if you are praised for something by a peer and then criticized for the same thing by your instructor. These things can and will happen, no matter how much time you spend developing universally accepted criteria for writing. Grades are not facts but judgments, and all judgments involve uncertainty. Students who are still learning the criteria for making judgments will sometimes apply those criteria differently than an instructor who has been working with them for years. But you should know too that two or more instructors might give you conflicting advice also, just as two or more doctors might give you different advice on what to do about the torn ligaments in your knee. In our view, the risks of misunderstanding are more than made up for by gains in understanding of the writing process, an understanding that comes from working in writing communities where everyone functions both as a writer and as a writing critic.

A third advantage to working in writing communities is closely related to the second advantage. The act of sharing your writing with other people helps you get beyond the bounds of egocentrism that limit all writers. By egocentrism, we don't mean pride or stuck-upness; we mean the failure to consider the needs of your readers. Unless you share your writing with another person, your audience is always a "mythical group," a fiction or a theory that exists only in your head. You must always try to anticipate the problems others will have in reading your work. But until others actually read it and share their reactions to it with you, you can never be fully sure you have understood your audience's point of view. Until another reads your writing critically, you can't be sure you aren't talking to yourself.

FORMING WRITING COMMUNITIES: SKILLS AND ROLES

Given that there are advantages to working in groups, just how do we go about forming writing communities in the classroom? We first have to decide how big to make the groups. From our experience, the best groups consist of either five to seven people or simply two people. Groups of three or four tend to polarize and become divisive, and larger groups tend to be unmanageable. Because working in five- to seven-person groups is quite different from working in pairs, we discuss each of these different-size groups in turn.

Working in Groups of Five to Seven People

The trick to successful group work is to consider the maximum number of viewpoints and concerns without losing focus. Because these two basic goals frequently conflict, you need some mechanisms for monitoring your progress. In particular, it's important that each group member is assigned to perform those tasks necessary to effective group functioning. (Some teachers assign roles to individual students, shifting the roles from day to day. Other teachers let the groups themselves determine the roles of individuals.) That is, the group must recognize that it has two objectives at all times: the stated objectives of a given task and the objective of making the group work well. It is very easy to get so involved with the given task that you overlook the second objective, generally known as "group maintenance."

The first role is group leader. We hesitate to call persons who fill this role "leaders" because we tend sometimes to think of leaders as know-it-alls who take charge and order people about. In classroom group work, however, being a group leader is a role you play, not a fixed part of your identity. The leader, above all else, keeps the group focused on agreed-on ends and protects the right of every group member to be heard. It's an important function, and group members should share the responsibility from task to task. Here is a list of things for the leader to do during a group discussion:

1. Ensure that everyone understands and agrees on the objectives of any given task and on what sort of final product is expected of the group (for example, a list of criteria, a brief written statement, or an oral response to a question).

2. Ask that the group set an agenda for completing the task, and have some sense of how much time the group will spend at each stage. (Your instructor should always make clear what time limits you have to operate within and when he or she expects your task to be completed. If a time limit isn't specified, you should request a reasonable estimate.)

3. Look for signs of getting off the track, and ask individual group members to clarify how their statements relate to agreed-on objectives.

4. Actively solicit everyone's contributions, and take care that all viewpoints are listened to and that the group does not rush to incomplete judgment.

5. Try to determine when the task has been adequately accomplished.

In performing each of these functions, the leader must be concerned to turn criticisms and observations into questions. Instead of saying to one silent and bored-looking member of the group, "Hey, Gormley, you haven't said diddly-squat here so far; say something relevant or take a hike," the leader might ask, "Irwin, do you agree with what Beth just said about this paper being disorganized?" Remember, every action in nature is met with an equal and opposite reaction—commands tend to be met with resistance, questions with answers.

A second crucial role for well-functioning groups is that of recorder. The recorder's function is to provide the group with a record of their deliberations so they can measure their progress. It is particularly important that the recorder write down the agenda and the solution to the problem in precise form. Because the recorder must summarize the deliberations fairly precisely, he must ask for clarifications. In doing this, he ensures that group members don't fall into the "ya know?" syndrome (a subset of clonethink) in which people assent to statements that are in fact cloudy to them. (Ya know?) At the completion of the task, the recorder should also ask whether there are any significant remaining disagreements or unanswered questions. Finally, the recorder is responsible for reporting the group's solutions to the class as a whole.*

If these two roles are conscientiously filled, the group should be able to identify and solve problems that temporarily keep it from functioning effectively. Maybe you are thinking that this sounds dumb. Whenever you've been in a group, everyone has known whether there were problems without leaders or recorders. Too often, however, a troubled group may sense that there is a problem without being perfectly clear about the nature of the problem or the solution. Let's say you are in a group with Elwood Lunt Jr., who is very opinionated and dominates the discussions. (For a sample of Elwood's cognitive style, see his essay "Good Writing and Computers for Today's American Youth of America," in Task 1 on page 454.) Group members may represent their problem privately to themselves with a statement such as "Lunt's such a jerk nobody can work with him. He talks constantly and none of the rest of us can get a word in." The group may devote all of its energies to punishing Lunt with ridicule or silence rather than trying to solve the problem. Although this may make you feel better for a short time, Lunt is unlikely to get any better, and the group is unlikely to get much done.

If Lunt is indeed bogging the group down by airing his opinions at great length, it is the leader's job to limit his dominance without excluding him. Because group members all realize that it is the group leader's role to handle such problems, the leader has a sort of license that allows her or him to deal directly with Lunt. Moreover, the leader also has the explicit responsibility to do so, so that each member is not forced to sit, silently seething and waiting for someone to do something.

The leader might control Lunt in one of several ways: (1) by keeping to the agenda ("Thanks, Elwood, hate to interrupt, but we're a bit behind schedule and we haven't heard from everyone on this point yet. Jack, shall we move on to you?"); (2) by simply asking Lunt to demonstrate how his remarks are relevant to the topic at hand. ("That's real interesting, Elwood, that you got to see Kurt Cobain in his last performance, but can you tell us how you see that relating to Melissa's point about ending welfare?"); or (3) by introducing more formal procedures such

---

*There is a debate among experts who study small-group communications about whether the roles of leader and recorder can be collapsed into one job. Your group may need to experiment until it discovers the structure that works best for bringing out the most productive discussions.

as asking group members to raise their hands and be called on by the chair. These procedures might not satisfy your blood lust, your secret desire to stuff Lunt into a Dumpster; however, they are more likely to let the group get its work done and perhaps, just maybe, to help Lunt become a better listener and participant.

The rest of the group members, though they have no formally defined roles, have an equally important obligation to participate fully. To ensure full participation, group members can do several things. They can make sure that they know all the other group members by their first names and speak to them in a friendly manner. They can practice listening procedures wherein they try not to dissent or disagree without first charitably summarizing the view with which they are taking issue. Most importantly, they can bring to the group as much information and as many alternative points of view as they can muster. The primary intellectual strength of group work is the ability to generate a more complex view of a subject. But this more complex view cannot emerge unless all individuals contribute their perspectives.

One collaborative task for writers that requires no elaborate procedures or any role playing is reading your essays aloud within the group. A good rule for this procedure is that no one responds to any one essay until all have been read. This is often an effective last step before handing in any essay. It's a chance to share the fruits of your labor with others and to hear finished essays that you may have seen in the draft stages. Hearing everyone else's final draft can also help you get a clearer perspective on how your own work is progressing. Listening to the essays read can both reassure you that your work is on a par with other people's and challenge you to write up to the level of the best student writing in your group.

Many of you may find this process a bit frightening at first. But the cause of your fright is precisely the source of the activity's value. In reading your work aloud, you are taking responsibility for that work in a special way. Writing specialist Kenneth Bruffee, whose work on collaborative learning introduced us to many of the ideas in this chapter, likens the reading of papers aloud to reciting a vow, of saying "I do" in a marriage ceremony. You are taking public responsibility for your words, and there's no turning back. The word has become deed. If you aren't at least a little nervous about reading an essay aloud, you probably haven't invested much in your words. Knowing that you will take public responsibility for your words is an incentive to make that investment—a more real and immediate incentive than a grade.

Working in Pairs

Working in pairs is another effective form of community learning. In our classes we use pairs at both the early-draft and the late-draft stages of writing. At the early-draft stage, it serves the very practical purpose of clarifying a student's ideas and sense of direction at the beginning of a new writing project. The interaction best takes place in the form of pair interviews. When you first sit down to interview each other, each of you should have done a fair amount of exploratory writing and thinking about what you want to say in your essay and how you're going to say it. Here is a checklist of questions you can use to guide your interview:

1. "What is your issue?" Your goal here is to help the writer focus an issue by formulating a question that clearly has alternative answers.

2. "What is your position on the issue, and what are alternative positions?" After you have helped your interviewee formulate the issue question, help her clarify this issue by stating her own position and show how that position differs from opposing ones. Your interviewee might say, for example, that "many of my friends are opposed to building more nuclear power plants, but I think we need to build more of them."

3. "Can you walk me through your argument step by step?" Once you know your interviewee's issue question and intended position, you can best help her by having her walk you through her argument talking out loud. You can ask prompting questions such as "What are you going to say first?" "What next?" and so on. At this stage your interviewee will probably still be struggling to discover the best way to support the point. You can best help by brainstorming along with her, both of you taking notes on your ideas. Often at this stage you can begin making a schematic plan for the essay and formulating supporting reasons as *because* clauses. Along the way give your interviewee any information or ideas you have on the issue. It is particularly helpful at this stage if you can provide counterarguments and opposing views.

The interview strategy is useful before writers begin their rough drafts. After the first drafts have been written, there are a number of different ways of using pairs to evaluate drafts. One practice that we've found helpful is simply to have writers write a one-paragraph summary of their own drafts and of their partner's. In comparing summaries, writers can often discover which, if any, of their essential ideas are simply not getting across. If a major idea is not in the reader's summary, writer and reader need to decide whether it's due to a careless reading or to problems within the draft. The nice thing about this method is that the criticism is given indirectly and hence isn't as threatening to either party. At other times, your instructor might also devise a checklist of features for you to consider, based on the criteria you have established for the assignment.

FOR CLASS DISCUSSION

1. As a group, consider the following quotation and then respond to the questions that follow: "In most college classrooms there is a reluctance to assume leadership. The norm for college students is to defer to someone else, to refuse

to accept the position even if it is offered. There is actually a competition in humility and the most humble person usually ends up as the leader."*

a. Do you think this statement is true?

b. On what evidence do you base your judgment of its truthfulness?

c. As a group, prepare an opening sentence for a paragraph that would report your group's reaction to this quotation.

2. Read the following statements about group interaction and decide as a group whether these statements are true or false.

a. Women are less self-assertive and less competitive in groups than are men.

b. There is a slight tendency for physically superior individuals to become leaders in a group.

c. Leaders are usually more intelligent than nonleaders.

d. Females conform to majority opinion more than males in reaching group decisions.

e. An unconventional group member inhibits group functioning.

f. An anxious group member inhibits group functioning.

g. Group members with more power are usually better liked than low-power group members.

h. Groups usually produce more and better solutions to problems than do individuals working alone.

With the assistance of the group, the recorder should write a four- to five-sentence description of the process your group used to reach agreement on the true-false statements. Was there discussion? Disagreement? Did you vote? Did every person give an opinion on each question? Were there any difficulties?

A SEVERAL-DAYS' GROUP PROJECT: DEFINING "GOOD ARGUMENTATIVE WRITING"

The problem we want you to address in this sequence of tasks is how to define and identify "good argumentative writing." This is a particularly crucial problem for developing writers insofar as you can't begin to measure your growth as a writer until you have some notion of what you're aiming for. To be sure, it's no easy task defining good argumentative writing. In order for even experienced teachers to reach agreement on this subject, some preliminary discussions

---

*Gerald Philips, Douglas Pederson, and Julia Wood, *Group Discussion: A Practical Guide to Participant Leadership* (Boston: Houghton Mifflin, 1979).

and no small amount of compromise are necessary. By the end of this task you will most certainly not have reached a universally acceptable description of good argumentative writing. (Such a description doesn't exist.) But you will have begun a dialog with each other and your instructor on the subject. Moreover, you will have developed a vocabulary for sharing your views on writing with each other.

For this exercise, we give you a sequence of four tasks, some homework, and other in-class group tasks. Please do the tasks in sequence.

Task 1 (Homework):
Preparing for the Group Discussion

Freewrite for five minutes on the question "What is good argumentation writing?" After finishing your freewrite, read fictional student Lunt's argument that follows and, based on the principles that Lunt seems to break, develop a tentative list of criteria for good argumentative writing.

Explanation   Before you come together with a group of people to advance your understanding and knowledge collectively, you first need to explore your own thoughts on the matter. Too often, groups collapse not because the members lack goodwill but because they lack preparation. To discharge your responsibility as a good group member, you must therefore begin by doing your homework. By using a freewriting exercise, you focus your thinking on the topic, explore what you already know or feel about it, and begin framing questions and problems.

To help you establish a standard for good argumentative writing, we've produced a model of bad arguing by a fictional student, one Elwood P. Lunt Jr. If you can figure out what's bad about Lunt's argument, then you can formulate the principles of good argument that he violates. Of course, no student of our acquaintance has ever written anything as bad as Lunt's essay. That's the virtue of this contrived piece. It's an easy target. In going over it critically, you may well find that Lunt violates principles of good writing you hadn't thought of in your freewrite. (We tried to ensure that he violated as many as possible.) Thus you should be sure to go back and modify your ideas from your freewrite accordingly.

A couple of important points to keep in mind here as you prepare to critique another person's work: (1) Remember the principle of charity. Try to look past the muddied prose to a point or intention that might be lurking in the background. Your critique should speak as much as possible to Lunt's failure to realize this intent. (2) Direct your critique to the prose, not the writer. Don't settle for "He just doesn't make sense" or "He's a dimwit." Ask yourself why he doesn't make sense and point to particular places where he doesn't make sense. In sum, give Lunt the same sort of reading you would like to get: compassionate and specific.

Good Writing and Computers for Today's Modern American Youth of America

(A partial fulfillment of writing an argument in the course in which I am attending)

1   In todays modern fast paced world computers make living a piece of cake. You can do a lot with computers which in former times took a lot of time and doing a lot of work. Learning to fly airplanes, for example. But there are no such things as a free lunch. People who think computers will do all the work for you need to go to the Iron Curtain and take a look around, that's the place for people who think they can be replaced by computers. The precious computer which people think is the dawn of a new civilization but which is in all reality a pig in a poke makes you into a number but can't even add right! So don't buy computers for two reasons.

2   The first reason you shouldn't buy a computer is writing. So what makes people think that they won't have to write just because they have a computer on his desk. "Garbage in and garbage out one philosopher said." Do you want to sound like garbage? I don't. That's why modern American fast paced youth must conquer this affair with computers and writing by ourselves is the answer to our dreams and not just by using a computer for that aforementioned writing. A computer won't make you think better and that's the problem because people think a computer will do your thinking for you. No way, Jose.

3   Another thing is grammar. My Dad Elwood P. Lunt Sr. hit the nail on the head; when he said bad grammar can make you sound like a jerk. Right on Dad. He would be so upset to think of all the jerks out there who wasted their money on a computer so that the computer could write for them. But do computers know grammar? So get on the bandwagon and write good and get rich with computers. Which can make you write right. You think any computer could catch the errors I just made? Oh, sure you do. Jerk. And according to our handbook on writing writing takes intelligence which computers don't have. Now I'm not against computers. I am just saying that computers have there place.

4   In conclusion there are two reasons why you shouldn't buy a computer. But if you want to buy one that is all right as long as you understand that it isn't as smart as you think.

Task 2 (In-Class Group Work): Developing a Master List of Criteria

As a group, reach a consensus on at least six or seven major problems with Lunt's argumentative essay. Then use that list to prepare a parallel list of criteria for a good written argument. Please have your list ready in thirty minutes.

Explanation   Your goal for this task is to reach consensus about what's wrong with Lunt's argument. As opposed to a "majority decision," in which more people agree than disagree, a "consensus" entails a solution that is generally acceptable to all members of the group. In deciding what is the matter with Lunt's essay, you should be able to reach consensus also on the criteria for a good argument. After each group has completed its list, recorders should report each group's consensus to the class as a whole. Your instructor will facilitate a discussion leading to the class's "master list" of criteria.

Task 3 (Homework):
Applying Criteria to Student Essays

At home, consider the following five samples of student writing. (This time they're real examples.) Rank the essays "1" through "5," with 1 being the best and 5 the worst. Once you've done this, develop a brief rationale for your ranking. This rationale should force you to decide which criteria you rank highest and which lowest. For example, does "quality of reasons" rank higher than "organization and development"? Does "colorful, descriptive style" rank high or low in your ranking system?

Explanation   The following essays were written as short arguments developing two or three reasons in support of a claim. Students had studied the argumentative concepts in Chapters 1–6 but had not yet studied refutation strategies. Although the students were familiar with classical argument structure, this introductory assignment asked them to support a claim/thesis with only two or three reasons. Summarizing and responding to opposing views was optional.

Bloody Ice

It is March in Alaska. The ocean-side environment is full of life and death. Man and animal share this domain but not in peace. The surrounding iceflows, instead of being cold and white, are steaming from the remains of gutted carcasses and stained red. The men are hunters and the animals are barely six weeks old. A slaughter has just taken place. Thousands of baby Harp seals lie dead on the ice and thousands more of adult mothers lay groaning over the death of their babies. Every year a total limit of 180,000 seals set by the U.S. Seal Protection Act is filled in a terrifying bloodbath. But Alaska with its limit of 30,000 is not alone. Canadians who hunt seals off the coast of Northern Newfoundland and Quebec are allowed 150,000 seals. The Norwegians are allowed 20,000 and native Eskimos of Canada and Greenland are allowed 10,000 seals per year. Although this act appears heartless and cruel, the men who hunt have done this for 200 years as a tradition for survival. They make many good arguments supporting their traditions. They feel the seals are in no immediate danger of extinction. Also seal furs can be used to line boots and gloves or merely traded for money and turned into robes or fur coats. Sometimes the meat is even used for food in the off hunting months when money is scarce. But are these valid justifications for the unmerciful killings? No, the present limit on Harp seal killings should be better regulated because the continued hunting of the seals will lead to eventual extinction and because the method of slaughter is so cruel and inhumane.

2   The Harp seal killing should be better regulated first because eventual extinction is inevitable. According to *Oceans* magazine, before the limit of 180,000 seals was established in 1950, the number of seals had dwindled from 3,300,000 to 1,250,000. Without these limitations hundreds of thousands were killed within weeks of birth. Now, even with this allotment, the seals are being killed off at an almost greater rate than they can remultiply. Adult female seals give birth once every year but due to pollution, disease, predation, whelping success and malnutrition they are already slowly dying on their own without being hunted. Eighty percent of the seals slaughtered are pups and the remaining twenty percent are adult seals and even sometimes mothers who try attacking the hunters after seeing their babies killed. The hunters, according to the Seal Protection Act, have this right.

3   Second, I feel the killing should be better regulated because of the inhumane method used. In order to protect the fur value of the seals, guns are not used. Instead, the sealers use metal clubs to bludgeon the seal to death. Almost immediately after being delivered a direct blow, the seals are gutted open and skinned. Although at this stage of life the seal's skull is very fragile, sometimes the seals are not killed by the blows but merely stunned; thus hundreds are skinned alive. Still others are caught in nets and drowned, which according to *America* magazine, the Canadian government continues to deny. But the worst of the methods used is when a hunter gets tired of swinging his club and uses the heel of his boot to kick the seal's skull in. Better regulation is the only way to solve this problem because other attempts seem futile. For example, volunteers who have traveled to hunting sites trying to dye the seals to ruin their fur value have been caught and fined heavily.

4   The plight of the Harp seals has been long and controversial. With the Canadian hunters feeling they have the right to kill the seals because it has been their industry for over two centuries, and on the other hand with humane organizations fearing extinction and strongly opposing the method of slaughter, a compromise must be met among both sides. As I see it, the solution to the problem is simple. Since the Canadians do occasionally use the whole seal and have been sealing for so long they could be allowed to continue but at a more heavily regulated rate. Instead of filling the limit of 180,000 every year and letting the numbers of seals decrease, Canadians could learn to ranch the seals as Montanans do cattle or sheep. The United States has also offered to help them begin farming their land for a new livelihood. The land is adequate for crops and would provide work all year round instead of only once a month every year. As a result of farming, the number of seals killed would be drastically cut down because Canadians would not be so dependent on the seal industry as before. This would in turn lead back to the ranching aspect of sealing and allow the numbers to grow back and keeping the tradition alive for future generations and one more of nature's creatures to enjoy.

RSS Should Not Provide Dorm Room Carpets

1   Tricia, a University student, came home exhausted from her work-study job. She took a blueberry pie from the refrigerator to satisfy her hunger and a tall glass of milk to quench her thirst. While trying to get comfortable on her bed, she tipped her snack over onto the

floor. She cleaned the mess, but the blueberry and milk stains on her brand new carpet could not be removed. She didn't realize that maintaining a clean carpet would be difficult and costly. Tricia bought her own carpet. Some students living in dorm rooms want carpeted rooms provided for them at the expense of the University. They insist that since they pay to live on campus, the rooms should reflect a comfortable home atmosphere. However, Resident Student Services (RSS) should not be required to furnish the carpet because other students do not want carpets. Furthermore, carpeting all the rooms totals into a very expensive project. And lastly, RSS should not have to provide the carpet because many students show lack of respect and responsibility for school property.

Although RSS considers the carpeting of all rooms a strong possibility, students like   2
Tricia oppose the idea. They feel the students should buy their own carpets. Others claim the permanent carpeting would make dorm life more comfortable. The carpet will act as insulation and as a sound proofing system. These are valid arguments, but they should not be the basis for changing the entire residence hall structure. Those students with "cold feet" can purchase house footwear, which cost less than carpet. Unfortunately carpeting doesn't muffle all the noise; therefore, some students will be disturbed. Reasonable quietness should be a matter of respect for other students' privacy and comfort. Those opposed to the idea reason out the fact that students constantly change rooms or move out. The next person may not want carpet. Also, if RSS carpets the rooms, the students will lose the privilege they have of painting their rooms any color. Paint stains cannot be removed. Some students can't afford to replace the carpet. Still another factor, carpet color may not please everyone. RSS would provide a neutral color like brown or gray. With tile floors, the students can choose and purchase their own carpets to match their taste.

Finally, another reason not to have carpet exists in the fact that the project can be expensive due to material costs, installation cost, and the maintenance cost caused mainly by the irresponsibility of many students. According to Rick Jones, Asst. Director of Housing Services, the cost will be $300 per room for the carpet and installation. RSS would also have to purchase more vacuum cleaners for the students use. RSS will incur more expense in order to maintain the vacuums. Also, he claims that many accidents resulting from shaving cream fights, food fights, beverage parties, and smoking may damage the carpet permanently. With floor tiles, accidents such as food spills can be cleaned up easier than carpet. The student's behavior plays an important role in deciding against carpeting. Many students don't follow the rules of maintaining their rooms. They drill holes into the walls, break mirrors, beds, and closet doors, and leave their food trays all over the floor. How could they be trusted to take care of school carpet when they violate the current rules? Many students feel they have the "right" to do as they please. This irresponsible and disrespectful behavior reflects their future attitude about carpet care.

In conclusion, the university may be able to afford to supply the carpets in each room,   4
but maintaining them would be difficult. If the students want carpets, they should pay and care for the carpets themselves. Hopefully, they will be more cautious and value it more. They should take the initiative to fundraise or find other financial means of providing this "luxury." They should not rely on the school to provide unnecessary room fixtures such as carpets. Also, they must remember that if RSS provides the carpet and they don't pay for the damages, they and future students will endure the consequences. What will happen???? Room rates will skyrocket!!!!!

Sterling Hall Dorm Food

1   The quality of Sterling Hall dorm food does not meet the standard needed to justify the high prices University students pay. As I watched a tall, medium-built University student pick up his Mexican burrito from the counter it didn't surprise me to see him turn up his nose. Johnny, our typical University student, waited five minutes before he managed to make it through the line. After he received his bill of $4.50 he turned his back to the cash register and walked away displeased with his meal.

2   As our neatly groomed University student placed his ValiDine eating card back into his Giorgio wallet, he thought back to the balance left on his account. Johnny had $24 left on his account and six more weeks left of school. He had been eating the cheapest meals he could and still receive a balanced meal, but the money just seemed to disappear. No student, not even a thrifty boy like Johnny, could possibly afford to live healthfully according to the University meal plan system.

3   Johnny then sat down at a dirty table to find his burrito only half way cooked. Thinking back to the long-haired cook who served him the burrito, he bit into the burrito and noticed a long hair dangling from his lips. He realized the cook's lack of preparation when preparing his burrito.

4   Since the food costs so much, yet the quality of the food remains low, University students do not get the quality they deserve. From the information stated I can conclude that using the ValiDine service system University students would be jeopardizing their health and wasting their hard-earned money. University students deserve something more than what they have now.

ROTC Courses Should Not Get College Credit

1   One of the most lucrative scholarships a student can receive is a four-year ROTC scholarship that pays tuition and books along with a living allowance. It was such a scholarship that allowed me to attend an expensive liberal arts college and to pursue the kind of well rounded education that matters to me. Of course, I am obligated to spend four years on active duty—an obligation that I accept and look forward to. What I am disappointed in, however, is the necessity to enroll in Military Science classes. Strong ROTC advocates argue that Military Science classes are essential because they produce good citizens, teach leadership skills, and provide practical experience for young cadets. Maybe so. But we could get the same benefits without having to take these courses for credit. Colleges should make ROTC training an extracurricular activity, not a series of academic courses taken for academic credit.

2   First of all, ROTC courses, unlike other college courses, do not stress inquiry and true questioning. The ROTC program has as its objective the preparation of future officers committed to the ideals and structure of the military. The structure of the military is based upon obediently following the orders of military superiors. Whereas all my other teachers stress

critical thinking and doing independent analysis, my ROTC instructors avoid political or social questions saying it is the job of civilian leaders to debate policies and the job of the military to carry them out. We don't even debate what role the military should play in our
country. My uncle, who was an ROTC cadet during the Vietnam war, remembers that not
only did ROTC classes never discuss the ethics of the war but that cadets were not allowed
to protest the war outside of their ROTC courses. This same obedience is demanded in my
own ROTC courses, where we are not able to question administration policies and examine openly the complexity of the situation in Iraq and Kuwait.

A second reason that Army ROTC courses do not deserve academic credit is that the   3
classes are not academically strenuous, thus giving cadets a higher GPA and an unfair
advantage over their peers. Much of what a cadet does for academic credit involves non-
academic activities such as physical training for an hour three days a week so that at least
some of a cadet's grade is based on physical activity, not mental activity. In conducting an
informal survey of 10 upper-classmen, I found out that none of them has ever gotten anything lower than an A in a Military Science class and they do not know of anyone who got
anything lower than an A. One third-year cadet stated that "the classes are basic. A monkey coming out of the zoo could get college credit for a Military Science class." He went on
to say that most of the information given in his current class is a brush-up to 8th grade U.S.
history. In contrast, a typical liberal arts college class requires much thought, questioning,
and analysis. The ROTC Military Science class is taught on the basis of "regurgitated knowledge," meaning that once you are given a piece of information you are required to know it
and reproduce it at any time without thought or question. A good example is in my class
Basic Officership. Our first assignment is to memorize and recite in front of the class the
Preamble to the Constitution of the United States. The purpose of doing so doesn't seem to
be to understand or analyze the constitution because we never talk about that. In fact, I
don't know what the purpose is. I just do it because I am told to. Because the "A" is so easy
to get in my ROTC class, I spend all my time studying for my other classes. I am a step
ahead of my peers in the competition for a high GPA, even though I am not getting as good
an education.

Finally, having to take ROTC classes means that I can't take other liberal arts courses   4
which would be more valuable. One of the main purposes for ROTC is to give potential officers a liberal education. Many cadets have the credentials to get into an armed forces academy, but they chose ROTC programs because they could combine military training with a
well-rounded curriculum. Unfortunately, by taking Military Science classes each quarter,
cadets find that their electives are all but eaten up by the time they are seniors. If ROTC
classes were valuable in themselves, I wouldn't complain. But they aren't, and they keep
me from taking upper division electives in philosophy, literature, and the humanities.

All of these reasons lead me to believe that Army ROTC cadets are getting short-   5
changed when they enroll for Military Science classes. Because cadets receive a lucrative
scholarship, they should have to take the required military science courses. But these
courses should be treated as extracurricular activities, like a work-study job or like athletics. Just as a student on a full-ride athletic scholarship does not receive academic credit for
football practices and games, so should a student on a full-ride ROTC scholarship have to
participate in the military education program without getting academic credit. By treating

ROTC courses as a type of extracurricular activity like athletics, students can take more elective credits that will expand their minds, better enabling them to have the knowledge to make moral decisions and to enjoy their world more fully.

Legalization of Prostitution

1   Prostitution . . . It is the world's oldest profession. It is by definition the act of offering or soliciting sex for payment. It is, to some, evil. Yet the fact is it exists.

2   Arguments are not necessary to prove the existence of prostitution. Rather, the argument arises when trying to prove something must be done to reduce the problems of this profession. The problems which exist are in the area of crime, of health, and of environment. Crime rates are soaring, diseases are spreading wildly, and the environment on the streets is rapidly decaying. Still, it has been generally conceded that these problems cannot be suppressed. However, they can be reduced. Prostitution should be legalized because it would reduce the wave of epidemics, decrease high crime rates, provide good revenue by treating it like other businesses, and get girls off the streets where sexual crimes often occur.

3   Of course, there are those who would oppose the legalization of prostitution stating that it is one of the main causes for the spread of venereal diseases. Many argue that it is inter-related with drug-trafficking and other organized crimes. And probably the most controversial is the moral aspect of the subject; it is morally wrong, and legalizing it would be enforcing, or even justifying, such an existence.

4   These points propose good arguments, but I shall counter each point and explain the benefits and advantages of legalizing prostitution. In the case of prostitution being the main cause for the spread of epidemics, I disagree. By legalizing it, houses would be set up which would solve the problem of girls working on the streets and being victims of sexual crimes. It would also provide regular health checks, as is successfully done in Nevada, Germany, and other parts of the U.S. and Europe, which will therefore cut down on diseases spreading unknowingly.

5   As for the increase of organized crime if prostitution is legalized, I disagree again. Firstly, by treating it like businesses, then that would make good state revenue. Secondly, like all businesses have regulations, so shall these houses. That would put closer and better control in policing the profession, which is presently a problem. Obviously, if the business of prostitution is more closely supervised, that would decrease the crime rates.

6   Now, I come to one of the most arguable aspects of legalizing prostitution: the moral issue. Is it morally wrong to legalize prostitution? That is up to the individual. To determine whether anything is "right or wrong" in our society is nearly impossible to do since there are various opinions. If a person were to say that prostitution is the root of all evil, that will not make it go away. It exists. Society must begin to realize that fear or denial will not make the "ugliness" disappear. It still exists.

7   Prostitution can no longer go ignored because of our societal attitudes. Legalizing it is beneficial to our society, and I feel in time people may begin to form an accepting attitude.

It would be the beginning of a more open-minded view of what is reality. Prostitution . . . it is the world's oldest profession. It exists. It is a reality.

Task 4 (In-Class Group Work):
Reaching Consensus on Ranking of Essays

Working again in small groups, reach consensus on your ranking of the five essays. Groups should report both their rankings and their justification for the rankings based on the criteria established in Task 2 or as currently modified by your group.

Explanation   You are now to reach consensus on how you rank the papers and why you rank them the way you do. Feel free to change the criteria you established earlier if they seem to need modification. Be careful in your discussions to distinguish between evaluation of the writer's written product and your own personal position on the writer's issue. In other words, there is a crucial difference between saying, "I don't like Pete's essay because I disagree with his ideas," and "I don't like Pete's essay because he didn't provide adequate support for his ideas." As each group reports back the results of its deliberations to the class as a whole, the instructor will highlight discrepancies among the groups' decisions and collate the criteria as they emerge. If the instructor disagrees with the class consensus or wants to add items to the criteria, he or she might choose to make these things known now. By the end of this stage, everyone should have a list of criteria for good argumentative writing established by the class.

A CLASSROOM DEBATE

In this exercise, you have an opportunity to engage in a variant of a formal debate. Although debates of this nature don't always lead to truth for its own sake, they are excellent forums for the development of analytical and organizational skills. The format for the debate is as follows.

First Hour   Groups will identify and reach consensus on "the most serious impediment to learning at this institution." Participants should have come to class prepared with their own individual lists of at least three problems. Once the class has reached consensus on the single most serious impediment to learning on your campus, your instructor will write it out as a formal statement. This statement constitutes the preliminary topic, which will eventually result in a proposition for your debate.

The instructor will then divide the class into an equal number of Affirmative and Negative teams (three to five members per team). Homework for all the Affirmative team members is to identify proposals for solving the problem identified by the class. Negative team members, meanwhile, will concentrate on reasons that the problem is not particularly serious and/or that the problem is "in the nature of things" and simply not solvable by any sort of proposal.

Second Hour   At the beginning of the period, the instructor will pair up each Affirmative team with a Negative team. The teams will be opponents during the actual debate, and there will be as many debates as there are paired teams. Each Affirmative team will now work on choosing the best proposal for solving the problem, while the Negative team pools its resources and builds its case against the seriousness and solvability of the problem. At the end of the period, each Affirmative team will share its proposal with its corresponding Negative team. The actual topic for each of the debates is now set: "Resolved: Our campus should institute Z (the Affirmative team's proposal) in order to solve problem X (the class's original problem statement)."

Homework for the next class is for each team to conduct research (interviewing students, gathering personal examples, polling students, finding data or expert testimony from the library, and so forth) to support its case. Each Affirmative team's research will be aimed at showing that the problem is serious and that the solution is workable. Each Negative team will try to show that the proposal won't work or that the problem isn't worth solving.

Third Hour   At this point each Affirmative team and each Negative team will select two speakers to represent their sides. During this hour each team will pool its ideas and resources to help the speakers make the best possible cases. Each team should prepare an outline for a speech supporting its side of the debate. Team members should then anticipate the arguments of the opposition and prepare a rebuttal.

Fourth (and Fifth) Hour(s)   The actual debates. (There will be as many debates as there are paired Affirmative and Negative teams.) Each team will present two speakers. Each speaker is limited to five minutes. The order of speaking is as follows:

FIRST AFFIRMATIVE:	Presents best case for the proposal
FIRST NEGATIVE:	Presents best case against the proposal
SECOND NEGATIVE:	Rebuts argument of First Affirmative
SECOND AFFIRMATIVE:	Rebuts argument of First Negative

Those team members who do not speak will be designated observers. Their task is to take notes on the debate, paying special attention to the quality of support for each argument and to those parts of the argument that are not rebutted by the opposition. By the next class period (fifth or sixth), they will have prepared a brief, informal analysis titled "Why Our Side Won the Debate."

Fifth or Sixth Hour   The observers will report to the class on their perceptions of the debates by using their prepared analysis as the basis of the discussion. The instructor will attempt to synthesize the main points of the debates and the most telling arguments for either side. At this point, your instructor may ask each of you to write an argument on the debate topic, allowing you to argue for or against any of the proposals presented.

credits

index

Checklist for Peer Reviewers

Understanding the Writer's Intentions

- What is the issue being addressed in this essay?
- What is the writer's major thesis/claim?
- Where does the writer present this thesis/claim? (See pp. 85–86, 165–68.)
- Who disagrees with this claim and why?
- Who is the primary audience for this argument? How resistant is this audience to the writer's claim? Does the writer regard this audience as supportive, undecided, or resistant? (See pp. 153–56.)
- Does the writer show awareness of the obstacles preventing the audience from accepting the writer's claim?
- If proposing an action, does the writer address a specific, appropriate group of decision makers? Is the writer aware of the constraints operating on these decision makers?

Reconstructing the Writer's Argument

- Can you summarize the writer's argument in your own words? Can you summarize it in one sentence as a claim with *because* clauses? (See pp. 83–86.) If you have trouble summarizing the argument, where is the source of difficulty?
- Can you make an outline, flowchart, or tree diagram of the writer's argument? If not, where do you have trouble perceiving the argument's structure?

Identifying the Argument's Claim Type

- Is the writer's main claim one of the claim types discussed in Part Three (category or definition, cause, resemblance, evaluation, proposal)?
- If so, does the writer use argumentative strategies appropriate to that claim type (for instance, using examples to support a categorical claim; using criteria-match arguing for definitional or evaluative claims; describing causal links for cause/consequence claims; arguing from category, consequence, or resemblance to support a proposal claim)?
- How well does the argument anticipate and respond to possible objections associated with each claim type?